Introduction to Property Testing

Property testing is concerned with the design of superfast algorithms for the structural analysis of large quantities of data. The aim is to unveil global features of the data, such as determining whether the data have a particular property or estimating global parameters. Remarkably, it is possible to achieve this aim by accessing only a small portion of the data. Property testing focuses on properties and parameters that go beyond simple statistics.

This book provides an extensive and authoritative introduction to property testing. It provides a wide range of algorithmic techniques for the design and analysis of tests for algebraic properties, properties of Boolean functions, graph properties, and properties of distributions.

Oded Goldreich is Professor of Computer Science at the Weizmann Institute of Science and holds the Meyer W. Weisgal Professorial Chair. He has made numerous contributions to property testing and to the theory of computation at large, and was awarded the 2017 Knuth Prize for this work. He is the author of several books, including the two-volume work *Foundations of Cryptography* and the book *Computational Complexity: A Conceptual Perspective*. He is an associate editor of the journal *Computational Complexity*, former editor of the *Journal of Cryptology* and *SIAM Journal on Computing*, and has been invited to speak at numerous conferences including the 1994 International Congress of Mathematicians.

Introduction to Property Testing

Oded Goldreich

Weizmann Institute of Science, Israel

CAMBRIDGE
UNIVERSITY PRESS

Shaftesbury Road, Cambridge CB2 8EA, United Kingdom

One Liberty Plaza, 20th Floor, New York, NY 10006, USA

477 Williamstown Road, Port Melbourne, VIC 3207, Australia

314–321, 3rd Floor, Plot 3, Splendor Forum, Jasola District Centre, New Delhi – 110025, India

103 Penang Road, #05–06/07, Visioncrest Commercial, Singapore 238467

Cambridge University Press is part of Cambridge University Press & Assessment,
a department of the University of Cambridge.

We share the University's mission to contribute to society through the pursuit of
education, learning and research at the highest international levels of excellence.

www.cambridge.org
Information on this title: www.cambridge.org/9781107194052

DOI: 10.1017/9781108135252

First published 2017

A catalogue record for this publication is available from the British Library

Library of Congress Cataloging-in-Publication data
Names: Goldreich, Oded, author.
Title: Introduction to property testing / Oded Goldreich, Weizmann Institute of Science, Israel.
Description: Cambridge, United Kingdom ; New York, NY, USA : Cambridge University Press, 2018. |
Includes bibliographical references and index.
Identifiers: LCCN 2017023051 | ISBN 9781107194052 (hardback : alk. paper)
Subjects: LCSH: Computer algorithms. | Structural analysis (Engineering)
Classification: LCC QA76.9.A43 G655 2018 | DDC 005.1 – dc23
LC record available at https://lccn.loc.gov/2017023051

ISBN   978-1-107-19405-2   Hardback

Contents

CONTENTS

Preface

Property testing is concerned with the design of superfast algorithms for structural analysis of huge amounts of data, where by structural analysis we mean an analysis aimed at unveiling global features of the data. Examples include determining whether the data as a whole have some property or estimating some global parameter of the data. The focus is on properties and parameters that go beyond simple statistics of the type that refers to the frequency of occurrence of various local patterns. The algorithms are given direct access to items of a huge data set, and determine whether this data set has some predetermined (global) property or is far from having this property. Remarkably, this decision is made by accessing only a small portion of the data set.

In other words, property testing is concerned with the design of *superfast algorithms for approximate decision making*, where the decision refers to properties or parameters of huge objects. In particular, we seek algorithms that inspect only relatively small portions of the huge object. Such algorithms must be randomized and can provide only approximate answers. Indeed, two salient aspects of property testing are that (1) it studies algorithms that can read only parts of the input, and (2) it focuses on algorithms that solve "approximate decision" problems. Both aspects are quite puzzling: What can one do without even reading the entire input? What does approximate decision mean?

The answer is that these two aspects are indeed linked: *Approximate decision* means distinguishing objects that have some predetermined property (i.e., reside in some predetermined set) from objects that are "far" from having the property (i.e., are far from any object having the property), where the notion of distance employed here is the relative number of different symbols in the descriptions of the objects. Such approximate decisions may be valuable in settings in which an exact decision is infeasible or very expensive or just considerably more expensive than obtaining an approximate decision.

The point is that, in many cases, an approximate decision can be achieved by means of *superfast randomized algorithms*. One well-known example is the common practice of estimating various statistics by sampling, which can be cast as a small collection of approximate decision problems (with respect to some threshold values). Research in property testing aims to extend this useful practice to properties that cannot be cast as statistics of values (which are associated with individual members of a large population). Examples in which this goal was achieved include testing properties of functions such as being a low-degree polynomial, being monotone, and depending on a specified number of attributes; testing properties of graphs such as being bipartite and being triangle-free, and testing properties of geometric objects and visual images such as being well clustered and being a convex body.

Objects as Functions and Their Exploration. Viewing the input object as a function is natural in the context of algorithms that do not read their entire input. Such algorithms must probe the input at locations of their choice, and such probing can be thought of as querying a function that represents the input. The key point here is that the number of probes (or queries) is smaller than the size of the input, and so decisions are taken after seeing only a small part of the input. However, the inspected positions are not fixed but rather are chosen at random by the algorithm, possibly based on answers obtained to prior queries. Thus, in general, these algorithms may "explore" the input, rather than merely obtain its value at a uniformly selected sample of locations. Such exploration is most appealing when the tested input is a graph, which may be represented by a function (e.g., by its adjacency predicate), but the notion of exploration applies also in other cases.

Wider Perspective and Connections. Research in property testing may be both algorithmic and complexity theoretic. This is reflected both in its goals, which may be either the design of better algorithms or the presentation of lower bounds on their complexity, and in its tools and techniques. Such research is related to several areas of computer science and mathematics including combinatorics, statistics, computational learning theory, computational geometry, and coding theory. Historically, property testing was closely associated with the study of Probabilistically Checkable Proofs (PCPs), and some connections do exist between the two, but property testing is not confined to PCPs (and/or to the study of "locally testable codes").

This Book. The current book aims to provide an introduction to property testing, by presenting some of the main themes, results, and techniques that characterize and are used in the area. As usual in such cases, *the choice of material reflects a judgment of what is most adequate for presentation in the context of such an introductory text*, and this selection does not reflect lack of appreciation of the omitted material but rather an opinion that it is less suitable for the intended purpose of the text.

In addition to the selection of material for this book, several choices were made regarding the organization of the material and the amount of interdependencies among its parts.

Organizational Choices. We chose to organize the material by the type of objects and the properties being tested. By the "type of object" we refer to the natural perception of the object; for example, whether it is most naturally perceived as a function or as a graph. Within the world of functions, the types correspond to the structure of the domain on which the function is defined (e.g., a group, a vector space, a Boolean hypercube, or a hypergrid). The structure of the domain is often reflected in the invariances that are satisfied by the properties that we consider (e.g., affine invariance, closure under graph isomorphism, etc.). Hence, our organization may be viewed as structurally oriented. (Possible alternatives to our organization include an organization by techniques (as in Ron [242]) or by complexity levels, for example, whether the complexity of testing is independent of the size of the object, is mildly dependent on it, is barely sublinear, or somewhere in between.)[1]

---

[1] Denoting the size of the object by n, one may distinguish bounds that are independent of n from bounds that are polylogarithmic in n, bounds that are expressed by a constant power of n (i.e., n^c for $c \in (0, 1)$), or are barely sublinear such as $n/\mathrm{poly}(\log n)$.

We chose to present the material with as few links between chapters as possible. Of course, all chapters depend on the core notions that are introduced in the first chapter, but additional interdependencies are rare and never heavily relied upon. Hence, the ordering of the other chapters is not very important, although we preferred a specific one (for reasons outlined in the Organization and Chapter Summaries section).

More Specific Choices. We chose to use (one-sided error) proximity-oblivious testers (POTs) *whenever possible*. This reflects our belief that when a tester (implicitly or explicitly) consists of repeating a POT for a number of times that depends on the proximity parameter, one should focus on the POT itself and rely on the generic transformation from POTs to standard testers.

For the sake of uniformity, n always denotes the size of the object in its natural representation (which is not grossly redundant). Hence, objects are typically viewed as functions $f : [n] \to R_n$. Consequently, Boolean functions are presented as $f : \{0, 1\}^\ell \to \{0, 1\}$, where $n = 2^\ell$ (rather than as having domain $\{0, 1\}^n$).

We made the choice of defining ϵ-far as the negation of ϵ-close. That is, a string x is ϵ-far from S if its relative distance from S is *strictly greater* than ϵ, and it is ϵ-close otherwise. We warn that in various sources different conventions are used regarding this minor issue.

The Use of Footnotes. We use footnotes quite heavily, and definitely much more often than is the norm in textbooks. Although this style is often criticized, it does offer the advantage of focusing on a main thread while deferring relevant elaborations of some related issues to an easy to locate place. We trust the reader to make the choice of whether to continue with the main thread or go for some elaborations of a point. Typical uses of such footnotes fall into two distinct categories. The first use is for the elaboration of technical details, which many readers may be willing to take on faith (and some may even figure out by themselves) but other readers may want to see fully justified before proceeding. The second use of footnotes is for advanced comments, which provide a somewhat wider perspective or refer to sources where such perspectives can be found.

Technical Style. At times, justifications for a sequence of (in)equalities appear after the sequence. This is typically done when we believe that these justifications are implicit in the text that preceded the sequence.

Teaching Note: The book contains several teaching notes, set as boxed text such as this.

Required Preliminaries. There are no required preliminaries for this text, but basic familiarity with some notions and results of the theory of computation and probability theory will be useful. These include

1. The notions of decision, search, and promise problems (see, e.g., [131, Sec. 1.2]);
2. Probabilistic algorithms (see, e.g., [131, Sec. 6.1] or [212]); and
3. Basic notions and facts regarding discrete probability distributions, including probabilistic inequalities such as the Union Bound and Chernoff Bound (see Appendix A,

although this material is covered in many textbooks, including [131, Apdx. D.1] and [212]).

Website for Notices Regarding This Book. We intend to maintain a website for this book, listing corrections and updates of various types. The site is located at

http://www.wisdom.weizmann.ac.il/~oded/pt-intro.html

Organization and Chapter Summaries

All chapters rely on a few core notions that are introduced in Sections 1.3.1 and 1.3.3. Although these parts of Section 1.3 provide a sufficient basis for reading any of the subsequent chapters, we strongly recommend reading the entire first chapter before proceeding to any other one.

In contrast to the central role of Chapter 1, no other chapter is essential for reading the other chapters. In particular, interdependencies between the other chapters are rare and never heavily relied on. The main dependencies are depicted in Figure 1, where thematic dependencies are marked by solid lines and technical dependencies by dashed lines.

Although the ordering of the chapters that follow Chapter 1 is not very important, a choice had to be made. We chose to start with simple properties of functions such as group homomorphism, low-degree polynomials, monotonicity (with respect to various partial orders), and depending on few variables (i.e., juntas). In all these cases, the correspondence between the object and its representation is transparent: *the function is the object*. In contrast, when moving to graph properties, the question of representation arises in an acute manner, and three different chapters are devoted to three different representations that correspond to three different testing models. Hence, from the perspective of property testing per se, it seems to make sense to start with functions and then move to graphs.

In accordance with the foregoing, the first cluster of chapters (Chapters 2–6) deals with testing properties of functions, whereas a second cluster (Chapters 8–10) deals with testing properties of graphs. A chapter on lower bound techniques (i.e., Chapter 7) is located in between these two clusters, since lower bounds are hardly mentioned in the first cluster, whereas they appear quite prominently in Chapters 9 and 10. The reason for this phenomenon is that these lower bounds are used to justify the significantly higher complexity of some testers that are presented in Chapters 9 and 10. Indeed, in the context of this book, we view lower bounds mainly as a justification for algorithms that may be considered to have a higher than expected complexity; the lower bounds assert that this impression is actually false, and that one cannot do significantly better.

Chapters 11–13 form a third cluster, which is actually a cluster of outliers with respect to the rest of this book. These chapters are indeed related to the previous chapters and yet they have a different flavor: Chapter 11 deals with testing properties of distributions, Chapter 12 explores a few variants of the basic setting (some of which were mentioned in Section 1.3.2), and Chapter 13 reviews locally testable codes and proofs. We stress that in Chapter 11 the tested objects are fundamentally different from those considered in all the other chapters, whereas in Chapter 13 we consider objects that are artificially designed so to offer superfast testing.

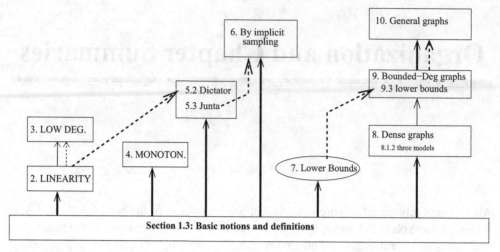

Figure 1: Dependencies among Chapters 1–10. Thicker lines represent greater dependency.

Chapter 1: The Main Themes (Approximate Decision and Sublinear Complexity).

This chapter introduces and illustrates the basic notions of property testing, emphasizing the themes of *approximate decision* and *sublinear complexity*. The chapter starts with a discussion of the potential benefits of property testing and culminates with a presentation of the definitions of (standard) testers and of proximity-oblivious testers (POTs). These definitions (and the relationship between them) are used extensively throughout the book. In addition, Chapter 1 discusses the key role of representation, points out the focus on properties that are not fully symmetric, and presents several general observations regarding POTs, testing, and learning.

Teaching Note: The conceptual framework put forward in Chapter 1 is pivotal for the rest of the book. It is essential that the main definitions (presented in Sections 1.3.1 and 1.3.3) and the rationales underlying them be internalized.

The following five chapters deal with properties of objects that are most naturally viewed as functions: Chapters 2 and 3 deal with algebraic properties, whereas Chapters 4–6 deal mostly with properties of Boolean functions. This distinction is quite fuzzy, and is reflected in the difference between the invariants that these properties satisfy: Algebraic properties are invariant under general affine transformations of the corresponding vector spaces, whereas the properties of Boolean functions that we consider are invariant only under transformations that permute the basis vectors.

Chapter 2: Testing Linearity (Group Homomorphism).

This chapter presents an analysis of a linearity tester that, on input a description of two groups G, H and oracle access to a function $f : G \to H$, queries the function at three points and satisfies the following conditions:

1. If f is a homomorphism from G to H, then the tester accepts with probability 1.
2. If f is δ-far from the set of all homomorphisms from G to H, then the tester rejects with probability at least $\min(0.5\delta, 0.1666)$.

The three queries are $x, y, x + y$, where x and y are selected uniformly at random in G. The archetypical case is that H is a finite field and G is a vector space over this field.

Chapter 3: Low-Degree Tests. For a finite field of prime cardinality $\mathcal{F}$, a degree bound $d < |\mathcal{F}|/2$, and number $m \in \mathbb{N}$, we consider the problem of testing whether a function $f : \mathcal{F}^m \to \mathcal{F}$ is a polynomial of total degree at most d. We present and analyze a low-degree tester that, given oracle access to $f : \mathcal{F}^m \to \mathcal{F}$, queries it at $d + 2$ points and satisfies the following conditions:

1. If f is an m-variate polynomial of (total) degree d, then the tester accepts with probability 1.
2. If f is δ-far from the set of m-variate polynomials of (total) degree d, then the tester rejects with probability at least $\min(0.5\delta, \Omega(d^{-2}))$.

The sequence of queries is generated by selecting at random $\bar{x}$ and $\bar{h}$ uniformly in $\mathcal{F}^m$, and using $\bar{x} + i\bar{h}$ as the ith query.

> **Teaching Note:** The analysis of the low-degree test is quite similar to the analysis of the linearity test, alas it is more complex (let alone that it depends on elementary preliminaries that are presented in Section 3.3). Hence, if short on time, then do consider skipping Chapter 3.

Chapter 4: Testing Monotonicity. For each n, we consider functions from a partially ordered set D_n to a totally ordered set R_n. Such a function $f : D_n \to R_n$ is called monotone if for every $x < y$ in D_n it holds that $f(x) \leq f(y)$, where $<$ denotes the partial order of D_n and $\leq$ refers to the total order in R_n. Two special cases of interest are

1. Boolean functions on the Boolean hypercube: In this case, D_n is the ℓ-dimensional Boolean hypercube (with the natural partial order), where $\ell = \log_2 n$, and $R_n = \{0, 1\}$. According to this partial order, $x_1 \cdots x_\ell \leq y_1 \cdots y_\ell$ if and only if $x_i \leq y_i$ for every $i \in [\ell]$.
2. Real functions on the discrete line: In this case, $D_n = [n]$ and $R_n = \mathbb{R}$, both with the natural total order.

Combining these two extremes, we also consider the case of the hypergrid domain $D_n = [m]^\ell$, for any $m, \ell \in \mathbb{N}$ such that $m^\ell = n$, and general ranges R_n. In all these cases, we present property testers of complexity $\text{poly}(\epsilon^{-1} \log n)$. In addition, we briefly survey relatively recent developments regarding the first case as well as known results regarding testing convexity, submodularity, and the Lipschitz property of functions from $[m]^\ell$ to $\mathbb{R}$.

> **Teaching Note:** Only parts of Chapter 4 (i.e., Sections 4.2.1 and 4.3.1) are recommended for teaching, and the rest is better left for optional independent reading.

Chapter 5: Testing Dictatorships, Juntas, and Monomials. We consider testing three basic properties of Boolean functions of the form $f : \{0, 1\}^\ell \to \{0, 1\}$:

1. Dictatorship: The case where the value of f depends on a single Boolean variable (i.e., $f(x) = x_i \oplus \sigma$ for some $i \in [\ell]$ and $\sigma \in \{0, 1\}$)

2. Junta (of size k): The case where the value of f depends on at most k Boolean variables (i.e., $f(x) = f'(x_I)$ for some k-subset $I \subset [\ell]$ and $f' : \{0, 1\}^k \to \{0, 1\}$)
3. Monomial (of size k): The case where the value of f is the conjunction of exactly k Boolean literals (i.e., $f(x) = \wedge_{i \in I}(x_i \oplus \sigma_i)$ for some k-subset $I \subseteq [\ell]$ and $\sigma_1, ..., \sigma_\ell \in \{0, 1\}$)

We present two different testers for dictatorship, where one generalizes to testing k-juntas and the other generalizes to testing k-monomials. (The presentation starts with the latter tester for dictatorship, sketches its generalization to testing k-monomials, and ends with the tester for k-juntas.)

> **Teaching Note:** We suggest leaving the overview section that discusses testing monomials (i.e., Section 5.2.2) for advanced independent reading.

Chapter 6: Testing by Implicit Sampling. Building on the junta tester, we present a general methodology for constructing testers for properties of Boolean functions (of the form $f : \{0, 1\}^\ell \to \{0, 1\}$) that can be approximated by small juntas. This methodology yields testers of low query complexity for many natural properties, which contain functions that depend on relatively few relevant variables; specifically, the query complexity is related to the size of the junta and is independent of the length of the input to the function (i.e., ℓ).

Chapter 7: Lower Bounds Techniques. We present and illustrate three techniques for proving lower bounds on the query complexity of property testers.

1. Showing a distribution on instances that have the property and a distribution on instances that are far from the property such that an oracle machine of low query complexity cannot distinguish these two distributions
2. Showing a reduction from communication complexity; that is, showing that a communication complexity problem of high complexity can be solved within communication complexity that is related to the query complexity of the property testing task that we are interested in
3. Showing a reduction from another testing problem; that is, showing a "local" reduction of a hard testing problem to the testing problem that we are interested in

We also present simplifications of these techniques for the cases of one-sided error probability testers and nonadaptive testers.

> **Teaching Note:** The first method (i.e., the method of "indistinguishability of distributions") is used much more often than the other two methods, and studying it should be at the highest priority.

The following three chapters deal with properties of objects that are most naturally viewed as graphs: These chapters consider three models that differ in the way that graphs are represented (and by the definition of relative distance between graphs).

> **Teaching Note:** Chapters 8–10 contain material that may occupy half the duration of a course that is based on the current book. Hence, painful choices will have to be made, unless a decision is made to spend this amount of time on studying the topic of testing graph properties, which is not an unreasonable decision in light of the ubiquitous presence of graphs in computer science. Our own (painful) choices regarding the material to be taught appear in the introductory sections of these chapters.

Chapter 8: Testing Graph Properties in the Dense Graph Model. Following a general introduction to testing graph properties, this chapter focuses on the dense graph model, where graphs are represented by their adjacency matrix (predicate). The highlights of this chapter include

1. A presentation of a natural class of graph properties that can each be tested within query complexity that is polynomial in the reciprocal of the proximity parameter. This class, called general graph partition problems, contains properties such as t-colorability (for any $t \geq 2$) and properties that refer to the density of the max-clique and to the density of the max-cut in a graph.
2. An exposition of the connection of testing (in this model) to Szemerédi's Regularity Lemma. The starting point and pivot of this exposition is the existence of constant-query (one-sided error) proximity-oblivious testers for all subgraph freeness properties.

We conclude this chapter with a taxonomy of known testers, organized according to their query complexity.

Chapter 9: Testing Graph Properties in the Bounded-Degree Graph Model. This chapter is devoted to testing graph properties in the bounded-degree graph model, where graphs are represented by their incidence lists (lumped together in an incidence function). The highlights of this chapter include

1. Upper and lower bounds on the complexity of testing Bipartiteness; specifically, we present a $\text{poly}(1/\epsilon) \cdot \widetilde{O}(\sqrt{k})$-time tester, and an $\Omega(\sqrt{k})$ lower bound on the query complexity of any tester for Bipartiteness.
2. A quasi-$\text{poly}(1/\epsilon)$-time tester for Planarity. The result extends to testing any minor-closed property (i.e., a graph property that is preserved under the omission of edges and vertices and under edge contraction).

We conclude this chapter with a taxonomy of known testers, organized according to their query complexity.

Chapter 10: Testing Graph Properties in the General Graph Model. This chapter is devoted to testing graph properties in the general graph model, where graphs are inspected via incidence and adjacency queries, and distances between graphs are normalized by their actual size (i.e., actual number of edges). The highlights of this chapter include

1. Demonstrating the derivation of testers for this model from testers for the bounded-degree graph model

2. Studying the tasks of estimating the number of edges in a graph and sampling edges uniformly at random

We conclude this chapter with some reflections regarding the three models of testing graph properties.

> **Teaching Note:** Although it is possible to study Chapter 10 without first studying Chapter 9, we strongly recommend not doing so. A basic familiarity with the bounded-degree graph model and some of the results regarding it will greatly facilitate the study of the general graph model. See further comments at the beginning of Chapter 10.

The last three chapters explore topics that are related to but significantly different from the topics studied in the previous chapters. Chapter 11 is most different in flavor, since it refers to a totally different type of objects and to a very different model of testing such objects. Chapter 13 seems more in line with the previous chapters, but it differs from them in considering objects that are artificially designed so to offer superfast testing. The topics explored in Chapter 12 are closest in spirit to those explored in previous chapters (and, indeed, some of these topics were mentioned in Section 1.3.2).

> **Teaching Note:** Chapter 11 can be read without reading any prior chapter (i.e., not even Sections 1.3.1 and 1.3.3), but some perspectives will be lost when doing so. Given the different flavor of this chapter, we recommend placing it at the end of a course based on the current book.

Chapter 11: Testing Properties of Distributions. This chapter provides an introduction to the study of testing properties of distributions, where the tester obtains samples of an unknown distribution (resp., samples from several unknown distributions) and is required to determine whether the distribution (resp., the tuple of distributions) has some predetermined property. We focus on the problems of testing whether an unknown distribution equals a fixed distribution and of testing equality between two unknown distributions. Our presentation is based on reductions from the general cases to some seemingly easier special cases. In addition, we also provide a brief survey of general results.

> **Teaching Note:** Chapters 12 and 13 are intended for optional independent reading. They both have more of the flavor of a survey than of a textbook. Chapter 12 follows up on topics that were mentioned briefly in prior chapters (including in Section 1.3.2). Chapter 13 focuses on topics that are somewhat related to property testing, while building on results presented in Chapters 2 and 3 (but doing so in a self-contained manner). Indeed, Chapter 13 can be read independently of the other chapters.

Chapter 12: Ramifications and Related Topics. We briefly review a few ramifications of the notion of property testers as well as related topics. The list includes tolerant testing and distance approximation; testing in the presence of additional promises on the input; sample-based testers; testing with respect to other distance measures; local computation algorithms; and noninteractive proofs of proximity (MAPs). The different sections of this chapter can be read independently of one another.

Chapter 13: Locally Testable Codes and Proofs. We survey known results regarding locally testable codes and locally testable proofs (known as PCPs). Local testability refers to approximately testing large objects based on a very small number of probes, each retrieving a single bit in the representation of the object. This yields superfast approximate testing of the corresponding property (i.e., being a codeword or being a valid proof). In terms of property testing, locally testable codes are error-correcting codes such that the property of being a codeword can be tested within low query complexity. As for locally testable proofs (PCPs), these can be viewed as massively parameterized properties that are testable within low query complexity such that the parameterized property is nonempty if and only if the corresponding parameter is in a predetermined set (of "valid statements"). Our first priority is minimizing the number of probes, and we focus on the case that this number is a constant. In this case (of a constant number of probes), we aim at minimizing the length of the constructs. That is, we seek locally testable codes and proofs of short length.

Appendix A: Probabilistic Preliminaries. This appendix presents background from probability theory, which is used extensively throughout the book. This background and preliminaries include conventions regarding random variables, basic notions and facts, and three useful probabilistic inequalities (i.e., Markov's Inequality, Chebyshev's Inequality, and Chernoff Bound).

Appendix B: A Mini-Compendium of General Results. This appendix restates several general results that were presented in this book, including deriving standard testers from POTs; positive results on the algebra of property testing; reducing testing to learning; the randomness complexity of testers; archetypical application of self-correction; and the effect of local reductions.

Appendix C: An Index of Specific Results. This appendix provides an index of all results regarding specific properties that were presented in this book. For each property, we provide only references to the sections (or statements) in which relevant results can be found.

Notation

Standard Notation

Sets and Sequences. We often consider the set $[n] = \{1, ..., n\}$, where n is a natural number. Likewise, we often consider the set

$$\Sigma^\ell = \{\sigma_1 \cdots \sigma_\ell : \sigma_1, ..., \sigma_\ell \in \Sigma\}$$

of all ℓ-long sequences over Σ, where often $\Sigma = \{0, 1\}$. For $x \in \Sigma^\ell$ and $i \in [\ell]$, we let x_i denote the ith symbol of x, and for $I = \{i_1, ..., i_t\} \subseteq [\ell]$ such that $i_1 < \cdots < i_t$, we let $x_I = x_{i_1} \cdots x_{i_t} \in \Sigma^t$.

For a set S and a natural number $t \leq |S|$, we denote by $\binom{S}{t}$ the set of all t-subsets of S; that is, $\binom{S}{t} = \{S' \subseteq S : |S'| = t\}$. Needless to say, the size of $\binom{S}{t}$ equals $\binom{|S|}{t}$. Likewise, the set of all subsets of S is denoted 2^S; that is, $2^S = \bigcup_{t \geq 0} \binom{S}{t}$, where $\binom{S}{0} = \emptyset$.

Graphs. Unless explicitly stated differently, a graph $G = (V, E)$, consists of a pair of finite sets V and $E \subseteq \binom{V}{2}$. The elements of V are called vertices, and the elements of E are called edges. (That is, we consider simple (undirected) graphs with no self-loops and no parallel edges.)[2] Each edge consists of a pair of vertices, called its endpoints.

Integrality Issues. We often ignore integrality issues, treating values such as $\log n$ and $\sqrt{n}$ as if they were integers. In such cases, rounding in an adequate manner will do.

Probabilistic Notation. We denote the probability that $\chi(e)$ holds when e is distributed according to D by $\mathbf{Pr}_{e \sim D}[\chi(e)]$. When D is the uniform distribution over a set S, we shall write $\mathbf{Pr}_{e \in S}[\chi(e)]$ instead of $\mathbf{Pr}_{e \sim D}[\chi(e)]$. Often, when S or D is understood from the context, we just omit it from the notation and write $\mathbf{Pr}_e[\chi(e)]$. For more probabilistic preliminaries, see Appendix A.

Asymptotic Notation. We use standard notation such as O, Ω, Θ, and their tilde versions. By writing $f(n) = O(g(n))$ (resp. $f(n) = \Omega(g(n))$) we mean that there exists a positive constant c such that $f(n) \leq c \cdot g(n)$ (resp., $f(n) \geq c \cdot g(n)$) holds for all $n \in \mathbb{N}$. Likewise, $f(n) = \widetilde{O}(g(n))$ (resp. $f(n) = \widetilde{\Omega}(g(n))$) means that there exists a positive

---

[2] In contrast, one may consider (nonsimple) graphs in which E is a multiset of edges, and each edge is a multiset of size 2. An edge that consists of two copies of the same vertex is called a self-loop, and identical edges are called parallel.

constant c such that $f(n) \leq c \cdot (\log n)^c \cdot g(n)$ (resp., $f(n) \geq c \cdot g(n)/(\log n)^{1/c}$) holds for all $n \in \mathbb{N}$. We write $f(n) = \tilde{\Theta}(g(n))$ (resp., $f(n) = \tilde{\Theta}(g(n))$) if both $f(n) = \tilde{O}(g(n))$ and $f(n) = \tilde{\Omega}(g(n))$ (resp., $f(n) = \tilde{O}(g(n))$ and $f(n) = \tilde{\Omega}(g(n))$) hold.

Common Abbreviations. We often use the following abbreviations:

e.g. for example
i.e. that is
iff if and only if
l.h.s. left hand side
r.h.s. right hand side
s.t. such that
w.h.p. with high probability
w.l.o.g. without loss of generality
w.r.t. with respect to
w.v.h.p. with very high probability

Typically, w.h.p. means with probability at least $1 - c$ for an arbitrary small constant $c > 0$, and w.v.h.p. means with probability at least $1 - \eta$ for a fastly decreasing function η in a relevant parameter.

Specific Notation Used Extensively

The following notions are redefined several times in this book (see, e.g., Sections 1.2.2 and 1.6).

The Notion of Distance. For $x, y \in \Sigma^n$, we consider their relative Hamming distance, denoted $\delta(x, y) \overset{\text{def}}{=} |\{i \in [n] : x_i \neq y_i\}|/n$. For $x \in \Sigma^n$ and $S \subseteq \Sigma^n$, we denote by $\delta_S(x)$ the relative Hamming distance of x from S; that is, $\delta_S(x)$ is the minimum, taken over all $z \in S \cap \{0, 1\}^{|x|}$, of $\delta(x, z)$. (If $S = \emptyset$, then $\delta_S(x) = \infty$.) We say that x is ϵ-far from S (resp., ϵ-close to S) if $\delta_S(x) > \epsilon$ (resp., $\delta_S(x) \leq \epsilon$). The same notations are used for functions from $[n]$ to Σ; that is, for $f, g : [n] \to \Sigma$, we let $\delta(f, g) \overset{\text{def}}{=} |\{i \in [n] : f(i) \neq g(i)\}|/n$.

Acknowledgments

We wish to thank Noga Alon, Clement Canonne, Constantinos Daskalakis, Ilias Diakonikolas, Zeev Dvir, Shafi Goldwasser, Robi Krauthgamer, Or Meir, Krzysztof Onak, Sofya Raskhodnikova, Dana Ron, Ronitt Rubinfeld, Madhu Sudan, and Theertha Suresh for offering advice regarding specific topics.

We also benefitted from comments on parts of the text offered by Ben Berger, Clement Canonne, Tom Gur, Yael Hitron, Nikolay Karpov, Akash Kumar, Inbal Livni, and Roei Tell. Special thanks to Clement and Roei, who proofread significant portions of prior versions.

The Main Themes: Approximate Decision and Sublinear Complexity

Summary: In this chapter, we introduce, discuss, and illustrate the conceptual framework of property testing, emphasizing the themes of *approximate decision* and *sublinear complexity*. In particular, we discuss the key role of representation, point out the focus on properties that are not fully symmetric, present the definitions of (standard) testers and of proximity-oblivious testers (POTs), and make some general observations regarding POTs, testing, and learning. To begin, we consider the potential benefits of testing (i.e., approximate decisions of sublinear complexity).

Section 1.1 provides a very brief introduction to property testing, sketching its basic definition and providing an overview of its flavor and potential benefits. The pace here is fast and sketchy, unlike that in the rest of this chapter. The technical material is presented in Sections 1.2 and 1.3, which constitutes the main part of this chapter. A more detailed account of the organization of this part is provided in Section 1.1.4.

1.1. Introduction

Big data is a broad term for data sets so large or complex that traditional data processing applications are inadequate.

Wikipedia entry on *Big Data*, February 17, 2016

Everyone talks of big data. Of course, the issue is making good use of large amounts of data, which requires analyzing it. But such an analysis may mean various things. At one extreme, it may mean locating tiny and possibly rare (but valuable) pieces of information. At the other extreme, it may means detecting global structures or estimating global parameters of the data as a whole.

It is the latter meaning that applies to the field of *property testing*. This field is concerned with the analysis of global features of the data, such as determining whether the data as a whole have some global property or estimating some global parameter of their structure. The focus is on properties and parameters that go beyond simple statistics that refer to the frequency of the occurrence of various local patterns. This is not to suggest that such simple statistics are not of value, but rather that not everything of interest can be reduced to them.

In general, the data are a set of records (or items) that may be interrelated in various ways. The contents and meaning of the data may be reflected not only in the individual items (or records), but also in the relations between them. In such a case, important aspects of the data are reflected in the structural relations between their items. In particular, the indication of which pairs of items are related may be such an aspect, and it can be modeled as a graph. Needless to say, this captures only one aspect of the data, but this aspect could be very significant. When such a model is used, checking whether the graph that arises has certain structural properties is of natural interest. Indeed, testing natural properties of huge graphs or estimating various parameters of such graphs is part of the agenda of *property testing*. More generally, *property testing* is concerned with testing structural properties of huge objects or estimating such structural parameters.

Important as it is, big data is not the only source of huge objects that are considered by *property testing*. Other types of huge objects are the functions that are computed by various programs or other computing devices. We stress that these objects do not appear in explicit form in reality; they are merely defined implicitly (and concisely) by these devices.

Our repeated reference to the huge size of the objects is meant to emphasize a salient feature of *property testing*. We refer to the fact that *property testing* seeks superfast algorithms that refrain from obtaining the full explicit description of the object. These algorithms inspect relatively small portions of the object and pass judgment based on such an inspection.

The reader may wonder how it is possible to say anything meaningful about an object without looking at all of it. On further thought, however, one may note that we are aware of such cases: All frequency statistics are of this form. It is worthwhile to highlight two features of these statistics: They are *approximate* rather than exact, and they are generated based on *random choices*. Indeed, a notion of approximation and the use of randomness are pivotal to *property testing*. (Yet, we stress again that property testing goes beyond frequency statistics.)

1.1.1. Property Testing at a Glance

As will be detailed in this chapter, property testing is primarily concerned with *superfact approximate decisions*, where the task is distinguishing between objects having a predetermined property and objects that are "far" from having this property. Related tasks such as estimating structural parameters of such objects or finding certain huge substructures inside them are also addressed. In all cases, the algorithms sought are of sublinear complexity (i.e., complexity that is sublinear in the size of the object), and in particular they inspect only relatively small portions of the object.

Typically, objects are modeled by functions, and distance between functions is measured as the fraction of the domain on which the functions differ. An object is considered far from having the property if its distance from any object that has the property exceeds a given *proximity parameter*. We consider (randomized) algorithms that may query the function at arguments of their choice, where this modeling allows for discussing algorithms that inspect only part of their input. In fact, our focus is on such algorithms, which make approximate decisions regarding their input (i.e., whether it has some property or is far from having it).

Cases in which such superfact approximate decisions are possible include testing properties of functions such as being a low-degree polynomial, being monotone, and depending on a specified number of attributes; testing properties of graphs such as being bipartite and triangle-free; and testing properties of visual images or geometric objects such as being well-clustered and being a convex body.

In the next section, we review the potential benefits of property testers. But before doing so, we wish to stress that, as with any theoretical research, the value of research in property testing is *not confined* to the actual use of the suggested algorithms (i.e., the resulting testers). The development and study of conceptual frameworks, let alone the development of algorithmic design and analysis techniques, is more important for the theory of computation at large as well as for computer practice. Although the impact on practice is typically hard to trace, the relations between property testing and the rest of the theory of computing are evident (and will be pointed out in relevant parts of this book).

1.1.2. On the Potential Benefits of Property Testers

Property testing is associated with approximate decision algorithms that run in sublinear time or at least make a sublinear number of queries to their input. The benefit of sublinear complexity is significant when the input is huge, but this benefit comes at the cost of having an approximate decision rather than an exact one. The question addressed in this section is whether (or rather when can) this *trading of accuracy for efficiency* be worthwhile. The answer is application dependent rather than universal: We discuss several different general settings in which such a trade-off is worthwhile.

It is infeasible to recover the object fully. This may be the case either because linear time is infeasible for the huge objects being considered in the application or because probes to the object are too expensive to allow inspecting all of it. In such settings, there is no choice but to use algorithms of sublinear query complexity and settle for whatever they can provide (of course, the more, the better).

Objects either have the property or are far from having it. Here we refer to applications in which we know *a priori* that the objects that we will encounter either have the property or are far from any object having the property. Intuitively, in such a case, objects are either perfect (i.e., have the property) or are very bad (i.e., far from it). In this case, we should not care about inputs that are neither in the set nor far from it, because such inputs correspond to objects that we are unlikely to encounter.

Objects that are close to having the property are good enough. Here we refer to applications in which the utility of objects that are close to having the property is almost as valuable as the utility of objects that have the property. Alternatively, it may be possible to modify the object at a cost related to its distance from having the property. In such cases, we may not care too much about ruling that the object has the property whereas in reality the object is only close to having this property.[1]

Testing as a preliminary step before deciding. Here we refer to the possibility of using the approximate decision procedure as a preliminary step, and using the more costly exact decision procedure only if the preliminary step was completed successfully (i.e.,

---

[1] **Advanced comment:** One may argue that in such cases, "tolerant testing" (see Section 1.3.2) is even more adequate. Yet, tolerant testing may be harder than standard testing (cf. [109]).

the approximate decider accepted the input). This is advantageous provided that objects that are far from having the property are not very rare, since we definitely save resources when rejecting such objects based on the preliminary step.

Testing as a preliminary step before reconstructing. This refers to settings in which we wish to recover the object fully, either by reading all of it or by running a learning algorithm, but we wish to do so only if the object has the property. Hence, before invoking the reconstruction procedure, we want to (approximately) decide whether the object has the property. (In the case of reconstruction by a learning algorithm, this makes sense only if the approximate decision procedure is more efficient than the learning algorithm.) Again, using the approximate decision procedure is advantageous provided that objects that are far from having the property are not very rare.

1.1.3. On the Flavor of Property Testing Research

Property testing seems to stand between algorithmic research and complexity theory. While the field's primary goal is the design of certain type of algorithms (i.e., ones of sub-linear complexity) for certain type of problems (i.e., approximate decision), it often needs to determine the limits of such algorithms, which is a question of lower bounds (having a complexity theoretic flavor). Furthermore, historically, property testing was associated with the study of Probabilistically Checkable Proofs (PCPs), and some connections do exist between the two areas, but property testing is not confined to PCPs (and/or to the study of "locally testable codes" [see Chapter 13]).

In addition to standing in between algorithmic research and complexity theory, the results of property testing have a flavor that makes them different from the mainstream results in both areas. Its positive results are not perceived as mainstream algorithmic research and its negative results are not perceived as mainstream complexity theory. In both cases, the specific flavor of property testing (i.e., approximate decision) makes its results stand out. But property testing is not the only research area that has this fate: The same can be said of machine learning and distributed computing, to mention just two examples.

One additional characteristic of property testing is that its positive results tend to be established by simple algorithms that are supported by a complex analysis. The simplic-ity of these algorithms has met a lack of respect among a few researchers, but this is a fundamental mistake on their part. The simplicity of algorithms is a virtue if one really considers using them, whereas the complexity of their analysis has no cost in terms of their applicability. Hence, simple algorithms that require a complex analysis are actually the greatest achievement that algorithmic research could hope for.

Like algorithmic research, property testing tends to split according to the "area" of the property and the "type" of objects being considered (i.e., the natural perception of the object). Indeed, the organization of the current book reflects this split, where Chapters 2–6 focus on (objects that are viewed as) functions and Chapters 8–10 focus on (objects that are viewed as) graphs. Furthermore, within the world of functions, one may distinguish types corresponding to the structure of the domain on which the function is defined (e.g., a group, a vector space, or a Boolean hypercube). The structure of the domain is often reflected by the invariances that are satisfied by the properties that one considers (e.g., affine invariance, closure under graph isomorphism, etc.). Still, conceptual frameworks, techniques, ideas, and inspiration do cross the borders between the parts of the foregoing splits.

Property testing has a clear potential for practical applications, although it seems not to have materialized so far. The most begging applications are to the practice in areas such as machine learning, compressed sensing, computer vision, statistics, and privacy preserving data analysis. To provide some illustration to this potential, we mention the experimental search-and-cluster engine [77], which is based on [177], which in turn uses [123, 98], which are informed by [121, 140]. (Indeed, a nondirect line of influence should be expected in the transportation of theoretical research to practice.) Applications that are more directly inspired by [140] are reported in [209, 163]. We also mention the connection between the study of testing visual images [230, 243] and finding matches between images [193, 194]. Lastly, we mention that research in the somewhat related area of "streaming algorithms" [15] has witnessed more interaction with practice (including computer networks and databases [213], compressed sensing (e.g., [80]), and numerical linear algebra [270]).

1.1.4. Organization and Some Notations

As stated previously, we view property testing as concerned primarily with approximate decisions, a notion discussed in Section 1.2.2. (For perspective, we recall in Section 1.2.1 the notion of approximate search problems.) Next, in Section 1.2.3, we discuss the second key feature of property testing – its focus on sublinear complexity. Then, in Section 1.2.4, we highlight yet another feature of property testing – its focus on properties that are not fully symmetric (i.e., are not invariant under arbitrary reordering of the sequence of values that represent the object). In general, the relation between objects and their representation is crucial in the context of property testing, and this issue is discussed in Section 1.2.5.

The core of this chapter is presented in Section 1.3. The basic notions, definitions, and goals of property testing are presented in Section 1.3.1 and used extensively throughout the entire book (with very few exceptions). In contrast, the ramifications discussed in Section 1.3.2 are used lightly (if at all), and ditto for the general observations made in Sections 1.3.4 and 1.3.5 (which refer to the "algebra of property testing" and to the testing-by-learning connection, respectively). In Section 1.3.3, we present another notion that is used extensively – that of a proximity-oblivious tester (POT).

Historical perspectives, suggestions for further reading, and exercises are provided in Sections 1.4 and 1.5. Finally, in Section 1.6 we reiterate some of issues discussed in the current chapter, in light of their importance to the rest of the book.

Some Notation. We shall be using the following *standard notations*:

- For $n \in \mathbb{N}$, we let $[n] \stackrel{\text{def}}{=} \{1, \ldots, n\}$.
- For $x \in \{0, 1\}^*$, we let $|x|$ denote the length of x and let x_i denote the ith bit of x; that is, if $n = |x|$, then $x = x_1 \cdots x_n$ such that $x_i \in \{0, 1\}$ for every $i \in [n]$.
- The Hamming weight of a string x, denoted $\text{wt}(x)$, is the number of locations that hold the value one; that is,

$$\text{wt}(x) = |\{i \in [|x|] : x_i = 1\}| = \sum_{i=1}^{|x|} x_i.$$

> **Teaching Note:** Section 1.2 provides a paced presentation of the mindframe that underlies property testing, illustrating key issues such as approximate decision and sublinear complexity. In case of time constraints, one can skip this section and go directly to Sections 1.3.1 and 1.3.3. Still, we recommend taking the slower pace and covering also Sections 1.3.4 and 1.3.5, although this may mean spending more than a single lecture on the current chapter. The ramifications discussed in Section 1.3.2 are discussed in greater detail in Chapter 12, but we believe that an early detour into these variants provides a good perspective on the main definition presented in Section 1.3.1 (while acknowledging that this may be too much for some readers).

1.2. Approximate Decisions

The notion of approximation is well known in the context of optimization problems, which are a special type of search problems. We start by recalling these notions, for the purpose of providing a wide perspective.

1.2.1. A Detour: Approximate Search Problems

Recall that search problems are defined in terms of binary relations, and consist of finding a "valid solution" y to a given instance x, where y is a valid solution to x if (x, y) satisfies the binary relation associated with the problem. Letting $R \subseteq \{0, 1\}^* \times \{0, 1\}^*$ denote such a relation, we say that y is a solution to x if $(x, y) \in R$, and the set of solutions for the instance x is denoted $R(x) \overset{\text{def}}{=} \{y : (x, y) \in R\}$. Hence, given x, the task is to find $y \in R(x)$, provided that $R(x) \neq \emptyset$. (The computation of a function corresponds to the special case in which all these sets are singletons.)

In optimization problems, the valid solutions are assigned a value (or a cost), captured by a function $v : \{0, 1\}^* \to \mathbb{R}$, and one is asked to find a solution of maximum value (resp., minimum cost); that is, given x, the task is to find $y \in R(x)$ such that $v(y) = \max_{z \in R(x)}\{v(z)\}$ (resp., $v(y) = \min_{z \in R(x)}\{v(z)\}$).[2]

A corresponding approximation problem is defined as finding a solution having value (resp., cost) close to the optimum; that is, given x the task is to find $y \in R(x)$ such that $v(y)$ is "close" to $\max_{z \in R(x)}\{v(z)\}$ (resp., to $\min_{z \in R(x)}\{v(z)\}$). One may also talk about the estimation problem, in which the task is to approximate the value of the optimal solution (rather than actually finding a solution that obtains that value).

The point we wish to make here is that, once a function v and a proximity parameter are fixed, *it is clear what one means by seeking an approximation solution for a search problem*. But, what do we mean when we talk about approximate decision problems?

1.2.2. Property Testing: Approximate Decision Problems

Indeed, *what can an approximate decision problem possibly mean?*

Unfortunately, there is no *decisive answer* to such questions; one can only propose an answer and articulate its natural appeal. Indeed, we believe that a natural notion of

---

[2]**Advanced comment:** Greater flexibility is achieved by allowing the value (resp., cost) to depend also on the instance; that is, use $v(x, y)$ rather than $v(y)$. Actually, this does not buy any additional generality, because we can always augment the solution y by the instance x and use $v'((y, x)) = v(x, y)$. On the other hand, using the more flexible formulation, one can get rid of the relation R by letting $v(x, y) = -\infty$ (resp., $v(x, y) = \infty$) if $(x, y) \notin R$.

approximate decision (or a natural relaxation of the decision problem) is obtained by ignoring "borderline" cases, which are captured by inputs that are close to the set but do not reside in it. That is, instead of asking whether an input x is in the set S, we consider the problem of distinguishing between the case that $x \in S$ and that of x being "far" from S. Hence, we consider a promise problem (cf. [105, 129] or [131, Sec. 2.4.1]), in which the YES-instances are the elements of S and the NO-instances are "far" from S.

Of course, we need to clarify what "far" means. To this end, we fix a metric, which will be the (relative) Hamming distance, and introduce a proximity parameter, denoted ϵ. Specifically, letting $\delta(x, z) = |\{i \in [|x|] : x_i \neq z_i\}|/|x|$ if $|x| = |z|$ and $\delta(x, z) = \infty$ otherwise, we define the distance of $x \in \{0, 1\}^*$ from S as $\delta_S(x) \stackrel{\text{def}}{=} \min_{z \in S}\{\delta(x, z)\}$. Now, for a fixed value of $\epsilon > 0$, the foregoing promise problem consists of distinguishing S from $\{x : \delta_S(x) > \epsilon\}$, which means that inputs in $\{x : 0 < \delta_S(x) \leq \epsilon\}$ are ignored.

Notation. Throughout the text, unless explicitly said differently, ϵ will denote a proximity parameter, which determines what is considered far. We shall say that x is ϵ-far from S if $\delta_S(x) > \epsilon$, and otherwise (i.e., when $\delta_S(x) \leq \epsilon$) we shall say that x is ϵ-close to S. Recall that $\delta_S(x)$ denotes the relative Hamming distance of x from S; that is, $\delta_S(x)$ is the minimum, taken over all $z \in S \cap \{0, 1\}^{|x|}$, of $|\{i \in [|x|] : x_i \neq z_i\}|/|x|$.

Lastly, we note that the set S will be associated with the property of being in it, which for simplicity will also be referred to as the property S. Approximate decision will be later called property testing; that is, *approximate decision for a set S corresponds to testing the property S*.

1.2.3. Property Testing: Sublinear Complexity

But *why did we relax standard decision problems into approximate decision problems?* The answer is that, as in the case of approximate search problems, this is done in order to allow for more efficient algorithms.

This answer is clear enough when the best known (or best possible) decision procedure requires more than linear time, let alone when the original decision problem is NP-Hard. But property testing deals also with properties that have linear-time algorithms. In these cases as well as in the former cases, the relaxation to approximate decision suggests the possibility of *sublinear-time algorithms*, that is, algorithms that do not even read their entire input. Such algorithms are particularly beneficial when the input is huge (see Section 1.1.2).

The latter suggestion requires a clarification. Talking about algorithms that do not read their entire input calls for a model of computation in which the algorithms have *direct access* to bits of the input. Unlike in complexity theory, such a model is quite common in algorithmic research: It is the standard RAM model. (For sake of abstraction, we will actually prefer to use the model of oracle machines, while viewing the oracle as the input device.)

Except in degenerate cases (in which the decision problem is essentially insensitive to almost all the bits in the input), the relaxation to an approximate decision seems necessary to avoid the reading of the entire input. For example, if S is the set of strings having even parity, then an exact decision procedure must read all the bits of the input (since flipping a single bit will change the decision), but the approximate decision problem is trivial (since each n-bit string is $1/n$-close to S). A more interesting case is presented next.

The Case of Majority**.** Let $\text{MAJ} = \{x : \sum_{i=1}^{|x|} x_i > |x|/2\}$. We shall show that the corresponding approximate decision problem can be solved by a (randomized) poly$(1/\epsilon)$-time algorithm (see Proposition 1.1), whereas no sublinear-time (randomized) algorithm can solve the corresponding (exact) decision problem (see Proposition 1.2). We shall also show that randomness is essential for the positive result (see Proposition 1.3).

> **Proposition 1.1** (A fast approximate decision procedure for MAJ): *There exists a randomized $O(1/\epsilon^2)$-time algorithm that decides whether x is in MAJ or is ϵ-far from MAJ.*

As usual in the context of randomized algorithms, deciding means outputting the correct answer with probability at least $2/3$.

> **Proof:** The algorithm queries the input x at $m = O(1/\epsilon^2)$ uniformly and independently distributed locations, denoted $i_1, \ldots, i_m$, and accepts if and only if the average value of these bits (i.e., $\sum_{j \in [m]} x_{i_j}/m$) exceeds $(1 - \epsilon)/2$. In the analysis, we use the Chernoff Bound (or alternatively Chebyshev's Inequality),[3] which implies that, with probability at least $2/3$, the average of the sample is within $\epsilon/2$ of the actual average; that is,
>
> $$\mathbf{Pr}_{i_1, \ldots, i_m \in [|x|]}\left[\left|\frac{\sum_{j \in [m]} x_{i_j}}{m} - \frac{\sum_{i=1}^{|x|} x_i}{|x|}\right| \leq \epsilon/2\right] \geq 2/3. \tag{1.1}$$
>
> We stress that Eq. (1.1) holds since $m = \Omega(1/\epsilon^2)$. It follows that the algorithm accepts each $x \in \text{MAJ}$ with probability at least $2/3$, since in this case $\sum_{i=1}^{|x|} x_i > |x|/2$. Likewise, it rejects each x that is ϵ-far from MAJ with probability at least $2/3$, since in this case $\sum_{i=1}^{|x|} x_i \leq (0.5 - \epsilon) \cdot |x|$. ∎

Teaching Note: We assume that the reader is comfortable with the assertion captured by Eq. (1.1); that is, the reader should find Exercise 1.1 easy to solve. If this is not the case, then we advise the reader to become comfortable with such assertions and arguments before continuing reading. Appendix A should suffice for readers who have basic familiarity with probability theory. Likewise, we assume that the reader is comfortable with the notion of a randomized algorithm; basic familiarity based on [131, Sec. 6.1] or any part of [212] should suffice.

> **Proposition 1.2** (Lower bound on decision procedures for MAJ): *Any randomized algorithm that exactly decides membership in MAJ must make $\Omega(n)$ queries, where n is the length of the input.*

Teaching Note: The following proof may be harder to follow than all other proofs in this chapter, with the exception of the proof of Proposition 1.11, which is also a lower bound. Some readers may prefer to skip these proofs at the current time, and return to them at a later time (e.g., after reading Chapter 7). We prefer to keep the proofs in place, but warn readers not to stall at them.

---

[3] **Advanced comment:** Indeed, both inequalities are essentially equivalent when one seeks constant error probability. See discussion in Appendix A.4.

Proof: For every $n \in \mathbb{N}$, we consider two probability distributions: A distribution X_n that is uniform over n-bit strings having Hamming weight $\lfloor n/2 \rfloor + 1$, and a distribution Z_n that is uniform over n-bit strings having Hamming weight $\lfloor n/2 \rfloor$. Hence, $\mathbf{Pr}[X_n \in \mathrm{MAJ}] = 1$ and $\mathbf{Pr}[Z_n \in \mathrm{MAJ}] = 0$. However, as shown in Claim 1.2.1, a randomized algorithm that queries either X_n or Z_n at $o(n)$ locations cannot distinguish these two cases with a probabilistic gap that exceeds $o(1)$, and hence must be wrong in one of the two cases.

(Note that the randomized decision procedure must be correct on each input. The proof technique employed here proceeds by showing that any "low-complexity" procedure fails even in the potentially simpler task of distinguishing between some distribution of YES-instances and some distribution of NO-instances. Failing to distinguish these two distributions implies that the procedure errs with too large probability on at least one of these two distributions, which in turn implies that there exists at least one input on which the procedure errs with too large probability.)

Claim 1.2.1 (Indistinguishability claim): *Let A be an algorithm that queries its n-bit long input at q locations. Then, $|\mathbf{Pr}[A(X_n) = 1] - \mathbf{Pr}[A(Z_n) = 1]| \leq q/n$.*

We stress that the claim holds even if the algorithm is randomized and selects its queries adaptively (based on answers to prior queries).

Proof: It is instructive to view X_n as generated by the following random process: First $i \in [n]$ is selected uniformly, then $y \in \{0, 1\}^n$ is selected uniformly among the strings of Hamming weight $\lfloor n/2 \rfloor$ that have 0 in position i, and finally X_n is set to $y \oplus 0^{i-1}10^{n-i}$. Likewise, Z_n is generated by letting $Z_n \leftarrow y$. (This is indeed a complicated way to present these random variables, but it greatly facilitates the following analysis.)[4] Now, observe that, as long as A does not query location i, it behaves in exactly the same way on X_n and Z_n, since in both cases it effectively queries the same random y. (Furthermore, conditioned on not having queried i so far, the distribution of i is uniform over all unqueried locations.) The claim follows. ∎

By the indistinguishability claim (Claim 1.2.1), if algorithm A queries its n-bit long input on less than $n/3$ locations, then $|\mathbf{Pr}[A(X_n) = 1] - \mathbf{Pr}[A(Z_n) = 1]| < 1/3$. Hence, either $\mathbf{Pr}[A(X_n) = 1] < 2/3$, which implies that A errs (w.p. greater than $1/3$) on some $x \in \mathrm{MAJ}$, or $\mathbf{Pr}[A(Z_n) = 1] > 1/3$, which implies that A errs (w.p. greater than $1/3$) on some $z \notin \mathrm{MAJ}$. The proposition follows. ∎

Proposition 1.3 (Randomization is essential for Proposition 1.1): *Any deterministic algorithm that distinguishes between inputs in* MAJ *and inputs that are 0.5-far from* MAJ *must make at least $n/2$ queries, where n is the length of the input.*

Proof: Fixing an arbitrary *deterministic* algorithm A that makes $q < n/2$ queries, we shall show that if A accepts each input in MAJ, then it also accepts the all-zero

---

[4] See Exercise 1.2 for details regarding the equivalence of the alternative and original definitions of X_n (resp., of Z_n).

string, which is 0.5-far from MAJ. It will follow that A fails to distinguish between some inputs in MAJ and some inputs that are 0.5-far from MAJ.

Relying on the hypothesis that A is deterministic, we consider the unique execution of A in which all queries of A are answered with 0, and denote the set of queried locations by Q. We now consider two different n-bit long strings that are consistent with these answers. The first string, denoted x, is defined such that $x_j = 1$ if and only if $j \notin Q$, and the second string is $z = 0^n$. Note that $x \in$ MAJ (since $\mathrm{wt}(x) = n - q > n/2$), whereas z is 0.5-far from MAJ. However, A behaves identically on x and z, since in both cases it obtains the answer 0 to each of its queries, which means that $A(x) = 1$ if and only if $A(z) = 1$. Hence, A errs either on x (which is in MAJ) or on z (which is 0.5-far from MAJ). The proposition follows. ∎

Digest. We have seen that sublinear time (in fact constant-time) algorithms for approximate decision problems exist in cases in which exact decision requires linear time. The benefit of the former is significant when the input is huge, although this benefit comes at the cost of having an approximate decision rather than an exact one (and using randomized algorithms rather than deterministic ones).

1.2.4. Symmetries and Invariants

The proof of Proposition 1.1 reflects the well-known practice of using sampling in order to estimate the average value of a function defined over a huge population. The same practice applies to any problem that refers to the statistics of binary values, while totally ignoring the identity of the entities to which these values are assigned. In other words, this refers to symmetric properties (of binary sequences), which are defined as *sets S such that for every $x \in \{0, 1\}^*$ and every permutation π over $[|x|]$ it holds that $x \in S$ if and only if $x_{\pi(1)} \cdots x_{\pi(|x|)} \in S$.*

Theorem 1.4 (Testing symmetric properties of binary sequences): *For every symmetric property* (of binary sequences), S, *there exists a randomized algorithm that makes $O(1/\epsilon^2)$ queries and decides whether x is in S or is ϵ-far from S.*

(The result can be generalized to symmetric properties of sequences over any fixed alphabet.[5] The result does not generalize to sequences over unbounded alphabet. In fact, there exist symmetric properties over unbounded alphabet for which the approximate decision problem requires a linear number of queries (see Exercise 1.3).)

Proof: The key observation is for every n there exists a set (of weights) $W_n \subseteq \{0, 1, \ldots, n\}$ such that for every $x \in \{0, 1\}^n$ it holds that $x \in S$ if and only if $\mathrm{wt}(x) \in W_n$, where $\mathrm{wt}(x) = |\{i \in [n] : x_i \neq 0\}|$. (In the case of MAJ, the set W_n is

---

[5] **Advanced comment:** When generalizing the result to the alphabet $\Sigma = \{0, 1, .., t\}$, consider the set (of "frequency patterns") $F_n \subseteq (\{0, 1, \ldots, n\})^t$ such that for every $x \in \Sigma^n$ it holds that $x \in S$ if and only if $(\#_1(x), \ldots, \#_t(x)) \in F_n$, where $\#_j(x) = |\{i \in [n] : x_i = j\}|$. The generalized tester will approximate each $\#_j(x)$ up to a deviation of $\epsilon/2t$.

$\{\lfloor n/2 \rfloor + 1, \ldots, n\}$.) Hence, deciding whether x is in S or is ϵ-far from S reduces to estimating $\mathrm{wt}(x)$ and comparing it to $W_{|x|}$. Specifically, on input x, the algorithm proceeds as follows:

1. Queries the input x at $m = O(1/\epsilon^2)$ uniformly and independently distributed locations, denoted $i_1, \ldots, i_m$, and computes the value $v = \sum_{j\in[m]} x_{i_j}/m$.
2. Accepts if and only if there exists $w \in W_{|x|}$ such that $|v - (w/|x|)| \le \epsilon/2$.
   Note that this step requires knowledge of $|x|$ (as well as of the set $W_{|x|}$) but no queries to x; its computational complexity depends on the "structure" of $W_{|x|}$ (or, equivalently, on the unary set $S \cap \{1\}^*$).

As in the proof of Proposition 1.1, the analysis of this algorithm reduces to (1) noting that $\mathbf{Pr}[|v - \mathrm{wt}(x)/|x|| \le \epsilon/2] \ge 2/3$, and (2) observing that the distance of x from S (i.e., $\delta_S(x) \cdot |x|$) equals $\min_{w\in W_{|x|}}\{|w - \mathrm{wt}(x)|\}$.[6] ∎

Beyond Symmetric Properties. Theorem 1.4 refers to properties that are defined in terms of the statistics of local patterns in an object (e.g., the frequency of the two bit-values in a string), while totally ignoring the identity of the locations in which these patterns occur (e.g., the location of the bit-values). These properties are symmetric in the sense that they are invariant under *all* permutation of these locations. In contrast, the focus of property testing is on properties that depend on the relationship between the values and the locations in which these values reside (although there are exceptions; see, e.g., [7]). That is, the focus is on asymmetric properties, which are properties that are *not* invariant under *all* permutation of the bit locations, although they may be invariant under some (nontrivial) permutations. In the extreme case the property is not invariant under any nontrivial permutation of the bit-locations; that is, $x \in S$ if and only if $x_{\pi(1)} \cdots x_{\pi(|x|)} \in S$ holds only when π is the identity permutation. This is the case for the "sorted-ness" property discussed next.

We say that a string $x \in \{0, 1\}^*$ is sorted if $x_i \le x_{i+1}$ for every $i \in [|x| - 1]$. Denote the set of sorted n-bit long strings by SORTED_n, and let $\mathrm{SORTED} = \cup_{n\in\mathbb{N}}\mathrm{SORTED}_n$. Although SORTED_n is not invariant under any nontrivial permutation of $[n]$, we present an $O(1/\epsilon)$-time approximate decision procedure for it.

Proposition 1.5 (A fast approximate decision procedure for SORTED): *There exists a randomized $O(\epsilon^{-1})$-time algorithm that decides whether a given string is in SORTED or is ϵ-far from SORTED.*

(The set SORTED can be defined with respect to sequences over any set that is equipped with a total order. This generalization will be considered in Section 4.3. We note that the algorithm presented next does not extend to this general case; see [101, 108].)

---

[6] To see (2), suppose that $z \in S$ satisfies $\delta_S(x) = \delta(x, z)$. Then, letting $n = |x| = |z|$, it holds that $\mathrm{wt}(z) \in W_n$, whereas $|\mathrm{wt}(x) - \mathrm{wt}(z)| \le \delta(x, z) \cdot n$, which implies $\min_{w\in W_n}\{|\mathrm{wt}(x) - w|\} \le \delta_S(x) \cdot n$. On the other hand, for every $x \in \{0, 1\}^n$ and $w \in \{0, 1, \ldots, n\}$, there exists $z \in \{0, 1\}^n$ such that $\mathrm{wt}(z) = w$ and $\delta(z, x) \cdot n = |\mathrm{wt}(z) - \mathrm{wt}(x)|$. Picking $w \in W_n$ that minimizes $|w - \mathrm{wt}(x)|$ and a suitable z (i.e., of weight w such that $\delta(z, x) \cdot n = |\mathrm{wt}(z) - \mathrm{wt}(x)|$), it follows that $\delta_S(x) \cdot n \le \min_{w\in W_n}\{|w - \mathrm{wt}(x)|\}$.

Proof: On input $x \in \{0, 1\}^n$, the algorithm proceeds as follows (assuming both $\epsilon n/2$ and $2/\epsilon$ are integers).

1. For $F = \{i\epsilon n/2 : i \in [2/\epsilon]\} \subseteq [n]$, query x at each $j \in F$.
   Let us denoted the retrieved $|F|$-bit long substring by y; that is, $y = x_{\epsilon n/2} x_{2\epsilon n/2} x_{3\epsilon n/2} \cdots x_n$.
2. Queries x at $m = O(1/\epsilon)$ uniformly and independently distributed locations, denoted $i_1, \ldots, i_m$.
3. Accept if and only if the induced substring is sorted; that is, letting $m' = |F| + m$ and $j_1 \leq j_2 \leq \cdots \leq j_{m'}$ such that $\{j_1, \ldots, j_{m'}\} = F \cup \{i_k : k \in [m]\}$ (as multi-sets), accept if and only if $x_{j_k} \leq x_{j_{k+1}}$ for every $k \in [m' - 1]$.

This algorithm always accepts any $x \in$ SORTED, since any substring of such a sorted x is also sorted. Now, suppose that x is ϵ-far from SORTED$_n$. We consider two cases:

Case 1: The $|F|$-bit long substring y retrieved in Step 1 is not sorted. In this case, the algorithm rejects in Step 3, regardless of the values retrieved in Step 2.

Case 2: The $|F|$-bit long substring y retrieved in Step 1 is sorted. In this case, the $|F|$-bit long substring $y = x_{\epsilon n/2} x_{\epsilon n} x_{3\epsilon n/2} \cdots x_n$, retrieved in Step 1, equals $0^t 1^{|F|-t}$ for some t. Now, if a sorted string z is "consistent" with y (i.e., $z_{i\epsilon n/2} = y_i$ for every $i \in [2/\epsilon]$), then z is determined up to the assignment of the bits residing in the $\epsilon n/2$-bit long interval $[t\epsilon n/2, (t + 1)\epsilon n/2]$, because $z_j = 0$ must hold if $j \leq t\epsilon/2$ whereas $z_j = 1$ must hold if $j \geq (t + 1)\epsilon/2$. But since x is ϵ-far from SORTED, with high probability, Step 2 chooses a location on which x differs from the determined value (i.e., the value as determined for any sorted string). Details follow.

As stated above, in the current case (i.e., sorted y), there exists a $t \in \{0, 1, \ldots, |F|\}$ such that $y = 0^t 1^{|F|-t}$; that is, for $i \in [t]$ it holds that $x_{i\epsilon/2} = 0$, and for $i \in [t + 1, |F|]$ it holds that $x_{i\epsilon/2} = 1$. Note that this determines the "nonviolating" values in locations $[t\epsilon n/2] \cup [(t + 1)\epsilon n/2, n]$; that is, if x is sorted, then $x_j = 0$ for every $j \in [t\epsilon n/2]$ since $x_j \leq x_{t\epsilon n/2} = 0$, and likewise $x_j = 1$ for every $j \in [(t + 1)\epsilon n/2, n]$ since $x_j \geq x_{(t+1)\epsilon n/2} = 1$. Hence, we say that location $j \in [n]$ is violating if either $j \in [t\epsilon n/2]$ and $x_j = 1$ or $j \in [(t + 1)\epsilon n/2, n]$ and $x_j = 0$. Note that any violating location j (which is not in $[t\epsilon n/2, (t + 1)\epsilon n/2]$) causes rejection at Step 3 (if chosen in Step 2).[7] On the other hand, there must be at least $\epsilon n/2$ violating locations, since otherwise x is ϵ-close to SORTED$_n$ (because we can make x sorted by modifying it at locations $V \cup [t\epsilon n/2, (t + 1)\epsilon n/2]$, where V denotes the set of violating locations). It follows that, in this case, the algorithm rejects with probability at least $1 - (1 - \epsilon/2)^m > 2/3$.

The proposition follows. ∎

Invariances (or Symmetries) versus Asymmetries. The properties MAJ and SORTED reside on opposite extremes of the invariance-versus-asymmetry axis: MAJ is invariant under each permutation of the domain $[n]$, which is totally symmetric w.r.t. MAJ, whereas SORTED refers to the domain $[n]$ as a totally ordered set (and admits no invariance except

---

[7] In the first case (i.e., $j \in [t\epsilon n/2]$ and $x_j = 1$) rejection is caused since $x_{t\epsilon n/2} = 0$, whereas in the second case (i.e., $j \in [(t + 1)\epsilon n/2, n]$ and $x_j = 0$) rejection is caused since $x_{(t+1)\epsilon n/2} = 1$.

the trivial one). In subsequent chapters, we shall see properties that are invariant under some nontrivial permutations but not under all permutations; that is, these properties are invariant under a nontrivial subgroup of the group of all permutations of [n]. Examples include low-degree multivariate polynomials (which are invariant under affine transformations of the domain) and graph properties (which are invariant under any relabelling of vertex names).[8]

Indeed, while the role of symmetries in property testing is often highlighted (see, e.g., [257, 143]), here we call attention to the fact that the focus of property testing is on properties that are not fully symmetric (i.e., are somewhat asymmetric). In these typical cases, the testers and their analyses do not reduce to estimating average values via a uniformly distributed sample.

1.2.5. Objects and Representation

So far we have referred to the instances of the (approximate) decision problems as abstract inputs, but it is time to recall that these instances are actually objects and that the inputs *represent* the description of these objects. The distinction between objects and their representation is typically blurred in computer science; nevertheless, this distinction is important. Indeed, reasonable and/or natural representations are always assumed either explicitly or implicitly (see, e.g., [131, Sec. 1.2.1]).[9]

The *specific choice* of a reasonable and/or natural representation becomes crucial when one considers the exact complexity of algorithms (as is common in algorithmic research), rather than their general "ball park" (e.g., being in the complexity class $\mathcal{P}$ or not). The representation is even more crucial in our context (i.e., in the study of property testing). This is the case for two reasons that transcend the standard algorithmic concerns:[10]

1. We shall be interested in sublinear time algorithms, which means that these algorithms query bits in the representation of the object. Needless to say, different representations mean different types of queries, and this difference is crucial when one does not fully recover the object by queries.
2. We shall be interested in the distance between objects (or, actually, in the distance between objects and sets of objects), whereas this distance will be measured in terms of the distance between their representations. In such a case, different representations of objects may yield vastly different distances between the same objects.

---

[8] **Advanced comment:** The role of invariances in property testing has been studied extensively, especially in the domain of algebraic properties (see [257]), but also beyond these (see [143]).

[9] For example, the computational problem that underlies the RSA cryptosystem is phrased as follows: Given integers N, e and y, find x such that $y \equiv x^e \pmod{N}$. This computational problem is believed to be hard when each of these integers is presented by its binary expansion, but it is easy when N is presented by its prime factorization. Likewise, factoring integers is believed to be hard when the integer is presented by its binary expansion, but it is easy when the integer is presented in unary (since this allows the solver to run in time that is exponential in the binary representation of the integer). Indeed, the alternative representations of integers used in these two examples are unnatural representations of the inputs.

[10] One standard concern, which is common to standard algorithmic research, is that complexity should be stated in terms of relevant parameters of the input. Hence, one either states complexities in terms of natural parameters of the object (e.g., the number of vertices and/or edges in a graph) or disallows overly redundant representations when complexities are stated in terms of the representation length.

To illustrate these concerns, suppose that the objects are represented by applying a good error correcting code to their standard representation, where a good error-correcting code is one of constant relative distance and constant rate.[11] (This is indeed a contrived representation, and it is merely used to illustrate the foregoing concerns.) Assuming that the code is efficiently decodable (even just in the case when no error occurs), the difference between this representation and the standard representation will have almost no impact on standard algorithmic research. But the difference between these representations is crucial in our context. On the one hand, under the nonstandard representation (by codewords), every two objects will be far apart, which means that approximate decision (w.r.t. this representation) will collapse to exact decision (w.r.t. the objects). On the other hand, it may be impossible to recover single bits in the standard representation by probing the codeword at a sublinear number of locations.

In light of the foregoing, when considering property testing, we always detail the exact representation of the objects. This representation will be presented either as a sequence, where the queries correspond to locations in the sequence, or as a function with queries corresponding to the elements in its domain. These two presentations are clearly equivalent via the obvious correspondence between sequences and functions (i.e., $x = (x_1, \ldots, x_n) \in \Sigma^n$ correspond to $f : [n] \to \Sigma$ such that $x_i = f(i)$ for every $i \in [n]$).

The choice of which presentation to use is determined either by the natural way we think of the corresponding objects or by mere technical convenience. For example, when discussing m-variate polynomials over a finite field $\mathcal{F}$, it is natural to present them as functions from $\mathcal{F}^m$ to $\mathcal{F}$. On the other hand, when discussing the set of strings that are accepted by a fixed finite-state automaton, it is natural to present each string as a sequence over $\{0, 1\}$.

The presentation of the object as a function is particularly appealing when the object has a concise implicit representation as a computing device (say a Boolean or Arithmetic circuit) that can be invoked on inputs of one's choice. Actually, in such a case, the function computed by this device is the explicit representation of the object. On the other hand, when the object is a huge database that one can query at will, both presentations seem equally appealing.

1.3. Notions, Definitions, Goals, and Basic Observations

Following the property testing literature, we shall refer to approximate decision algorithms by the name "(property) testers." Likewise, we shall talk about "properties" rather than about sets. That is, a tester for property Π is an approximate decision algorithm for the set Π, where in both cases we refer to the same notion of distance and to the same proximity parameter ϵ.

The basic notions, definitions, and goals of property testing are presented in Section 1.3.1, and are used extensively throughout the entire book (with very few exceptions). In contrast, the ramifications discussed in Section 1.3.2 will be lightly used (if at all), and ditto for the general observations made in Sections 1.3.4 and 1.3.5. In Section 1.3.3, we shall present another notion that will be used quite a lot – that of a proximity-oblivious tester (POT).

---

[11] An error-correcting code of relative distance $\gamma \in (0, 1]$ and rate $\rho \in (0, 1]$ is a mapping $C : \{0, 1\}^{\rho n} \to \{0, 1\}^n$ such that every two images of C are at relative Hamming distance at least γ.

> **Teaching Note:** Sections 1.3.1 and 1.3.3 are by far more important than anything else in this chapter, let alone the other parts of Section 1.3. In fact, one may consider skipping Sections 1.3.2, 1.3.4, and 1.3.5 on first reading (or when teaching), and return to them at a later point.

1.3.1. Basics

The properties that we shall focus on are properties of functions, which represent objects that we can probe by querying the function at the corresponding points. The size of the domain of these functions is a key parameter, denoted n. Without loss of generality, we consider the domain $[n]$. The range may also depend on n, and is denoted R_n. Hence, a property is a set Π_n of functions from $[n]$ to R_n.

The Inputs. For the sake of algorithmic uniformity and asymptotic analysis,[12] we let n vary, and consider testers for $\Pi = \cup_{n \in \mathbb{N}} \Pi_n$, while providing these testers with the parameter n as explicit input (i.e., the tester can read this input at no cost). Hence, the same algorithm (tester) is used for all values of n. The *main input* of the tester is a function $f : [n] \to R_n$, which is viewed as an oracle to which the tester has query access; that is, the tester is an oracle machine and f is its oracle (i.e., query $i \in [n]$ to the oracle $f : [n] \to R_n$ is answered with the value $f(i)$). Another explicit input that is given to the tester is the *proximity parameter*, denoted ϵ. Indeed, this means that the tester is uniform across all possible values of $\epsilon > 0$.

These conventions make positive results more useful; in contrast, when presenting (query complexity) lower bounds, we will typically consider also nonuniform algorithms that may depend arbitrarily on n and ϵ. Indeed, in exceptional cases, typically in lower bounds, we may consider testers that operate only for some fixed value of the proximity parameter ϵ. We shall refer to such testers as ϵ-testers.

(In some other cases, for the sake of usefulness, we may wish to have testers that are uniform also across other parameters of the property at stake. For example, when considering properties of graphs of bounded degree, we may wish the same tester to apply to all values of the degree bound, and in this case we provide the tester with the degree bound. Likewise, when we consider properties of functions defined over a finite field, we may provide the tester with a representation of this finite field. (A more acute need for providing such an auxiliary input arises in the context of massively parameterized properties.)[13] For the sake of simplicity, in this chapter we consider the basic case in which no auxiliary inputs of the aforementioned type are given.)

---

[12] By *algorithmic uniformity* we mean presenting a single algorithm for all instances of the problem, rather than presenting a different algorithm per each value of the size parameter n (and/or the proximity parameter ϵ). By *asymptotic analysis* we mean a functional presentation of complexity measures in terms of the size and proximity parameters, while ignoring constant multiplicative factors (i.e., using the $O(\cdot)$ and $\Omega(\cdot)$ notation).

[13] **Advanced comment:** For example, one may consider the property of being isomorphic to an explicitly given graph, which is viewed as a parameter. In this case, one graph is a parameter, while another graph (of the same size) is considered the main input: the tester is given free access to the parameter, and oracle access (for which it is charged) to the main input. See survey on massively parameterized problems [216].

Distance. In accordance with the discussion in Section 1.2, we consider the relative distance between functions, denoted δ. Specifically, for $f, g : [n] \to R_n$, we let $\delta(f, g) = |\{i \in [n] : f(i) \neq g(i)\}|/n$; that is,

$$\delta(f, g) \overset{\text{def}}{=} \mathbf{Pr}_{i \in [n]}[f(i) \neq g(i)], \tag{1.2}$$

where i is uniformly distributed in $[n]$. For $f : [n] \to R_n$ and $\Pi = \cup_{n \in \mathbb{N}} \Pi_n$ such that Π_n contains functions defined over $[n]$, we let $\delta_\Pi(f)$ denote the distance of f from Π_n; that is,

$$\delta_\Pi(f) \overset{\text{def}}{=} \min_{g \in \Pi_n} \{\delta(f, g)\} \tag{1.3}$$

where $\delta_\Pi(f) \overset{\text{def}}{=} \infty$ if $\Pi_n = \emptyset$.

Oracle Machines. We model the testers as probabilistic oracle machines that access their main input via queries. Hence, the output of such a machine, denoted T, when given explicit inputs n and ϵ, and oracle access to $f : [n] \to R_n$, is a random variable, denoted $T^f(n, \epsilon)$. We shall associate the output 1 (resp., 0) with the decision to accept (resp., reject) the main input. We are now ready to present the main definition of property testing.

Definition 1.6 (A tester for property Π): *Let $\Pi = \cup_{n \in \mathbb{N}} \Pi_n$ such that Π_n contains functions of the form $f : [n] \to R_n$. A* tester *for Π is a probabilistic oracle machine, denoted T, that, on input parameters n and ϵ and oracle access to a function $f : [n] \to R_n$, outputs a binary verdict that satisfies the following two conditions.*

1. *T accepts inputs in Π: For every $n \in \mathbb{N}$ and $\epsilon > 0$, and for every $f \in \Pi_n$, it holds that $\mathbf{Pr}[T^f(n, \epsilon) = 1] \geq 2/3$.*
2. *T rejects inputs that are ϵ-far from Π: For every $n \in \mathbb{N}$ and $\epsilon > 0$, and for every $f : [n] \to R_n$ such that $\delta_\Pi(f) > \epsilon$, it holds that $\mathbf{Pr}[T^f(n, \epsilon) = 0] \geq 2/3$.*

If the first condition holds with probability 1 (i.e., $\mathbf{Pr}[T^f(n, \epsilon) = 1] = 1$), then we say that T has one-sided error; *otherwise, we say that T has* two-sided error.

Indeed, the *error probability* of the tester is bounded by $1/3$. As with the definition of $\mathcal{BPP}$ (and co$\mathcal{RP}$), the choice of the error bound is rather arbitrary as long as it is a constant smaller than $1/2$; the error can be decreased by repeated application of the tester (while ruling by majority; see Exercise 1.4). Specifically, by using t repetitions, the error can be reduced to $\exp(-\Omega(t))$.

Focus: Query Complexity. Our main focus will be on the *query complexity* of the tester, when considered as a function of n and ϵ: We say that the tester has query complexity $q : \mathbb{N} \times (0, 1] \to \mathbb{N}$ *if, on input n, ϵ and oracle access to any $f : [n] \to R_n$, the tester makes at most $q(n, \epsilon)$ queries.* Clearly, any property can be tested in query complexity $q(n, \epsilon) = n$. The first priority is to have the query complexity be sublinear in n, and the slower it grows with n, the better. The ultimate goal, which is not always achievable, is to have the query complexity be independent of n. We shall also care about the dependence of the query complexity on ϵ, and in particular whether it is $O(1/\epsilon)$, or poly$(1/\epsilon)$ or worse.

The *time complexity* of the tester will be our secondary focus, although it is obviously important. We shall say that a tester is efficient *if its time complexity is almost linear in its query complexity*. As in algorithmic research, we allow standard manipulation of the symbols (i.e., elements of R_n) and addresses (i.e., elements of $[n]$) at unit costs; for example, uniformly selecting $i \in [n]$ or comparing $f(i)$ to $v \in R_n$ are considered as performed in a single computational step.

Illustrating the Foregoing Terminology. Let us rephrase some of the results presented in Section 1.2 using the forgoing terminology.

- Proposition 1.1: There exists a $O(1/\epsilon^2)$-time tester for MAJ.
- Proposition 1.3: Every deterministic tester for MAJ has query complexity $\Omega(n)$. This holds even for deterministic 0.5-testers.
- Theorem 1.4: Every symmetric property of Boolean functions can be tested in query complexity $O(1/\epsilon^2)$.
- Proposition 1.5: There exists a $O(1/\epsilon)$-time one-sided error tester for SORTED.

Nonadaptivity. We also distinguish between adaptive and nonadaptive testers, where a tester is called nonadaptive if it determines all its queries based on its explicit inputs and internal coin tosses, independently of the specific function to which it is given oracle access. In contrast, an adaptive tester may determine it $i + 1^{\text{st}}$ query based on the answers it has received to the prior i queries. Note the all the aforementioned testers (i.e., the testers presented in Section 1.2) are nonadaptive.

A nonadaptive tester T can be decomposed into two modules, denoted Q and D, such that Q uses the randomness r of T in order to generate queries $i_1, \ldots, i_q$, whereas D decides according to r and the answers obtained; that is, $T^f(n, \epsilon; r) = D(r, f(i_1), \ldots, f(i_q))$, where $(i_1, \ldots, i_q) \leftarrow Q(n, \epsilon; r)$.

Global versus Local. Property testers of "low" query complexity give rise to a global-versus-local phenomenon. In this case, a global property of the function $f : [n] \to R_n$ (i.e., its belonging to Π_n) is reflected by its "local behavior" (i.e., the pattern seen in the portion of f that is inspected by the tester (as determined by the random outcome of its coin tosses)).[14] This perspective is more appealing when the tester is nonadaptive. In this case, and using the foregoing decoupling, the "local behavior" refers to the values of f on the points in the sequence $(i_1, \ldots, i_q) \leftarrow Q(n, \epsilon; r)$, where each choice of r corresponds to a different portion of $[n]$. This perspective is even more appealing when the tester has one-sided error and its final decision (i.e., $D(r, f(i_1), \ldots, f(i_q))$) depends only on the answers obtained (i.e., is independent of r).

Common Abuses. When describing specific testers, we often neglect to mention their explicit inputs (i.e., n and ϵ), which are always clear from the context. Likewise, even when we discuss auxiliary parameters (such as degree bounds for graphs or descriptions of finite fields), we neglect to write them as explicit inputs of the tester. Finally, for simplicity, we often use Π rather than Π_n, even when we refer to inputs of length n. Likewise,

---

[14] Indeed, the portions of $[n]$ observed when considering all possible outcomes of the tester's randomness are likely to cover $[n]$, but the tester's decision on a specific outcome depends only on the function's values on the corresponding portion of $[n]$.

we may define Π as a finite set consisting of functions over a fixed domain $[n]$ and a fixed range. In any case, unless explicitly stated differently, the value of the size parameter n has to be thought of as generic (and ditto for the value of the proximity parameter ϵ).

1.3.2. Ramifications

Recall that distance between functions (having the same domain $[n]$) was defined in Eq. (1.2) as the probability that they disagree on a *uniformly distributed point in their domain*. A more general definition may refer to the disagreement with respect to an arbitrary distribution $\mathcal{D}_n$ over $[n]$; that is, we may define

$$\delta_{\mathcal{D}_n}(f, g) \overset{\text{def}}{=} \mathbf{Pr}_{i \sim \mathcal{D}_n}[f(i) \neq g(i)], \tag{1.4}$$

where $i \sim \mathcal{D}_n$ means that i is distributed according to $\mathcal{D}_n$. In such a case, for a "distribution ensemble" $\mathcal{D} = \{\mathcal{D}_n\}$, we let $\delta_{\Pi,\mathcal{D}}(f) \overset{\text{def}}{=} \min_{g \in \Pi_n} \{\delta_{\mathcal{D}_n}(f, g)\}$. This leads to a definition of *testing with respect to an arbitrary distribution ensemble* $\mathcal{D}$, where Definition 1.6 is viewed as a special case in which $\mathcal{D}_n$ is the uniform distribution over $[n]$.

One step further is to consider *distribution-free testers*. Such a tester should satisfy the foregoing requirement for all possible distributions $\mathcal{D}$, and it is typically equipped with a special device that provides it with samples drawn according to the distribution in question (i.e., the distribution $\mathcal{D}_n$ used in the definition of distance). That is, a distribution-free tester for Π is an oracle machine that can query the function $f : [n] \to R_n$ as well as obtain samples drawn from *any* distribution $\mathcal{D}_n$, and its performance should refer to $\delta_{\Pi,\mathcal{D}}(f)$ (i.e., the distance of f from Π_n as measured according to the distribution $\mathcal{D}_n$).[15] In such a case, one may consider both the tester's query complexity and its sample complexity.[16]

The aforementioned use of samples raises the question of what can be done, even with respect to the uniform distribution, when the tester obtains only ("labeled") samples; that is, when the tester obtains the function's values at some sampled points but cannot query the function on points of its choice. We call such a tester sample-based, and clarify that, when testing a function $f : [n] \to R_n$, this tester is given a sequence of f-labeled samples, $((i_1, f(i_1)), \ldots, (i_s, f(i_s)))$, where $i_1, \ldots, i_s$ are drawn independently and uniformly in $[n]$. As we shall see in subsequent chapters, the ability to make queries is very powerful: even when the queries are selected nonadaptively, they may be selected to depend on one another. In contrast, a sample-based tester is quite restricted (i.e., it cannot obtain related samples); nevertheless sample-based testers are desirable in many applications where obtaining samples is far more feasible than obtaining answers to queries of one's choice. (An extensive study of sample-based testers was initiated by Goldreich and Ron [153]; see further details in Section 12.3.)

---

[15] Specifically, a distribution-free tester for Π is a probabilistic oracle machine, denoted T, such that for every $n \in \mathbb{N}$ and every distribution $\mathcal{D}_n$ over $[n]$, the following two conditions hold:

1. For every $f \in \Pi_n$, it holds that $\mathbf{Pr}[T^{f,\mathcal{D}_n}(n, \epsilon) = 1] \geq 2/3$.

2. For every $f : [n] \to R_n$ such that $\delta_{\Pi,\mathcal{D}}(f) > \epsilon$, it holds that $\mathbf{Pr}[T^{f,\mathcal{D}_n}(n, \epsilon) = 0] \geq 2/3$.

In both items, $T^{f,\mathcal{D}_n}(n, \epsilon)$ denotes the output of T when given oracle access to $f : [n] \to R_n$ as well as access to samples from $\mathcal{D}_n$ (and explicit inputs n and ϵ).

[16] In particular, one may also consider the case that the tester does not query the function on each sample obtained from $\mathcal{D}_n$; see [30].

Testing Distributions. A seemingly related, but actually different, notion is that of testing properties of distributions. Here we do not test properties of functions (with respect to a distance defined according to some distribution), but rather test properties of distributions, when given samples drawn independently from a target distribution. Note that the formalism presented so far does not apply to this notion, and a different formalism will be used. (The study of testing properties of distributions was initiated by Batu *et al.* [35], and will be discussed in Chapter 11.)

Tolerant Testing. Getting back to the basic framework of Definition 1.6 and recalling some of the settings discussed in Section 1.1.2, we note that a natural generalization of testing refers to distinguishing between objects that are ϵ'-close to the property and objects that are ϵ-far from the property, for parameters $\epsilon' < \epsilon$. Indeed, standard property testing refers to the case of $\epsilon' = 0$, and tolerant testing may be viewed as "tolerating" small deviation of the object from having the property.[17] (The study of tolerant testing properties of functions was initiated by Parnas, Ron, and Rubinfeld [225]; see further details in Section 12.1.)

Other Distance Measures. Almost all research in property testing refers to the distance measure defined in Eq. (1.2), which corresponds to the relative Hamming distance between sequences. We already saw a deviation from this archetypical case in Eq. (1.4). Different distance measures, which are natural in some settings, include the edit distance and the $\mathcal{L}_1$-distance. (The study of property testing with respect to the edit distance was initiated by Batu *et al.* [33], and a study of testing with respect to the $\mathcal{L}_p$-distance was initiated by Berman, Raskhodnikova, and Yaroslavtsev [50].)

1.3.3. Proximity-Oblivious Testers (POTs)

How does the tester use the proximity parameter?

In the examples presented in Section 1.2, the proximity parameter was used to determine the number of queries. These testers were quite simple, and it was not clear how to decompose them to repetitions of even simpler testers. Nevertheless, as we shall see in subsequent chapters, in many cases such a decomposing is conceptually helpful. Furthermore, in many cases the basic testers do not use the proximity parameter at all (see Proposition 1.8), but are rather repeated for a number of times that depend on this parameter. This leads to the notion of a proximity-oblivious tester (POT), which is defined next.

Below, we present a general notion of a POT, which allows two-sided error probability. The notion of a one-sided error POT, obtained as a special case by setting the threshold $\tau = 1$, emerges much more naturally in applications in the sense that one may actually first think of a POT and then get to a standard tester (as per Definition 1.6) from this POT. In contrast, two-sided error POTs seem quite contrived, and may be viewed as an afterthought or as an exercise. Indeed, the reader may want to focus on the one-sided error version (and just substitute τ by 1), at least on first reading.

---

[17] Tolerant testing is related to distance approximation, where no proximity parameter is given and the tester is required to output an approximation (up to a given parameter) of the distance of the object to the property. Typically, the term "tolerant testing" is used when the parameter ϵ' is a fixed function of ϵ (e.g., $\epsilon' = \epsilon/2$), and "distance approximation" is used when one seeks an approximation scheme that is governed by an approximation parameter (which corresponds to $\epsilon - \epsilon'$ when the sought approximation is additive and to ϵ/ϵ' when it is multiplicative).

We stress that the POT does not obtain a proximity parameter as input, but its rejection probability is a function of the distance of the tested object from the property. In the case of one-sided error, the rejection probability is zero when the object has the property, and it increases with the distance of the object from the property. In the case of two-sided error, the rejection probability is at most $1 - \tau$ when the object has the property, and it increases above $1 - \tau$ with the distance of the object from the property. In the following definition, we refer to the acceptance probability of the POT, and state that it decreases below τ as a function of the distance of the object from the property. The latter function is denoted ϱ.

Definition 1.7 (Proximity-oblivious tester): *Let $\Pi = \cup_{n \in \mathbb{N}} \Pi_n$ such that Π_n contains functions defined over $[n]$ (as in Definition 1.6). Let $\tau \in (0, 1]$ be a constant and $\varrho : (0, 1] \to (0, 1]$ be monotonically nondecreasing. A* proximity-oblivious tester (POT) with threshold probability τ and detection probability ϱ *for Π is a probabilistic oracle machine, denoted T, that satisfies the following two conditions.*

1. *T accepts inputs in Π with probability at least τ: For every $n \in \mathbb{N}$ and every $f \in \Pi_n$, it holds that $\mathbf{Pr}[T^f(n) = 1] \geq \tau$.*
2. *T accepts inputs that not in Π with probability that decreases below τ as a function of their distance from Π: For every $n \in \mathbb{N}$ and every $f : [n] \to R_n$ that is not in Π, it holds that $\mathbf{Pr}[T^f(n) = 1] \leq \tau - \varrho(\delta_\Pi(f))$, where δ_Π is as in Eq. (1.3).*

When $\tau = 1$, we say that T has one-sided error.

Hence, $f \notin \Pi$ is rejected with probability at least $(1 - \tau) + \varrho(\delta_\Pi(f))$. The postulate that ϱ is monotonically nondecreasing means that *any function that is ϵ-far from Π is rejected with probability at least $(1 - \tau) + \varrho(\epsilon)$*; that is, if $\delta_\Pi(f) \geq \epsilon$ (and not only if $\delta_\Pi(f) = \epsilon$), then f is rejected with probability at least $(1 - \tau) + \varrho(\epsilon)$. This postulate is natural (and it can be enforced in general by redefining $\varrho(\epsilon) \leftarrow \inf_{\delta \geq \epsilon}\{\varrho(\delta)\}$).

Note that if $\tau < 1$, then it is not necessarily the case that all $f \in \Pi$ are accepted with the same probability (e.g., τ); it may be that some functions are accepted with probability τ and others are accepted with probability greater than τ (see [156]). We also mentioned that Definition 1.7 can be generalized such that both the detection probability function ϱ and the threshold τ depend on n, but we shall not use this generalization. Before making any additional comments, let us see an example of a proximity-oblivious tester.

Proposition 1.8 (A two-query POT for SORTED): *There exists a (one-sided error) proximity-oblivious tester for* SORTED *using two queries and having quadratic detection probability, where* SORTED *is as in Proposition 1.5.*

Proof: (Here it will be more convenient to view the input as a bit string.) On input n and oracle access to $x \in \{0, 1\}^n$, the tester selects uniformly $i, j \in [n]$ such that $i < j$ and accepts if and only if $x_i \leq x_j$. Clearly, each sorted string is accepted with probability 1. To lower-bound the detection probability of this tester, we consider an arbitrary $x \in \{0, 1\}^n$ at distance $\delta_S(x) > 0$ from $S \overset{\text{def}}{=}$ SORTED.

Observing that $x' = 0^{n-\text{wt}(x)}1^{\text{wt}(x)}$ is the sorted version of x, consider the disagreements between x and x'. Specifically, let D_1 denote the set of locations in the $(n - \text{wt}(x))$-bit long prefix of x that hold 1's (i.e., $D_1 = \{i \in [n - \text{wt}(x)] : x_i = 1\}$).

Likewise, denote the set of locations in the $\text{wt}(x)$-bit long suffix of x that hold 0's by D_0 (i.e., $D_0 = \{i \in [n - \text{wt}(x) + 1, n] : x_i = 0\}$), and note that $|D_0| = |D_1|$. Now, on the one hand, $\delta_S(x) \leq \delta(x, x') = (|D_1| + |D_0|)/n$, which implies that $d \stackrel{\text{def}}{=} |D_1| \geq \delta_S(x) \cdot n/2$.[18] On the other hand, for each pair $(i, j) \in D_1 \times D_0$, it holds that $1 \leq i < j \leq n$ and $x_i = 1 > 0 = x_j$. Hence,

$$\mathbf{Pr}_{i,j\in[n]:i<j}[x_i > x_j] \geq \frac{|D_1| \cdot |D_0|}{\binom{n}{2}}$$

$$= \frac{d^2}{n(n-1)/2}$$

$$> \frac{(\delta_S(x) \cdot n/2)^2}{n^2/2}$$

$$= 0.5 \cdot \delta(x)^2.$$

The proposition follows. ∎

General Observations about POTs. The query complexity of POTs is stated as a function of n, and at times – as in Proposition 1.8 – their query complexity will be a constant (independent of n). All POTs we shall see in this book have one-sided error.[19] Nevertheless, we mention that *the threshold in two-sided error POTs is immaterial*, as long as it is a constant in $(0, 1)$: See Exercise 1.7. More importantly, we show how to derive standard testers out of POTs, while noting that for one-sided testers (resp., two-sided error) the resulting tester has query complexity that is linear (resp., quadratic) in $1/\varrho$:

Theorem 1.9 (Deriving standard testers from POTs):

1. *If Π has a one-sided error POT of query complexity q with detection probability ϱ, then Π has a one-sided error tester of query complexity q' such that $q'(\epsilon) = O(q/\varrho(\epsilon))$.*
2. *If Π has a POT of query complexity q with threshold probability $\tau \in (0, 1)$ and detection probability ϱ, then Π has a tester of query complexity q' such that $q'(\epsilon) = O(q/\varrho(\epsilon)^2)$.*

The time complexity of the derived tester relates to that of the POT in a similar manner. If the POT is nonadaptive, then so is the derived tester.

Proof: On input proximity parameter $\epsilon > 0$, the standard tester invokes the POT for a number of times that depends on $\varrho(\epsilon)$. Specifically, if the POT has one-sided error, then the tester invokes it for $O(1/\varrho(\epsilon))$ times and accepts if and only if all invocations accepted. If the POT has threshold probability $\tau \in (0, 1)$, then the tester invokes it for $O(1/\varrho(\epsilon)^2)$ times and accepts if and only if at least a $\tau - 0.5 \cdot \varrho(\epsilon)$ fraction of the invocations accepted. The analysis of this tester reduces to observing

---

[18] **Advanced comment:** The fact that $\delta_S(x) \geq d/n$ is not used here, but proving it is a good exercise (see Exercise 1.6).

[19] Rather contrived exceptions are presented in Exercises 1.8 and 1.9.

that a function that is ϵ-far from Π is accepted by the POT with probability at most $\tau - \varrho(\epsilon)$ (whereas any function in Π is accepted with probability at least τ).[20] ∎

Discussion. Note that the standard tester for SORTED obtained from the POT of Proposition 1.8 (by applying Theorem 1.9) is inferior to the tester of Proposition 1.5. This is not a singular case (see [152]). Furthermore, some properties have good testers, but do not have good POTs at all; that is, there exist natural properties that have poly($1/\epsilon$)-time testers but have no constant-query POTs (see Exercise 1.10).

1.3.4. The Algebra of Property Testing

In this section we show that (asymptotic complexity classes of) testable properties are closed under union but not under intersection (and complementation). That is, if Π' and Π'' are testable within some complexity bounds, then so is $\Pi' \cup \Pi''$ (up to a constant factor), but $\Pi' \cap \Pi''$ may be much harder to test.[21] Details follow.

Unions. The basic idea is that if Π' and Π'' are testable by algorithms T' and T'', respectively, then one may test $\Pi' \cup \Pi''$ by invoking both testers and accepting if and only if at least one of these invocations accepted. This procedure doubles the error probability of ordinary testers and squares the detection probability of one-sided error POTs, so in the former case we should first apply error reduction.

Theorem 1.10 (Testing the union of properties):

1. *If Π' and Π'' are each testable within query complexity q, then $\Pi' \cup \Pi''$ is testable within query complexity $O(q)$. Furthermore, one-sided error testing is preserved.*
2. *Suppose that Π' has a q-query one-sided error POT with detection probability $\varrho : (0, 1] \to (0, 1]$, and ditto for Π''. Then, $\Pi' \cup \Pi''$ has a $2q$-query one-sided error POT with detection probability ϱ^2.*

Furthermore, the time complexity is preserved up to a constant factor.

(Indeed, it is unclear how to handle the case of two-sided error POTs. The issue is that, in this case, inputs in $\Pi' \setminus \Pi''$ may be rejected by the foregoing procedure with probability $1 - \tau$, where τ is the threshold probability.[22] On the other hand, inputs that are at distance δ from $\Pi' \cup \Pi''$ may be rejected with probability $(1 - \tau + \varrho(\delta))^2$. But for $\tau < 1$ and sufficiently small $\delta > 0$, it holds that $1 - \tau > (1 - \tau + \varrho(\delta))^2$. In contrast, for $\tau = 1$ and any $\delta > 0$, it holds that $1 - \tau = 0 < (1 - \tau + \varrho(\delta))^2$.)

---

[20] The first assertion relies on the postulation that ϱ is monotonically nondecreasing. This postulate implies that any function that is ϵ-far from Π (rather than only functions that are at distance exactly ϵ from Π) is rejected with probability at least $(1 - \tau) + \varrho(\epsilon)$.

[21] This is a general result in the sense that the positive part holds for all Π' and Π'' whereas the negative part indicates a failure for some Π' and Π''. In contrast, in some cases, both $\Pi' \cup \Pi''$ and $\Pi' \cap \Pi''$ may be much easier to test than Π' and Π''.

[22] This is because an input in $\Pi' \setminus \Pi''$ may be rejected by the tester of Π' with probability exactly $1 - \tau$, and may be rejected by the tester of Π'' with probability 1.

Proof: The key point is that being far from $\Pi' \cup \Pi''$ implies being far from both Π' and Π''. The theorem follows by noting that the combined tester rejects an input if and only if the two testers that it invokes reject. Details follow.

By the hypothesis of Part 1, each of the two properties is testable within query complexity q, but these testers may have error probability as large as $1/3$. Hence, we first obtain corresponding testers of error probability at most $1/6$, by invoking each of the original testers for a constant number of times. Combining the two resulting testers, as described above, we establish Part 1. Specifically, inputs in $\Pi' \cup \Pi''$ are accepted with probability at least $5/6$ (due to residing in one of the sets), whereas inputs that are far from $\Pi' \cup \Pi''$ are rejected with probability at least $(5/6)^2 > 2/3$.

Turning to Part 2, we note that no error reduction is needed here; the claimed result follows by merely lower-bounding the probability that both testers reject when the input is at distance δ from $\Pi' \cup \Pi''$; that is, this input is rejected with probability at least $\varrho(\delta') \cdot \varrho(\delta'')$, where $\delta' \geq \delta$ denotes its distance from Π', and $\delta'' \geq \delta$ denotes its distance from Π''. (On the other hand, inputs in $\Pi' \cup \Pi''$ are accepted with probability 1 (due to residing in one of the sets).) ∎

Hardness for Testing. The negative results regarding intersection and complementation rely on properties that are hard to test. For concreteness we start by presenting one such hardness result.

Proposition 1.11 (Hardness of testing membership in a linear code): *Let G be a $0.5n$-by-n Boolean matrix in which every $0.05n$ columns are linearly independent and every nonempty linear combination of the rows has Hamming weight at least $0.1n > 1$. Let $\Pi = \{xG : x \in \{0, 1\}^{0.5n}\}$ be the linear code generated by G. Then, 0.1-testing Π requires more than $0.05n$ queries.*

The existence of a matrix G that satisfies the hypothesis can be proved using the probabilistic method (see Exercise 1.12). The proof of Proposition 1.11 only uses the fact that every $0.05n$ columns are linearly independent (and that there are $0.5n$ rows). The fact that the code has distance greater than 1 will be used later (when using Π to show the negative result regarding complementation).

> **Teaching Note:** See the teaching note that follows Proposition 1.2. In short, some readers may prefer to skip the following proof, and return to it at a later time (e.g., after reading Chapter 7).

Proof: We shall use the following two observations.

Observation 1: An algorithm that makes $0.05n$ queries cannot distinguish the case that its input is uniformly distributed in Π from the case that its input is uniformly distributed in $\{0, 1\}^n$.

This is the case since, for a uniformly distributed $x \in \{0, 1\}^{0.5n}$, each $0.05n$-bit long subsequence of xG is uniformly distributed in $\{0, 1\}^{0.05}$ (see Exercise 1.13). Observe that this implies that an adaptive algorithm that makes at most $0.05n$ queries to xG sees uniformly and independently distributed bits.

Observation 2: All but at most $2^{0.99n}$ of the strings in $\{0, 1\}^n$ are 0.1-far from Π.

This follows by straightforward counting (see Exercise 1.14).

Observation 2 implies that a 0.1-tester must reject a uniformly distributed n-bit string with probability at least $(1 - 2^{-0.01n}) \cdot 2/3 > 0.6$. On the other hand, such a tester must accept any string in Π with probability at least 2/3 (and so reject it with probability at most 1/3). But Observation 1 asserts that no gap in the rejection probability is possible when making at most $0.05n$ queries. ∎

Intersection (and Complementation). Proposition 1.11 yields an example in which the complexity of testing a property is vastly different from the complexity of testing its complement. Specifically, consider the property $\Pi' = \{0, 1\}^n \setminus \Pi$, where Π is as in Proposition 1.11. Note that every n-bit string is $1/n$-close to Π' (since each string is either in Π' or is surrounded by strings in Π')[23]; hence, testing Π' is trivial (i.e., if $\epsilon \geq 1/n$, then we may accept the input without examining it at all, and otherwise reading the entire input means making at most $1/\epsilon$ queries). But, testing the complement of Π' (i.e., testing Π) is extremely hard (i.e., requires a linear number of queries)!

A small twist on the foregoing argument allows proving the following result.

Theorem 1.12 (On testing the intersection of properties): *There exist Π' and Π'' such that the following hold:*

1. *Each of these two properties is testable within query complexity $1/\epsilon$; actually, they are each testable with query complexity q such that $q(n, \epsilon) = 0$ if $\epsilon \geq 1/n$ and $q(n, \epsilon) = n$ otherwise.*
2. *Testing $\Pi' \cap \Pi''$ requires a linear number of queries; actually, 0.1-testing $\Pi' \cap \Pi''$ requires more than $0.05n$ queries.*

Proof: Starting with Π as in Proposition 1.11, we consider $\Pi' = \Pi \cup \{0x' : x' \in \{0, 1\}^{n-1}\}$ and $\Pi'' = \Pi \cup \{1x' : x' \in \{0, 1\}^{n-1}\}$. Part 1 follows from the fact that every n-bit string is $1/n$-close to Π' (resp., Π''). Part 2 follows from the fact that $\Pi' \cap \Pi'' = \Pi$. ∎

Digest. The proof of Theorem 1.12 introduces sets Π' and Π'' such that every string is (very) close to each of these sets, but some strings are far from the intersection of the two sets.[24] Indeed, the fact that x is close to both Π' and Π'' does not imply that x is close to $\Pi' \cap \Pi''$; see illustration in Figure 1.1. As shown next, this cannot happen in case the sets are "monotone."

The Case of Monotone Properties. We say that $\Pi \subseteq \{0, 1\}^*$ is monotone if for every $x \in \Pi$ and $w \in \{0, 1\}^{|x|}$ it holds that $x \vee w = (x_1 \vee w_1, \ldots, x_n \vee w_n)$ is in Π; that is, Π is preserved under resetting any of the bits to 1. We first note that the discrepancy between the complexity of testing a property and the complexity of testing its complement

---

[23] Here we use the hypothesis that strings in Π are at (Hamming) distance at least two apart.

[24] **Advanced comment:** An interesting question (raised by Inbal Livni) is whether Theorem 1.12 holds for sets Π' and Π'' that do not have this feature (i.e., there exist strings that are far from Π', and ditto for Π'').

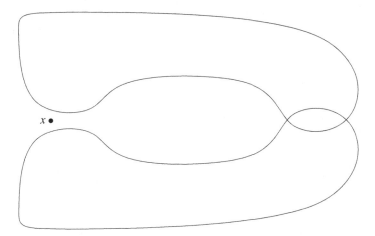

$x \bullet$

Figure 1.1: Being close to two sets versus being close to their intersection.

is maintained also for monotone properties (see Exercise 1.16). More importantly, in contrast to Theorem 1.12, we have

Theorem 1.13 (Testing the intersection of monotone properties): *Let Π' and Π'' be monotone properties.*

1. *If Π' and Π'' are testable within query complexity q' and q'', respectively, then, for every $\epsilon' \in (0, \epsilon)$, the property $\Pi' \cap \Pi''$ is ϵ-testable within query complexity $q(n, \epsilon) = O(q'(n, \epsilon') + q''(n, \epsilon - \epsilon'))$. Furthermore, one-sided error testing is preserved.*
2. *Suppose that Π' has a q-query one-sided error POT with detection probability $\varrho : (0, 1] \to (0, 1]$, and ditto for Π''. Then, $\Pi' \cap \Pi''$ has a $2q$-query one-sided error POT with detection probability $\varrho'(\delta) = \varrho(\delta/2)$.*

Furthermore, the time complexity is preserved up to a constant factor.

Theorem 1.13 is generalized and abstracted in Exercise 1.17. A totally different case in which testability is preserved under intersection is presented in Theorem 5.11.

Proof: The basic idea is that if Π' and Π'' are testable by algorithms T' and T'', respectively, then one may test $\Pi' \cap \Pi''$ by invoking both testers and accepting if and only if both these invocations accepted.[25] While this procedure fails for general properties, we show that it works for monotone ones. The key observation is that, for monotone properties Π' and Π'', if x is ϵ'-close to Π' and ϵ''-close to Π'', then x is $(\epsilon' + \epsilon'')$-close to $\Pi' \cap \Pi''$. This is shown next.

We first show that *if $\Pi \subseteq \{0, 1\}^n$ is monotone* (and nonempty), *then, for every $x \in \{0, 1\}^n$ there exists $w \in \{0, 1\}^n$ such that $x \vee w \in \Pi$ and* $\mathrm{wt}(w) = \delta_\Pi(x) \cdot n$. This is the case because, by monotonicity, when modifying x into a string in Π it never helps to reset bits to 0, since keeping them intact will do. Specifically, if $x \wedge w \in \Pi$ then $x \in \Pi$ (since $x = (x \wedge w) \vee (x \wedge \overline{w})$, whereas the latter is in Π by

---

[25] In the case of two-sided error tester, this is done after reducing the error probability to $1/6$. In any case, for Part 1 and any $\epsilon' \in (0, \epsilon)$, the ϵ-tester invokes the ϵ'-tester for Π' and the $(\epsilon - \epsilon')$-tester for Π''.

monotonicity). Hence, letting $w_1, w_0 \in \{0, 1\}^n$ be such that $(x \vee w_1) \wedge (1^n \oplus w_0) \in \Pi$ and $\mathrm{wt}(w_1) + \mathrm{wt}(w_0) = \delta_\Pi(x) \cdot n$, we infer that $x \vee w_1 \in \Pi$ and the claim follows (since $\mathrm{wt}(w_0) \geq 0$).[26]

Now, we show that, for every $x \in \{0, 1\}^n$ it holds $\delta_{\Pi' \cap \Pi''}(x) \leq \delta_{\Pi'}(x) + \delta_{\Pi''}(x)$. Let w' (resp., w'') be such that $x \vee w' \in \Pi'$ and $\mathrm{wt}(w') = \delta_{\Pi'}(x) \cdot n$ (resp., $x \vee w'' \in \Pi''$ and $\mathrm{wt}(w'') = \delta_{\Pi''}(x) \cdot n$). Then, by using monotonicity again, we have $x \vee w' \vee w'' \in \Pi'$ and $x \vee w' \vee w'' \in \Pi''$, whereas $\mathrm{wt}(w' \vee w'') \leq \mathrm{wt}(w') + \mathrm{wt}(w'')$. The theorem follows. ∎

Two Final Comments about the Algebra of Testing Properties. We first mention that a notion of strong complementation underlies the definition of *testing dual properties* [259]. Specifically, a dual property is defined based on a property Π and a constant $\delta > 0$, and it consists of all objects that are δ-far from Π. Lastly, we warn that the complexity of property testing does not necessarily increase or decrease when considering a subset (or a superset) of some property:[27] The nonmonotonicity of the complexity of testing is evident from the fact that Π may be hard to test (e.g., if Π is as in Proposition 1.11) but testing $\emptyset$ and $\{0, 1\}^n$ is trivial (whereas $\emptyset \subset \Pi \subset \{0, 1\}^n$).

1.3.5. Testing via Learning

A general observation, which is seldom used, is that property testing reduces to learning. The reason that this observation is seldom used is that one typically seeks testers that are more efficient than the corresponding learners. Still, for sake of perspective, we detail the aforementioned reduction.

To streamline the presentation, we use the terminology of Definition 1.6 in our definition of learning. (In the learning literature (cf., e.g., [184]), the set Π is called a concept class, the functions $f : [n] \to R_n$ are called concepts, and one usually focuses on $R_n = \{0, 1\}$ and $n = 2^\ell$, while viewing ℓ as the main parameter. More importantly, as in Definition 1.6 we provide the learner with oracle access to the function (rather than with labeled examples as is standard in the learning literature), focus on the uniform distribution (rather than on the distribution-free case), and fix the error probability to equal $1/3$ (rather than using an additional parameter).)[28]

Definition 1.14 (Learning and proper learning for Π, following [262] and [227]): *Let $\Pi = \cup_{n \in \mathbb{N}} \Pi_n$ such that Π_n contains functions defined over $[n]$. A* learner *for Π is a probabilistic oracle machine, denoted L, such that for every $n \in \mathbb{N}$ and every $f \in \Pi_n$, with probability at least $2/3$, it holds that $L^f(n, \epsilon)$ is a description of a*

---

[26] In fact, $\mathrm{wt}(w_0) = 0$, since otherwise $\mathrm{wt}(w_1) < \delta_\Pi(x) \cdot n$, in contradiction to the definition of $\delta_\Pi(x)$.

[27] **Advanced comment:** For perspective, recall that the computational complexity of decision problems does not always decrease or increase when considering decision problems that correspond to subsets of the original set. In contrast, a promise problem, $(S_{\mathrm{yes}}, S_{\mathrm{no}})$, never becomes harder (resp., easier) when taking subsets (resp., supersets) of both S_{yes} and S_{no}. The point is for $S' \subset S$, moving from the promise problem $(S, \{0, 1\}^* \setminus S)$ to the promise problem $(S', \{0, 1\}^* \setminus S')$ means moving the border between yes-instances and no-instances, rather than omitting instances from the promise set (which equals $\{0, 1\}^*$ in both cases).

[28] **Advanced comment:** The last deviation from the standard presentation of learning algorithms weakens the definition, since error reduction is not available in this context (akin to the situation with randomized algorithms for search problems; cf. [131, Sec. 6.1.2]). Specifically, if we invoke the learner t times and obtain hypotheses $h_1, \ldots, h_t$, then it is not clear how to combine the h_i's in order to obtain (with probability $1 - \exp(-\Omega(t))$) a function that is ϵ-close to the target function f, although we expect a majority of the h_i's to be ϵ-close to f.

function that is ϵ-close to f. If the output function always belongs to Π, then we say that L performs proper learning.

Note that, in contrast to testing, nothing is required in case f is ϵ-far from Π (let alone when it only holds that $f \notin \Pi$). On the other hand, and again in contrast to testing, when $f \in \Pi$, the learner is required to output a function (called a hypothesis) that is ϵ-close to the target function f (and not only say "yes").

When considering the computational complexity of the learner, one typically requires that the learner outputs a concise representation of the function, and in case of proper learning this representation should fit the prescribed representation of functions in Π.

We note that every Π can be properly learned within query complexity $q(n, \epsilon) = \min(n, O(\epsilon^{-1} \log |\Pi_n|))$, where the second bound follows by an algorithm that scans all possible $h \in \Pi_n$ and uses the same sample of $O(\epsilon^{-1} \log |\Pi_n|)$ random points in order to estimate the distance between each $h \in \Pi$ and the target function f (see Exercise 1.18). Such an estimation procedure is pivotal for establishing the following result.

Theorem 1.15 (Learning implies testing): *Let $\Pi = \cup_{n \in \mathbb{N}} \Pi_n$ be as in Definition 1.14, and suppose that Π can be learned within query complexity $q(n, \epsilon)$. Then, Π can be tested within query complexity $q'(n, \epsilon) = q(n, 0.3\epsilon) + O(1/\epsilon)$. Furthermore, if the learning algorithm is proper, runs in time $t(n, \epsilon)$, and outputs descriptions of functions such that evaluating these functions and checking their membership in Π can be done in time $T(n)$, then Π can be tested within query complexity $q'(n, \epsilon) = q(n, 0.7\epsilon) + O(1/\epsilon)$ and time complexity $t'(n, \epsilon) = t(n, 0.7\epsilon) + O(T(n)/\epsilon)$.*

We mention that similar results hold with respect to a variety of models including sample-based learning and testing and distribution-free learning and testing. Note that in the case of nonproper learning we invoke the learner with a proximity parameter that is strictly smaller than $\epsilon/2$, whereas in the case of proper learning we may use a proximity parameter that is larger than $\epsilon/2$ (as long as it is strictly smaller than ϵ). More importantly, the stated bound on the time complexity (i.e., $t'(n, \epsilon) = t(n, 0.7\epsilon) + O(T(n)/\epsilon)$) does not hold in the case of nonproper learning (see [140, Sec. 3.2]). We also note that *the resulting tester has two-sided error probability.*

Proof: On input f and proximity parameter ϵ, the tester proceeds as follows:

1. The tester invokes the nonproper (resp., proper) learner on f with proximity parameter 0.3ϵ (resp., 0.7ϵ), obtaining a description of a hypothesis $h : [n] \to R_n$.
   (If $f \in \Pi_n$, then, with probability at least $2/3$, the nonproper (resp., proper) learner outputs a function h that is 0.3ϵ-close (resp., 0.7ϵ-close) to f. Furthermore, in the proper case it holds that $h \in \Pi$. In both cases, if $f \notin \Pi$, then nothing is guaranteed, which means that h may be arbitrary.)
2. The tester checks whether h is 0.3ϵ-close to Π_n (resp., is in Π_n):
   Case of nonproper learning: The tester checks whether h is 0.3ϵ-close to Π_n, and if the answer is negative it rejects.
   This step requires no access to f, but it may require going over all functions in Π_n and comparing each of them to h.

Case of proper learning: The tester checks whether $h \in \Pi_n$, and if the answer is negative it rejects.

This step can be implemented in time $T(n)$, and requires no access to f.

(If the tester did not reject, then it proceeds to the next step.)

3. The tester uses an auxiliary sample of $O(1/\epsilon)$ elements of $[n]$ in order to estimate the distance between h and f up to an additive term of 0.1ϵ (or just indicate that this distance is greater than ϵ), with error probability 0.1.

Case of nonproper learning: The tester accepts if and only if according to this estimate, the distance between h and f is at most 0.5ϵ.

Case of proper learning: The tester accepts if and only if according to this estimate, the distance between h and f is at most 0.85ϵ.

(In the case of proper learning, the estimate is performed in time $O(1/\epsilon) \cdot T(n)$.)

This algorithm satisfies the complexity bounds stated in the theorem, and so we turn to analyze its behavior.

We start with the case of nonproper learning. If $f \in \Pi_n$, then, with probability at least $2/3$, the hypothesis h is 0.3ϵ-close to f, and in this case, with probability at least 0.9, the tester will accept (since h is 0.3ϵ-close to Π_n and with high probability the estimated distance between h and f is at most 0.4ϵ). On the other hand, if f is ϵ-far from Π_n, then either h is 0.3ϵ-far from Π_n or h is 0.7ϵ-far from f, since otherwise f is $(0.7\epsilon + 0.3\epsilon)$-close to Π. In the first case (i.e., h is 0.3ϵ-far from Π_n) Step 2 rejects, whereas in the second case (i.e., h is 0.7ϵ-far from f), with probability at least 0.9, Step 3 will reject (since in this case h is estimated to be 0.6ϵ-far from f).

We now turn to the case of proper learning. If $f \in \Pi_n$, then, with probability at least $2/3$, the hypothesis $h \in \Pi_n$ is 0.7ϵ-close to f, and in this case, with probability at least 0.9, the tester will accept (since h is estimated to be 0.8ϵ-close to f). On the other hand, if f is ϵ-far from Π_n, then either $h \notin \Pi_n$ or $h \in \Pi_n$ is ϵ-far from f, and in the latter case, with probability at least 0.9, the tester will reject (since in the latter case h is estimated to be 0.9ϵ-far from f).

Hence, in both cases, the tester accepts any $f \in \Pi_n$ with probability at least $(2/3) \cdot 0.9 = 0.6$, and rejects any f that is ϵ-far from π with probability at least 0.9. By modifying the tester such that with probability 0.2 it accepts obliviously of the input, we obtain a tester than accepts functions in Π with probability at least $0.2 + 0.8 \cdot 0.6 > 2/3$ and rejects ϵ-far functions with probability greater than $0.8 \cdot 0.9 > 2/3$. ∎

1.4. Historical Notes

Property testing emerged, implicitly, in the work of Blum, Luby, and Rubinfeld [59], which presents, among other things, a tester for linearity (or rather group homomorphism). This line of research was pursued in [124, 245], culminating in the work of Rubinfeld and Sudan [246], where the approach was abstracted and captured by the notion of a *robust characterization*.

The starting point of Rubinfeld and Sudan [246] is the observation that the (algebraic) properties considered in [59, 124, 245] have a *local characterization*; that is, a function f has the property Π if and only if the values assigned by f to every "admissible local neighborhood" satisfy some local property. Hence, the definition of a local characterization specifies a set of local neighborhoods (i.e., $O(1)$-long sequences of elements in the function's domain) as well as a local property (i.e., a set of corresponding $O(1)$-long sequences of values that are admissible for each local neighborhood), and $f \in \Pi$ if and only if the values assigned by f to each local neighborhood satisfy the local property.

A robust characterization is then defined as a local characterization in which the distance of a function from the property is reflected by the number of local conditions that it violates. That is, an (ϵ, ρ)-robust characterization of Π is a local characterization of Π such that every function that is ϵ-far from Π violates at least a ρ fraction of the local conditions (i.e., the values assigned by f to at least a ρ fraction of the local neighborhoods violate the corresponding local property).

As noted by Rubinfeld and Sudan [246], the existence of a (ϵ, ρ)-robust characterization of Π implies an ϵ-tester for Π, which samples $2/\rho$ random neighborhoods, queries the function values at the corresponding points, and accepts if and only if the corresponding local conditions are all satisfied. Note that the resulting tester is *nonadaptive* and has *one-sided error probability*. Hence, the notion of robust characterization captures only a special case of property testing.

A general and systematic study of property testers was initiated by Goldreich, Goldwasser, and Ron [140]. Their notion of a tester allows for adaptive queries and two-sided error probability, while viewing nonadaptivity and one-sided error probability as special cases. The bulk of their paper [140] focuses on testing graph properties (see [140, Sec. 5–10]), but the paper also contains general results (see [140, Sec. 3–4]). It is worth mentioning that their main point of reference was the model of PAC learning [262]; that is, they viewed property testing as complementary to PAC learning and taking place within the same setting (in which the target entities are huge functions that may only be probed at relatively few locations).

The work of Goldreich, Goldwasser, and Ron [140] advocated viewing *property testing as a new type of computational problems*, rather than as a tool towards program checking [58] (as viewed in [59]) or towards the construction of PCP systems (see later). The instances of these problems were viewed as descriptions of actual objects; that is, objects that arise from some application. Consequently, the representation of these objects as functions became a non-obvious step, which required justification. For example, in the case of testing graph properties, the starting point is the graph itself, and its representation as a function is an auxiliary conceptual step.[29]

The distinction between objects and their representations became more clear when alternative representations of graphs were studied in [147, 148, 180]. At this point, query complexity that is polynomially related to the size of the object (e.g., its square root) was no longer considered inhibiting. This is related to the "shift in scale" that is discussed next.

Initially, property testing was viewed as referring to functions that are implicitly defined by some succinct programs (as in the context of program checking) or by "transcendental" entities (as in the context of PAC learning). From this perspective the yardstick for efficiency is being polynomial in the length of the query, which means being polylogarithmic in the size of the object. In contrast, when viewing property testing as

---

[29] In [140] graphs are represented by their adjacency relation (or matrix), which is not overly redundant when dense graphs are concerned. In contrast, in [147] bounded-degree graphs are considered and they are represented by their sequence of incidence lists.

being applied to (huge) objects that may exist in explicit form in reality, the size of these objects becomes the point of reference, and any algorithm of sublinear complexity may be beneficial.

Proximity Oblivious Testers. The notion of (one-sided error) proximity-oblivious testing is implicit in many works, starting with [59]. Its systematic study was initiated by Goldreich and Ron [152]. The notion of two-sided error proximity-oblivious testing was defined and studied in [156].

Ramifications. Property testing with respect to general distributions as well as distribution-free testing, sample-based testing, and tolerant testing were all mentioned in [140, Sec. 2]. However, the focus of Goldreich, Goldwasser, and Ron [140] as well as of almost all subsequent works was on the basic framework of Definition 1.6 (i.e., using queries in testing w.r.t. the uniform distribution). An explicit study of the various ramifications started (later) in [167, 153, 225], respectively. Further discussion of these and other ramifications appears in Chapter 12.

The PCP Connection. All known PCP constructions rely on testing codewords of some code. In the "first generation" of PCP constructions (i.e., [29, 28, 107, 25, 24]), the relevant codes were the Hadamard code and (generalized) Reed–Muller codes, which led to the use of linearity testers and low-degree tests, respectively. In the "second generation" of PCP constructions (e.g., [37, 170, 171]), the use and testing of the long-code (suggested for these applications by [37]) became pivotal.[30] Some works that belong to the "third generation" of PCP constructions return to (generalized) Reed–Muller codes (e.g., [157, 44, 210, 93]), whereas for some (e.g., [92]) any "basic PCPP" will do.[31] In all cases, the focus is on testing membership in codes, which are designed to support extremely local testing; that is, the tested objects do not arise from some application, but are rather designed to be used in some application. Such codes are called *locally testable*, and their systematic study was initiated in [157]. Locally testable codes are reviewed in Chapter 13, which also reviews PCPs, while viewing them as closely related to the notion of *locally testable proofs*.

1.5. Suggested Reading and Exercises

Needless to say, this book covers only a tiny fraction of the research in the area of property testing, let alone research in areas that are closely related to it. We mention that a forthcoming book by Bhattacharyya and Yoshida [56] seems to have a small intersection

---

[30] Our periodicity scheme defines the first generation of constructions as those culminating in the (original proof of the) PCP Theorem [25, 24], and the second generation of constructions as the subsequent PCPs that are aimed at optimizing parameters of the (binary) query complexity (e.g., [37, 170, 171, 249]). The works of the "third generation" tend to focus on other considerations such as proof length (e.g., [157, 44]), combinatorial constructions (e.g., [94, 92]), and lower error via few multivalued queries (e.g., [210, 93]). Alternatively, the second generation may be characterized as focusing on the optimization of the "inner verifier" (while relying on an "outer verifier" derived by applying the Parallel Repetition Theorem [234] to a two-prover system derived from the PCP Theorem), whereas works of the third generation also pay attention to the construction of the "outer verifier" (placing works such as [95, 186, 189, 187] in the third generation).

[31] In her alphabet reduction, Dinur [92] can use any "PCP of Proximity" (as defined in [44, 94]) for membership in a code of constant relative distance.

with the current book. In addition, several surveys of property testing and subareas of it have appeared in the past. A collection of such surveys appears in [134], which contains also some examples of contemporary research (dated 2010). Two more extensive surveys were written by Ron [241, 242]: The first offers a computational learning theoretic perspective [241], and the second is organized according to techniques [242].

Most current research in property testing is listed and annotated in the *Property Testing Review* (http://ptreview.sublinear.info/). (This is a good opportunity to thank its initiators, Eric Blais, Sourav Chakraborty, and C. Seshadhri, for their service to the property testing community.)[32] Some property testing works that have a complexity theoretic flavor are also posted on *ECCC* (http://eccc.weizmann.ac.il/).

The Benefit of Adaptivity. One natural question regarding property testing refers to the benefit of adaptive queries over nonadaptive ones. Indeed, the same question arises in any query-based model. Adaptive queries can always be emulated at exponential cost; that is, q adaptive queries to a function $f : [n] \to R$ can be emulated by less than $|R|^q$ nonadaptive queries (see Exercise 1.19).[33] The question is whether a cheaper emulation is possible. Within the context of property testing, the answer seems to vary according to the type of property. Types of properties for which the emulation has no overhead are shown in [47, 108]. In the context of graph properties, the answer varies according to the specific model: See [158, 151] versus [233].

One-sided versus Two-sided Error. Another natural question regarding property testing refers to the difference between one-sided and two-sided error probability. Needless to say, the same question arises in any model of probabilistic computation (see, e.g., $\mathcal{BPP}$-versus-$\mathcal{RP}$). Interestingly, in the context of property testing, a huge gap may exist between these two versions. For example, Proposition 1.1 asserts an $O(1/\epsilon^2)$-time tester of two-sided error probability for MAJ, whereas any one-sided error tester for MAJ must make a linear number of queries (see Exercise 1.11). Gaps exist also in models of testing graphs properties (see the results regarding ρ-Clique in [140] and the results regarding cycle-freeness in [147, 81]).

We mention that the "reverse type of one-sided error" testing, where the tester is required to always reject (i.e., reject with probability 1) objects that are far from the property, has not been studied for a good reason (see [259, Prop. 5.6] or [260]).

Hierarchy. Complexity hierarchies are known in many computational models (see, e.g., the classical computational complexity hierarchies [131, Chap. 4]). It turns out that such hierarchies (i.e., query hierarchies) exist also in property testing [144].

Basic Exercises

Most of the following exercises detail some claims that were made in the main text.

Exercise 1.1 (Details for the proof of Proposition 1.1): Use the Chernoff Bound (or alternatively Chebyshev's Inequality) to prove that the average value of the sample points

---

[32] Currently, the team of moderators includes the initiators as well as Clement Canonne and Gautam Kamath, and our thanks extend to the latter too.

[33] **Advanced comment:** Alternatively, the number of queries can be preserved at the cost of decreasing the distinguishing gap of the tester by a factor of $|R|^q$ (see Exercise 1.20).

approximates the average value of all x_i's. The details involve defining m random variables, and using the aforementioned inequality.

Exercise 1.2 (Details for the proof of Claim 1.2.1): Prove that X_n (resp., Z_n) as redefined in the proof of Claim 1.2.1 is uniformly distributed over n-bit strings of Hamming weight $\lfloor n/2 \rfloor + 1$ (resp., $\lfloor n/2 \rfloor$).

> **Guideline:** A crude solution amounts to computing the probability mass given to each string according to each of the definitions. A nicer solution is to show that the redefined processes yield output distributions that are symmetric with respect to the indices.

Exercise 1.3 (On testing symmetric properties of sequences over an unbounded alphabet):[34] The goal of this advanced exercise is to show that there are symmetric properties of sequences over an unbounded alphabet for which testing requires a linear number of queries. Specifically, we shall consider properties of n-long sequences over $[p]$, where $p > n^2$ is a prime. For $k = \Omega(n)$, we start with a sample space $S_n \subset [p]^n$ of size p^{k+1} over $[p]$ that is k-wise independent (see, e.g., [78]); that is, for every set $K \subset [n]$ of size k, taking a uniformly distributed element of S_n and projecting it on the coordinates K results in the uniform distribution over $[p]^k$. Let Π_n denote all sequences obtained by permuting sequences of S_n arbitrarily; that is, $(\sigma_1, \ldots, \sigma_n) \in \Pi_n$ if and only if there exists a permutation $\pi : [n] \to [n]$ such that $(\sigma_{\pi(1)}, \ldots, \sigma_{\pi(n)}) \in S_n$. Show that for $\epsilon = 0.1$ and $k = n/3$, almost all sequences in $[p]^n$ are ϵ-far from Π_n, and conclude that testing Π_n requires more than k queries. Observe that the argument extents to any $\epsilon > 0$ and $k < n$ such that $\epsilon < (n - k)/n - \Omega(1)$, provided that p is large enough.

> **Guideline:** Show that $|\Pi_n| \leq n! \cdot |S_n| < n^n \cdot p^{k+1}$ and upper-bound the number of sequences that are ϵ-close to Π_n by $\binom{n}{\epsilon n} \cdot p^{\epsilon n} \cdot |\Pi_n|$. On the other hand, observe that an algorithm that makes k queries cannot distinguish the uniform distribution over S_n from the uniform distribution over $[p]^n$. (Indeed, the strategy used here combines elements of the proof of Proposition 1.11 with an idea presented in the guideline of Exercise 1.16.)

Exercise 1.4 (Error reduction for testers): Show that the error probability of a property tester can be reduced to 2^{-t} at the cost of increasing its query (and time) complexity by a factor of $O(t)$, and while preserving one-sided error.

> **Guideline:** Invoke the original tester t times, while using independent randomness in each invocations, and accept if and only if the majority of these invocations accepted. The analysis reduces to showing that if we repeat an experiment that succeeds with probability $2/3$ for t times, then, with probability $1 - \exp(-\Omega(t))$, the majority of the trials succeed.

Exercise 1.5 (On size-oblivious query complexity): Let $\Pi = \cup_{n \in \mathbb{N}} \Pi_n$ such that Π_n contains functions defined over $[n]$, and let $q : (0, 1] \to \mathbb{N}$. Suppose that for every $\epsilon > 0$

---

[34] Inspired by [140, Sec. 10.2.3].

and all sufficiently large $n \in \mathbb{N}$, the property Π_n can be ϵ-tested by making $q(\epsilon)$ queries. Show that Π has a property tester of query complexity that is upper-bounded by a function of ϵ only.

Guideline: For each $\epsilon > 0$, let n_ϵ be such that for every $n \geq n_\epsilon$ the property Π_n can be ϵ-tested by making $q(\epsilon)$ queries. Consider a tester that on input parameters (n, ϵ), determines n_ϵ, activates the original tester if $n \geq n_\epsilon$, and reads the entire n-long input otherwise. Note that this yields a query complexity bound of $\max(q(\epsilon), n_\epsilon)$, which is effective if the mapping $\epsilon \mapsto n_\epsilon$ is effective (e.g., as in the case $n_\epsilon = \mathrm{poly}(1/\epsilon)$ or $n_\epsilon = 2^{1/\epsilon}$).

Exercise 1.6 (On the distance to SORTED versus the distance to the sorted version):Let S denote the set of sorted n-bit long strings, and let $x \in \{0, 1\}^n$ and $x' = 0^{n-\mathrm{wt}(x)} 1^{\mathrm{wt}(x)}$. Noting that $\delta_S(x) \leq \delta(x, x')$, prove that $\delta_S(x) \geq \delta(x, x')/2$, and show that this lower bound is tight.

Guideline: Letting D_1 and D_0 be as in the proof of Proposition 1.8, consider a matching between D_1 and D_0, and observe that any string in S must differ from x on at least one endpoint of each pair in the matching. To show that this lower bound is tight, consider the case of $x = 0^{n-w-d} 1^d 0^d 1^{w-d}$.

Exercise 1.7 (On the threshold probability of POTs): Show that, for every $\tau \in (0, 1]$ and $\tau' \in (0, 1)$, and for every $\rho : (0, 1] \to (0, 1]$ and $q : \mathbb{N} \to \mathbb{N}$, if Π has a q-query POT with threshold probability τ and detection probability ϱ, then Π has a q-query POT with threshold probability τ' and detection probability $\varrho' = \Omega(\varrho)$.

Guideline: Consider a POT that invokes the given POT with probability p (to be determined as a function of τ and τ'), and accepts (or rejects) otherwise.

Exercise 1.8 (A two-sided error POT for MAJ): Show that the following algorithm constitutes a two-sided error POT with linear detection probability for MAJ. For odd n, on input $x \in \{0, 1\}^n$, the algorithm selects uniformly $i \in [n]$, and outputs x_i. For even n, a small modification is required so that we can still use the threshold probability $\tau = 1/2$.

Guideline: The probability that x is accepted is $\mathrm{wt}(x)/|x|$. For an even n, reducing the acceptance probability by a factor of $1 - n^{-1}$ will do, since $(1 - n^{-1}) \cdot (0.5 + n^{-1}) \geq 0.5$ (whereas $(1 - n^{-1}) \cdot 0.5 < 0.5$).

Exercise 1.9 (A less trivial two-sided error POT): Since the example provided by Exercise 1.8 is quite disappointing, we consider the following set $\mathrm{BAL} = \{x : \mathrm{wt}(x) = |x|/2\}$ (of "balanced" strings). Show that the following algorithm constitutes a two-sided error POT with threshold probability 0.5 and quadratic detection probability for BAL. On input $x \in \{0, 1\}^n$, the algorithm selects uniformly $i, j \in [n]$, and accepts if and only if $x_i \neq x_j$. Note that the same algorithm constitutes a POT also for $S_c = \{x : c \cdot |x| \leq \mathrm{wt}(x) \leq (1 - c) \cdot |x|\}$, for every constant $c \in (0, 0.5)$, but the threshold probability and the detection probability are different in this case.

Guideline: The probability that x is accepted equals $2 \cdot \mathrm{wt}(x) \cdot (|x| - \mathrm{wt}(x))/|x|^2$, which is smaller than $1/2$ if and only if $\mathrm{wt}(x) \neq |x|/2$. In the case of S_c, the threshold probability is $2c(1 - c)$, and the detection probability function is linear.

Exercise 1.10 (Easily testable properties that have no POT): For a generic n, let Π denote the set of functions $f : [n] \to [n]$ that have no odd-length cycles, where a cycle of length ℓ in f is a sequence of distinct elements $i_0, \ldots, i_{\ell-1} \in [n]$ such that $f(i_j) = i_{j+1 \bmod \ell}$ for every $j \in \{0, 1 \ldots, \ell - 1\}$. In other words, f is not in Π (i.e., has an odd-length cycle) if for some $i \in [n]$ and odd j it holds that $f^j(i) = i$, where $f^0(i) = i$ and $f^j(i) = f(f^{j-1}(i))$. (It may be helpful to depict $f : [n] \to [n]$ as a directed graph with edges going from i to $f(i)$, and observe that this graph consists of vertex-disjoint directed cycles and directed trees that "feed" into them.)

1. Show that Π can be tested in query complexity $O(1/\epsilon^2)$.
2. Show that Π has no constant-query proximity-oblivious tester.

Part 2 holds even if the tested function is guaranteed to be a permutation.

Guideline: For Part 1, consider an algorithm that selects uniformly a set I of $m = O(1/\epsilon)$ elements in $[n]$, and obtains the values of $f(i), \ldots, f^m(i)$, for each $i \in I$. This algorithm rejects f if and only if it sees an odd-length cycle (i.e., if $f^s(i) = f^t(i)$ for any $i \in I$ and $s, t \in \{0, 1, \ldots, m\}$ such that $|s - t|$ is odd). Calling i bad if the values $f(i), \ldots, f^m(i)$ contain an odd-length cycle, prove that *if at most $2n/m$ of the i's are bad, then f is ϵ-close to Π* (and observe that otherwise the algorithm accepts with probability at most $(1 - (2/m))^m < 1/3$).[35] In Part 2, consider first the case of one-sided error POTs. Assuming that such an algorithm makes q queries, let $\ell = 2 \cdot \lceil q/2 \rceil + 1$, and consider its execution when given access to a permutation that consists of ℓ-cycles. Note that a POT is required to reject this permutation with positive probability, although it does not see a cycle in it (and so it also rejects a permutation in Π with nonzero probability). Handling the two-sided error case amounts to showing that a q-query algorithm cannot distinguish a random permutation that consists of ℓ-cycles from a random permutation that consists of 2ℓ-cycles (assuming $n/2\ell$ is an integer).[36]

Exercise 1.11 (On one-sided error testers for MAJ): Prove that MAJ has no one-sided error tester of sublinear query complexity.

Guideline: Consider an arbitrary sublinear algorithm T and an execution (i.e., selection of randomness for T) in which T rejects the string 0^n, which is 0.5-far from MAJ. (Such an execution exists since $\mathbf{Pr}[T^{0^n}(n, 0.5) = 0] \geq 2/3 > 0$.) Denoting by Q the set of locations queried in *this execution*, consider the string $x \in \{0, 1\}^n$ such that

---

[35] In order to prove the (italicized) claim, consider the directed graph obtained by omitting the edges that go out from bad vertices as well as omitting a single edge from each directed cycle that has odd length that exceeds m. Observe that at most $2n/m + n/m$ edges were omitted, whereas the resulting directed graph has no odd-length cycles and has at most $3n/m$ vertices that have no outgoing edge. Lastly, show that it is possible to add a single outgoing edge to each of the latter vertices without forming odd-length cycles (e.g., these edges can be directed to arbitrary vertices that reside on cycles in the residual graph if such vertices exist, and otherwise we can connect all directed paths in a way that forms a single n-cycle (and make a last modification if n is odd)).

[36] This is shown by observing that in each of the two cases, the value of the random function f at a newly queried point x is uniformly distributed among all values that neither occurred as previous images of f nor are values that form an f-path to x. (Depicting the query-answer pairs as directed edges, the query x is answered with a vertex that neither has an ingoing edge nor is the endpoint of a directed path that leads to x.) Since the indistinguishability is perfect, it suffices to note that the first permutation is not in Π (i.e., there is no need to use the fact that this permutation is actually $\Omega(1/q)$-far from Π).

$x_i = 0$ if and only if $i \in Q$, and note that $\mathbf{Pr}[T^x(n, \epsilon) = 1] < 1$. On the other hand, if $|Q| < n/2$, then $x \in$ MAJ.

Exercise 1.12 (The existence of good linear codes): Show that there exists a $0.5n$-by-n Boolean matrix in which every $0.05n$ columns are linearly independent and every nonempty linear combination of the rows has Hamming weight at least $0.1n$.

> **Guideline:** Using the probabilistic method (see [22]), upper-bound the probability that a random matrix does not satisfy the foregoing conditions.

Exercise 1.13 (Detail for the proof of Proposition 1.11): Let G be an m-by-n Boolean matrix in which every t columns are linearly independent. Prove that for a uniformly distributed $x \in \{0, 1\}^m$, each t-bit long subsequence of xG is uniformly distributed in $\{0, 1\}^t$.

> **Guideline:** Consider the corresponding m-by-t matrix G', and note that each image of the map $x \mapsto xG'$ has 2^{m-t} preimages.

Exercise 1.14 (Another detail for the proof of Proposition 1.11): Let G be an $0.5n$-by-n Boolean matrix. Prove that, for sufficiently large n, the number of n-bit strings that are 0.1-close to $\{xG : x \in \{0, 1\}^{0.5n}\}$ is at most $2^{0.99n}$.

Exercise 1.15 (Testability is preserved under intersection with a trivially testable property): We say that $\Psi = \cup_{n \in \mathbb{N}} \Psi_n$ is trivially testable if, for every $n \in \mathbb{N}$, either $\Psi_n = \emptyset$ or Ψ_n contains all functions defined over $[n]$. Prove that, if Ψ is trivially testable, then, for every $\Pi = \cup_{n \in \mathbb{N}} \Pi_n$ such that Π_n contains functions defined over $[n]$, the query complexity of testing $\Pi \cap \Psi$ is upper-bounded by that of testing Π.

Exercise 1.16 (The testability of monotone properties is not closed under complementation): Show that there is a monotone property Π such that testing Π is trivial (any n-bit string is $1/n$-close to Π), but 0.001-testing $\{0, 1\}^* \setminus \Pi$ requires a linear number of queries.

> **Guideline:** Let G' be a $0.05n$-by-$(n - 1)$ Boolean matrix in which every $0.001n$ columns are linearly independent and every nonempty linear combination of the rows has Hamming weight at least $0.1n$. (Indeed, the existence of such a matrix can be proved analogously to Exercise 1.12.) Let $\Pi' = \{xG' : x \in \{0, 1\}^{0.05n} \setminus \{0^{0.05n}\}\}$ and $\Pi'' = \{w' \vee w'' : w' \in \Pi' \wedge w'' \in \{0, 1\}^{n-1}\}$; that is, Π' is the linear code generated by G' *with the exception of the all-zero string*, and Π'' is its "monotone closure." Letting $\Pi = \{0, 1\}^n \setminus \{1w : w \in \Pi''\}$, note that each string is $1/n$-close to Π, whereas $\{0, 1\}^n \setminus \Pi = \{1w : w \in \Pi''\}$ is hard to test.[37] The latter claim is proved (analogously to the proof of Proposition 1.11) by establishing the following two facts:
>
> 1. The uniform distribution on Π' is perfectly indistinguishable (by $0.001n$ queries) from the uniform distribution on $\{0, 1\}^{n-1}$.
> 2. The set Π'' has low density: $|\Pi''| \le 2^{0.9n} \cdot |\Pi'| < 2^{0.95n}$, where the first inequality is due to the fact that each string in Π' has Hamming weight at least $0.1n$.

---

[37] Indeed, Π is anti-monotone (i.e., it is preserved under resetting bits to zero), so one may consider $\{1^n \oplus w : w \in \Pi\}$ instead.

(Note that the uniform distribution over Π' serves here as an arbitrary distribution over Π''.)

Exercise 1.17 (Generalization of Theorem 1.13): Let Π' and Π'' be properties of functions defined over the same domain, D.

1. Prove that if, for every $f : D \to \{0, 1\}^*$, it holds that $\delta_{\Pi' \cap \Pi''}(f) \leq \delta_{\Pi'}(f) + \delta_{\Pi''}(f)$, then, for every $\epsilon' \in (0, \epsilon)$, the property $\Pi' \cap \Pi''$ is ϵ-testable within query complexity $q(n, \epsilon) = O(q'(n, \epsilon') + q''(n, \epsilon - \epsilon'))$, where q' and q'' denote the query complexities of testing the properties Π' and Π'', respectively.
2. Show that if Π' and Π'' are monotone properties, then $\delta_{\Pi' \cap \Pi''}(f) \leq \delta_{\Pi'}(f) + \delta_{\Pi''}(f)$ holds for any function f.
3. Generalizing Part 1, suppose that for $F : (0, 1] \times (0, 1] \to (0, 1]$ it holds that $\delta_{\Pi' \cap \Pi''}(f) \leq F(\delta_{\Pi'}(f), \delta_{\Pi''}(f))$, for every f. Show that, for every $\epsilon > 0$, if $F(\epsilon', \epsilon'') \leq \epsilon$, then the property $\Pi' \cap \Pi''$ is ϵ-testable within query complexity $O(q'(n, \epsilon') + q''(n, \epsilon''))$.
4. Show that a function as in Part 3 does not exist for the properties used in the proof of Theorem 1.12.

   Guideline: Parts 1–3 are implicit in the proof of Theorem 1.13. Part 4 can be proved either by direct inspection of these properties or by arguing that the contrary hypothesis contradicts Theorem 1.12.

Exercise 1.18 (A generic learning algorithm): Show that every $\Pi = \cup_{n \in \mathbb{N}} \Pi_n$ can be properly learned within query complexity $q(n, \epsilon) = \min(n, O(\epsilon^{-1} \log |\Pi_n|))$.

   Guideline: The key observation that a sample of $O(t/\epsilon)$ random points allows for approximating the distance between two functions up to an additive term of $\epsilon/2$ (or just indicate that this distance is greater than ϵ)[38] with error probability 2^{-t}. The bound of $O(\epsilon^{-1} \log |\Pi_n|)$ follows by observing that the same sample can be used to estimate the distance of each $h \in \Pi_n$ to the target function f, and applying a union bound.

Additional Exercises

The following exercises present a few useful observations regarding oracle machines in general.

Exercise 1.19 (Straightforward emulation of adaptive queries): Show that the execution of any oracle machine that makes q (possibly adaptive) queries to an unknown function $f : [n] \to R$ can be emulated by a nonadaptive machine that makes at most $\sum_{i=0}^{q-1} |R|^i$ queries.

   Guideline: Fixing the internal coin tosses of the machine, consider a tree that describes all its possible q-long sequences of queries, where the vertices correspond to queries and the edges correspond to possible answers.

---

[38] Note that if the distance is $\Omega(\epsilon)$, then a constant factor approximation suffices, and such an approximation can be obtained (with probability $1 - 2^{-t}$) based on $m = O(t/\epsilon)$ random points. Hence, outputting the fraction of points of disagreement seen in the sample, we obtain an $\epsilon/2$-additive approximation if the actual value is below 2ϵ, and a factor of 2 approximation otherwise (which provides the correct indication that the actual value is above ϵ).

Exercise 1.20 (An alternative emulation of adaptive queries): Let Π be a property of functions from $[n]$ to R, and suppose that T is a q-query POT for property Π with threshold probability τ and detection probability ϱ. Show that Π has a q-query *non-adaptive* POT with threshold probability τ and detection probability $\varrho/|R|^q$.

> **Guideline:** Select uniformly at random a sequence of internal coin tosses ω for T and a sequence of values $(v_1, \ldots, v_q) \in R^q$. Consider the execution of T on coins ω, when its jth query is answered with the value v_j, and let $i_1, \ldots, i_q$ denote the corresponding queries. We stress that the i_j's are determined without making any query to the oracle (i.e., i_j is the jth query made on coins ω, assuming that the previous queries were answered with $v_1, \ldots, v_{j-1}$). Next, query the oracle f at $i_1, \ldots, i_q$. If for every $j \in [q]$ it holds that $f(i_j) = v_j$, then rule according to the verdict of T. Otherwise, accept with probability τ (and reject otherwise).

Exercise 1.21 (Upper bound on the randomness complexity of oracle machines):[39] Let Π be a promise problem regarding functions from $[n]$ to R, where ϵ-testing a property of such functions is a special case (in which the YES-instances are functions having the property and the NO-instances are functions that are ϵ-far from the property). Suppose that M is a randomized oracle machine that solves the problem Π with error probability at most $1/4$, while making q queries. Assuming that n is sufficiently large, show that Π can be solved by a randomized oracle machine that makes at most q queries, tosses at most $\log_2 n + \log_2 \log_2 |R| + O(1)$ coins, and has error probability at most $1/3$. Note that the randomness-efficient machine derived here is not necessarily computationally efficient.

> **Guideline:** Suppose that M tosses r coins, and observe that the number of possible functions that M is required to decide about is at most $|R|^n$. Using the probabilistic method, show that there exists a $O(\log |R|^n)$-set $S \subseteq \{0, 1\}^r$, such that for every function $f : [n] \to R$ it holds that
>
> $$|\mathbf{Pr}_{\omega \in S}[M^f(\omega) = 1] - \mathbf{Pr}_{\omega \in \{0,1\}^r}[M^f(\omega) = 1]| < 1/12.$$
>
> Then, a randomness-efficient machine may select ω uniformly in S, and emulate M while providing it with ω (as the outcome of the internal coin tosses used by M).

Exercise 1.22 (On the tightness of the bound provided in Exercise 1.21):[40] Let Π be a promise problem regarding functions from $[n]$ to R. We say that Π is ρ-evasive if there exists a function $f : [n] \to R$ such that for every $Q \subset [n]$ of density ρ, there exists a YES-instance (*of* Π) denoted f_1 and a NO-instance denoted f_0 such that for every $x \in Q$ it holds that $f_1(x) = f_0(x) = f(x)$. Show that if a ρ-evasive Π can be decided (say, with error probability $1/3$) by an oracle machine M that makes q queries, then this machine must toss at least $\log_2(\rho n/q)$ coins. Note that for many natural properties and for sufficiently small constant $\epsilon > 0$, the problem of ϵ-testing the property is $\Omega(1)$-evasive.[41]

> **Guideline:** Suppose that M solve Π while tossing r coins, and let f be a function as in the ρ-evasive condition. Consider all 2^r possible executions of M^f, and let Q denote

---

[39] Based on [155].

[40] Based on [155].

[41] A partial list includes sets of low-degree polynomials, any code of linear distance, monotonicity, juntas, and various graph properties (e.g., $f \equiv 0$ and $f_1 = f$ will do in many cases). Indeed, this list is confined to examples that will appear in subsequent chapters.

the set of queries made in these executions. Then, $|Q| \leq 2^r \cdot q$. On the other hand, $|Q| > \rho \cdot n$, since otherwise these executions cannot distinguish the corresponding functions f_1 and f_0 that are guaranteed by the ρ-evasive condition.

1.6. Digest: The Most Important Points

Given that this is quite a long chapter, it seems good to list some of the points that will be instrumental for the subsequent chapters. Needless to say, the definition of a property tester (i.e., Definition 1.6) is pivotal for all that follows. The notion of a proximity-oblivious tester (see Definition 1.7) will also be used a lot (sometimes only implicitly). Two important points that underly the study of such testers are:

- Representation. The tested objects will be (typically) represented in a natural and concise manner, and n will denote their size. They will be presented either as sequences over an alphabet Σ (e.g., $x \in \Sigma^n$) or as functions from $[n]$ to Σ (i.e., in such a case we consider the function $x : [n] \to \Sigma$).

  Indeed, here we seized the opportunity to present these notions while referring to an arbitrary alphabet rather than only to the binary alphabet (i.e., $\Sigma = \{0, 1\}$), as done in previous sections.

- The (standard) notion of distance. For $x, y \in \Sigma^n$, we consider their relative Hamming distance, denoted $\delta(x, y) \overset{\text{def}}{=} |\{i \in [n] : x_i \neq y_i\}|/n$. For $x \in \Sigma^n$ and $S \subseteq \Sigma^n$, we denote by $\delta_S(x)$ the relative Hamming distance of x from S; that is, $\delta_S(x)$ is the minimum, taken over all $z \in S \cap \{0, 1\}^{|x|}$, of $\delta(x, z)$.

  We shall say that x is ϵ-far from S if $\delta_S(x) > \epsilon$, and otherwise (i.e., when $\delta_S(x) \leq \epsilon$) we shall say that x is ϵ-close to S. Indeed, typically, ϵ will denote a proximity parameter, which determines what is considered far.

Our main focus will be on the *query complexity* of standard testers (i.e., as in Definition 1.6), measured in terms of the size of the tested object, denoted n, and the proximity parameter, denoted ϵ. The first priority is to have *query complexity that is sublinear in n*, and the slower this complexity grows with n, the better. At times, especially when discussing lower bounds, we may fix the value of the proximity parameter (i.e., set ϵ to be a small positive constant), and consider the complexity of the residual tester, called an ϵ-tester, as a function of n only. The ultimate goal, which is not always achievable, is to have the query complexity be independent of n. We shall also care about the dependence of the query complexity on ϵ, and in particular whether it is $O(1/\epsilon)$, or poly$(1/\epsilon)$, or worse.

The *time complexity* of the tester will be our secondary focus, although it is obviously important. We shall say that a tester is efficient if its time complexity is almost linear in its query complexity.

The foregoing refers to standard testers (i.e., as in Definition 1.6). In contrast, the complexity of proximity-oblivious testers (as in Definition 1.7) only depends on n, and their rejection probability is related to the distance of the tested object from the property. The latter relation is captured by a monotonically nondecreasing function, typically denoted ϱ. As shown in Theorem 1.9, a proximity-oblivious tester yields an ordinary tester by repeating the former for $O(1/\varrho^c(\epsilon))$ times, where $c = 1$ in case of one-sided error testing (and $c = 2$ otherwise), and ϵ is the proximity parameter (given to the ordinary tester). This brings us to the last point in this section.

- One-sided error probability refers to the case that the tester always accepts any object that has the property, but may accept with bounded probability objects that are far from the property (which means that it errs with some bounded probability).[42] General testers (a.k.a two-sided error testers) may err, with bounded probability, both in the case the object has the property and in the case it is far from the property.

---

[42] Recall that a property is associated with the set of objects having the property.

CHAPTER TWO

Testing Linearity
(Group Homomorphism)

Summary: We present and analyze a proximity-oblivious tester for linearity (or rather homomorphism between groups). On input a description of two groups G, H and oracle access to a function $f : G \to H$, the tester queries the function at three points and satisfies the following conditions:

1. If f is a homomorphism from G to H, then the tester accepts with probability 1.
2. If f is δ-far from the set of all homomorphisms from G to H, then the tester rejects with probability at least $\min(0.5\delta, 0.1666)$.

The three queries are $x, y, x + y$, where x and y are selected uniformly at random in G.

This chapter is based on the work of Blum, Luby, and Rubinfeld [59], which pioneered the study of property testing.

2.1. Preliminaries

Let G and H be two groups. For simplicity, we denote by $+$ the group operation in each of these groups. A function $f : G \to H$ is called a (group) homomorphism if for every $x, y \in G$ it holds that $f(x + y) = f(x) + f(y)$.

One important special case of interest is when H is a finite field and G is a vector space over this field; that is, $G = H^m$ for some natural number m. In this case and assuming that H has prime order, a homomorphism f from G to H can be presented as $f(x_1, \ldots, x_m) = \sum_{i=1}^{m} c_i x_i$, where $x_1, \ldots, x_m, c_1, \ldots, c_m \in H$; that is, f is a linear function over H^m. This explains why testing group homomorphism is often referred to as linearity testing.

Group homomorphisms are among the simplest and most basic sets of finite functions. They may indeed claim the title of the most natural algebraic functions. This chapter addresses the problem of testing whether a given function is a group homomorphism or is far from any group homomorphism.

2.2. The Tester

The definition of being a homomorphism is presented as a conjunction of $|G|^2$ local conditions, where each local condition refers to the value of the function on three points.

Interestingly, this definition is robust in the sense that the fraction of satisfied local conditions can be related to the distance of the function from being a homomorphism. In other words, a tester for this property is obtained by checking a single local condition that is selected at random.

Algorithm 2.1 (Testing whether f is a homomorphism): *Select uniformly $x, y \in G$, query f at the points $x, y, x + y$, and accept if and only if $f(x + y) = f(x) + f(y)$.*

It is clear that this tester accepts each homomorphism with probability 1, and that each non-homomorphism is rejected with positive probability. The non-obvious fact is that, in the latter case, the rejection probability is linearly related to the distance of the function from the set of all homomorphisms. We first prove a weaker lower bound on the rejection/detection probability.

Proposition 2.2 (A partial analysis of Algorithm 2.1): *Suppose that $f : G \to H$ is at distance δ from the set of homomorphisms from G to H. Then, Algorithm 2.1 rejects f with probability at least $3\delta - 6\delta^2$.*

The lower bound $3\delta - 6\delta^2 = 3(1 - 2\delta) \cdot \delta$ increases with δ only when $\delta \in [0, 1/4]$. Furthermore, this lower bound is useless when $\delta \geq 1/2$ (and for this reason the corresponding analysis was called "partial"). Thus, an alternative lower bound is needed when δ approaches $1/2$ (or is larger than it). Such a bound is provided in Theorem 2.3; but, let us prove Proposition 2.2 first.

Proof: Suppose that h is a homomorphism closest to f (i.e., $\delta = \mathbf{Pr}_{x \in G}[f(x) \neq h(x)]$). We first observe that the rejection probability (i.e., $\mathbf{Pr}_{x,y \in G}[f(x) + f(y) \neq f(x + y)]$) is lower-bounded by

$$\mathbf{Pr}_{x,y \in G}[f(x) \neq h(x) \wedge f(y) = h(y) \wedge f(x + y) = h(x + y)] \tag{2.1}$$

$$+\mathbf{Pr}_{x,y \in G}[f(x) = h(x) \wedge f(y) \neq h(y) \wedge f(x + y) = h(x + y)] \tag{2.2}$$

$$+\mathbf{Pr}_{x,y \in G}[f(x) = h(x) \wedge f(y) = h(y) \wedge f(x + y) \neq h(x + y)], \tag{2.3}$$

because these three events are disjoint, whereas $f(x) + f(y) \neq f(x + y)$ mandates that f and h disagree on some point in $\{x, y, x + y\}$ (since $h(x) + h(y) = h(x + y)$).[1] We lower-bound Eq. (2.1), while noting that Eqs. (2.2) and (2.3) can be lower-bounded analogously.

$\mathbf{Pr}_{x,y}[f(x) \neq h(x) \wedge f(y) = h(y) \wedge f(x + y) = h(x + y)]$

$= \mathbf{Pr}_{x,y}[f(x) \neq h(x)] - \mathbf{Pr}_{x,y}[f(x) \neq h(x) \wedge (f(y) \neq h(y) \vee f(x + y) \neq h(x + y))]$

$\geq \mathbf{Pr}_{x,y}[f(x) \neq h(x)]$

$\quad - (\mathbf{Pr}_{x,y}[f(x) \neq h(x) \wedge f(y) \neq h(y)] + \mathbf{Pr}_{x,y}[f(x) \neq h(x) \wedge f(x + y) \neq h(x + y)])$

$= \delta - \delta^2 - \delta^2,$

where the last equality follows since x and y are independently and uniformly distributed in G (and ditto w.r.t. x and $x + y$). ∎

---

[1] **Advanced comment:** Indeed, this lower bound is typically not tight, since we ignored the event in which f and h disagree on more than one point, which may also lead to rejection. For example, if H is the two-element set with addition modulo 2, then disagreement on three points (i.e., $f(x) \neq h(x) \wedge f(y) \neq h(y) \wedge f(x + y) \neq h(x + y)$) also leads to rejection (since in this case $f(x) + f(y) - f(x + y) = h(x) + 1 + h(y) + 1 - (h(x + y) + 1) = 1$).

Theorem 2.3 (Full analysis of Algorithm 2.1): *Algorithm 2.1 is a* (one-sided error) *proximity-oblivious tester with detection probability* $\min(0.5\delta, 1/6)$, *where* δ *denotes the distance of the given function from being a homomorphism from* G *to* H.

Proof: Let ρ denote the probability that f is rejected by the test, and suppose that $\rho < 1/6$ (since otherwise we are done). We shall show that in this case f is 2ρ-close to some homomorphism (and $\rho \geq \delta/2$ follows).[2]

The intuition underlying the proof is that the hypothesis regarding f (i.e., that it is rejected with probability $\rho < 1/6$) implies that f can be modified (or "corrected") into a homomorphism by modifying f on relatively few values (i.e., on at most $2\rho|G|$ values). Specifically, the hypothesis that $\mathbf{Pr}_{x,y \in G}[f(x) = f(x+y) - f(y)] = 1 - \rho > 5/6$ suggests that a "corrected" version of f, denoted f', that is determined such that $f'(x)$ is the most frequent value of $f(x+y) - f(y)$, when considering all possible choices of $y \in G$, is a homomorphism that is relatively close to f.

Suppose, *for illustration*, that f is obtained by selecting an arbitrary homomorphism h and corrupting it on relatively few points (say on less than one fourth of G). Then, f' (i.e., the corrected version of f) equals h (since for every $x \in G$ it holds that $\mathbf{Pr}_{y \in G}[f(x+y) - f(y) = h(x+y) - h(y)] > 1/2$), and both claims hold (i.e., $f' = h$ is a homomorphism and it is relatively close to f). Needless to say, we cannot start with the foregoing assumption (that f is 0.249-close to some homomorphism)[3], but should rather start from an arbitrary f that satisfies

$$\mathbf{Pr}_{x,y \in G}[f(x) = f(x+y) - f(y)] = 1 - \rho > 5/6. \tag{2.4}$$

We now turn to the actual proof.

Define the vote of y regarding the value of f at x as $\phi_y(x) \stackrel{\text{def}}{=} f(x+y) - f(y)$, and define $\phi(x)$ as the corresponding plurality vote (with ties broken arbitrarily); that is,

$$\phi(x) \stackrel{\text{def}}{=} \text{argmax}_{v \in H}\{|\{y \in G : \phi_y(x) = v\}|\}. \tag{2.5}$$

We shall show that ϕ is 2ρ-close to f, and that ϕ is a homomorphism.

Claim 2.3.1 (Closeness): *The function ϕ is 2ρ-close to f.*

Proof: This is merely an averaging argument, which counts as bad any point x such that $f(x)$ disagrees with at least half of the votes (regarding the value of f at x), while noting that otherwise f agrees with ϕ on x. Specifically, denoting $B = \{x \in G : \mathbf{Pr}_{y \in G}[f(x) \neq \phi_y(x)] \geq 1/2\}$, we get

$$\rho = \mathbf{Pr}_{x,y}[f(x) \neq f(x+y) - f(y)]$$

$$= \mathbf{Pr}_{x,y}[f(x) \neq \phi_y(x)]$$

$$\geq \mathbf{Pr}_x[x \in B] \cdot \min_{x \in B}\{\mathbf{Pr}_y[f(x) \neq \phi_y(x)]\}$$

$$\geq \frac{|B|}{|G|} \cdot \frac{1}{2},$$

---

[2] Hence, either $\rho \geq 1/6$ or $\rho \geq \delta/2$, which implies $\rho \geq \min(0.5\delta, 1/6)$ as claimed.

[3] The gap between the foregoing illustration and the actual proof is reflected in the fact that the illustration refers to $\delta < 1/4$, whereas the actual proof uses $\rho < 1/6$.

which implies that $|B| \leq 2\rho \cdot |G|$. On the other hand, if $x \in G \setminus B$, then $f(x) = \phi(x)$ (since $\mathbf{Pr}_y[f(x) = \phi_y(x)] > 1/2$, whereas $\phi(x)$ equals the most frequent vote (among the votes $\phi_y(x)$ regarding the value of f at x)). ∎

Recall that $\phi(x)$ was defined to equal the most frequent vote (i.e., the most frequent $\phi_y(x)$ over all possible $y \in G$). Hence, $\phi(x)$ occurs as a vote with frequency at least $1/|H|$. Actually, we just saw (in the proof of Claim 2.3.1) that on at least $1 - 2\rho$ of the x's it holds that $\phi(x)$ is the majority value. We next show that $\phi(x)$ is much more frequent: it occurs in a strong majority (for all x's).

> **Teaching Note:** The rest of the analysis is easier to verify in the case of Abelian groups, since in this case one does not need to be careful about the order of summations.

Claim 2.3.2 (Strong majority): *For every $x \in G$, it holds that $\mathbf{Pr}_y[\phi_y(x) = \phi(x)] \geq 1 - 2\rho$.*

Proof: Fixing x, we consider the random variable $Z_x = Z_x(y) \overset{\text{def}}{=} f(x+y) - f(y)$, while noting that $\phi(x)$ was defined as the most frequent value that this random variable assumes. We shall show that the collision probability of Z_x (i.e., $\sum_v \mathbf{Pr}[Z_x = v]^2$) is high, and it will follow that Z_x must assume its most frequent value (which is indeed $\phi(x)$) with high probability.

Recalling that the collision probability of a random variable equals the probability that two independent copies of it assume the same value, we observe that the collision probability of Z_x equals

$$\mathbf{Pr}_{y_1, y_2}[Z_x(y_1) = Z_x(y_2)] = \mathbf{Pr}_{y_1, y_2}[f(x+y_1) - f(y_1) = f(x+y_2) - f(y_2)]. \tag{2.6}$$

Toward lower-bounding Eq. (2.6), we call a pair (y_1, y_2) good if both $f(y_1) + f(-y_1 + y_2) = f(y_2)$ and $f(x+y_1) + f(-y_1 + y_2) = f(x+y_2)$ hold. (Note that $y_1 + (-y_1 + y_2) = y_2$ and $(x+y_1) + (-y_1 + y_2) = (x+y_2)$.) Now, on the one hand, a random pair is good with probability at least $1 - 2\rho$, since

$$\mathbf{Pr}_{y_1, y_2}[f(y_1) + f(-y_1 + y_2) = f(y_1 + (-y_1 + y_2))] = 1 - \rho$$

and

$$\mathbf{Pr}_{y_1, y_2}[f(x+y_1) + f(-y_1 + y_2) = f((x+y_1) + (-y_1 + y_2))] = 1 - \rho,$$

where the equalities rely on the fact that the pair $(y_1, -y_1 + y_2)$ (resp., the pair $(x + y_1, -y_1 + y_2)$) is uniformly distributed in G^2 when (y_1, y_2) is uniformly distributed in G^2. On the other hand, for a good (y_1, y_2), it holds that $Z_x(y_1) = Z_x(y_2)$, since

$$Z_x(y_2) = f(x+y_2) - f(y_2)$$
$$= (f(x+y_1) + f(-y_1 + y_2)) - (f(y_1) + f(-y_1 + y_2))$$
$$= f(x+y_1) - f(y_1) = Z_x(y_1).$$

It follows that the collision probability of Z_x is lower-bounded by $1 - 2\rho$. Observing that $\sum_v \mathbf{Pr}[Z_x = v]^2 \leq \max_v\{\mathbf{Pr}[Z_x = v]\}$, it follows that $\mathbf{Pr}[Z_x = \phi(x)] \geq 1 - 2\rho$, since $\phi(x)$ is the most frequent value assigned to Z_x. ∎

Claim 2.3.3 (ϕ is a homomorphism): *For every $x, y \in G$, it holds that $\phi(x) + \phi(y) = \phi(x + y)$.*

Proof: Fixing any $x, y \in G$, we prove that $\phi(x) + \phi(y) = \phi(x + y)$ holds by considering the somewhat fictitious expression $p_{x,y} \stackrel{\text{def}}{=} \mathbf{Pr}_{r \in G}[\phi(x) + \phi(y) \neq \phi(x + y)]$, and showing that $p_{x,y} < 1$ (which implies that $\phi(x) + \phi(y) \neq \phi(x + y)$ is false).[4] We prove that $p_{x,y} < 1$, by showing that

$$p_{x,y} \leq \mathbf{Pr}_r \left[\begin{array}{l} \phi(x) \neq f(x + r) - f(r) \\ \vee \ \phi(y) \neq f(r) - f(-y + r) \\ \vee \ \phi(x + y) \neq f(x + r) - f(-y + r) \end{array} \right] \tag{2.7}$$

and upper-bounding the probability of each of the three events in the r.h.s. of Eq. (2.7) holds by $2\rho < 1/3$. Details follow.

We first observe that if none of the three events in the r.h.s. of Eq. (2.7) holds (i.e., if $\phi(x) = f(x + r) - f(r)$, $\phi(y) = f(r) - f(-y + r)$, and $\phi(x + y) = f(x + r) - f(-y + r)$ hold), then $\phi(x) + \phi(y) = \phi(x + y)$ holds. Hence, $\phi(x) + \phi(y) \neq \phi(x + y)$ mandates that at least one of the three events in the r.h.s. of Eq. (2.7) holds.

We upper-bound the probability that each of the three events in Eq. (2.7) holds by using Claim 2.3.2 (and some variable substitutions). Specifically, recall that Claim 2.3.2 asserts that for every $z \in G$ it holds that $\mathbf{Pr}_s[\phi(z) = f(z + s) - f(s)] \geq 1 - 2\rho$. It follows that

$$\mathbf{Pr}_r[\phi(x) \neq f(x + r) - f(r)] \leq 2\rho$$

$$\mathbf{Pr}_r[\phi(y) \neq f(r) - f(-y + r)] = \mathbf{Pr}_s[\phi(y) \neq f(y + s) - f(s)] \leq 2\rho$$

$$\mathbf{Pr}_r[\phi(x + y) \neq f(x + r) - f(-y + r)] = \mathbf{Pr}_s[\phi(x + y) \neq f(x + y + s) - f(s)] \leq 2\rho,$$

where in both equalities we use $s = -y + r$ (equiv., $r = y + s$). Hence, $p_{x,y} \leq 3 \cdot 2\rho < 1$, and the claim follows. ∎

Combining Claims 2.3.1 and 2.3.3, the theorem follows. ∎

Digest. The proof of Theorem 2.3, which provides an analysis of Algorithm 2.1, is based on the *self-correction paradigm* (cf. [59]). In general, this paradigm refers to functions f for which the value of f at any fixed point x can be reconstructed based on the values of f at a few random points. We stress that each of these points is uniformly distributed in the function's domain, but they are not independent of one another. For example, in the proof of Theorem 2.3 (specifically, in the proof of Claim 2.3.2), we use the fact that, when f is close to a linear function f', the value of $f'(x)$ can be reconstructed from $\phi_y(x) = f(x + y) - f(y)$, where y is uniformly distributed in G. (Note that, in this case, $x + y$ is uniformly distributed in G, but $x + y$ depends on y, since x is fixed.) Specifically,

---

[4] Indeed, the definition of $p_{x,y}$ is fictitious, since the event $\phi(x) + \phi(y) \neq \phi(x + y)$ does not depend on r. In particular, $p_{x,y} \in \{0, 1\}$. An alternative presentation starts with the event $E_{x,y,r}$ captured by Eq. (2.7) and deduces from the existence of $r \in G$ that satisfies $\neg E_{x,y,r}$ that $\phi(x) + \phi(y) = (f(x + r) - f(r)) + (f(r) - f(-y + r)) = f(x + r) - f(-y + r) = \phi(x + y)$.

if f is ϵ-close to the linear function f', then $\mathbf{Pr}_{y \in G}[f'(x) = \phi_y(x)] \geq 1 - 2\epsilon$ for every $x \in G$. We note that here self-correction is used only in the analysis of an algorithm (see the proof of Claim 2.3.2), whereas in other cases (see, e.g., Section 5.2) it is used in the algorithm itself. Furthermore, self-correction is used for reducing worst-case to average-case (see, e.g., [131, Sec. 7.1.3] and [131, Sec. 7.2.1.1]), and some of these applications predate the emergence of property testing.

2.3. Chapter Notes

As stated previously, Algorithm 2.1 was suggested and first analyzed by Blum, Luby, and Rubinfeld [59], in a work that pioneered the study of property testing. The proof of Proposition 2.2 is due to [38], whereas the proof of Theorem 2.3 follows the ideas of [59]. Recall that these results establish lower bounds on the detection probability of Algorithm 2.1.

The True Behavior of Algorithm 2.1. Fixing groups G and H, for every $f : G \to H$, we denote by $\delta_{G,H}(f)$ the distance of f from the set of homomorophisms, and by $\rho_{G,H}(f)$ the probability that Algorithm 2.1 rejects f. Recall that Proposition 2.2 asserts that $\rho_{G,H}(f) \geq 3\delta_{G,H}(f) - 6\delta_{G,H}(f)^2$, whereas Theorem 2.3 asserts that $\rho_{G,H}(f) \geq \min(0.5\delta_{G,H}(f), 1/6)$. These are not the best bounds known. In particular, it is known that $\rho_{G,H}(f) \geq 2/9$ for every f such that $\delta_{G,H}(f) \geq 1/4$ (see [36, 59]). Hence, for every f it holds that $\rho_{G,H}(f) \geq \beta(\delta_{G,H}(f))$, where

$$\beta(x) \overset{\text{def}}{=} \begin{cases} 3x - 6x^2 & \text{if } x \leq \tau \\ 2/9 & \text{if } x \geq \tau \end{cases} \tag{2.8}$$

and $\tau = 0.25 + \sqrt{33}/36 \approx 0.41$ is the positive root of $3x - 6x^2 = 2/9$ (cf. [36]). This bound is depicted in Figure 2.1. Surprisingly enough, for some groups G and H, the bound $\rho_{G,H}(f) \geq \beta(\delta_{G,H}(f))$ is tight in the sense that for every $v \in [0, 5/16]$ there exists f such that $\delta_{G,H}(f) \approx v$ and $\rho_{G,H}(f) = \beta(v) = 3\delta_{G,H}(f) - 6\delta_{G,H}(f)^2$ (cf. [36]). Hence, in these groups, the decrease of β in the interval $[1/4, 5/16]$ represents the actual behavior of the tester: The detection probability of Algorithm 2.1 does *not* necessarily increase with the distance of the function from being homomorphic.

In the special case where H is the two-element field GF(2) and $G = GF(2)^m$, Bellare et al. [36] showed that $\rho_{G,H}(f) \geq \delta_{G,H}(f)$ and that $\rho_{G,H}(f) \geq 45/128$ for every f such that $\delta_{G,H}(f) \geq 1/4$. Thus, for every f it holds that $\rho_{G,H}(f) \geq \beta'(\delta_{G,H}(f))$, where

$$\beta'(x) \overset{\text{def}}{=} \begin{cases} 3x - 6x^2 & \text{if } x \leq 5/16 \\ 45/128 & \text{if } x \in [5/16, 45/128] \\ x & \text{if } x \geq 45/128. \end{cases} \tag{2.9}$$

(This three-segment bound is depicted in Figure 2.2.) Furthermore, Bellare et al. [36] showed that the bound $\rho_{G,H}(f) \geq \beta'(\delta_{G,H}(f))$ is also tight for every value of $\rho_{G,H}(f) \in [0, 5/16]$; that is, the first segment of the bound β', which decreases in the interval $[1/4, 5/16]$, represents the actual behavior of the tester. In contrast, it is known

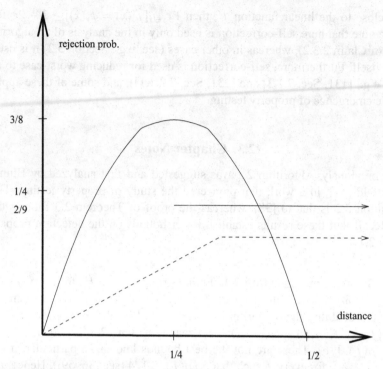

Figure 2.1: The lower bounds on the rejection probability of f as a function of the distance of f from a homomorphism, for general groups. The two solid lines show the bounds underlying $\beta(\cdot)$, whereas the broken dashed line shows the bound $\min(0.5x, 1/6)$.

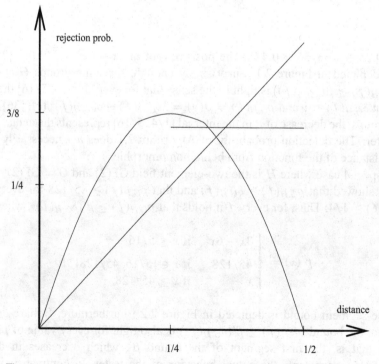

Figure 2.2: The three lower bounds on the rejection probability of f as a function of distance of f from a homomorphism, for $H = \mathrm{GF}(2)$ and $G = \mathrm{GF}(2)^m$.

that the bound $\rho_{G,H}(f) \geq \beta'(\delta_{G,H}(f))$ is *not* tight in the interval $(44.997/128, 0.5)$; in fact, $\rho_{G,H}(f) \geq (1 + \mathrm{poly}(1 - 2\delta_{G,H}(f))) \cdot \delta_{G,H}(f)$, where the extra term is really tiny (see [181]).[5] Still, this indicates that the known bounds used in the second and third segments of β' do not represent the actual behavior of the tester. Determining the exact behavior of $\rho_{G,H}(f)$ as a function of $\delta_{G,H}(f)$ is an open problem (even in this special case where $H = \mathrm{GF}(2)$ and $G = \mathrm{GF}(2)^m$).

Open Problem 2.4 (Determining the exact behavior of Algorithm 2.1): *For any two groups G and H, and for every $x \in (0, 1]$, what is the minimum value of $\rho_{G,H}(f)$ when taken over all $f : G \to H$ such that $\delta_{G,H}(f) = x$?*

Note that for some groups G and H, the bound $\rho_{G,H}(f) \geq \beta(\delta_{G,H}(f))$ may not be tight even for $\delta_{G,H}(f) < 5/16$.

The PCP Connection. We mention that the foregoing linearity test (i.e., Algorithm 2.1) has played a key role in the construction of Probabilistically Checkable Proof (PCP) systems, starting with [24]. Furthermore, a good analysis of this test was important in some of these constructions (see, e.g., [37, 170, 171][6]). For further details, the interested reader is referred to Chapter 13 (see, especially, Section 13.3.1).

Variations. A natural variant of linearity testing consists of testing affine homomorphisms (also known as translations of homomorphisms). A function $f : G \to H$ is called an affine homomorphism if there exists a group homomorphism $h : G \to H$ such that $f(x) = h(x) + f(0)$. (An equivalent definition requires that for every $x, y \in G$, it holds that $f(x + y) = f(x) - f(0) + f(y)$.)[7] Testing whether f is an affine homomorphism reduces to testing whether $h(x) \stackrel{\mathrm{def}}{=} f(x) - f(0)$ is a homomorphism: If f is an affine homomorphism then h is a homomorphism, whereas if f is ϵ-far from being an affine homomorphism then h is ϵ-far from being a homomorphism.[8]

A different variant of linearity testing was considered by David *et al.* [85]. Referring to the special case where $H = \mathrm{GF}(2)$ and $G = \mathrm{GF}(2)^m$, for any $k \in [m]$, they consider functions $f : W_k \to H$, where W_k is the set of m-dimensional Boolean vectors of weight k, and seek to test whether f agrees with a group homomorphism. That is, given oracle access to a function $f : W_k \to H$, the task is to test whether there exists a homomorphism $h : G \to H$ such that $f(x) = h(x)$ for every $x \in W_k$.

Linearity testing has served as a benchmark for several questions concerning PCPs. The fact that the randomness complexity is a key parameter in PCP led to studies of the randomness complexity of linearity testing, which culminated in [254]. We mention that, while the randomness complexity of Algorithm 2.1 is $2 \log_2 |G|$, a saving of randomness

---

[5] The additive $\mathrm{poly}(1 - 2\delta_{G,H}(f))$ term is always smaller than 0.0001.

[6] Actually, Hastad [170, 171] relies on a good analysis of the Long Code (suggested by [37]), but such an analysis would have been inconceivable without a good analysis of linearity tests (i.e., tests of the Hadamard code).

[7] On the one hand, if $f(x) = h(x) + f(0)$ holds for some homomorphism h and all $x \in G$, then $f(x + y) = h(x + y) + f(0) = h(x) + h(y) + f(0) = f(x) - f(0) + f(y)$ for all $x, y \in G$. On the other hand, if $f(x + y) = f(x) - f(0) + f(y)$ holds for all $x, y \in G$, then defining $h(x) \stackrel{\mathrm{def}}{=} f(x) - f(0)$ we get $h(x + y) = f(x + y) - f(0) = f(x) - f(0) + f(y) - f(0) = h(x) + h(y)$ for all $x, y \in G$.

[8] Suppose that h is ϵ-close to a homomorphism h'. Then, f is ϵ-close to f' such that $f'(x) = h'(x) + f(0)$, which means that f' is an affine homomorphism (since $f(0) = h'(0) + f(0) = f'(0)$).

is possible; that is, $\log_2 |G| + \log\log |H| + O(1)$ bits suffice (see Exercise 1.21). This claim ignores the computational complexity of the tester. On the other hand, we note that $\log_2(|G|/q) - O(1)$ random bits are necessary for any tester that makes q queries (see Exercise 1.22). The problem of providing a computationally efficient analogue of the positive result is extensively studied in [254].

CHAPTER THREE

Low-Degree Tests

Summary: We present and analyze a proximity-oblivious tester for the set of polynomials of bounded degree. Specifically, for a finite field of prime cardinality $\mathcal{F}$, a degree bound $d < |\mathcal{F}|/2$, and a number $m \in \mathbb{N}$, we consider a tester that, given oracle access to a function $f : \mathcal{F}^m \to \mathcal{F}$, queries the function at $d + 2$ points and satisfies the following conditions:

1. If f is an m-variate polynomial of (total) degree d, then the tester accepts with probability 1.
2. If f is δ-far from the set of m-variate polynomials of (total) degree d, then the tester rejects with probability at least $\min(0.5\delta, \Omega(d^{-2}))$.

The sequence of queries is generated by selecting at random $\bar{x}$ and $\bar{h}$ uniformly in $\mathcal{F}^m$, and using $\bar{x} + i\bar{h}$ as the ith query.

This chapter is based on the work of Rubinfeld and Sudan [246]; specifically, Section 3.4 is based on [246, Sec. 4], whereas Section 3.3 is based on [246, Apdx.].

3.1. A Brief Introduction

Polynomials of bounded individual degree and of bounded total degree are the most natural sets of functions over the vector space $\mathcal{F}^m$, where $\mathcal{F}$ is a finite field and $m \in \mathbb{N}$. Indeed, such polynomials are ubiquitous in this context, and linear functions over $\mathcal{F}$ are an important special case.

For a finite field $\mathcal{F}$ and any $m \in \mathbb{N}$, any function $f : \mathcal{F}^m \to \mathcal{F}$ can be written as a polynomial of individual degree $|\mathcal{F}| - 1$, that is, as a polynomial that has degree at most $|\mathcal{F}| - 1$ in each variable, and hence has total degree $m \cdot (|\mathcal{F}| - 1)$ (see Exercise 3.1). Thus, one may say that f is a low-degree polynomial if it has degree that is significantly lower than that. Specifically, in this chapter, we call f a low-degree polynomial if it has (total) degree at most d, where $d < |\mathcal{F}|/2$ is a parameter. Testing whether a function is a low-degree polynomial is a natural computational problem, which has direct applications to several areas of the theory of computation, most notably to the design of Probabilistically Checkable Proofs (PCPs) and error correcting codes.

Notation: Fixing a finite field $\mathcal{F}$ and an integer m, we often distinguish m-dimensional vectors over $\mathcal{F}$ from elements of $\mathcal{F}$ by overlining the former. In particular, $\overline{ev}$ denotes the scalar multiplication of the vector $\bar{v} \in \mathcal{F}^m$ by the scalar $e \in \mathcal{F}$; that is, if $\bar{v} = (v_1, \ldots, v_m)$, then $e\bar{v} = (ev_1, \ldots, ev_m)$.

Organization: The tester itself is presented and analyzed in Section 3.4, which relies only on Corollary 3.3 (which is stated at the end of Section 3.3). Still, readers may benefit from the intuition provided in Section 3.2. The proof of Corollary 3.3 is presented in Section 3.3.

> **Teaching Note:** We strongly recommend leaving the contents of Section 3.3 (i.e., the proof of Corollary 3.3) for optional independent reading. We are undecided regarding the question of whether or not to present the intuition provided in Section 3.2 before focusing on the core material presented in Section 3.4.

3.2. A Kind of Intuition (which may be skipped)

In this section, we attempt to provide some intuition for the construction of low-degree tests. We start with the univariate case, and then move to the multivariate case.

3.2.1. The Univariate Case

For $d \ll |\mathcal{F}|$, a natural way of testing whether $f : \mathcal{F} \to \mathcal{F}$ is a (univariate) polynomial of degree (at most) d is to check that the values of f at $d + 2$ distinct random points match some degree d polynomial. Before analyzing this tester, note that it uses $d + 2$ queries to the function f, whereas the size of the field $\mathcal{F}$ may be much larger. Note that this tester can be viewed as first finding (by extrapolation) the (unique) degree d polynomial that fits the values of f on the first $d + 1$ points, and then checking that this polynomial agrees with f on the $d + 2^{\text{nd}}$ point.

The analysis of this tester relies on the fact that the distance of f from the set of polynomials of degree d is upper-bounded by the distance of f to the (unique) degree d polynomial f' that fits the values of f on the first $d + 1$ points. Now, since the $d + 2^{\text{nd}}$ point is uniformly distributed among the other $|\mathcal{F}| - (d + 1)$ points of $\mathcal{F}$, it follows that this point hits a point of disagreement (between f and f') with probability at least $\frac{\delta(f,f') \cdot |\mathcal{F}|}{|\mathcal{F}| - (d+1)} > \delta(f, f')$, which is at least the distance of f from being a polynomial of degree d. (Indeed, the foregoing analysis is oblivious of the distribution of the first $d + 1$ points, which may even be fixed; it only requires that the $d + 2^{\text{nd}}$ point is uniformly distributed (conditioned on being different from the prior points).)

An Alternative Low-Degree Test. Confining ourselves to the case of finite fields of prime cardinality (where the field $\mathcal{F}$ consists of the set $\mathbb{Z}_{|\mathcal{F}|} = \{0, 1, \ldots, |\mathcal{F}| - 1\}$ with addition and multiplication modulo $|\mathcal{F}|$), we consider an alternative low-degree test (for the univariate case). This test, which will be implicitly used later, selects uniformly $r, s \in \mathcal{F}$, and checks that the values of f at $r, r + s, \ldots, r + (d + 1) \cdot s$ match some degree d polynomial. For starters, one can show that, for any $s \neq 0$, it holds that f is a degree d polynomial if and only if for every $r \in \mathcal{F}$ the values of f at $r, r + s, \ldots, r + (d + 1) \cdot s$

match some degree d polynomial.[1] But *how does the rejection probability of this tester relate to the distance of f from the set of degree d polynomials of degree d?*

The answer to the foregoing question follows as a special case of the analysis of the tester outlined below for the set of low-degree m-variate polynomials. Indeed, we would welcome a simpler analysis of the univariate case (or an indication that this special case is not simpler, say, by a *simple* reduction of the multivariate case to the univariate case). But, at this point, we wish to proceed with the intuition.

3.2.2. The Multivariate Case

We now turn to the case of m-variate functions $f : \mathcal{F}^m \to \mathcal{F}$. The first observation here is that f is a degree d polynomial if and only if its values on each line in $\mathcal{F}^m$ can be described by a univariate polynomial of degree d, where a line in $\mathcal{F}^m$ is a ($|\mathcal{F}|$-long) sequence of the form $(\bar{x} + i\bar{h})_{i \in \mathcal{F}}$ such that $\bar{x}, \bar{h} \in \mathcal{F}^m$. One can readily verify that if $f : \mathcal{F}^m \to \mathcal{F}$ is a degree d polynomial, then its values on each line can be described by a univariate polynomial of degree d; that is, the function $f_{\bar{x},\bar{h}} : \mathcal{F} \to \mathcal{F}$ defined as $f_{\bar{x},\bar{h}}(z) = f(\bar{x} + z\bar{h})$ is a polynomial of degree d in z. The opposite direction is less obvious, but it is indeed true (see Theorem 3.1).

At this point, a natural suggestion is to test that $f : \mathcal{F}^m \to \mathcal{F}$ is of degree d by considering the values of f on a random line in $\mathcal{F}^m$. Recall that if f is not of degree d, then there exists a line such that the values of f on this line do not fit a degree d polynomial. But *if f is ϵ-far from being a degree d polynomial, then how far are its values on a random line from fitting a degree d univariate polynomial?*

The answer to the latter question is not obvious. Nevertheless, it is known that the expected distance (of these values from a univariate polynomial) is $\Omega(\epsilon)$, where the expectation is over all possible lines with uniform probability distribution (cf. [120, 26, 165]). In Section 3.4, we will show a lower bound of $\min(\Omega(\epsilon), \Omega(d^{-2}))$, but we have no real intuition to offer (beyond attempting to present the technical proof in words, an attempt we shall not venture). The actual analysis of the foregoing (low-degree) tester mimics the analysis of the linearity tester, but is more complex (in some of its details). Specifically, we define a "self-corrected" version of the tested function and show that if the test rejects with small probability, then this corrected version is a polynomial of degree d that is close to the tested function.[2]

---

[1] Obviously, if f has degree d, then its values at any subset of $\mathcal{F}$ match a degree d polynomial. As would be the case throughout this chapter, the opposite direction is considerably less obvious, and its proof is outlined next. Recall that we wish to show that, for any $s \in \mathcal{F} \setminus \{0\}$, if for every $r \in \mathcal{F}$ the values of f at the $d + 2$ points $r, r + s, \ldots, r + (d + 1) \cdot s$ match some degree d polynomial, then f is a polynomial of degree d. We start by letting f_r denote the (unique) degree d polynomial that agrees with f on the $d + 1$ points $r, r + s, \ldots, r + d \cdot s$, and observe that (by the hypothesis) it holds that $f_r(r + (d + 1) \cdot s) = f(r + (d + 1) \cdot s)$. This implies that $f_r = f_{r+s}$, since $f_{r+s}(r + s + d \cdot s) = f(r + s + d \cdot s)$ (by the definition of f_{r+s}), whereas f_r and f_{r+s} are degree d polynomials (which were shown to agree on the $d + 1$ points $r + s, \ldots, r + (d + 1) \cdot s$). Using the fact that $(r - r')/s \in \mathcal{F}$ for every $r, r' \in \mathcal{F}$, we infer that all the f_r's are identical, and the claim follows since $f(r) = f_r(r)$ for each $r \in \mathcal{F}$ (by the definition of f_r). We mention that this local characterization of low-degree polynomials (which refers to a fixed $s \in \mathcal{F} \setminus \{0\}$) does *not* yield a good tester: see Exercise 3.2.

[2] The following outline of the actual analysis is not supposed to be verifiable at this point. It is provided here mainly in order to evoke the analogy to the analysis of the linearity tester (which was presented in Chapter 2).

Assuming that f is rejected with probability $\rho < 1/O(d^2)$, we shall show that f is 2ρ-close to a low-degree polynomial, by taking the following steps (as in the analysis of the linearity tester):

As in the case of linearity testing, the only intuition we shall offer is an illustration as to why the "self-corrected" version of the function is a low-degree polynomial that is relatively close to the function. The illustration will refer to a function that is obtained by slightly corrupting a low-degree polynomial, and so it will only illustrate that the voting scheme employed when constructing the self-corrected version makes sense.

3.2.3. Linking the Above Intuition to the Actual Proof

The actual tester, presented in Section 3.4, tests that a function $f : \mathcal{F}^m \to \mathcal{F}$ is a polynomial of degree (at most) d by checking whether the values of the function restricted to a random line fit a degree d univariate polynomial, where the latter check is performed by considering the values of this restriction on the first $d + 2$ points. However, the fact that this line is random means that its starting point as well as the gap between its points are random. Specifically, considering the first $d + 2$ values of f on the line $(\overline{x} + i\overline{h})_{i \in \mathcal{F}}$ is analogous to considering the values of f at the points $(\overline{x}' + (r + i \cdot s) \cdot \overline{h}')_{i=0,\dots,d+1}$ such that $\overline{x}' = \overline{x} - r \cdot \overline{h}'$ and $\overline{h}' = s^{-1} \cdot \overline{h}$ (i.e., the points $(r + is)_{i=0,\dots,d-1}$ on the line $(\overline{x}' + j\overline{h}')_{j \in \mathcal{F}}$, assuming $s \neq 0$).[3] Hence, the tester for the m-variate case actually invokes the ("alternative") tester of the univariate case. Furthermore, we use an explicit expression (i.e., Eq. (3.2)) that captures the decision of the latter tester; that is, we spell out the relation among the aforementioned $d + 2$ values of a univariate function such that this relation holds if and only if the univariate function has degree (at most) d.

The analysis of the tester for the m-variate case combines *elements of a reduction* to the univariate case *with an analysis of a specific tester for the univariate case*. Moreover, we refer to the specific expression (i.e., Eq. (3.2)) used by the univariate tester in making its decision. We stress that this analysis does not present an explicit reduction of the m-variate case to the univariate case, although such reductions can be found elsewhere (see, e.g. [120, 26, 165]). These choices are made in order to make the analysis more concrete and hopefully more clear.

Note: For the sake of simplicity, we focus on the case of finite fields of prime cardinality. In this case, the field $\mathcal{F}$ consists of the set $\mathbb{Z}_{|\mathcal{F}|} = \{0, 1, \dots, |\mathcal{F}| - 1\}$ with addition and multiplication modulo $|\mathcal{F}|$. In the general case (of arbitrary finite fields), the sequence $(\overline{x} + i\overline{h})_{i=0}^{d+1}$ is replaced by the sequence $(\overline{x} + e\overline{h}, \overline{x} + e_1\overline{h}, \dots, \overline{x} + e_{d+1}\overline{h})$, where e is

---

- First we define a "self-corrected" version, denoted f', of the function f such that $f'(x)$ is the most frequent vote cast by the lines passing through x.
- Next, we show that f' is 2ρ-close to f, by using the fact that the vote of a specific line regarding $x \in \mathcal{F}^m$ was defined such that it equals $f(x)$ if and only if the test does not reject when examining (the values on) this line.
- Then, we show that there is a strong majority among the votes (for each point), by lower bounding the collision probability of the random variable that represents a vote of a random line.
- Finally, we show that f' is a low-degree polynomial.

The last two steps are performed by showing that each of the corresponding claims can be written as the conjunction of relatively few events that are each related to the check performed by the tester, and using the hypothesis that the rejection probability of the tester (i.e., ρ) is sufficiently small.

[3] Indeed, if $\overline{x}, \overline{h}$ are uniformly distributed in $\mathcal{F}^m$, then so are $\overline{x}', \overline{h}'$. The point made here is that although the test is described as inspecting the points $0, 1, \dots, d + 1$ on a random line, it is actually equivalent to a test that inspects the points $r, r + s, \dots, r + (d + 1) \cdot s$ on a random line, where $s \neq 0$ and r are uniformly and independently distributed in $\mathcal{F}$.

uniformly distributed in $\mathcal{F}$, the e_i's are fixed (distinct) field elements, and the α_i's used in the extrapolation formula (i.e., Eq. (3.2)) are determined accordingly.

Teaching Note: Section 3.3 provides proofs of two basic facts about polynomials (specifically, Theorems 3.1 and 3.2); it is highly technical and offers no intuition (since the author has none to offer). Unfortunately, these two facts (or rather their combination stated in Corollary 3.3) are necessary preliminaries for Section 3.4, which presents the analysis of the tester (which was outlined above). Fortunately, reading Section 3.4 only requires reading the statement of Corollary 3.3, and the reader may skip its proof, which is the bulk of Section 3.3.

3.3. Background

Throughout this chapter, $\mathcal{F}$ is a finite field of prime cardinality, and d, m are integers such that $d < |\mathcal{F}|/2$. We consider functions $f : \mathcal{F}^m \to \mathcal{F}$, and the set $\mathcal{P}_{m,d}$ of m-variate polynomials of total degree (at most) d. Such functions are called low-degree polynomials, because their (total) degree is significantly smaller than $|\mathcal{F}|$.

As shown next, f is in $\mathcal{P}_{m,d}$ if and only if its restriction to each line in $\mathcal{F}^m$ can be represented as a univariate polynomial of degree d, where a line in $\mathcal{F}^m$ is a sequence of the form $L_{\bar{x},\bar{h}} \stackrel{\text{def}}{=} (\bar{x} + i\bar{h})_{i \in \mathcal{F}}$ for $\bar{x}, \bar{h} \in \mathcal{F}^m$, and saying that the restriction of f to the line $L_{\bar{x},\bar{h}}$ is represented by the univariate polynomial p means that $p(i) = f(\bar{x} + i\bar{h})$ for every $i \in \mathcal{F}$. Hence, *the global condition of being a degree d polynomial is characterized as the conjunction of $|\mathcal{F}^m|^2$ local conditions*, where each local condition refers to the value of the function on $|\mathcal{F}|$ points (on a line in $\mathcal{F}^m$).

Theorem 3.1 (Local characterization of multivariate polynomials): *Let $|\mathcal{F}| > 2d$. The function $f : \mathcal{F}^m \to \mathcal{F}$ is in $\mathcal{P}_{m,d}$ if and only if for every $\bar{x}, \bar{h} \in \mathcal{F}^m$ there exists a degree-d univariate polynomial $p_{\bar{x},\bar{h}}$ such that $p_{\bar{x},\bar{h}}(i) = f(\bar{x} + i\bar{h})$ for every $i \in \mathcal{F}$.*

Proof: Clearly, the restriction of $f \in \mathcal{P}_{m,d}$ to any line in $\mathcal{F}^m$ can be represented as a univariate polynomial of degree d, since for every fixed $\bar{x} = (x_1, \ldots, x_m) \in \mathcal{F}^m$ and $\bar{h} = (h_1, \ldots, h_m) \in \mathcal{F}^m$ it holds that $f(\bar{x} + z\bar{h}) = f(x_1 + zh_1, \ldots, x_m + zh_m)$ is a univariate polynomial of degree d in z.

The opposite direction is not straightforward: it asserts that if the restriction of f to each line in $\mathcal{F}^m$ can be represented as a univariate polynomial of degree d, hereafter referred to as the lines-condition, then $f \in \mathcal{P}_{m,d}$. This claim is proved by induction on m, where the base case (of $m = 1$) is trivial. In the induction step (i.e., going from $m - 1$ to m), given an m-variate polynomial $f : \mathcal{F}^m \to \mathcal{F}$ that satisfies the lines-condition, we need to show that $f \in \mathcal{P}_{m,d}$. Towards this end, for every fixed $e \in \mathcal{F}$, we consider the $(m - 1)$-variate polynomial f_e defined by $f_e(x_1, \ldots, x_{m-1}) = f(x_1, \ldots, x_{m-1}, e)$. By the induction hypothesis, f_e is an $(m - 1)$-variate polynomial of degree d (since the restriction of f_e to any line in $\mathcal{F}^{m-1}$ is a degree d univariate polynomial).[4] The following claim implies that f is a polynomial of total degree at most $2d$.

---

[4] This is the case since the restriction of f_e to any line in $\mathcal{F}^{m-1}$ constitutes a restriction of f to a corresponding line in $\mathcal{F}^m$, whereas f satisfies the lines-condition. In other words, if f satisfies the lines-condition, then so does f_e.

Claim 3.1.1 (The degree of f is at most $2d$): *For every $e \in \{0, 1, \ldots, d\}$, let δ_e be the unique degree d univariate polynomial that satisfies $\delta_e(e) = 1$ and $\delta_e(e') = 0$ for every $e' \in \{0, 1, \ldots, d\} \setminus \{e\}$. Then, $f(\overline{x}) = \sum_{e=0}^{d} \delta_e(x_m) f_e(x_1, \ldots, x_{m-1})$. Hence, f has degree at most d in x_m, whereas its total degree in $x_1, \ldots, x_{m-1}$ is at most d.*

(The fact that δ_e has degree d is shown in Exercise 3.1.)

Proof: Fixing any $e_1, \ldots, e_{m-1} \in \mathcal{F}$, we first observe that $g_{e_1,\ldots,e_{m-1}}(x) \stackrel{\text{def}}{=} f(e_1, \ldots, e_{m-1}, x)$ is a degree d univariate polynomial in x, since $g_{e_1,\ldots,e_{m-1}}$ describes the restriction of f to the line $L_{(e_1,\ldots,e_{m-1},0),(0,\ldots,0,1)}$ (and f satisfies the lines-condition). Next, we show that $f(e_1, \ldots, e_{m-1}, x) = \sum_{e=0}^{d} \delta_e(x) f_e(e_1, \ldots, e_{m-1})$. This holds since each side of the equation is a degree d univariate polynomial in x, whereas these two polynomials agree on $d + 1$ points (specifically, for every $e' \in \{0, 1, \ldots, d\}$, it holds that $\sum_{e=0}^{d} \delta_e(e') f_e(e_1, \ldots, e_{m-1})$ equals $f_{e'}(e_1, \ldots, e_{m-1}) = f(e_1, \ldots, e_{m-1}, e')$). Having shown that $f(e_1, \ldots, e_{m-1}, x) = \sum_{e=0}^{d} \delta_e(x) f_e(e_1, \ldots, e_{m-1})$, for every $e_1, \ldots, e_{m-1} \in \mathcal{F}$, the claim follows. ∎

To show that f is actually of degree d, we consider for each $\overline{h} \in \mathcal{F}^m$ the univariate polynomial $g_{\overline{h}}(z) = f(z\overline{h})$. On the one hand, $\deg(g_{\overline{h}}) \leq d$ for every $\overline{h} \in \mathcal{F}^m$, since $g_{\overline{h}}$ describes the values of f on the line $L_{\overline{0},\overline{h}}$. On the other hand, we shall show next that $\deg(g_{\overline{h}}) = \deg(f)$ for some $\overline{h} \in \mathcal{F}^m$, and $\deg(f) \leq d$ will follow.

Claim 3.1.2 (The degree of some $g_{\overline{h}}$ equals the degree of f): *There exists $\overline{h} \in \mathcal{F}^m$ such that $\deg(g_{\overline{h}}) = \deg(f)$.*

Proof: We actually prove that, with probability at least $1 - \frac{\deg(f)}{|\mathcal{F}|} > 0$ over the choice of $\overline{h} \in \mathcal{F}^m$, it holds that $\deg(g_{\overline{h}}) = \deg(f)$, where the inequality uses $\deg(f) \leq 2d < |\mathcal{F}|$ (established by Claim 3.1.1). We may assume that f is a nonzero polynomial, or else the claim is trivial. Now, to prove this claim, consider the coefficient of $z^{\deg(f)}$ in $f(z\overline{h})$. This coefficient is a nonzero polynomial in $\overline{h}$ of total degree at most $\deg(f)$, whereas any nonzero polynomial of degree d' evaluates to zero on at most a $d'/|\mathcal{F}|$ fraction of the points (see Exercise 3.3). Hence, with probability at least $1 - \frac{\deg(f)}{|\mathcal{F}|} > 0$ over the choice of $\overline{h} \in \mathcal{F}^m$, the coefficient of $z^{\deg(f)}$ in $g_{\overline{h}}(z)$ is nonzero. ∎

Having proved Claim 3.1.2, the theorem follows (since for this $\overline{h}$ it holds that $\deg(f) = \deg(g_{\overline{h}}) \leq d$). ∎

Theorem 3.1 characterizes low-degree multivariate polynomials in terms of low-degree univariate polynomials. Specifically, the global condition regarding the multivariate function $f : \mathcal{F}^m \to \mathcal{F}$ was shown equivalent to the conjunction of $|\mathcal{F}|^{2m}$ local conditions, where each of these conditions asserts that some univariate function (defined based on f) is of low degree. But these conditions are not "ultimately" local, since each of them refers to $|\mathcal{F}|$ values of f. We now show that the condition of being a univariate polynomial of degree at most $d \ll |\mathcal{F}|$ over $\mathcal{F}$ can be expressed as a conjunction of $|\mathcal{F}|$ conditions such that each condition refers only to $d + 2$ values.[5] These conditions have a very explicit form in the case that $\mathcal{F}$ has prime cardinality.

Notation. For $i = 0, 1, \ldots, d + 1$, let $\alpha_i = (-1)^{i+1} \cdot \binom{d+1}{i}$. The α_i's (or rather their values reduced modulo $|\mathcal{F}|$) are viewed as elements of $\mathcal{F}$.

Theorem 3.2 (Local characterization of univariate polynomials): *A univariate polynomial* $g : \mathcal{F} \to \mathcal{F}$ *has degree* $d < |\mathcal{F}|$ *if and only if for every* $e \in \mathcal{F}$ *it holds that*

$$\sum_{i=0}^{d+1} \alpha_i \cdot g(e + i) = 0. \tag{3.1}$$

We view Eq. (3.1) as an extrapolation formula: it determines the value of g at a point based on its value at $d + 1$ other points (i.e., we rewrite Eq. (3.1) as $g(e) = \sum_{i=1}^{d+1} \alpha_i \cdot g(e + i)$, while using $\alpha_0 = -1$). This formula refers to $d + 2$ specific points (and to specific extrapolation coefficients given by the α_i's). This specific formula relies on the hypothesis that $0, 1, \ldots, d + 1$ are distinct field elements, which holds since $|\mathcal{F}|$ is postulated to be a *prime* (and $|\mathcal{F}| \geq d + 2$).[6] In the general case (i.e., for an arbitrary finite field $\mathcal{F}$ of size at least $d + 2$), the sequence $(e + i)_{i=0}^{d+1}$ is replaced by the sequence $(e, e_1, \ldots, e_{d+1})$, where the e_i's are fixed (distinct) field elements, e varies, and the α_i's used in Eq. (3.1) are determined accordingly (depending on the e_i's and e).[7] In both cases, the global condition of being a degree d univariate polynomial is characterized as the conjunction of $|\mathcal{F}|$ local conditions, where each local condition refers to the value of the function at $d + 2$ points (whereas d may be much smaller than $|\mathcal{F}|$).

Proof: We shall first show that g has degree exactly $d > 0$ if and only if (its "derivative" function) $g'(x) \stackrel{\text{def}}{=} g(x + 1) - g(x)$ has degree exactly $d - 1$, and then use this fact in order to establish the main claim (i.e., the claim of the theorem) by induction on d.

Claim 3.2.1 (The degree of g is determined by the degree of g'): *For* $g : \mathcal{F} \to \mathcal{F}$, *let* $g' : \mathcal{F} \to \mathcal{F}$ *be defined by* $g'(x) \stackrel{\text{def}}{=} g(x + 1) - g(x)$. *Then,* g *has degree exactly* $d > 0$ *if and only if* g' *has degree exactly* $d - 1$.

Proof: Writing $g(x) = \sum_{j=0}^{d} c_j \cdot x^j$, where $c_d \neq 0$, we get

$$g'(x) = \sum_{j=0}^{d} c_j \cdot (x + 1)^j - \sum_{j=0}^{d} c_j \cdot x^j$$

---

[5] **Advanced comment:** In contrast, note that such a characterization cannot be based on the values of the function at $d + 1$ points, since the values of a random univariate polynomial of degree d at any $d + 1$ points are indistinguishable from the values of a random function (from $\mathcal{F}$ to $\mathcal{F}$) at these points.

[6] The case of $|\mathcal{F}| = d + 1$ holds trivially, since every function over $\mathcal{F}$ is a polynomial of degree at most $|\mathcal{F}| - 1$.

[7] See Exercise 3.4. Indeed, in the case that $|\mathcal{F}|$ is a prime, we used $e_i = e + i$ for every $i = 1, \ldots, d + 1$, and the α_i's were independent of e. Hence, in that case we used e_i's that vary with e rather than fixed e_i's. This difference mirrors the difference between the two different testers for the univariate case presented in Section 3.2.

$$= \sum_{j=0}^{d} c_j \cdot ((x+1)^j - x^j)$$

$$= \sum_{j=1}^{d} c_j \cdot \sum_{k=0}^{j-1} \binom{j}{k} \cdot x^k.$$

It follows that the degree of g' is at most $d - 1$, whereas the coefficient of x^{d-1} equals $c_d \cdot \binom{d}{d-1} = c_d \cdot d \neq 0$, where the inequality uses $c_d \neq 0$ and $d \in \{1, \ldots, |\mathcal{F}| - 1\}$. The claim follows. ∎

Teaching Note: The rest of the proof can be made more transparent by explicitly introducing iterative derivatives, proving that g is of degree d if and only if its $d + 1^{\text{st}}$ derivative is identically zero, and showing that this derivative equals $\sum_{i=0}^{d+1}(-1)^{d+1-i} \cdot \binom{d+1}{i} \cdot g(x+i)$. This strategy is detailed in Exercise 3.5. The author prefers not to introduce an additional notion for the sake of a proof of a highly technical nature, and notes that the actual arguments are analogous.

We now prove the main claim (i.e., the characterization of univariate polynomials via Eq. (3.1)) by induction on d. For the base case (i.e., $d = 0$) we observe that g is a constant function if and only if $-g(e) + g(e+1) = 0$ holds for every $e \in \mathcal{F}$. For the induction step (i.e., going from $d - 1$ to d), we use the fact that g has degree $d > 0$ if and only if g' has degree $d - 1$. Using the induction hypothesis, the latter condition coincides with $\sum_{i=0}^{d}(-1)^{i+1} \cdot \binom{d}{i} \cdot g'(e+i) = 0$ for every $e \in \mathcal{F}$. Hence, g has degree d if and only if (for every $e \in \mathcal{F}$)

$$\sum_{i=0}^{d}(-1)^{i+1} \cdot \binom{d}{i} \cdot (g(e+i+1) - g(e+i)) = 0.$$

Finally, note that

$$\sum_{i=0}^{d}(-1)^{i+1} \cdot \binom{d}{i} \cdot (g(e+i+1) - g(e+i))$$

$$= \sum_{i=0}^{d}(-1)^{i+1} \cdot \binom{d}{i} \cdot g(e+i+1) - \sum_{i=0}^{d}(-1)^{i+1} \cdot \binom{d}{i} \cdot g(e+i)$$

$$= \sum_{j=1}^{d+1}(-1)^{j} \cdot \binom{d}{j-1} \cdot g(e+j) + \sum_{i=0}^{d}(-1)^{i} \cdot \binom{d}{i} \cdot g(e+i)$$

$$= g(e) + (-1)^{d+1} \cdot g(e+d+1) + \sum_{i=1}^{d}(-1)^{i} \cdot \left(\binom{d}{i-1} + \binom{d}{i}\right) \cdot g(e+i)$$

$$= -\sum_{i=0}^{d+1}(-1)^{i+1} \binom{d+1}{i} \cdot g(e+i)$$

and the inductive claim follows. ∎

Combining Theorems 3.1 and 3.2, we get:

Corollary 3.3 *Let $|\mathcal{F}| > 2d$ and $\alpha_i = (-1)^{i+1} \cdot \binom{d+1}{i}$. The function $f : \mathcal{F}^m \to \mathcal{F}$ is in $\mathcal{P}_{m,d}$ if and only if for every $\bar{x}, \bar{h} \in \mathcal{F}^m$ it holds that*

$$\sum_{i=0}^{d+1} \alpha_i \cdot f(\bar{x} + i\bar{h}) = 0. \tag{3.2}$$

Proof: Clearly (by Theorem 3.2)[8], any $f \in \mathcal{P}_{m,d}$ satisfies Eq. (3.2), for every $\bar{x}, \bar{h} \in \mathcal{F}^m$. When proving the opposite direction, for every line $L = L_{\bar{x},\bar{h}}$, we use Eq. (3.2) on the sequence $((\bar{x} + e\bar{h}) + i\bar{h})_{i=0}^{d+1}$, for each $e \in \mathcal{F}$, and infer (by Theorem 3.2) that the restriction of f to L is a univariate polynomial of degree d. Specifically, for every line $L = L_{\bar{x},\bar{h}}$, we consider the function $g_L(z) = f(\bar{x} + z\bar{h})$ and infer $\sum_{i=0}^{d+1} \alpha_i g_L(e + i) = 0$ (for each $e \in F$) by using Eq. (3.2) on the points $(\bar{x} + e\bar{h} + i\bar{h})_{i=0}^{d+1}$ (i.e., using $\sum_{i=0}^{d+1} \alpha_i f((\bar{x} + e\bar{h}) + i\bar{h}) = 0$). We complete the proof by using the non-obvious direction of Theorem 3.1. ∎

3.4. The Tester

Recall that we consider functions $f : \mathcal{F}^m \to \mathcal{F}$, where $\mathcal{F}$ be a finite field of prime cardinality, and the set $\mathcal{P}_{m,d}$ of m-variate polynomials of total degree d, which is considered "low" since $d < |\mathcal{F}|/2$.

The characterization provided in Corollary 3.3 asserts that the global condition $f \in \mathcal{P}_{m,d}$ can be decomposed into $|\mathcal{F}^m|^2$ local conditions, where each local condition refers to the value of f at $d + 2$ points in $\mathcal{F}^m$. Such a decomposition, yielding a characterization via a conjunction of many local conditions, is a highly non-obvious phenomenon. It is even more non-obvious that the corresponding characterization is robust in the sense that the fraction of unsatisfied local conditions is related to the distance of the object from the global condition.[9]

A Parenthetical Discussion. Note that while a characterization states a qualitative dichotomy (i.e., X holds if and only if Y holds), a robust characterization is a quantitative version that relates the "level of violation" of each of its "sides" (i.e., X is "δ-close to being satisfied" if and only if Y is "ρ-close to being satisfied"). The notion of closeness used here need not coincide with the notion of closeness used throughout this book. Still, in the specific case discussed here there is a correspondence: What we shall show is that f is δ-close to $\mathcal{P}_{m,d}$ if and only if a $1 - \Theta_d(\delta)$ fraction of the local conditions concerning f are satisfied, where the notation Θ_d hides factors that depend (polynomially) on d. Actually, we shall only show that if $f \in \mathcal{P}_{m,d}$ then all local conditions are satisfied, whereas if

---

[8] Indeed, we also use the obvious direction of Theorem 3.1.

[9] Artificial examples where a local characterization is not robust are easy to generate; for example, we can augment any local characterization by many copies of the same local conditions (or insignificant variants of the same condition). Natural examples also exist: one such example is provided by Exercise 3.2.

f is δ-far from $\mathcal{P}_{m,d}$ then at least a $\min(\Omega(\delta), \Omega_d(1))$ fraction of the local conditions are unsatisfied.[10]

The foregoing discussion leads to the following tester, which selects a local condition at random among the $|\mathcal{F}^m|^2$ conditions referred to in Corollary 3.3.

Algorithm 3.4 (Testing whether f is in $\mathcal{P}_{m,d}$): *Select uniformly $\bar{x}, \bar{h} \in \mathcal{F}^m$, query f at the points $\bar{x}, \bar{x} + \bar{h}, \ldots, \bar{x} + (d+1)\bar{h}$, and accept if and only if these values satisfy Eq. (3.2). That is, the tester accepts if and only if*

$$\sum_{i=0}^{d+1} \alpha_i \cdot f(\bar{x} + i\bar{h}) = 0, \tag{3.3}$$

where $\alpha_i = (-1)^{i+1} \cdot \binom{d+1}{i}$.

Essentially, the test checks whether the degree d univariate polynomial that interpolates the values of f on the first $d + 1$ points on a random line agrees with the value assigned by f to the $d + 2^{\text{nd}}$ point (on that line). In other words, the test checks whether the value extrapolated for the $d + 2^{\text{nd}}$ point based on the first $d + 1$ points matches the actual value of that point (according to f itself). The fact that we use "evenly spaced" points as the $d + 2$ points on the (random) line is inessential to the validity of this tester, but it allows to present an explicit extrapolation formula (in the case that $|\mathcal{F}|$ is prime).

3.4.1. Analysis of the Tester

Recall that (by Corollary 3.3) $f \in \mathcal{P}_{m,d}$ if and only if Eq. (3.3) holds for every $\bar{x}, \bar{h} \in \mathcal{F}^m$. At times, it will be useful to write Eq. (3.3) as $f(\bar{x}) = \sum_{i=1}^{d+1} \alpha_i \cdot f(\bar{x} + i\bar{h})$, which asserts that the value of $f \in \mathcal{P}_{m,d}$ at $\bar{x}$ is determined (via extrapolation) by the value of f on $d + 1$ other points on the line $L_{\bar{x},\bar{h}} = (\bar{x} + i\bar{h})_{i \in \mathcal{F}}$.

Theorem 3.5 (Analysis of Algorithm 3.4): *Let $\delta_0 = 1/(d+2)^2$. Then, Algorithm 3.4 is a (one-sided error) proximity-oblivious tester with detection probability $\min(\delta, \delta_0)/2$, where δ denotes the distance of the given function from $\mathcal{P}_{m,d}$.*

> **Teaching Note:** The following proof uses the strategy used in the ("full") analysis of the linearity tester of Blum, Luby, and Rubinfeld [59], as presented in the proof of Theorem 2.3. Indeed, the implementation of this strategy is more complex in the current setting (of low-degree testing).

Proof: By (the easier direction of) Corollary 3.3, each $f \in \mathcal{P}_{m,d}$ is accepted by the tester with probability 1. Hence, the theorem follows by proving that if f is at distance δ from $\mathcal{P}_{m,d}$, then it is accepted by the tester with probability at most $1 - \min(\delta, \delta_0)/2$. Towards this goal, we denote by ρ the probability that f is rejected,

---

[10] The reader can easily verify that if f is δ-close to $\mathcal{P}_{m,d}$, then at most a $O_d(\delta)$ fraction of the local conditions is unsatisfied. This follows from the fact that each of the $d + 2$ queries made by the following tester is uniformly distributed in $\mathcal{F}^m$.

and show that if $\rho < \delta_0/2$, then f is 2ρ-close to $\mathcal{P}_{m,d}$.[11] This is shown by presenting a function g, and proving that g is 2ρ-close to f and that g is in $\mathcal{P}_{m,d}$.

The intuition underlying the proof is that the hypothesis regarding f (i.e., that it is rejected with probability $\rho < \delta_0/2$) implies that f can be modified (or "corrected") into a low-degree polynomial by modifying f on relatively few values (i.e., on at most $2\rho \cdot |\mathcal{F}^m|$ values). Specifically, the hypothesis that $\mathbf{Pr}_{\bar{x},\bar{h} \in \mathcal{F}^m}[f(\bar{x}) \neq \sum_{i \in [d+1]} \alpha_i \cdot f(\bar{x} + i\bar{h})] = \rho < 1/2(d+2)^2$ suggests that a "corrected" version of f that is determined (at each $\bar{x} \in \mathcal{F}^m$) according to the most frequent value of $\sum_{i \in [d+1]} \alpha_i \cdot f(\bar{x} + i\bar{h})$, when considering all possible choices of $\bar{h} \in \mathcal{F}^m$, is a polynomial of degree d that is relatively close to f. Suppose, *for illustration*, that f is obtained by selecting an arbitrary degree d polynomial p and corrupting it on relatively few points (say on fewer than $|\mathcal{F}^m|/2(d+1)$ points). Then, the corrected version of f will equal p (since for a random $\bar{h} \in \mathcal{F}^m$, with probability at least $1 - (d+1) \cdot \rho > 1/2$ it holds that $\sum_{i \in [d+1]} \alpha_i \cdot f(\bar{x} + i\bar{h}) = \sum_{i \in [d+1]} \alpha_i \cdot p(\bar{x} + i\bar{h})$ which equals $p(\bar{x})$ (by Corollary 3.3)), and both claims hold (i.e., p is a polynomial of degree d that is relatively close to f). Needless to say, we cannot start with the foregoing assumption,[12] but should rather start from an arbitrary f that satisfies

$$\mathbf{Pr}_{\bar{x},\bar{h} \in \mathcal{F}^m}\left[\sum_{i=0}^{d+1} \alpha_i \cdot f(\bar{x} + i\bar{h}) = 0\right] = 1 - \rho, \tag{3.4}$$

where $\rho < \delta_0/2 = 1/2(d+2)^2$. We now turn to the actual proof, while recalling that the expression in Eq. (3.4) is equivalent to $f(\bar{x}) = \sum_{i=1}^{d+1} \alpha_i \cdot f(\bar{x} + i\bar{h})$.

Recall that assuming that $\rho < \delta_0/2$, we intend to present a function $g : \mathcal{F}^m \to \mathcal{F}$, and prove that g is 2ρ-close to f and that g is in $\mathcal{P}_{m,d}$. In accordance with the foregoing discussion, we define $g(\bar{x})$ as the most likely value of $\sum_{i=1}^{d+1} \alpha_i \cdot f(\bar{x} + i\bar{h})$, when $\bar{h}$ is uniformly distributed. In other words, letting $\mathrm{MFO}_{e \in S}\{v_e\}$ denote the *most frequently occurring* value of v_e when $e \in S$ (with ties broken arbitrarily), we define

$$g(\bar{x}) \overset{\text{def}}{=} \mathrm{MFO}_{\bar{h} \in \mathcal{F}^m}\left\{\sum_{i=1}^{d+1} \alpha_i \cdot f(\bar{x} + i\bar{h})\right\}. \tag{3.5}$$

Indeed, by Eq. (3.4), the function g is likely to agree with f on a random $\bar{x} \in \mathcal{F}^m$, and so g is likely to satisfy Eq. (3.3) on random $\bar{x}, \bar{h} \in \mathcal{F}^m$. However, we need much stronger assertions than the one just made, and stronger assertions will indeed be provided by the following claims.

Claim 3.5.1 (Closeness): *The function g is 2ρ-close to f.*

Proof: This is merely an averaging argument, which counts as bad any point $\bar{x}$ such that Eq. (3.3) is satisfied by at most half of the possible $\bar{h}$'s, while noting that otherwise g agrees with f on $\bar{x}$. Details follow.

---

[11] Hence, either $\rho \geq \delta_0/2$ or $\rho \geq \delta/2$, which implies $\rho \geq \min(\delta, \delta_0)/2$, as claimed.

[12] The gap between this illustration and the actual proof is reflected in the fact that the illustration refers to $\delta < 1/2(d+1)$, whereas the actual proof uses $\rho < 1/2(d+2)^2$.

Let B denote the set of $\bar{x}$'s such that Eq. (3.3) is satisfied by at most half of the possible $\bar{h}$'s; that is, $\bar{x} \in B$ if and only if

$$\mathbf{Pr}_{\bar{h} \in \mathcal{F}^m} \left[\sum_{i=0}^{d+1} \alpha_i \cdot f(\bar{x} + i\bar{h}) = 0 \right] \leq 0.5.$$

Now, on the one hand, $\mathbf{Pr}_{\bar{x} \in \mathcal{F}^m}[\bar{x} \in B] \leq 2\rho$, because otherwise $\mathbf{Pr}_{\bar{x}, \bar{h} \in \mathcal{F}^m}[\sum_{i=0}^{d+1} \alpha_i \cdot f(\bar{x} + i\bar{h}) \neq 0]$ is greater than $2\rho \cdot 0.5$ (in contradiction to Eq. (3.4)). On the other hand, for every $\bar{x} \in \mathcal{F}^m \setminus B$, it holds that

$$\mathbf{Pr}_{\bar{h} \in \mathcal{F}^m} \left[f(\bar{x}) = \sum_{i=1}^{d+1} \alpha_i \cdot f(\bar{x} + i\bar{h}) \right] > 0.5,$$

which implies that $f(\bar{x})$ is the majority value (obtained by the r.h.s. of the foregoing random variable) and hence $f(\bar{x}) = g(\bar{x})$. ∎

Recall that $g(\bar{x})$ was defined to equal the most frequent value of $\sum_{i=1}^{d+1} \alpha_i \cdot f(\bar{x} + i\bar{h})$, where frequencies were taken over all possible $\bar{h} \in \mathcal{F}^m$. Hence, $g(\bar{x})$ occurs with frequency at least $1/|\mathcal{F}|$ (yet, we saw, in the proof of Claim 3.5.1, that on at least $1 - 2\rho$ of the $\bar{x}$'s it holds that $g(\bar{x})$ is the majority value). We next show that $g(\bar{x})$ is much more frequent: it occurs in a strong majority (for every $\bar{x}$).

Claim 3.5.2 (Strong majority): *For every $\bar{x} \in \mathcal{F}^m$, it holds that*

$$\mathbf{Pr}_{\bar{h} \in \mathcal{F}^m} \left[g(\bar{x}) = \sum_{i=1}^{d+1} \alpha_i \cdot f(\bar{x} + i\bar{h}) \right] \geq 1 - 2(d+1)\rho.$$

Proof: For each $\bar{x} \in \mathcal{F}^m$, we consider the random variable $Z_{\bar{x}}(\bar{h})$ defined to equal $\sum_{i=1}^{d+1} \alpha_i \cdot f(\bar{x} + i\bar{h})$, where the probability space is uniform over the choice of $\bar{h} \in \mathcal{F}^m$. By Eq. (3.4), we have $\mathbf{Pr}_{\bar{x} \in \mathcal{F}^m}[f(\bar{x}) = Z_{\bar{x}}] = 1 - \rho$, which means that for typical $\bar{x}$ the value $Z_{\bar{x}}$ is almost always a fixed value (i.e., $f(\bar{x})$), which implies that $Z_{\bar{x}} = g(\bar{x})$ with high probability. However, we want to establish such a statement for any $\bar{x}$, not only for typical ones.

Fixing any $\bar{x} \in \mathcal{F}^m$, the idea is to lower-bound the collision probability of $Z_{\bar{x}}$, which equals $\mathbf{Pr}_{\bar{h}_1, \bar{h}_2 \in \mathcal{F}^m}[Z_{\bar{x}}(\bar{h}_1) = Z_{\bar{x}}(\bar{h}_2)]$. (If this lower bound is greater than half, then the same lower bound would hold for $\mathbf{Pr}[Z_{\bar{x}} = g(\bar{x})]$.) Recalling that $Z_{\bar{x}}(\bar{h}) = \sum_{i=1}^{d+1} \alpha_i \cdot f(\bar{x} + i\bar{h})$, we consider

$$\mathbf{Pr}_{\bar{h}_1, \bar{h}_2 \in \mathcal{F}^m} \left[\sum_{i=1}^{d+1} \alpha_i \cdot f(\bar{x} + i\bar{h}_1) = \sum_{i=1}^{d+1} \alpha_i \cdot f(\bar{x} + i\bar{h}_2) \right]. \tag{3.6}$$

The key observation is that each point (except $\bar{x}$) on each of these two lines (i.e., on the lines $L_{\bar{x}, \bar{h}_1}$ and $L_{\bar{x}, \bar{h}_2}$)[13] is uniformly distributed in $\mathcal{F}^m$, and hence we can apply Eq. (3.4) to each such point (i.e., to $\bar{x} + i\bar{h}_j$ for any $i \neq 0$ and $j \in \{1, 2\}$) using a random direction. Furthermore, we can use the direction $\bar{h}_2$ (resp., $\bar{h}_1$) for the points on $L_{\bar{x}, \bar{h}_1}$ (resp., $L_{\bar{x}, \bar{h}_2}$), which means that, for every $i \in [d+1]$, we apply Eq. (3.4) to the points $((\bar{x} + i\bar{h}_1) + j\bar{h}_2)_{j=0}^{d+1}$ (resp., $((\bar{x} + i\bar{h}_2) + j\bar{h}_1)_{j=0}^{d+1}$). Doing so allows to

---

[13] Recall that $L_{\bar{x}, \bar{h}} = (\bar{x} + i\bar{h})_{i \in \mathcal{F}}$.

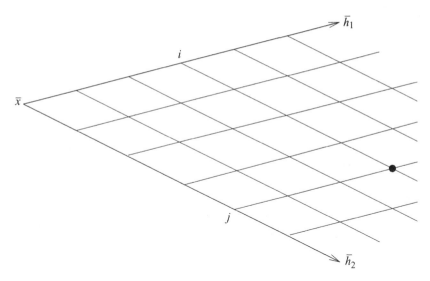

Figure 3.1: The lattice spanned by $\bar{h}_1$ and $\bar{h}_2$, and the point $\bar{x} + i\bar{h}_1 + j\bar{h}_2$.

express each of the two sums in Eq. (3.6) by the same double summation, since (as illustrated by Figure 3.1) the jth point on the line $L_{\bar{x}+i\bar{h}_1,\bar{h}_2}$ coincides with the ith point on the line $L_{\bar{x}+j\bar{h}_2,\bar{h}_1}$ (i.e., $(\bar{x} + i\bar{h}_1) + j\bar{h}_2 = (\bar{x} + j\bar{h}_2) + i\bar{h}_1$). As shown below, it follows that the collision probability of $Z_{\bar{x}}$ is lower bounded by $1 - 2(d + 1) \cdot \rho$, and consequently the most frequent value of $Z_{\bar{x}}$, which is $g(\bar{x})$, occurs with probability at least $1 - 2(d + 1)\rho$.

We now turn to the actual proof, where an arbitrary $\bar{x} \in \mathcal{F}^m$ is fixed (for the entire proof). For every $i, j \in [d + 1]$, if $\bar{h}_1$ and $\bar{h}_2$ are uniformly and independently distributed in $\mathcal{F}^m$, then so are $\bar{x} + i\bar{h}_1$ and $j\bar{h}_2$ (resp., $\bar{x} + j\bar{h}_2$ and $i\bar{h}_1$). Hence, by Eq. (3.4), for every $i \in [d + 1]$, it follows that,

$$\mathbf{Pr}_{\bar{h}_1,\bar{h}_2 \in \mathcal{F}^m}\left[f(\bar{x} + i\bar{h}_1) = \sum_{j=1}^{d+1} \alpha_j \cdot f((\bar{x} + i\bar{h}_1) + j\bar{h}_2) \right] = 1 - \rho, \tag{3.7}$$

and likewise for every $j \in [d + 1]$,

$$\mathbf{Pr}_{\bar{h}_1,\bar{h}_2 \in \mathcal{F}^m}\left[f(\bar{x} + j\bar{h}_2) = \sum_{i=1}^{d+1} \alpha_i \cdot f((\bar{x} + j\bar{h}_2) + i\bar{h}_1) \right] = 1 - \rho. \tag{3.8}$$

Hence, using a union bound (over $i \in [d + 1]$ (resp., $j \in [d + 1]$)), we have

$$\mathbf{Pr}_{\bar{h}_1,\bar{h}_2 \in \mathcal{F}^m}\left[\sum_{i=1}^{d+1} \alpha_i f(\bar{x} + i\bar{h}_1) = \sum_{i=1}^{d+1}\sum_{j=1}^{d+1} \alpha_i\alpha_j \cdot f(\bar{x} + i\bar{h}_1 + j\bar{h}_2) \right] \geq 1 - (d + 1) \cdot \rho \tag{3.9}$$

$$\mathbf{Pr}_{\bar{h}_1,\bar{h}_2 \in \mathcal{F}^m}\left[\sum_{j=1}^{d+1} \alpha_j f(\bar{x} + j\bar{h}_2) = \sum_{j=1}^{d+1}\sum_{i=1}^{d+1} \alpha_i\alpha_j \cdot f(\bar{x} + i\bar{h}_1 + j\bar{h}_2) \right] \geq 1 - (d + 1) \cdot \rho, \tag{3.10}$$

which implies (by a union bound on Eq. (3.9)&(3.10)) that

$$\mathbf{Pr}_{\bar{h}_1, \bar{h}_2 \in \mathcal{F}^m} \left[\sum_{i=1}^{d+1} \alpha_i f(\bar{x} + i\bar{h}_1) = \sum_{j=1}^{d+1} \alpha_j f(\bar{x} + j\bar{h}_2) \right] \geq 1 - 2(d+1)\rho. \qquad (3.11)$$

Note that the two summations in Eq. (3.11) represent two independent (and identically distributed) random variables, which are functions of $\bar{h}_1$ and $\bar{h}_2$ respectively. Furthermore, each of these summations is distributed identically to the random variable $Z_{\bar{x}}(\bar{h}) \stackrel{\text{def}}{=} \sum_{i=1}^{d+1} \alpha_i f(\bar{x} + i\bar{h})$, which is a function of a uniformly distributed $\bar{h} \in \mathcal{F}^m$. This means that the collision probability of $Z = Z_{\bar{x}}$ (which equals $\sum_u \mathbf{Pr}[Z = u]^2$) is at least $1 - 2(d+1)\rho$, which implies that the most frequent value occurs in Z with probability at least $1 - 2(d+1)\rho$ (since if v is the most frequent value assigned to Z then $\sum_u \mathbf{Pr}[Z = u]^2 \leq \sum_u \mathbf{Pr}[Z = v] \cdot \mathbf{Pr}[Z = u] = \mathbf{Pr}[Z = v]$). Recalling that $g(\bar{x})$ was defined as the most frequent value of $Z_{\bar{x}}$, the claim follows. ∎

Using Claim 3.5.2, we now show that $g \in \mathcal{P}_{m,d}$. This follows by combining Claim 3.5.3 with the characterization of $\mathcal{P}_{m,d}$.

Claim 3.5.3 $(g \in \mathcal{P}_{m,d})$: *For every* $\bar{x}, \bar{h} \in \mathcal{F}^m$, *it holds that* $\sum_{i=0}^{d+1} \alpha_i \cdot g(\bar{x} + i\bar{h}) = 0$.

Proof: As in the proof of the analogous claim in the analysis of the linearity test, we prove the claim by considering a fictitious probabilistic expression regarding the event $\sum_{i=0}^{d+1} \alpha_i \cdot g(\bar{x} + i\bar{h}) = 0$, when $\bar{x}$ and $\bar{h}$ are fixed. That is, fixing any $\bar{x}, \bar{h} \in \mathcal{F}^m$, we prove that $\sum_{i=0}^{d+1} \alpha_i \cdot g(\bar{x} + i\bar{h}) = 0$ by showing that $\mathbf{Pr}_{\bar{h}_1, \bar{h}_2} [\sum_{i=0}^{d+1} \alpha_i \cdot g(\bar{x} + i\bar{h}) = 0] > 0$. (The random directions $\bar{h}_1$ and $\bar{h}_2$ will be used to set up a lattice of random points and argue about them in a way that is similar to the proof of Claim 3.5.2, although the specific lattice and the arguments will be different.)[14]

Fixing any $\bar{x}, \bar{h} \in \mathcal{F}^m$ and using Claim 3.5.2, we infer that, for each $i \in \{0, 1, \ldots, d+1\}$, it holds that

$$\mathbf{Pr}_{\bar{h}' \in \mathcal{F}^m} \left[g(\bar{x} + i\bar{h}) = \sum_{j=1}^{d+1} \alpha_j \cdot f((\bar{x} + i\bar{h}) + j\bar{h}') \right] \geq 1 - 2(d+1)\rho. \qquad (3.12)$$

Rather than using the same direction $\bar{h}'$ for each i, we use pairwise independent directions such that the direction $\bar{h}_1 + i\bar{h}_2$ is used for approximating $g(\bar{x} + i\bar{h})$, which means that we extrapolate (at the point $\bar{x} + i\bar{h}$) according to the line $L_i = L_{\bar{x}+i\bar{h}, \bar{h}_1 + i\bar{h}_2}$. Hence, the jth point on the line L_i is $(\bar{x} + i\bar{h}) + j \cdot (\bar{h}_1 + i\bar{h}_2)$, which can be written as $(\bar{x} + j\bar{h}_1) + i \cdot (\bar{h} + j\bar{h}_2)$; see Figure 3.2. Now, by Eq. (3.4), for every $j \in [d+1]$ it holds that

$$\mathbf{Pr}_{\bar{h}_1, \bar{h}_2 \in \mathcal{F}^m} \left[\sum_{i=0}^{d+1} \alpha_i \cdot f((\bar{x} + j\bar{h}_1) + i \cdot (\bar{h} + j\bar{h}_2)) = 0 \right] = 1 - \rho, \qquad (3.13)$$

---

[14] In particular, in the proof of Claim 3.5.2 we used the lattice points $\bar{x} + i\bar{h}_1 + j\bar{h}_2$ for $i, j \in [d+1]$, whereas here we shall use the lattice points $\bar{x} + i\bar{h} + j\bar{h}_1 + ij\bar{h}_2$ for $(i, j) \in \{0, 1, \ldots, d+1\} \times [d+1]$.

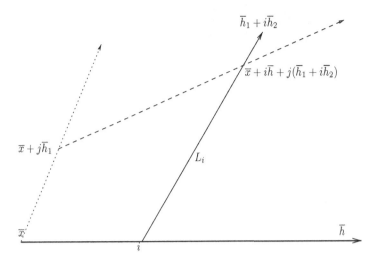

Figure 3.2: The jth point on the (solid) line $L_i = L_{\bar{x}+i\bar{h},\bar{h}_1+i\bar{h}_2}$ is reached as the ith point on the (dashed) line $L_{\bar{x}+j\bar{h}_1,\bar{h}+j\bar{h}_2}$, which is totally random. Recall that the line $L_{\bar{x},\bar{h}}$ is fixed.

since $\bar{x} + j\bar{h}_1$ and $\bar{h} + j\bar{h}_2$ are uniformly and independently distributed in $\mathcal{F}^m$. (This fact as well as the rest of the argument will be further detailed below.) Now, when all equalities captured in Eqs. (3.12) and (3.13) hold, which happens with probability at least $1 - (d + 2) \cdot 2(d + 1)\rho - (d + 1) \cdot \rho$, we get

$$\sum_{i=0}^{d+1} \alpha_i \cdot g(\bar{x} + i\bar{h}) = \sum_{i=0}^{d+1} \alpha_i \cdot \sum_{j=1}^{d+1} \alpha_j \cdot f((\bar{x} + i\bar{h}) + j \cdot (\bar{h}_1 + i\bar{h}_2))$$

$$= \sum_{j=1}^{d+1} \alpha_j \cdot \sum_{i=0}^{d+1} \alpha_i \cdot f((\bar{x} + j\bar{h}_1) + i \cdot (\bar{h} + j\bar{h}_2))$$

$$= \sum_{j=1}^{d+1} \alpha_j \cdot 0,$$

where the first equality uses Eq. (3.12) with $\bar{h}' = \bar{h}_1 + i\bar{h}_2$, and the last one uses Eq. (3.13). The claim follows by noting that the event in question (i.e., $\sum_{i=0}^{d+1} \alpha_i \cdot g(\bar{x} + i\bar{h}) = 0$) is fixed, and so if it occurs with positive probability (according to an analysis carried through in some auxiliary probability space), then it simply holds.

We now turn to the actual proof, which just repeats the foregoing argument while using more explicit formulations. Fixing arbitrary $\bar{x}, \bar{h} \in \mathcal{F}^m$, let $\bar{h}_1$ and $\bar{h}_2$ be uniformly and independently distributed in $\mathcal{F}^m$. For every $i \in \{0, 1, \ldots, d + 1\}$, using Claim 3.5.2, while noting that $\bar{h}_1 + i\bar{h}_2$ is uniformly distributed in $\mathcal{F}^m$, we get

$$\mathbf{Pr}_{\bar{h}_1, \bar{h}_2 \in \mathcal{F}^m} \left[g(\bar{x} + i\bar{h}) = \sum_{j=1}^{d+1} \alpha_j \cdot f((\bar{x} + i\bar{h}) + j(\bar{h}_1 + i\bar{h}_2)) \right] \geq 1 - 2(d + 1)\rho.$$

$$(3.14)$$

On the other hand, for every $j \in [d+1]$, noting that $\bar{x} + j\bar{h}_1$ and $\bar{h} + j\bar{h}_2$ are uniformly and independently distributed in $\mathcal{F}^m$, and using Eq. (3.4), we get

$$\mathbf{Pr}_{\bar{h}_1, \bar{h}_2 \in \mathcal{F}^m}\left[\sum_{i=0}^{d+1} \alpha_i \cdot f((\bar{x} + j\bar{h}_1) + i(\bar{h} + j\bar{h}_2)) = 0\right] = 1 - \rho. \tag{3.15}$$

Note that, in Eq. (3.15), the argument to f (i.e., $(\bar{x} + j\bar{h}_1) + i(\bar{h} + j\bar{h}_2)$) can be written as $(\bar{x} + i\bar{h}) + j(\bar{h}_1 + i\bar{h}_2)$. Taking an adequate linear combination of the equalities captured by Eq. (3.15), we get

$$\mathbf{Pr}_{\bar{h}_1, \bar{h}_2 \in \mathcal{F}^m}\left[\sum_{j=1}^{d+1} \alpha_j \sum_{i=0}^{d+1} \alpha_i \cdot f((\bar{x} + i\bar{h}) + j(\bar{h}_1 + i\bar{h}_2)) = 0\right] \geq 1 - (d+1) \cdot \rho. \tag{3.16}$$

Combining Eqs. (3.14) and (3.16), we get

$$\mathbf{Pr}_{\bar{h}_1, \bar{h}_2 \in \mathcal{F}^m}\left[\sum_{i=0}^{d+1} \alpha_i g(\bar{x} + i\bar{h}) = \sum_{i=0}^{d+1} \alpha_i \sum_{j=1}^{d+1} \alpha_j \cdot f((\bar{x} + i\bar{h}) + j(\bar{h}_1 + i\bar{h}_2)) = 0\right]$$
$$\geq 1 - (d+2) \cdot 2(d+1)\rho - (d+1) \cdot \rho.$$

Using $(2d+5) \cdot (d+1)\rho < 1$ (which follows from $\rho \leq 1/2(d+2)^2$), we get

$$\mathbf{Pr}_{\bar{h}_1, \bar{h}_2 \in \mathcal{F}^m}\left[\sum_{i=0}^{d+1} \alpha_i g(\bar{x} + i\bar{h}) = 0\right] > 0 \tag{3.17}$$

and the claim follows (since $\sum_{i=0}^{d+1} \alpha_i g(\bar{x} + i\bar{h}) = 0$ is independent of the choice of $\bar{h}_1, \bar{h}_2 \in \mathcal{F}^m$).[15] ∎

Combining Claims 3.5.1 and 3.5.3 with the characterization of $\mathcal{P}_{m,d}$ (i.e., Corollary 3.3)[16], it follows that f is 2ρ-close to $\mathcal{P}_{m,d}$. ∎

3.4.2. Digest (or an Abstraction)

We wish to spell out what is actually being used in the proof of Theorem 3.5. The proof refers to a test for functions of the form $f : D \rightarrow R$, where in our application $D = \mathcal{F}^m$ and $R = \mathcal{F}$ (and $t = d + 1$), that checks a condition of the form $f(x) = F(f(y_1), \ldots, f(y_t))$, where x is uniformly distributed in D and F is a fixed function. Indeed, at this point we assume nothing about the distribution of $(y_1, \ldots, y_t)$ conditioned on x, hereafter denoted Y_x. First, a self-corrected version of f, denoted g, is defined by letting $g(x)$ be the most frequent value of $F(f(y_1), \ldots, f(y_t))$, when $(y_1, \ldots, y_t) \leftarrow Y_x$. Claim 3.5.1 holds in this generic setting; that is, if the test rejects with probability ρ, then g is 2ρ-close to f. In the proofs of Claims 3.5.2 and 3.5.3, we used additional features of Y_x, detailed next.

---

[15] Recall that $\bar{x}, \bar{h} \in \mathcal{F}^m$ are fixed. Hence, the probability in Eq. (3.17) is either 0 or 1, whereas the lower bound rules out 0.

[16] Indeed, here we use the harder direction of Corollary 3.3.

One such feature, which is used in both proofs, is that for every $x \in D$ and $i \in [t]$, the ith element in Y_x is uniformly distributed in D. To state the other feature used in the proof of Claim 3.5.2, we let $Y_x(\omega)$ denote the value of Y_x when ω is a point in the probability space Ω that underlies Y_x (i.e., $Y_x : \Omega \to D'$). The proof of Claim 3.5.2 boils down to lower-bounding the collision probability of $F(Y_x)$, for any x, and it uses the hypothesis (which is a fact in our application) that for every $i, j \in [t]$ and $\omega_1, \omega_2 \in \Omega$ it holds that *the ith element of $Y_v(\omega_1)$ equals the jth element of $Y_u(\omega_2)$, where u is the ith element of $Y_x(\omega_1)$ and v is the jth element of $Y_x(\omega_2)$.* This feature holds when $D = \Omega$ is an additive (Abelian) group and the ith element of $Y_x(\omega)$ equals $x + i\omega$, which is indeed the case in our application.[17]

In the proof of Claim 3.5.3 we use a more complex feature, which presumes that $D = \Omega$ and views it is an additive (Abelian) group. The actual feature is that for every $i, j \in [t]$ and $\omega, \omega_1, \omega_2 \in \Omega$ it holds that the jth element of $Y_{x+i\omega}(\omega_1 + i\omega_2)$ equals the ith element of $Y_{x+j\omega_1}(\omega + j\omega_2)$, which holds when the ith element of $Y_x(\omega)$ equals $x + i\omega$ (since $(x + i\omega) + j(\omega_1 + i\omega_2)$ equals $(x + j\omega_1) + i(\omega + j\omega_2)$).

3.5. Chapter Notes

We mention that low-degree tests play a key role in the construction of PCP systems, starting with the "first generation" of such constructions [29, 28, 107, 25, 24]. For further details, the interested reader is referred to Chapter 13 (see, especially, Section 13.3.2).

The analysis of Algorithm 3.4 provided in Theorem 3.5 is probably not tight. An improved analysis of a related low-degree tester appeared in [120]. This tester selects uniformly $\bar{x}, \bar{h} \in \mathcal{F}^m$ and $i \in \mathcal{F}$, queries f at $\bar{x}, \bar{x} + \bar{h}, \ldots, \bar{x} + d\bar{h}$ and $\bar{x} + i\bar{h}$, and accepts if and only if there exists a degree d univariate polynomial that agrees with these $d + 2$ values (i.e., a polynomial p such that $p(j) = f(\bar{x} + j\bar{h})$ for every $j \in \{0, 1, \ldots, d, i\}$).[18] Friedl and Sudan [120] showed that the foregoing tester is a (one-sided error) proximity-oblivious tester with detection probability $\min(0.124, \delta/2)$, where δ denotes the distance of the given function from $\mathcal{P}_{m,d}$ (and 0.124 can be replaced by any constant c_0 smaller than $1/8$).[19]

The Low-Error Regime. Our presentation has focused on the "high-error regime"; that is, we have only guaranteed small detection probability (e.g., in [120] the detection probability is smaller than $1/8$). Equivalently, we asserted that if f is accepted with high probability (i.e., $\alpha = 1 - \rho > 7/8$), then it is close (i.e., 2ρ-close) to $\mathcal{P}_{m,d}$. Subsequent research regarding low-degree testing refers to the "low-error regime" where one asks what can

---

[17] In that case, $v + i\omega_1 = (x + j\omega_2) + i\omega_1 = (x + i\omega_1) + j\omega_2 = u + j\omega_2$.

[18] **Advanced comment:** Alternatively, this tester may be viewed as checking whether the degree d univariate polynomial that fits the values of the first $d + 1$ points on the (random) line agrees with the value assigned to a random point on this line. In the context of PCP, this tester is often described as having access to two oracles: the function $f : \mathcal{F}^m \to \mathcal{F}$, which is called a "point oracle," and a "line oracle" that assigns a degree d univariate polynomial to each line in $\mathcal{F}^m$ (i.e., the line-oracle is a function from $(\mathcal{F}^m)^2$ to $\mathcal{F}^{d+1}$). In such a case, it is called a line-vs-point tester. We mention that a plane-vs-point tester was also considered (cf. [235]): The plane-oracle assigns to each plane in $\mathcal{F}^m$ (which is described by three points in $\mathcal{F}^m$) a degree d bivariate polynomial, which is supposed to describe the value of f when restricted to this plane.

[19] In addition, it is required that $|\mathcal{F}| > c \cdot d$ (rather than $|\mathcal{F}| > 2d$), where c is a constant that depends on c_0.

be said about a function that is accepted with probability at least 0.01 (or so).[20] It turns out that in this case the function is 0.9934-close to $\mathcal{P}_{m,d}$; that is, if f is accepted with probability at least 0.01, then it agree with some degree d polynomial on at least 0.0066 fraction of the domain. In general, as shown in [26, 235] (using different tests of query complexity poly(d)), if f is accepted with probability at least α, then f is $(1 - \Omega(\alpha))$-close to $\mathcal{P}_{m,d}$ (i.e., f agree with some degree d polynomial on at least $\Omega(\alpha)$ fraction of the domain).[21]

Small Fields. So far, we have focused on the case of large fields; that is, we assumed that the field is larger than the degree bound (i.e., $|\mathcal{F}| > d$).[22] But, for multivariate polynomials, the case of small fields makes sense too. Alon et al. [11] studied the case of the two-element field, denoted GF(2), and presented a low-degree tester of query complexity that is exponential in the degree bound.[23] They also observed that exponential (in the degree bound) query complexity is required in this case. The case of fields of intermediate size (i.e., $|\mathcal{F}| \in (2, d]$) was studied by Kaufman and Ron [182] and Jutla et al. [174], who showed that the query complexity in this case is $|\mathcal{F}|^{\Theta(\ell)}$, where $\ell = \lceil (d+1)/(|\mathcal{F}| - 1) \rceil$ if $|\mathcal{F}|$ is a prime (and $\ell = \lceil (d+1)/(p^s - p^{s-1}) \rceil$ if $|\mathcal{F}| = p^s$ for a prime p).[24]

Robust Characterization. We have alluded to the notion of a robust characterization in some of our intuitive discussions (most conspicuously at the beginning of Section 3.4), but refrained from using it in the actual proofs. The notions of local characterization and its robustness were put forward by Rubinfeld and Sudan [246], and are briefly reviewed in Section 1.4. The interested reader is referred to these two texts.[25] We mention that some subsequent studies of low-degree tests are conducted in terms of the "robustness" of various local characterizations (see, e.g., [120, 26, 235]). For example, the robustness of the "line tester" was defined as the minimum, over all $f \notin \mathcal{P}_{m,d}$, of the ratio of the expected distance of the restriction of f to a random line from $\mathcal{P}_{1,d}$ (i.e., univariate degree d polynomials) versus the distance of f from $\mathcal{P}_{m,d}$.

Invariances. The set $\mathcal{P}_{m,d}$ is invariant under full rank affine transformations on the functions' domain. That is, for every $f : \mathcal{F}^m \to \mathcal{F}$ and any full rank affine transformation

---

[20] The terms "high" and "low" ("error regimes"), refer to the case that $f \notin \mathcal{P}_{m,d}$ and (rightfully) consider the acceptance probability in these cases as an error probability. Hence, accepting a function (not in $\mathcal{P}_{m,d}$) with probability 0.9 is considered to be in the high-error regime, whereas accepting this function with probability 0.01 is in the low-error regime.

[21] **Advanced comment:** These results assume that $|\mathcal{F}| \geq$ poly(d), whereas [120] assumes only $|\mathcal{F}| \geq \Theta(d)$. We mention that [165] requires only $|\mathcal{F}| \geq (1 + \Omega(1)) \cdot d$, but this comes at the cost of a larger hidden constant in the agreement rate (i.e., in $\Omega(\alpha)$).

[22] Actually, we focused on the case that $|\mathcal{F}| > 2d$, which does not cover the special case of $|\mathcal{F}| = 2$ and $d = 1$. We mention that this special case (of $|\mathcal{F}| = 2$ and $d = 1$) can be viewed as a special case of group homomorphism testing, which is considered in the previous chapter (i.e., the homomorphism is from the group $\mathcal{F}^m$ to the group $\mathcal{F}$).

[23] **Advanced comment:** They actually presented a proximity-oblivious tester that, for a degree bound d, makes 2^{d+1} queries and has detection probability $\delta/2^q$, where δ denotes the distance of the tested function from being a degree d polynomial. It turns our that their tester has detection probability $\Omega(\delta)$; see [51] (as well as [168] which presents an analogous result for fields of intermediate size).

[24] The latter case is analyzed only in [182].

[25] **Advanced comment:** In Section 1.4 the notion of locality was presented as referring to constant size neighborhoods, but the notion extends to neighborhoods of size poly(d). Actually, the notion extends to neighborhoods of any size that is significantly smaller than the tested object.

$T : \mathcal{F}^m \to \mathcal{F}^m$ it holds that $f \in \mathcal{P}_{m,d}$ if and only if $f \circ T \in \mathcal{P}_{m,d}$. A general study of the complexity of testing properties that are invariant under affine transformations was initiated by Kaufman and Sudan [183], and is surveyed in [257].[26]

Exercises

The following exercises elaborate on comments made in the main text.

Exercise 3.1 (Low-degree extensions): Show that for a finite field $\mathcal{F}$ and any $m \in \mathbb{N}$, any function $f : \mathcal{F}^m \to \mathcal{F}$ can be written as a polynomial of individual degree $|\mathcal{F}| - 1$. More generally, show that for any $H \subseteq \mathcal{F}$ and any function $f : H^m \to \mathcal{F}$ there exists a polynomial $p : \mathcal{F}^m \to \mathcal{F}$ of individual degree $|H| - 1$ such that $p(\bar{x}) = f(\bar{x})$ for every $\bar{x} \in H^m$.

> **Guideline:** For every $a \in H$, let $\delta_a : \mathcal{F} \to \mathcal{F}$ be such that $\delta_a(z) = \prod_{b \in H \setminus \{a\}} (x - b)/(a - b)$. Consider $p(x_1, \dots, x_m) = \sum_{a_1, \dots, a_m \in H} f(a_1, \dots, a_m) \cdot \prod_{i \in [m]} \delta_{a_i}(x_i)$.

Exercise 3.2 (A failed attempt for testing low-degree univariate polynomials): Note that in the case of $m = 1$, Algorithm 3.4 amounts to selecting $r, s \in \mathcal{F}$ uniformly at random, and checking that the values of $f : \mathcal{F} \to \mathcal{F}$ at $r, r + s, \dots, r + (d + 1) \cdot s$ match some degree d polynomial. Consider the algorithm that selects r uniformly in $\mathcal{F}$, and checks that the values of f at $r, r + 1, \dots, r + d + 1$ match some degree d polynomial. Show that this algorithm does not yield a good tester in the sense that, for $|\mathcal{F}| \gg d$, there exists a function $f : \mathcal{F} \to \mathcal{F}$ that is 0.499-far from being of degree d, whereas the algorithm rejects it with probability $O(d/|\mathcal{F}|)$. Generalize the counterexample to the case of an algorithm that checks that the values of f at $r, r + s, \dots, r + (d + 1) \cdot s$, for any fixed $s \in \mathcal{F}$ (and uniformly distrubuted $r \in \mathcal{F}$).

> **Guideline:** Let $p_1, p_2 : \mathcal{F} \to \mathcal{F}$ be two distinct polynomials of degree d, and let $f(x) = p_1(x)$ if $x \in \{1, \dots, \lfloor |\mathcal{F}|/2 \rfloor\}$ and $f(x) = p_2(x)$ otherwise. Then, f is $(0.5 - (d + 1)/|\mathcal{F}|)$-far from being a polynomial of degree d, whereas the algorithm rejects f with probability at most $2(d + 1)/|\mathcal{F}|$.[27]

Exercise 3.3 (The Schwartz–Zippel Lemma [250, 276, 86]):[28] Let $p : \mathcal{F}^m \to \mathcal{F}$ be a nonzero m-variate polynomial of total degree d over a finite field $\mathcal{F}$. Prove that $\mathbf{Pr}_{x \in \mathcal{F}^m}[p(x) = 0] \leq d/|\mathcal{F}|$.

> **Guideline:** Use induction on the number of variables, m. The base case of $m = 1$ follows by the fact that $p \not\equiv 0$ has at most d roots. In the induction step, assuming that p depends on its last variable, write $p(x) = \sum_{i=0}^{d} p_i(x_1, \dots, x_{m-1}) \cdot x_m^i$, where p_i is an $(m - 1)$-variate polynomial of degree at most $d - i$, and let t be the largest integer such that p_t is nonzero. Then, using $x' = (x_1, \dots, x_{m-1})$, observe that
>
> $$\mathbf{Pr}_{x \in \mathcal{F}^m}[p(x) = 0]$$
>
> $$\leq \mathbf{Pr}_{x' \in \mathcal{F}^{m-1}}[p_t(x') = 0] + \mathbf{Pr}_{x' \in \mathcal{F}^{m-1}}[p_t(x') \neq 0] \cdot \mathbf{Pr}_{x \in \mathcal{F}^m}[p(x) = 0 | p_t(x') \neq 0],$$

---

[26] Be warned that there have been many subsequent (to [257]) developments in this direction.

[27] The first claim holds because for every polynomial p of degree d there exists $i \in \{1, 2\}$ such that p agrees with p_i on at most d points, which implies that $\delta(p, f) \geq \delta(p, p_i) - \lceil |\mathcal{F}|/2 \rceil / |\mathcal{F}| \geq (\lfloor |\mathcal{F}|/2 \rfloor - d)/|\mathcal{F}|$. The second claim holds because the algorithm may reject only if $\{r, r + 1, \dots, r + d + 1\}$ has a nontrivial intersection with $\{1, \dots, |\mathcal{F}|/2\}$.

[28] A more general version is presented in Exercise 5.1.

and that, for any fixed x' such that $p_t(x') \neq 0$, the function $f_{x'}(x_m) \overset{\text{def}}{=} p(x', x_m) = p(x)$ is a nonzero (univariate) polynomial of degree t in x_m.

Exercise 3.4 (Local characterization of low-degree univariate polynomials in the case of general finite fields): Let $\mathcal{F}$ be an arbitrary finite field and $d < |\mathcal{F}| - 1$. Suppose that $e_1, \ldots, e_{d+1}$ are distinct field elements. Prove that there exist a sequence of tuples $(\alpha_1^{(e)}, \ldots, \alpha_{d+1}^{(e)})_{e \in \mathcal{F}}$, where $\alpha_i^{(e)} \in \mathcal{F}$, such that $g : \mathcal{F} \to \mathcal{F}$ is a univariate polynomial of degree d if and only if for every $e \in \mathcal{F}$ it holds that

$$g(e) = \sum_{i=1}^{d+1} \alpha_i^{(e)} \cdot g(e_i). \tag{3.18}$$

Guideline: First, show that there exists a unique degree d polynomial p that agrees with g on $e_1, \ldots, e_{d+1}$, by writing $p(x) = \sum_{i=0}^{d} c_i x^i$ and observing that

$$\begin{pmatrix} g(e_1) \\ g(e_2) \\ \vdots \\ g(e_{d+1}) \end{pmatrix} = \begin{pmatrix} 1 & e_1 & \cdots & e_1^d \\ 1 & e_2 & \cdots & e_2^d \\ \vdots & \vdots & \cdots & \vdots \\ 1 & e_d & \cdots & e_{d+1}^d \end{pmatrix} \begin{pmatrix} c_0 \\ c_1 \\ \vdots \\ c_d \end{pmatrix} \tag{3.19}$$

holds.[29] Furthermore, the c_i's can be expressed as a linear combination of the $g(e_i)$'s. Next, observe that g is a degree d polynomial if and only if $g(e) = \sum_{i=0}^{d} c_i \cdot e^i$ for every $e \in \mathcal{F}$. Finally, set the $\alpha_i^{(e)}$'s accordingly.

Exercise 3.5 (Iterative derivatives and Theorem 3.2)[30]: Recall that the proof of Theorem 3.2 referred to the derivatives of functions $g : \mathcal{F} \to \mathcal{F}$. Here we explicitly define iterative derivatives, denoted $\partial^{(i)}$, such that the value of $\partial^{(1)} g = \partial g$ at x equals $g(x + 1) - g(x)$ and $\partial^{(i+1)} g = \partial \partial^{(i)} g$ (where $\partial^{(0)} g = g$). Recall that in the first part of the proof of Theorem 3.2 we showed that, for every $d > 0$, it holds that g has degree d if and only if ∂g has degree $d - 1$. Prove the following two facts:

1. For every $d \geq 0$ and $g : \mathcal{F} \to \mathcal{F}$, it holds that g has degree d if and only if the function $\partial^{(d+1)} g$ is identically zero.
2. For every $k \geq 0$ and $g : \mathcal{F} \to \mathcal{F}$, it holds that the value of $\partial^{(k)} g$ at x equals

$$\sum_{i=0}^{k} (-1)^{k-i} \cdot \binom{k}{i} \cdot g(x + i).$$

Observe that the combination of these facts establishes Theorem 3.2.

Guideline: Both facts can be proved by induction (on d and k, resp.).

---

[29] Recall that the matrix in Eq. (3.19), which is the Vandermonde matrix, is full rank.

[30] The following alternative presentation of the second part of the proof of Theorem 3.2 was suggested to us by Roei Tell.

CHAPTER FOUR

Testing Monotonicity

Summary: For each n, we consider functions from a partially ordered set D_n to a totally ordered set R_n. Such a function $f : D_n \to R_n$ is called monotone if for every $x < y$ in D_n it holds that $f(x) \le f(y)$, where $<$ denotes the partial order of D_n and $\le$ refers to the total order in R_n. We shall focus on two special cases:

1. Boolean functions on the Boolean hypercube: In this case, D_n is the ℓ-dimensional Boolean hypercube (with the natural partial order), where $\ell = \log_2 n$, and $R_n = \{0, 1\}$. According to this partial order, $x_1 \cdots x_\ell \le y_1 \cdots y_\ell$ if and only if $x_i \le y_i$ for every $i \in [\ell]$.
2. Real functions on the discrete line: In this case, $D_n = [n]$ and $R_n = \mathbb{R}$, both with the natural total order.

We shall later consider also the case of the hypergrid domain $D_n = [m]^\ell$, for any $m, \ell \in \mathbb{N}$ such that $m^\ell = n$, and general ranges R_n. In all these cases, we present property testers of complexity $\mathrm{poly}(\epsilon^{-1} \log n)$.

In addition, we briefly survey relatively recent developments regarding the Boolean case as well as known results regarding testing convexity, submodularity, and the Lipschitz property of functions from $[m]^\ell$ to $\mathbb{R}$.

This chapter is based on the works of Goldreich *et al.* [139] (for case 1), Ergun *et al.* [101] (for case 2), and Dodis *et al.* [96] (for their "interpolation").

Notation: The Hamming weight of a binary string $x \in \{0, 1\}^\ell$, denoted $\mathrm{wt}(x)$, is the number of locations that hold a nonzero value; that is, $\mathrm{wt}(x) = |\{i \in [\ell] : x_i \ne 0\}|$.

4.1. Introduction

Leaving the land of algebraic functions behind us, we find the notion of a monotone function most appealing. The definition of this notion presumes a partial order on the domain of the function and a total order on its range. We say that $f : D \to R$ is monotone if, for every $x, y \in D$ if $x < y$ (according to the partial order on D), then $f(x) \le f(y)$ (according to the order on R).

The most natural partially ordered domains are the total order on the "line" $[n] = \{1, 2, \ldots, n\}$ and the partial order on the hypercube $\{0, 1\}^\ell$. Interpolating these two case, we consider the partial order on the hypergrid $[m]^\ell$, where $(x_1, \ldots, x_\ell) < (y_1, \ldots, y_\ell)$ if $x_i \leq y_i$ for all $i \in [\ell]$ and $(x_1, \ldots, x_\ell) \neq (y_1, \ldots, y_\ell)$.

We shall consider testing monotonicity in all these cases, both when the range is Boolean and when it is arbitrary. In all cases, we shall consider pair tests, which are (non-adaptive) two-query proximity-oblivious testers (POTs) that, when given oracle access to $f : D \to R$, select a pair $(x, y) \in D^2$ such that $x < y$ and accept if and only if $f(x) \leq f(y)$. The focus will be on choosing a distribution on these pairs, and analyzing the detection probability of the resulting POT.

Organization. In Section 4.2 we consider the case of Boolean functions defined on the Boolean hypercube $\{0, 1\}^\ell$. Its core is Section 4.2.1, which provides a detailed analysis of a simple tester. An alternative tester is reviewed in Section 4.2.2, but this part is merely an overview of advanced material that is only meant for optional reading. In Section 4.3 we study the case of multivalued functions on the discrete line $[n]$; the core of this section is Section 4.3.1, whereas Section 4.3.2 presents additional results that are not used elsewhere in this chapter. Lastly, in Section 4.4, we consider multivalued functions on the hypergrid $[m]^\ell$, which generalizes the previous two cases.

Teaching Note: We recommend teaching only the core material, presented in Sections 4.2.1 and 4.3.1, while leaving the rest of the material for advanced reading.

4.2. Boolean Functions on the Boolean Hypercube

We consider Boolean functions of the form $f : \{0, 1\}^\ell \to \{0, 1\}$. Such a function f is called monotone if for every $x < y$ in $\{0, 1\}^\ell$ it holds that $f(x) \leq f(y)$, where $x_1 \cdots x_\ell \leq y_1 \cdots y_\ell$ if and only if $x_i \leq y_i$ for every $i \in [\ell]$ (and, indeed, $x_1 \cdots x_\ell = y_1 \cdots y_\ell$ if and only if $x_i = y_i$ for every $i \in [\ell]$).

It is instructive to think of $\{0, 1\}^\ell$ (with the above partial order) as a directed version of the Boolean hypercube. The Boolean hypercube of dimension ℓ is a graph with vertex set $\{0, 1\}^\ell$ and edge set $\{\{u, v\} : \mathrm{wt}(v \oplus u) = 1\}$; that is, u is adjacent to v if and only if they differ on a single bit. In the directed version, which we consider, the edge $\{u, v\}$ is directed from the vertex of smaller Hamming weight to the vertex with higher (by 1) weight.

4.2.1. The Edge Test

We show that the natural algorithm that selects uniformly an edge of the Boolean hypercube and compares the values of the function at its end-points constitutes a good proximity-oblivious tester. Such an edge corresponds to a pair (x, y) such that $x < y$ and x differs from y in a single bit (i.e, $\mathrm{wt}(x \oplus y) = 1$), and the algorithm accepts if and only if $f(x) \leq f(y)$. Specifically, we refer to the following algorithm.

Algorithm 4.1 (Testing whether $f : \{0, 1\}^\ell \to \{0, 1\}$ is monotone): *Select uniformly $v \in \{0, 1\}^\ell$ and $i \in [\ell]$, query f at v and $v \oplus 0^{i-1}10^{\ell-i}$, and accept if and only if f is monotone on this pair; that is, letting $\{x, y\} = \{v, v \oplus 0^{i-1}10^{\ell-i}\}$ such that $x < y$, the algorithm accepts if and only if $f(x) \leq f(y)$.*

Let Π_n denote the set of monotone of Boolean functions over $\{0, 1\}^\ell$, where $n = 2^\ell$.

Theorem 4.2 (Algorithm 4.1 is a POT for monotonicity): *Algorithm 4.1 is a* (one-sided error) *proximity-oblivious tester for* Π_n *with detection probability* δ/ℓ, *where* δ *denotes the distance of the given function from being monotone.*

We comment that this analysis of Algorithm 4.1 is asymptotically tight in a strong sense: for every $\alpha \in (\exp(-\Omega(\ell)), 0.5)$, there exists a function $f : \{0, 1\}^{\ell} \to \{0, 1\}$ that is at distance $\delta \in [\alpha, 2\alpha]$ from being monotone such that Algorithm 4.1 rejects f with probability at most $2\delta/\ell$ (see [139, Prop. 4, Part 1]). For example, $f(x) \stackrel{\text{def}}{=} x_1 \oplus 1$ is at distance 0.5 from being monotone but is rejected with probability $1/\ell$.

Proof: Algorithm 4.1 accepts each monotone function with probability 1, since the set of all possible executions corresponds to a set of conditions that is a subset of the local conditions used in the definition of monotonicity (i.e., the set of edges constitutes a subset of the set of all pairs (x, y) such that $x < y$).[1] The point, however, is showing that if $f : \{0, 1\}^{\ell} \to \{0, 1\}$ is at distance δ from being monotone, then it is rejected with probability at least δ/ℓ. We shall prove the counterpositive. That is, assuming that f is accepted with probability $1 - \rho$, we shall show that f is $(\ell \cdot \rho)$-close to being monotone.

We shall show that f can be made monotone by modifying its values on at most $\rho\ell \cdot 2^{\ell}$ points. We shall proceed in iterations such that in the ith iteration we make f "monotone in the ith direction," while preserving its monotonicity in the prior directions.

Definition 4.2.1 (Monotonicity in direction i): *Let $f : \{0, 1\}^{\ell} \to \{0, 1\}$ and $i \in [\ell]$. We say that f is monotone in direction i if for every $v' \in \{0, 1\}^{i-1}$ and $v'' \in \{0, 1\}^{\ell-i}$ it holds that $f(v'0v'') \leq f(v'1v'')$.*

We make f monotone in direction i by applying a corresponding "switching operator," denoted S_i, which maps Boolean functions to Boolean functions by switching the values of the endpoints of some of the edges in direction i.

Definition 4.2.2 (Switch in direction i): *For every $i \in [\ell]$, the switch operator S_i is defined such that for every function $f : \{0, 1\}^{\ell} \to \{0, 1\}$ the function $S_i(f) : \{0, 1\}^{\ell} \to \{0, 1\}$ is monotone in direction i and satisfies $\{S_i(f)(v'0v''), S_i(f)(v'1v'')\} = \{f(v'0v''), f(v'1v'')\}$ for every $v' \in \{0, 1\}^{i-1}$ and $v'' \in \{0, 1\}^{\ell-i}$. (Indeed, $S_i(f)(x)$ denotes the value of the function $S_i(f)$ at the point x.)*

That is, for every $v' \in \{0, 1\}^{i-1}$ and $v'' \in \{0, 1\}^{\ell-i}$, if $f(v'0v'') \leq f(v'1v'')$, then S_i leaves the values at these two points intact (i.e., $S_i(f)(v'0v'') = f(v'0v'')$ and $S_i(f)(v'1v'') = f(v'1v'')$); otherwise (i.e., $f(v'0v'') > f(v'1v'')$) the two values are switched (i.e., $S_i(f)(v'0v'') = f(v'1v'')$ and $S_i(f)(v'1v'') = f(v'0v'')$). Either way, it holds that $S_i(f)(v'0v'') \leq S_i(f)(v'1v'')$.

---

[1] **Advanced comment:** Actually, the only functions that are accepted by Algorithm 4.1 with probability 1 are monotone, since the subset of local conditions checked by the algorithm imposes all the local conditions in the definition. To see this, consider, for every $x < y$, a (shortest) directed path (in the hypercube), denoted $x^{(0)} = x, x^{(1)}, \ldots, x^{(t)} = y$, leading from x to y, and use $f(x^{(0)}) \leq f(x^{(1)}) \leq \cdots \leq f(x^{(t)})$. Indeed, w.l.o.g., $x^{(i)} = x_1 \cdots x_j y_{j+1} \cdots y_{\ell}$, where j is the location of the ith nonzero bit in $x \oplus y$. (See the related Exercise 4.1.)

Now, assuming that f is accepted with probability $1 - \rho$, we shall consider the sequence of functions $f_0, \ldots, f_\ell$ such that $f_0 = f$ and $f_i = S_i(f_{i-1})$ for $i = 1, \ldots, \ell$. We shall show that f_ℓ is monotone and that $\sum_{i \in [\ell]} \delta(f_i, f_{i-1}) \le \ell \cdot \rho$, where $\delta(g, h) = \mathbf{Pr}_x[g(x) \ne h(x)]$ is the standard distance between functions. The fact that $f_i = S_i(f_{i-1})$ is monotone in direction i follows by the definition of the switch operator, whereas the fact that f_i preserves the monotonicity of f_{i-1} in each direction $j < i$ needs to be proved. This will follow as a special case of a general claim that will also allow us to establish $\sum_{i \in [\ell]} \delta(f_i, f_{i-1}) \le \ell \cdot \rho$. Towards this claim, we shall need the following definition.

Definition 4.2.3 (Violation in direction i): *Let $g : \{0, 1\}^\ell \to \{0, 1\}$ and $i \in [\ell]$. For $v' \in \{0, 1\}^{i-1}$ and $v'' \in \{0, 1\}^{\ell-i}$, the directed edge $(v'0v'', v'1v'')$ is a violating edge of g in direction i if $g(v'0v'') > g(v'1v'')$. We denote by $V_i(g)$ the set of violating edges of g in direction i.*

Clearly, g is monotone in direction i if and only if it has no violating edges in direction i (i.e., $V_i(g) = \emptyset$). We are now ready to state our main claim, which asserts that applying the switch operator in direction i does not increase the number of violations in direction j.

Claim 4.2.4 (The effect of the switch operator on the set of violations): *Let $g : \{0, 1\}^\ell \to \{0, 1\}$ and $i, j \in [\ell]$. Then, $|V_j(S_i(g))| \le |V_j(g)|$.*

It follows that if g is monotone in direction j, then so is $S_i(g)$. The fact that $\sum_{i \in [\ell]} \delta(f_i, f_{i-1}) \le \ell\rho$ will follow by using two additional observations (see Facts 1 and 2 below).[2]

Proof: The case of $i = j$ is trivial (since $V_i(S_i(g)) = \emptyset$), and so, we consider $i \ne j$. For the sake of notational simplicity and without loss of generality, we may consider the case of $i = 1$ and $j = 2$. The key observation is that the analysis of the effect of S_i on the violations of g in direction j can be reduced to the effects on the violations of the functions obtained (from g) by all possible restrictions of the other $\ell - 2$ coordinates. That is, for every $u \in \{0, 1\}^{\ell-2}$, we consider the residual function $g_u(\sigma\tau) = g(\sigma\tau u)$, and observe that $|V_2(g)| = \sum_{u \in \{0,1\}^{\ell-2}} |V_2(g_u)|$ (and $|V_2(S_1(g))| = \sum_{u \in \{0,1\}^{\ell-2}} |V_2(S_1(g_u))|$).[3] Hence, it suffices

---

[2] Specifically, we shall show that $\sum_{i \in [\ell]} |V_i(f)| = \rho \cdot \ell \cdot 2^{\ell-1}$ (Fact 1) and $\delta(f_i, f_{i-1}) = 2^{-(\ell-1)} \cdot |V_i(f_{i-1})|$ (Fact 2). Combining these facts with Claim 4.2.4, it follows that

$$\sum_{i \in [\ell]} \delta(f_i, f_{i-1}) = 2^{-(\ell-1)} \cdot \sum_{i \in [\ell]} |V_i(f_{i-1})|$$

$$\le 2^{-(\ell-1)} \cdot \sum_{i \in [\ell]} |V_i(f)|$$

$$= \rho \cdot \ell$$

as claimed.

[3] This is because the question of whether the edge $(\sigma 0u, \sigma 1u)$ is violating depends only on the values at its endpoints, whereas S_1 satisfies $\{S_1(g)(0\tau u), S_1(g)(1\tau u)\} = \{g(0\tau u), g(1\tau u)\}$. Hence, the contributions of the edges $(00u, 01u)$ and $(10u, 11u)$ to $V_2(g)$ and $V_2(S_1(g))$ depend only on the values of g and $S_1(g)$ on $00u, 01u, 10u$, and $11u$.

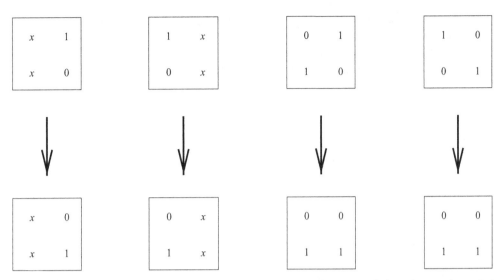

Figure 4.1: The remaining four cases in the proof of Claim 4.2.4. In the first two (leftmost) cases the sorted column equals $(xx)^\top$, whereas in the other two cases the sorted column is $(01)^\top$.

to prove that $|V_2(S_1(g_u))| \leq |V_2(g_u)|$ *holds for every u*. This can be verified by a case analysis, but it is instructive to make a picture.[4]

Pictorially, consider a 2-by-2 Boolean matrix M such that the (σ, τ)-entry corresponds to $g_u(\sigma\tau)$. The foregoing claim (i.e., $|V_2(S_1(g_u))| \leq |V_2(g_u)|$) asserts that *if we sort the columns of M, then the number of unsorted rows may only decrease*. The only cases worthy of consideration are those in which at least one of the columns of M is unsorted, since otherwise sorting the columns has no effect. Now, if both columns are unsorted, then they are both equal to the vector $(10)^\top$, and sorting the columns only means permuting the rows, which means that the number of violations (which is zero) is preserved. We are left with four cases, depicted in Figure 4.1, in which exactly one column is sorted. In the first two cases (where the sorted column is monochromatic), sorting the columns means permuting the rows (which again preserves the number of violations). In the other two cases (where the sorted column is $(01)^\top$), sorting the columns means eliminating all violations (since the resulting columns will both equal $(01)^\top$). ∎

By repeated applications of Claim 4.2.4, we obtain

Corollary 4.2.5 (On the sets of violations in the sequence of f_i's):

1. *For every $i \in [\ell]$, the function f_i is monotone in each direction $j \leq i$. In particular, f_ℓ is monotone.*
2. *For every $i, j \in [\ell]$, it holds that $|V_j(f_i)| \leq |V_j(f)|$.*

---

[4]**Advanced comment:** Yet another alternative, which is generalized in Secrion 4.4.1, also refers to the same picture but proceeds as follows. Specifically, considering a 2-by-2 Boolean matrix M such that the (σ, τ)-entry corresponds to $g_u(\sigma\tau)$, we show that *if we sort the columns of M, then the number of unsorted rows may only decrease*. This is shown by letting t_c denote the number of 1's in column c, and observing that the number of unsorted rows is at least $\max(t_1 - t_2, 0)$ and that this value is obtained when the columns are sorted.

Proof: Recalling that $f_i = S_i(f_{i-1})$ and applying Claim 4.2.4 (with $g = f_{i-1}$), we get that, for every $i, j \in [\ell]$, it holds that $|V_j(f_i)| \leq |V_j(f_{i-1})|$. Hence, for every $j \in [\ell]$ and $0 \leq i_1 < i_2 \leq \ell$, it holds that $|V_j(f_{i_2})| \leq |V_j(f_{i_1})|$. Now, Item 1 follows because $|V_j(f_i)| \leq |V_j(f_j)| = 0$ (for every $j < i$), whereas Item 2 follows because $|V_j(f_i)| \leq |V_j(f_0)|$ (for every $i > 0$).[5] ∎

We now establish the two facts mentioned above (i.e., right after Claim 4.2.4):[6]

Fact 1: $2 \cdot \sum_{i \in [\ell]} |V_i(f)| = \rho \cdot \ell 2^\ell$.

This follows since the random choice $(v, i) \in \{0, 1\}^\ell \times [\ell]$ makes Algorithm 4.1 reject f if and only if the (directed version of the) edge $\{v, v \oplus 0^{i-1} 10^{\ell-i}\}$ is violating (for f in direction i).[7] (Indeed, each such violating edge $(v'0v'', v'1v'')$ contributes to two choices of Algorithm 4.1 (i.e., to the choices $(v'0v'', |v'| + 1)$ and $(v'1v'', |v'| + 1)$).)

Fact 2: $2^\ell \cdot \delta(f_i, f_{i-1}) = 2 \cdot |V_i(f_{i-1})|$.

This is a special case of $2^\ell \cdot \delta(S_i(g), g) = 2 \cdot |V_i(g)|$, which holds because $S_i(g)(x) \neq g(x)$ if and only if the (directed version of the) edge $\{x, x \oplus 0^{i-1} 10^{\ell-i}\}$ is violating (for g in direction i).[8] (Indeed, each such violating edge contributes two units to $2^\ell \cdot \delta(f_i, f_{i-1})$.)

By combining these two facts with Item 2 of Corollary 4.2.5 we get

$$\delta(f, f_\ell) \leq \sum_{i \in [\ell]} \delta(f_{i-1}, f_i)$$

$$= \sum_{i \in [\ell]} 2^{-(\ell-1)} \cdot |V_i(f_{i-1})|$$

$$\leq 2^{-(\ell-1)} \cdot \sum_{i \in [\ell]} |V_i(f)|$$

$$= \ell \cdot \rho,$$

where the first equality follows by Fact 2, the second inequality follows by Item 2 of Corollary 4.2.5, and the second equality follows by Fact 1. Recalling that (by Item 1 of Corollary 4.2.5) the function f_ℓ is monotone, we conclude that f is $\ell\rho$-close to monotone. The theorem follows. ∎

---

[5] Recall that $f_0 = f$.

[6] See also footnote 2, which also provides a preview of their use.

[7] Formally,

$$\rho = \mathbf{Pr}_{(v,i) \in \{0,1\}^\ell \times [\ell]} \left[f(v_{[i-1]} 0 v_{[i+1,\ell]}) > f(v_{[i-1]} 1 v_{[i+1,\ell]}) \right]$$

$$= \frac{1}{\ell} \cdot \sum_{i \in [\ell]} \mathbf{Pr}_{(v',v'') \in \{0,1\}^{i-1} \times \{0,1\}^{\ell-i}} \left[f(v'0v'') > f(v'1v'') \right]$$

$$= \frac{1}{\ell} \cdot \sum_{i \in [\ell]} \frac{|V_i(f)|}{2^{\ell-1}},$$

where the second equality uses the fact that the value of the bit v_i is irrelevant to the event being analyzed.

[8] Formally, $\delta(S_i(g), g) = \mathbf{Pr}_{x \in \{0,1\}^\ell}[S_i(g)(x) \neq g(x)]$, which equals the probability that x is an endpoint of an edge in $V_i(g)$, which in turn equals $(2 \cdot |V_i(g)|)/2^\ell$.

Digest. The proof of Theorem 4.2 shows that the *absolute* distance of f from being monotone, denoted $\Delta_M(f)$, is upper-bounded by twice the number of violating edges (of f). Denoting the latter set by $V(f)$, it is tempting to think that $\Delta_M(f) \leq |V(f)|$, since each violation can be corrected by modifying one endpoint of the violating edge, but this ignores the possibility that the correction of one violation may cause other violations. Indeed, in the proof of Theorem 4.2, we performed modifications with more care: We proceed in iterations such that in the ith iteration, we eliminate a subset of violations in f_i, denoted $V_i(f_i)$, while making sure that the number of violations in the resulting function, denoted f_{i+1}, does not exceed $|V(f_i) \setminus V_i(f_i)|$. We stress that $V(f_{i+1})$ is not necessarily a subset of $V(f_i) \setminus V_i(f_i)$, yet $|V(f_{i+1})| \leq |V(f_i) \setminus V_i(f_i)|$. Recall that *the set of violations $V_i(f_i)$, which constitutes a matching, was not eliminated by modifying f_i at one endpoint of each edge, but rather by switching the pair of values at the endpoints of each violating edge.* (Thus, $|\{x : f_i(x) \neq f_{i+1}(x)\}| = 2 \cdot |V_i(f_i)|$, rather than half this amount.) This "wasteful" method of modifying f_i enables proving that $|V(f_{i+1})| \leq |V(f_i) \setminus V_i(f_i)|$, and it follows that $\Delta_M(f) \leq 2 \cdot |V(f)|$.

On the Tightness of the Analysis. Recall that the *relative* distance of f from being monotone, denoted $\delta_M(f)$, equals $\Delta_M(f)/2^\ell$, whereas the probability that Algorithm 4.1 rejects f, denoted $\rho(f)$, equals $\frac{|V(f)|}{\ell \cdot 2^\ell/2}$. Hence, $\Delta_M(f) \leq 2 \cdot |V(f)|$ translates to $\delta_M(f) \leq 2^{-\ell+1} \cdot |V(f)| = \ell \cdot \rho(f)$. As stated upfront, the upper bound $\delta_M(f) = O(\ell \cdot \rho(f))$ is tight: For every $\alpha \in (\exp(-\Omega(\ell)), 0.5)$, there exists a function $f : \{0, 1\}^\ell \to \{0, 1\}$ such that $\delta_M(f) \in [\alpha, 2\alpha]$ and $\delta_M(f) = \Omega(\ell \cdot \rho(f))$ (see [139, Prop. 4, Part 1]). For example, for $f(x) = 1 - x_1$ it holds that $\delta_M(f) = 0.5$ and $\rho(f) = 1/\ell$.

On the other hand, $\delta_M(f) = \Omega(\ell \cdot \rho(f))$ does not hold for all f's: For every $\alpha \in (\exp(-\Omega(\ell)), 0.5)$, there exists a function $f : \{0, 1\}^\ell \to \{0, 1\}$ such that $\delta_M(f) \in [\alpha, 2\alpha]$ and $\delta_M(f) = \Theta(\rho(f))$ (see [139, Prop. 4, Part 2]). For example, for $f(x) = \text{wt}(x) \bmod 2$ it holds that $\delta_M(f) \approx 0.5$ and $\rho(f) \approx 0.5$ (see Exercise 4.2).

4.2.2. Path Tests

The fact that the analysis of the rejection probability of Algorithm 4.1 is tight (i.e., there are nonmonotone functions f that this algorithm rejects with probability $O(\delta_M(f)/\ell)$), does not mean that one cannot do better, even when using two-query tests. Algorithm 4.1 checks the values at the endpoints of a uniformly selected edge of the hypercube, which seems a natural thing to do. Indeed, this is the best choice for tests that examine the values at the endpoints of an edge selected according to any distribution.[9]

Of course, there is no reason to restrict two-query testers to examine the values at the endpoints of an edge of the hypercube. Indeed, without loss of generality, the two queries made by the test must be comparable (or else it makes no sense to compare the answers), but these two queries may reside on the endpoints of a path of (almost) arbitrary length. Also, for the purpose of ϵ-testing, little is lost when restricting the random path to have both endpoints be strings of Hamming weight in $[(\ell/2) \pm O(\sqrt{\ell \log(1/\epsilon)})]$, since vertices with Hamming weight that deviates from this interval occupy at most a 0.1ϵ

---

[9] Consider such an algorithm and let $i \in [\ell]$ denote the direction that is selected with the lowest probability, where the direction of an edge $\{u, v\}$ is the coordinate on which u and v differ. Then, the function $f(x) = 1 - x_i$ is rejected with probability at most $1/\ell$, while it is 0.5-far from being monotone.

fraction of the hypercube. (Also, little is lost by restricting the tester to be nonadaptive: see Exercise 1.20.)

To see the benefit of this generalization, for a generic $i \in [\ell]$, consider the function $f(x) = 1 - x_i$, which is at distance 0.5 from being monotone. While the edge test rejects this function with probability $1/\ell$, a tester that examines the endpoints of a random path of length $\sqrt{\ell}$ (which starts at a uniformly distributed vertex) rejects this function with probability $1/\sqrt{\ell}$. It turns out that rejection probability $\widetilde{\Theta}_\delta(1/\sqrt{\ell})$ is achievable and is optimal for two-query testers, where the $\widetilde{\Theta}_\delta$ notation hides arbitrary dependencies on the distance (denoted δ) of the function from being monotone. We mention that this dependence cannot be linear (i.e., the rejection probability of such two-query testers cannot have the form $\Omega(\delta/\ell^{0.5+o(1)})$); actually, if, for some function $F : \mathbb{N} \to \mathbb{N}$, a two-query proximity-oblivious tester (with one-sided error) rejects f with probability $\delta_M(f)/F(\ell)$, then $F(\ell) = \Omega(\ell/\log \ell)$ (cf. [65]).

Following is a description of a generic "path tester": In light of the foregoing, this tester selects a "random path" (i.e., a pair of comparable vertices) such that each of its endpoints is almost uniformly distributed. This is done by selecting the first vertex, denoted u, uniformly, and selecting the second vertex, denoted v, uniformly among all vertices that are at distance d from u, where the distance is selected according to some distribution, denoted $\mathcal{D}_\ell$. One specific suggestion that works well (see Theorem 4.4) is to have $\mathcal{D}_\ell$ be uniform over the set $\{2^i : i \in \{0, 1, \ldots, \lfloor \log \ell \rfloor\}\}$.

Algorithm 4.3 (The generic path test, parameterized by a distribution $\mathcal{D}_\ell$ over $[\ell]$):

1. *Select comparable $u, v \in \{0, 1\}^\ell$ by the following process. First, select u uniformly in $\{0, 1\}^\ell$, and then select $d \leftarrow \mathcal{D}_\ell$ and $\sigma \in \{-1, +1\}$ uniformly. Now, select v uniformly among all ℓ-bit long strings of weight $\mathrm{wt}(u) + \sigma \cdot d$ that are comparable to u (i.e., either $u < v$ or $u > v$, depending on σ).[10] Specifically, if $\sigma = 1$, then v is selected uniformly in $\{z > u : \mathrm{wt}(z) = \mathrm{wt}(u) + d\}$, else v is selected uniformly in $\{z < u : \mathrm{wt}(z) = \mathrm{wt}(u) - d\}$. Indeed, if $\mathrm{wt}(u) + \sigma \cdot d \notin \{0, 1, \ldots, \ell\}$, then no vertex v is selected and the algorithm halts accepting.*
2. *Query f at u and v and accept if and only if f is monotone on this pair; that is, letting $\{x, y\} = \{v, u\}$ such that $x < y$, the algorithm accepts if and only if $f(x) \leq f(y)$.*

Indeed, having $\mathcal{D}_\ell \equiv 1$ corresponds to the edge test of Algorithm 4.1. We now consider two alternative choices for the distribution $\mathcal{D}_\ell$:

The pure path tester: One natural choice is to have $\mathcal{D}_\ell$ represent the deviation from $\ell/2$ of the Hamming weight of a uniformly distributed ℓ-bit long string;[11] that is, $\mathcal{D}_\ell$ is distributed identically to $|\mathrm{wt}(U_\ell) - (\ell/2)|$, where U_ℓ denotes the uniform distribution on $\{0, 1\}^\ell$. In this case, $\mathcal{D}_\ell$ resides in $[\Theta(\sqrt{\ell})]$ with constant probability, and equals 1 with probability $\Theta(1/\sqrt{\ell})$. Hence, the corresponding tester (which typically uses long paths) is called the pure path tester.

---

[10] Indeed, in this case the vertex v is not uniformly distributed among the vertices that are comparable to u and at distance d from it, except when $\mathrm{wt}(u) = \ell/2$. This is because σ is selected uniformly in $\{-1, +1\}$, rather than being selected in proportion to the numbers of such vertices. Still, the deviation from the former distribution is relatively small when $\mathrm{wt}(u) \approx \ell/2$, which is typically the case.

[11] **Advanced comment:** A related alternative is to have $\mathcal{D}_\ell$ be uniform over $[O(\sqrt{\ell \log(1/\epsilon)})]$.

The combined path and edge tester: In contrast, letting $\mathcal{D}_\ell$ be uniform over the set $\{2^i : i \in \{0, 1, \ldots, \lfloor \log \ell \rfloor\}\}$ yields a distribution in which both the values 1 and $2^{0.5\lfloor \log \ell \rfloor} \approx \sqrt{\ell}$ occur with probability $1/\log \ell$. Hence, the corresponding tester (i.e., that uses this "skewed" $\mathcal{D}_\ell$) is called the combined path and edge tester.

While a tight analysis of the pure path tester is currently unknown, an almost tight analysis of the combined (path and edge) tester is known.

Theorem 4.4 (Analysis of the combined edge and path tester [188]): *Algorithm 4.3, with $\mathcal{D}_\ell$ that is uniform over $\{2^i : i \in \{0, 1, \ldots, \lfloor \log \ell \rfloor\}\}$, constitutes a (one-sided error) proximity-oblivious tester for monotonicity with detection probability $\widetilde{\Omega}(\delta^2/\sqrt{\ell})$, where δ denotes the distance of the given function from being monotone.*

Note that the detection probability bound provided by Theorem 4.4 is quadratic in δ and linear in $1/\sqrt{\ell}$, whereas the bound in Theorem 4.2 is linear in both δ and $1/\ell$. Indeed, the point of Theorem 4.4 is obtaining an improved performance in terms of ℓ; in fact, this improved performance is optimal (up to polylogarithmic factors).[12] It is conjectured that the pure path test also achieves the bound stated in Theorem 4.4. More generally, we pose the following question.

Open Problem 4.5 (Which path testers are best for constant δ?): *For which choices of the distribution $\mathcal{D}_\ell$ does Algorithm 4.3 constitute a (one-sided error) proximity-oblivious tester for monotonicity with detection probability $\widetilde{\Omega}(\mathrm{poly}(\delta)/\sqrt{\ell})$, where δ denotes the distance of the given function from being monotone.*

4.3. Multivalued Functions on the Discrete Line

Here we consider multivalued functions of the form $f : [n] \to R_n$, where R_n is an arbitrary totally ordered set (e.g., any subset of the real numbers). Such a function f is called monotone if for every $x < y$ in $[n]$ it holds that $f(x) \le f(y)$. Recall that a special case of this problem, where $R_n = \{0, 1\}$, was studied in Chapter 1 (see Propositions 1.5 and 1.8).

4.3.1. A Tester Based on Binary Search

It will be instructive to view the values of $f : [n] \to R_n$ as residing in an array of n cells and to assume that all values of f are distinct (i.e., $|\{f(i) : i \in [n]\}| = n$). Consider the following tester for monotonicity that selects $i \in [n]$ uniformly at random, and then tries to find the value $f(i)$ in the said array by conducting a binary search. If f is indeed (strictly) monotone, then this search will succeed in finding $f(i)$ in location i. Hence, this (binary-search) tester performs $1 + \lceil \log_2 n \rceil$ queries, and accepts if and only if $f(i)$ is found in this binary search. (In order to waive the requirement that f has distinct values,

---

[12] **Advanced comment:** More generally, if a pair tester has detection probability $\Omega(\delta^b/\ell^a)$, then $2a + b \ge 3$ (see [188]). Hence, both Theorems 4.2 and 4.4 meet this lower bound, at $(a, b) = (1, 1)$ and $(a, b) = (0.5, 2)$, respectively.

when comparing values of f, we augment $f(i)$ to $((f(i), i)$, while using the lexicographic order on pairs.)[13]

As noted above, this tester always accepts monotone functions, and the point is lower-bounding the rejection probability of the tester as a function of the distance of f from being monotone. We shall show that if $f : [n] \to R_n$ is δ-far from monotone, then the foregoing tester rejects it with probability greater than δ. We shall actually prove the counterpositive.

Claim 4.6 (On the rejection probability of the binary search tester): *If the binary search tester accepts* $f : [n] \to R_n$ *with probability* $1 - \delta$, *then* f *is* δ-*close to monotone.*

Teaching Note: The foregoing tester as well as the following proof are presented in a somewhat loose style, since we shall later provide a more rigorous presentation and analysis of a related tester (see Algorithm 4.7 and its analysis). In fact, the reader may skip the following proof and proceed directly to Algorithm 4.7 (and later derive a proof of Claim 4.6 by minor modifications to the proof of Lemma 4.8).

Proof: Note that the only *random choice* performed by the tester is the choice of $i \in [n]$ made at its very first step. We call $i \in [n]$ good if an execution that starts with choosing i is completed with acceptance. For simplicity, we assume that all values in f are distinct or alternatively consider an execution in which f is replaced by f' such that $f'(i) = (f(i), i)$. The binary search for the value v starts with the eligible interval $[1, n]$. In each step, the eligible interval $[s, e]$ is divided into two halves at a pivot location $p = \lceil (s + e)/2 \rceil$, and the search takes the first half (i.e., resets the current interval to $[s, p]$) if and only if $v \le f(p)$; otherwise, the search takes $[p_1 + 1, b]$.

We first claim that if $i < j$ are both good, then $f(i) < f(j)$. To prove this claim, we consider the pair of binary searches conducted for $f(i)$ and for $f(j)$. Since both i and j are good, the first binary search ended at location i and the second binary search ended at j. Let $t \in [\lceil \log_2 n \rceil]$ be the first step in which these two binary searchers took different halves after comparing the "sought for" value against a pivot value associated with location p_t (which is at the end of the first half of the currently eligible interval). Since the two searches took different halves (of the current interval) and ended at i and j, respectively, and since $i < j$, the search for $f(i)$ took the first half whereas the search for $f(j)$ took the second half. But due to the comparisons made at this step, it follows that $f(i) \le f(p_t)$ and $f(j) > f(p_t)$. Hence, $f(i) < f(j)$, as claimed.

Finally, we observe that the restriction of f to the set of good points yields a monotone function. Hence, by modifying f on the non-good points, we obtain a monotone function over $[n]$. Recalling that there are $(1 - \delta) \cdot n$ good points, the claim follows. ∎

---

[13] That is, instead of comparing $f(i)$ to $f(j)$, we compare $(f(i), i)$ to $(f(j), j)$ and say that $(f(i), i)$ is (strictly) smaller than $(f(j), j)$ if either $f(i) < f(j)$ or both $f(i) = f(j)$ and $i < j$ hold.

A Related Tester. The foregoing tester was presented as if the tester is adaptive. Specifically, after selecting a random $i \in [n]$, the tester takes choices that supposedly depend on the values of f that it obtains. However, a closer look reveals that the correct choices (of which half-interval to take) can be determined *a priori* (by the value of i), and if the examined values of f do not match these choices, then it is safe to reject immediately. This observation leads to the following nonadaptive tester, where the sequence of intervals and pivot points is determined *a priori* in Step 2.

> **Algorithm 4.7** (Testing whether $f : [n] \to R_n$ is monotone): *Let $\ell = \lceil \log_2 n \rceil$ and $[a_0, b_0] = [1, n]$.*
>
> 1. *Uniformly select $i \in [n]$.*
> 2. *For $t = 1, \ldots, \ell$, let $p_t = \lceil (a_{t-1} + b_{t-1})/2 \rceil$ and*
>
> $$[a_t, b_t] = \begin{cases} [a_{t-1}, p_t] & \text{if } i \leq p_t \\ [p_t + 1, b_{t-1}] & \text{otherwise} \end{cases} \tag{4.1}$$
>
> *Note that $a_\ell = b_\ell = i$.*
> 3. *Query f at i as well as at $p_1, \ldots, p_\ell$.*
> 4. *For $t = 1, \ldots, \ell$, if $i \leq p_t$ and $f(i) > f(p_t)$, then reject. Likewise, for $t = 1, \ldots, \ell$, if $i > p_t$ and $f(i) < f(p_t)$, then reject.*
> *(Indeed, in case $i > p_t$, we only reject if $f(i) < f(p_t)$, since we do not assume here that all values of f are distinct.)*[14]
>
> *If the algorithm did not reject in Step 4, then it accepts.*

Algorithm 4.7 performs $1 + \lceil \log_2 n \rceil$ queries and always accepts a monotone function. To complete its analysis, we show that if $f : [n] \to R_n$ is δ-far from being monotone, then Algorithm 4.7 rejects it with probability greater than δ.

> **Lemma 4.8** (On the rejection probability of Algorithm 4.7): *If Algorithm 4.7 accepts $f : [n] \to R_n$ with probability $1 - \delta$, then f is δ-close to monotone.*

The proof is analogous to the proof of Claim 4.6, but it is more rigorous due to the more detailed description of the algorithm, which facilitates clear references to its steps. (The main clarification is in the second paragraph of the proof.)

> **Proof:** Note that the only random choice performed by Algorithm 4.7 is the choice of $i \in [n]$ made in Step 1, and call $i \in [n]$ good if an execution that starts with choosing i is completed with acceptance.
>   We first claim that if $i < j$ are *both good*, then $f(i) \leq f(j)$. Let $t \in [\ell]$ be the smallest integer for which the tth interval (i.e., $[a_t, b_t]$) determined (in Step 2) for i

---

[14] That is, the acceptance condition asserts that, for every $t \in [\ell]$, if $i \leq p_t$ then $f(i) \leq f(p_t)$ must hold, and otherwise (i.e., if $i > p_t$) then $f(i) \geq f(p_t)$ must hold. Hence, here the value of i determines the condition on f, whereas in the description of the binary search the value of f determined the condition on i. This is the reason that identical values of f pose no difficulty here.

is different from the tth interval determined for j. (Such t exists since the final intervals are different singletons.) It follows that p_t is assigned the same value in both executions, but exactly one element in $\{i, j\}$ took the first half in the tth iteration. Therefore, exactly one of these two elements is smaller or equal to p_t, and it follows that $i \leq p_t$ and $j > p_t$, since $i < j$. Now, by the corresponding part of Step 4, it follows that $f(i) \leq f(p_t)$ and $f(j) \geq f(p_t)$, or else the corresponding execution would have rejected (in contradiction to the hypothesis that both i and j are good). Hence, $f(i) \leq f(j)$, as claimed.

Denoting the set of good choices by G, we observe that the restriction of f to G yields a monotone function. Hence, by modifying f only on points in $[n] \setminus G$, we obtain a monotone function over $[n]$. (For example, we can modify f at $i \in [n] \setminus G$ such that $f(i) = f(j)$, where j is the smallest element in G that is greater than i, and if no such element exists we set $f(i)$ to equal the largest element in R_n.) Using $|G| = (1 - \delta) \cdot n$, the lemma follows. ∎

Corollaries. Let Π_n denote the set of monotone functions with domain $[n]$ and range R_n. Then, by Lemma 4.8, we have

Theorem 4.9 (Algorithm 4.7 is a POT for monotonicity): *Algorithm 4.7 is a (one-sided error) $(1 + \lceil \log_2 n \rceil)$-query proximity-oblivious tester for Π_n with detection probability δ, where δ denotes the distance of the given function from being monotone.*

Observing that Algorithm 4.7 rejects if and only if at least one of the checks of Step 4 rejects, we obtain a two-query POT with detection probability δ/ℓ. Specifically, we refer to a version of Algorithm 4.7 in which Steps 3 and 4 are replaced by selecting $t \in [\ell]$ uniformly at random, and comparing $f(i)$ to $f(p_t)$; that is, the test rejects if and only if either $i \leq p_t$ and $f(i) > f(p_t)$ or $i > p_t$ and $f(i) < f(p_t)$.

Theorem 4.10 (A two-query nonadaptive POT for monotonicity): *The foregoing algorithm is a (one-sided error) two-query proximity-oblivious tester for Π_n with detection probability δ/ℓ, where δ denotes the distance of the given function from being monotone and $\ell = \lceil \log_2 n \rceil$.*

We mention that $O(\delta/\log n)$ in an upper bound on the detection probability of any two-query test (for Π_n).[15] Recall that in the special case of Boolean functions (i.e., $R_n = \{0, 1\}$), we have seen (in Proposition 1.8) a two-query POT with detection probability $\Omega(\delta^2)$.

Proof: Using the terminology of Lemma 4.8, we observe that if i is not good (w.r.t. Algorithm 4.7), then the two-query algorithm rejects with probability at least $1/\ell$ (since at least one of the ℓ relevant checks fails). On the other hand, by Lemma 4.8, a function that is at distance δ from Π_n must have at least $\delta \cdot n$ points $i \in [n]$ that are not good. ∎

---

[15] Actually, for some $\epsilon > 0$, any ϵ-tester for Π_n has query complexity $\Omega(\log n)$; see [101, 108].

4.3.2. Other Testers

Theorem 4.10 presents a two-query POT with detection probability $\delta/\lceil\log_2 n\rceil$ for monotone functions over $[n]$ (i.e., for the property Π_n). An alternative proof of a similar lower bound follows as a special case of the following result.

Theorem 4.11 (General analysis of two-query nonadaptive POTs for monotonicity): *Let $G = ([n], E)$ be a connected multigraph such that for every $1 \le i < j \le n$ either $\{i, j\} \in E$ or there exists $k \in (i, j)$ such that $\{i, k\}, \{k, j\} \in E$. Consider an algorithm that, on input $f : [n] \to R_n$, selects an edge $\{i, j\} \in E$ uniformly at random, and accepts if and only if $f(i) \le f(j)$, where $i < j$. Then, this algorithm constitutes a* (one-sided error) *two-query proximity-oblivious tester for Π_n with detection probability at least $\frac{n}{2|E|} \cdot \delta$, where δ denotes the distance of the given function from being monotone.*

Theorem 4.10 follows as a special case by noting that the $n \cdot \ell$ pairs of possible queries (of the corresponding two-query version of Algorithm 4.7) define a graph that satisfies the hypothesis of Theorem 4.11, since every $i < j$ are connected via p_t (for an adequate t). (It also follows that the algorithm that compares the values at random pair of points $(i, j) \in [n]^2$ is a POT with detection probability δ/n.)[16]

Proof: Fix $f \notin \Pi_n$ and let δ denote the distance of f from Π_n. We say that a pair $(i, j) \in [n]^2$ such that $i < j$ is a violation if $f(i) > f(j)$. Viewing the set of violating edges as a graph, denoted G^f, we observe that G^f has no vertex cover of size smaller than δn, since the restriction of f to any independent set is a monotone function (and so f can be made monotone by modifying its value at the vertices of the vertex cover).[17] It follows that G^f has a matching of size at least $\delta n/2$; in fact, each maximal matching in G^f must have such a size (or else we obtain a vertex cover of size smaller than δn).

Note, however, that this matching, denoted M^f, need not be a subset of E, since M^f is a matching in the ("violation") graph G^f and E is the edge-set of the ("query") graph G. Nevertheless, by the hypothesis regarding G, for each $\{i, j\} \in M^f \setminus E$ such that $i < j$ there exists $k \in \{i + 1, \ldots, j - 1\}$ such that $\{i, k\}, \{k, j\} \in E$. It follows that either $f(i) > f(k)$ or $f(k) > f(j)$, since otherwise $f(i) \le f(k) \le f(j)$, in contradiction to the hypothesis that the pair (i, j) is a violation. In other words, each violating pair in M^f yields a violating pair in E, and the latter pairs are distinct since M^f is a matching. Hence, the tester rejects with probability at least $\frac{|M^f|}{|E|} \ge \frac{\delta n}{2|E|}$. ∎

Comments. It turns out that a graph satisfying the hypothesis of Theorem 4.11 must have $\Omega(n \log n)$ edges. (See [231] for a proof as well as a wider perspective.) On the other

---

[16] **Advanced comment:** The analysis of this naive tester is asymptotically optimal: Consider, for example, the function $f : [n] \to [n]$ such that $f(i) = 2 \cdot \lceil i/2 \rceil + (i \bmod 2) - 1 \in \{2\lceil i/2 \rceil - 1, 2\lceil i/2 \rceil\}$, which is at distance 0.5 from being monotone, but has only $n/2$ violating pairs (and hence is rejected with $\frac{n/2}{\binom{n}{2}} \approx 1/n$). It is even easier to see that the analysis of the two-query POT referred to by Theorem 4.10 is asymptotically optimal: Consider, for example, the function $f : [n] \to \{0, 1\}$ such that $f(i) = 1$ if and only if $i < n/2$.

[17] Indeed, the same observation is implicit in the proof of Lemma 4.8. The argument is generalized to any partially ordered set in Exercise 4.3.

hand, some two-query POTs for Π_n are not covered by Theorem 4.11: For example, an algorithm that selects $i \in [n-1]$ uniformly and accepts if and only if $f(i) \le f(i+1)$ rejects each $f \notin \Pi_n$ with probability at least $1/(n-1)$.

4.4. Multivalued Functions on the Hypergrid

Generalizing the two previous cases, we now consider the case of $D_n = [m]^\ell$, for any $m, \ell \in \mathbb{N}$ such that $m^\ell = n$, and general R_n. (Indeed, in Section 4.2 we had $m = 2$ and $R_n = \{0, 1\}$, whereas in Section 4.3 we had $m = n$.) That is, we consider functions of the form $f : [m]^\ell \to R_n$. Such a function f is called monotone if for every $x < y$ in $[m]^\ell$ it holds that $f(x) \le f(y)$, where $x = x_1 \cdots x_\ell \le y = y_1 \cdots y_\ell$ if and only if $x_i \le y_i$ for every $i \in [\ell]$ (and, indeed, $x_1 \cdots x_\ell = y_1 \cdots y_\ell$ if and only if $x_i = y_i$ for every $i \in [\ell]$).

It turns out that testing monotonicity in this case reduces to testing monotonicity in the one-dimensional case. The proof of this fact (for the case of $R_n = \{0, 1\}$) generalizes the proof of Theorem 4.2 and may be viewed as a "robust" extension[18] of the observation that $f : [m]^\ell \to R_n$ is monotone if and only if f is monotone in each direction (i.e., if and only if for every $\alpha \in [m]^{i-1}$ and $\beta \in [m]^{\ell-i}$ the function $f'(z) = f(\alpha z \beta)$ is monotone in z).[19] The extension from the special case of $R_n = \{0, 1\}$ to general R_n is based on a different argument. Hence, we consider the following algorithmic schema.

Algorithm 4.12 (Testing whether $f : [m]^\ell \to R_n$ is monotone):

1. *Select uniformly $i \in [\ell]$, as well as $\alpha \in [m]^{i-1}$ and $\beta \in [m]^{\ell-i}$.*
2. *Invoke a monotonicity tester for functions from $[m]$ to R_n, while providing it with oracle access to the function f' such that $f'(z) = f(\alpha z \beta)$.*

Algorithm 4.12 preserves the query complexity of the tester used in Step 2. Also, by the foregoing characterization, it follows that if a one-sided error tester is used in Step 2, then Algorithm 4.12 has one-sided error. The analysis of the rejection probability of this testing schema combines two reductions (which refer only to two-query POTs). The first reduction refers only to Boolean functions, and lower-bounds the rejection probability of the schema in terms of the rejection probability of the (two-query) tester used in Step 2.

Lemma 4.13 (Dimension reduction for the Boolean case): *Let T be a two-query one-sided error POT for monotonicity, and let ϱ_m denotes its detection probability function; that is, if h is at distance δ from a monotone Boolean function, then $\Pr[T^h(m) = 0] \ge \varrho_m(\delta)$. Suppose that ϱ_m is convex, and that when T makes the queries $x < y$ to $h : [m] \to \{0, 1\}$ it accepts if and only if $h(x) \le h(y)$. Then, using T in Step 2 of Algorithm 4.12 yields a two-query POT for monotonicity of Boolean functions over $[m]^\ell$ with detection probability function $\varrho(\delta) = \varrho_m(\delta/2\ell)$; that is, if $g : [m]^\ell \to \{0, 1\}$ is at distance δ from a monotone Boolean function, then the algorithm rejects it with probability at least $\varrho_m(\delta/2\ell)$.*

---

[18] Here robustness is used in the sense of robust characterization, as discussed in Sections 1.4 and 3.4.
[19] See Exercise 4.1.

(The proof of Lemma 4.13 is presented in Section 4.4.1.) In particular, using the POT of Theorem 4.10 in Step 2, we obtain a POT for monotone Boolean functions over $[m]^\ell$ such that functions that are at distance δ from monotone are rejected with probability at least $\frac{\delta/\lceil \log_2 m \rceil}{2\ell} = \Omega(\delta/\log n)$, where $n = m^\ell$.

The second reduction refers to functions over any partial order, and it relates the performance of any two-query POT in the case of a general range to the performance of the same POT on a binary range. Specifically, the probability that this POT rejects a general function that is δ-far from the set of monotone functions (with general range) is lower-bounded in terms of the probability that this very POT rejects any Boolean function that is δ-far from the set of monotone (Boolean) functions. (This is reminiscent of the "0-1 principle for sorting network" that states that a comparison-based sorting network that works on binary inputs also works on general inputs, except that here the "extension of the range" does *not* come for free.)

Lemma 4.14 (Range reduction): *Let P be an arbitrary partial order set over n elements, and R be an arbitrary totally ordered set. Let $\mathcal{D}$ be an arbitrary distribution over pairs $(x, y) \in P \times P$ such that $x < y$ (according to the partial order P). Suppose that for some linear function $\varrho : (0, 1] \to (0, 1]$ and for every Boolean function $g : P \to \{0, 1\}$ it holds that*

$$\mathbf{Pr}_{(x,y)\sim\mathcal{D}}[g(x) > g(y)] \geq \varrho(\delta_2(g)),$$

where $\delta_2(g)$ denotes the distance of g from the set of Boolean monotone functions. Then, for every function $f : P \to R$ it holds that

$$\mathbf{Pr}_{(x,y)\sim\mathcal{D}}[f(x) > f(y)] \geq \frac{\varrho(\delta(f))}{\lceil \log_2 |R| \rceil},$$

where $\delta(f)$ denotes the distance of f from the set of monotone functions (with range R).

(An overview of the proof of Lemma 4.14 is presented in Section 4.4.2.) Note that we lose a factor of $\log_2 |R|$ in the detection probability, where without loss of generality we may use R as the range of the tested function (and so $|R| \leq n$, see Exercise 4.4). The linearity condition (regarding ϱ) can be replaced by subadditivity, but the lemma does not hold otherwise (see Exercise 4.5). Letting Π_n denote the set of all monotone functions from $[m]^\ell$ to R_n, where $n = m^\ell$, and combining all the foregoing, we get

Corollary 4.15 (A two-query POT for multivalue monotonicity over $[m]^\ell$): *There exists an efficient (one-sided error) two-query proximity-oblivious tester for Π_n with detection probability $\Omega(\delta/\log^2 n)$, where δ denotes the distance of the given function from being monotone.*

Indeed, the foregoing lower bound is a simplification of $\frac{\delta}{2\ell \cdot \lceil \log_2 m \rceil \cdot \lceil \log_2 |R_n| \rceil}$.

Proof: Starting with the POT for Boolean functions over $[m]$ that is provided by Theorem 4.10, we first apply Lemma 4.13 and obtain a POT for Boolean functions over $[m]^\ell$. Then, we apply Lemma 4.14 and obtain a POT for multivalued functions over $[m]^\ell$, as asserted by the corollary. ∎

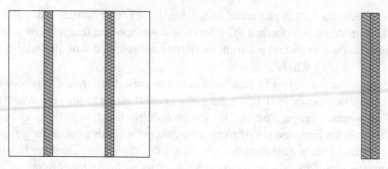

Figure 4.2: A two-dimensional slice of g and a generic corresponding function $g_\gamma^{\tau_1,\tau_2}$.

4.4.1. Dimension Reduction (Proof of Lemma 4.13)

This proof generalizes the proof of Theorem 4.2. Specifically, monotonicity in direction $i \in [\ell]$ is defined in the natural manner (extending Definition 4.2.1), whereas the switch operator is replaced by a sorting operator; that is, for every $i \in [\ell]$, the sorting operator S_i is defined such that for every function $f : [m]^\ell \to \{0, 1\}$ the function $S_i(f) : [m]^\ell \to \{0, 1\}$ is monotone in direction i and preserves the Hamming weight of each line in direction i (i.e., satisfies $\sum_{\tau \in [m]} S_i(f)(\alpha\tau\beta) = \sum_{k \in [m]} f(\alpha\tau\beta)$ for every $\alpha \in [m]^{i-1}$ and $\beta \in [m]^{\ell-i}$).[20]

When counting violations in direction i we shall use a more refined extension of Definition 4.2.3. Specifically, for every $i \in [\ell]$, $\alpha \in [m]^{i-1}$ and $\beta \in [m]^{\ell-i}$, we have $\binom{m}{2}$ directed pairs (of the form $(\alpha\tau_1\beta, \alpha\tau_2\beta)$ where $\tau_1 < \tau_2$) rather than one: For $1 \le \tau_1 < \tau_2 \le m$, the directed pair $(\alpha\tau_1\beta, \alpha\tau_2\beta)$ is called a violating (τ_1, τ_2)-pair of g in direction i if $g(\alpha\tau_1\beta) > g(\alpha\tau_2\beta)$. We denote by $V_i^{\tau_1,\tau_2}(g)$ the set of violating (τ_1, τ_2)-pairs of g in direction i.

Our generalization of Claim 4.2.4 asserts that *for every* $g : [m]^\ell \to \{0, 1\}$ *and* $i, j \in [\ell]$ *and* $1 \le \tau_1 < \tau_2 \le m$, *it holds that* $|V_j^{\tau_1,\tau_2}(S_i(g))| \le |V_j^{\tau_1,\tau_2}(g)|$. This is proved by fixing $i = 1$, $j = 2$, $\tau_1 < \tau_2$ and $\gamma \in [m]^{\ell-2}$, and considering the function $g_\gamma^{\tau_1,\tau_2} : [m] \times [2] \to \{0, 1\}$ such that $g_\gamma^{\tau_1,\tau_2}(\sigma, b) = g(\sigma\tau_b\gamma)$, as depicted in Figure 4.2. The key observation is that the effect of S_1 on $V_2^{\tau_1,\tau_2}$ can be decomposed among the various $g_\gamma^{\tau_1,\tau_2}$'s (since S_1 sorts the values that reside on each line in direction 1 (i.e., each line of the form $(\sigma\tau\gamma)_{\sigma \in [m]}$), operating separately on each such line). Furthermore, considering an m-by-2 Boolean submatrix, note that the number of unsorted rows may only decrease when the columns are sorted. This is the case, because the minimal number of unsorted rows in a submatrix with t_c ones in column c is $\max(t_1 - t_2, 0)$, and this minimum is obtained when the columns are sorted.

Now, starting with an arbitrary Boolean function $f_0 : [m]^\ell \to \{0, 1\}$, we consider the (analogous) sequence of f_i's defined by $f_i = S_i(f_{i-1})$. Generalizing Corollary 4.2.5, we infer that f_ℓ is monotone and that $|V_j^{\tau_1,\tau_2}(f_i)| \le |V_j^{\tau_1,\tau_2}(f_0)|$, for every $i, j \in [\ell]$ and $1 \le \tau_1 < \tau_2 \le m$. Letting $\delta_{i,\alpha,\beta}$ denote the (relative) distance of the sequence

---

[20] Indeed, this generalizes Definition 4.2.2, since for $b_1, b_2 \in \{0, 1\}$ there is a bijection between the three possible values of the integer $b_1 + b_2$ and the three possible values of the set $\{b_1, b_2\}$.

$(f_{i-1}(\alpha 1\beta), \ldots, f_{i-1}(\alpha m\beta))$ from a monotone sequence, we get

$$\delta(f_0, f_\ell) \leq \sum_{i\in[\ell]} \delta(f_{i-1}, f_i)$$

$$= \sum_{i\in[\ell]} \mathbb{E}_{(\alpha,\beta)\in[m]^{i-1}\times[m]^{\ell-i}} \left[|\{\tau \in [m] : f_{i-1}(\alpha\tau\beta) \neq f_i(\alpha\tau\beta)\}|/m \right]$$

$$= \sum_{i\in[\ell]} \mathbb{E}_{(\alpha,\beta)\in[m]^{i-1}\times[m]^{\ell-i}} \left[|\{\tau \in [m] : f_{i-1}(\alpha\tau\beta) \neq S_i(f_{i-1})(\alpha\tau\beta)\}|/m \right]$$

$$\leq \sum_{i\in[\ell]} \mathbb{E}_{(\alpha,\beta)\in[m]^{i-1}\times[m]^{\ell-i}} \left[2 \cdot \delta_{i,\alpha,\beta} \right],$$

where the last inequality follows by observing that the distance of a Boolean sequence $s = (e_1, \ldots, e_m)$ from its sorted version (i.e., $0^{m-\mathrm{wt}(s)} 1^{\mathrm{wt}(s)}$) is at most twice the distance of s to being monotone.[21] Hence:

$$\delta(f_0, f_\ell) \leq 2\ell \cdot \mathbb{E}_{i\in[\ell]}\mathbb{E}_{(\alpha,\beta)\in[m]^{i-1}\times[m]^{\ell-i}} \left[\delta_{i,\alpha,\beta} \right]. \tag{4.2}$$

On the other hand, the probability, denoted ρ, that Algorithm 4.12 rejects f_0, when using T in Step 2, where T selects pairs of queries according to the distribution $\mathcal{D}$, is

$$\rho = \mathbb{E}_{i\in[\ell]}\mathbb{E}_{(\alpha,\beta)\in[m]^{i-1}\times[m]^{\ell-i}} \left[\mathbf{Pr}_{(\tau_1,\tau_2)\sim\mathcal{D}}[f_0(\alpha\tau_1\beta) > f_0(\alpha\tau_2\beta)] \right]$$

$$= \mathbb{E}_{i\in[\ell]} \left[m^{-(\ell-1)} \cdot \mathbb{E}_{(\tau_1,\tau_2)\sim\mathcal{D}}[|V_i^{\tau_1,\tau_2}(f_0)|] \right]$$

$$\geq \mathbb{E}_{i\in[\ell]} \left[m^{-(\ell-1)} \cdot \mathbb{E}_{(\tau_1,\tau_2)\sim\mathcal{D}}[|V_i^{\tau_1,\tau_2}(f_{i-1})|] \right],$$

where the first equality is due to the definition of Algorithm 4.12 (when using T which uses the distribution $\mathcal{D}$), the second equality is due to the definition of $V_i^{\tau_1,\tau_2}$, and the inequality is due to the (second item of the) generalization of Corollary 4.2.5. Using the definitions of T (when given access to $f'(\tau) = f_{i-1}(\alpha\tau\beta)$) and ϱ_m, we get

$$\rho \geq \mathbb{E}_{i\in[\ell]}\mathbb{E}_{(\alpha,\beta)\in[m]^{i-1}\times[m]^{\ell-i}} \left[\varrho_m(\delta_{i,\alpha,\beta}) \right]. \tag{4.3}$$

Combining Eqs. (4.2) and (4.3) and using the convexity of ϱ_m, we get

$$\rho \geq \mathbb{E}_{i\in[\ell]}\mathbb{E}_{(\alpha,\beta)\in[m]^{i-1}\times[m]^{\ell-i}} \left[\varrho_m(\delta_{i,\alpha,\beta}) \right]$$

$$\geq \varrho_m \left(\mathbb{E}_{i\in[\ell]}\mathbb{E}_{(\alpha,\beta)\in[m]^{i-1}\times[m]^{\ell-i}}[\delta_{i,\alpha,\beta}] \right)$$

$$\geq \varrho_m(\delta(f_0, f_\ell)/2\ell).$$

Recalling that f_ℓ in monotone (by the first item of the generalization of Corollary 4.2.5), the lemma follows (since f_0 is at distance at most $\delta(f_0, f_\ell)$ from being monotone).

4.4.2. Range Reduction (Overview of the Proof of Lemma 4.14)

Without loss of generality, we assume that $R = [r]$ and that r is a power of 2. The key idea is that the values assigned to the two endpoints of a violating edge are either both at the same half of the interval $[1, r]$ or are in different halves (i.e., one value is in $[1, 0.5r]$ and the other is in $[0.5r + 1, r]$). The first type of edges can be represented by edges that have

---

[21] This assertion relies on the hypothesis that the sequence is binary and does not hold otherwise; see Exercise 4.6.

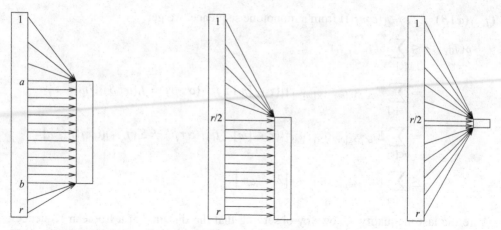

Figure 4.3: The generic filter $F_{a,b}$ (on the left), and the cases of $F_{1,0.5r}$ and $F_{0.5r,0.5r+1}$.

both their endpoints in the same interval of length $r/2$, whereas the edges of the second type can be represented by edges that have both their endpoints in the same interval of length 2 (where these two values represent the two halves). This suggests a reduction of the testing problem for range $[r]$ to two disjoint problems for range $[r/2]$ and another disjoint problem that refers to the range $\{1, 2\}$, where each violating edge (for range $[r]$) appears in exactly one of the instances. Needless to say, these separate instances should be handled in a way that allows for their later integration.

Towards this end, for every $1 \leq a < b \leq r$, we define a squashing filter $F_{a,b}$ such that for every function $f : P \to [r]$ the function $F_{a,b}(f) : P \to [a, b]$ satisfies

$$F_{a,b}(f)(x) = \begin{cases} a & \text{if } f(x) \leq a \\ b & \text{if } f(x) \geq b \\ f(x) & \text{otherwise (i.e., if } f(x) \in [a, b]) \end{cases} \quad (4.4)$$

(see Figure 4.3). Hence, the first type of violations with respect to f appear either in $F_{1,0.5r}(f)$ or in $F_{0.5r+1,r}(f)$, whereas violations of the second type appear in $F_{0.5r,0.5r+1}(f)$. In order to facilitate the aforementioned integration, we introduce a corresponding discarding operator $D_{a,b}$, which allows ignoring the modifications that are required for making $F_{a,b}(f)$ monotone and focusing on what is required beyond this in order to make f itself monotone. In other words, $D_{a,b}$ changes the value at x only if making $F_{a,b}(f)$ monotone (while using as few modifications as possible) requires changing the value of $F_{a,b}(f)$ at x. Specifically, for every function $f : P \to [r]$, we fix a monotone function $g : P \to [a, b]$ that is closest to $F_{a,b}(f)$, and define

$$D_{a,b}(f)(x) = \begin{cases} g(x) & \text{if } F_{a,b}(f)(x) \neq g(x) \\ f(x) & \text{otherwise (i.e., if } F_{a,b}(f)(x) = g(x)). \end{cases} \quad (4.5)$$

In other words, $D_{a,b}(f)$ agrees with the monotone function g that is closest to $F_{a,b}(f)$ on all points on which these two functions (i.e., g and $F_{a,b}(f)$) differ, but $D_{a,b}(f)$ maintains the value of f on points on which g and $F_{a,b}(f)$ agree. We stress that if $F_{a,b}(f)(x) = g(x)$, then the value of $D_{a,b}(f)(x)$ equals $f(x)$ rather than $F_{a,b}(f)(x)$, which makes a difference when $f(x) \notin [a, b]$ (since then $f(x) \neq F_{a,b}(f)(x)$). Now, given an arbitrary function $f : P \to [r]$, we consider the following sequence of auxiliary functions:

1. $f' = F_{0.5r, 0.5r+1}(f)$, which ranges over $\{0.5r, 0.5r + 1\}$.
2. $f'' = F_{1, 0.5r}(D_{0.5r, 0.5r+1}(f))$, which ranges over $[1, 0.5r]$.
3. $f''' = F_{0.5r+1, r}(D_{1, 0.5r}(D_{0.5r, 0.5r+1}(f)))$, which ranges over $[0.5r + 1, r]$.

Denoting by $\delta_{[a,b]}(g)$ the relative distance of $g : P \to [a, b]$ from the set of monotone functions over P with range $[a, b]$, one can prove the following claims.

Claim 1: $\delta_{[1,r]}(f) \leq \delta_{[0.5r, 0.5r+1]}(f') + \delta_{[1, 0.5r]}(f'') + \delta_{[0.5r+1, r]}(f''')$.
Claim 2: $\mathbf{Pr}_{(x,y) \sim \mathcal{D}}[f(x) > f(y)] \geq \mathbf{Pr}_{(x,y) \sim \mathcal{D}}[f'(x) > f'(y)]$.
Claim 3: $\mathbf{Pr}_{(x,y) \sim \mathcal{D}}[f(x) > f(y)] \geq \mathbf{Pr}_{(x,y) \sim \mathcal{D}}[f''(x) > f''(y)] + \mathbf{Pr}_{(x,y) \sim \mathcal{D}}[f'''(x) > f'''(y)]$.

Claim 2 is quite easy to establish (see Exercise 4.7). Claims 1 and 3 seem quite intuitive, but they do require proofs, which are a bit tedious (and are omitted here). Once all claims are proved, the lemma can be proved by induction. The induction step proceeds as follows, when $s = \log_2 r$:

$$\mathbf{Pr}_{(x,y) \sim \mathcal{D}}[f(x) > f(y)] \geq \frac{1}{s} \cdot \mathbf{Pr}_{(x,y) \sim \mathcal{D}}[f'(x) > f'(y)]$$

$$+ \frac{s-1}{s} \cdot \left(\mathbf{Pr}_{(x,y) \sim \mathcal{D}}[f''(x) > f''(y)] \right.$$

$$\left. + \mathbf{Pr}_{(x,y) \sim \mathcal{D}}[f'''(x) > f'''(y)] \right)$$

$$\geq \frac{1}{s} \cdot \varrho(\delta_{[0.5r, 0.5r+1]}(f')) + \frac{s-1}{s}$$

$$\cdot \left(\frac{\varrho(\delta_{[1, 0.5r]}(f''))}{s-1} + \frac{\varrho(\delta_{[0.5r+1, r]}(f'''))}{s-1} \right)$$

$$= \frac{\varrho(\delta_{[0.5r, 0.5r+1]}(f') + \delta_{[1, 0.5r]}(f'') + \delta_{[0.5r+1, r]}(f'''))}{s}$$

$$\geq \frac{\varrho(\delta_{[1,r]}(f))}{s},$$

where the first inequality uses Claims 2 and 3, the second inequality uses the induction hypothesis, the equality uses the linearity of ϱ, and the last inequality uses Claim 1.

4.5. Chapter Notes

4.5.1. History and Credits

Monotonicity testing was first considered by Goldreich *et al.* [139] and Ergün *et al.* [101]: While Goldreich *et al.* [139] considered Boolean functions over the partial order associated with the hypercube, Ergun *et al.* [101] considered multivalued functions over the total order associated with the line (see Sections 4.2.1 and 4.3.1, respectively).[22] The interpolation of both cases, presented in Section 4.4, refers to multivalued functions over the partial order associated with the hypergrid $[m]^{\ell}$. This case is reduced to the case of Boolean functions over $[m]^{\ell}$, which is then reduced to the case of Boolean functions over $[m]$. The range reduction is due to Dodis *et al.* [96], whereas the dimension reduction

---

[22] The focus of Goldreich *et al.* [139] was on monotonicity testing, whereas the investigation of Ergun *et al.* [101] was far broader than that.

appears in [139, 96]. Recall that the resulting two-query POT has detection probability at least $\delta/O(\log n \cdot \log |R_n|)$, where $n = m^\ell$ and R_n denotes the range of these functions (see Corollary 4.15, and recall that δ denotes the distance of the tested function from monotonicity). An improved bound of $\delta/O(\log n)$ was recently obtained in [72], and this is optimal.[23] We mention that a study of monotonicity testing in general partially ordered sets was initiated by Fischer et al. [113].

The exact complexity of testing monotonicity of Boolean functions over the Boolean hypercube has attracted much attention for over a decade. In particular, the focus was on whether the detection probability of a two-query POT must decrease linearly with the dimension ℓ. In fact, it was conjectured that the detection probability may decrease linearly with the square root of the dimension (i.e., that it has the form $\Omega(\mathrm{poly}(\delta)/\sqrt{\ell})$). This conjecture was established, up to polylogarithmic factors (see Theorem 4.4), by Khot, Minzer, and Safra [188]. Their result improved over a prior result of Chakrabarty and Seshadhri [71], which established a sublinear dependence on the dimension. Interestingly, the $\widetilde{\Omega}(\mathrm{poly}(\delta)/\sqrt{\ell})$ lower bound is almost tight [75] (improving over [76]).[24] For other related results regarding the complexity of testing monotonicity (and related problems), the reader is referred to [108, 72].

4.5.2. Related Problems

Two properties of functions that are related to monotonicity via their reference to a (partially) ordered domain as well as the specific domains considered are the property of satisfying the *Lipschitz condition* and *submodularity*. In both cases, we consider the domain $[m]^\ell$ as well as special cases in which either $m = 2$ or $\ell = 1$.

Lipschitz Functions. A function $f : [m]^\ell \to \mathbb{R}$ is called c-Lipschitz if for every $x, y \in [m]^\ell$ it holds that $|f(x) - f(y)| \le c \cdot \|x - y\|_1$, where $\|x - y\|_1 = \sum_{i \in [\ell]} |x_i - y_i|$. The study of testing (and reconstructing) Lipschitz functions was initiated by Jha and Raskhodnikova [173], who were motivated by applications to data privacy. Although it seem that testing Lipschitz functions cannot be reduced to testing monotonicity, Chakrabarty and Seshadhri presented a uniform framework that covers both problems [72], and obtained a two-query POT of detection probability $\delta/O(\ell \log m)$ for both problems.[25]

Submodular Functions. A function $f : [m]^\ell \to \mathbb{R}$ is called submodular if for every $x = (x_1, \ldots, x_\ell)$ and $y = (y_1, \ldots, y_\ell)$ in $[m]^\ell$ it holds that

$$f(\max(x, y)) - f(\min(x, y)) \le (f(x) - f(\min(x, y))) + (f(y) - f(\min(x, y))),$$
(4.6)

[23] This claim of optimality refers to two-query POTs. We mention that standard $O(1)$-testers for monotonicity must have query complexity $\Omega(\log n)$ both in the special case of $\ell = \log_2 n$ and $|R_n| = \Omega(\sqrt{\ell})$ (see [54] or Exercise 7.9) and in the special case of $\ell = 1$ and $|R_n| = \Omega(n)$ (see [101, 108]).

[24] **Advanced comment:** The lower bound is actually stronger, since it refers to the query complexity of standard testers with two-sided error (alas nonadaptive ones). Specifically, any nonadaptive $\Omega(1)$-tester for monotonicity of Boolean functions must have query complexity $\Omega(\ell^\alpha)$, for every constant $\alpha < 1/2$. A recent result of [39] establishes an $\widetilde{\Omega}(\ell^{1/4})$ lower bound for general (i.e., possibly adaptive) testers.

[25] Throughout this section, δ denotes the distance of the tested function from the property.

where $\max((x_1, \ldots, x_\ell), (y_1, \ldots, y_\ell)) = (\max(x_1, y_1), \ldots, \max(x_\ell, y_\ell))$ and ditto for $\min(x, y)$. Indeed, Eq. (4.6) is equivalent to $f(\max(x, y)) + f(\min(x, y)) \leq f(x) + f(y)$, and it is meaningless for $\ell = 1$. The study of testing submodularity was initiated by Parnas, Ron, and Rubinfeld [224], who focused on the case of $\ell = 2$ (which corresponds to "Monge matrices"), and presented a $O(1)$-query POT that has detection probability $\Omega(\delta / \log^2 m)$.[26] Seshadhri and Vondrak [252] considered the case of $m = 2$ (which corresponds to "modular set functions"), and showed a natural four-query POT of detection probability $\delta^{\tilde{O}(\sqrt{\ell})}$.

Convex Functions. Another property considered in [224] is convexity. A function $f : [m]^\ell \to \mathbb{R}$ is called convex if for every $x, y \in [m]^\ell$ and every $\alpha \in [0, 1]$ such that $z = \alpha x + (1 - \alpha)y \in [m]^\ell$ it holds that $f(z) \leq \alpha \cdot f(x) + (1 - \alpha) \cdot f(y)$. While submodularity refers to the "rectangle spanned by x and y" (along with $\max(x, y)$ and $\min(x, y)$), convexity refers to the line that connects x and y. Focusing on the case of $\ell = 1$, a $O(1)$-query POT was shown in [224] to have detection probability $\Omega(\delta / \log m)$.[27]

Invariances. We note that all properties studied in this chapter are invariant under a permutation of the variables; that is, for each of these properties Π, the function $f : [m]^\ell \to R$ is in Π if and only if for every permutation $\pi : [\ell] \to [\ell]$ the function $f_\pi(x_1, \ldots, x_\ell) = f(x_{\pi(1)}, \ldots, x_{\pi(\ell)})$ is in Π.

4.5.3. Exercises

The following exercises detail some claims that were made in the main text. In addition, Exercise 4.7 calls for proving Claims 1–3 of Section 4.4.2.

Exercise 4.1 (Characterization of monotonicity over the hypergrid): Prove that the function $f : [m]^\ell \to R_n$ is monotone if and only if it is monotone in each direction (i.e., if and only if for every $i \in [\ell]$ and for every $\alpha \in [m]^{i-1}$ and $\beta \in [m]^{\ell-i}$, the function $f'(z) = f(\alpha z \beta)$ is monotone in z).

> **Guideline:** For the less obvious direction, given $x = x_1 \cdots x_\ell < y = y_1 \cdots y_\ell$ in $[m]^\ell$, consider the sequence of points $x_1 \cdots x_i y_{i+1} \cdots y_\ell \in [m]^\ell$ for $i = \ell, \ldots, 1, 0$.

Exercise 4.2 (A typical case in which Algorithm 4.1 is asymptotically optimal): Recall that $\delta_M(f)$ denotes the relative distance of $f : \{0, 1\}^\ell \to \{0, 1\}$ from being monotone, whereas $\rho(f)$ denotes the probability that Algorithm 4.1 rejects f. Note that $\rho(f) \leq 2\delta_M(f)$ for every f. Show that for $f(x) = \mathrm{wt}(x) \bmod 2$ it holds that $\delta_M(f) \approx 0.5$ and $\rho(f) \approx 0.5$

> **Guideline:** Consider the set of edges between strings of odd Hamming weight and strings that are one unit heavier (i.e., the edge (x, y) is in this set if and only if $\mathrm{wt}(x)$ is odd and $\mathrm{wt}(y) = \mathrm{wt}(x) + 1$). Note that Algorithm 4.1 rejects f if and only if it selected

---

[26] The property tester presented in [224, Alg. 3] employs a $O(\log^2 m)$-query POT of detection probability $\Omega(\delta)$, but this POT conducts $O(\log^2 m)$ unrelated checks, which are determined nonadaptively, such that each check uses only $O(1)$ queries (see [224, Def. 9] and [224, Clm. 4]). (See the analogous move from Theorem 4.9 to Theorem 4.10.)

[27] The property tester presented in [224, Alg. 1] employs a $O(\log m)$-query POT of detection probability $\Omega(\delta)$, but this POT (see [224, Proc. 1]) proceeds in $\log_2 m$ iterations that are actually nonadaptive and check unrelated conditions, where each condition refers to $O(1)$ values of the function. (See an analogous move in footnote 26.)

such an edge, and that this set of edges contains approximately half of all the edges (and contains a matching of size $\approx 2^{\ell-1}$).

Exercise 4.3 (Vertex covers in the graph of violating pairs): Let P be an arbitrary partial order set over n elements, and suppose that $f : P \to R$ is at distance δ from the set of monotone functions over P (with range R). Consider the graph G^f such that $\{x, y\}$ is an edge if $x < y$ but $f(x) > f(y)$. Then, G^f has no vertex cover of size smaller than δn.

Guideline: Since the restriction of f to any independent set of G^f is a monotone function, f can be made monotone by modifying its values at the vertex cover.

Exercise 4.4 (Distance to monotone functions with the same range): Let P be an arbitrary partial order set over n elements, and suppose that $f : P \to R$ is at distance δ from the set of monotone functions over P (with range R). Show that $f : P \to R$ is at distance δ from the set of monotone functions over P with range $\{f(x) : x \in P\}$.

Guideline: Let $f' : P \to R$ be a monotone function that is at distance δ from f. Letting $R_f \overset{\text{def}}{=} \{f(x) : x \in P\}$, observe that $\{x : f'(x) \notin R_f\}$ is a subset of $\{x : f'(x) \neq f(x)\}$. Denoting the distinct values in R_f by $v_1 < \cdots < v_t$, define $f''(x) = v_i$ if $f'(x) \in [v_i, v_{i+1})$ and $f''(x) = v_1$ if $f'(x) < v_1$ (resp., $f''(x) = v_t$ if $f'(x) \geq v_t$). Note that f'' is monotone, and that it agrees with f' on R_f.

Exercise 4.5 (On the linearity of ϱ in Lemma 4.14): Show that Lemma 4.14 holds for any sub-additive function $\varrho : (0, 1] \to (0, 1]$ (rather than only for linear ones) and that it does not hold otherwise.

Guideline: For the positive part, note that the linearity of ϱ is used only in the final calculation, and that it can be replaced there by subadditivity. For the negative part, consider the two-query POT for monotonicity of Boolean functions presented in the proof of Proposition 1.8. Recall that in the Boolean case this POT has detection probability $\varrho(\delta) = \Omega(\delta^2)$, and observe that this POT rejects the function $f : [n] \to [n]$ such that $f(i) = 2\lceil i/2 \rceil - (i + 1 \bmod 2)$ with probability $O(1/n)$ (although f is $\Omega(1)$-far from monotone).

Exercise 4.6 (Distance to monotone versus distance to the sorted version): Prove that the distance of a sequence $\bar{s} = (e_1, \ldots, e_m) \in R^m$ to its sorted version is at most $|R|$ times the distance of $\bar{s}$ to a monotone m-sequence over R. Show that this upper bound is tight.

Guideline: As a warm-up consider the case of $R = \{0, 1\}$. Suppose that $\bar{s}$ has z zeros and let t denote the number of ones in the z-bit long prefix of $\bar{s}$. Then, $\bar{s}$ is at distance $2t$ from its sorted version, and at distance at least t from any monotone sequence, where the last assertion is proved by considering a matching between the t ones in the z-bit long prefix of $\bar{s}$ and the t zeros in its $(m - z)$-bit long suffix.

For a general R, suppose that $\bar{s}$ has m_i occurrences of the value $i \in R$ and let $m_i' = \sum_{j \leq i} m_j$. Let $D_i^+ \subseteq [m_{i-1}' + 1, m_i']$ (resp., $D_i^- \subseteq [m_{i-1}' + 1, m_i']$) be the set of positions that hold the value i in the sorted version of $\bar{s}$ but hold a value larger (resp., smaller) than i in $\bar{s}$ itself. (In the warm-up, $D_0^+ \subseteq [1, z]$ had size t, and ditto $D_1^- \subseteq [z + 1, m]$.) Note that $\bar{s}$ differs from its sorted version on $\sum_i |D_i^+ \cup D_i^-|$ positions, whereas the distance of $\bar{s}$ to the set of monotone m-sequences over R is lower-bounded by the size of any matching in $\cup_{i<j} D_i^+ \times D_j^-$. The claimed upper bound follows by showing that $\cup_{i<j} D_i^+ \times D_j^-$ contains a matching of size $\sum_i |D_i^+ \cup D_i^-|/|R|$. (This can be shown by considering the cycle structure of a permutation that sorts $\bar{s}$ by moving a

minimal number of elements, and observing that each such cycle has at least one edge in $\cup_{i<j} D_i^+ \times D_j^-$, whereas (w.l.o.g.) it has at most one position in each interval $[m'_{i-1} + 1, m'_i].)^{28}$

To see that the upper bound is tight consider the sequence $(m, 1, 2, \ldots, m - 1)$.

Exercise 4.7 (Claims 1–3 of Section 4.4.2): Prove Claims 1–3 of Section 4.4.2. Claim 2 is proved by showing that the squashing filter never increases the set of violating pairs. As a warm-up towards proving Claims 1 and 3, prove the following weaker analogues:

Claim 1w: $\delta_{[1,r]}(f) \leq \delta_{[0.5r, 0.5r+1]}(f) + \delta_{[1,0.5r]}(f) + \delta_{[0.5r+1,r]}(f)$.
Claim 3w: $\mathbf{Pr}_{(x,y) \sim \mathcal{D}}[f(x) > f(y)]$ is lower-bounded by

$$\mathbf{Pr}_{(x,y) \sim \mathcal{D}}[F_{1,0.5r}(f)(x) > F_{1,0.5r}(f)(y)] + \mathbf{Pr}_{(x,y) \sim \mathcal{D}}[F_{0.5r+1,r}(f)(x) > F_{0.5r+1,r}(f)(y)].$$

Claims 1–3 appear as items of [96, Lem. 14], using somewhat different notations, and their proofs appear in [96, Sec. 4.1–4.2].

> **Guideline:** Moving from the warm-up claims to the actual claims requires establishing some features of the operator $D_{a,b}$. Denoting the set of violating pairs for g by $V(g)$, the most useful features include
>
> 1. $V(D_{a,b}(h)) \subseteq V(h)$;
> 2. if $(x, y) \in V(h)$ and $|\{h(x), h(y)\} \cap [a, b]| = 2$, then $(x, y) \notin V(D_{a,b}(h))$;
> 3. if $(x, y) \in V(D_{a,b}(h))$, then $[D_{a,b}(h)(y), D_{a,b}(h)(x)] \subseteq [h(y), h(x)]$.
>
> These facts appear as items of [96, Lem. 13].

---

[28] That is, we claim that at least one vertex on each such cycle must be modified to make $\bar{s}$ monotone, whereas each cycle has size at most $|R|$. A simpler proof of the upper bound is indeed welcomed.

CHAPTER FIVE

Testing Dictatorships, Juntas, and Monomials

Summary: We consider testing three basic properties of Boolean functions of the form $f : \{0, 1\}^\ell \to \{0, 1\}$:

1. Dictatorship: The case where the value of f depends on a single Boolean variable (i.e., $f(x) = x_i \oplus \sigma$ for some $i \in [\ell]$ and $\sigma \in \{0, 1\}$).
2. Junta (of size k): The case where the value of f depends on at most k Boolean variables (i.e., $f(x) = f'(x_I)$ for some k-subset $I \subset [\ell]$ and $f' : \{0, 1\}^k \to \{0, 1\}$).
3. Monomial (of size k): The case where the value of f is the conjunction of exactly k Boolean literals (i.e., $f(x) = \wedge_{i \in I}(x_i \oplus \sigma_i)$ for some k-subset $I \subseteq [\ell]$ and $\sigma_1, \ldots, \sigma_\ell \in \{0, 1\}$).

We present two different testers for dictatorship, where one generalizes to testing k-Juntas and the other generalizes to testing k-Monomials.

This chapter is based on the works of Parnas, Ron, and Samorodnitsky [226][1] and Fischer, Kindler, Ron, Safra, and Samorodnitsky [111].

5.1. Introduction

We view Boolean functions $f : \{0, 1\}^\ell \to \{0, 1\}$ as functions of ℓ Boolean variables; that is, we view the ℓ-bit long argument to f as an assignment of Boolean values to ℓ Boolean variables. Boolean functions f that depend on very few of their Boolean variables are of interest in many applications. Such variables are called *relevant variables*, and they arise in the study of natural phenomena, where there are numerous variables (or attributes) that describe the phenomena but only few of them are actually relevant.

Typically, one does not know *a priori* which of the ℓ variables are relevant, and a natural task is to try to find this out. But before setting out to find the relevant variables, one may want to find out how many variables are actually relevant. Furthermore, in some cases (as shown in Chapter 6) just knowing a good upper bound on the number of influential variables is valuable.

---

[1] See discussions regarding the relation to testing the Long Code and the work of Bellare, Goldreich, and Sudan [37].

Assuming that there are $k \leq \ell$ influential variables, finding the set of influential variables requires making $\Omega(2^k + k \log \ell)$ queries to the function, because the number of functions $f : \{0, 1\}^\ell \to \{0, 1\}$ that have k influential variables is of the order of $\binom{\ell}{k} \cdot 2^{2^k}$. Our goal is to test whether f has k influential variables (or is ϵ-far from having this property) using only poly(k/ϵ) queries; in particular, the complexity we seek is independent of ℓ, which is especially valuable when ℓ is very large compared to k.

Functions having at most k influential variables will be called k-juntas, and in case of $k = 1$ they will be called *dictatorships* (unless they are constant functions). We shall start with the latter case: in Section 5.2 we present a tester of dictatorships, while viewing dictatorships as linear functions that depend on one variable. Hence, this tester will first check whether the function is linear, and then check (via self-correction) whether this linear function is a dictatorship. This approach is abstracted in Section 5.2.3, which is highly recommended.

Section 5.3 deals with the more general problem of testing whether a function is a k-junta, where $k \geq 1$ is a parameter that is given to the tester. This tester uses different ideas, and thus it yields an alternative tester for dictatorship. (The analysis of this tester is more complex than the analysis of the tester for dictatorship presented in Section 5.2.)

Teaching Note: We suggest leaving the (overview) section that discusses testing monomials (i.e., Section 5.2.2) for advanced independent reading.

5.2. Testing Dictatorship via Self-correction

We consider testing two related properties of Boolean functions $f : \{0, 1\}^\ell \to \{0, 1\}$, called *dictatorship* and *monotone dictatorship*. First, we note that the object being tested is of size $n = 2^\ell$, and so query complexity that is logarithmic in ℓ (which can be obtained via proper learning (see Section 1.3.5))[2] is definitely sublinear. Still, we shall seek testers of lower complexity; specifically, we seek complexity that is independent of the size of the object.

Definition 5.1 (Dictatorship and monotone dictatorship): *A function $f : \{0, 1\}^\ell \to \{0, 1\}$ is called a* monotone dictatorship *if for some $i \in [\ell]$ it holds that $f(x) = x_i$. It is called a* dictatorship *if for some $i \in [\ell]$ and $\sigma \in \{0, 1\}$ it holds that $f(x) = x_i \oplus \sigma$.*

Note that f is a dictatorship if and only if either f or $f \oplus 1$ is a monotone dictatorship. Hence, the set of dictatorships is the union of Π and $\{f : f \oplus 1 \in \Pi\}$, where Π is the set of monotone dictatorships. Using the closure of property testing under unions (see Section 1.3.4), we may reduce testing dictatorship to testing monotone dictatorship.[3] Thus, we shall focus on the latter task.

A Detour: Dictatorship and the Long Code. The Long Code, which was introduced in [37] and plays a pivotal role in many Probabilistically Checkable Proof (PCP)

---

[2] This uses the fact that there are only 2ℓ different dictatorship functions.
[3] In fact, we also use the fact that testing $\{f : f \oplus 1 \in \Pi\}$ reduces to testing Π. Indeed, this holds for any property Π of Boolean functions.

constructions (see, e.g., [37, 170, 171, 249, 95, 186, 187, 211])[4], encodes k-bit long strings by 2^{2^k}-bit long strings such that $x \in \{0, 1\}^k$ is encoded by the sequence of the evaluations of all $n = 2^{2^k}$ Boolean functions $g : \{0, 1\}^k \to \{0, 1\}$ at x. That is, the gth location of the codeword $C(x) \in \{0, 1\}^n$ equals $g(x)$. Now, look at $f_x = C(x)$ as a function from $\{0, 1\}^{2^k}$ to $\{0, 1\}$ such that $f_x(\langle g \rangle) = g(x)$, where $\langle g \rangle \in \{0, 1\}^{2^k}$ denotes the truth-table of $g : \{0, 1\}^k \to \{0, 1\}$. Note that the 2^k (bit) locations in $\langle g \rangle$ correspond to k-bit strings, where the bit corresponding to location $x \in \{0, 1\}^\ell$ in $\langle g \rangle$, denoted $\langle g \rangle_x$, holds the value $g(x)$. Thus, the function $f_x : \{0, 1\}^{2^k} \to \{0, 1\}$ is a monotone dictatorship, since its value at any input $\langle g \rangle$ equals $\langle g \rangle_x$ (i.e., $f_x(\langle g \rangle) = g(x) = \langle g \rangle_x$ for every $\langle g \rangle$). Hence, the Long Code (encoding k-bit strings) is the set of monotone dictatorship functions from $\{0, 1\}^{2^k}$ to $\{0, 1\}$, which means that the Long Code corresponds to the case that ℓ is a power of 2.

5.2.1. The Tester

One key observation towards testing monotone dictatorships is that these functions are linear; that is, they are parity functions (where each parity function is the exclusive-or of a subset of its Boolean variables). Hence, we may first test whether the input function $f : \{0, 1\}^\ell \to \{0, 1\}$ is linear (or rather close to linear), and rejects otherwise. (Indeed, a suitable test was presented in Chapter 2.) Assuming that f is close to the linear function f', we shall test whether f' is a (monotone) dictatorship, by relying on the following dichotomy, where $x \wedge y$ denotes the bit-by-bit AND of the ℓ-bit strings x and y:

- On the one hand, if f' is a monotone dictatorship, then

$$\Pr_{x,y \in \{0,1\}^\ell}[f'(x) \wedge f'(y) = f'(x \wedge y)] = 1. \tag{5.1}$$

This holds since if $f'(x) = x_i$, then $f'(y) = y_i$ and $f'(x \wedge y) = x_i \wedge y_i$.
- On the other hand, if $f'(x) = \oplus_{i \in I} x_i$ for $|I| > 1$, then

$$\Pr_{x,y \in \{0,1\}^\ell}[f'(x) \wedge f'(y) = f'(x \wedge y)]$$

$$= \Pr_{x,y \in \{0,1\}^\ell}[(\oplus_{i \in I} x_i) \wedge (\oplus_{i \in I} y_i) = \oplus_{i \in I}(x_i \wedge y_i)]$$

$$= \Pr_{x,y \in \{0,1\}^\ell}[\oplus_{i,j \in I}(x_i \wedge y_j) = \oplus_{i \in I}(x_i \wedge y_i)]. \tag{5.2}$$

Our aim is to show that Eq. (5.2) is strictly smaller than 1. It will be instructive to analyze this expression by moving to the arithmetics of the two-element field. Hence, Eq. (5.2) can be written as

$$\Pr_{x,y \in \{0,1\}^\ell}\left[\sum_{i,j \in I : i \neq j} x_i \cdot y_j = 0\right]. \tag{5.3}$$

Observing that the expression in Eq. (5.3) is a nonzero polynomial of degree 2, we conclude that it equals zero with probability at most $3/4$ (see Exercise 5.1). It follows

[4] **Advanced comment:** The Long Code is pivotal especially in PCP constructions aimed at optimizing parameters of the query complexity, which are often motivated by the desire to obtain tight inapproximability results. We refer to this line of research as the "second generation" of PCP constructions, which followed the "first generation" that culminated in the establishing of the PCP Theorem [25, 24]. In contrast, the Long Code is not used (or need not be used) in works of the "third generation" that focus on other considerations such as proof length (e.g., [157, 44]), combinatorial constructions (e.g., [94, 92]), and lower error via few multivalued queries (e.g., [210, 93]).

that in this case

$$\Pr_{x,y \in \{0,1\}^\ell}[f'(x) \wedge f'(y) = f'(x \wedge y)] \leq 3/4. \tag{5.4}$$

The gap between Eq. (5.1) and Eq. (5.4) should allow us to distinguish these two cases. However, there is also a third case; that is, the case that f' is the all-zero function. This pathological case can be discarded by checking that $f'(1^\ell) = 1$, and rejecting otherwise.

The foregoing description presumes that we can query f' at arguments of our choice, but this is not the case, since we have no access to f' (but rather to f). Nevertheless, assuming that f' is close to f, we can obtain the value of f' at any desired point by using "self-correction" (on f) as follows. When seeking the value of $f'(z)$, we select uniformly at random $r \in \{0,1\}^\ell$, query f at r and at $r \oplus z$, and use the value $f(r) \oplus f(r \oplus z)$. Indeed, the value $f(r) \oplus f(r \oplus z)$ can be thought of as a random vote regarding the value of $f'(z)$. If f' is ϵ-close to f, then this vote equals the value $f'(z)$ with probability at least $\Pr_r[(f'(r) = f(r)) \& (f'(r \oplus z) = f(r \oplus z))] \geq 1 - 2\epsilon$, since $f'(r) \oplus f'(r \oplus z) = f'(z)$ by linearity of f'.

This discussion leads to a natural tester for monotone dictatorship, which first checks whether f is linear and if so checks that the linear function f' that is close to f is a monotone dictatorship. We check that f' is a dictatorship by checking that $f'(x \wedge y) = f'(x) \wedge f'(y)$ for uniformly distributed $x, y \in \{0,1\}^\ell$ and that $f'(1^\ell) = 1$, where in both cases we use self-correction (for the values at $x \wedge y$ and 1^ℓ).[5] Indeed, in Step 2 (below), the random strings r and s are used for self-correction of the values at $x \wedge y$ and 1^ℓ, respectively.

Below, we assume for simplicity that $\epsilon \leq 0.01$. This assumption can be made, without loss of generality, by redefining $\epsilon \leftarrow \min(\epsilon, 0.01)$. (It follows that any function f is ϵ-close to *at most one* linear function, since the linear functions are at distance $1/2$ from one another whereas $\epsilon < 0.25$.)[6]

Algorithm 5.2 (Testing monotone dictatorship): *On input $n = 2^\ell$ and $\epsilon \in (0, 0.01]$, when given oracle access to a function $f : \{0,1\}^\ell \to \{0,1\}$, proceed as follows.*

1. *Invoke the linearity tester on input f, while setting the proximity parameter to ϵ. If the linearity test rejected, then halt rejecting.*
   Recall that the known linearity tester, presented in Chapter 2, makes $O(1/\epsilon)$ queries to f.
2. *Repeat the following check for $O(1/\epsilon)$ times.[7]*
   (a) Select $x, y, r, s \in \{0,1\}^\ell$ uniformly at random.
   (b) Query f at the points x, y, r, s as well as at $r \oplus (x \wedge y)$ and $s \oplus 1^\ell$.
   (c) If $f(x) \wedge f(y) \neq f(r) \oplus f(r \oplus (x \wedge y))$, then halt rejecting.
   (d) If $f(s) \oplus f(s \oplus 1^\ell) = 0$, then halt rejecting.

If none of the iterations rejected, then halt accepting.

---

[5] Values at these points require self-correction, since these points are not uniformly distributed in $\{0,1\}^\ell$. In contrast, no self-correction is required for the values at the uniformly distributed points x and y. See Section 5.2.3 for a general discussion of the self-correction technique.

[6] **Advanced comment:** The uniqueness of the linear function that is ϵ-close to f is not used explicitly in the analysis, but the analysis does require that $\epsilon < 1/16$ (see proof of Theorem 5.4).

[7] Step 2 is a self-corrected form of the test $f(x) \wedge f(y) \overset{?}{=} f(x \wedge y)$, whereas Step 2 is a self-corrected form of the test $f(1^\ell) \overset{?}{=} 1$.

(Actually, in Step 2, we can use r instead of s, which means that we can reuse the same randomization in both invocations of the self-correction.)[8] Recalling that linearity testing is performed by invoking a three-query proximity-oblivious tester for $O(1/\epsilon)$ times, it is begging to consider the following proximity-oblivious tester (POT) instead of Algorithm 5.2.

Algorithm 5.3 (POT for monotone dictatorship): *On input $n = 2^\ell$ and oracle access to a function $f : \{0, 1\}^\ell \to \{0, 1\}$, proceed as follows.*

1. *Invoke the three-query proximity-oblivious tester* (of linear detection probability) *for linearity.[9] If the linearity test rejected, then halt rejecting.*
2. *Check closure to bit-by-bit conjunction.*
   (a) *Select $x, y, r \in \{0, 1\}^\ell$ uniformly at random.*
   (b) *Query f at the points x, y, r and $r \oplus (x \wedge y)$.*
   (c) *If $f(x) \wedge f(y) \neq f(r) \oplus f(r \oplus (x \wedge y))$, then reject.*
3. *Check that f is not the all-zero function.*
   (a) *Select $s \in \{0, 1\}^\ell$ uniformly at random.*
   (b) *Query f at the points s and $s \oplus 1^\ell$.*
   (c) *If $f(s) \oplus f(s \oplus 1^\ell) = 0$, then reject.*

If none of the foregoing steps rejected, then halt accepting.

As shown next, Algorithm 5.3 is a nine-query POT with linear detection probability. The same holds for a four-query algorithm that performs one of the three steps at random (i.e., each step is performed with probability $1/3$).[10]

Theorem 5.4 (Analysis of Algorithm 5.3): *Algorithm 5.3 is a one-sided error proximity-oblivious tester for monotone dictatorship with rejection probability $\varrho(\delta) = \Omega(\delta)$.*

Proof: The proof merely details the foregoing discussion. First, suppose that $f : \{0, 1\}^\ell \to \{0, 1\}$ is a monotone dictatorship, and let $i \in [\ell]$ such that $f(x) = x_i$. Then, f is linear, and so Step 1 never rejects. Furthermore, $f(x) \wedge f(y) = x_i \wedge y_i = f(x \wedge y)$, which implies that Step 2 never rejects (since $f(r) \oplus f(r \oplus z) = f(z)$ for all r, z). Lastly, in this case, $f(1^\ell) = 1$, which implies that Step 3 never rejects. It follows that Algorithm 5.3 always accepts f.

Now, suppose that f is at distance $\delta > 0$ from being a monotone dictatorship. Letting $\delta' = \min(0.9\delta, 0.01)$, we consider two cases.[11]

1. If f is δ'-far from being linear, then Step 1 rejects with probability $\Omega(\delta') = \Omega(\delta)$.
2. If f is δ'-close to being linear, then it is δ'-close to some linear function, denoted f'. Note that f' cannot be a dictatorship function, since this would mean that f is δ'-close to a monotone function whereas $\delta' < \delta$.

---

[8] This takes advantage of the fact that, in the analysis, for each possible f we rely only on *one* of the three rejection options.

[9] Such a POT, taken from [59], is presented in Chapter 2.

[10] See Exercise 5.2.

[11] **Advanced comment:** Any choice of $\delta' \leq 0.01$ such that is $\delta' \in [\Omega(\delta), \delta)$ will do. In fact, 0.01 can be replaced by any constant in $(0, 1/16)$.

We first note that if f' is the all-zero function (i.e., $f'(z) = 0$ for every $z \in \{0, 1\}^\ell$), then Step 3 rejects with probability greater than $1 - 2 \cdot 0.01 = \Omega(\delta)$, since

$$\mathbf{Pr}_s[f(s) \oplus f(s \oplus 1^\ell) = 0] \geq \mathbf{Pr}_s[(f(s) = f'(s)) \& (f(s \oplus 1^\ell) = f'(s \oplus 1^\ell))]$$

$$\geq 1 - \mathbf{Pr}_s[f(s) \neq f'(s)] - \mathbf{Pr}_s[f(s \oplus 1^\ell) \neq f'(s \oplus 1^\ell)]$$

$$\geq 1 - 2 \cdot \delta',$$

where the first inequality uses the fact that $f(s) = 0 \& f(s \oplus 1^\ell) = 0$ implies $f(1^\ell) = 0$, and the last inequality is due to the hypothesis that f is δ'-close to f'.

Hence, we are left with the case that $f'(x) = \oplus_{i \in I} x_i$, where $|I| \geq 2$. Relying on the hypothesis that f is 0.01-close to f' and using $f'(r) \oplus f'(r \oplus (x \wedge y)) = f'(x \wedge y)$, we observe that the probability that Step 2 rejects equals

$$\mathbf{Pr}_{x,y,r}[f(x) \wedge f(y) \neq f(r) \oplus f(r \oplus (x \wedge y))]$$

$$\geq \mathbf{Pr}_{x,y,r}[f'(x) \wedge f'(y) \neq f'(r) \oplus f'(r \oplus (x \wedge y))]$$

$$- \mathbf{Pr}_{x,y,r}[(f(x) \neq f'(x)) \vee (f(y) \neq f'(y)) \vee (f(r) \neq f'(r))$$

$$\vee (f(r \oplus (x \wedge y)) \neq f'(r \oplus (x \wedge y)))]$$

$$\geq \mathbf{Pr}_{x,y}[f'(x) \wedge f'(y) \neq f'(x \wedge y)] - 4 \cdot \mathbf{Pr}_z[f(z) \neq f'(z)]$$

$$\geq 0.25 - 4 \cdot 0.01,$$

where the second inequality uses a union bound as well as $f'(r) \oplus f'(r \oplus (x \wedge y)) = f'(x \wedge y)$, and the last inequality is due to Eq. (5.4). Hence, in this case, Step 2 rejects with probability greater than $0.2 = \Omega(\delta)$.

To summarize, in each of the two cases, the algorithm rejects with probability $\Omega(\delta)$, and the theorem follows. ∎

Digest. Note that self-correction was applied for obtaining the values of $f'(x \wedge y)$ and $f'(1^\ell)$, but not for obtaining $f'(x)$ and $f'(y)$, where x and y were uniformly distributed in $\{0, 1\}^\ell$. Indeed, there is no need to apply self-correction when seeking the value of f' at a uniformly distributed point. In contrast, the points 1^ℓ and $x \wedge y$ are *not* uniformly distributed: the point 1^ℓ is fixed, whereas $x \wedge y$ is selected from a distribution of ℓ-bit long strings in which each bit is set to 1 with probability $1/4$ (rather than $1/2$), independently of all other bits. For further discussion of the self-correction paradigm, see Section 5.2.3.

5.2.2. Testing Monomials

The ideas that underlie the foregoing testers of (monotone) dictatorship can be extended towards testing the set of functions that are (monotone) k-monomials, for any $k \geq 1$.

Definition 5.5 (Monomial and monotone monomial): *A function* $f : \{0, 1\}^\ell \to \{0, 1\}$ *is called a* k-monomial *if for some k-subset* $I \subseteq [\ell]$ *and* $\sigma = \sigma_1 \cdots \sigma_\ell \in \{0, 1\}^\ell$ *it holds* $f(x) = \wedge_{i \in I}(x_i \oplus \sigma_i)$. *It is called a* monotone k-monomial *if* $\sigma = 0^\ell$.

Indeed, the definitions of (regular and monotone) dictatorship coincide with the notions of (regular and monotone) 1-monomials. (In particular, f is a dictatorship if and only if either f or $f'(x) = f(x \oplus 1^\ell)$ is a monotone dictatorship).

Teaching Note: Alternative procedures for testing (regular and monotone) monomials are presented in Chapter 6. These alternative procedures are obtained by a simple application of a general paradigm, as opposed to the direct approach that is outlined here. In light of these facts, the reader may skip the current section and proceed directly to Section 5.2.3.

5.2.2.1. A Reduction to the Monotone Case

Note that f is a k-monomial if and only if for some $\sigma \in \{0, 1\}^\ell$ the function $f_\sigma(x) = f(x \oplus \sigma)$ is a monotone k-monomial. Actually, it suffices to consider only σ's such that $f(\sigma \oplus 1^\ell) = 1$, since if f_σ is a monotone monomial, then $f_\sigma(1^\ell) = 1$ must hold. This suggests the following reduction of testing k-monomials to testing monotone k-monomials.

Algorithm 5.6 (Reducing testing monomials to the monotone case): *Given parameters k and ϵ and oracle access to a function $f : \{0, 1\}^\ell \to \{0, 1\}$, proceed as follows if $\epsilon < 4 \cdot 2^{-k}$.*

1. *Select uniformly a random $O(2^k)$-subset of $\{0, 1\}^\ell$, denoted S, and for each $\sigma \in S$ query f at $\sigma \oplus 1^\ell$. If for every $\sigma \in S$ it holds that $f(\sigma \oplus 1^\ell) = 0$, then reject. Otherwise, pick any $\sigma \in S$ such that $f(\sigma \oplus 1^\ell) = 1$, and proceed to Step 2.*
2. *Invoke the ϵ-tester for monotone k-monomials, while proving it with oracle access to f' such that $f'(x) = f(x \oplus \sigma)$.*

If $\epsilon \geq 4 \cdot 2^{-k}$, then use $O(1/\epsilon)$ samples in order to distinguish the case of $|f^{-1}(1)| \leq 0.25\epsilon \cdot 2^\ell$ from the case of $|f^{-1}(1)| \geq 0.75\epsilon \cdot 2^\ell$. Accept in the first case and reject in the second case. (That is, accept if less than a 0.5ϵ fraction of the sample evaluates to 1, and reject otherwise.)

Note that the restriction of the actual reduction to the case that $\epsilon < 2^{-k+2}$ guarantees that the (additive) overhead of the reduction, which is $O(2^k)$, is upper-bounded by $O(1/\epsilon)$. On the other hand, when $\epsilon \geq 2^{-k+2}$, testing is reduced to estimating the density of $f^{-1}(1)$, while relying on the facts that any k-monomial is at distance exactly 2^{-k} from the all-zero function. In both cases, the reduction yields a tester with *two-sided error* (even when using a tester of one-sided error for monotone monomials).

Theorem 5.7 (Analysis of Algorithm 5.6): *If the ϵ-tester for monotone k-monomials invoked in Step 2 has error probability at most $1/4$, then Algorithm 5.6 constitutes a tester for k-monomials.*

Proof: We start with the (main) case of $\epsilon < 2^{-k+2}$. Note that if $|f^{-1}(1)| < 2^{\ell-k}$, then f cannot be a k-monomial, and it is OK to reject it. Otherwise (i.e., $|f^{-1}(1)| \geq 2^{\ell-k}$), with probability at least 0.9, Step 1 finds σ such that $f(\sigma \oplus 1^\ell) = 1$. Now, if f is a k-monomial, then f' as defined in Step 2 (i.e., $f'(x) = f(x \oplus \sigma)$) is a monotone k-monomial, since all strings in $f^{-1}(1)$ agree on the values of the bits in

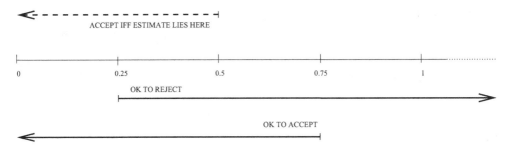

Figure 5.1: Detail for the proof of Theorem 5.7. The algorithmic decision is depicted by a dashed arrow that refers to the estimated value (in multiples of $\epsilon 2^\ell$), and the analysis is depicted by solid arrows that refers to the real value of $|f^{-1}(1)|$.

location I, where I denotes the indices of the variables on which f depends.[12] Thus, any k-monomial is accepted by the algorithm with probability at least $0.9 \cdot 0.75 > 2/3$ (since the tester used in Step 2 has error probability at most $1/4$).

On the other hand, if f is ϵ-far from being a k-monomial, then either Step 1 rejects or (as shown next) f' is (also) ϵ-far from being a (monotone) k-monomial, and Step 2 will reject it with probability at least $3/4 > 2/3$. To see that f' is ϵ-far from being a k-monomial (let alone ϵ-far from being a monotone k-monomial), we consider a k-monomial g' that is supposedly ϵ-close to f' and derive a contradiction by considering the function g such that $g(x) = g'(x \oplus \sigma)$, where σ is as in Step 2 (i.e., satisfies $f'(x) = f(x \oplus \sigma)$). Specifically, g maintains the k-monomial property of g', whereas $\delta(f, g) = \delta(f', g') \leq \epsilon$ (in contradiction to the hypothesis that f is ϵ-far from being a k-monomial).

We complete the proof by considering the case of $\epsilon \geq 2^{-k+2}$. In this case, if $|f^{-1}(1)| > 0.25\epsilon \cdot 2^\ell$, which implies $|f^{-1}(1)| > 2^{\ell-k}$, then f is not a k-monomial, and it is OK to reject it. On the other hand, if $|f^{-1}(1)| \leq 0.75\epsilon \cdot 2^\ell$, then f is 0.75ϵ-close to the all-zero function, which is 2^{-k}-close to a k-monomial, and so it is OK to accept f, because f is ϵ-close to a k-monomial (since $0.75\epsilon + 2^{-k} \leq \epsilon$). Indeed, when $|f^{-1}(1)| \in (0.25\epsilon 2^\ell, 0.75\epsilon 2^\ell]$, any decision is fine (see Figure 5.1). Hence, it suffices to guarantee rejection (w.p. $2/3$) when $|f^{-1}(1)| \geq 0.75\epsilon 2^\ell$ and acceptance (w.p. $2/3$) when $|f^{-1}(1)| \leq 0.25\epsilon 2^\ell$, as the algorithm does. ∎

5.2.2.2. Testing Monotone k-Monomials – An Overview

We start by interpreting the dictatorship tester in a way that facilitates its generalization. If f is a monotone dictatorship, then $f^{-1}(1)$ is an $(\ell - 1)$-dimensional affine subspace (of the ℓ-dimensional space $\{0, 1\}^\ell$). Specifically, if $f(x) = x_i$, then this subspace is $\{x \in \{0, 1\}^\ell : x_i = 1\}$. In this case, the *linearity tester* could be thought of as testing that $f^{-1}(1)$ is an arbitrary $(\ell - 1)$-dimensional subspace, whereas the "conjunction test" verifies that this subspace is an affine translation by 1^ℓ of a linear space that is spanned by $\ell - 1$ unit vectors (i.e., vectors of Hamming weight 1).[13]

---

[12] To see this claim, let $f(x) = \wedge_{i \in I}(x_i \oplus \tau_i)$, for some k-set $I \subseteq [\ell]$ and $\tau \in \{0, 1\}^\ell$. Then, $f(\sigma \oplus 1^\ell) = 1$ if and only if $\wedge_{i \in I}(\sigma_i \oplus 1 \oplus \tau_i) = 1$, which holds if and only if $\sigma_i = \tau_i$ for every $i \in I$. Hence, $f'(x) = f(x \oplus \sigma) = f(x \oplus \tau)$ is a monotone monomial.

[13] That is, we requires that this subspace has the form $\{1^\ell + \sum_{j \in ([\ell] \setminus \{i\})} c_j e_j : c_1, \ldots, c_\ell \in \{0, 1\}\}$, where $e_1, \ldots, e_\ell \in \{0, 1\}^\ell$ are the ℓ unit vectors (i.e., vectors of Hamming weight 1).

Turning to the general case (of $k \geq 1$), we observe that if f is a monotone k-monomial, then $f^{-1}(1)$ is an $(\ell - k)$-dimensional affine subspace of a specific form (i.e., it has the form $\{x \in \{0, 1\}^{\ell} : (\forall i \in I) x_i = 1\}$, for some k-subset I). So the idea is to first test that $f^{-1}(1)$ is an $(\ell - k)$-dimensional affine subspace, and then test that it is an affine subspace of the right form. Following is an outline of the treatment of these two tasks.

Testing Affine Subspaces. Suppose that the alleged affine subspace $H \subseteq \{0, 1\}^{\ell}$ is presented by a Boolean function $h : \{0, 1\}^{\ell} \to \{0, 1\}$ such that $h(x) = 1$ if and only if $x \in H$. (Indeed, in our application, $h = f$.) We wish to test that H is indeed an affine subspace.

(Actually, we are interested in testing that H has a given dimension, but this extra condition can be checked easily by estimating the density of H in $\{0, 1\}^{\ell}$, since we are willing to have complexity that is inversely proportional to the designated density (i.e., 2^{-k}).)[14]

This task is related to linearity testing and it was indeed solved in [226] using a tester and an analysis that resemble the standard linearity tester of [59]. Specifically, the tester selects uniformly $x, y \in H$ and $z \in \{0, 1\}^{\ell}$ and checks that $h(x + y + z) = h(z)$ (i.e., that $x + y + z \in H$ if and only if $z \in H$). Indeed, we uniformly sample H by repeatedly sampling $\{0, 1\}^{\ell}$ and checking whether the sampled element is in H.

Note that, for co-dimension $k > 1$ (of H), the function $h : \{0, 1\}^{\ell} \to \{0, 1\}$ is not affine; in particular, $|h^{-1}(1)| = 2^{\ell-k} < 2^{\ell-1}$. Still, testing affine subspaces can be reduced to testing linearity (see [138, Sec. 4] or Exercises 5.9–5.11), providing an alternative to the presentation of [226].

Testing That an Affine Subspace Is a Translation by 1^{ℓ} of a Linear Subspace Spanned by Unit Vectors. Suppose that an affine subspace H' is presented by a Boolean function, denoted h', and that we wish to test that H' has the form $\{1^{\ell} + \sum_{i \in [\ell] \setminus I} c_i e_i : c_1, \ldots, c_{\ell} \in \{0, 1\}\}$, where $e_1, \ldots, e_{\ell} \in \{0, 1\}^{\ell}$ are unit vectors, and $I \subseteq [\ell]$ is arbitrary. That is, we wish to test that $h'(x) = \wedge_{i \in I} x_i$.

This can be done by picking uniformly $x \in H'$ and $y \in \{0, 1\}^{\ell}$, and checking that $h'(x \wedge y) = h'(y)$ (i.e., $x \wedge y \in H'$ if and only if $y \in H'$). Note that if H' has the form $1^{\ell} + L$, where L is a linear subspace spanned by the unit vectors (i.e., $L = \{e_i : i \in [\ell] \setminus I\}$ for some I), then $h'(z) = \wedge_{i \in I} z_i$ holds for all $z \in \{0, 1\}^{\ell}$ and $h'(x \wedge y) = h'(x) \wedge h'(y)$ holds for all $x, y \in \{0, 1\}^{\ell}$. On the other hand, as shown in [226], if H' is an affine subspace that does not have the foregoing form, then the test fails with probability at least 2^{-k-1}.

However, as in the case of $k = 1$, we do not have access to h' but rather to a Boolean function h that is (very) close to h'. So we need to obtain the value of h' at specific points by querying h at uniformly distributed points. Specifically, the value of h' at z is obtained by uniformly selecting $r, s \in h^{-1}(1)$ and using the value $h(r + s + z)$. In other words, we self-correct h at any desired point z by using the value of h at a point obtained by shifting z by the sum of two random elements of $h^{-1}(1)$, while hoping that the latter points actually reside in the affine subspace H'. This hope is likely to materialize when h is $0.01 \cdot 2^{-k}$-close to h'.

The foregoing is indeed related to the conjunction check performed in Step 2 of Algorithm 5.3, and the test and the analysis in [226] resemble the corresponding parts in

---

[14] Recall that if $\epsilon < 2^{-k+2}$, then $O(2^k) = O(1/\epsilon)$, and otherwise (i.e., for $\epsilon \geq 2^{-k+2}$) we can proceed as in Algorithm 5.6.

Section 5.2.1. An alternative approach, which essentially reduces the general case (of any $k \geq 1$) to the special case (of $k = 1$), appears in [138, Sec. 5].

Conclusion. To recap, the overall structure of the resulting tester resembles that of Algorithm 5.3, with the exception that we perform a density test in order to determine the dimension of the affine subspace. We warn, however, that the analysis is significantly more involved (and the interested reader is referred to [226]).[15] Lastly, we stress that the tester of monotone k-monomials has two-sided error probability, which is due to its estimation of the density of the affine subspace. We wonder whether this is inherent.

> **Open Problem 5.8** (One-sided error testers for monomials): *For any constant $k \geq 2$, is there a one-sided error tester for monotone k-monomials with query complexity that depends only on the proximity parameter? Ditto for testing k-monomials.*

It seems that when the arity of the monomial (i.e., k) is not specified (i.e., when testing monomials of arbitrary arity), one-sided testing is possible by modifying the tester of [226] such that the density check is avoided. Indeed, in such a case, one may fail to sample $f^{-1}(1)$ using $O(1/\epsilon)$ random queries, but we can avoid rejection in this case because it occurs with noticeable probability only when the function f is 0.5ϵ-close to the all-zero function, which implies that f is ϵ-close to the monotone ℓ-monomial (provided that $2^{-\ell} \leq 0.5\epsilon$).[16]

5.2.3. The Self-correction Paradigm: An Abstraction

Recall that self-correction was used in the *analysis* of the linearity and low-degree tests, whereas in Section 5.2.1 we used this paradigm as part of the tester. We now abstract the self-correction paradigm, viewing it as an algorithmic paradigm (rather than as a tool of analysis).

In general, the self-correction of a function f that is close to a function g is based on a "random self-reduction" feature of g, which is the ability to easily recover the value of g at any fixed z in g's domain based on the values of g at few uniformly distributed points in g's domain. We stress that each of these points is uniformly distributed in g's domain, but *they are not necessarily independent of one another*.

The foregoing description of (the notion of) a random self-reduction is lacking, because, for a single function g, nothing prevents the recovery algorithm from just computing $g(z)$. In the context of complexity theory this is avoided by requiring the recovery algorithm to have lower *computational complexity* than any algorithm that computes g. In the current context, where the focus is information theoretic (i.e., on the query complexity), we cannot use this possibility. Instead, here we avoid this trivial (and useless) solution by defining random self-reducibility for sets of functions. In such a case, typically, the value of $g(z)$ cannot be found without querying g.

> **Definition 5.9** (Random self-reduction): *Let Π be a set of functions defined over D. We say that* functions in Π are randomly self-reducible by q queries *if there exist a*

---

[15] Recall that an alternative presentation appears in [138].
[16] Otherwise (i.e., if $\epsilon < 2^{-\ell+1}$), we can just recover f by making $2^\ell = O(1/\epsilon)$ queries.

randomized (query generating) *algorithm Q and a* (recovery) *algorithm R such that for every $g \in \Pi$ and every $z \in D$ the following two conditions hold:*

1. Recovery: *For every sequence of queries $(r_1, \ldots, r_q)$ generated by $Q(z)$, it holds that*

$$R(z, r_1, \ldots, r_q, g(r_1), \ldots, g(r_q)) = g(z).$$

2. Query distribution: *For each $i \in [q]$, the ith element in $Q(z)$ is uniformly distributed in D; that is, for every $e \in D$, it holds that*

$$\mathbf{Pr}_{(r_1,\ldots,r_q)\leftarrow Q(z)}[r_i = e] = \frac{1}{|D|}.$$

Indeed, various generalizations are possible.[17] For example, we may allow the recovery algorithm to be randomized and require (only) that it is correct with probability 2/3. Likewise, one may require the query distribution to be only "sufficiently random" (e.g., require only that $\mathbf{Pr}_{(r_1,\ldots,r_q)\leftarrow Q(z)}[r_i = e] \leq 2/|D|$ for every $i \in [q]$ and $e \in D$).

The self-correction paradigm amounts to using such a random self-reduction, while observing that *if f is ϵ-close to some $g \in \Pi$* (rather than $f = g \in \Pi$), *then, with probability at least $1 - q \cdot \epsilon$, the value obtained by applying R on the answers obtained by querying f on $Q(z)$ matches $g(z)$.* This observation is captured by the following theorem.

Theorem 5.10 (Self-correction): *Let Π be a set of functions defined over D. Suppose that functions in Π are randomly self-reducible by q queries, and denote the corresponding query-generating and recovery algorithms by Q and R, respectively. Then, for every f that is ϵ-close to some $f' \in \Pi$ and for every $z \in D$, it holds that*

$$\mathbf{Pr}_{(r_1,\ldots,r_q)\leftarrow Q(z)}[R(z, r_1, \ldots, r_q, f(r_1), \ldots, f(r_q)) = f'(z)] \geq 1 - q \cdot \epsilon.$$

It follows that f cannot be at distance smaller than $1/2q$ from two different functions in Π. Hence, functions in Π must be at mutual distance of at least $1/q$; in fact, *if Π is random self-reducible by q queries, then for every distinct $f, g \in \Pi$ it holds that $\delta(f, g) \geq 1/q$* (see Exercise 5.4).

(Indeed, Theorem 5.10 and its proof are implicit in Section 5.2.1 as well as in the analysis of the linearity and low-degree tests.)

Proof: By the (recovery condition of the) hypothesis, we know that for every sequence of queries $(r_1, \ldots, r_q)$ generated by Q, it holds that $R(z, r_1, \ldots, r_q, f'(r_1), \ldots, f'(r_q)) = f'(z)$. Hence,

$$\mathbf{Pr}_{(r_1,\ldots,r_q)\leftarrow Q(z)}[R(z, r_1, \ldots, r_q, f(r_1), \ldots, f(r_q)) = f'(z)]$$

$$\geq \mathbf{Pr}_{(r_1,\ldots,r_q)\leftarrow Q(z)}[(\forall i \in [q]) \quad f(r_i) = f'(r_i)]$$

---

[17] **Advanced comment:** One generalization, which matters only when one considers the computational efficiency of the recovery algorithm R, is providing R with the coins used by Q (rather than with the generated q-long sequence of queries). Needless to say, the recovery algorithm still gets z as well as the oracle answers $g(r_1), \ldots, g(r_q)$. That is, denoting by $Q(z; \omega)$ the output of Q on input z, when using coins ω, we replace the recovery condition by $R(z, \omega, g(r_1), \ldots, g(r_q)) = g(z)$ for every ω, where $(r_1, \ldots, r_q) = Q(z; \omega)$.

$$\geq 1 - \sum_{i\in[q]} \mathbf{Pr}_{(r_1,\ldots,r_q)\leftarrow Q(z)}[f(r_i) \neq f'(r_i)]$$

$$= 1 - q \cdot \mathbf{Pr}_{r\in D}[f(r) \neq f'(r)],$$

where the equality uses the (the query distribution condition of the) hypothesis by which each of the queries generated by Q is uniformly distributed in D. Recalling that f is ϵ-close to f', the claim follows. $\blacksquare$

An Archetypical Application. In the following result, we refer to the general notion of solving a promise problem. Recall that a promise problem is specified by two sets, P and Q, where P is the promise and Q is the question. The problem, denoted (P, Q), is define as *given an input in P, decide whether or not the input is in Q* (where standard decision problems use the trivial promise in which P consists of the set of all possible inputs). Equivalently, the problem consists of distinguishing between inputs in $P \cap Q$ and inputs in $P \setminus Q$, and indeed promise problems are often presented as pairs of nonintersecting sets (i.e., the set of YES-instances and the set of NO-instances). Lastly, note that here we consider solving such promise problems by probabilistic oracle machines, which means that the answer needs to be correct (only) with probability at least $2/3$.

Specifically, we shall refer to the promise problem (Π', Π''), where Π' is randomly self-reducible and *testable* within some given complexity bounds. We shall show that if (Π', Π'') is *solvable* within some complexity, then $\Pi' \cap \Pi''$ is *testable* within complexity that is related to the three given bounds.

Theorem 5.11 (Testing intersection with a self-correctable property): *Let Π' and Π'' be sets of functions defined over D. Suppose that functions in Π' are randomly self-reducible by q queries, that Π' is ϵ-testable using $q'(\epsilon)$ queries, and that the promise problem (Π', Π'') can be solved in query complexity q'' (i.e., a probabilistic q''-query oracle machine can distinguish between inputs in $\Pi' \cap \Pi''$ and inputs in $\Pi' \setminus \Pi''$). Then, $\Pi' \cap \Pi''$ is ϵ-testable using $O(q'(\min(\epsilon, 1/3q))) + q \cdot \widetilde{O}(q'')$ queries.*

(Indeed, Theorem 5.11 and its proof are implicit in Section 5.2.1.) We stress that Theorem 5.11 does not employ a tester for Π'', but rather employs a decision procedure for the promise problem (Π', Π''). However, as shown in Exercise 5.5, such a decision procedure is implied by any ϵ''-tester for Π'' for any $\epsilon'' < 1/q$, since Π' has distance at least $1/q$ (see Exercise 5.4).[18]

Proof: We propose the following tester for $\Pi' \cap \Pi''$. On input f, the tester proceeds in two steps:

1. It invokes the $\min(\epsilon, 1/3q)$-tester for Π' on input f and rejects if this tester rejects.

---

[18] **Advanced comment:** In light of the latter fact, we would have gained nothing by considering a promise problem version of *testing* Π'' when the promise is that the input is in Π' (rather than a tester for Π'' or a solver for (Π', Π'')). By such a version we mean the task of distinguishing between inputs in $\Pi' \cap \Pi''$ and inputs in Π' that are ϵ-far from Π'', where ϵ is a given proximity parameter as in standard testing problems. As stated above, if $\epsilon < 1/q$, then all inputs in $\Pi' \setminus \Pi''$ are ϵ-far from $\Pi'' \cap \Pi'$.

2. Otherwise, it invokes the decision procedure for the promise problem (Π', Π''), while providing this procedure with answers obtained from f via the self-correction procedure (for Π') guaranteed by Theorem 5.10. Specifically, let Q and R be the query-generating and recovery algorithms guaranteed by Theorem 5.10. Then, the query z is answered with the value $R(z, r_1, \ldots, r_q, f(r_1), \ldots, f(r_q))$, where $(r_1, \ldots, r_q) \leftarrow Q(z)$. Needless to say, the tester decides according to the verdict of the decision procedure.

By using error reduction, we may assume that both the tester of Π' and the solver of (Π', Π'') have error probability at most 0.1. Likewise, we assume that the self-correction procedure has error probability at most $0.1/q''$ (when invoked on any input that is $1/3q$-close to Π').[19] Hence, Step 1 can be implemented using $O(q'(\min(\epsilon, 1/3q)))$ queries, whereas Step 2 can be implemented using $q'' \cdot O(q \cdot \log q'')$ queries.

We now turn to the analysis of the proposed tester. If $f \in \Pi' \cap \Pi''$, then Step 1 rejects with probability at most 0.1, and otherwise we proceed to Step 2, which accepts with probability at least 0.9 (since in this cases all answers provided by the self-correction procedure are always correct). On the other hand, if f is ϵ-far from $\Pi' \cap \Pi''$, then we consider two cases.

Case 1: f is $\min(\epsilon, 1/3q)$-far from Π'. In this case, Step 1 rejects with probability at least 0.9.

Case 2: f is $\min(\epsilon, 1/3q)$-close to Π'. Let $f' \in \Pi'$ be $\min(\epsilon, 1/3q)$-close to f, and note that $f' \notin \Pi''$ (since otherwise f would have been ϵ-close to $\Pi' \cap \Pi''$). Hence, the decision procedure employed in Step 2 would have rejected f' with probability at least 0.9, since $f' \in \Pi' \setminus \Pi''$. However, this procedure is not invoked with f', but is rather provided with answers according to the self-correction procedure for Π'. Still, since f is $1/3q$-close to f', each of these answers agrees with f' with probability at least $1 - 0.1/q''$, which implies that with probability at least 0.9 all q'' answers agree with $f' \in \Pi' \setminus \Pi''$. We conclude that Step 2 rejects with probability at least $0.9 \cdot 0.9$.

Combining the two cases, we infer that any function that is ϵ-far from $\Pi' \cap \Pi''$ is rejected with probability greater than 0.8, and the theorem follows. ∎

Detour: On the Complexity of Testing Self-correctable Properties. An interesting feature of self-correctable properties is that the complexity of testing them is inversely proportional to the proximity parameter. This is due to the fact that testing a property that is randomly self-reducible by t queries reduces to checking whether the target function equals its self-corrected version (after $1/2t$-testing the property).[20]

Theorem 5.12 (Proximity parameter reduction for self-correctable properties): *Suppose that the functions in Π are randomly self-reducible by t queries, and that Π has a tester of query complexity $q : \mathbb{N} \times (0, 1] \to \mathbb{N}$. Then, Π has a tester of query*

---

[19] Specifically, we invoke the self-correction procedure for $O(\log q'')$ times and take the value that appears most frequently. Note that each invocation returns the correct value with probability at least $1 - q \cdot 1/3q = 2/3$.

[20] **Advanced comment:** Actually, we can use a c/t-tester, for any constant $c \in (0, 1)$. The point is that, when the function is c/t-close to the property, we only need the self-corrector to yield the correct value with positive probability (rather than with probability greater than $1/2$).

complexity $q' : \mathbb{N} \times (0, 1] \to \mathbb{N}$ *such that* $q'(n, \epsilon) = q(n, 1/2t) + O(t/\epsilon)$. *Furthermore, one-sided error probability is preserved.*

Proof Sketch: On input f, the new tester proceeds as follows.[21]

1. Invoke the tester (hereafter denoted T) guaranteed by the hypothesis with proximity parameter $1/2t$. If T rejects, then the new tester rejects.
2. Uniformly select a sample S of $O(1/\epsilon)$ elements in the domain of f, and compare the value of f on each of these points to the value obtained via the self-correction procedure (which relies on the random self-reducibility of Π).
   Specifically, let Q and R denote the query-generating and recovery algorithms guaranteed by the hypothesis. Then, for each $x \in S$, we compare the value of $f(x)$ to $R(x, r_1, \ldots, r_t, f(r_1), \ldots, f(r_t))$, where $(r_1, \ldots, r_t) \leftarrow Q(x)$, and accept if and only if no mismatch is found.

Note that when Step 2 is employed to any $f \in \Pi$, no mismatch is ever found. On the other hand, any function that is $1/2t$-far from Π is rejected in Step 1 with probability at least $2/3$. Lastly, suppose that the distance of f from Π, denoted δ, resides in the interval $(\epsilon, 1/2t]$. Let $f' \in \Pi$ be at distance δ from f, and let D denote the domain of f. In this case, we have

$$\mathbf{Pr}_{x \in D, (r_1, \ldots, r_t) \leftarrow Q(x)}[f(x) \neq R(x, r_1, \ldots, r_t, f(r_1), \ldots, f(r_t))]$$

$$\geq \mathbf{Pr}_{x \in D, (r_1, \ldots, r_t) \leftarrow Q(x)}[f(x) \neq f'(x) = R(x, r_1, \ldots, r_t, f(r_1), \ldots, f(r_t))]$$

$$\geq \mathbf{Pr}_{x \in D}[f(x) \neq f'(x)]$$

$$\quad \cdot \min_{x \in D} \left\{ \mathbf{Pr}_{(r_1, \ldots, r_t) \leftarrow Q(x)}[f'(x) = R(x, r_1, \ldots, r_t, f(r_1), \ldots, f(r_t))] \right\}$$

$$\geq \epsilon \cdot (1 - t \cdot \delta),$$

which is at least $\epsilon/2$. Hence, in this case (where $\delta \in (\epsilon, 1/2t]$), f is rejected by each iteration of Step 2 with probability at least $\epsilon/2$, and the theorem follows. $\blacksquare$

5.3. Testing Juntas

Here we consider testing a property of Boolean functions $f : \{0, 1\}^\ell \to \{0, 1\}$ called k-junta, which consists of functions that depend on at most k of their variables. Indeed, the notion of a k-junta generalizes the notion of a dictatorship, which corresponds to the special case of $k = 1$ (provided we ignore the constant functions). For $k \geq 2$, the set of k-juntas is a proper superset of the set of k-monomials, which (of course) says nothing about the relative complexity of testing these two sets.

Definition 5.13 (k-juntas): *A function* $f : \{0, 1\}^\ell \to \{0, 1\}$ *is called a* junta of size k *(or a* k-junta*) if there exist* k *indices* $i_1, \ldots, i_k \in [\ell]$ *and a Boolean function* $f' : \{0, 1\}^k \to \{0, 1\}$ *such that* $f(x) = f'(x_{i_1} \cdots x_{i_k})$ *for every* $x = x_1 \cdots x_\ell \in \{0, 1\}^\ell$.

---

[21] An alternative presentation views Step 2 as repeating a $(t + 1)$-query proximity-oblivious tester of detection probability $\varrho(\delta) = 1 - t \cdot \delta$ (see Exercise 5.6) for $O(1/\epsilon)$ times. Indeed, we can obtain a $(q(n, 1/2t) + t + 1)$-query proximity-oblivious tester of detection probability $\varrho(\delta) = \Omega(\delta)$ for Π.

In order to facilitate the exposition, let us recall some notation: For $I = \{i_1, \ldots, i_t\} \subseteq [\ell]$ such that $i_1 < \cdots < i_t$ and $x \in \{0, 1\}^\ell$, we denote by x_I the t-bit long string $x_{i_1} \cdots x_{i_t}$. Then, the condition in Definition 5.13 can be restated as asserting that *there exists a k-set* $I \subseteq [\ell]$ *and a function* $f' : \{0, 1\}^k \to \{0, 1\}$ *such for every* $x \in \{0, 1\}^\ell$ *it holds that* $f(x) = f'(x_I)$. In other words, for every $x, y \in \{0, 1\}^\ell$ that satisfy $x_I = y_I$, it holds that $f(x) = f(y)$. An alternative formulation of this condition asserts that *there exists a $(\ell - k)$-set* $U \subseteq [\ell]$ *that has zero influence on* f, where the influence of a subset S on f equals the probability that $f(x) \neq f(y)$ when x and y are selected uniformly subject to $x_{[\ell]\setminus S} = y_{[\ell]\setminus S}$ (see Definition 5.15.1). Indeed, the two alternatives are related via the correspondence between U and $[\ell] \setminus I$.

Note that the number of k-juntas is at most $\binom{\ell}{k} \cdot 2^{2^k}$, and so this property can be ϵ-tested by $O(2^k + k \log \ell)/\epsilon$ queries via proper learning (see Section 1.3.5). Our aim is to present an ϵ-tester of query complexity poly$(k)/\epsilon$.

The key observation is that if f is a k-junta, then any partition of $[\ell]$ will have at most k subsets that have positive influence. On the other hand, as will be shown in the proof of Theorem 5.15, *if f is δ-far from being a k-junta, then a random partition of $[\ell]$ into $O(k^2)$ subsets is likely to result in more than k subsets that each have $\Omega(\delta/k^2)$ influence on the value of the function*. To gain some intuition regarding the latter fact, suppose that f is the exclusive-or of $k + 1$ variables. Then, with high constant probability, the locations of these $k + 1$ variables will reside in $k + 1$ different subsets of a random $O(k^2)$-way partition, and each of these subsets will have high influence. The same holds if f has $k + 1$ variables that are each quite influential (but this is not necessarily the case, in general, and the proof will have to deal with that issue). In any case, the aforementioned dichotomy leads to the following algorithm.

Algorithm 5.14 (Testing k-juntas): *On input parameters ℓ, k and ϵ, and oracle access to a function $f : \{0, 1\}^\ell \to \{0, 1\}$, proceed as follows, while setting $t = O(k^2)$.*

1. *Select a random t-way partition of $[\ell]$ by assigning to each $i \in [\ell]$ a uniformly selected $j \in [t]$, which means that i is placed in the jth part.*
   Let $(R_1, \ldots, R_t)$ denote the resulting partition.
2. *For each $j \in [t]$, estimate the influence of R_j on f, or rather check whether R_j has positive influence on f. Specifically, for each $j \in [t]$, select uniformly $m \overset{\text{def}}{=} \tilde{O}(t)/\epsilon$ random pairs (x, y) such that x and y agree on the bit positions in $\overline{R_j} = [\ell] \setminus R_j$ (i.e., $x_{\overline{R_j}} = y_{\overline{R_j}}$), and mark j as influential if $f(x) \neq f(y)$ for any of these pairs (x, y).*
3. *Accept if and only if at most k indices were marked influential.*

The query complexity of Algorithm 5.14 is $t \cdot m \cdot 2 = \tilde{O}(t^2)/\epsilon = \tilde{O}(k^4)/\epsilon$.

Theorem 5.15 (Analysis of Algorithm 5.14): *Algorithm 5.14 is a one-sided tester for k-juntas.*

Proof: For the sake of good order, we start by formally presenting the definition of the influence of a set on a Boolean function.[22]

---

[22] Recall that, for $S \subseteq [\ell]$ and $x \in \{0, 1\}^\ell$, we let x_S denote the $|S|$-bit long string $x_{i_1} \cdots x_{i_s}$, where $S = \{i_1, \ldots, i_s\}$ and $i_1 < \cdots < i_s$. Also, $\overline{S} = [\ell] \setminus S$.

Definition 5.15.1 (Influence of a set):[23] *The influence of a subset $S \subseteq [\ell]$ on the function $f : \{0, 1\}^\ell \to \{0, 1\}$, denoted $I_S(f)$, equals the probability that $f(x) \neq f(y)$ when x and y are selected uniformly subject to $x_{\bar{S}} = y_{\bar{S}}$; that is,*

$$I_S(f) \stackrel{\text{def}}{=} \mathbf{Pr}_{x,y \in \{0,1\}^\ell : x_{\bar{S}} = y_{\bar{S}}}[f(x) \neq f(y)]. \tag{5.5}$$

Note that the substrings x_S and y_S are uniformly and independently distributed in $\{0, 1\}^{|S|}$, whereas the substring $x_{\bar{S}} = y_{\bar{S}}$ is uniformly distributed in $\{0, 1\}^{|\bar{S}|}$ (independently of x_S and y_S). Hence, $I_S(f)$ equals the probability that the value of f changes when the argument is "re-randomized" in the locations that correspond to S, while fixing the random value assigned to the locations in $\bar{S}$. In other words, $I_S(f)$ equals the expected value of $\mathbf{Pr}_{x,y \in \Omega_{\bar{S},r}}[f(x) \neq f(y)]$, where $\Omega_{\bar{S},r} \stackrel{\text{def}}{=} \{z \in \{0, 1\}^\ell : z_{\bar{S}} = r\}$ and the expectation is taken uniformly over all possible choices of $r \in \{0, 1\}^{|\bar{S}|}$; that is,

$$I_S(f) = \mathbb{E}_{r \in \{0,1\}^{|\bar{S}|}}\left[\mathbf{Pr}_{x,y \in \{0,1\}^\ell : x_{\bar{S}} = y_{\bar{S}} = r}[f(x) \neq f(y)]\right]. \tag{5.6}$$

The following two facts are quite intuitive, but their known proofs are quite tedious:[24]

Fact 1 (monotonicity): $I_S(f) \leq I_{S \cup T}(f)$.

Fact 2 (subadditivity): $I_{S \cup T}(f) \leq I_S(f) + I_T(f)$.

Now, if f is a k-junta, then there exists a k-subset $J \subseteq [\ell]$ such that $[\ell] \setminus J$ has zero influence on f (since $f(x)$ depends only on x_J), and so Algorithm 5.14 always accepts f (since, for every partition of $[\ell]$, at most k parts intersect J, whereas the other parts have zero influence).[25] On the other hand, we first show (see Claim 5.15.2) that if f is δ-far from a k-junta, then for every k-subset $J \subseteq [\ell]$ it holds that $[\ell] \setminus J$ has influence greater than δ on f. This, by itself, does not suffice for concluding that Algorithm 5.14 rejects f (w.h.p.), but it will be used towards establishing the latter claim.

Claim 5.15.2 (Influences of large sets versus distance from small juntas): *If there exists a k-subset $J \subseteq [\ell]$ such that $[\ell] \setminus J$ has influence at most δ on f, then f is δ-close to being a k-junta.*

Proof: Fixing J as in the hypothesis, let $g(x) \stackrel{\text{def}}{=} \text{maj}_{u:u_J = x_J}\{f(u)\}$. Then, on the one hand, g is a k-junta, since the value of $g(x)$ depends only on x_J. On the other hand, we shall show that f is δ-close to g. Let $g' : \{0, 1\}^k \to \{0, 1\}$ be such that $g(x) = g'(x_J)$

---

[23] In many sources, the influence of a set is defined as twice the quantity in Eq. (5.5). This is done in order to have this definition extend the definition of the "influence of a variable" as the probability that $f(x) \neq f(x')$, where x is uniformly distributed in $\{0, 1\}^\ell$ and x' is obtained from x by flipping the value of the variable (rather than re-randomizing it). We believe that Definition 5.15.1 is more natural in the current context.

[24] See [111, Prop. 2.4] or Exercise 5.12. An alternative proof appears in [52, Cor. 2.10], which relies on [52, Prop. 2.9]. Indeed, a simpler proof will be appreciated.

[25] This uses Fact 1. Specifically, for R such that $R \cap J = \emptyset$ (i.e., $R \subseteq [\ell] \setminus J$), it holds that $I_R(f) \leq I_{[\ell] \setminus J}(f) = 0$.

for every x. Then

$$\mathbf{Pr}_{x\in\{0,1\}^\ell}[f(x) = g(x)] = \mathbf{Pr}_{x\in\{0,1\}^\ell}[f(x) = g'(x_J)]$$

$$= \mathbb{E}_{\alpha\in\{0,1\}^k}[\mathbf{Pr}_{x:x_J=\alpha}[f(x) = g'(\alpha)]]$$

$$= \mathbb{E}_{\alpha\in\{0,1\}^k}[p_\alpha],$$

where $p_\alpha \overset{\text{def}}{=} \mathbf{Pr}_{x:x_J=\alpha}[f(x) = g'(\alpha)]$. Fixing any $\alpha \in \{0,1\}^k$, let Z denote the uniform distribution over $\{z \in \{0,1\}^\ell : z_J = \alpha\}$. Then, $p_\alpha = \mathbf{Pr}[f(Z) = g'(\alpha)] = \max_v\{\mathbf{Pr}[f(Z) = v]\}$, by the definition of g' (and g). It follows that the collision probability of $f(Z)$, which equals $\sum_v \mathbf{Pr}[f(Z) = v]^2 = p_\alpha^2 + (1 - p_\alpha)^2$, is at most p_α. Hence,

$$\mathbf{Pr}_{x\in\{0,1\}^\ell}[f(x) = g(x)] = \mathbb{E}_{\alpha\in\{0,1\}^k}[p_\alpha]$$

$$\geq \mathbb{E}_{\alpha\in\{0,1\}^k}\left[\sum_v \mathbf{Pr}_{z:z_J=\alpha}[f(z) = v]^2\right]$$

$$= \mathbb{E}_{\alpha\in\{0,1\}^k}[\mathbf{Pr}_{x,y:x_J=y_J=\alpha}[f(x) = f(y)]]$$

$$= \mathbf{Pr}_{x,y:x_J=y_J}[f(x) = f(y)]$$

$$= 1 - I_J(f).$$

Recalling that $I_J(f) \leq \delta$, it follows that f is δ-close to g, and recalling that g is a k-junta the claim follows. ∎

Recall that our goal is to prove that any function that is ϵ-far from being a k-junta is rejected by Algorithm 5.14 with probability at least $2/3$. Let us fix such a function f for the rest of the proof, and shorthand $I_S(f)$ by I_S. By Claim 5.15.2, every $(\ell - k)$-subset has influence greater than ϵ on f. This noticeable influence may be due to one of two cases:

1. There are at least $k + 1$ elements in $[\ell]$ that have each a noticeable influence (i.e., each singleton that consists of one of these elements has noticeable influence). Fixing such a collection of $k + 1$ influential elements, a random t-partition is likely to have these elements reside in different parts (since, say, $t > 10 \cdot (k + 1)^2$), and in such a case each of these parts will have a noticeable influence, which will be detected by the algorithm and cause rejection.

2. Otherwise (i.e., at most k elements have noticeable influence), the set of elements that are individually noninfluential is of size at least $\ell - k$, and thus contains an $(\ell - k)$-subset, which (by Claim 5.15.2) must have noticeable influence. It is tempting to think that the t parts in a random t-partition will each have noticeable influence, but proving this fact is not straightforward at all (see the proof of Lemma 5.15.3). Furthermore, this fact is true only because, in this case, we have a set that has noticeable influence but consists of elements that are each of small individual influence.

Towards making the foregoing discussion precise, we fix a threshold $\tau = c \cdot \epsilon/t$, where $c > 0$ is a universal constant (e.g., $c = 0.01$ will do), and consider the set of elements H that are "heavy" (w.r.t. individual influence); that is,

$$H \overset{\text{def}}{=} \{i \in [\ell] : I_{\{i\}} > \tau\}. \tag{5.7}$$

The easy case is when $|H| > k$. In this case (and assuming $t \geq 3 \cdot (k+1)^2$), with probability at least $5/6$, the partition selected in Step 1 has more than k parts that intersect H (i.e., $\mathbf{Pr}_{(R_1,\ldots,R_t)}[|\{i \in [t] : R_i \cap H \neq \emptyset\}| > k] \geq 5/6$).[26] On the other hand, for each $j \in [t]$ such that $R_j \cap H \neq \emptyset$, it holds that $\mathtt{I}_{R_j} \geq \min_{i \in H}\{\mathtt{I}_{\{i\}}\} > c\epsilon/t$, where the first inequality uses Fact 1. Hence, with probability at least $1 - (1 - c\epsilon/t)^m \geq 1 - (1/6t)$, Step 2 (which estimates $\mathtt{I}_{R_j}$ by $m = \widetilde{O}(t)/\epsilon$ experiments) will mark j as influential, and consequently Step 3 will reject with probability at least $(5/6)^2 > 2/3$.

We now turn to the other case, in which $|H| \leq k$. By Claim 5.15.2 (and possibly Fact 1)[27], we know that $\mathtt{I}_{\overline{H}} > \epsilon$. Our aim is to prove that, with probability at least $5/6$ over the choice of the random t-partition $(R_1, \ldots, R_t)$, there are at least $k+1$ indices j such that $\mathtt{I}_{R_j} > c\epsilon/t$. In fact, we prove something stronger.[28]

Lemma 5.15.3 (On the influence of a random part): *Let H be as in Eq. (5.7) and $\mathtt{I}_{\overline{H}} > \epsilon$. Then, for every $j \in [t]$, it holds that* $\mathbf{Pr}[\mathtt{I}_{R_j \cap \overline{H}} > \epsilon/2t] > 0.9$.

(We comment that essentially the same proof establishes that $\mathbf{Pr}[\mathtt{I}_{R_j \cap \overline{H}} = \Omega(\epsilon/t \log t)] > 1 - (1/6t)$, which implies that with probability at least $5/6$ each R_j has influence $\Omega(\epsilon/t \log t)$.)[29] Calling j good if $\mathtt{I}_{R_j} > c\epsilon/t$, Lemma 5.15.3 implies that the expected number of good j's is at least $0.9t$. Using an averaging argument[30] it follows that, with probability at least $5/6$, there exist at least $\frac{0.9t-(5/6)t}{1/6} = 0.4t > k$ good j's, and the bound on the rejection probability of the algorithm holds (just as in the easy case).

Proof: Denote $R = R_j$, and recall that each $i \in [\ell]$ is placed in R with probability $1/t$, independently of all other choices. Things would have been simple if influence was additive; that is, if it were the case that $\mathtt{I}_S = \sum_{i \in S} \mathtt{I}_{\{i\}}$. In this case, applying a multiplicative Chernoff Bound (see Eq. (A.15) in Appendix A) would have yielded the desired bound. Specifically, defining random variables, $\zeta_1, \ldots, \zeta_\ell$, such that $\zeta_i \stackrel{\text{def}}{=} \zeta_i(R)$ equals $\mathtt{I}_{\{i\}}$ if $i \in (R \setminus H)$ and zero otherwise, and observing that $\sum_{i \in [\ell]} \mathbb{E}[\zeta_i] > \epsilon/t$ and $\zeta_i \in [0, \tau]$, we would have obtained

$$\mathbf{Pr}_R\left[\sum_{i \in [\ell]} \zeta_i(R) < \epsilon/2t\right] < \exp(-\Omega(\tau^{-1}\epsilon/t)),$$

which is smaller than 0.1 when $c = t\tau/\epsilon > 0$ is small enough. Unfortunately, $\mathtt{I}_S = \sum_{i \in S} \mathtt{I}_{\{i\}}$ does not hold in general, and for this reason the proof of the current lemma

---

[26] Let H' be an arbitrary $(k+1)$-subset of H. Then, the probability that some R_j has more than a single element of H' is upper bounded by $\binom{k+1}{2} \cdot 1/t < (k+1)^2/2t$.

[27] Fact 1 is used in case $|H| < k$. In this case we consider an arbitrary k-superset $H' \supset H$ and use $\mathtt{I}_{\overline{H}} \geq \mathtt{I}_{\overline{H'}} > \epsilon$. Alternatively, one could have stated Claim 5.15.2 with respect to a set of size at most k, while observing that its current proof would have held intact.

[28] The significant strengthening is in arguing on each individual R_j rather than on some (i.e., $k+1$) of them. The fact that the lemma refers to $\mathtt{I}_{R_j \cap \overline{H}}$ rather than to $\mathtt{I}_{R_j}$ is less significant. While the weaker form suffices for our application, we believe that the stronger form is more intuitive (both as a statement and as a reflection of the actual proof).

[29] Using this bound would have required to use (in Step 2) a value of m that is a factor of $\log t$ larger.

[30] Specifically, suppose that with probability at least $1/6$ there are at most t' good j's. Then, $\frac{5}{6} \cdot t + \frac{1}{6} \cdot t' \geq 0.9t$, which solves to $t' \geq \frac{0.9t-(5/6)t}{1/6} = 5.4t - 5t$.

is not so straightforward. In particular, instead of the unsupported assumption that the influence of sets is additive (i.e., $I_S = \sum_{i \in S} I_{\{i\}}$), we shall use the following fact about the influence of sets.

Fact 3 (diminishing marginal gain): For every $S, T, M \subseteq [\ell]$ and every f, it holds that $I_{S \cup T \cup M}(f) - I_{S \cup T}(f) \leq I_{S \cup M}(f) - I_S(f)$.

(This fact may not be as intuitive as Facts 1 and 2, but it is quite appealing; see Exercise 5.13 or [111, Prop. 2.5].)

Now, we consider the following (less straightforward) sequence of random variables, $\zeta_1, \ldots, \zeta_\ell$, such that $\zeta_i \overset{\text{def}}{=} \zeta_i(R)$ equals $I_{[i] \backslash H} - I_{[i-1] \backslash H}$ if $i \in R$ and zero otherwise.[31] Observe that

1. The ζ_i's are independent random variables, since the value of ζ_i depends only on whether or not $i \in R$.
2. Each ζ_i is assigned values in the interval $[0, \tau]$, since $0 \leq I_{[i] \backslash H} - I_{[i-1] \backslash H} \leq \tau$, where the first inequality is due to Fact 1 and the second inequality follows by combining Fact 2 with $I_{\{i\} \backslash H} \leq \tau$. (Indeed, if $i \in H$, then $I_{\{i\} \backslash H} = I_\emptyset = 0$, and otherwise $I_{\{i\} \backslash H} = I_{\{i\}} \leq \tau$ (by definition of $\overline{H}$).)
3. The expected value of $\sum_{i \in [\ell]} \zeta_i$ equals $I_{\overline{H}}/t$, since $\mathbb{E}[\zeta_i] = (I_{[i] \backslash H} - I_{[i-1] \backslash H})/t$ whereas $\sum_{i \in [\ell]}(I_{[i] \backslash H} - I_{[i-1] \backslash H})$ equals $I_{[\ell] \backslash H} - I_\emptyset = I_{\overline{H}}$.
4. As shown next, for every fixed set F, it holds that

$$\sum_{i \in [\ell]} \zeta_i(F) \leq I_{F \cap \overline{H}}. \tag{5.8}$$

(Therefore, $\mathbf{Pr}_R[I_{R \cap \overline{H}} \leq \epsilon/2t] \leq \mathbf{Pr}_R[\sum_{i \in [\ell]} \zeta_i(R) \leq \epsilon/2t]$, and so upper-bounding the latter probability suffices for establishing the lemma.)

The proof of Eq. (5.8) uses Fact 3, and proceeds as follows (see further justifications below):

$$\sum_{i \in [\ell]} \zeta_i(F) = \sum_{i \in F}(I_{[i] \backslash H} - I_{[i-1] \backslash H})$$

$$= \sum_{i \in F \backslash H}(I_{([i-1] \backslash H) \cup \{i\}} - I_{[i-1] \backslash H})$$

$$\leq \sum_{i \in F \backslash H}(I_{(([i-1] \backslash H) \cap F) \cup \{i\}} - I_{([i-1] \backslash H) \cap F})$$

$$= \sum_{i \in [\ell]}(I_{([i] \backslash H) \cap F} - I_{[i-1] \backslash H) \cap F})$$

$$= I_{([\ell] \backslash H) \cap F}$$

$$= I_{F \cap \overline{H}}.$$

[31] Indeed, we define $[0] = \emptyset$, which implies $I_{[0] \backslash H} = I_\emptyset = 0$.

where the inequality uses Fact 3 (with $S = ([i-1] \setminus H) \cap F$, $T = ([i-1] \setminus H) \cap \overline{F}$ and $M = \{i\}$, which implies $S \cup T = [i-1] \setminus H$).[32]

Hence, $\zeta = \sum_{i \in [\ell]} \zeta_i$ is the sum of ℓ independent random variables, each ranging in $[0, c\epsilon/t]$, such that $\mathbb{E}[\zeta] > \epsilon/t$. Applying a multiplicative Chernoff Bound (see Eq. (A.15) in Appendix A) implies that under these conditions it holds that $\mathbf{Pr}[\zeta \leq \epsilon/2t] < \exp(-\Omega(1/c)) < 0.1$, and the lemma follows (by Eq. (5.8), when using $F = R$ and recalling that $\zeta_i = \zeta_i(R)$). ■

Let us recap. Assuming that f is ϵ-far from being a k-junta, we defined the set H (in Eq. (5.7)). We first disposed of the easy case in which $|H| > k$, showing that in this case the algorithm rejects with probability at least $5/6$. Turning to the complementary case, we showed that if $|H| \leq k$, then (by Claim 5.15.2) the hypothesis of Lemma 5.15.3 holds, and it follows that $\mathbf{Pr}[\mathbf{I}_{R_j} > \epsilon/2t] > 0.9$ for each $j \in [t]$. As shown right after the statement of Lemma 5.15.3, this implies that the algorithm rejects with probability at least $5/6$ also in this case. The theorem follows. ■

Digest. The main difficulty is establishing Theorem 5.15 is captured by the proof of Lemma 5.15.3, which can be abstracted as follows. For a function $v : 2^{[\ell]} \to [0, 1]$ assigning values to subsets of $[\ell]$ such that $v([\ell]) \geq \epsilon$ and $\max_{i \in [\ell]}\{v(\{i\})\} \leq \tau \ll \epsilon/t$, we wish to show that $\mathbf{Pr}_R[v(R) < \epsilon/2t]$ is small, when R is selected at random by picking each element with probability $1/t$ independently of all other elements.[33] Of course, this is not true in general, and some conditions must be made on v such that $\mathbf{Pr}_R[v(R) < \epsilon/2t]$ is small. The conditions we have used are (1) monotonicity, (2) subadditivity, and (3) diminishing marginal gain. These conditions correspond to Facts 1–3, respectively, which were established for $v(S) \stackrel{\text{def}}{=} \mathbf{I}_S(f)$. We comment that Condition (3) is often called submodularity. Hence, we actually established the following (which is meaningful only for $\tau \ll \epsilon/t$).

Lemma 5.16 (Lemma 5.15.3, generalized): *Let $v : 2^{[\ell]} \to [0, 1]$ be monotone, sub-additive, and submodular (i.e., has diminishing marginal gain) such that $v([\ell]) \geq \epsilon$ and $\max_{i \in [\ell]}\{v(\{i\})\} \leq \tau$. Suppose that R is selected at random by picking each element with probability $1/t$ independently of all other elements. Then, $\mathbf{Pr}_R[v(R) < \epsilon/2t] < \exp(-\Omega(\tau^{-1}\epsilon/t))$.*

Recall that $v : 2^{[\ell]} \to \mathbb{R}$ is monotone if $v(S \cup T) \geq v(S)$ for all $S, T \subseteq [\ell]$, it is subadditive if $v(S \cup T) \leq v(S) + v(T)$ for all $S, T \subseteq [\ell]$, and it is submodular (i.e., has diminishing marginal gain) if $v(S \cup T \cup M) - v(S \cup T) \leq v(S \cup M) - v(S)$ for all $S, T, M \subseteq [\ell]$. We comment that subadditivity implies $v(\emptyset) \geq 0$, whereas submodularity and $v(\emptyset) \geq 0$ imply subadditivity (see Exercise 5.8).

---

[32] In addition, the second equality (i.e., moving from summation over F to summation over $F \setminus H$) uses the fact that for every $i \in H$ it holds that $[i] \setminus H = [i-1] \setminus H$. Likewise, the third equality (i.e., moving from summation over $F \setminus H$ to summation over $[\ell]$) uses the fact that for every $i \in H \cup \overline{F}$ it holds that $([i] \setminus H) \cap F = ([i-1] \setminus H) \cap F$.

[33] Indeed, this formulation refers to the case of $H = \emptyset$, and captures the essence of Lemma 5.15.3.

5.4. Chapter Notes

The presentation of testing dictatorship via self-correction (Section 5.2.1) is based on the work of Parnas, Ron, and Samorodnitsky [226]. As noted in Section 5.2.1, the Long Code (presented by Bellare, Goldreich, and Sudan [37]) yields a family of Boolean functions that coincide with the set of dictatorship functions when ℓ is a power of 2. Interestingly, the monotone dictatorship tester of [226] is almost identical to the tester of the Long Code presented in [37]. This tester has played a pivotal role in the PCP constructions of [37] as well as in numerous subsequent PCP constructions including those in [170, 171, 249, 95, 186, 187, 211].

The problem of testing monomials was also studied by Parnas, Ron, and Samorodnitsky [226], and the overview provided in Section 5.2.2 is based on their work. An alternative procedure for testing monomials is presented in Chapter 6.

The problem of testing juntas was first studied by Fischer, Kindler, Ron, Safra, and Samorodnitsky [111], and the presentation provided in Section 5.3 is based on their work. Recall that the query complexity of the k-junta tester presented as Algorithm 5.14 is $\tilde{O}(k^4)/\epsilon$. Several alternative testers are known, culminating in a tester of Blais [52] that has query complexity $O(k/\epsilon) + \tilde{O}(k)$, which is almost optimal. For further discussion, see the survey [53].

Self-correction. The self-correction paradigm, as an algorithmic tool toward the construction of property testers, was introduced by Blum, Luby, and Rubinfeld [59]. The self-correction paradigm has been used extensively in constructions of PCP schemes, starting with [29]. As explained in Section 5.2.3, this paradigm is based on random self-reducibility, which seems to have first appeared in the "index calculus" algorithms [4, 206, 229] for the Discrete Logarithm Problem. Random self-reducibility was extensively used in (the complexity theoretic foundations of) cryptography, starting with the work of Goldwasser and Micali [160]. (These applications, which have a hardness amplification flavor, may be viewed as applying self-correction to a hypothetical adversary, yielding an algorithm that is postulated not to exist, and thus establishing specific limitations on the success probability of efficient adversaries. For example, a hypothetical adversary that approximates a ("hard-core") predicate yields an algorithm that inverts the underlying one-way function [145]. Subsequently, the use of random self-reducibility for hardness amplification became quite prevalent in complexity theory at large.)

Invariances. We note that all properties considered in this chapter are invariant under a permutation of the variables; that is, for each of these properties Π, the function $f : \{0, 1\}^\ell \to \{0, 1\}$ is in Π if and only if for every permutation $\pi : [\ell] \to [\ell]$ the function $f_\pi(x_1, \ldots, x_\ell) = f(x_{\pi(1)}, \ldots, x_{\pi(\ell)})$ is in Π. (Note that such permutations of the ℓ variables induce a permutation of the domain $\{0, 1\}^\ell$; that is, the permutation $\pi : [\ell] \to [\ell]$ induces a permutation $T_\pi : \{0, 1\}^\ell \to \{0, 1\}^\ell$ such that $T_\pi(x) = (x_{\pi(1)}, \ldots, x_{\pi(\ell)})$.)

Basic Exercises

Exercise 5.1 states a well-known and widely used classic.

Exercise 5.1 (The Schwartz–Zippel Lemma [250, 276, 86]): Prove the following two claims.

Large-field version: Let $p : \mathcal{F}^m \to \mathcal{F}$ be a *nonzero* m-variate polynomial of total
degree d over a finite field $\mathcal{F}$. Then, $\mathbf{Pr}_{x \in \mathcal{F}^m}[p(x) = 0] \leq d/|\mathcal{F}|$.

Small-field version: Let $p : \mathcal{F}^m \to \mathcal{F}$ be a *nonzero* m-variate polynomial of total
degree d over a finite field $\mathcal{F}$. Then, $\mathbf{Pr}_{x \in \mathcal{F}^m}[p(x) = 0] \leq 1 - |\mathcal{F}|^{-d/(|\mathcal{F}|-1)}$.

Note that the individual degree of p is at most $|\mathcal{F}| - 1$, and so $d \leq m \cdot (|\mathcal{F}| - 1)$. The
large-field version, which is meaningful only for $|\mathcal{F}| > d$, is called the Schwartz–
Zippel Lemma.[34] When establishing Eq. (5.4), we used the small field version with
$|\mathcal{F}| = 2$.

> **Guideline:** Both versions are proved by induction on the number of variables, m.
> The base case of $m = 1$ follows by the fact that $p \not\equiv 0$ has at most d roots, whereas
> in the small field version we use the fact that $\frac{d}{|\mathcal{F}|} \leq 1 - |\mathcal{F}|^{-d/(|\mathcal{F}|-1)}$ for every $d \in$
> $[0, |\mathcal{F}| - 1]$ (which is trivial for $|\mathcal{F}| = 2$).[35] In the induction step, assuming that p
> depends on all its variables, write $p(x) = \sum_{i=0}^{d} p_i(x_1, \ldots, x_{m-1}) \cdot x_m^i$, where p_i is an
> $(m - 1)$-variate polynomial of degree at most $d - i$, and let t be the largest integer
> such that p_t is nonzero. Then, using $x' = (x_1, \ldots, x_{m-1})$, observe that
>
> $$\mathbf{Pr}_{x \in \mathcal{F}^m}[p(x) = 0]$$
>
> $$\leq \mathbf{Pr}_{x' \in \mathcal{F}^{m-1}}[p_t(x') = 0] + \mathbf{Pr}_{x' \in \mathcal{F}^{m-1}}[p_t(x') \neq 0] \cdot \mathbf{Pr}_{x \in \mathcal{F}^m}[p(x) = 0 | p_t(x') \neq 0].$$
>
> Using the induction hypothesis, prove the induction claim (in both versions).[36]

Exercise 5.2 (A variant of Algorithm 5.3): Consider a variant of Algorithm 5.3 in which
one selects uniformly $i \in [3]$ and performs only Step i of Algorithm 5.3, while accepting if and only if this step did not reject. Show that this four-query algorithm is a
one-sided error proximity-oblivious tester for monotone dictatorship with rejection
probability $\varrho(\delta) = \Omega(\delta)$.

> **Guideline:** Reduce the analysis to the statement of Theorem 5.4.

Exercise 5.3 (Generalizing Theorem 5.10): Consider a relaxation of Definition 5.9 in
which R is allowed to be randomized as long as it recovers the correct value with
probability at least $2/3$. Suppose that functions in Π are randomly self-reducible by q
queries, in this relaxed sense. Prove that for every f that is ϵ-close to some $f' \in \Pi$ and
for every $z \in D$, self-correction succeeds with probability at least $\frac{2}{3} \cdot (1 - q \cdot \epsilon)$; that
is,

$$\mathbf{Pr}_{(r_1, \ldots, r_q) \leftarrow Q(z)}[R(z, r_1, \ldots, r_q, f(r_1), \ldots, f(r_q)) = f'(z)] \geq \frac{2}{3} \cdot (1 - q \cdot \epsilon).$$

---

[34] There is also a version for infinite fields. It asserts that for every finite set S such that $S \subseteq \mathcal{F}$, where $\mathcal{F}$ is an
arbitrary field (which is possibly infinite), and for any *nonzero* m-variate polynomial $p : \mathcal{F}^m \to \mathcal{F}$ of total degree d,
it holds that $\mathbf{Pr}_{x \in S^m}[p(x) = 0] \leq d/|S|$.

[35] In general, for $a = 1/|\mathcal{F}|$ and $b = (\ln |\mathcal{F}|)/(|\mathcal{F}| - 1)$, we need to show that $f(x) \stackrel{\text{def}}{=} 1 - ax - e^{-bx}$ is non-
negative for every integer $x \in [0, |\mathcal{F}| - 1]$. This can be shown by observing that f decreases at x if and only if
$x > \tau \stackrel{\text{def}}{=} (1/b) \ln(b/a)$. Since $\tau > 0$, this means that $\min_{x \in [0, |\mathcal{F}| - 1]} \{f(x)\}$ equals $\min(f(0), f(|\mathcal{F}| - 1)) = 0$.

[36] A rather careless approach suffices for the large-field case (i.e., we can use $\mathbf{Pr}_x[p(x) = 0] \leq \mathbf{Pr}_{x'}[p_t(x') = 0] +$
$\mathbf{Pr}_x[p(x) = 0 | p_t(x') \neq 0]$), but not for the small-field case (where one better keep track of the effect of
$\mathbf{Pr}_{x'}[p_t(x') \neq 0]$).

Exercise 5.4 (Random self-reducibility mandates distance): Prove that if Π is random self-reducible by q queries, then for every distinct $g, h \in \Pi$ it holds that $\delta(g, h) \geq 1/q$.

> **Guideline:** This can be proved by invoking Theorem 5.10 twice (with z on which g and h disagree): In the first invocation we use $f = f' = g$ and $\epsilon = 0$, and in the second invocation $(f, f') = (g, h)$ and $\epsilon = \delta(g, h)$. By the first invocation we derive $\mathbf{Pr}[R^g(z) = g(z)] = 1$, whereas by the second invocation we derive $\mathbf{Pr}[R^g(z) = h(z)] \geq 1 - q \cdot \delta(g, h)$, where $R^g(z)$ denotes $R(z, r_1, \ldots, r_q, g(r_1), \ldots, g(r_q))$ with $(r_1, \ldots, r_q) \leftarrow Q(z)$. Hence, $1 - q \cdot \delta(g, h) \leq 0$ must hold (since $g(z) \neq h(z)$).

Exercise 5.5 (Testing intersection with a self-correctable property): Let Π' and Π'' be sets of functions. Suppose that functions in Π' are randomly self-reducible by q queries, and that Π' and Π'' are ϵ-testable using $q'(\epsilon)$ and $q''(\epsilon)$ queries, respectively. Show that, for every $\epsilon_0 < 1/q$ and $\epsilon > 0$, the property $\Pi' \cap \Pi''$ is ϵ-testable using $O(q'(\min(\epsilon, 1/3q))) + q \cdot \tilde{O}(q''(\epsilon_0))$ queries.

> **Guideline:** Using the fact that Π' has distance at least $1/q$ (see Exercise 5.4), observe that any element of $\Pi' \setminus \Pi''$ is ϵ_0-far from $\Pi' \cap \Pi''$, and infer that the tester for Π'' implies that the promise problem (Π', Π'') can be solved in query complexity $q''(\epsilon_0)$. Finally, invoke Theorem 5.11.

Exercise 5.6 (POTs for self-correctable properties – take 1):[37] Show that if the functions in Π are randomly self-reducible by t queries, then Π has a $(t + 1)$-query proximity-oblivious tester of detection probability $\varrho(\delta) = (1 - t \cdot \delta) \cdot \delta$. (Indeed, this is meaningful only for functions that are $1/t$-close to Π, and Π may be hard to test in general (i.e., for $\delta \geq 1/t$).)[38]

> **Guideline:** The POT selects uniformly a random element z in the function's domain and compares the value of the function at z to the value obtained (for z) via the self-correction procedure. (For f at distance δ from Π, letting $f' \in \Pi$ be a function at distance δ from f, note that the tester rejects if $f(z) \neq f'(z)$ but all t points used by the self-corrector lie in $\{x : f(x) = f'(x)\}$.)

Exercise 5.7 (POTs for self-correctable properties – take 2): In continuation to Exercise 5.6, suppose again that the functions in Π are randomly self-reducible by t queries. Furthermore, suppose that the recovery algorithm is extremely sensitive to the function values in the sense that for every sequence $(z, r_1, \ldots, r_1, v_1, \ldots, v_1)$ and for every $i \in [t]$, the mapping

$$v \mapsto R(z, r_1, \ldots, r_t, v_1, \ldots, v_{i-1}, v, v_{i+1}, \ldots, v_t)$$

is a bijection. Show that Π has a $(t + 1)$-query proximity-oblivious tester of detection probability $\varrho(\delta) = (t + 1) \cdot (1 - t \cdot \delta) \cdot \delta$. (Indeed, Proposition 2.2 follows as a special case.)

> **Guideline:** The tester is the same as in Exercise 5.6, but detection is due not only to the case that the value of the function at the selected pointong (and the t values retrieved by the self-corrector are all correct) but also to the case that the value of the function at the selected point is correct and exactly one of the t queries

---

[37] See proof of Theorem 5.12.
[38] See Theorem 7.10 regarding k-linearity, which is randomly self-reducible by two queries.

made by the self-corrector returned a wrong answer. (In other words, here we lower-bound $\mathbf{Pr}_{z,(r_1,\ldots,r_t)\leftarrow Q(z)}[f(z) \neq R(z, r_1, \ldots, r_t, f(r_1), \ldots, f(r_t))]$ by the probability that exactly one of the $t + 1$ points (i.e., $z, r_1, \ldots, r_t$) resides in $\{x : f(x) \neq f'(x)\}$, where $f' \in \Pi$ is closest to f.)

Exercise 5.8 (On properties of set functions): Let $v : 2^{[\ell]} \to \mathbb{R}$ be an arbitrary set function. Show that

1. If v is subadditive, then $v(\emptyset) \geq 0$.
2. If v is submodular and $v(\emptyset) \geq 0$, then v is subadditive.
3. If v is monotone and $v(\emptyset) \geq 0$, then v is nonnegative.

Guideline: In each case, let one of the sets be the empty set.

Additional Exercises

The following exercises actually present proof sketches of various results and facts. Exercises 5.9–5.11 outline reductions of the task of testing affine subspaces to the task of testing linearity. They are highly recommended. Exercises 5.12 and 5.13 call for proving Facts 1–3 that were used in the proof of Theorem 5.15. These facts are of independent interest, and proofs that are simpler and/or more intuitive than those presented in our guidelines will be greatly appreciated.

Exercise 5.9 (Testing affine subspaces – a reduction to the linear case):[39] Show that testing whether a Boolean function $h : \{0, 1\}^\ell \to \{0, 1\}$ describes a $(\ell - k)$-dimensional affine subspace (i.e., whether the set $h^{-1}(1)$ is such an affine space) can be reduced to testing whether a Boolean function $h' : \{0, 1\}^\ell \to \{0, 1\}$ describes a $(\ell - k)$-dimensional linear subspace (i.e., whether $\{x : h'(x) = 1\}$ is such a linear space), where the reduction introduces an additive overhead of $O(2^k)$ queries.

> **Guideline:** Note that if h describes a $(\ell - k)$-dimensional affine subspace, then (w.h.p.) a sample of $O(2^k)$ random points in $\{0, 1\}^\ell$ contains a point on which h evaluates to 1. On the other hand, for any u such that $h(u) = 1$, consider the function $h'(x) \stackrel{\text{def}}{=} h(x + u)$.

Exercise 5.10 (Reducing testing linear subspaces to testing linearity):[40] Let $h : \{0, 1\}^\ell \to \{0, 1\}$ be a Boolean function. Show that testing whether $h^{-1}(1)$ is an $(\ell - k)$-dimensional linear subspace is reducible to testing linearity, while increasing the complexities by a factor of 2^k. Specifically, define a function $g : \{0, 1\}^\ell \to \{0, 1\}^k \cup \{\perp\}$ such that if $H \stackrel{\text{def}}{=} h^{-1}(1)$ is linear then g (ranges over $\{0, 1\}^k$ and) is linear and $g^{-1}(0^k) = H$. The definition of g is based on any fixed sequence of linearly independent vectors $v^{(1)}, \ldots, v^{(k)} \in \{0, 1\}^\ell$ such that for every nonempty $I \subseteq [k]$ it holds that $\sum_{i \in I} v^{(i)} \notin H$. (If H is an $(\ell - k)$-dimensional linear space, then these $v^{(i)}$'s form a basis for a k-dimensional linear space that complements H.) Fixing such a sequence, define $g : \{0, 1\}^\ell \to \{0, 1\}^k \cup \{\perp\}$ such that $g(x) = (c_1, \ldots, c_k)$ if $(c_1, \ldots, c_k) \in \{0, 1\}^k$ is the unique sequence that satisfies $x + \sum_{i \in [k]} c_i v^{(i)} \in H$ and

---

[39] Based on [138, Sec. 4.1].
[40] Based on [138, Sec. 4.2]. The argument can be generalized to the case of affine subspaces, while also using a reduction of testing affinity to testing linearity (of functions); but, in light of Exercise 5.9, such a generalization is not needed.

let $g(x) = \perp$ otherwise. (Whenever we say that g is linear, we mean, in particular, that it never assumes the value $\perp$.)[41]

- Show that H is an $(\ell - k)$-dimensional linear space if and only if g (*as defined above*) is a surjective linear function.
- Show that if H is an $(\ell - k)$-dimensional linear space, then a sequence as underlying the definition of g can be found (*w.h.p.*) by making $O(2^k)$ queries to h.
- Assuming that g is linear, show that testing whether it is surjective can be done by making $O(2^k)$ queries to h. (It is indeed easier to perform such a check by using $O(2^k)$ queries to g.)

Combining the foregoing ideas, present the claimed reduction. Note that this reduction has two-sided error, and that the resulting tester has query complexity $O(2^k/\epsilon)$ (rather than $O(1/\epsilon)$, all in case that $\epsilon < 2^{-k+2}$).[42]

> **Guideline:** Let V be a k-by-ℓ full rank matrix such that $cV \in H$ implies $c = 0^k$ (i.e., the rows of V are the $v^{(i)}$'s of the hypothesis). Recall that $g : \{0, 1\}^\ell \to \{0, 1\}^k \cup \{\perp\}$ is defined such that $g(x) = c$ if $c \in \{0, 1\}^k$ is the unique vector that satisfies $x + cV \in H$ (and $g(x) = \perp$ if the number of such vectors is not 1). Note that $g^{-1}(0^k) \subseteq H$ always holds (since $g(x) = c$ implies $x + cV \in H$), and that equality holds if g never assumes the value $\perp$ (since in this case $x + cV \in H$ implies that $g(x) = c$).
>
> Now, on the one hand, if H is an $(\ell - k)$-dimensional linear space, then, for some full-rank $(\ell - k)$-by-ℓ matrix G, it holds that $H = \{yG : y \in \{0, 1\}^{\ell-k}\}$. In this case, g is a surjective linear function (since for every x there exists a *unique* representation of x as $yG + cV$, which implies $x + cV = yG \in H$, and so $g(x) = c$). On the other hand, if g is a surjective linear function (i.e., $g(x) = xT$ for some full-rank ℓ-by-k matrix T), then $H = \{x : g(x) = 0^k\}$, which implies that H is an $(\ell - k)$-dimensional linear subspace. It follows that if g is ϵ-close to being a surjective linear function, then $g^{-1}(0^k)$ is ϵ-close to being an $((\ell - k)$-dimensional) linear space (i.e., the indicator functions of these sets are ϵ-close). In light of the foregoing facts, consider the following algorithm.
>
> 1. Using $O(2^k)$ queries to h, try to find a k-by-ℓ matrix V such that for any nonzero $c \in \{0, 1\}^k$ it holds that $cV \notin H$. (The matrix V can be found in k iterations such that in the ith iteration we try to find a vector $v^{(i)}$ such that $\sum_{j \in [i]} c_j v^{(j)} \notin H$ holds for every $(c_1, \ldots, c_i) \in \{0, 1\}^i \setminus \{0^i\}$.) If such a matrix V is found, then proceed to the next step. Otherwise, reject.
> 2. Test whether the function $g : \{0, 1\}^\ell \to \{0, 1\}^k \cup \{\perp\}$ (defined based on this V) is linear, and reject if the linearity tester rejects. When the tester queries g at x, query h on $x + cV$ for all $c \in \{0, 1\}^k$, and answer accordingly; that is, the answer is c if c is the unique vector satisfying $h(x + cV) = 1$, otherwise (i.e., $g(x) = \perp$) the execution is suspended and the algorithm rejects.
> 3. Test whether g is surjective. Assuming that g is linear, the task can be performed as follows.
>   (a) Select uniformly at random a target image $c \in \{0, 1\}^k$.
>   (b) Select uniformly at random a sample S of $O(2^k)$ elements in $\{0, 1\}^\ell$, and accept if and only if there exists $x \in S$ such that $x + cV \in H$ (i.e., $g(x) = c$).

---

[41] Indeed, when emulating g for the linearity tester, we shall reject if we ever encounter the value $\perp$.

[42] Needless to say, we would welcome a one-sided error reduction. Note that the case $\epsilon \geq 2^{-k+2}$ can be handled as in Algorithm 5.6. A complexity improvement for the main case (of $\epsilon < 2^{-k+2}$) appears in Exercise 5.11.

We stress that we do not compute g at x, which would have required 2^k queries to h, but rather check whether $g(x) = c$ by making a single query to h (i.e., we query h at $x + cV$).

Exercise 5.11 (Improving the efficiency of the reduction of Exercise 5.10):[43] Let $h : \{0, 1\}^\ell \to \{0, 1\}$ be a Boolean function. In Exercise 5.10, we reduced ϵ-testing whether $h^{-1}(1)$ is an $(\ell - k)$-dimensional linear subspace to ϵ-testing the linearity of a function g, where the value of g at any point can be computed by making 2^k queries to h. (Indeed, that reduction made $O(2^k)$ additional queries to h.) This yields an ϵ-tester of time complexity $O(2^k/\epsilon)$ for testing linear subspaces. Recall that, for every $\epsilon_0 < 1/4$, if g is ϵ_0-close to being a linear function, then it is ϵ_0-close to a unique linear function g', which can be computed by self-correction of g (where each invocation of the self-corrector makes two queries to g and is correct with probability at least $1 - 2\epsilon_0$). This suggests the following algorithm.

1. Invoke the algorithm of Exercise 5.10 with proximity parameter set to a sufficiently small constant $\epsilon_0 > 0$. If the said invocation rejects, then reject. Otherwise, let V be the matrix found in Step 1 of that invocation, and let g be the corresponding function. Let g' denote the linear function closest to g.
2. Test that h is ϵ-close to $h' : \{0, 1\}^\ell \to \{0, 1\}$, where $h'(x) = 1$ if and only if $g'(x) = 0^k$.
   We implement this step in complexity $\widetilde{O}(1/\epsilon)$ by taking a sample of $m = O(1/\epsilon)$ *pairwise independent* points in $\{0, 1\}^\ell$ such that evaluating g' on these m points can be done in time $O(m + 2^k \cdot \widetilde{O}(\log m))$. Specifically, for $t = \lceil \log_2(m + 1) \rceil$, we select uniformly $s^{(1)}, \ldots, s^{(t)} \in \{0, 1\}^\ell$, compute each $g'(s^{(j)})$ via self-correcting g, with error probability $0.01/t$, and use the sample points $r^{(J)} = \sum_{j \in J} s^{(j)}$ for all nonempty subsets $J \subseteq [t]$. That is, for each such J, we check whether $h(r^{(J)}) = h'(r^{(J)})$ by querying h at $r^{(J)}$ and computing $h'(r^{(J)})$ (based on the obtained values of the $g'(s^{(j)})$'s), and reject if and only if we find a point $r^{(J)}$ of disagreement.

Assuming that g' is surjective, show that the foregoing algorithm constitutes an ϵ-tester of time complexity $O(\epsilon^{-1} + 2^k \cdot \widetilde{O}(\log(1/\epsilon)))$ for $(\ell - k)$-dimensional linear subspaces. The assumption can be removed by slightly augmenting the algorithm.

Guideline: Note that $g'(\sum_{j \in J} s^{(j)}) = \sum_{j \in J} g'(s^{(j)})$, and show that the $r^{(J)}$'s are pairwise independent.

Exercise 5.12 (The influence of sets is monotone and subadditive): Prove that for every $S, T \subseteq [\ell]$ and every $f : \{0, 1\}^\ell \to \{0, 1\}$ it holds that

1. $I_S(f) \le I_{S \cup T}(f)$.
2. $I_{S \cup T}(f) \le I_S(f) + I_T(f)$.

Guideline: The key observation is that $I_S(f)$ equals twice the expectation over r of $V_{z \in \{0,1\}^\ell : z_{\overline{S}} = r_{\overline{S}}}[f(z)]$, where r is distributed uniformly in $\{0, 1\}^\ell$; that is,

$$0.5 \cdot I_S(f) = \mathbb{E}_{r \in \{0,1\}^\ell} \left[V_{z \in \{0,1\}^\ell : z_{\overline{S}} = r_{\overline{S}}}[f(z)] \right]. \tag{5.9}$$

---

[43] Based on [138, Sec. 4.3], which in turn is inspired by [145] (as presented in [131, Sec. 7.1.3]). Again, the argument can be generalized to the case of affine subspaces.

This is the case since

$$\mathbb{I}_S(f) = \mathbb{E}_{r \in \{0,1\}^\ell} \left[\mathbf{Pr}_{x,y \in \{0,1\}^\ell : x_{\overline{S}} = y_{\overline{S}} = r_{\overline{S}}} [f(x) \neq f(y)] \right]$$
$$= \mathbb{E}_{r \in \{0,1\}^\ell} [2 \cdot p_r \cdot (1 - p_r)],$$

where $p_r \stackrel{\text{def}}{=} \mathbf{Pr}_{z \in \{0,1\}^\ell : z_{\overline{S}} = r_{\overline{S}}} [f(z) = 1]$, while observing that $\mathbb{V}_{z \in \{0,1\}^\ell : z_{\overline{S}} = r_{\overline{S}}} [f(z)] = p_r \cdot (1 - p_r)$. The two parts of the exercise are proven by manipulation of the relevant quantities when expressed as expectation of variances (i.e., as in Eq. (5.9)).

Part 1 is proved by considering, without loss of generality, the case that S and T are disjoint (since otherwise we can use S and $T \setminus S$). When proving it, use the "law of total variance," which considers a random variable Z that is generated by first picking $x \leftarrow X$ and outputting Z_x, where X and the Z_x's are independent random variables. The said law asserts that the variance of Z (i.e., $\mathbb{V}[Z]$) equals $\mathbb{E}_{x \leftarrow X}[\mathbb{V}[Z_x]] + \mathbb{V}_{x \leftarrow X}[\mathbb{E}[Z_x]]$ (and its proof is via striaghtforward manipulations, which use only the definition of variance).[44] Now, assume, for simplicity of notation, that $S = [1, a]$ and $T = [a + 1, b]$, and consider selecting uniformly $w \in \{0, 1\}^{\ell - b}$ and $(u, v) \in \{0, 1\}^a \times \{0, 1\}^{b-a}$. Then, we have

$$0.5 \cdot \mathbb{I}_{S \cup T}(f)$$
$$= \mathbb{E}_{w \in \{0,1\}^{\ell-b}} [\mathbb{V}_{uv \in \{0,1\}^b} [f(uvw)]]$$
$$= \mathbb{E}_{w \in \{0,1\}^{\ell-b}} \left[\mathbb{E}_{v \in \{0,1\}^{b-a}} [\mathbb{V}_{u \in \{0,1\}^a} [f(uvw)]] + \mathbb{V}_{v \in \{0,1\}^{b-a}} [\mathbb{E}_{u \in \{0,1\}^a} [f(uvw)]] \right]$$
$$\geq \mathbb{E}_{w \in \{0,1\}^{\ell-b}} \left[\mathbb{E}_{v \in \{0,1\}^{b-a}} [\mathbb{V}_{u \in \{0,1\}^a} [f(uvw)]] \right]$$
$$= \mathbb{E}_{vw \in \{0,1\}^{\ell-a}} \left[\mathbb{V}_{u \in \{0,1\}^a} [f(uvw)] \right]$$
$$= 0.5 \cdot \mathbb{I}_S(f).$$

In Part 2 we again assume that S and T are disjoint, but now the justification is by Part 1 (which implies $\mathbb{I}_{T \setminus S}(f) \leq \mathbb{I}_T(f)$). In the proof itself, using the same notations as in the proof of Part 1, we have

$$0.5 \cdot \mathbb{I}_{S \cup T}(f)$$
$$= \mathbb{E}_{w \in \{0,1\}^{\ell-b}} \left[\mathbb{E}_{v \in \{0,1\}^{b-a}} [\mathbb{V}_{u \in \{0,1\}^a} [f(uvw)]] + \mathbb{V}_{v \in \{0,1\}^{b-a}} [\mathbb{E}_{u \in \{0,1\}^a} [f(uvw)]] \right]$$
$$\leq \mathbb{E}_{w \in \{0,1\}^{\ell-b}} \left[\mathbb{E}_{v \in \{0,1\}^{b-a}} [\mathbb{V}_{u \in \{0,1\}^a} [f(uvw)]] + \mathbb{E}_{u \in \{0,1\}^a} [\mathbb{V}_{v \in \{0,1\}^{b-a}} [f(uvw)]] \right]$$
$$= \mathbb{E}_{vw \in \{0,1\}^{\ell-a}} \left[\mathbb{V}_{u \in \{0,1\}^a} [f(uvw)] \right] + \mathbb{E}_{uw \in \{0,1\}^{a+\ell-b}} \left[\mathbb{V}_{v \in \{0,1\}^{b-a}} [f(uvw)] \right]$$
$$= 0.5 \cdot \mathbb{I}_S(f) + 0.5 \cdot \mathbb{I}_T(f),$$

---

[44] The proof is as follows:

$$\mathbb{V}[Z] = \mathbb{E}[Z^2] - \mathbb{E}[Z]^2$$
$$= \mathbb{E}_{x \leftarrow X}[\mathbb{E}[Z_x^2]] - \mathbb{E}_{x \leftarrow X}[\mathbb{E}[Z_x]]^2$$
$$= \mathbb{E}_{x \leftarrow X}[\mathbb{V}[Z_x] + \mathbb{E}[Z_x]^2] - \mathbb{E}_{x \leftarrow X}[\mathbb{E}[Z_x]]^2$$
$$= \mathbb{E}_{x \leftarrow X}[\mathbb{V}[Z_x]] + \mathbb{E}_{x \leftarrow X}[\mathbb{E}[Z_x]^2] - \mathbb{E}_{x \leftarrow X}[\mathbb{E}[Z_x]]^2$$
$$= \mathbb{E}_{x \leftarrow X}[\mathbb{V}[Z_x]] + \mathbb{V}_{x \leftarrow X}[\mathbb{E}[Z_x]],$$

where the last equality refers to a random variables that is assigned the value $\mathbb{E}[Z_x]$ with probability $\mathbf{Pr}[X = x]$.

where the inequality is proved by using the definition of variance.[45] Indeed, we could have assumed, w.l.o.g., that $b = \ell$ (and avoided taking the expectation over w), since for every $A \subseteq S \cup T$ it holds that $I_A(f) = \mathbb{E}_w[I_A(f_w)]$, where $f_w(uv) = f(uvw)$.

Exercise 5.13 (The influence of sets has diminishing marginal gain): Prove that for every $S, T, M \subseteq [\ell]$ and every f, it holds that

$$I_{S \cup T \cup M}(f) - I_{S \cup T}(f) \leq I_{S \cup M}(f) - I_S(f).$$

Guideline: As shown next, we may focus on the case that S, T and M are disjoint. Considering only T and M that are disjoint of S is without loss of generality, since we may consider $T \setminus S$ and $M \setminus S$, respectively. Focusing on disjoint M and T is justified by monotonicity (i.e., Part 1 of Exercise 5.12). Furthermore, we can assume, w.l.o.g., that $S \cup T \cup M = [\ell]$ (see comment at the end of the guideline for Exercise 5.12).

Now, assume, for simplicity of notation, that $S = [1, a]$, $T = [a + 1, b]$, and $M = [b + 1, \ell]$, and consider selecting uniformly $(u, v, w) \in \{0, 1\}^a \times \{0, 1\}^{b-a} \times \{0, 1\}^{\ell-b}$. Then, using Eq. (5.9), we have

$$0.5 \cdot I_{S \cup M}(f) - 0.5 \cdot I_S(f)$$

$$= \mathbb{E}_{v \in \{0,1\}^{b-a}}[\mathbb{V}_{uw \in \{0,1\}^{a+\ell-b}}[f(uvw)]] - \mathbb{E}_{vw \in \{0,1\}^{\ell-a}}[\mathbb{V}_{u \in \{0,1\}^a}[f(uvw)]]$$

$$= \mathbb{E}_{v \in \{0,1\}^{b-a}}[\mathbb{V}_{w \in \{0,1\}^{\ell-b}}[\mathbb{E}_{u \in \{0,1\}^a}[f(uvw)]] + \mathbb{E}_{w \in \{0,1\}^{\ell-b}}[\mathbb{V}_{u \in \{0,1\}^a}[f(uvw)]]]$$

$$- \mathbb{E}_{vw \in \{0,1\}^{\ell-a}}[\mathbb{V}_{u \in \{0,1\}^a}[f(uvw)]]$$

$$= \mathbb{E}_{v \in \{0,1\}^{b-a}}[\mathbb{V}_{w \in \{0,1\}^{\ell-b}}[\mathbb{E}_{u \in \{0,1\}^a}[f(uvw)]]],$$

where the second equality uses the "law of total variance" (see guideline to Exercise 5.12). Similarly,

$$0.5 \cdot I_{S \cup T \cup M}(f) - 0.5 \cdot I_{S \cup T}(f) = \mathbb{V}_{w \in \{0,1\}^{\ell-b}}[\mathbb{E}_{uv \in \{0,1\}^b}[f(uvw)]].$$

Letting $g(vw) = \mathbb{E}_{u \in \{0,1\}^a}[f(uvw)]$, we have

$$0.5 \cdot I_{S \cup M}(f) - 0.5 \cdot I_S(f)$$

$$= \mathbb{E}_{v \in \{0,1\}^{b-a}}[\mathbb{V}_{w \in \{0,1\}^{\ell-b}}[g(vw)]]$$

$$\geq \mathbb{V}_{w \in \{0,1\}^{\ell-b}}[\mathbb{E}_{v \in \{0,1\}^{b-a}}[g(vw)]]$$

$$= 0.5 \cdot I_{S \cup T \cup M}(f) - 0.5 \cdot I_{S \cup T}(f),$$

where the inequality is proved by using the definition of variance (as in footnote 45).

---

[45] For any $w \in \{0, 1\}^{\ell-b}$, letting $f_w(uv) = f(uvw)$, prove that

$$\mathbb{V}_{v \in \{0,1\}^{b-a}}[\mathbb{E}_{u \in \{0,1\}^a}[f_w(uv)]] \leq \mathbb{E}_{u \in \{0,1\}^a}[\mathbb{V}_{v \in \{0,1\}^{b-a}}[f_w(uv)]],$$

using $\mathbb{V}[Z] = \mathbb{E}[(Z - \mathbb{E}[Z])^2] = \mathbb{E}[Z^2] - \mathbb{E}[Z]^2$ and $\mathbb{E}[Z]^2 \leq \mathbb{E}[Z^2]$ (which is implied by it). Specifically, we have

$$\mathbb{V}_{v \in \{0,1\}^{b-a}}[\mathbb{E}_{u \in \{0,1\}^a}[f_w(uv)]] = \mathbb{E}_v[(\mathbb{E}_u[f_w(uv)] - \mathbb{E}_{v'}[\mathbb{E}_u[f_w(uv')]])^2]$$

$$= \mathbb{E}_v[(\mathbb{E}_u[f_w(uv)] - \mathbb{E}_u[\mathbb{E}_{v'}[f_w(uv')]])^2]$$

$$= \mathbb{E}_v[\mathbb{E}_u[f_w(uv) - \mathbb{E}_{v'}[f_w(uv')]]^2]$$

$$\leq \mathbb{E}_v[\mathbb{E}_u[(f_w(uv) - \mathbb{E}_{v'}[f_w(uv')])^2]]$$

$$= \mathbb{E}_u[\mathbb{E}_v[(f_w(uv) - \mathbb{E}_{v'}[f_w(uv')])^2]]$$

$$= \mathbb{E}_u[\mathbb{V}_v[f_w(uv)]].$$

CHAPTER SIX
Testing by Implicit Sampling

Summary: Building on the junta tester, we present a general methodology for constructing testers for properties of Boolean functions (of the form $f : \{0, 1\}^\ell \to \{0, 1\}$) that can be approximated by small juntas. This methodology yields testers of low query complexity for many natural properties, which contain functions that depend on relatively few relevant variables; specifically, the query complexity is related to the size of the junta and is independent of the length of the input to the function (i.e., ℓ).

This chapter is based on the work of Diakonikolas, Lee, Matulef, Onak, Rubinfeld, Servedio, and Wan [91]. The paradigm introduced in their work is often called *testing by implicit learning* (see, e.g., [251]), but we prefer the term "implicit sampling" for reasons that will be clarified later. This chapter builds on the junta tester presented in Section 5.3; thus, the latter section is a prerequisite to the current chapter.

6.1. Introduction

As in Chapter 5, we view Boolean functions $f : \{0, 1\}^\ell \to \{0, 1\}$ as functions of ℓ Boolean variables. The natural interest in Boolean functions that have few relevant variables leads to an interest in functions of this type that have additional properties; that is, for a parameter k, we consider properties that are subsets of the set of all k-juntas. Such properties may refer both to the set of relevant variables and on the residual function (applied to the relevant variables).

We focus on the case that these additional properties are only properties of the residual function (and are independent of the identity of the relevant variables).[1] That is, we are interested in properties of the form $\Pi \subseteq \{f : \{0, 1\}^\ell \to \{0, 1\}\}$ such that there exists $\Pi' \subseteq \{f' : \{0, 1\}^k \to \{0, 1\}\}$ so that $f \in \Pi$ if and only if for some k-subset I and $f' \in \Pi'$ it holds that $f(x) = f'(x_I)$. For example, k-linearity is the set of linear Boolean functions

---

[1] Hence, these properties are invariant under any permutation of the variables; that is, for each of these properties Π, the function $f : \{0, 1\}^\ell \to \{0, 1\}$ is in Π if and only if for every permutation $\pi : [\ell] \to [\ell]$ the function $f_\pi(x_1, \ldots, x_\ell) = f(x_{\pi(1)}, \ldots, x_{\pi(\ell)})$ is in Π. (Note that such permutations of the ℓ variables induce a permutation of the domain $\{0, 1\}^\ell$; that is, the permutation $\pi : [\ell] \to [\ell]$ induces a permutation $T_\pi : \{0, 1\}^\ell \to \{0, 1\}^\ell$ such that $T_\pi(x) = (x_{\pi(1)}, \ldots, x_{\pi(\ell)})$.) In contrast, properties that refer to the set of relevant variables (e.g., the set of functions that depend only on k out of the first $3k$ variables) are not invariant under all permutations of the variables.

that depend on exactly k variables (i.e., $f : \{0, 1\}^\ell \to \{0, 1\}$ is k-linear iff $f(x) = \oplus_{i \in I} x_i$ for some k-subset I).

The study of testers for such properties leads to a technique that illustrates the usefulness of partial information of the type that is provided by property testers. We refer to information of the form "the set S contains no relevant variables" (of the function f). Specifically, given oracle access to f such that $f(x) = f'(x_I)$ for some small but unknown $I \subset [\ell]$, we show how to use partial information of the foregoing type in order to efficiently generate random pairs of the form $(z, f'(z))$, which can be used for testing whether f' has the desired property. We stress that the generation of such random pairs is performed without knowing I and without trying to find it.

Organization. Section 6.2 constitutes the core of this chapter; it presents the technique of "testing by implicit sampling" and focuses on testing properties of the foregoing type (i.e., subclasses of juntas that are defined in terms of properties of the residual function). Section 6.3 extends the results to properties that are approximated by the foregoing properties.

Teaching Note: We suggest focusing on Section 6.2, and leaving Section 6.3 for advanced independent reading.

6.2. Testing Subsets of k-Juntas

Recall that a function $f : \{0, 1\}^\ell \to \{0, 1\}$ is called a k-junta if there exist k indices $i_1, \ldots, i_k \in [\ell]$ and a Boolean function $f' : \{0, 1\}^k \to \{0, 1\}$ such that $f(x) = f'(x_{i_1} \cdots x_{i_k})$ for every $x = x_1 \cdots x_\ell \in \{0, 1\}^\ell$. Here, we assume, without loss of generality, that $i_1 < \cdots < i_k$. In other words, $f(x) = f'(x_I)$, where $I = \{i_1, \ldots, i_k\} \subseteq [\ell]$ such that $i_1 < \cdots < i_k$ and x_I denotes the k-bit long string $x_{i_1} \cdots x_{i_k}$. Natural subsets of k-juntas arise when restricting f' to reside in a predetermined set of functions. Specifically, we refer to the following definition.

Definition 6.1 $((k, \Phi)$-juntas$)$: *Let Φ be a set of Boolean functions over $\{0, 1\}^k$. A function $f : \{0, 1\}^\ell \to \{0, 1\}$ is called a (k, Φ)-junta if there exist a k-subset I and a Boolean function $f' : \{0, 1\}^k \to \{0, 1\}$ in Φ such that $f(x) = f'(x_I)$ for every $x \in \{0, 1\}^\ell$.*

Properties of this form (i.e., (k, Φ)-juntas) may be viewed as properties of functions that have only k relevant inputs (called "relevant attributes" in the machine learning literature). Hence, it is reasonable to hope that computational tasks related to these properties will have query complexity that does not depend on ℓ, and may only depend on $k \ll \ell$.

A natural way to test whether a function is a (k, Φ)-junta is to first check that it is a k-junta, then find the corresponding set I, and finally test whether the corresponding f' is in Φ. The point (of "testing by implicit sampling") is that we want to avoid finding the set I, since in general finding the set I requires more than $\log \binom{\ell}{k}$ queries (see Exercise 6.1), whereas we may wish the query complexity to be independent of ℓ. The paradigm of implicit sampling offers a way of skipping the second step (of finding I), and generating a random sample of labeled k-tuples that can be used for testing f'. Note, however, that the testing of f' is performed by samples only; that is, we invoke a tester for Φ that

---

uses only f'-labeled samples (and makes no queries to f').[2] The relevant definition of such testers was briefly mentioned in Section 1.3.2; they are called *sample-based*, and are defined as follows.

Definition 6.2 (Sample-based tester for property Φ): *Let $\Phi = \cup_{n \in \mathbb{N}} \Phi_n$ such that Φ_n contains functions defined over $[n]$, and $s : \mathbb{N} \times (0, 1] \to \mathbb{N}$. A sample-based tester of (sample) complexity s for Φ is a probabilistic machine, denoted T, that satisfies the following two conditions.*

1. *T accepts inputs in Φ: For every $n \in \mathbb{N}$ and $\epsilon > 0$, and for every $f \in \Phi_n$, it holds that $\mathbf{Pr}[T(n, \epsilon; ((i_1, f(i_1)) \ldots, (i_s, f(i_s)))) = 1] \geq 2/3$, where $s = s(n, \epsilon)$, and $i_1, \ldots, i_s$ are drawn independently and uniformly in $[n]$.*
2. *T rejects inputs that are ϵ-far from Φ: For every $n \in \mathbb{N}$ and $\epsilon > 0$, and for every f with domain $[n]$ such that $\delta_\Phi(f) > \epsilon$, it holds that $\mathbf{Pr}[T(n, \epsilon; ((i_1, f(i_1)) \ldots, (i_s, f(i_s)))) = 0] \geq 2/3$, where $\delta_\Phi(f)$ denotes the distance of f from Φ, and $i_1, \ldots, i_s$ are as in Item 1.*

If the first condition holds with probability 1, then we say that T has one-sided error.

The sequence $((i_1, f(i_1)) \ldots, (i_s, f(i_s)))$ is called an f-labeled sample of s points (in the domain of f). Recall that any set $\Phi = \cup_{n \in \mathbb{N}} \Phi_n$ can be tested by using a sample of size $O(\epsilon^{-1} \log |\Phi_n|)$, via reducing (sample-based) testing to (sample-based) proper learning (see Section 1.3.5). Now, we are ready to state a general result that is obtained by the "implicit sampling" paradigm.

Theorem 6.3 (Testing by implicit sampling):[3] *Let Φ be a property of k-variate Boolean functions (i.e., functions from $\{0, 1\}^k$ to $\{0, 1\}$) such that Φ is invariant under permuting the bits of the argument to the function (i.e., $f' \in \Phi$ if and only if for every permutation $\pi : [k] \to [k]$ it holds that $f'_\pi(y) = f'(y_{\pi(1)}, \ldots, y_{\pi(k)})$ is in Φ). Suppose that there exists a sample-based tester of sample complexity $s_k : (0, 1] \to \mathbb{N}$ for Φ such that $s_k(\epsilon) \geq 1/\epsilon$. Then, (k, Φ)-juntas can be tested within query complexity $q(n, \epsilon) = \text{poly}(k) \cdot \widetilde{O}(s_k(0.9\epsilon)^2)$. Furthermore, each of the queries made by this tester is uniformly distributed in $\{0, 1\}^\ell$.*

Needless to say, this result is beneficial only when $k \ll \ell$ (since we can always find the junta within complexity $\widetilde{O}(k \log \ell / \epsilon)$; see Exercise 6.2). Note that all properties of ℓ-variate Boolean functions discussed in prior chapters are invariant in the foregoing sense (i.e., they are invariant under renaming of the variables; see Exercise 6.3). In contrast, properties that do not satisfy this condition refer to the identity of the variables (e.g., all Boolean functions that are influenced by their first variable), and seem less natural (especially in the current context).

Proof: Recall that we plan to test whether $f : \{0, 1\}^\ell \to \{0, 1\}$ is a (k, Φ)-junta by first testing whether f is a k-junta, which means that $f(x) = f'(x_I)$ for some k-subset I and $f' : \{0, 1\}^k \to \{0, 1\}$, and then testing whether f' is in Φ. We have seen a junta tester in Section 5.3, so the real challenge here is to test f' for

---

[2] The reason that we cannot support queries will be clarified in the proof of Theorem 6.3.
[3] The constant 0.9 can be replaced by any constant in $(0, 1)$.

membership in Φ while only having access to f. Recall that passing the k-junta test only assures us that f is close to being a k-junta (rather than actually being a k-junta). Nevertheless, let us assume for a moment that f is a k-junta. Furthermore, suppose that we are given a k-partition of $[\ell]$, denoted $(S_1, \ldots, S_k)$, such that each part has exactly one member of the junta (i.e., $|S_j \cap I| = 1$ for every $j \in [k]$).

In such a case, things would have been easy. We could have emulated a *standard* tester for Φ as follows. When the tester issues a query $y = y_1 \cdots y_k$, we would query f on the string z such that for every $j \in [k]$ and $i \in S_j$ it holds that $z_i = y_j$. This relies on the hypothesis that $f(x) = f'(x_I)$, which implies that z_I equals $y_{\pi(1)} \cdots y_{\pi(k)}$ for some permutation $\pi : [k] \to [k]$, and on the hypothesis that membership in Φ is invariant under permuting the bits of the argument to f'.

Unfortunately, the k-junta test only assures us that f is close to being a k-junta, and so we cannot rely on the answers that f provides on the 2^k possible z's used in the foregoing construction. In other words, after verifying that $f : \{0, 1\}^\ell \to \{0, 1\}$ is close to being a k-junta, denoted g (such that $g(x) = g'(x_I)$ for some I and $g' : \{0, 1\}^k \to \{0, 1\}$), we can safely obtain the value of g only at uniformly distributed points. We shall show that this suffices for generating g'-labeled samples (in the domain of g'), which is far from being obvious. (For this reason, we can emulate a *sample-based* tester, but not a tester that makes queries.)

The key question, indeed, is how can we generate these g'-labeled samples, without knowing I. Suppose that f is ϵ'-close to a k-junta g (such that $g(x) = g'(x_I)$ for some k-subset I), and suppose again that we are given a k-partition of $[\ell]$, denoted $(S_1, \ldots, S_k)$, such that each part has exactly one member of the junta (i.e., $|S_j \cap I| = 1$ for every $j \in [k]$). Note that the difference from the first paragraph (of the proof) is that this junta (i.e., I) refers to g, not to f (which is only close to g). Now suppose that we pick $x \in \{0, 1\}^\ell$ uniformly at random, and obtain $f(x)$, which equals $g(x) = g'(x_I)$ with probability at least $1 - \epsilon'$. So we got the g'-label of x_I, but we do not know x_I (although we do know x), since we don't know I. Actually, having $x_{S_1 \cap I} \cdots x_{S_k \cap I}$ is good enough, since we can consider testing $g'_\pi(z) = g'(z_{\pi(1)} \cdots z_{\pi(k)})$ (for a suitable π)[4] whose distance from Φ equals the distance of g' from Φ. Hence, for each $j \in [k]$, we wish to obtain $x_{S_j \cap I}$.

In other words, given $x \in \{0, 1\}^\ell$ and $S = S_j \subset [\ell]$ such that exactly one bit-location in S influences the value of g (i.e., $|S \cap I| = 1$), we wish to find out the value assigned to this bit-location in x. We can determine this value by finding out whether $S^0 = S \cap \{i : x_i = 0\}$ influences g, since if the answer is positive then $S^0 \cap I = S \cap I$ and $x_{S \cap I} = 0$, and otherwise $x_{S \cap I} = 1$ holds (since we have assumed that S does influence g). Furthermore, the influence of S on g is closely related to the influence of S on f (i.e., these influences differ by at most $2\epsilon'$), since g is close (i.e., ϵ'-close) to f. Finally, recall that we know how to test whether a set of locations influences a function; this is part of the junta tester (presented in Section 5.3). We review this part next.

Algorithm 6.3.1 (Testing influence of a set of locations on a function f): *On input a set $S \subseteq [\ell]$ and a parameter m, and oracle access to $f : \{0, 1\}^\ell \to \{0, 1\}$, select uniformly m random pairs (r, s) such that r and s agree on bit positions $[\ell] \setminus S$ (i.e.,*

---

[4] If $I = \{i_1, \ldots, i_k\}$ such that $i_1 < \cdots < i_k$, then π is defined such that $\{i_j\} = S_{\pi(j)} \cap I$. Hence, $z_{\pi(j)} = x_{S_{\pi(j)} \cap I} = x_{i_j}$.

$r_{\bar{S}} = s_{\bar{S}}$), and indicate that S is influential *if and only if $f(r) \neq f(s)$ for any of these pairs (r, s). Actually, output the fraction of pairs (r, s) such that $f(r) \neq f(s)$ as an estimate of the influence of S.*

Recalling that the influence of S on f, denoted $I_S(f)$, equal the probability that a single pair yields different values (i.e., $\mathbf{Pr}_{r,s:r_{\bar{S}}=s_{\bar{S}}}[f(r) \neq f(s)]$), it follows that S is deemed influential with probability $1 - (1 - I_S(f))^m$, which equals $1 - \exp(-\Theta(m \cdot I_S(f)))$ if $I_S(f) > 0$ (and zero otherwise). Furthermore, the estimate output by Algorithm 6.3.1 distinguishes, with success probability $1 - \exp(-\Omega(m \cdot \nu))$, between the case that $I_S(f) \geq 2\nu$ and the case that $I_S(f) \leq \nu$. This is done by ruling according to whether or not the said estimate (i.e., the fraction of pairs (r, s) such that $f(r) \neq f(s)$) exceeds 1.5ν.

Returning to the foregoing k-partition $(S_1, \ldots, S_k)$, we observe that a procedure for finding such a k-partition is also implicit in the k-junta tester we saw (in Section 5.3): It amounts to selecting a $O(k^2)$-partition at random, and testing whether more than k of the parts influence f. If the answer is positive, then we shall reject, and otherwise we can use this $O(k^2)$-partition for our purposes (either by merging the $O(k^2)$ parts into k sets such that each set contains at most one influential part or by just using the influential parts and ignoring the rest).

There is one problem with the forgoing suggestion. Taking a close look at the paragraph preceding Algorithm 6.3.1, note that we have assumed that each S_j contains a single influential variable; that is, we assumed that the singleton $I \cap S_j$ has positive influence on f. This is not necessarily the case. For starters, it may be that g is actually a $(k-1)$-junta. Moreover, even if g depends on all variables in I, it may be the case that some of these variables have negligible influence on g. Lastly, recall that we are estimating the influence of sets on f rather than on g, and the difference is not necessarily zero, although it is small. The reason that these cases pose a problem is that if we determine the jth bit in the k-bit sample (i.e., $x_{S_j \cap I}$) according to the influence of S_j^0 on f, then we may almost always set this value to 1 when $S_j \cap I$ has negligible influence on f. In such a case we shall end up invoking the sample-based tester on a sample that is not uniformly distributed.

The foregoing problem is resolved by estimating the influence of S_j on f. If this influence is noticeable, then we set the jth bit of the sample as suggested (i.e., we set it to 0 if and only if S_j^0 has positive influence of f). Otherwise (i.e., when S_j has negligible influence on f), we just set this bit at random (i.e., to be 0 with probability $1/2$). The foregoing ideas yield the following algorithmic schema, which utilizes a sample-based tester of complexity s_k for Φ. Specifically, Steps 1 and 2 of this schema correspond to a k-junta tester (and are indeed identical to Algorithm 5.14), but the partition generated in Step 1 is also used in the subsequent steps. In particular, Step 3 provides a finer estimate of the influence of the k relevant parts of the partition, Step 4 uses such estimates towards generating labeled samples for the Φ-tester, and Step 5 invokes this tester. We note that the proximity parameters for the "tests of influence" (denoted ϵ_2 and ϵ_3) are set to values that are smaller than ϵ (but related to it).

Algorithm 6.3.2 (Testing (k, Φ)-juntas): *Let $c > 0$ be a sufficiently small constant (e.g., $c = 0.01$). On input parameters ℓ and ϵ, and oracle access to a function f : $\{0, 1\}^\ell \rightarrow \{0, 1\}$, the tester sets $t = \Theta(k^2)$, and proceeds as follows.*

1. *Select a random t-way partition of $[\ell]$, denoted $(R_1, \ldots, R_t)$, by assigning each $i \in [\ell]$ a uniformly selected $j \in [t]$, which means that i is assigned to R_j.*

2. *For each $j \in [t]$, check whether R_j influences f (i.e., R_j has positive influence on f). The aim is distinguishing, with success probability at least $1 - c/t$, between the case that $\mathrm{I}_{R_j}(f) = 0$ and the case that $\mathrm{I}_{R_j}(f) \geq \epsilon_2 \stackrel{\text{def}}{=} c/(2t \cdot k \cdot s_k(0.9\epsilon))$. This is done by using Algorithm 6.3.1, while setting the parameter m to $m_2 \stackrel{\text{def}}{=} O(\epsilon_2^{-1} \log t)$, and asserting that R_j influences f if and only if the estimate output by the algorithm is positive.*

   Let J denote the set of j's for which R_j was found to influence f. If $|J| > k$, then the algorithm rejects. Otherwise, assume, without loss of generality, that $|J| = k$, by possibly considering a k-superset of J. For notational simplicity, we assume that $J = [k]$.[5]

3. *For each $j \in J$, estimate the influence of R_j on f with the aim of distinguishing, with success probability at least $1 - c/k$, between the case that $\mathrm{I}_{R_j}(f) \geq 4\epsilon_3$ and the case that $\mathrm{I}_{R_j}(f) < 3\epsilon_3$, where $\epsilon_3 \stackrel{\text{def}}{=} 4t\epsilon_2 = 2c/(k \cdot s_k(0.9\epsilon)) \leq 2c \cdot \epsilon$. This is done by using Algorithm 6.3.1, while setting the parameter m to $m_3 \stackrel{\text{def}}{=} O(\epsilon_3^{-1} \log k)$, and deciding based on the estimate that it outputs.*

   Let $J' \subseteq J$ denote the set of j's for which the foregoing estimate exceeds $3.5\epsilon_3$.

4. *Generate $s_k(0.9\epsilon)$ labeled samples for the (sample-based) tester of Φ, where each labeled sample is generated as follows.*

   a. *Select uniformly $x \in \{0, 1\}^\ell$ and query f at x.*

   b. *For every $j \in J'$, estimate the influence of R_j^x on f, where $R_j^x = \{i \in R_j : x_i = 0\}$. Here the aim is to distinguish, with success probability at least $1 - c/(k \cdot s_k(0.9\epsilon))$, between the case that $\mathrm{I}_{R_j^x}(f) \leq \epsilon_3$ and the case that $\mathrm{I}_{R_j^x}(f) \geq 2\epsilon_3$. This is done by using Algorithm 6.3.1, while setting the parameter m to $m_4 \stackrel{\text{def}}{=} O(\epsilon_3^{-1} \log(k \cdot s_k(0.9\epsilon)))$, and asserting that R_j^x has a high influence on f if and only if the output estimate exceeds $1.5\epsilon_3$. In the first case (i.e., R_j^x was asserted to have high influence), set $y_j = 0$ and otherwise set $y_j = 1$.*

   c. *For every $j \in J \setminus J'$, select y_j uniformly at random in $\{0, 1\}$. The labeled sample is $(y_1 \cdots y_k, f(x))$.*

5. *Invoke the sample-based tester for Φ, while using proximity parameter 0.9ϵ, and assuming it has error probability at most c. Provide this tester with the $s_k(0.9\epsilon)$ labeled sample generated in Step 4, and output its verdict (i.e., accept if and only if the latter tester has accepted).*

We first note that each query made by Algorithm 6.3.2 is uniformly distributed in $\{0, 1\}^\ell$. The query complexity of the algorithm is $t \cdot 2m_2 + k \cdot 2m_3 + s_k(0.9\epsilon) \cdot (1 + k \cdot 2m_4)$, where the first term is due to Step 2, the second term is due to Step 3, and the third term is due to Step 4. (We may ignore the second term since it is dominated by the first.) Using $m_2 = O(\epsilon_2^{-1} \log t) = \widetilde{O}(tk) \cdot s_k(0.9\epsilon)$ and $m_4 = O(\epsilon_3^{-1} \log(k \cdot s_k(0.9\epsilon))) = \widetilde{O}(s_k(0.9\epsilon) \cdot k)$, we obtain a complexity bound of

$$O(t \cdot m_2 + s_k(0.9\epsilon) \cdot k \cdot m_3) = \widetilde{O}(k^5 \cdot s_k(0.9\epsilon) + k^2 \cdot s_k(0.9\epsilon)^2).$$

We now turn to the analysis of Algorithm 6.3.2.

---

[5] In general, one should use a one-to-one mapping $\phi : J \to [k]$. In this case, in Step 4b, for every $j \in J$, we set $y_{\phi(j)}$ according to R_j^x.

First, suppose that f is a (k, Φ)-junta. Let $f' \in \Phi$ be such that $f(x) = f'(x_I)$ for some k-subset I and all $x \in \{0, 1\}^\ell$. Then, with probability at least $1 - c$ over the choice of the t-partition (selected in Step 1), it holds that $|R_j \cap I| \leq 1$ for each $j \in [t]$. In this case, with probability at least $1 - c$, the set J determined in Step 2 contains all j's such that $I_{R_j}(f) \geq \epsilon_2$ (which implies that it contains contains all j's such that $I_{R_j}(f) \geq 4\epsilon_3$). Likewise, with probability at least $1 - c$, the set J' determined in Step 3 satisfies

$$\{j \in [t] : I_{R_j}(f) \geq 4\epsilon_3\} \subseteq J' \subseteq \{j \in [t] : I_{R_j}(f) > 3\epsilon_3\}. \tag{6.1}$$

Now, for each x selected in Step 4 and for each $j \in J'$, with probability at least $1 - c/(k \cdot s_k(0.9\epsilon))$, the algorithm determines y_j such that $y_j = x_{R_j \cap I}$.[6] As for $j \in J \setminus J'$, with probability at least $1 - 4\epsilon_3$ (over the choice of x), it holds that replacing $x_{R_j \cap I}$ by y_j does not affect the value of f. Hence (using $\epsilon_3 = 2c/(ks_k(0.9\epsilon))$), with probability at least $(1 - c)^3 \cdot (1 - c/(k \cdot s_k(0.9\epsilon)))^{k \cdot s_k(0.9\epsilon)} - k \cdot s_k(0.9\epsilon) \cdot 4\epsilon_3 > (1 - c)^4 - 8c > 1 - 12c$, the sample-based tester for Φ is invoked with a uniformly distributed f'-labeled sample. It follows that f is accepted with probability at least $(1 - 12c) \cdot (1 - c) > 2/3$.

Next, we consider the case that f is ϵ-far from being a (k, Φ)-junta. As shown in Section 5.3, if f is $2t\epsilon_2$-far from being a k-junta, then it will be rejected in Step 2 (with high probability over the choice of the t-partition and the execution of Step 2). Hence, we focus on the case that f is $2t\epsilon_2$-close to a k-junta g, which in turn is $(\epsilon - 2t\epsilon_2)$-far from being a (k, Φ)-junta; that is, $g(x) = g'(x_I)$ for some $g' \notin \Phi$ and some k-subset I (and all $x \in \{0, 1\}^\ell$). It follows that g' is $(\epsilon - 2t\epsilon_2)$-far from Φ. Now, as before, with probability at least $1 - c$ over the partition selected in Step 1, it holds that $|R_j \cap I| \leq 1$ for each $j \in [t]$. Furthermore, with probability at least $1 - c$, either Step 2 rejects or the set J' determined in Step 3 satisfies Eq. (6.1). Using the fact that *the influence of a set on the function g is within an additive distance of $2 \cdot 2t\epsilon_2$ from the influence of the same set on the function f* (see Exercise 6.4)) and $4t\epsilon_2 \leq \epsilon_3$, we have

$$\{j \in [t] : I_{R_j}(g) \geq 5\epsilon_3\} \subseteq J' \subseteq \{j \in [t] : I_{R_j}(g) > 2\epsilon_3\}. \tag{6.2}$$

Hence, for every $j \in J'$ it holds that $I_{R_j}(g) > 2\epsilon_3$, whereas for every $i \in I \setminus \bigcup_{j \in J'} R_j$ it holds that $I_{\{i\}}(g) \leq 5\epsilon_3$.

Now, note that, with probability at least $1 - s_k(0.9\epsilon) \cdot 2t\epsilon_2 > 1 - c$, it holds that $f(x) = g(x)$ (which equals $g'(x_I)$) *for all x's generated in Step 4*, since each x is uniformly distributed in $\{0, 1\}^\ell$ (and f is $2t\epsilon_2$-close to g). Again, for each x generated in Step 4 and each $j \in J'$, with probability at least $1 - c/(k \cdot s_k(0.9\epsilon))$, the algorithm determines correctly the jth bit of x_I. As before, the random setting of the bits in positions $J \setminus J'$ has limited effect. Hence (using $\epsilon_3 = 2c/(ks_k(0.9\epsilon))$), with probability at least $(1 - c)^3 \cdot (1 - c) \cdot (1 - 0.1/(k \cdot s_k(0.9\epsilon)))^{k \cdot s_k(0.9\epsilon)} - k \cdot s_3(0.9\epsilon) \cdot 5\epsilon_3 > (1 - c)^5 - 10c > 1 - 15c$, either Step 2 rejects or the sample-based tester

---

[6] This description assumes, for notational simplicity, that $J = [k]$ and that $R_j \cap I = \{i_j\}$ where $I = \{i_1, \ldots, i_k\}$ and $i_1 < \cdots < i_k$. Eliminating the first assumption requires using $y_{\phi(j)}$ instead of y_j, where ϕ is as in footnote 5. Eliminating the second assumption requires referring to f'_π (rather than to f') for an adequate permutation π over $[k]$ (i.e., π sorts the k-sequence $(R_j \cap I)_{j \in J}$), as in the motivating discussion. The same comment applies to the next couple of paragraphs (which deals with f that is ϵ-far from being a (k, Φ)-junta).

for Φ is invoked with a uniformly distributed g'-labeled sample. Since g' is $(\epsilon - 2t\epsilon_2)$-far from Φ and $\epsilon - 2t\epsilon_2 \geq \epsilon - c/s_k(0.9\epsilon) > 0.9\epsilon$, it follows that, in this case, f is rejected with probability at least $(1 - 15c) \cdot (1 - c) > 2/3$. The theorem follows. ∎

Applications. To illustrate the applicability of Theorem 6.3, we consider the problems of testing whether a function $f : \{0, 1\}^k \to \{0, 1\}$ is a (monotone and general) k-monomial, which were studied in Section 5.2.2. Clearly, the set of k-monomials is a subset of k-juntas, and testing that a Boolean function $f' : \{0, 1\}^k \to \{0, 1\}$ is a k-monomial is quite straightforward (since there are only 2^k such functions that are k-monomials (and a single monotone k-monomial)). Hence, invoking Theorem 6.3, we get

Corollary 6.4 (Testing monotone and general k-monomials): *The following two properties of Boolean functions over $\{0, 1\}^\ell$ can be tested within query complexity* poly(k/ϵ):

1. *The set of monotone k-monomials; that is, functions $f : \{0, 1\}^\ell \to \{0, 1\}$ such that for some k-subset $I \subseteq [\ell]$ it holds that $f(x) = \wedge_{i \in I} x_i$.*
2. *The set of k-monomials; that is, functions $f : \{0, 1\}^\ell \to \{0, 1\}$ such that for some k-subset $I \subseteq [\ell]$ and $\sigma = \sigma_1 \cdots \sigma_\ell \in \{0, 1\}^\ell$ it holds $f(x) = \wedge_{i \in I}(x_i \oplus \sigma_i)$.*

Furthermore, each query is uniformly distributed in $\{0, 1\}^\ell$.

Proof: Starting with the set of monotone k-monomials, let Φ denote the set of k-variate functions that are monotone k-monomials. Indeed, Φ is a singleton; that is, there is only one such function. Hence, testing whether $f' : \{0, 1\}^k \to \{0, 1\}$ is in Φ amounts to estimating the distance of f' from the unique monotone k-monomial, which can be done by using $O(1/\epsilon)$ random samples. Applying Theorem 6.3, Part 1 follows.

Turning to the set of k-monomials, let Φ denote the set of k-variate functions that are k-monomials. Indeed, Φ is of size 2^k, and we can estimate the distance of f' from each of them by using $O(k/\epsilon)$ random samples. Again, applying Theorem 6.3, Part 2 follows.[7] ∎

Preservation of Computational Complexity. Theorem 6.3 is proved by a transformation (captured by Algorithm 6.3.2) that preserves the computational complexity of the sample-based tester that is provided in its hypothesis. Hence, obtaining computationally efficient testers for (k, Φ)-juntas calls for using computationally efficient sample-based testers for Φ, which means that one should avoid the reduction of testing Φ to the "generic learning" of Φ (via ruling out all functions in Φ that are far from the input function). Hence, the tester in Exercise 6.5 should be preferred over the one outlined in the proof of Corollary 6.4.

---

[7] Note, however, that the running time of this straightforward tester is exponential in k, since it is based on estimating 2^k quantities. An alternative tester is presented in Exercise 6.5.

6.3. Extension to Properties Approximated by Subsets of k-Juntas

In this section we extend the result of the previous section to properties that can be approximated by sets of (k, Φ)-juntas, for adequate choices of k and Φ. The notion of approximation is defined next.

Definition 6.5 (Approximation of a property): *The property Π is δ-approximated by the property Π' if each function in Π is δ-close to some function in Π', and vice versa.*

For example, the set of (monotone) monomials of unbounded arity is 2^{-k}-approximated by the set of (monotone) monomials of arity at most k, which in turn is a subset of k-juntas. Specifically, any monomial can be replaced by a monomial that contains at most k of the original literals. Note that in this case the approximation error decreases exponentially with k, whereas the query complexity of testing the relevant subset of k-juntas (i.e., the set of i-monomials for $i \le k$) increases polynomially with k. Hence, for sufficiently large k, the approximation error is smaller than the reciprocal of the query complexity. In other words, the complexity of testing the set Π' that δ-approximates Π is sub-linear in $1/\delta$. This is the setting envisioned in the following general result.

Theorem 6.6 (Testing via an approximating property):[8] *Let $\Pi = \cup_{n \in \mathbb{N}} \Pi_n$ such that Π_n contains functions defined over $[n]$. Suppose that for every $\delta > 0$ there exists a property $\Pi^{\delta} = \cup_{n \in \mathbb{N}} \Pi_n^{\delta}$ and a function $q_{\delta} : \mathbb{N} \times (0, 1] \to \mathbb{N}$ such that*

1. *Π_n is δ-approximated by Π_n^{δ}; and*
2. *Π_n^{δ} can be ϵ'-tested by using $q_{\delta}(n, \epsilon')$ queries that are* each uniformly distributed in $[n]$.

If there exists a function $\Delta : (0, 1] \to (0, 1)$ such that for every $\epsilon \in (0, 1]$ it holds that $\Delta(\epsilon) < 0.1\epsilon$ and $q_{\Delta(\epsilon)}(n, 0.9\epsilon) < 0.1/\Delta(\epsilon)$, then Π can be tested within query complexity $q(n, \epsilon) = O(q_{\Delta(\epsilon)}(n, 0.9\epsilon))$.

We mention that the transformation presented in the following proof does not preserve one-sided error probability. Using Theorem 6.6 calls for presenting a sequence of parameterized properties (i.e., $(\Pi^{\delta})_{\delta>0}$) such that the approximation distance (to Π) equals this parameter (i.e., the parameter δ of the property Π^{δ}). It is likely that the query complexity of testing (i.e., testing Π^{δ}) increases with that parameter (i.e., with δ), and using Theorem 6.6 requires that the rate in which the query complexity increases is slower than the rate in which the approximation distance decreases (as reflected in the condition $q_{\Delta(\epsilon)}(n, 0.9\epsilon) < 0.1/\Delta(\epsilon)$). See further discussion following the proof.

Proof: On input parameters n, ϵ and oracle access to f, we set $\delta = \Delta(\epsilon)$ and invoke the guaranteed tester for Π^{δ}, denoted T, providing it with the parameters n and 0.9ϵ as well as with access to f, and output whatever T does. The analysis of $T^f(n, 0.9\epsilon)$

---

[8] Again, the constant 0.9 can be replaced by any constant $c \in (0, 1)$, but in such a case the condition $\Delta(\epsilon) < 0.1\epsilon$ should be replaced by the condition $\Delta(\epsilon) < (1 - c) \cdot \epsilon$.

is based on the observation that if f is δ-close to some function f', then

$$|\mathbf{Pr}[T^f(n, 0.9\epsilon) = 1] - \mathbf{Pr}[T^{f'}(n, 0.9\epsilon) = 1]| \leq q_\delta(n, 0.9\epsilon) \cdot \delta, \qquad (6.3)$$

since (by the hypothesis) each query is uniformly distributed in $[n]$.

Suppose that $f \in \Pi_n$. Then, there exists $f' \in \Pi_n^\delta$ that is δ-close to f, and T accepts f' with probability at least $2/3$. By Eq. (6.3), it follows that T accepts f with probability at least $2/3 - 0.1 > 0.55$, since $q_\delta(n, 0.9\epsilon) \cdot \delta < 0.1$ by the hypothesis (when recalling that $\delta = \Delta(\epsilon)$).

On the other hand, for f that is ϵ-far from Π_n, we observe that f must be $(\epsilon - \delta)$-far from Π_n^δ, because otherwise f is $(\epsilon - \delta)$-close to a function $g' \in \Pi_n^\delta$, which is δ-close to some $g \in \Pi_n$, which implies that f is $((\epsilon - \delta) + \delta)$-close to Π_n. Using $\epsilon - \delta > 0.9\epsilon$, where the inequality is due to the hypothesis $\delta = \Delta(\epsilon) < 0.1\epsilon$, it follows that f is 0.9ϵ-far from Π^δ, and so T must reject f with probability at least $2/3$. Using error reduction, the theorem follows. ∎

Applications. In the current context, we approximate a given property Π by a sequence of $(k, \cdot)$-junta properties such that the approximation distance to Π decreases with the junta-size parameter k. It is likely that the query complexity increases with k, and using Theorem 6.6 requires that the rate at which the query complexity increases is slower than the rate in which the approximation distance decreases. In many cases (see examples in Diakonikolas *et al.* [91]), the approximation distance decreases exponentially with k, whereas the query complexity only grows polynomially with k. In such cases, we can apply Theorem 6.6.

As with Theorem 6.3, we shall illustrate this application by considering the set of functions that are (monotone or general) monomials, but this time we refer to monomials of unbounded arity. Clearly, the set of (monotone or general) monomials is 2^{-k}-approximated by the corresponding set of monomials of size at most k. The latter set is merely the union of k sets that are each easily testable (i.e., the sets of i-monomials, for $i \in [k]$). Hence, we get

Corollary 6.7 (Testing monotone and general monomials): *The following two properties of Boolean functions over $\{0, 1\}^\ell$ can be tested within query complexity* $\mathrm{poly}(1/\epsilon)$:

1. *The set of monotone monomials; that is, functions $f : \{0, 1\}^\ell \to \{0, 1\}$ such that for some set $I \subseteq [\ell]$ it holds that $f(x) = \wedge_{i \in I} x_i$.*
2. *The set of monomials; that is, functions $f : \{0, 1\}^\ell \to \{0, 1\}$ such that for some set $I \subseteq [\ell]$ and $\sigma = \sigma_1 \cdots \sigma_\ell \in \{0, 1\}^\ell$ it holds $f(x) = \wedge_{i \in I}(x_i \oplus \sigma_i)$.*

Proof: As stated above, the relevant set of monomials, denoted Π, is 2^{-k}-approximated by the corresponding set of monomials of size at most k, denoted Π'. The latter set is the union over $i \in [k]$ of the sets of corresponding i-monomials. Hence, by Corollary 6.4 (and the closure of testability under unions)[9], the set Π' can be ϵ'-tested using $\mathrm{poly}(k/\epsilon)$ queries, which are each uniformly distributed in $\{0, 1\}^\ell$. Setting $k = O(\log(1/\epsilon))$ and applying Theorem 6.6, while noting that $2^{-k} < 0.1\epsilon$ and $\mathrm{poly}(k/\epsilon) < 0.1/2^{-k}$, the corollary follows. ∎

---

[9] See Section 1.3.4.

More generally, combining Theorems 6.3 and 6.6, we get

Corollary 6.8 (Testing via an approximating $(\cdot, \cdot)$-juntas property): *Let* $\Pi = \cup_{n \in \mathbb{N}} \Pi_n$ *such that* Π_n *contains functions defined over* $[n]$. *Suppose that there exists a function* $\kappa : (0, 1] \to \mathbb{N}$ *and a sequence of properties* $(\Phi_k)_{k \in \mathbb{N}}$ *such that* $\Phi_k \subseteq \{f' : \{0, 1\}^k \to \{0, 1\}\}$ *and it holds that*

1. *For every* $k \in \mathbb{N}$, *the property* Φ_k *is invariant under permuting the bits of the argument to the function[10] and* Φ_k *has a sample-based tester of sample complexity* $s_k : (0, 1] \to \mathbb{N}$ *such that* $s_k(\epsilon) \leq s_{k+1}(\epsilon)$ *for all* $\epsilon > 0$.
2. *There exists a function* $\delta : \mathbb{N} \to (0, 1]$ *such that for every* $\epsilon \in (0, 1]$, *the property* Π_n *is* $\delta(\kappa(\epsilon))$-*approximated by the union over* $i \in [\kappa(\epsilon)]$ *of the sets of* (i, Φ_i)-*juntas and*

$$\delta(\kappa(\epsilon)) < \min\left(0.1 \cdot \epsilon, \frac{0.1}{\text{poly}(\kappa(\epsilon)) \cdot \widetilde{O}(s_{\kappa(\epsilon)}(0.81\epsilon))^2}\right).$$

Then, Π *can be tested within query complexity* $\text{poly}(\kappa(\epsilon)) \cdot \widetilde{O}(s_{\kappa(\epsilon)}(0.81\epsilon))^2$.

Note that the two conditions correspond to the hypotheses in Theorems 6.3 and 6.6, respectively. In many cases, $s_k(\epsilon) = \text{poly}(k/\epsilon)$ and $\delta(k) = \exp(-k^{\Omega(1)})$, which allows setting $\kappa(\epsilon) = \text{poly}(\log(1/\epsilon))$.

Proof: By Theorem 6.3 and the first hypothesis, for each i we can test (i, Φ_i)-juntas by a tester that makes $\text{poly}(i) \cdot \widetilde{O}(s_i(0.9\epsilon)^2)$ uniformly distributed queries. The same holds with respect to the union of the first k such properties; that is, it can be ϵ'-tested using $\text{poly}(k) \cdot \widetilde{O}(s_k(0.9\epsilon')^2)$ uniformly distributed queries.[11] Fixing any $\epsilon > 0$, let Π'_n be the union of the first $\kappa = \kappa(\epsilon)$ foregoing properties. Then, by the foregoing, Π'_n can be ϵ'-tested using $q'(\epsilon') = \text{poly}(\kappa) \cdot \widetilde{O}(s_\kappa(0.9\epsilon'))^2$ uniformly distributed queries. By the second hypothesis, Π_n is $\delta(\kappa)$-approximated by Π'_n, whereas

$$\delta(\kappa) < \frac{0.1}{\text{poly}(\kappa) \cdot \widetilde{O}(s_\kappa(0.81\epsilon))^2}$$

$$= \frac{0.1}{q'(0.9\epsilon)},$$

where the equality uses $q'(0.9\epsilon) = \text{poly}(\kappa) \cdot \widetilde{O}(s_\kappa(0.9 \cdot 0.9\epsilon))^2$. Recalling that $\kappa = \kappa(\epsilon)$ and $\delta(\kappa) < 0.1\epsilon$, we apply Theorem 6.6, and infer that Π_n can be tested within query complexity $q(n, \epsilon) = O(q'(0.9\epsilon)) = \text{poly}(\kappa) \cdot \widetilde{O}(s_\kappa(0.9^2\epsilon))^2$. The corollary follows. ∎

---

[10] As in Theorem 6.3, this means that $f' \in \Phi_k$ if and only if for every permutation $\pi : [k] \to [k]$ it holds that $f'_\pi(y) = f'(y_{\pi(1)}, \ldots, y_{\pi(k)})$ is in Φ_k.

[11] See Section 1.3.4 (for the closure of testability under unions).

6.4. Chapter Notes

The "testing by implicit sampling" methodology originates in the work of Diakonikolas, Lee, Matulef, Onak, Rubinfeld, Servedio, and Wan [91], which presents numerous applications of it. In particular, their paper uses this methodology to derive testers for several natural properties including sets of functions computable by *bounded size* devices such as decision trees, branching programs, Boolean formulas, and Boolean circuits.

This methodology is often called *testing by implicit learning* (see, e.g., [251]), but we prefer the term "implicit sampling" for reasons that are closely related to the fact that our presentation of the said methodology differs from the one in [91] in several aspects. First, we decouple the *reduction of testing a property* Π *to testing* $(\cdot, \cdot)$-*junta properties that approximate* Π from the actual *testing of* $(\cdot, \cdot)$-*junta properties*: The former reduction is captured by Theorem 6.6, which is actually more general, whereas the testing of $(\cdot, \cdot)$-junta properties is captured by Theorem 6.3.

Second, we reduce the testing of (k, Φ)-junta properties to *testing* Φ, which is a property of k-variate functions, where the testing task is performed by sample-based testers. In contrast, Diakonikolas *et al.* [91] reduce the testing of (k, Φ)-junta properties to the *proper learning* of Φ (also via sample-based algorithms). Indeed, such a learning algorithm implies a sample-based tester of about the same sample complexity (see Section 1.3.5), but there is no reason to restrict the methodology to this special case (since sample-based testing may be easier than learning, see, e.g., [153]). For this reason we prefer to avoid a term that associates this methodology with learning. Furthermore, the core of the methodology is the technique of generating a labeled sample that refers to the (unknown) relevant variables, and it is nice to reflect this fact in the name of the methodology.

On Testing Problems Associated with Sets of Boolean Functions

We seize the opportunity to distinguish between two different types of testing problems that are commonly associated with sets of Boolean functions.

Testing a Property of the Input Function. In this case, we refer to a property Π of Boolean functions, where the input is a Boolean function $f : \{0, 1\}^\ell \to \{0, 1\}$, and the tester is required to determine whether $f \in \Pi$ or f is far from Π. Indeed, in the case, the tested object has size $n = 2^\ell$.

The testing problems studied in this chapter (as well as in Chapters 2–5) are all of this type.

Testing That the Input Evaluates to 1 Under a Fixed Function. In this case, we fix a Boolean function $f : \{0, 1\}^n \to \{0, 1\}$, and consider a property of n-bit strings that consists of the set of all strings that evaluate to 1 under f. Hence, f is a fixed parameter determining the property $f^{-1}(1)$, the input is a n-bit string, denoted x, and the tester is required to determine whether $x \in f^{-1}(1)$ (i.e., $f(x) = 1$) or x is far from $f^{-1}(1)$.

Studies of this type are typically not confined to a single function f, but rather consider any function f in a set of functions Π. In these cases, one does not test whether f is in Π; the function f is given to the tester explicitly, and it is guaranteed to be in Π. What is being tested is whether a string, to which the tester is given oracle access, has a property defined by f (i.e., is in $f^{-1}(1)$).

Since we did not discuss such problems so far, let us mention that testing whether a given string is in the set generated by a fixed regular expression (see [14]) belongs to this category. In this case, the same regular expression (or the finite automaton computing the corresponding indicator function) is used for all input lengths. One may also consider fixing a sequence of finite functions $f_n : \{0, 1\}^n \to \{0, 1\}$, and testing whether the input x is in $f_{|x|}^{-1}(1)$. For example, for any fixed w and any family of oblivious read-once branching programs $\{p_n : \{0, 1\}^n \to \{0, 1\}\}_{n \in \mathbb{N}}$ of width w, testing membership in the corresponding set (i.e., $\cup_{n \in \mathbb{N}} p_n^{-1}(1)$) was considered in [215]. Such a testing problem falls within the framework of massively parameterized properties (see [216]).

We stress that both types of problems may arise with respect to Boolean functions that are associated with computing devices. Specifically, testing whether a given function can be computed by a branching program of a given size (see [91]) is a notable example of the first type, whereas the aforementioned problem of testing membership in the set of strings accepted by a fixed branching program is a notable example of the second type.

Exercises

Exercise 6.1 (On the complexity of finding the junta – a lower bound): For each k-subset $I \subseteq [\ell]$, consider the function $f_I : \{0, 1\}^\ell \to \{0, 1\}$ defined by $f_I(x) = \oplus_{i \in I} x_i$. Prove that finding I requires at least $\log_2 \binom{\ell}{k} - 1$ queries, when given access to an arbitrary f_I, even if one is allowed to fail with probability at most $1/3$.

> **Guideline:** Consider first the case of deterministic algorithms. The computation of such an algorithm is captured by a decision tree in which the vertices correspond to queries, and the edges represent the corresponding answers. Hence, a deterministic algorithm that finds the set I corresponds to a decision tree that has at least $\binom{\ell}{k}$ different leaves (which implies that its depth is at least $\log_2 \binom{\ell}{k}$). Turning to randomized algorithms, note that each such algorithm can be viewed as a distribution on such decision trees, and that, in expectation, a random tree in this distribution corresponds to a deterministic algorithm that succeeds on at least a $2/3$ fraction of the possible functions. Hence, this distribution must contain a tree (that corresponds to an algorithm) that succeeds on at least a $2/3$ fraction of the functions, which means that this tree must have at least $\frac{2}{3} \cdot \binom{\ell}{k}$ different leaves.

Exercise 6.2 (On the complexity of finding the junta – an upper bound): Present a randomized algorithm that when given access to a k-junta $f : \{0, 1\}^\ell \to \{0, 1\}$ in which each relevant variable has influence at least ϵ (i.e., $f(x) = f'(x_I)$ for some k-subset I and $I_{\{i\}}(f) \geq \epsilon$ for every $i \in I$), finds the junta with probability at least $2/3$ while making $O(k) \cdot (\log \ell)/\epsilon$ queries.

> **Guideline:** On input f, for $t = O(k^2)$, we first select a random t-partition, $(R_1, \ldots, R_t)$, as in Step 1 of Algorithm 6.3.2, and find $J = \{j \in [\ell] : I_{R_j}(f) \geq \epsilon\}$. Next, for each $j \in J$, we find $i \in R_j$ such that $I_{\{i\}}(f) \geq \epsilon$ by a binary search, while using Algorithm 6.3.1 to estimate the influence of the various relevant subsets. This

algorithm makes $(\widetilde{O}(t) + \widetilde{O}(k)\log\ell)/\epsilon$ queries, but the first step can be made more efficient (yielding the claimed bound).[12]

Exercise 6.3 (Properties of Boolean functions that are invariant under renaming of variables): Prove that all properties of ℓ-variate Boolean functions studied in prior chapters are invariant under renaming of the variables; that is, $f : \{0, 1\}^\ell \to \{0, 1\}$ has the property if for every permutation $\pi : [\ell] \to [\ell]$ it holds that $f_\pi(x) = f(x_{\pi(1)}, \ldots, x_{\pi(\ell)})$ has the property. Specifically, consider the following properties: linearity (and being a low-degree polynomial), monotonicity, being a monotone dictatorship, being a (monotone or general) monomial, and being a k-junta.

Exercise 6.4 (The influences of a set on functions that are close to each other): Prove that if $f : \{0, 1\}^\ell \to \{0, 1\}$ is ϵ-close to $g : \{0, 1\}^\ell \to \{0, 1\}$, then $|\mathbf{I}_S(f) - \mathbf{I}_S(g)| \le 2 \cdot \epsilon$ for every $S \subseteq [\ell]$.

Guideline: Fixing S, let D_f (resp., D_g) denote the set of pairs $(r, s) \in \{0, 1\}^\ell \times \{0, 1\}^\ell$ such that $r_{\bar{S}} = s_{\bar{S}}$ and $f(r) \ne f(s)$ (resp., $g(r) \ne g(s)$). Observe that the absolute value of $|D_f| - |D_g|$ is upper-bounded by the size of the symmetric difference between D_f and D_g, denoted $D_f \triangledown D_g$. It follows that

$$|\mathbf{I}_S(f) - \mathbf{I}_S(g)| \le \mathbf{Pr}_{r,s:r_{\bar{S}}=s_{\bar{S}}}[(r, s) \in D_f \triangledown D_g]$$
$$= \mathbf{Pr}_{r,s:r_{\bar{S}}=s_{\bar{S}}}[f(r) - f(s) \ne g(r) - g(s)]$$
$$\le \mathbf{Pr}_{r,s:r_{\bar{S}}=s_{\bar{S}}}[f(r) \ne g(r) \vee g(s) \ne g(s)].$$

Exercise 6.5 (Testing general k-monomials): In continuation to Corollary 6.4, present a tester for k-monomials of time complexity $\mathrm{poly}(k/\epsilon)$.

Guideline: For $\epsilon \le 3 \cdot 2^{-k}$, the tester presented in the proof of Corollary 6.4 would do (since $2^k = O(1/\epsilon)$ in this case). Hence, we focus on the case of $\epsilon > 3 \cdot 2^{-k}$, and observe that a k-monomial evaluates to 1 on a $2^{-k} < \epsilon/3$ fraction of its domain. On the other hand, every function that evaluates to 1 on at most an $2\epsilon/3$ fraction of its domain is ϵ-close to a k-monomial. Thus, using $O(1/\epsilon)$ random samples, we estimate the fraction of points on which the input function evaluates to 1, and accept if and only if this estimate is at most $\epsilon/2$.

Exercise 6.6 (An easy case of approximation): Show that the set of functions that are ϵ-close to Π is ϵ-approximated by Π.

Exercise 6.7 (Another easy case of approximation): Suppose that any two functions in Π are at distance at least ϵ of one another, and let Π' be the set of functions that are at distance approximately $\epsilon/2$ from Π (i.e., $\Pi' = \{f : \delta_\Pi(f) \in [0.4\epsilon, 0.6\epsilon]\}$). Show that Π' is 0.6ϵ-approximated by Π.

[12] Place $R_1, \ldots, R_t$ at the t leaves of a balanced binary tree and let each internal vertex hold the union of the sets placed at its children. Now conduct a DFS from the root while continuing only on vertices that were found to hold an influential set.

CHAPTER SEVEN

Lower Bounds Techniques

Summary: We present and illustrate three techniques for proving lower bounds on the query complexity of property testers.

1. Showing a pair of distributions, one on instances that have the property and the other on instances that are far from the property, such that an oracle machine of low query complexity cannot distinguish these two distributions.
2. Showing a reduction from communication complexity. That is, showing that a communication complexity problem of high complexity can be solved within communication complexity that is related to the query complexity of the property testing task that we are interested in.
3. Showing a reduction from another testing problem. That is, showing a "local" reduction of a hard testing problem to the testing problem that we are interested in.

We also present simplifications of these techniques for the cases of one-sided error probability testers and nonadaptive testers.

The methodology of reducing from communication complexity was introduced by Blais, Brody, and Matulef [54], and our description of it is based on [136].

Teaching Note: The order of the sections in this chapter happens to reflect our priority regarding teaching. In particular, the method of *indistinguishability of distributions* (presented in Section 7.2) is used much more often than the other two methods, and studying it should be at the highest priority. The method of *reducing from communication complexity* (see Section 7.3) is most interesting, and studying it is highly recommended. Sections 7.4 and 7.5 may be left for optional independent reading.

7.1. Introduction

Our perspective in this book is mainly algorithmic. Hence, we view complexity lower bounds mainly as justifications for the failure to provide better algorithms (i.e., algorithms of lower complexity). The lower bounds that we shall be discussing are lower bounds on the query complexity of testers. These lower bounds are of an information theoretic nature, and so they cannot (and do not) rely on computational assumptions.

We start with two brief preliminary discussions. The first discussion is very abstract and vague: it concerns the difficulty of establishing lower bounds. The second discussion is very concrete: it highlights the fact that computational complexity considerations play no role in this chapter, a fact that is most evident in the avoidance of the uniformity condition.

What Makes Lower Bounds Hard to Prove? Proving lower bounds is often more challenging than proving upper bounds, since one has to defeat all possible methods (or algorithms) rather than show that one of them works. Indeed, it seems harder to cope with a universal quantifier than with an existential one, but one should bear in mind that a second quantifier of opposite nature follows the first one. That is, a complexity lower bound has the form "every method fails on some instance" (i.e., $\forall\exists$), whereas an algorithmic upper bound has the form "(there) exists a method that succeeds on all instances" (i.e., $\exists\forall$). Still, the $\forall\exists$ template seems harder to argue about than the $\exists\forall$ template. Furthermore, the universal quantifier in a typical complexity lower bound refers to a class of objects that is defined *in terms of externalities* (i.e., resource bounds) rather than in terms of *internal structure* (as when studying a standard mathematical object (e.g., a finite field)).

On the Uniformity Condition. Recall that when presenting testers, we have presented them in terms of uniform algorithms that get the size parameter n and a proximity parameter ϵ as inputs. That is, the same algorithm is used for all values of n and ϵ, making it potentially more useful, especially when it is relatively efficient in terms of computational complexity (i.e., when its running time is closely related to its query complexity). In contrast, when seeking query complexity lower bounds, we drop the computational complexity requirement, and even allow the potential tester to be nonuniform (i.e., depend arbitrarily on n and ϵ).[1] This makes the lower bound results stronger, clarifying that they are due only to "information theoretic" considerations; but the truth is that the techniques presented in this chapter cannot capitalize on uniformity conditions.

7.2. Indistinguishability of Distributions

A popular methodology for proving lower bounds on the complexity of solving computational problems consists of presenting a distribution of instances on which every algorithm that has lower complexity (i.e., lower than claimed) fails to solve the problem at hand. In the context of randomized algorithms (of error probability at most $1/3$), this means presenting a distribution X such that, for every algorithm A having lower complexity, it holds that $A(X)$ is wrong about X with probability greater than $1/3$, where the probability is taken over both X and the internal coin tosses of A. (Typically, X cannot

---

[1] In other words, we allow to present a different algorithm for each possible value of n and ϵ, making no requirements regarding the dependence of this algorithm on these values (or about the "uniformity" of this sequence of algorithms).

be concentrated on a single instance, since for every instance there exists a "special purpose" algorithm that solves it.)[2]

The foregoing methodology seems to make the job of proving lower bounds harder. Rather than having total freedom in choosing for each "low complexity" algorithm a designated instance (or a distribution of instances) on which this algorithm fails, the prover is required to find a single distribution of instances on which all (low complexity) algorithms fail. Proving lower bounds this way is certainly valid (since if each algorithm fails on the selected distribution then for each algorithm there exists an instance on which it fails), but one may wonder about the rationale of restricting the freedom of the lower bound prover. Note, however, that such a restriction is manifested in any proof technique; that is, any proof technique represents a restriction of the possible proof strategies to a single one. The point is that a restriction has the benefit of focusing attention, which is often beneficial. In other words, the restriction may turn out to be a simplification, especially when we recall the thesis that the $\exists\forall$ template (underlying the existence of a distribution that foils any algorithm) seems simpler (or more intuitive to handle) than the $\forall\exists$ template (which underlies the task of finding a bad instance for each algorithm).[3]

In the context of nonuniform complexity, as is the case when we only care about the query complexity of oracle machines, we can take a "without loss of generality" simplification step. Specifically, when lower-bounding the error probability of algorithms (of bounded complexity) on a single input-distribution X, it suffices to consider deterministic algorithms (of the same bounded complexity). This is because a randomized algorithm A is a convex combination of deterministic machines of the same complexity; in other words, the error probability of A equals the expected error probability of the corresponding deterministic algorithms. Specifically, for every x, let $\eta_x : \{0, 1\}^* \to \{0, 1\}$ indicates the incorrectness of a solution for instance x; that is, $\eta_x(y)$ holds if and only if y is not a correct solution for instance x. Then, the probability that $A(x)$ errs (i.e., $\mathbf{Pr}[\eta_x(A(x))]$) equals $\mathbb{E}_r[\eta_x(A'(x, r))]$, where $A'(x, r)$ denotes the output of A on input x when the outcome of A's internal coin tosses equals r. Considering the (nonuniform) deterministic algorithm A_r defined by $A_r(x) = A'(x, r)$, and using $\mathbb{E}[\eta_X(A(X))] = \mathbb{E}_{x\leftarrow X}[\mathbb{E}_r[\eta_x(A'(x, r))]] = \mathbb{E}_r[\mathbb{E}_{x\leftarrow X}[[\eta_x(A_r(x))]]]$, it follows that there exists an r such that $\mathbb{E}[\eta_X(A_r(X))] \leq \mathbb{E}[\eta_X(A(X))]$. This means that the error probability of A on X is lower-bounded by the error probability of the best A_r on X (i.e., $\mathbb{E}[\eta_X(A(X))] \geq \min_r\{\mathbb{E}[\eta_X(A_r(X))]\}$).

We wish to stress that the foregoing discussion refers to two steps. Starting with the goal of proving a lower bound on the complexity of algorithms that have bounded error probability (say $1/3$), we formulated this goal as showing that *every* algorithm of "low complexity" must err with higher (than $1/3$) probability on *some* input x. The first step was confining ourselves to the selection of one input distribution X, with the aim of showing that every algorithm of low complexity errs with higher (than $1/3$) probability on the distribution X. That is, we consider the expected error probability of the algorithm, where the expectation is taken over X (as well as over the internal coins tosses of the

---

[2] This assertion refers to nonuniform models of computation. In contract, in the context of uniform models of computation, one may encounter (lower bound or impossibility) arguments that identify a single instance per each length, although in these cases one refers to an infinite sequence of such instances (whereas the same uniform machine must handle all lengths).

[3] Furthermore, in the context of nonuniform complexity, this methodology is actually "complete" in the sense that any valid lower bound can be proved by presenting a single distribution that foils all "low-complexity" algorithms. See further discussion following the statement of Theorem 7.1.

algorithm). The second step was observing that, without loss of generality, it suffices to prove the latter for deterministic algorithms (i.e., lower-bound the error probability of such algorithms).

7.2.1. The Actual Method

Let us detail the foregoing argument in the concrete setting of property testing. Recall that in this setting we deal with randomized algorithms, which are allowed error probability at most $1/3$, for solving a promise problem (i.e., distinguishing instances that have the property from instances that are far from the property). Hence, the algorithm (i.e., a potential tester) fails only if it outputs a wrong answer, with probability exceeding $1/3$, on an instance that *satisfies the promise*. As stated above, rather than seeking, for each algorithm of low complexity, an instance (that satisfies the promise) on which this algorithm fails, we shall seek a single distribution (on inputs that satisfy the promise) such that the each algorithm of low complexity fails on this distribution. That is, the algorithm errs with probability exceeding $1/3$, where the probability is taken both over the distribution and the internal coin tosses of the algorithm. Furthermore, fixing such a distribution of instances, it will suffice to consider deterministic algorithms. (Lastly, for greater flexibility, we allow arbitrary distributions but only consider errors that occur on inputs that satisfy the promise.)

Theorem 7.1 (The query complexity of randomized algorithms is lower bounded by the "distributional" query complexity of deterministic algorithms): *Let $\Pi = \cup_{n \in \mathbb{N}} \Pi_n$ such that Π_n contains functions from $[n]$ to R_n, and let $q : \mathbb{N} \times (0, 1] \to \mathbb{N}$. Suppose that for some $\epsilon > 0$ and $n \in \mathbb{N}$, there exists a distribution F of functions from $[n]$ to R_n such that for every deterministic oracle machine M that makes at most $q(n, \epsilon)$ queries it holds that*

$$\mathbf{Pr}[F \in \Pi_n \wedge M^F(n, \epsilon) \neq 1] + \mathbf{Pr}[F \in \Gamma_\epsilon(\Pi_n) \wedge M^F(n, \epsilon) \neq 0] > \frac{1}{3} \qquad (7.1)$$

where $\Gamma_\epsilon(\Pi_n)$ denotes the set of functions (from $[n]$ to R_n) that are ϵ-far from Π_n. Then, the query complexity of ϵ-testing Π is greater than $q(\cdot, \epsilon)$.

The term "distributional complexity" that appears in the title of Theorem 7.1 refers to the query complexity of deterministic algorithms that are only required to solve the problem "on the average" (or rather on random instances drawn from some fixed distribution). The method underlying Theorem 7.1 was first employed by Yao [273], and it turns out that it is "complete" in the sense that any valid lower bound can be proved by using it; that is, if Π has query complexity greater than q, then there exists a distribution as in the hypothesis of Theorem 7.1. (The latter claim is far more difficult to establish; it requires employing von Neumann's Minimax Theorem [269].)[4]

Proof: Suppose toward the contradiction that T is an ϵ-tester of query complexity $q(\cdot, \epsilon)$ for Π. Then, for any $n \in \mathbb{N}$ and every $f \in \Pi_n$ it holds that $\mathbf{Pr}[T^f(n, \epsilon) \neq 1] \leq 1/3$, whereas for every $f : [n] \to R_n$ that is ϵ-far from Π_n it holds that $\mathbf{Pr}[T^f(n, \epsilon) \neq 0] \leq 1/3$, since T has error probability at most $1/3$. On the other

---

[4] See discussion in [135, Apdx. A.1].

hand, for every distribution F of functions from $[n]$ to R_n, it holds that

$$\mathbf{Pr}[F \in \Pi_n \wedge T^F(n, \epsilon) \neq 1] \leq \mathbf{Pr}[F \in \Pi_n] \cdot \max_{f \in \Pi_n}\{\mathbf{Pr}[T^f(n, \epsilon) \neq 1]\} \quad (7.2)$$

$$\mathbf{Pr}[F \in \Gamma_\epsilon(\Pi_n) \wedge T^F(n, \epsilon) \neq 0] \leq \mathbf{Pr}[F \in \Gamma_\epsilon(\Pi_n)] \cdot \max_{f \in \Gamma_\epsilon(\Pi_n)}\{\mathbf{Pr}[T^f(n, \epsilon) \neq 0]\}.$$
$$(7.3)$$

(Each of these inequalities represents an averaging argument over the distribution F; specifically, it reflects the fact that for every predicate χ and set S, and for independent random variables X and R, it holds that $\mathbf{Pr}[\chi(X, R)|X \in S] \leq \max_{x \in S}\{\mathbf{Pr}[\chi(x, R)]\}$.)[5] Recalling that each of the "max-factors" in Eqs. (7.2) and (7.3) is upper-bounded by $1/3$, we get

$$\mathbf{Pr}[F \in \Pi_n \wedge T^F(n, \epsilon) \neq 1] + \mathbf{Pr}[F \in \Gamma_\epsilon(\Pi_n) \wedge T^F(n, \epsilon) \neq 0] \leq \frac{1}{3} \quad (7.4)$$

since $\mathbf{Pr}[F \in \Pi_n] + \mathbf{Pr}[F \in \Gamma_\epsilon(\Pi_n)] \leq 1$.

Teaching Note: Recall that Eqs. (7.2) and (7.3) were derived by an averaging argument over the distribution F. In contrast, in the following paragraph we shall employ an averaging argument over the internal coin tosses of T.

Denoting by T_r the residual deterministic machine that is obtained by fixing the internal coin tosses of T to r, it follows (by an averaging argument on r)[6] that there exists an r such that

$$\mathbf{Pr}[F \in \Pi_n \wedge T_r^F(n, \epsilon) \neq 1] + \mathbf{Pr}[F \in \Gamma_\epsilon(\Pi_n) \wedge T_r^F(n, \epsilon) \neq 0] \leq \frac{1}{3}, \quad (7.5)$$

which contradicts Eq. (7.1), since T_r is a deterministic oracle machine that makes at most $q(n, \epsilon)$ queries. ∎

A More Convenient Form – Indistinguishability. Another simplification step is obtained by considering a distribution F (of functions from $[n]$ to R_n) such that $\mathbf{Pr}[F \in \Pi_n] = \mathbf{Pr}[F \in \Gamma_\epsilon(\Pi_n)] = 1/2$. In this case, it suffices to show that no deterministic

---

[5] Here X represents F and R represents the internal coin tosses of T. In Eq. (7.2) we used $S = \Pi$ and $\chi(x, R) = 1$ iff $T^F \neq 1$ (under coins R), whereas in Eq. (7.3) we used $S = \Gamma_\epsilon(\Pi)$ and $\chi(x, R) = 1$ iff $T^F \neq 0$ (under coins R).

[6] We stress that Eq. (7.5) is proved by viewing the l.h.s. of Eq. (7.4) as an expected value of the l.h.s. of Eq. (7.5), where the expectation is taken over all possible choices of r. That is, we argue as follows

$$\mathbf{Pr}[F \in \Pi_n \wedge T^F(n, \epsilon) \neq 1] + \mathbf{Pr}[F \in \Gamma_\epsilon(\Pi_n) \wedge T^F(n, \epsilon) \neq 0]$$

$$= \mathbb{E}_r\left[\mathbf{Pr}[F \in \Pi_n \wedge T_r^F(n, \epsilon) \neq 1] + \mathbf{Pr}[F \in \Gamma_\epsilon(\Pi_n) \wedge T_r^F(n, \epsilon) \neq 0]\right]$$

$$\geq \min_r\left\{\mathbf{Pr}[F \in \Pi_n \wedge T_r^F(n, \epsilon) \neq 1] + \mathbf{Pr}[F \in \Gamma_\epsilon(\Pi_n) \wedge T_r^F(n, \epsilon) \neq 0]\right\},$$

where the key point that we wish to stress here is that r is selected such that it minimizes the sum of the two terms in the l.h.s. of Eq. (7.4). (In contrast, we cannot just pick an r_1 that minimized the first term in the l.h.s. of Eq. (7.4) and an r_2 that minimizes the second term.)

oracle machine M that makes at most $q(n, \epsilon)$ queries can distinguish the case of $F \in \Pi_n$ from the case of $F \in \Gamma_\epsilon(\Pi_n)$ with a gap of at least $1/3$.

Theorem 7.2 (The method of indistinguishability of distributions): *Let $\Pi = \cup_{n \in \mathbb{N}} \Pi_n$ and $\Gamma_\epsilon(\Pi_n)$ be as in Theorem 7.1, and let $q : \mathbb{N} \times (0, 1] \to \mathbb{N}$. Suppose that for some $\epsilon > 0$ and $n \in \mathbb{N}$, there exists a distribution F_1 of functions in Π_n and a distribution F_0 of functions in $\Gamma_\epsilon(\Pi_n)$ such that for every deterministic oracle machine M that makes at most $q(n, \epsilon)$ queries it holds that*

$$\left| \mathbf{Pr}[M^{F_1}(n, \epsilon) = 1] - \mathbf{Pr}[M^{F_0}(n, \epsilon) = 1] \right| < \frac{1}{3}. \tag{7.6}$$

Then, the query complexity of ϵ-testing Π is greater than $q(\cdot, \epsilon)$.

The quantity on the l.h.s. of Eq. (7.6) is called the **distinguishing gap** of M. (The method captured by Theorem 7.2 is also complete in the sense that any valid lower bound can be proved by using it; see Exercise 7.3.)

Proof: Fixing any deterministic oracle machine M of query complexity q, for every $i \in \{0, 1\}$, let p_i denote the probability that $M^{F_i}(n, \epsilon)$ equals 1. Then, by Eq. (7.6), we have $|p_1 - p_0| < 1/3$. Now, let F equal F_1 with probability $1/2$, and equal F_0 otherwise. Then, the probability that $M^F(n, \epsilon)$ errs (i.e., either outputs 0 when $F = F_1$ or outputs 1 when $F = F_0$) is $0.5 \cdot (1 - p_1) + 0.5 \cdot p_0 \geq 0.5 - 0.5 \cdot |p_1 - p_0| > 1/3$. Hence, F satisfies the hypothesis of Theorem 7.1, and the current claim follows. ∎

A More Flexible Form. The reasoning underlying Theorem 7.2 remains valid also if we allow F_1 and F_0 to reside outside their designated sets with small probability. In such a case, we should reduce the gap accordingly. This yields the following more flexible version, when in typical applications (which are asymptotic) one can make all η_i's arbitrarily small positive constants.

Corollary 7.3 (A more flexible form of Theorem 7.2): *Let $\Pi = \cup_{n \in \mathbb{N}} \Pi_n$, $\Gamma_\epsilon(\Pi_n)$, and $q : \mathbb{N} \times (0, 1] \to \mathbb{N}$ be as in Theorem 7.2. Suppose that for some $\epsilon > 0$, $\eta_0, \eta_1, \eta_2 > 0$ and $n \in \mathbb{N}$, there exist distributions F_1 and F_0 such that $\mathbf{Pr}[F_1 \in \Pi_n] \geq 1 - \eta_1$ and $\mathbf{Pr}[F_0 \in \Gamma_\epsilon(\Pi_n)] \geq 1 - \eta_0$, and for every deterministic oracle machine M that makes at most $q(n, \epsilon)$ queries it holds that*

$$\left| \mathbf{Pr}[M^{F_1}(n, \epsilon) = 1] - \mathbf{Pr}[M^{F_0}(n, \epsilon) = 1] \right| \leq \eta_2. \tag{7.7}$$

If $\eta_0 + \eta_1 + \eta_2 < 1/3$, then the query complexity of ϵ-testing Π is greater than $q(\cdot, \epsilon)$.

Proof: Let F_1' (resp., F_0') denote the distribution of F_1 (resp., F_0) conditioned on $F_1 \in \Pi_n$ (resp., $F_0 \in \Gamma_\epsilon(\Pi_n)$). Then, for each $i \in \{0, 1\}$, the statistical distance between F_i' and F_i is at most η_i (since the statistical distance between X and "X conditioned on $X \in S$" equals $\mathbf{Pr}[X \notin S]$).[7] Hence, if (F_1, F_0) satisfies Eq. (7.7) and

[7] Denoting the latter distribution by X', recall that the statistical distance between X and X' equals $\max_T \{\mathbf{Pr}[X \in T] - \mathbf{Pr}[X' \in T]\}$, and observe that in the current case this maximum is obtained at $T = \bar{S}$.

$\eta_0 + \eta_1 + \eta_2 < 1/3$, then (F_1', F_0') satisfies Eq. (7.6),[8] and the proof is completed by applying Theorem 7.2. ∎

7.2.2. Illustrating the Application of the Method

We have already used the method of indistinguishability of distributions (twice) in the first chapter (i.e., in the proofs of Propositions 1.2 and 1.11). Here we reproduce the proof of the existence of properties that are hard to test, while explicitly using Corollary 7.3.

Proposition 7.4 (Hardness of testing membership in a linear code, restating Proposition 1.11): *Let G be a 0.5n-by-n Boolean matrix in which every 0.05n columns are linearly independent. Let $\Pi = \{xG : x \in \{0, 1\}^{0.5n}\}$ be the linear code generated by G. Then, for all sufficiently large n's, 0.1-testing Π requires more than 0.05n queries.*

Proof: Let X denote the uniform distribution on Π, and Y denote the uniform distribution on $\{0, 1\}^n$. We shall use the following two observations, which were already justified in the proof of Proposition 1.11.

1. An algorithm that makes at most $0.05n$ queries cannot distinguish X from Y; that is, for any oracle machine M that makes at most $0.05n$ queries, it holds that $\mathbf{Pr}[M^X = 1] = \mathbf{Pr}[M^Y = 1]$.
   (Recall that this follows from the fact that the restriction of each of the two distributions to any $0.05n$ coordinates is uniformly distributed in $\{0, 1\}^{0.05n}$.)[9]
2. For all sufficiently large n, with probability at least $1 - 2^{-0.01n}$, it holds that Y is 0.1-far from Π.
   (Recall that this follows from a counting argument that relies on the exponentially vanishing density of Π (and on the volume of a Hamming ball of radius $0.1n$).)

Invoking Corollary 7.3, with $q(n) = 0.05n$, $\epsilon = 0.1$, $\eta_1 = \eta_2 = 0$, and $\eta_0 = 0.3$ (and sufficiently large n), the claim follows. (Indeed, $\eta_0 = 2^{-0.01n} < 0.3$ follows by Observation 2 (and $n \geq 200$), $\eta_2 = 0$ follows by Observation 1, and $\eta_1 = 0$ follows by the definition of X.) ∎

Digest: On the Simplicity of the Foregoing Proof. The simplicity of the proof of Proposition 7.4 is due to the fact that the projections of the two distributions on any set of q

---

[8] This holds since

$$\left|\mathbf{Pr}[M^{F_1'}(n, \epsilon) = 1] - \mathbf{Pr}[M^{F_0'}(n, \epsilon) = 1]\right| \leq \left|\mathbf{Pr}[M^{F_1'}(n, \epsilon) = 1] - \mathbf{Pr}[M^{F_1}(n, \epsilon) = 1]\right|$$

$$+ \left|\mathbf{Pr}[M^{F_1}(n, \epsilon) = 1] - \mathbf{Pr}[M^{F_0}(n, \epsilon) = 1]\right|$$

$$+ \left|\mathbf{Pr}[M^{F_0}(n, \epsilon) = 1] - \mathbf{Pr}[M^{F_0'}(n, \epsilon) = 1]\right|,$$

which is at most $\eta_1 + \eta_2 + \eta_0 < 1/3$.

[9] As shown in Exercise 7.4, the distinguishing gap of an algorithm that makes q adaptive queries (to a Boolean function) is at most 2^q times larger than the distinguishing gap of a corresponding nonadaptive algorithm (which makes q nonadaptive queries). Note that in the current case the two distributions are perfectly indistinguishable by nonadaptive algorithms of low query complexity (i.e., the corresponding distinguishing gap is zero).

coordinates are identically distributed, where $q + 1$ is the lower bound established by the proof. In more complicated cases, this strong assertion does not hold, and only weaker assertions can be proved. For example, if for some small $\eta > 0$, one can prove that the projections of the two distributions on any fixed set of $i \leq q$ coordinates are within statistical distance of at most $i \cdot \eta$, then we can only infer that a *nonadaptive* algorithm that makes q queries has a distinguishing gap of at most $q \cdot \eta$ (and it follows that nonadaptive testers must make $\Omega(1/\eta)$ queries). A lower bound on the query complexity of general (i.e., adaptive) testers follows by a straightforward emulation of adaptive oracle machines by nonadaptive ones (see Exercise 1.19), but better bounds may be obtained by a direct analysis of the distinguishing gap of adaptive oracle machines.

Another simple aspect in the proof of Proposition 7.4 is that F_1 was taken to be uniform over Π_n, whereas F_0 was close to being uniform over $\Gamma_\epsilon(\Pi_n)$. Typical cases in which other distributions are used were presented in Exercises 1.3 and 1.16. In the latter cases, the property Π_n is the closure (under some operation) of some basic property Φ_n, and the distribution F_1 is uniform over Φ_n.

7.2.3. Further Reflections

The fact that Theorems 7.1 and 7.2 (and Corollary 7.3) allow restricting the attention to deterministic algorithms (rather than considering all randomized algorithms) is less useful than one may think. In fact, many arguments that use these results can be generalized to relate to the distinguishing gap of randomized algorithms (see, e.g., the proof of Proposition 7.4). The *important aspect of the method is the focus on the distinguishing gap* (between a distribution concentrated on instances that have the property and a distribution concentrated on inputs that are far from the property). Still, in some cases the argument (or its presentation) is simplified by restricting attention to deterministic algorithm. (Note, however, that the proof of Theorem 7.1 would not have been much simpler if we were to relax it and refer to the behavior of randomized algorithms.)[10]

As just stated, the important aspect of the method is not the apparent gain obtained by restricting attention to deterministic algorithms (rather than randomized ones), but rather the apparent loss that arises when confining ourselves to a single distribution of instances (and showing that all "low-complexity" algorithms fail on this distribution). We stress that potentially we gave up on the possibility of tailoring a hard instance (or distribution of instances) to each potential algorithm, although in retrospect it turns out that nothing was lost (since the method is "complete" in the sense that any valid lower bound can be proved by using it). Nevertheless, as is often the case in mathematics and science, proving a stronger statement and/or using more restricted methods is sometimes easier.

Final Digest. The path we have taken (towards presenting Corollary 7.3) consisted of four steps, where the first two steps are packed into Theorem 7.1, and the last two steps are captured by Theorem 7.2 and Corollary 7.3, respectively. These four steps are abstracted as follows.

1. Requiring the lower bound prover to present a single distribution that foils all algorithms of low complexity.

---

[10] Also note that the proofs of Theorem 7.2 and Corollary 7.3 would remain intact, since Theorem 7.2 is proved by a reduction to Theorem 7.1, whereas Corollary 7.3 is proved by reduction to Theorem 7.2.

Recall that potentially this makes the task of the prover harder, since the claim being established is seemingly stronger, but as argued above, such a step may turn out to be beneficial. Furthermore, in the context of nonuniform complexity, this seemingly harder task is actually equivalent to the original task (i.e., the seemingly stronger claim is actually equivalent to the original one).

2. Showing that it suffices to establish the foregoing (foiling) claim for deterministic algorithms rather than for randomized ones.
   This step simplifies the presentation of lower bound proofs, but in many cases it is less helpful than one may imagine.

3. Requiring the lower bound prover to prove the foiling claim by showing that low-complexity algorithms cannot distinguish (a distribution over) instances that should be accepted from (a distribution over) instances that should be rejected.
   As with Step 1, potentially this makes the task of the prover harder, since the claim being established is seemingly stronger, but again such a step may turn out beneficial, and again the claim it seeks to establish is actually not stronger.

4. Showing that it suffices to establish a relaxed version of the indistinguishability claim. Like Step 2, the current step simplifies the presentation of lower bound proofs, freeing the prover from the need to deal with some issues either implicitly or explicitly. In the current case, we free the prover from presenting distributions that perfectly fit two corresponding sets, and allow it to present distributions that approximately fit these sets.

Hence, Steps 1 and 3 make the proving task potentially harder, although they actually help to focus attention on a task that is more intuitive and easier to think about. In contrast, Steps 2 and 4 simplify the proving task either by restricting its scope (see Step 2) or by relaxing the requirements (see Step 4).

7.3. Reduction from Communication Complexity

A somewhat unexpected methodology for proving lower bounds on the query complexity of property testing problems consists of reducing communication complexity problems to property testing problems. This is quite surprising because we reduce between two very different models. Specifically, property testing problems have no "topology" that can be naturally 2-partitioned to fit the two-party setting of communication complexity.

Teaching Note: Readers who are not familiar with communication complexity may want to skip the following paragraph. On the other hand, readers who are familiar with the communication complexity background may skim through Section 7.3.1 with the sole purpose of picking the specific notations that we shall use.

The Reduction at a Glance. In order to derive a lower bound on testing the property Π, one presents a mapping F of pairs of inputs $(x, y) \in \{0, 1\}^{\ell+\ell}$ for a two-party communication problem Ψ to $n(\ell)$-bit long inputs for Π such that $(x, y) \in \Psi$ implies $F(x, y) \in \Pi$ and $(x, y) \notin \Psi$ implies that $F(x, y)$ is ϵ-far from Π. Let $f_i(x, y)$ be the ith bit of $F(x, y)$, and suppose that B is an *upper bound* on the (deterministic) communication complexity of each f_i, and that C is a *lower bound* on the randomized communication complexity of Ψ. Then, ϵ-testing Π requires at least C/B queries.

Tedious Comments. For the sake of simplicity, we focus on problems that refer to the binary representation of objects (i.e., the objects are represented as sequences over a binary alphabet).[11] Also, our main presentation refers to finite problems that correspond to bit strings of fixed lengths, denoted ℓ and $n = n(\ell)$, respectively. The reader should think of these lengths as generic (or varying), and interpret the O-notation (as well as similar notions) as hiding universal constants (which do not depend on any parameter of the problems discussed).

7.3.1. Communication Complexity

We refer to the standard setting of communication complexity, and specifically to randomized two-party protocols in the model of shared randomness (cf. [195, Sec. 3]). The basic setting consists of two parties, each obtaining a private input, who wish to decide whether their input-pair resides in some set. We stress that it is required that both parties reach the same decision. Towards this end, they communicate with one another, based on some shared randomness (which is available to both parties, free of charge), and the issue is minimizing the amount of communication. We denote by $\langle A(x), B(y)\rangle(r)$ the (joint) output of the two parties, when the first party uses strategy A and gets input x, the second party uses strategy B and gets input y, and both parties have free access to the shared randomness r. Since many of the known reductions that use the methodology surveyed here actually reduce from promise problems, we present communication problems in this more general setting. The standard case of decision problems is obtained by using a trivial promise (i.e., $P = \{0, 1\}^{2\ell}$).[12]

Definition 7.5 (Two-party communication complexity): *Let* $\Psi = (P, S)$ *such that* $P, S \subseteq \{0, 1\}^{2\ell}$, *and* $\eta \geq 0$. *A two-party protocol that solves* Ψ *with error at most* η *is a pair of strategies* (A, B) *such that the following hold (w.r.t. some* $\rho = \rho(\ell)$):*

1. *If* $(x, y) \in P \cap S$, *then* $\mathbf{Pr}_{r \in \{0,1\}^{\rho}}[\langle A(x), B(y)\rangle(r) = 1] \geq 1 - \eta$.
2. *If* $(x, y) \in P \setminus S$, *then* $\mathbf{Pr}_{r \in \{0,1\}^{\rho}}[\langle A(x), B(y)\rangle(r) = 0] \geq 1 - \eta$.

The communication complexity of this protocol *is the maximum number of bits exchanged between the parties when the maximization is over all* $(x, y) \in P$ *and* $r \in \{0, 1\}^{\rho}$. *The* η-error communication complexity of Ψ, *denoted* $\mathsf{CC}_{\eta}(\Psi)$, *is the minimum communication complexity of all protocols that solve* Ψ *with error at most* η.

For a Boolean function $f : \{0, 1\}^{2\ell} \to \{0, 1\}$, the two-party communication problem of computing f is the promise problem $\Psi_f \overset{\text{def}}{=} (\{0, 1\}^{2\ell}, f^{-1}(1))$. Abusing notation, we let $\mathsf{CC}_{\eta}(f)$ denote $\mathsf{CC}_{\eta}(\Psi_f)$.

Note that randomized complexity with zero error (i.e., $\eta = 0$) collapses to deterministic complexity.[13] This is one reason that we kept η as a free parameter rather than setting it

---

[11] **Advanced comment:** For two different treatments of the general case of nonbinary alphabets, see [136, Sec. 6] and Exercise 7.5. Either way, the bottom line is that little is lost by considering only the binary representation.

[12] In general, P denotes the promise and S denotes the set of YES-instances. The task is to distinguish between instances in $P \cap S$ and instances in $P \setminus S$.

[13] **Advanced comment:** Note that $\mathsf{CC}_0(\cdot)$ is different from the *standard* notion of zero-error randomized communication complexity, since in the latter one considers the expected number of bits exchanged on the worst-case pair of inputs (where the expectation is over the shared randomness), whereas we consider the worst-case over both the

to a small constant (e.g., $\eta = 1/3$), as is the standard. Another reason for our choice is to allow greater flexibility in our presentation (cf., e.g., Theorem 7.7, where we use several different values of η). For the same reason, as seen next, we take the rather unusual choice of making the error probability explicit also in the context of property testing (where we also denote it by η).

7.3.2. The Methodology

For the sake of clarity, we spell out the version of the definition of property testing that we shall refer to. In this definition, as in most work on *lower bounds* in property testing, we fix the proximity parameter (denoted ϵ). As stated in the previous paragraph, in contrast to this fixing (of ϵ), we treat the error probability as a free parameter (rather than having it fixed to $1/3$).

Definition 7.6 (Property testing, redefined): *Let* $\Pi \subseteq \{0, 1\}^n$, *and* $\epsilon, \eta > 0$. *An* ϵ-tester with error η for Π *is a randomized oracle machine* T *that satisfies the following two conditions.*

1. *If* $z \in \Pi$, *then* $\mathbf{Pr}[T^z(n) = 1] \geq 1 - \eta$.
2. *If* $z \in \{0, 1\}^n$ *is* ϵ-far from Π, *then* $\mathbf{Pr}[T^z(n) = 0] \geq 1 - \eta$.

The query complexity of T *is the maximum number of queries that* T *makes, when the maximization is over all* $z \in \{0, 1\}^n$ *and all possible outcomes of the coin tosses of* T. *The* η-error query complexity of ϵ-testing Π, *denoted* $Q_\eta(\epsilon, \Pi)$, *is the minimum query complexity of all* ϵ-testers with error η for Π.

For any property Π and any constant $\eta > 0$, it holds that $Q_\eta(\epsilon, \Pi) = O(Q_{1/3}(\epsilon, \Pi))$, where the O-notation hides a $\log(1/\eta)$ factor. Thus, establishing a lower bound on the ϵ-testing query complexity of Π for any constant error probability yields the same asymptotic lower bound for the (standard) error level of $1/3$. In light of this fact, we may omit the constant error from our discussion; that is, when we say the query complexity of ϵ-testing Π we mean the $1/3$-error query complexity of ϵ-testing Π. Hence, we denote $Q(\epsilon, \Pi) = Q_{1/3}(\epsilon, \Pi)$.

With the foregoing preliminaries in place, we are ready to state the main result, which captures the methodology of obtaining lower bounds on the query complexity of property testing based on lower bounds on communication complexity. Using this methodology towards establishing a lower bound on the query complexity of testing the property Π requires finding a suitable communication complexity problem Ψ (for which adequate lower bounds are known) and presenting a reduction that satisfies the hypothesis of Theorem 7.7.

Theorem 7.7 (Property testing lower bounds via communication complexity): *Let* $\Psi = (P, S)$ *be a promise problem such that* $P, S \subseteq \{0, 1\}^{2\ell}$, *and let* $\Pi \subseteq \{0, 1\}^n$ *be a property. For* $\epsilon, \eta > 0$, *suppose that there exists a mapping* $F : \{0, 1\}^{2\ell} \to \{0, 1\}^n$ *that satisfies the following two conditions:*

shared randomness and the pair of inputs. While the difference between the expected complexity and the worst-case complexity is not very significant in the case of $\Theta(1)$-error communication complexity, it is crucial in the case of zero-error.

1. *For every $(x, y) \in P \cap S$, it holds that $F(x, y) \in \Pi$.*
2. *For every $(x, y) \in P \setminus S$, it holds that $F(x, y)$ is ϵ-far from Π.*

Then, $Q_\eta(\epsilon, \Pi) \geq CC_{2\eta}(\Psi)/B$, where $B = \max_{i \in [n]}\{CC_{\eta/\ell}(f_i)\}$ and $f_i(x, y)$ is the ith bit of $F(x, y)$. Furthermore, if $B = \max_{i \in [n]}\{CC_0(f_i)\}$, then $Q_\eta(\epsilon, \Pi) \geq CC_\eta(\Psi)/B$.

Hence, the reduction F "creates a gap" (between inputs $(x, y) \in P \cap S$ and inputs $(x, y) \in P \setminus S$) while merging the two parts of the input (i.e., x and y) into one string (i.e., $F(x, y)$). The fact that the parties in the communication complexity setting may have no direct access to bits of $F(x, y)$ is accounted for by the protocols for computing the bits of $F(x, y)$.

Proof: Given an ϵ-tester with error η for Π and communication protocols for the f_i's, we present a two-party protocol for solving Ψ. The key idea is that, using their shared randomness, the two parties (holding x and y, respectively) can emulate the execution of the ϵ-tester, while providing it with virtual access to $F(x, y)$. Specifically, when the tester queries the ith bit of the oracle, the parties provide it with the value of $f_i(x, y)$ by first executing the corresponding communication protocol. Details follow.

The protocol for solving Ψ proceeds as follows: On local input x (resp., y) and shared randomness $r = (r_0, r_1, \ldots, r_n) \in (\{0, 1\}^*)^{n+1}$, the first (resp., second) party invokes the ϵ-tester on randomness r_0, and answers the tester's queries by interacting with the other party. That is, each of the two parties invokes a local copy of the tester's program, but both copies are invoked on the same randomness (i.e., r_0), and are fed with identical answers to their (identical) queries. Specifically, when the tester issues a query $i \in [n]$, the parties compute the value of $f_i(x, y)$ by using the corresponding communication protocol, and feed $f_i(x, y)$ to (their local copy of) the tester. Specifically, denoting the latter protocol (i.e., pair of strategies) by (A_i, B_i), the parties answer with $\langle A_i(x), B_i(y) \rangle (r_i)$. When the tester halts, each party outputs the very output it has obtained from (its local copy of) the tester.

Turning to the analysis of this protocol, we note that the two local executions of the tester are identical, since they are fed with the same randomness and the same answers (to the same queries).[14] The total number of bits exchanged by the two parties is at most B times the query complexity of ϵ-tester; that is, the communication complexity of this protocol is at most $B \cdot q$, where q denotes the query complexity of the ϵ-tester.

Let us consider first the furthermore clause; that is, suppose that $B = \max_{i \in [n]}\{CC_0(f_i)\}$. In this case, the parties always provide the ϵ-tester, denoted T, with the correct answers to all its queries. Now, if $(x, y) \in P \cap S$, then $F(x, y) \in \Pi$, which implies that $\Pr[T^{F(x,y)}(n) = 1] \geq 1 - \eta$ (since T has error at most η), which in turn implies that the parties output 1 with probability at least $1 - \eta$. On the other hand, if $(x, y) \in P \setminus S$, then $F(x, y)$ is ϵ-far from Π, which implies that $\Pr[T^{F(x,y)}(n) = 0] \geq 1 - \eta$, which in turn implies that the parties output 0 with probability at least $1 - \eta$. Hence, in this case (assuming that T has query complexity $Q_\eta(\epsilon, \Pi)$), we get $CC_\eta(\Psi) \leq B \cdot Q_\eta(\epsilon, \Pi)$.

---

[14] Each of these answers is correct with a certain probability that depends on the corresponding subprotocols (A_i, B_i), but by convention both parties always obtain the same answer (from these subprotocols).

Turning to the main claim, we may assume that $q \stackrel{\text{def}}{=} Q_\eta(\epsilon, \Pi) \leq \ell$, since otherwise we can just use the trivial communication protocol for Ψ (which has complexity ℓ). Recall that if $(x, y) \in P \cap S$, then $\mathbf{Pr}[T^{F(x,y)}(n) = 1] \geq 1 - \eta$. However, in the emulation, T is given access to bits that are each correct only with probability $1 - (\eta/\ell)$, and hence the probability that the protocol outputs 1 is at least $1 - \eta - q \cdot (\eta/\ell) \geq 1 - 2\eta$. On the other hand, if $(x, y) \in P \setminus S$, then $\mathbf{Pr}[T^{F(x,y)}(n) = 0] \geq 1 - \eta$. Again, taking account of the errors in computing the f_i's, we conclude that the probability that the protocol outputs 0 in this case is at least $1 - 2\eta$. The claim follows (i.e., $CC_{2\eta}(\Psi) \leq B \cdot Q_\eta(\epsilon, \Pi)$, where $B = \max_{i \in [n]}\{CC_{\eta/\ell}(f_i)\}$). $\blacksquare$

7.3.3. Illustrating the Application of the Methodology

Recall that the set of ℓ-variate linear functions over GF(2) is ϵ-testable within query complexity $O(1/\epsilon)$. In contrast, we shall show that, for every even $k \leq \ell/2$, the set of linear (ℓ-variate) functions that depend on exactly k of their ℓ variables, called k-linear functions, cannot be 0.499-tested using $o(k)$ queries.[15] This will be shown by a reduction from the communication complexity of the $k/2$-disjointness function (in which the two parties are each given a $k/2$-subset of $[\ell]$ and need to determine whether these subsets are disjoint). We start by defining the k-linear property and the communication complexity known as $k/2$-disjointness.

Definition 7.8 (k-linearity): *A function $f : \mathrm{GF}(2)^\ell \to \mathrm{GF}(2)$ is called k-linear if it is linear and depends on exactly k of its variables; that is, $f(z) = \sum_{i \in I} z_i$ for some $I \subseteq [\ell]$ of cardinality k.*

In the following definition, one should think of ℓ-bit long strings as representing subsets of $[\ell]$. Hence, k-subsets are represented by strings of Hamming weight k, and set disjointness is represented by strings that share no bit position that holds the value 1. (Recall that the Hamming weight of z is denoted $\mathrm{wt}(z)$; that is, $\mathrm{wt}(z) = |\{i \in [|z|] : z_i = 1\}|$.)

Definition 7.9 ($k/2$-disjointness): *For $k : \mathbb{N} \to \mathbb{N}$, the communication problem called $k/2$-disjointness consists of solving $\{\mathrm{DISJ}_\ell^{(k)} = (P_\ell, S_\ell)\}_{\ell \in \mathbb{N}}$, where $P_\ell, S_\ell \subseteq \{0, 1\}^{2\ell}$ such that $(x, y) \in P_\ell$ if $\mathrm{wt}(x) = \mathrm{wt}(y) = k(\ell)/2$, and $(x, y) \in S_\ell$ if $I(x, y) \stackrel{\text{def}}{=} \{i \in [\ell] : x_i = y_i = 1\}$ is empty.*

Indeed, recalling that x and y are indicators of sets, the set $I(x, y)$ is the intersection of these sets.

For $k(\ell) \leq \ell/2$, using the celebrated result $CC_{1/3}(\mathrm{DISJ}_\ell^{(k)}) = \Omega(k(\ell))$, which is implicit in [176] (see also [54, Lem. 2.6]), we shall prove that 0.499-testing k-linearity requires $\Omega(k)$ queries, for every even $k \leq \ell/2$. This will be done by invoking Theorem 7.7.

Theorem 7.10 (On the complexity of k-linearity): *For every even $k(\ell) \leq \ell/2$, the query complexity of 0.499-testing $k(\ell)$-linearity is $\Omega(k(\ell))$.*

---

[15] The cases of odd k and $k > \ell/2$ will be treated in Section 7.4.

Proof: We present a reduction from the communication complexity problem $\{\text{DISJ}_\ell^{(k)} = (P_\ell, S_\ell)\}_{\ell \in \mathbb{N}}$ to testing $k(\ell)$-linearity of ℓ-variate functions, where in this case the size of the tested object is $n = 2^\ell$. The reduction $F : \{0, 1\}^{2\ell} \to \{0, 1\}^n$ maps pairs (x, y) of the communication problem to a function $g_{x,y} : \{0, 1\}^\ell \to \{0, 1\}$, which may be described by its truth-table $T_{x,y} \in \{0, 1\}^n$, such that $g_{x,y}(\zeta) = \sum_{i \in [\ell]} (x_i + y_i) \cdot \zeta_i$, where the arithmetics is mod 2. Indeed, $g_{x,y}(\zeta) = \sum_{i : x_i + y_i = 1} \zeta_i$, which means that $g_{x,y}$ is $|\{i \in [\ell] : x_i + y_i = 1\}|$-linear.

Let $k = k(\ell)$. Then, if $(x, y) \in P_\ell \cap S_\ell$ (i.e., x and y are "disjoint"), then $F(x, y) = g_{x,y}$ is k-linear, since $|\{i \in [\ell] : x_i + y_i = 1\}| = \text{wt}(x) + \text{wt}(y) = k$. On the other hand, if $(x, y) \in P_\ell \setminus S_\ell$, then $F(x, y) = g_{x,y}$ is $(k - 2 \cdot |I(x, y)|)$-linear, since

$$|\{i \in [\ell] : x_i + y_i = 1\}| = |\{i \in [\ell] : x_i = 1 \wedge y_i = 0\}| + |\{i \in [\ell] : x_i = 0 \wedge y_i = 1\}|$$

$$= \text{wt}(x) + \text{wt}(y) - 2 \cdot |\{i \in [\ell] : x_i = y_i = 1\}|,$$

which equals $k - 2 \cdot |I(x, y)|$. Hence, in this case $g_{x,y}$ is a linear function that is not k-linear. Using the fact that different linear functions are at distance $1/2$ of one another, it follows that $F(x, y) = g_{x,y}$ is 0.499-far from being k-linear.[16] Hence, F satisfies the conditions of Theorem 7.7.

We now consider the communication complexity of the functions that correspond to the bits of $F(x, y)$. Associating $[n]$ with $\{0, 1\}^\ell$ means that the bit associated with $\alpha \in \{0, 1\}^\ell$ in $F(x, y)$, denoted $F(x, y)_\alpha$ or $f_\alpha(x, y)$, is $g_{x,y}(\alpha) = \sum_{i \in [\ell]} (x_i + y_i) \cdot \alpha_i$. The key observation is that

$$\sum_{i \in [\ell]} (x_i + y_i) \cdot \alpha_i = \left(\sum_{i \in [\ell]} x_i \cdot \alpha_i \right) + \left(\sum_{i \in [\ell]} y_i \cdot \alpha_i \right).$$

This means that $f_\alpha(x, y) = F(x, y)_\alpha = \sum_i x_i \alpha_i + \sum_i y_i \alpha_i$. Hence, $f_\alpha(x, y)$ can be computed by the two-party protocol in which the first party (who holds x) sends $\sum_{i \in [\ell]} \alpha_i \cdot x_i$ to the second party, who (holds y and) responds with $\sum_{i \in [\ell]} \alpha_i \cdot y_i$. That is, the bit sent by each party is the inner product (mod 2) of the desired location α and its own input, and each party outputs the XOR of the two communicated bits.

Invoking the furthermore part of Theorem 7.7, with $B = 2$, it follows that the query complexity of 0.499-testing $k(\ell)$-linearity is at least $\text{CC}_{1/3}(\text{DISJ}_\ell^{(k)})/2 = \Omega(k(\ell))$. ∎

A Generalization, which May Further Clarify the Argument. Theorem 7.10 is a special case of the following result that refers to properties that are subsets of linear codes (i.e., nonlinear sub-codes of linear codes). Specifically, for any linear code of constant relative distance, we consider the set of codewords that correspond to the encoding of (ℓ-bit long) strings of a specific Hamming weight (i.e., $k(\ell)$). Theorem 7.10 refers to the special case in which the code is the Hadamard code (i.e., $n = 2^\ell$).

Theorem 7.11 (On the complexity of testing some sets of codewords in linear codes): *Let $\{C_\ell : \{0, 1\}^\ell \to \{0, 1\}^n\}_{\ell \in \mathbb{N}}$ be a family of* linear *codes (i.e., $C_\ell(x \oplus y) = C_\ell(x) \oplus C_\ell(y)$) of constant relative distance. Then, for some constant $\epsilon > 0$ and any*

---

[16] Recall that ϵ-far (from Π) was defined as being at distance (from Π) that is strictly larger than ϵ. Indeed, the constant 0.499 can be replaced by any constant in $(0, 0.5)$.

function $k : \mathbb{N} \to \mathbb{N}$ *such that* $k(\ell)$ *is even and* $k(\ell) \leq \ell/2$, *the query complexity of* ϵ-*testing the property*

$$\Pi_n \stackrel{\text{def}}{=} \{C_\ell(z) : z \in \{0, 1\}^\ell \wedge \text{wt}(z) = k(\ell)\} \tag{7.8}$$

is $\Omega(k(\ell))$. *That is,* $\mathsf{Q}(\epsilon, \Pi_n) = \Omega(k(\ell))$. *Furthermore,* $\epsilon > 0$ *may be any constant that is smaller than the relative distance of the code* C_ℓ.

Note that Π_n is a code; actually, it is a subcode of the (linear) code C, but Π_n is not necessarily a linear code (i.e., $w, w' \in \Pi_n$ does not necessarily imply $w \oplus w' \in \Pi_n$). In the special case that C is the Hadamard code, the property Π_n is $k(\ell)$-linearity; that is, the codewords of the Hadamard code correspond to linear functions (from $\text{GF}(2)^\ell$ to $\text{GF}(2)$) and the codewords of Π_n are $k(\ell)$-linear functions.[17] We stress that testing Π_n is hard although testing the original linear code (i.e., C_ℓ) may be easy. The following proof is very similar to the proof of Theorem 7.10, but it may be more clear because Π_n is now viewed as a property of n-bit strings (rather than as a property of Boolean functions on the domain $[n] \equiv \{0, 1\}^\ell$).

Proof: Again, we reduce from the communication problem $\{\text{DISJ}_\ell^{(k)} = (P_\ell, S_\ell)\}_{\ell \in \mathbb{N}}$, and invoke Theorem 7.7. The reduction maps (x, y) to $F(x, y) = C_\ell(x \oplus y)$, and the ith bit of $C_\ell(x \oplus y) = C_\ell(x) \oplus C_\ell(y)$ can be computed by exchanging the ith bits of $C_\ell(x)$ and $C_\ell(y)$.

We again observe that for every $(x, y) \in P_\ell$ it holds that $\text{wt}(x \oplus y) = k(\ell) - 2 \cdot |I(x, y)|$, where $I(x, y) = \{i \in [\ell] : x_i = y_i = 1\}$. Hence, if $(x, y) \in P_\ell \cap S_\ell$ (i.e., x and y are "disjoint"), then $\text{wt}(x \oplus y) = k(\ell)$ and $F(x, y) = C_\ell(x \oplus y)$ is in Π_n. On the other hand, if $(x, y) \in P_\ell \setminus S_\ell$, then $\text{wt}(x \oplus y) \neq k(\ell)$ and $F(x, y) = C_\ell(x \oplus y)$ is ϵ-far from Π_n, where $\epsilon > 0$ is any constant that is smaller than the relative distance of the code C_ℓ.

Finally, we invoke again the furthermore part of Theorem 7.7 with $B = 2$, and it follows that the query complexity of ϵ-testing Π_n is at least $\text{CC}_{1/3}(\text{DISJ}_\ell^{(k)})/2 = \Omega(k(\ell))$. ∎

Another Implication of Theorem 7.11. As stated previously, Theorem 7.10 follows as a special case of Theorem 7.11. Another result that follows easily from Theorem 7.11 is a generalization of Theorem 7.10 to the case of k-sparse homogeneous polynomials of degree d (i.e., polynomials that have exactly k monomials such that each monomial is the product of d variables). We state the latter result for polynomials over $\text{GF}(2)$, but it can be proved also for larger finite fields (while losing a factor that is logarithmic in the field size).[18]

Corollary 7.12 (On the complexity of k-sparse polynomials): *Let* $d, m, k \in \mathbb{N}$ *and* Π_n *denote the set* m-*variate homogeneous polynomials of degree* d *over* $\text{GF}(2)$ *having exactly* k *monomials, where* $n = 2^m$. *Then, if* $k \leq \binom{m}{d}/2$ *is even, then the query complexity of* $0.99 \cdot 2^{-d}$-*testing* Π_n *is* $\Omega(k)$.

---

[17] **Advanced comment:** Indeed, in this case Π_n is not a linear code; that is, if f and g are k-linear functions, then the linear function $f + g$ is not necessarily k-linear.

[18] See Exercise 7.6.

Proof: For $\ell = \binom{m}{d}$, consider the Reed–Muller code of order d, which maps the ℓ-bit long description of an m-variate polynomial of degree d over GF(2) to its evaluation at all points of GF(2)^m. This code has relative distance 2^{-d}, and so the claim follows by Theorem 7.11. ∎

7.4. Reduction among Testing Problems

A natural method for obtaining lower bounds is via reductions. Indeed, this method is common practice in computability as well as in the theory of NP-completeness and in the study of other computational complexity classes (see, e.g., [131]). In each case, the definition of a reduction should preserve the relevant notion of feasible computation. Hence, when using reductions in the context of property testing, we should use reductions that preserve easy testability. Specifically, when we reduce the testing property of Π to the testing property of Π', it should be possible to answer each query to the reduced instance by making few queries to the original instance. In addition, the reduction should preserve the distance to the property, at least to some extent.

Teaching Note: For the sake of simplicity, we confine ourselves to many-to-one reductions; that is, reductions that map an instance of the original problem to a single instance of the reduced problem such that YES-instances are mapped to YES-instances and NO-instances are mapped to NO-instances. (In the context of property testing, instances in Π are mapped to instances in Π' and instances that are far from Π are mapped to instances that are far from Π'.) That is, we consider the analogue of Karp-reductions rather than the analogue of Cook-reduction in which the reduction is a machine that given an instance of the original problem may issue queries to various instances of the reduced problem (see [131, Sec. 2.2.1]).

Definition 7.13 (Local reductions): *Let $\Pi = \cup_{n\in\mathbb{N}}\Pi_n$ and $\Pi' = \cup_{n\in\mathbb{N}}\Pi'_n$ be such that Π_n and Π'_n contains functions from $[n]$ to R_n and R'_n, respectively. A mapping F_n from the set of functions $\{f : [n] \to R_n\}$ to the set of functions $\{f' : [n'] \to R'_{n'}\}$ is called a q-local (ϵ, ϵ')-reduction of Π_n to $\Pi'_{n'}$ if for every $f : [n] \to R_n$ the following conditions hold.*

1. Locality (local reconstruction): *The value of $F_n(f)$ at any point $i \in [n']$ is determined by the value of f at q points in $[n]$; that is, there exist functions $Q_n : [n'] \to [n]^q$ and $V_n : [n'] \times R_n^q \to R'_{n'}$ such that $V_n(i, f(i_1), \ldots, f(i_q)) = (F_n(f))(i)$, where $(i_1, \ldots, i_q) = Q_n(i)$.*
2. Preservation of the properties: *If $f \in \Pi_n$, then $F_n(f) \in \Pi'_{n'}$.*
3. Partial preservation of distance to the properties: *If f is ϵ-far from Π_n, then $F_n(f)$ is ϵ'-far from $\Pi'_{n'}$.*

For $q : \mathbb{N} \to \mathbb{N}$, the ensemble $\{F_n\}_{n\in\mathbb{N}}$ is called a q-local (ϵ, ϵ')-reduction of Π to Π' if there exists a function $L : \mathbb{N} \to \mathbb{N}$ such that for every $n \in \mathbb{N}$ it holds that F_n is a $q(n)$-local (ϵ, ϵ')-reduction of Π_n to $\Pi'_{L(n)}$. In such a case we say that Π is q-locally (ϵ, ϵ')-reducible to Π' (with length function L).

Indeed, Definition 7.13 corresponds to a deterministic reduction, and this suffices in many cases. Nevertheless, we shall present a randomized version of Definition 7.13 at a later stage. But before doing so, let us examine the effect of such reductions.

Theorem 7.14 (Local reductions preserve testability): *Let $\Pi = \cup_{n\in\mathbb{N}}\Pi_n$ and $\Pi' = \cup_{n'\in\mathbb{N}}\Pi'_{n'}$ be as in Definition 7.13. Suppose that Π is q-locally (ϵ, ϵ')-reducible to Π' with length function L. Then, if Π' can be ϵ'-tested with $q'(n', \epsilon')$ queries, then Π can be ϵ-tested with $q(n) \cdot q'(L(n), \epsilon')$ queries.*

Theorem 7.14 states the positive effect of a local reduction, but in the context of proving lower bounds one uses its counterpositive, which asserts that *if the query complexity of ϵ-testing Π exceeds $B(n, \epsilon)$, then the query complexity of ϵ'-testing $\Pi' = \cup_{n'}\Pi'_{n'}$ exceeds $B'(n', \epsilon') = B(n, \epsilon)/q(n)$ for any $n \in L^{-1}(n')$.* We shall state this counterpositive below, after proving Theorem 7.14.

Proof: Let us fix any $n \in \mathbb{N}$ and let $n' = L(n)$. Given an ϵ'-tester T' for $\Pi'_{n'}$ as in the hypothesis, we construct an ϵ-tester for Π_n as follows. On input $f : [n] \to R_n$, the new tester invokes T' and answers each of its queries by using the local reconstruction procedure (i.e., Q_n and V_n) that is associated with the local reduction, denoted F_n. That is, the query $i \in [n']$ is answered by querying f at $i_1, \ldots, i_q$, where $(i_1, \ldots, i_q) = Q_n(i)$, and providing the value $V_n(i, f(i_1), \ldots, f(i_q))$. Hence, this tester, denoted T, makes $q(n)$ queries per each of the $q'(n', \epsilon')$ queries issued by T'. When T' halts, T just outputs the verdict provided by T'.

Turning to the analysis of T, we first observe that, on input f, algorithm T answers each query of T' according to $F_n(f)$. Hence, if $f \in \Pi_n$, then $F_n(f)$ is in $\Pi'_{n'}$, and T' will accept (with probability at least $2/3$) and so will T. On the other hand, if f is ϵ-far from Π_n, then $F_n(f)$ is ϵ'-far from $\Pi'_{n'}$, and T' will reject (with probability at least $2/3$) and so will T. The theorem follows. ∎

Corollary 7.15 (Lower bounds via local reductions, a counterpositive of Theorem 7.14): *Let $\Pi = \cup_{n\in\mathbb{N}}\Pi_n$ and $\Pi' = \cup_{n'\in\mathbb{N}}\Pi'_{n'}$ be as in Definition 7.13. Suppose that Π is q-locally (ϵ, ϵ')-reducible to Π' with length function L. Then, if the query complexity of ϵ-testing Π exceeds $B(n, \epsilon)$, then the query complexity of ϵ'-testing $\Pi' = \cup_{n'}\Pi'_{n'}$ exceeds $B'(n', \epsilon') = \max_{n:L(n)=n'}\{B(n, \epsilon)/q(n)\}$.*

Typically, $L : \mathbb{N} \to \mathbb{N}$ is nondecreasing and one-to-one, and so we get $B'(n', \epsilon') = \frac{B(L^{-1}(n'), \epsilon)}{q(L^{-1}(n'))}$ for any n' in the image of L.

Illustrating the Application of the Method. Recall that Theorem 7.10 provides a lower bound on the query complexity of testing k-linearity (of ℓ-variate Boolean functions) only in the case that $k(\ell) \leq \ell/2$ is even. Using two simple reductions, we establish the following.

Proposition 7.16 (Theorem 7.10, extended): *For every $k : \mathbb{N} \to \mathbb{N}$, the query complexity of 0.499-testing k-linearity is $\Omega(\min(k(\ell), \ell - k(\ell)))$.*

Proof Sketch: We first reduce ϵ-testing k-linearity of ℓ-variate Boolean functions to ϵ-testing $(k + 1)$-linearity of $(\ell + 2)$-variate Boolean functions. (This reduction allows to switch the parity of the linearity parameter.)[19] The reduction just maps

---

[19] We reduce to $(\ell + 2)$-variate functions, rather than to $(\ell + 1)$-variate functions, in order to have $k + 1 \leq (\ell + 2)/2$ whenever $k \leq \ell/2$. (But, actually, this is not really crucial.)

$f : \{0, 1\}^\ell \to \{0, 1\}$ to $f' : \{0, 1\}^{\ell+2} \to \{0, 1\}$ such that $f'(x_1 \cdots x_\ell x_{\ell+1} x_{\ell+2}) = f(x_1 \cdots x_\ell) + x_{\ell+1}$. Hence, each query to f' can be answered by making a single query to f (i.e., the query $\sigma_1 \cdots \sigma_{\ell+1} \sigma_{\ell+2}$ is answered by querying f at $\sigma_1 \cdots \sigma_\ell$ and returning $f(\sigma_1 \cdots \sigma_\ell) + \sigma_{\ell+1}$). Observe the distance of f from being k-linear equals the distance of f' from being $(k+1)$-linear. In particular, this yields a 1-local $(0.499, 0.499)$-reduction (with length function $L(2^\ell) = 4 \cdot 2^\ell$) from the case of even $k \le \ell/2$ to the case of odd $(k + 1) \le (\ell/2) + 1 = (\ell + 2)/2$. Hence, applying Corollary 7.15, the lower bound of Theorem 7.10 is extended to the case of an odd linearity parameter.

The second reduction is from testing k-linearity of ℓ-variate Boolean functions (when $k \le \ell/2$) to testing $(\ell - k)$-linearity of ℓ-variate Boolean functions (when $\ell - k \ge \ell/2$). The reduction just maps $f : \{0, 1\}^\ell \to \{0, 1\}$ to $f' : \{0, 1\}^\ell \to \{0, 1\}$ such that $f'(x) = f(x) + \sum_{i \in [\ell]} x_i$, where $x = x_1 \cdots x_\ell$. Again, each query to f' can be answered by making a single query to f. In this case the distance of f from being k-linear equals the distance of f' from being $(\ell - k)$-linear. In particular, this yields a 1-local $(0.499, 0.499)$-reduction of k-linearity to $(\ell - k)$-linearity. Hence, applying Corollary 7.15, the $\Omega(k)$ lower bound for testing k-linearity when $k \le \ell/2$, yields a lower bound of $\Omega(k)$ for testing $(\ell - k)$-linearity when $\ell - k \ge \ell/2$. ∎

Randomized Reductions (Advanced Comment). Definition 7.13 captures only deterministic reductions. This is reflected in the main deterministic mapping F_n as well as in the auxiliary functions Q_n and V_n (used in the locality condition). Allowing randomized auxiliary algorithms in the locality condition is straightforward (and one should just require that they yield the correct value with probability at least $2/3$). More care should be taken when allowing a randomized mapping F_n: In such a case, its randomness should be handed over to the algorithms used in the locality condition, or else different invocations of (the local reconstruction procedure captured by) these algorithms may not yield values that are consistent with a single function $f' : [n'] \to R'_{n'}$ (but may rather yield values that fit different functions $f' : [n'] \to R'_{n'}$).[20] For the sake of simplicity, in the following definition, we view the randomized mapping as a distribution of (deterministic) mappings and allow the auxiliary algorithms to depend on the specific mapping chosen from that distribution.

Definition 7.17 (Randomized local reductions): *Let $\Pi = \cup_{n \in \mathbb{N}} \Pi_n$ and $\Pi' = \cup_{n \in \mathbb{N}} \Pi'_n$ be as in Definition 7.13. A distribution of mappings $\mathcal{F}_n$ from the set of functions $\{f : [n] \to R_n\}$ to the set of functions $\{f' : [n'] \to R'_{n'}\}$ is called a* randomized *q-local (ϵ, ϵ')-reduction of Π_n to $\Pi'_{n'}$ if for every $f : [n] \to R_n$ the following conditions hold with probability at least $5/6$ when the mapping F_n is selected according to the distribution $\mathcal{F}_n$.*

1. Locality (local reconstruction): *There exist randomized algorithms $Q_n : [n'] \to [n]^q$ and $V_n : [n'] \times R_n^q \to R'_{n'}$, which may depend on F_n, such that for every $i \in [n']$ it holds that*

$$\mathbf{Pr}_{(i_1, \ldots, i_q) \leftarrow Q_n(i)}[V_n(i, f(i_1), \ldots, f(i_q)) = (F_n(f))(i)] \ge 2/3. \qquad (7.9)$$

2. Preservation of the properties: *If $f \in \Pi_n$, then $F_n(f) \in \Pi'_{n'}$.*

---

[20] A similar issue arises in the general definition of local computation algorithms, to be discussed in Section 12.5.

3. Partial preservation of distance to the properties: *If f is ϵ-far from Π_n, then $F_n(f)$ is ϵ'-far from $\Pi'_{n'}$.*

Randomized local reduction of Π to Π' are defined analogously to Definition 7.13.

Hence, if $f \in \Pi_n$ (resp., if f is ϵ-far from Π_n), then, with probability at least 5/6, over the choice of F_n, Conditions 1 and 2 both hold (resp., Conditions 1 and 3 both hold). When applying such a reduction, the error probability of the algorithms guaranteed by the locality condition (i.e., Condition 1) should be reduced according to the application (see Exercise 7.10).[21] (The error probability of the ϵ'-tester for Π' should also be reduced, say, to 0.1.)

Another Type of Reductions. We reinterpret a result that appeared in Chapter 5 as a reduction among (related) property testing problems. Specifically, we refer to Exercise 5.5, which for a "random self-reducible" property Π' reduces testing $\Pi' \cap \Pi''$ to testing both Π' and Π''. When Π' is easy to test, this yields a reduction of testing $\Pi' \cap \Pi''$ to testing Π''. For the sake of clarity, we first restate the foregoing result, which refers to the notion of random self-reducibility as defined in Section 5.2.3.

Theorem 7.18 (Exercise 5.5, restated):[22] *Let Π' and Π'' be sets of functions defined over D. Suppose that functions in Π' are randomly self-reducible by q queries, and that Π' and Π'' are ϵ-testable using $q'(\epsilon)$ and $q''(\epsilon)$ queries, respectively. Then, for every $\epsilon_0 < 1/q$ and $\epsilon > 0$, the property $\Pi' \cap \Pi''$ is ϵ-testable using $O(q'(\min(\epsilon, 1/3q))) + q \cdot \widetilde{O}(q''(\epsilon_0))$ queries.*

The positive application of this result yields a tester for $\Pi' \cap \Pi''$ when given testers for Π' and Π''. Here, we present a negative application: Given a lower bound on the query complexity of $\Pi' \cap \Pi''$ and assuming that q and $q'(\epsilon)$ are both relatively small, we derive a lower bound on the query complexity of Π''.

Corollary 7.19 (Negative application of Theorem 7.18): *Let Π' be a set of functions defined over D such that functions in Π' are randomly self-reducible by q queries, and Π' is ϵ-testable using $q'(\epsilon)$ queries. Suppose that $Q(\epsilon)$ is a lower bound on the query complexity of ϵ-testing $\Pi \cap \Pi''$, where Π'' is also a set of functions defined over D. Then, for every $\epsilon_0 < 1/q$, the query complexity of ϵ_0-testing Π'' is $\max_{\epsilon \in (0, 1/3q]}\{\widetilde{\Omega}((Q(\epsilon) - O(q'(\epsilon)))/q)\}$.*[23]

---

[21] Specifically, if the ϵ'-tester for Π' makes q' queries, then the error probability of these algorithms should be reduced to $1/10q'$.

[22] Recall that Exercise 5.5 is proved based on Theorem 5.11, which postulates the existence of a decision procedure for the promise problem (Π', Π'') rather than a tester for Π'' as postulated here. But as suggested in the guideline for Exercise 5.5, for any $\epsilon_0 < 1/q$, a tester of query complexity $q''(\epsilon)$ for Π'' yields a procedure of query complexity $q''(\epsilon_0)$ for distinguishing inputs in $\Pi' \cap \Pi''$ from inputs in $\Pi' \setminus \Pi''$. This is because every input in $\Pi' \setminus \Pi''$ is at distance at least $1/q$ from Π'' (since self-reducibility by q queries implies that distinct functions in Π' are at distance at least $1/q$ apart). Note that we need to invoke the tester for Π'' with a proximity parameter smaller than $1/q$ so to guarantee that inputs at distance exactly $1/q$ are rejected (w.h.p.).

[23] The polylogarithmic factor in the $\widetilde{\Omega}$-notation is merely a logarithmic factor. We stress that all constants are universal (i.e., they are independent of Π' and Π''). Note that we lower-bounded $\max_{\epsilon \in (0,1]}\{\widetilde{\Omega}((Q(\epsilon) - O(q'(\min(\epsilon, 1/3q))))/q)\}$ by $\max_{\epsilon \in (0, 1/3q]}\{\widetilde{\Omega}((Q(\epsilon) - O(q'(\epsilon)))/q)\}$, losing nothing in the typical cases in which $Q(1/3q) \geq \max_{\epsilon \in [1/3q, 1]}\{Q(\epsilon)\}$.

As an illustration to the application of Corollary 7.19, we use it to derive a lower bound on testing k-juntas. Toward this application, we consider the set of $k^{\leq}$-linear functions defined as the union of the sets of i-linear function for $i = 0, 1, \ldots, k$, and note that the lower bound for k-linearity holds also for $k^{\leq}$-linearity (see Exercise 7.7). The key observation is that the set of $k^{\leq}$-linear functions is the intersection of the set of linear functions and the set of k-juntas.

Corollary 7.20 (A lower bound on the query complexity of testing k-juntas): *For every $k(\ell) \leq (\ell/2) - 2$, the complexity of 0.499-testing k-juntas is $\widetilde{\Omega}(k)$.*

We comment that a linear (in k) lower bound can be obtained by direct reduction from a communication complexity problem; see Exercise 7.8.

Proof: We let Π' denote the set of linear functions, and Π'' denote the set of $k(\ell)$-juntas. Recall that the set of linear functions is randomly self-reducible by two queries, and that it ϵ-testable by $O(1/\epsilon)$ queries. Observing that $\Pi' \cap \Pi''$ is the set of $k(\ell)^{\leq}$-linear functions, we use the fact that 0.499-testing this set requires $\Omega(k(\ell))$ queries (see Exercise 7.7). Now, invoking Corollary 7.19, we infer that 0.499-testing Π'' requires $\widetilde{\Omega}((k(\ell) - O(1))/2)$ queries. ∎

7.5. Lower Bounds for Restricted Testers

Restricted algorithms may have higher complexity than general ones, and proving lower bounds regarding their complexity may be easier (even when these lower bounds are higher). Two natural restrictions in the context of property testing are the restriction to one-sided error probability and the restriction to nonadaptive queries. We mention that separations between such restricted testers and general testers are known in many (natural) cases (see, e.g., testing graph properties in the bounded-degree model), but there are also (natural) cases in which the restriction does not increase the complexity of testing (e.g., testing linear properties [47]).[24]

7.5.1. One-Sided Error Testers

When analyzing one-sided error testers, the ("indistinguishability") method captured by Corollary 7.3 takes a simpler form. The point is that in this case, any function f having the property Π must be accepted by the tester with probability 1 (since the tester is allowed no error when $f \in \Pi$). Hence, it suffices to find a distribution F_0 of functions that are (typically) far from Π such that no low-complexity machine that accepts each $f \in \Pi$ with probability 1 can reject F_0 with probability greater than $1/2$.[25]

---

[24] As shown in Theorem 9.2, nonadaptive testers are very restricted in the bounded-degree graph model (e.g., when compared to the adaptive testers presented in Section 9.2). The bounded-degree model also features a dramatic gap between the complexity of one-sided error and two-sided error testers for cycle-freeness (see Section 9.2.5 versus Theorem 9.17). In contrast, when testing linear properties, nonadaptivity and one-sided error can be obtained at no extra cost [47].

[25] Here we assume that "typically" means with probability greater than $5/6$; that is, we assume that $\mathbf{Pr}[F_0 \in \Gamma_\epsilon(\Pi_n)] \geq 5/6$.

Theorem 7.21 (The method of indistinguishability, a one-sided error version): *Let $\Pi = \cup_{n\in\mathbb{N}}\Pi_n$, $\Gamma_\epsilon(\Pi_n)$, and $q : \mathbb{N} \times (0, 1] \to \mathbb{N}$ be as in Theorem 7.2. Suppose that for some $\epsilon > 0$, $\eta_0 > 0$ and $n \in \mathbb{N}$, there exist a distribution F_0 such that $\mathbf{Pr}[F_0 \in \Gamma_\epsilon(\Pi_n)] \geq 1 - \eta_0$, and for every deterministic oracle machine M that makes at most $q(n, \epsilon)$ queries and accepts each $f \in \Pi$ with probability 1 (i.e., $|\mathbf{Pr}[M^f(n, \epsilon) = 1] = 1$ for each $f \in \Pi_n$) it holds that $\mathbf{Pr}[M^{F_0}(n, \epsilon) = 1] > \frac{1}{3} + \eta_0$. Then, the query complexity of ϵ-testing Π with one-sided error probability is greater than $q(\cdot, \epsilon)$.*

Considering a machine M as postulated in Theorem 7.21, note that such a machine cannot reject a function when its partial view of it (i.e., the sequence of query and answer pairs)[26] matches a partial view of a function in Π. Hence, the probability that M accepts F_0 (i.e., $\mathbf{Pr}[M^{F_0}(n, \epsilon) = 1]$) may be replaced by the probability that M sees a partial view of F_0 that matches some function in Π.[27] Thus, the hypothesis of Theorem 7.21 may be reformulated as follows: *There exists a distribution F_0 such that $\mathbf{Pr}[F_0 \in \Gamma_\epsilon(\Pi_n)] \geq 1 - \eta_0$, and for every deterministic oracle machine M that makes at most $q(n, \epsilon)$ queries it holds that the probability that M sees a partial view of F_0 that matches some function in Π is greater than $\frac{1}{3} + \eta_0$.*

Proof Sketch: Suppose that T is a one-sided error probability tester for Π, and let F_0' denote the distribution F_0 conditioned on $F_0 \in \Gamma_\epsilon(\Pi_n)$. Then, $\mathbf{Pr}[T^{F_0'}(n, \epsilon) = 1] \leq 1/3$. Let T_r denote a residual deterministic machine (obtained by fixing the coins of T to r) such that $\mathbf{Pr}[T_r^{F_0'}(n, \epsilon) = 1] \leq 1/3$. Then, $\mathbf{Pr}[T_r^{F_0}(n, \epsilon) = 1] < 1/3 + \eta_0$, whereas $T_r^f(n, \epsilon) = 1$ for every $f \in \Pi$ (since $\mathbf{Pr}[T^f(n, \epsilon) = 1] = 1$). It follows that T must have query complexity greater than $q(\cdot, \epsilon)$. ∎

The Actual Methodology. As hinted in the discussion following the statement of Theorem 7.21, the methodology that arises here is to find distribution F_0 such that $\mathbf{Pr}[F_0 \in \Gamma_\epsilon(\Pi_n)] \geq 1 - \eta_0$, and to show that any oracle machine that makes at most $q(n, \epsilon)$ queries sees, with probability greater than $\frac{1}{3} + \eta_0$ over the choice of F_0, a partial view that matches some function in Π.

Reduction from Communication Complexity. The methodology described in Section 7.3 can be adapted to provide a reduction among the *one-sided error probability versions* of the two types of problems. For details see [54, 136].

7.5.2. Nonadaptive Testers

When analyzing nonadaptive testers, we can also obtain a simplification of the ("indistinguishability") method captured by Corollary 7.3. In this case, it suffices to consider nonadaptive *deterministic* machines, which is the same as just considering the projection of the relevant distributions on any size-bounded subset of the function domain.

---

[26] The partial view that M has of f is the sequence of pairs $((i_1, f(i_1)), \ldots, (i_q, f(i_q)))$, where i_{j+1} is the $j + 1^{\mathrm{st}}$ query made by M after receiving the oracle answers $f(i_1), \ldots, f(i_j)$.

[27] Note that the one-sided error condition only mandates that M must accept if its partial view of the input function matches some function in Π, but it need not reject otherwise. Nevertheless, M may well reject if its partial view does not match any function in Π.

Theorem 7.22 (The method of indistinguishability, a nonadaptive version): *Let* $\Pi = \cup_{n \in \mathbb{N}} \Pi_n$, $\Gamma_\epsilon(\Pi_n)$, *and* $q : \mathbb{N} \times (0, 1] \to \mathbb{N}$ *be as in Theorem 7.2. Suppose that for some* $\epsilon > 0$, $\eta_0, \eta_1, \eta_2 > 0$ *and* $n \in \mathbb{N}$, *there exist distributions* F_1 *and* F_0 *such that* $\mathbf{Pr}[F_1 \in \Pi_n] \geq 1 - \eta_1$ *and* $\mathbf{Pr}[F_0 \in \Gamma_\epsilon(\Pi_n)] \geq 1 - \eta_0$, *and for every set* $Q \subset [n]$ *of size* $q(n, \epsilon)$ *it holds that the projection of* F_1 *on* Q *is* η_2-close *to the projection of* F_0 *on* Q; *that is, for* $q = q(n, \epsilon)$ *and every* $i_1, \ldots, i_q \in [n]$, *it holds that*

$$\frac{1}{2} \cdot \sum_{v_1, \ldots, v_q \in R_n} |\mathbf{Pr}[F_1(i_1) \cdots F_1(i_q) = v_1 \cdots v_q]$$

$$- \mathbf{Pr}[F_0(i_1) \cdots F_0(i_q) = v_1 \cdots v_q]| \leq \eta_2. \tag{7.10}$$

If $\eta_0 + \eta_1 + \eta_2 < 1/3$, *then the* nonadaptive *query complexity of* ϵ-testing Π *is greater than* $q(\cdot, \epsilon)$.

Proof Sketch: Following the argument that led to Corollary 7.3, observe that it implies that *if the distinguishing gap of deterministic nonadaptive machines that make at most* $q(n, \epsilon)$ *queries is at most* η_2, *then the current claim follows.* To establish the former condition, note that, on input parameters n and ϵ, any deterministic nonadaptive machine M (of query complexity $q = q(n, \epsilon)$) queries each function at the same q positions, denoted $i_1^{M,n,\epsilon}, \ldots, i_q^{M,n,\epsilon}$. Hence, M's distinguishing gap between F_1 and F_0 is upper-bounded by the statistical distance between $(F_1(i_1^{M,n,\epsilon}), \ldots, F_1(i_q^{M,n,\epsilon}))$ and $(F_0(i_1^{M,n,\epsilon}), \ldots, F_0(i_q^{M,n,\epsilon}))$, which is captured in Eq. (7.10). ∎

Reduction from Communication Complexity. Adapting the methodology described in Section 7.3 to nonadaptive testers yields a method for lower-bounding their query complexity based on lower bounds on the complexity of *one-way communication protocols*.[28] Actually, it is even more natural to reduce from an even weaker model of communication protocols, known as the *simultaneous model*. In this model, each of the two parties holding an input sends a single message to an auxiliary party, called the referee (who has access only to the common random string), and the referee is the sole producer of output (see Figure 7.1). The proof of Theorem 7.7 is easily adapted to yield the following result, where Q^{na} and $\mathsf{CC}^{\mathrm{sim}}$ denote the corresponding complexity measures (i.e., the query complexity of nonadaptive testers and the communication complexity of simultaneous protocols).

Theorem 7.23 (The communication complexity method, a nonadaptive version): *Let* $\Psi = (P, S)$ *be a promise problem such that* $P, S \subseteq \{0, 1\}^{2\ell}$, *and let* $\Pi \subseteq \{0, 1\}^n$ *be a property. For* $\epsilon, \eta > 0$, *suppose that there exists a mapping* $F : \{0, 1\}^{2\ell} \to \{0, 1\}^n$ *that satisfies the following two conditions:*

1. *For every* $(x, y) \in P \cap S$, *it holds that* $F(x, y) \in \Pi$.
2. *For every* $(x, y) \in P \setminus S$, *it holds that* $F(x, y)$ *is* ϵ-far *from* Π.

---

[28] In such protocols the first party sends a single message to the second party, who produces the output.

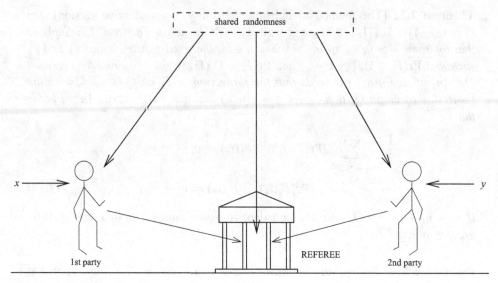

Figure 7.1: The simultaneous communication model.

Then, $Q_\eta^{na}(\epsilon, \Pi) \geq CC_{2\eta}^{sim}(\Psi)/B$, where $B = \max_{i \in [n]}\{CC_{\eta/\ell}^{sim}(f_i)\}$ and $f_i(x, y)$ is the ith bit of $F(x, y)$. Furthermore, if $B = \max_{i \in [n]}\{CC_0^{sim}(f_i)\}$, then $Q_\eta^{na}(\epsilon, \Pi) \geq CC_\eta^{sim}(\Psi)/B$.

Proof Sketch: Given a nonadaptive ϵ-tester with error η for Π and simultaneous communication protocols for the f_i's, we present a simultaneous protocol for solving Ψ. The key idea is that, using their shared randomness, the two parties (holding x and y, respectively) and the referee can emulate an execution of the nonadaptive tester, while providing it with virtual access to $F(x, y)$. Specifically, if the tester queries the ith bit of the oracle, then the two parties provide the referee with messages that allow it to obtain the value of $f_i(x, y)$. The referee feeds all answers to the tester, and outputs whatever it has output.

The main difference between this emulation and the one that is carried out in the proof of Theorem 7.7 is that the tester is nonadaptive, and this fact allows its emulation in the simultaneous communication model. Specifically, the tester generates all its queries as a function of its internal coin tosses (and n) only, which means that both parties obtain these queries based on the shared randomness only (i.e., without interacting). Each party then sends the referee a message that corresponds to the execution of the suitable protocol; that is, if location i in $F(x, y)$ is queried, then each party sends the message that allows for the computation of $f_i(x, y)$ in the simultaneous protocol. The referee gets all these messages, reconstructs the corresponding $f_i(x, y)$'s, feeds them to the tester, obtains its verdict, and outputs it. Hence, the two parties only invoke the query-generation stage of the tester, whereas the referee invokes its decision stage. (All invocations use the same randomness, which is read from the shared randomness of the three parties.)[29] ∎

---

[29] Other parts of the shared randomness are used for the executions of the protocols for computing the f_i's.

7.6. Chapter Notes

The methodology captured in Theorems 7.1 and 7.2 suggests proving lower bounds on the worst-case complexity of randomized algorithms (e.g., property testers) by proving lower bounds on the "distributional complexity" of corresponding deterministic algorithms (which are only required to solve the problem "on the average"). This methodology is commonly attributed to Yao [273], who employed it in the context of several nonuniform models of computation such as Boolean circuits and communication complexity. It was first employed in the context of property testing by Goldreich, Goldwasser, and Ron [140, Sec. 4.1].

Recall that this methodology is "complete" in the sense that any valid lower bound can be proved by using it. The latter assertion, which can be traced to an earlier work of Yao [272] and is proved by employing von Neumann's Minimax Theorem [269], is often confused with the methodology itself. That is, results derived via Theorems 7.1 and 7.2 use the methodology of Yao [273], not the "Minimax principle" of von Neumann [269] as employed by Yao [272]. For further discussion of this point, the interested reader is referred to [135, Apdx. A.1].

The methodology of deriving lower bounds on the query complexity of property testing problems based on communication complexity lower bounds was introduced by Blais, Brody, and Matulef [54]. As noted in Section 7.3, we find this connection quite surprising, since property testing problems have no "topology" that can be naturally 2-partitioned to fit the two-party setting of communication complexity. Nevertheless, using this methodology, Blais *et al.* [54] were able to resolve a fair number of open problems (cf., e.g., [54, Thms. 1.1–1.3]). Our presentation of their methodology is based on [136], which generalizes the presentation of Blais *et al.* [54].[30] (We believe that the more general formulation of the methodology is easier to use as well as more intuitive than the original one.)

Our discussion of reduction among property testing problems (cf. Section 7.4) was confined to many-to-one reductions. Formulating a general notion of reductions among such problems is possible, albeit such a formulation will have to address the issues that arise when defining general reductions among promise problems (cf. [129, Sec. 1.2]).

Exercises

Exercise 7.1 (Generalization of Theorem 7.1): Let Π and q be as in Theorem 7.1. Suppose that for some $p \in (0, 0.5)$, $\epsilon > 0$ and $n \in \mathbb{N}$, the hypothesis of Theorem 7.1 holds except that $1/3$ is replaced (in Eq. (7.1)) by p; that is, there exists a distribution F of functions from $[n]$ to R_n such that for every deterministic oracle machine M that makes at most $q(n, \epsilon)$ queries it holds that

$$\mathbf{Pr}[F \in \Pi_n \wedge M^F(n, \epsilon) \neq 1] + \mathbf{Pr}[F \in \Gamma_\epsilon(\Pi_n) \wedge M^F(n, \epsilon) \neq 0] > p.$$

Prove that, in this case, any ϵ-tester of error probability p for Π_n makes more than $q(n, \epsilon)$ queries.

---

[30] Loosely speaking, the formulation of Blais *et al.* [54] refers to the special case (of Theorem 7.7) in which each $f_i(x, y)$ is a function of the ith bit of x and the ith bit of y (i.e., x_i and y_i). Indeed, in that case, $n = \ell$ and $B = 2$ (by the straightforward protocol in which the two parties exchange the relevant bits (i.e., x_i and y_i)). Typically, using this restricted formulation requires reducing the original communication (complexity) problem into an auxiliary one, and applying the reduction on the latter. Our formulation frees the user from this maneuver, and makes the reduction from the original (communication) problem (to property testing) more transparent. See further discussion in [136].

Exercise 7.2 (Generalization of Theorem 7.2): Let Π and q be as in Theorem 7.2. Suppose that for some $\eta \in (0, 1)$, $\epsilon > 0$ and $n \in \mathbb{N}$, the hypothesis of Theorem 7.2 holds except that $1/3$ is replaced (in Eq. (7.6)) by η; that is, the relevant distinguishing gap is smaller than η. Prove that, in this case, any ϵ-tester of error probability $(1 - \eta)/2$ for Π_n makes more than $q(n, \epsilon)$ queries.

Exercise 7.3 (On the completeness of Theorem 7.2). Recall that Theorem 7.1 is complete in the sense that any valid lower bound can be proved by using it. Show that essentially the same assertion holds with respect to Theorem 7.2. Specifically, show that if Π satisfies the hypothesis of Theorem 7.1, then it satisfies the hypothesis of Theorem 7.2 (possibly with a threshold of $1/2$ rather than $1/3$).[31]

> **Guideline:** Let F be as the hypothesis of Theorem 7.1, and let F_1 (resp., F_0) denote the distribution of F conditioned on $F \in \Pi$ (resp., $F \in \Gamma_\epsilon(\Pi)$). Suppose, for simplicity, that $\Pr[F \in \Pi] = \Pr[F \in \Gamma_\epsilon(\Pi)] = 1/2$. Then, by the hypothesis of Theorem 7.1, $\frac{1}{2} \cdot (1 - \Pr[M^{F_1} = 1]) + \frac{1}{2} \cdot \Pr[M^{F_0} = 1] > 1/3$, which is equivalent to $\Pr[M^{F_1} = 1] - \Pr[M^{F_0} = 1] < 1/3$. By considering the machine that complements the output of M, we also have $\Pr[M^{F_0} = 1] - \Pr[M^{F_1} = 1] < 1/3$, and the hypothesis of Theorem 7.2 follows. In general, for $q_1 \stackrel{\text{def}}{=} \Pr[F \in \Pi]$ and $q_0 \stackrel{\text{def}}{=} \Pr[F \in \Gamma_\epsilon(\Pi)]$, it holds that $q_1 \cdot (1 - \Pr[M^{F_1} = 1]) + q_0 \cdot \Pr[M^{F_0} = 1] > 1/3$. Observing that $q_0, q_1 \in (1/3, 2/3)$ (since otherwise a trivial algorithm violates the hypothesis), we get $\frac{2}{3} \cdot (1 - \Pr[M^{F_1} = 1]) + \frac{2}{3} \cdot \Pr[M^{F_0} = 1] > 1/3$, which is equivalent to $\Pr[M^{F_1} = 1] - \Pr[M^{F_0} = 1] < 1/2$. (Using the "complementing" machine, we also have $\Pr[M^{F_0} = 1] - \Pr[M^{F_1} = 1] < 1/2$.)[32]

Exercise 7.4 (On the distinguishing gap of adaptive testers): Let $\eta \geq 0$ and suppose that X and Y are random variables distributed over $\{0, 1\}^n$ such that, for every fixed $I \subseteq [n]$ of size at most q, the statistical difference between X_I and Y_I is at most η.

1. Prove that for any (adaptive) oracle machine M that makes q queries, it holds that

$$|\Pr[M^X = 1] - \Pr[M^Y = 1]| \leq 2^q \cdot \eta.$$

   Note that this holds also for $\eta = 0$, which means that if for any q-subset $I \subset [n]$ the distributions X_I and Y_I are identically distributed, then no q-query oracle machine can distinguish X from Y with any positive gap.
2. Demonstrate that the upper bound provided in Part 1 is quite tight by considering the following two distributions X and Y that are each uniform over $\{0, 1\}^n$ except that the first $\log_2 n$ bits indicate a bit-position that is set to 0 in X and to 1 in Y. That is, for $n = q - 1 + 2^{q-1}$, let X (resp., Y) be the uniform distribution except the bit that corresponds to location $q + \sum_{j \in [q-1]} 2^{j-1} X_j$ is set to 0 (resp., location $q + \sum_{j \in [q-1]} 2^{j-1} Y_j$ is set to 1).

---

[31] Note that this good enough for claiming "completeness," since an indistinguishability gap of $1/2$ yields that each algorithm is wrong with probability at least $1/4$ (see Exercise 7.2). Still, we would welcome a converse that has no slackness, although we do not know if it is possible. Note that the argument outlined in the guideline is tight (see footnote 32).

[32] **Advanced comment:** Note that the current argument is tight in the sense that there exists a machine M that errs (on $F \in \Pi \cup \Gamma_\epsilon(\Pi)$) with probability greater than $1/3$ whereas the gap $|\Pr[M^{F_1} = 1] - \Pr[M^{F_0} = 1]|$ is almost $1/2$. Consider, for example, for any $\mu \in (0, 1/12)$, the case of $\Pr[M^{F_1} = 1] = 0.5$ and $\Pr[M^{F_0} = 1] = 2\mu$, when $q_1 = \frac{2}{3} - \mu$ and $q_0 = 1 - q_1$.

We stress that the proof of Part 1 is generic, and better bounds can be obtained in many cases (i.e., for specific pairs (X, Y)).

> **Guideline:** Part 1 is proved by fixing the coins of M and considering all 2^q possible answers to the corresponding sequence of q queries. (Indeed, each possible sequence of answers uniquely determines a sequence of queries (made by the residual deterministic machine).) By the hypothesis, the difference in the probability that each such sequence of answers occurs in the two distributions is at most η, and the claim follows.[33] Part 2 follows by observing that an adaptive q-query machine can perfectly distinguish between X and Y (i.e., has distinguishing gap 1), whereas for every fixed $I \subseteq [n]$ of size at most q the statistical difference between X_I and Y_I is at most $|I|/(n - (q - 1)) = O(q/2^q)$.

Exercise 7.5 (Theorem 7.7, generalized): Let $\Psi = (P, S)$ be a promise problem such that $P, S \subseteq \{0, 1\}^{2\ell}$, and let $\Pi \subseteq \Sigma^n$ be a property where Σ is an arbitrary finite set. (Indeed, the generalization is from $\Sigma = \{0, 1\}$ to arbitrary Σ.) For $\epsilon, \eta > 0$, suppose that there exists a mapping $F : \{0, 1\}^{2\ell} \to \Sigma^n$ that satisfies the following two conditions:

1. For every $(x, y) \in P \cap S$, it holds that $F(x, y) \in \Pi$.
2. For every $(x, y) \in P \setminus S$, it holds that $F(x, y)$ is ϵ-far from Π, where $z \in \Sigma^n$ is ϵ-far from Π if $\min_{w \in \Pi}\{|\{i \in [n] : z_i \neq w_i\}|\} > \epsilon \cdot n$.

---

[33] For $\alpha \in \{0, 1\}^q$ and $i \in [q]$, let $M'(\alpha_{[i-1]})$ denote the ith query of the residual deterministic machine when getting the sequence of answers $\alpha_{[i-i]} = (\alpha_1, \ldots, \alpha_{i-1})$, and $M'(\alpha)$ denote the corresponding final output. Then, $M^z = 1$ if and only if $M'(\alpha) = 1$ where $\alpha \in \{0, 1\}^q$ is such that $\alpha_i = z_{M'(\alpha_{[i-1]})}$ for every $i \in [q]$. It follows that

$$
\left| \mathbf{Pr}[M^X = 1] - \mathbf{Pr}[M^Y = 1] \right|
$$

$$
= \left| \sum_{\alpha \in \{0,1\}^q : M(\alpha)=1} \mathbf{Pr}[(\forall i \in [q]) X_{M'(\alpha_{[i-1]})} = \alpha_i] - \sum_{\alpha \in \{0,1\}^q : M(\alpha)=1} \mathbf{Pr}[(\forall i \in [q]) Y_{M'(\alpha_{[i-1]})} = \alpha_i] \right|
$$

$$
\leq \sum_{\alpha \in \{0,1\}^q} \left| \mathbf{Pr}[(\forall i \in [q]) X_{M'(\alpha_{[i-1]})} = \alpha_i] - \mathbf{Pr}[(\forall i \in [q]) Y_{M'(\alpha_{[i-1]})} = \alpha_i] \right|
$$

$$
= \sum_{\alpha \in \{0,1\}^q} \left| \mathbf{Pr}[X_{M'(\lambda)} \cdots X_{M'(\alpha_{[q-1]})} = \alpha] - \mathbf{Pr}[Y_{M'(\lambda)} \cdots Y_{M'(\alpha_{[q-1]})} = \alpha] \right|
$$

$$
\leq \sum_{\alpha \in \{0,1\}^q} \max_{I \subseteq [n] : |I|=q} \max_{\beta \in \{0,1\}^q} \{|\mathbf{Pr}[X_I = \beta] - \mathbf{Pr}[Y_I = \beta]|\},
$$

which is at most $2^q \cdot \eta$. We wish to highlight two points regarding the foregoing proof.

1. The last inequality holds per each $\alpha \in \{0, 1\}^q$, and in particular for α that maximizes $|\mathbf{Pr}[X_{M'(\lambda)} \cdots X_{M'(\alpha_{[q-1]})} = \alpha] - \mathbf{Pr}[Y_{M'(\lambda)} \cdots Y_{M'(\alpha_{[q-1]})} = \alpha]|$. Letting V^z denote the view of an arbitrary deterministic q-query adaptive machine when querying the oracle z, the foregoing inequality can be interpreted as saying that for every α it holds that $|\mathbf{Pr}[V^X = \alpha] - \mathbf{Pr}[V^Y = \alpha]|$ is upper-bounded by $\max_{I:|I|=q}\{|\mathbf{Pr}[X_I = \alpha] - \mathbf{Pr}[Y_I = \alpha]|\}$, which in turn is upper-bounded by $\max_{I:|I|=q} \max_\beta \{|\mathbf{Pr}[X_I = \beta] - \mathbf{Pr}[Y_I = \beta]|\}$. (Recall that the upper bound is proved by setting I to equal the sequence of locations queried by the machine when answered according to α.)

2. We have upper-bounded the max-norm distance between the random variables X_I and Y_I by their total variation distance.

Note that the fixing of M's coins does simplify the exposition of the argument, and it can be justified as in the proof of Theorem 7.1. Alternatively, Theorem 7.2 asserts that, for the purpose of proving query complexity lower bounds, it suffices to consider the distinguishing gap of deterministic testers.

Then, $Q_\eta(\epsilon, \Pi) \geq CC_{2\eta}(\Psi)/B$, where $B = \max_{i \in [n]}\{CC_{\eta/\ell}(f_i)\}$ and $f_i(x, y)$ is the ith symbol of $F(x, y)$. (Indeed, applying CC to f_i requires a straightforward generalization of communication complexity to the context of computing functions that range over Σ rather than Boolean functions, where the communication itself is still measured in bits.)[34] Furthermore, if $B = \max_{i \in [n]}\{CC_0(f_i)\}$, then $Q_\eta(\epsilon, \Pi) \geq CC_\eta(\Psi)/B$.

Exercise 7.6 (On the complexity of k-sparse polynomials, revisited): Let p be a prime power, $d, m, k \in \mathbb{N}$ such that $d < p$ and $k \leq \binom{m}{d}/2$ is even. For $n = p^m$, let Π_n denote the set of m-variate polynomials of degree d over GF(p) having exactly k monomials such that each monomial is the product of d variables. Then, for every $\epsilon \in (0, 1 - (d/p))$, the query complexity of ϵ-testing Π_n is $\Omega(k/\log p)$.

> **Guideline:** The main step is extending Theorem 7.11 to linear codes $C_\ell : \Sigma^\ell \to \Sigma^n$ for any finite $\Sigma \supseteq \{0, 1\}$ that is associated with an additive group. To prove this extension, invoke Exercise 7.5, while using the reduction $F(x, y) = C_\ell(x - y)$ and noting that $C_\ell(x - y) = C_\ell(x) - C_\ell(y)$. The exercise now follows analogously to Corollary 7.12.

Exercise 7.7 (A lower bound for testing $k^{\leq}$-linearity): A function $f : \text{GF}(2)^\ell \to \text{GF}(2)$ is called $k^{\leq}$-linear if it is linear and depends on at most k of its variables. Show that for every $k(\ell) \leq (\ell/2) - 2$, the query complexity of 0.499-testing $k(\ell)^{\leq}$-linearity is $\Omega(k(\ell))$.

> **Guideline:** We reduce from the communication complexity problem that is the complement of $\{\text{DISJ}_\ell^{(k)}\}_{\ell \in \mathbb{N}}$; that is, the YES-instances are pairs (x, y) such that $I(x, y) \stackrel{\text{def}}{=} \{i \in [\ell] : x_i = y_i = 1\} \neq \emptyset$. Note that the communication complexity of problems remains unchanged by complementation. Finally, note that the reduction used in the proof of Theorem 7.10 maps intersecting pairs to $(k - 2)^{\leq}$-linear functions, and non-intersecting pairs to k-linear functions, which are 0.499-far from being $(k - 2)^{\leq}$-linear.[35]

Exercise 7.8 (A lower bound for testing k-juntas): Show that for every even $k(\ell) \leq (\ell/2) - 2$, the complexity of 0.499-testing k-juntas is $\Omega(k)$.

> **Guideline:** Just use the same reduction as in Exercise 7.7, while noting that $(k - 2)^{\leq}$-linear functions are $(k - 2)$-junta, whereas k-linear functions are 0.499-far from being k-juntas.

Exercise 7.9 (A lower bound for testing monotonicity):[36] Recall that $f : \{0, 1\}^\ell \to R_\ell$ is called monotone if $f(x) \leq f(y)$ for every $x < y$ (per the lexicographic order). Prove that 0.1-testing monotonicity, even when $|R_\ell| = O(\ell)$, requires $\Omega(\ell)$ queries.

> **Guideline:** Using Exercise 7.5, reduce from the communication complexity of solving $\{\text{DISJ}_\ell^{(k)} = (P_\ell, S_\ell)\}_{\ell \in \mathbb{N}}$, where $k(\ell) = \ell/2$. Specifically, map the instance $(x, y) \in P_\ell$

---

[34] That is, $CC_{\eta'}(f_i)$ denotes the number of *bits* that are communicated in the best two-party protocol that computes f_i with error probability at most η' (i.e., a pair of strategies (A, B) such that for every (x, y) it holds that $\Pr_r[\langle A(x), B(y)\rangle(r) = f_i(x, y)] \geq 1 - \eta'$). Letting Σ be encoded by t-bit long strings, where $t = \log_2 |\Sigma|$, and defining $f_{i,j}(x, y)$ as the jth bit in the encoding of $f_i(x, y)$, we have $CC_{\eta'}(f_i) \leq \sum_{j \in [t]} CC_{\eta'/t}(f_{i,j})$.

[35] All the above refers to the case of even k; the case of odd k can be handled as in the proof of Proposition 7.16.

[36] Based on [54, Sec. 4], which proves a stronger result (i.e., allowing even $|R_\ell| = O(\sqrt{\ell})$).

to the instance $f_{x,y} : \{0, 1\}^{\ell} \to [2\ell + 3]$ such that

$$f_{x,y}(z) = 2\mathrm{wt}(z) + 1 + (-1)^{\sum_{i\in[\ell]} x_i z_i} + (-1)^{\sum_{i\in[\ell]} y_i z_i}.$$

Observe that, for every $j \in [\ell]$, $u \in \{0, 1\}^{j-1}$ and $w \in \{0, 1\}^{\ell-j}$, letting $z' = u0w$, it holds that

$$f_{x,y}(u1w) - f_{x,y}(u0w) = 2 + ((-1)^{x_j} - 1) \cdot (-1)^{\sum_{i\in[\ell]} x_i z_i'}$$
$$+ ((-1)^{y_j} - 1) \cdot (-1)^{\sum_{i\in[\ell]} y_i z_i'}.$$

Finally, observe that if $x_j y_j = 0$ for every $j \in [\ell]$, then $f_{x,y}(u1w) - f_{x,y}(u0w) \geq 0$ for every $u \in \{0, 1\}^{j-1}$ and $w \in \{0, 1\}^{\ell-j}$, whereas if for some j it holds that $x_j = y_j = 1$, then $f_{x,y}(u1w) - f_{x,y}(u0w) = -2$ for one fourth of the pairs $(u, w) \in \{0, 1\}^{j-1} \times \{0, 1\}^{\ell-j}$.

Exercise 7.10 (Randomized local reductions preserve testability): Let $\Pi = \cup_{n\in\mathbb{N}} \Pi_n$ and $\Pi' = \cup_{n'\in\mathbb{N}} \Pi'_{n'}$ be as in Definition 7.13. Suppose that Π is randomly q-local (ϵ, ϵ')-reducible to Π' with length function L. Show that if Π' can be ϵ'-tested with $q'(n', \epsilon')$ queries, then Π can be ϵ-tested with $q(n) \cdot \tilde{O}(q'(L(n), \epsilon'))$ queries.

> **Guideline:** Extend the proof of Theorem 7.14. Note that the error probability of the local computation algorithms should be reduced to $1/10q'$ (or so). Likewise, the error probability of the ϵ'-tester for Π' should also be reduced to 0.1 (or so). Under these choices, the error probability of the derived tester is at most $\frac{1}{6} + \frac{5}{6} \cdot (q' \cdot \frac{1}{10q'} + 0.1) = \frac{1}{3}$.

CHAPTER EIGHT

Testing Graph Properties in the Dense Graph Model

Summary: Following a general introduction to testing graph properties, this chapter focuses on the dense graph model, where graphs are represented by their adjacency matrix (predicate). The highlights of this chapter include:

1. A presentation of a natural class of graph properties that can each be tested within query complexity that is polynomial in the reciprocal of the proximity parameter. This class, called general graph partition problems, contains properties such as t-Colorability (for any $t \geq 2$) and properties that refer to the density of the max-clique and to the density of the max-cut in a graph.
2. An exposition of the connection of testing (in this model) to Szemerédi's Regularity Lemma. The starting point and pivot of this exposition is the existence of constant-query (one-sided error) proximity-oblivious testers for all subgraph freeness properties.

We conclude this chapter with a taxonomy of known testers, organized according to their query complexity.

The current chapter is based on many sources; see Section 8.6.1 for details.

Organization. The current chapter is the first of a series of three chapters that cover three models for testing graph properties. In each model, we spell out the definition of property testing (when specialized to that model), present some of the known results, and demonstrate some of the ideas involved in the construction of testers (by focusing on testing Bipartiteness, which seems a good benchmark).

We start the current chapter with a general introduction to testing graph properties, which includes an overview of the three models (see Section 8.1.2). We then present and illustrate the "dense graph model" (Section 8.2), which is the focus of the current chapter. The main two sections (i.e., Sections 8.3 and 8.4) cover the two topics that are mentioned in the foregoing summary: Section 8.3 deals with testing arbitrary graph partition properties, as illustrated by the example of testing Bipartitness. Section 8.4 deals with the connection between property testing in this model and Szemerédi's Regularity Lemma, as illustrated by testing subgraph-freeness. The last two sections (i.e., Sections 8.5 and 8.6) are descriptive in nature: Section 8.5 presents a taxonomy of the known results, whereas Section 8.6 presents final comments.

> **Teaching Note:** Much of this chapter (e.g., Sections 8.5 and 8.6) is intended for optional independent reading. We recommend basing the actual teaching on Sections 8.1.2–8.3, with the possibility of leaving Section 8.3.2 for independent reading. (If under time pressure, one may be forced to skip Sections 8.2.3–8.2.4.) We do share the temptation to cover also Section 8.4 in class, but think that teaching the material presented in the previous sections should have a higher priority.

8.1. The General Context: Introduction to Testing Graph Properties

> Graph theory has long become recognized as one of the more useful mathematical subjects for the computer science student to master. The approach which is natural in computer science is the algorithmic one; our interest is not so much in existence proofs or enumeration techniques, as it is in finding efficient algorithms for solving relevant problems, or alternatively showing evidence that no such algorithms exist. Although algorithmic graph theory was started by Euler, if not earlier, its development in the last ten years has been dramatic and revolutionary.
>
> Shimon Even, *Graph Algorithms*, 1979

Meditating on these facts, one may ask what is the source of this ubiquitous use of graphs in computer science. The most common answer is that graphs arise naturally as a model (or an abstraction) of numerous natural and artificial objects. Another answer is that graphs help visualize binary relations over finite sets. These two different answers correspond to two types of models of testing graph properties that will be discussed below. But before doing so, let us recall some basic background.

> **Teaching Note:** We believe that most readers can afford skipping Section 8.1.1, which presents the basic notions and terminology regarding graphs. The vocabulary includes terms such as vertex, edge, simple graph, incident, adjacent, degree, path, cycle, subgraph, induced graph, and isomorphism between graphs.

8.1.1. Basic Background

A simple graph $G = (V, E)$ consists of a *finite* set of vertices V and a finite set of edges E, where each edge is an *unordered pair* of vertices; that is, $E \subseteq \binom{V}{2} \overset{\text{def}}{=} \{\{u, v\} : u, v \in V \wedge u \neq v\}$. This formalism does not allow self-loops and parallel edges, which are allowed in general (i.e., nonsimple) graphs, where E is a multiset that may contain (in addition to two-element subsets of V also) singletons (i.e., self-loops). Unless explicitly stated differently, *we shall only consider simple graphs; that is, typically, a graph means a simple graph.*

The relationship between edges and vertices yields a few basic notions: The vertex u is called an endpoint of the edge $\{u, v\}$, and the edge $\{u, v\}$ is said to be incident at u (and at v). In such a case we say that u and v are adjacent in the graph, and that u is a neighbor of v. The degree of a vertex in G is defined as the number of edges that are incident at this vertex.

We will consider various substructures of graphs, the simplest one being paths. A path in a graph $G = (V, E)$ is a sequence of vertices $(v_0, \ldots, v_\ell)$ such that for every $i \in [\ell] \stackrel{\text{def}}{=} \{1, \ldots, \ell\}$ it holds that v_{i-1} and v_i are adjacent in G. Such a path is said to have length ℓ. A simple path is a path in which each vertex appears at most once, which implies that the longest possible simple path in G has length $|V| - 1$. The graph is called connected if there exists a path between each pair of vertices in it.

A cycle is a path in which the last vertex equals the first one (i.e., $v_\ell = v_0$). The cycle $(v_0, \ldots, v_\ell)$ is called simple if $\ell > 2$ and $|\{v_0, \ldots, v_\ell\}| = \ell$ (i.e., $v_i = v_j$ holds only for $v_0 = v_\ell$, whereas the cycle (u, v, u) is *not* considered simple). A graph is called acyclic (or cycle-free or a forest) if it has no simple cycles, and if it is also connected then it is called a tree. Note that $G = (V, E)$ is a tree if and only if it is connected and $|E| = |V| - 1$; also, G is a tree if and only if there is a unique simple path between each pair of vertices in it.

A subgraph of the graph $G = (V, E)$ is any graph $G' = (V', E')$ satisfying $V' \subseteq V$ and $E' \subseteq E$. Note that a simple cycle in G is a connected subgraph of G in which each vertex has degree exactly 2. An induced subgraph of the graph $G = (V, E)$ is any subgraph $G' = (V', E')$ that contains all edges of G that have both endpoints in V'. In such a case, we say that G' is the subgraph induced by V'.

Two graphs, $G_1 = (V_1, E_1)$ and $G_2 = (V_2, E_2)$, are said to be isomorphic if there exists a bijection $\phi : V_1 \to V_2$ such that $E_2 = \{\{\phi(u), \phi(v)\} : \{u, v\} \in E_1\}$; that is, $\phi(u)$ is adjacent to $\phi(v)$ in G_2 if and only if u is adjacent to v in G_1.

8.1.2. Three Models of Testing Graph Properties

The fact that we call the objects of our study "graphs" is meaningless unless our study refers to characteristics of these objects, which are not be shared by other objects. The feature that distinguishes the edge set E of a graph $G = (V, E)$ from any other set of similar cardinality is that we can refer to E via V; that is, E is a binary relation over V, and so the existence of two edges that share a common endpoint (i.e., $\{u, v_1\}$ and $\{u, v_2\}$) is different from the existence of two edges that do not share an endpoint. Likewise, a cycle of length t is not an arbitrary sequence of t elements of E, but rather one with a specific structure. Furthermore, we are interested in properties that are invariant under renaming of the vertices. Such properties are called *graph properties*.

Definition 8.1 (Graph properties): *A graph property is a set of graphs that is closed under graph isomorphism. That is, Π is a graph property if, for every graph $G = (V, E)$ and every bijection $\pi : V \to V'$, it holds that $G \in \Pi$ if and only if $\pi(G) \in \Pi$, where $\pi(G)$ is the graph obtained from G by relabeling the vertices according to π; that is,*

$$\pi(G) \stackrel{\text{def}}{=} (V', \{\{\pi(u), \pi(v)\} : \{u, v\} \in E\}). \tag{8.1}$$

For the sake of simplicity, we shall consider only graphs $G = (V, E)$ with vertex set $V = \{1, \ldots, |V|\}$. (Wishing to reserve n for the size of the representation of the tested object, we shall often denote the number of vertices by $k = |V|$.)

In light of what we have seen so far, a tester for a graph property Π is a randomized algorithm that is given oracle access to a graph, $G = (V, E)$, and has to determine whether the graph is in Π or is far from being in Π. But the foregoing falls short from constituting a sound definition. We have to specify what does it mean to be given oracle access to a graph, and when are two graphs considered to be far from one another. That is, we have to specify the meaning of "oracle access to a graph" (i.e., the type of queries that are allowed to the graph) as well as the distance measure (between pairs of graphs). Recall that, as stated in Section 1.2.5, these (pair of) choices are of key importance. There are at least three natural (pairs of) choices, and each of them yields a different model. These three models are reviewed next.

The Dense Graphs (a.k.a. Adjacency Predicate) Model. In this model, the graph $G = (V, E)$ is represented by the *adjacency predicate* $g : \binom{V}{2} \to \{0, 1\}$ such that $g(\{u, v\}) = 1$ if and only if $\{u, v\} \in E$. Hence, oracle access to G means oracle access to g, and the distance between graphs (with vertex set V) is defined as the distance between their corresponding representations (which have size $\binom{|V|}{2}$); that is, if the graphs G and G' are represented by the functions g and g', then their relative distance is the fraction of pairs $\{u, v\}$ such that $g(\{u, v\}) \neq g'(\{u, v\})$ (i.e., $|\{\{u, v\} : g(\{u, v\}) \neq g'(\{u, v\})\}|/\binom{|V|}{2}$).

It will be more convenient to represent the graph $G = (V, E)$ by the symmetric function $g : V \times V \to \{0, 1\}$ such that $g(u, v) = 1$ if and only if $\{u, v\} \in E$. This representation is slightly redundant, since $g(u, v) = g(v, u)$ and $g(v, v) = 0$ always holds, but it is less cumbersome. Note that representing G and G' by $g : V \times V \to \{0, 1\}$ and $g' : V \times V \to \{0, 1\}$ means that the relative distance between G and G' is the fraction of ordered pairs on which g and g' differ (i.e., $|\{(u, v) : g(u, v) \neq g'(u, v)\}|/|V|^2$).[1]

Note that saying that $G = (V, E)$ is ϵ-far from the graph property Π means that for every $G' \in \Pi$ it holds that G is ϵ-far from G'. Since Π is closed under graph isomorphism, this means that G is ϵ-far from any isomorphic copy of G'; that is, for every permutation π over V, it holds that $|\{(u, v) : g(u, v) \neq g'(\pi(u), \pi(v))\}| > \epsilon \cdot |V|^2$, where $g : V^2 \to \{0, 1\}$ and $g' : V^2 \to \{0, 1\}$ are as in the previous paragraph.

Finally, note that this notion of distance between graphs is most meaningful in the case that the graphs are dense (since in this case dividing by the number of possible vertex pairs is closely related to dividing by the actual number of edges). Thus, this model is often called the *dense graph model*.

The Bounded-Degree Graph (a.k.a. Incidence Function) Model. In this model, for some fixed upper bound d on the degrees of vertices in G, the graph $G = (V, E)$ is represented by the *incidence function* $g : V \times [d] \to V \cup \{\bot\}$ such that $g(u, i) = v$ if $\{v, u\}$ is the ith edge incident at u, and $g(u, i) = \bot$ if the degree of u smaller than i. In other words, $g(u, i) = v$ if v is the ith neighbor u and $g(u, i) = \bot$ if u has less than i neighbors. Indeed, this representation assumes and/or induces an order on the neighbors of each vertex in G, and it is redundant since each edge is represented twice.[2]

As before, oracle access to G means oracle access to g, but g is different here. Likewise, the distance between graphs (with vertex set V) is defined as the distance between their corresponding representations (which have size $|V| \cdot d$); that is, if the graphs G and G' are represented by the functions g and g', then their relative distance is the fraction of pairs (u, i) such that $g(u, i) \neq g'(u, i)$.

Indeed, only graphs of degree at most d can be represented in this model, which is called the *bounded-degree graph model*.

---

[1] Indeed, there is a small difference between this fraction and the fraction defined in the previous paragraph.

[2] That is, we always assume that $g(u, i) = v$ if and only if there exists a $j \in [d]$ such that $g(v, j) = u$. We stress that j does not necessarily equal i.

Again, saying that $G = (V, E)$ is ϵ-far from the graph property Π means that for every $G' \in \Pi$ it holds that G is ϵ-far from G'. Since Π is closed under graph isomorphism and the ordering of the vertices incident at each vertex is arbitrary, this means that for every permutation π over V, it holds that

$$\sum_{u \in V} |\{v : \exists i \; g(u, i) = v\} \triangle \{v : \exists i \; g'(\pi(u), i) = \pi(v)\}| > \epsilon dN,$$

where g and g' are the incidence functions of G and G', and $\triangle$ denotes the symmetric difference (i.e., $A \triangle B = (A \cup B) \setminus (A \cap B)$).

We stress that both in the dense graph model and in the bounded-degree graph model, the (relative) distance between graphs is measured according to the representation of these graphs as functions, but the representation is different in the two models (and so the (relative) distances are different in the two models). In contrast to the foregoing two models in which the oracle queries and the (relative) distances between graphs are linked to the representation of graphs as functions, in the following model the representation is blurred and the query types and distance measure are decoupled.

The General Graph Model. In this model, the graphs are redundantly represented by both their adjacency predicate and their incidence functions (while not assuming a degree bound (except for the obvious bound of $|V| - 1$)). This representation is implicit in the type of queries allowed (i.e., the algorithm can make queries of both types) and does not affect the distance measure. Instead, the relative distance between the graphs $G = (V, E)$ and $G' = (V, E')$ is defined as $\frac{|E \triangle E'|}{\max(|E|, |E'|)}$; that is, the absolute distance is normalized by the actual number of edges rather than by an absolute upper bound (on the number of edges) such as $\binom{|V|}{2}$ or $d|V|/2$.

Needless to say, the general graph model is the most general one, and it is indeed closest to actual algorithmic applications. In other words, this model is relevant for most applications, since these seem to refer to general graphs (which model various natural and artificial objects). In contrast, the dense graph model is relevant to applications that refer to (dense) binary relations over finite sets, whereas the bounded-degree graph model is relevant only to applications in which the vertex degree is bounded.

The fact that the *general graph model* has received relatively little attention (so far) merely reflects the fact that its study is overly complex. Given that current studies of the other models still face formidable difficulties (and that these models offer a host of interesting open problems), it is natural that researchers shy away from yet another level of complication.

Teaching Note: While the following comment applies to property testing at large, it seems appropriate to make it (and stress it) in the context of testing graph properties, since this context seems closest to standard algorithmic research.

The Current Focus on Query Complexity. Although property testing is motivated by referring to superfast algorithms, research in the area tends to focus on the *query complexity* of testing various properties. This focus should be viewed as providing an initial estimate of the actual complexity of the testing problems involved; certainly, query-complexity lower bounds imply corresponding bounds on the time complexity, whereas the latter is typically at most exponential in the query complexity. Furthermore, in many cases, the time complexity is polynomial (or even linear) in the query complexity, and this fact is typically stated. Thus, we will follow the practice of focusing on the query complexity of testing, but also mention time complexity upper bounds whenever they are of interest.

Digest: The Issue of Representation in Light of the Three Models. As stated in Section 1.2.5, the distinction between objects and their representation is typically blurred in computer science; nevertheless, this distinction is important. Indeed, reasonable and/or natural representations are always assumed either explicitly or implicitly (see, e.g., [131, Sec. 1.2.1]). The specific choice of a reasonable and/or natural representation becomes crucial when one considers the exact complexity of algorithms (as is common in algorithmic research), rather than their general "ball park" (e.g., being in the complexity class $\mathcal{P}$ or not).

The representation is even more crucial in our context (i.e., in the study of property testing). This is the case for two reasons, which transcend the standard algorithmic concerns:

1. We are interested in sublinear time algorithms, which means that these algorithms query bits in the representation of the object. Needless to say, different representations mean different types of queries, and this difference is crucial when one does not fully recover the object by queries.
2. We are interested in the distance between objects (or, actually, in the distance between objects and sets of objects), whereas this distance may be measured in terms of the distance between their representations. In such a case, different representations of objects may yield vastly different distances between the same objects.

In light of the foregoing, when considering property testing, we always detail the exact representation of the objects. This is exactly what has been done here: The three foregoing models use different representations of the same objects, which means that the algorithms in the different models have different query capacities and their performance is evaluated with respect to different distance measures. We believe that the types of queries allowed in each model constitute the natural choice for that model. In the first two models, the underlying representation also provides a natural basis for the definition of a distance measure between objects, whereas in the third model the definition of the distance measure is decoupled from the representation of the objects (and refers to their "actual size").

8.2. The Dense Graph Model: Some Basics

In this section we spell out the actual definition of "testing graph properties in the dense graph model" (Section 8.2.1) and discuss a couple of simple testers, which are based on artifacts of this specific model (Section 8.2.2). In contrast, in Section 8.2.3, we illustrate how the fact that we deal with graphs complicates the analysis of a seemingly simple tester.

8.2.1. The Actual Definition

In the adjacency matrix model (a.k.a. the dense graph model), a k-vertex graph $G = ([k], E)$ is represented by the Boolean function $g : [k] \times [k] \to \{0, 1\}$ such that $g(u, v) = 1$ if and only if u and v are adjacent in G (i.e., $\{u, v\} \in E$). Distance between graphs is measured in terms of their aforementioned representation (i.e., as the fraction of (the number of) different matrix entries (over k^2)), but occasionally one uses the more intuitive notion of the fraction of (the number of) unordered vertex pairs over $\binom{k}{2}$.[3]

Recall that we are interested in *graph properties*, which are sets of graphs that are closed under isomorphism; that is, Π is a graph property if for every graph $G = ([k], E)$ and every permutation π of $[k]$ it holds that $G \in \Pi$ if and only if $\pi(G) \in \Pi$, where $\pi(G) \overset{\text{def}}{=} ([k], \{\{\pi(u), \pi(v)\} : \{u, v\} \in E\})$. We now spell out the meaning of property testing in this model.[4]

Definition 8.2 (Testing graph properties in the adjacency matrix model): *A tester for a graph property Π is a probabilistic oracle machine that, on input parameters k and ϵ and access to (the adjacency predicate of) a k-vertex graph $G = ([k], E)$, outputs a binary verdict that satisfies the following two conditions.*

1. *If $G \in \Pi$, then the tester accepts with probability at least $2/3$.*
2. *If G is ϵ-far from Π, then the tester accepts with probability at most $1/3$, where G is ϵ-far from Π if for every k-vertex graph $G' = ([k], E') \in \Pi$ it holds that the symmetric difference between E and E' has cardinality that is greater than $\epsilon \cdot k^2/2$ (equiv., the representations of G and G' as adjacency predicates differ on more than $\epsilon \cdot k^2$ vertex-pairs).[5]*

If the tester accepts every graph in Π with probability 1, then we say that it has one-sided error; *otherwise, we say that it has* two-sided error. *A tester is called* nonadaptive *if it determines all its queries based solely on its internal coin tosses (and the parameters k and ϵ); otherwise, it is called* adaptive.

The query complexity of a tester is the number of queries it makes to any k-vertex graph, as a function of the parameters k and ϵ.[6] We say that a tester is efficient if it runs in time that is linear in its query complexity, where basic operations on elements of $[k]$ (and in particular, uniformly selecting an element in $[k]$) are counted at unit cost.

We stress that testers are defined as (uniform) algorithms that are given the size parameter k and the distance (or proximity) parameter ϵ as explicit inputs.[7] This uniformity (over the values of the distance parameter) makes the positive results stronger and more appealing (especially in light of a separation result shown in [21]). In contrast, negative results typically refer to a fixed value of the distance parameter.

Representing graphs by their adjacency predicate is very natural, but it is quite problematic if the input graph is not dense (i.e., if $|E| = o(k^2)$). In such a case (i.e., when

---

[3] Indeed, there is a tiny discrepancy between these two measures, but it is immaterial in all discussions. Note that, for the sake of technical convenience, we chose to use a redundant representation (i.e., $g(u, v) = g(v, u)$ and $g(v, v) = 0$), and that we denote the number of vertices by k in order to maintain the convention that n denotes the size of the representation (i.e., $n = k^2$).

[4] Indeed, we slightly deviate from the conventions of Definition 1.6 by providing the tester with k (which denotes the number of vertices in G) rather than with $n = k^2$ (which denotes the size of the domain of the function g).

[5] Indeed, it is more natural to consider the symmetric difference between E and E' as a fraction of $\binom{k}{2}$, but it is more convenient to adopt the alternative normalization.

[6] As in footnote 4, we deviated from the convention of presenting the query complexity as a function of $n = k^2$ and ϵ.

[7] That is, we refer to the standard (uniform) model of computation (cf., e.g., [131, Sec. 1.2.3]), which does not allow for hard-wiring of some parameters (e.g., input length) into the computing device (as done in the case of nonuniform circuit families).

G is not dense), queries to the oracle are likely to be uninformative (e.g., a uniformly distributed query is answered with 0 with probability $1 - o(1)$). On the other hand, each nondense graph is $o(1)$-close to the empty graph, so if the latter has the property (and we are guaranteed that the tested graph is nondense), then testing is trivial (for any constant $\epsilon > 0$). All these reservations are not applicable when the tested graph is dense, as is the case when the graph is used to represent a (symmetric) binary relation that is satisfied quite frequently (say, with constant frequency).

8.2.2. Abuses of the Model: Trivial and Sparse Properties

In continuation of the foregoing discussion, we note that graph properties can be trivial to test also when the input graph is dense. One such case is when every k-vertex graph is ϵ-close to the property (for some $\epsilon > k^{-\Omega(1)}$). This is the case with many natural graph properties: for example, every k-vertex graph is $O(1/k)$-close to being connected (or even Hamiltonian and Eulerian), and ditto with respect to being unconnected.

Proposition 8.3 (Trivially testable properties (in the dense graph model)): *Let Π be a graph property and $c > 0$. If every k-vertex graph is k^{-c}-close to Π, then ϵ-testing Π with one-sided error can be done with zero queries if $\epsilon \geq k^{-c}$ and with $(1/\epsilon)^{2/c}$ queries otherwise.*

Proof: If $\epsilon \geq k^{-c}$, then the tester accepts the graph without making any query (since, in this case, the graph is ϵ-close to Π). Otherwise (i.e., $\epsilon < k^{-c}$), the tester just retrieves the entire graph and decides accordingly, but in this case $k^2 < (1/\epsilon)^{2/c}$. ∎

Another case when testing is easy, alas not that trivial, is when the property is satisfied only by sparse graphs. For example, consider being *planar* or being *cycle-free*.[8] In such a case, testing the property (typically) reduces to checking that the graph is sparse enough.

Proposition 8.4 (Testing "sparse graph" properties in the dense graph model): *Let Π be a graph property and $c < 2$. If every k-vertex graph in Π has at most k^c edges, then ϵ-testing Π can be done in $\mathrm{poly}(1/\epsilon)$ many queries. In particular, if $\epsilon \geq 3k^{-(2-c)}$ then $O(1/\epsilon)$ queries suffice.*

(Note that this tester has two-sided error.)

Proof Sketch: If $\epsilon \geq 3k^{-(2-c)}$, then the tester uses $O(1/\epsilon)$ random queries to estimate the edge density of the graph such that it distinguishes between density at least $2\epsilon/3$ and density at most $\epsilon/3$.[9] In the first case the tester rejects (since the graph is far enough from being sufficiently sparse), and in the second case the tester accepts (since the graph is close enough to the empty graph, which is close enough to Π). Otherwise (i.e., when $\epsilon < 3k^{-(2-c)}$), the tester just retrieves the entire graph and decides accordingly, but in this case $k^2 < (3/\epsilon)^{2/(2-c)}$. ∎

---

[8] Recall that any k-vertex planar graph has at most $\max(k - 1, 3k - 6)$ edges, whereas any (k-vertex) cycle-free graph has at most $k - 1$ edges.

[9] The analysis uses a multiplicative Chernoff Bound. We also assume, for the sake of simplicity, that Π contains some k-vertex graph, for each k.

8.2.3. Testing Degree Regularity

A case in which the fact that we deal with graphs actually makes life harder is that of testing *degree regularity*. A graph is called regular if all its vertices have the same degree; that is, $G = ([k], E)$ is regular if there exists an integer d such that $d_G(u) \overset{\text{def}}{=} |\{v : \{u, v\}|$ equals d for every $u \in [k]$. In such a case we say that G is d-regular.

> **Theorem 8.5** (Testing degree regularity in the dense graph model): *Degree regularity can be tested by using $O(1/\epsilon^2)$ nonadaptive queries. Furthermore, the tester is efficient.*

We note that this upper bound is tight (see Exercise 8.1). As further discussed in the proof, the tester is identical to one that could be used to test that a k-by-k Boolean matrix has rows of equal Hamming weight, but its analysis is more complex in the current setting (in which the matrix must be symmetric and lack 1-entries on its diagonal). The point is that it is not obvious that if the average deviation of the degrees of vertices in the graph (from some value) is small, then the graph is close to being regular (see Claim 8.5.1). (In contrast, it is obvious that if the average deviation of the weights of rows in a matrix (from some value) is small, then the matrix is close to having equal weight rows.)

> **Proof:** We start by reviewing a simpler tester of query complexity $\tilde{O}(1/\epsilon^3)$. This tester selects $O(1/\epsilon)$ random vertices, and estimates the degree of each of them up to $\pm 0.01\epsilon k$ using a sample of $s = \tilde{O}(1/\epsilon^2)$ random vertices (and making the corresponding s queries).[10] The tester accepts if and only if all these estimates are at most $0.02\epsilon k$ apart.
>
> If G is regular (i.e., d-regular), then the tester will accept G with high probability (since, with high probability, all degree estimates will fall in $[d \pm 0.01\epsilon k]$). On the other hand, if the tester accepts G with high probability, then we can infer that there exists an integer d such that all but at most $0.02\epsilon k$ of the vertices have degree $d \pm (0.02\epsilon k + 1)$. (This can be shown by considering the $0.01\epsilon k$ vertices of highest degree and $0.01\epsilon k$ vertices of lowest degree.)[11] The analysis is completed by proving that in this case the graph G is ϵ-close to regular.
>
> **Claim 8.5.1** (Local versus global distance to degree regularity): *If $d < k$ and $dk/2$ are natural numbers and $\sum_{v \in [k]} |d_G(v) - d| \le \epsilon' \cdot k^2$, then G is $6\epsilon'$-close to the set of d-regular k-vertex graphs.*

(Indeed, $\sum_{v \in [k]} |d_G(v) - d|$ represents the "local" distance of G from being regular, whereas we are interested in the "global" distance as captured by Definition 8.2.)

Note that a version of Claim 8.5.1 that refers to general k-by-k Boolean matrices, where $d_G(v)$ denotes the Hamming weight of row v in the matrix G, is trivial. In

---

[10] Recall that we can the estimate of the average value of a function $f : [k] \to \{0, \dots, k - 1\}$ by a sample of size $O(t/\epsilon^2)$ such that, with probability at least $1 - 2^{-t}$, the estimate is within an additive deviation of $0.01\epsilon k$ from the actual value.

[11] Let L and H be the corresponding sets; that is, let L (resp., H) be a set of $0.01\epsilon k$ vertices having the lowest (resp., highest) degree in G. For $\ell \overset{\text{def}}{=} \max_{v \in L}\{d_G(v)\}$ and $h \overset{\text{def}}{=} \min_{v \in H}\{d_G(v)\}$, if $h - \ell \le 0.04\epsilon k$, then each vertex in $[k] \setminus (L \cup H)$ has degree that resides in $\{\ell, \dots, h\}$, and the claim follows (since these degrees are all within $\pm(0.02\epsilon k + 1)$ from $\lfloor (\ell + h)/2 \rfloor$). On the other hand, if $h - \ell > 0.04\epsilon k$, then the tester rejects with high probability (by having seen at least one vertex in L and one vertex in H, and having estimated their degrees well enough).

that case (of general Boolean matrices), the matrix G is ϵ'-close to a matrix in which all rows have weight d. But the latter matrix is not necessarily symmetric and may have 1-entries on the diagonal (i.e., it does not necessarily correspond to an adjacency matrix of a graph). Turning back to our application, note if there exists an integer d such that all but at most $0.02\epsilon k$ of the vertices in the graph G have degree $d \pm (0.03\epsilon k)$, then $\sum_{v \in [k]} |d_G(v) - d| < 0.02\epsilon k \cdot (k-1) + k \cdot 0.03\epsilon k < 0.05\epsilon k^2$, and it follows that G is 0.3ϵ-close to being d-regular. (This assumes that dk is even; otherwise we can use $d - 1$ instead of d.)[12]

Teaching Note: The proof of Claim 8.5.1 is purely combinatorial and can be left for independent reading. The complexity saving captured by Algorithm 8.5.2 is far more important to the contents of the course.

Proof: We modify G in three stages, while keeping track of the number of edge modifications. In the first stage we reduce all vertex degrees to at most d, by scanning all vertices and omitting at most $d_G(v) - d$ edges incident at each vertex $v \in H \stackrel{\text{def}}{=} \{u : d_G(u) > d\}$. Specifically, when handling a vertex v, we consider its degree $d'(v)$ in the current graph and omit $\max(0, d'(v) - d)$ of its edges. Since $\sum_{v \in H} (d_G(v) - d) \le \epsilon' k^2$, we obtain a graph G' that is $\frac{\epsilon' k^2}{k^2/2}$-close to G such that $d_{G'}(v) \le d$ holds for each vertex v. Furthermore, $\sum_{v \in [k]} |d_{G'}(v) - d| \le \epsilon' \cdot k^2$, because each omitted edge $\{u, v\}$ reduces either $|d'(u) - d|$ or $|d'(v) - d|$ (while possibly increasing the other quantity by one unit, where $d'(\cdot)$ denotes the degrees at the time this edge is omitted).

In the second stage, we insert an edge between each pair of vertices that are currently nonadjacent and have both degrees smaller than d. Thus, we obtain a graph G'' such that $\{v : d_{G''}(v) < d\}$ is a clique in G'' (and $d_{G''}(v) \le d$ for all v). Furthermore, G'' is $\frac{\epsilon' k^2/2}{k^2/2}$-close to G' and $\sum_{v \in [k]} |d_{G''}(v) - d| \le \epsilon' \cdot k^2$.

In the third stage, we iteratively increase the degrees of vertices that have degree lower than d while preserving the degrees of all other vertices. Denoting by $\Gamma(v)$ the current set of neighbors of vertex v, we distinguish two cases.

Case 1: There exists a single vertex of degree lower than d. Denoting this vertex by v, we note that $|\Gamma(v)| \le d - 2$ must hold (since $\sum_{u \in [k]} |\Gamma(u)|$ must be even, whereas in this case this sum equal $(k-1) \cdot d + |\Gamma(v)| = kd - (d - |\Gamma(v)|)$), and by the hypothesis kd is even). We shall show that there exist two vertices u and w such that $\{u, w\}$ is an edge in the current graph but $u, w \notin \Gamma(v) \cup \{v\}$. Adding the edges $\{u, v\}$ and $\{w, v\}$ to the graph, while omitting the edge $\{u, w\}$, we increase $|\Gamma(v)|$ by 2, while preserving the degrees of all other vertices. We show the existence of two such vertices by recalling that $|\Gamma(v) \cup \{v\}| \le d - 1$, whereas all other $k - 1 \ge d$ vertices in the graph have degree d. Considering an arbitrary vertex $u \notin \Gamma(v) \cup \{v\}$, we note that u has d neighbors (since $u \ne v$), and these neighbors cannot all be in $\Gamma(v) \cup \{v\}$ (which has size at most $d - 1$). Thus, there exists $w \in \Gamma(u) \setminus (\Gamma(v) \cup \{v\})$, and we are done.

---

[12] Being even more nitpicking, we note that using $d - 1$ instead of d yields an additional loss of k edges, which is OK provided $k \le 0.01\epsilon k^2$. On the other hand, if $\epsilon < 100/k$, then we can just retrieve the entire graph using $\binom{k}{2} = O(1/\epsilon^2)$ queries.

Case 2: There exist at least two vertices of degree lower than d. Let v_1 and v_2 be two vertices such that $|\Gamma(v_i)| \le d - 1$ holds for both $i \in \{1, 2\}$. Note that $\{v_1, v_2\}$ is an edge in the current graph, since the set of vertices of degree less than d constitute a clique. We shall show that there exist two vertices $u_1 \in [k] \setminus \{v_1\}$ and $u_2 \in [k] \setminus \{v_2\}$ such that $\{u_1, u_2\}$ is an edge in the current graph but neither $\{v_1, u_1\}$ nor $\{v_2, u_2\}$ are edges (and so $|\Gamma(u_1)| = |\Gamma(u_2)| = d$). Adding the edges $\{u_1, v_1\}$ and $\{u_2, v_2\}$ to the graph, while omitting the edge $\{u_1, u_2\}$, we increase $|\Gamma(v_i)|$ by 1 (for each $i \in \{1, 2\}$), while preserving the degrees of all other vertices.

We show the existence of two such vertices by starting with an arbitrary vertex $u_1 \notin (\Gamma(v_1) \cup \{v_1, v_2\})$. Such a vertex exists since $v_2 \in \Gamma(v_1)$ and so $|\Gamma(v_1) \cup \{v_1, v_2\}| = |\Gamma(v_1) \cup \{v_1\}| \le d < k$. We now make the following two observations.

- Vertex u_1 has d neighbors (see above).[13] Obviously, $v_1 \notin \Gamma(u_1)$ (since $u_1 \notin \Gamma(v_1)$).
- The set $(\Gamma(v_2) \cup \{v_2\}) \setminus \{v_1\}$ has size at most $d - 1$, since $v_1 \in \Gamma(v_2)$ and $|\Gamma(v_2)| < d$.

It follows that $\Gamma(u_1)$ cannot be contained in $\Gamma(v_2) \cup \{v_2\}$, since $|\Gamma(u_1) \setminus \{v_1\}| = d$ whereas $|(\Gamma(v_2) \cup \{v_2\}) \setminus \{v_1\}| \le d - 1$. Hence, there exists $u_2 \in \Gamma(u_1) \setminus (\Gamma(v_2) \cup \{v_2\})$.

Thus, in each step of the third stage, we decrease $\sum_{v \in [N]} |d_{G''}(v) - d|$ by *two units*, while preserving both invariances established in the second stage (i.e., $\{v : d_{G''}(v) < d\}$ is a clique and $d_{G''}(v) \le d$ for all v). Since in each step we modified three edges (and there are at most $\epsilon' k^2 / 2$ steps), we conclude that G'' is $\frac{3\epsilon' k^2 / 2}{k^2 / 2}$-close to a d-regular graph, and the claim follows (by recalling that G is $3\epsilon'$-close to G''). ∎

Reducing the Query Complexity. The wasteful aspect in the aforementioned tester is that it samples $O(1/\epsilon)$ vertices and estimates the degree of each of these vertices up to an additive term of $0.01\epsilon k$. This tester admits a straightforward analysis by which if $\sum_{v \in [k]} |d_G(v) - d| > 0.05\epsilon k^2$, then at least $0.02\epsilon k$ of the vertices have degree outside the interval $[d \pm 0.03\epsilon k]$. In this analysis a vertex is defined as "exceptional" if its degree deviates from the average value by more than $0.03\epsilon k$, but when lower-bounding the number of exceptional vertices we use k as an upper bound on the contribution of each exceptional vertex (to the sum of deviations). That is, the threshold for being considered "exceptional" is minimalistic (i.e., it considers an extremely mild deviation as exceptional), but when analyzing the number of exceptional vertices we considered the maximal possible deviation.

Obviously, we must take into account both these extreme cases (i.e., both mild deviations and large deviations of individual degrees), but we may treat vertices with different levels of deviation differently. Specifically, if all exceptional vertices "deviate by much" (i.e., their degrees deviate from the average by at least $\delta k \gg \epsilon k$), then fewer samples suffice for detecting their deviation (i.e., $O(1/\delta^2) \ll O(1/\epsilon^2)$

---

[13] This is because $u_1 \notin \Gamma(v_1)$, whereas all vertices of degree lower than d are neighbors of v_1 (since the vertices of lower degree form a clique).

samples suffice). On the other hand, if the exceptional vertices only "deviate by little" (i.e., their degrees deviates from the average by at most $\delta k = O(\epsilon k)$ (or so)), then it suffices to sample less vertices in order to encounter such a vertex (i.e., it suffices to sample $O(\delta/\epsilon)$ vertices). Of course, we do not know which case holds, and in fact we may have a mix of several cases. Still, we can handle all cases concurrently.

Specifically, assuming that the total deviation is $\Omega(\epsilon k^2)$ and letting $\ell = \log_2(O(1)/\epsilon)$, we observe that there exists $i \in [\ell]$ such that at least $\Omega(2^{-i} \cdot k)$ of the vertices have degrees that deviate from the average by $\Theta(2^i \epsilon \cdot k/\log(1/\epsilon))$ units, since otherwise the total deviation would have been

$$\sum_{i \in [\ell]} o(2^{-i} \cdot k) \cdot \Theta(2^i \epsilon \cdot k/\log(1/\epsilon)) = \sum_{i \in [\ell]} o(\epsilon k^2/\log(1/\epsilon)) = o(\epsilon k^2),$$

in contradiction to the hypothesis. Hence, for every $i \in [\ell]$, we attempt to detect a $\Omega(2^{-i})$ fraction of the vertices that have degrees that deviate from the average by $\Theta(2^i \epsilon \cdot k/\log(1/\epsilon))$ units, where the total amount of work involved in performing the relevant estimates is

$$\sum_{i \in [\ell]} O(2^{-i})^{-1} \cdot \Theta(2^i \epsilon/\log(1/\epsilon))^{-2} = \sum_{i \in [\ell]} 2^{-i} \cdot O(\log(1/\epsilon)/\epsilon)^2 = \tilde{O}(1/\epsilon^2).$$

Actually, we shall obtain a slightly better result by setting the parameters differently; specifically, by attempting to detect a $\Omega(2^{-i})$ fraction of the vertices that have degrees that deviate from the average by $\Theta(2^{4i/5} \epsilon \cdot k)$ units. (The analysis of this choice will appear within (and after) the presentation of Algorithm 8.5.2.)[14] In addition, we simplify the analysis by introducing an auxiliary step in which we estimate the average degree of the vertices in the graph.

Algorithm 8.5.2 (The actual tester): *For a sufficiently large constant c, let $\ell \stackrel{\text{def}}{=} \log_2(c/\epsilon)$.*

1. *The tester estimates the average degree of the graph by making $O(1/\epsilon^2)$ uniformly distributed queries. This allows to estimate the average degree up to $\pm \epsilon \cdot k/c$, with probability at least $5/6$. Let $\tilde{d}$ denote the estimated average.*
2. *For every $i \in [\ell]$, the tester attempts to find a vertex with degree outside the interval $[\tilde{d} \pm 2^{1+(4i/5)} \epsilon \cdot k/c]$, by taking a sample of $c \cdot 2^i$ vertices, and estimating their degree up to $\pm 2^{4i/5} \epsilon \cdot k/c$. Specifically:*
   (a) *The tester selects uniformly $c \cdot 2^i$ vertices, and estimates the degree of each of these vertices up to $\pm 2^{4i/5} \cdot k/c$ units by using a sample of $s_i \stackrel{\text{def}}{=} c^3 \cdot 2^{-3i/2} \epsilon^{-2} \gg (2^{4i/5} \epsilon/c)^{-2}$ random vertices. Note that with probability at least*

$$1 - c \cdot 2^i \cdot \exp(-2 \cdot s_i \cdot (2^{4i/5} \epsilon/c)^2) = 1 - c \cdot 2^i \cdot \exp(-2 \cdot c^3 2^{-3i/2} \epsilon^{-2} \cdot 2^{8i/5} \epsilon^2/c^2)$$
$$= 1 - c \cdot 2^i \cdot \exp(-2c \cdot 2^{i/10})$$
$$> 1 - 2^{-i-c}$$

all these estimates are as desired.

---

[14] **Advanced comment:** We note that the same analysis will hold when setting the deviation level to $\Theta(2^{\alpha i} \epsilon \cdot k)$, for any $\alpha \in (0.5, 1)$, where here we used $\alpha = 4/5$. In such a case, we set $s_i = \Theta(2^{-\beta i} \epsilon^{-2})$, for any $\beta \in (1, 2\alpha)$, where here we used $\beta = 3/2$.

(b) If any of these estimates is outside the interval $[\tilde{d} \pm 2^{1+(4i/5)}\epsilon \cdot k/c]$, then the tester rejects.

If the tester did not reject in any of these ℓ iterations, then it accepts.

The query complexity of Algorithm 8.5.2 is $O(1/\epsilon^2) + \sum_{i\in[\ell]} c2^i \cdot c^3 2^{-3i/2}\epsilon^{-2} = O(1/\epsilon^2)$. The probability that any of the estimates performed in (any of the iterations of) Step 2 deviates by more than desired is $\sum_{i\in[\ell]} 2^{-i-c} = 2^{-c} < 1/10$.

We first observe that Algorithm 8.5.2 accepts each regular graph with probability at least $2/3$. This is the case since $\Pr[|\tilde{d} - d| \leq \epsilon k/c] \geq 0.9$, where d denotes the degree of each vertex in the graph, and with probability at least 0.9 for each $i \in [\ell]$ each of the degree estimates performed in (the ith iteration of) Step 2 fell inside the interval $[d \pm 2^{4i/5}\epsilon \cdot k/c]$, which is contained in $[\tilde{d} \pm 2^{1+(4i/5)}\epsilon \cdot k/c]$.

On the other hand, if a graph G is accepted with probability at least $1/3$, then (as detailed next), for every $i \in [\ell]$, it holds that all but at most a 2^{-i} fraction of the vertices have degree that is within $2^{2+(4i/5)}\epsilon \cdot k/c$ of the average degree of G, denoted d.

Claim: If, for some $i \in [\ell]$, more than a 2^{-i} fraction of the vertices have degree that deviates from d by more than $2^{2+(4i/5)}\epsilon \cdot k/c$, then Algorithm 8.5.2 rejects with probability greater than $2/3$.

Proof: We first observe that, with probability at least 0.9, such a deviating vertex, denoted v, is selected in the ith iteration of Step 2. Now, with probability at least 0.9, the degree of v is estimated within $\pm 2^{4i/5}\epsilon \cdot k/c$ of its correct value. Recalling that $\Pr[|\tilde{d} - d| < \epsilon k/c] \geq 0.9$, we conclude that, with probability at least 0.7, the estimated degree of v deviates from $\tilde{d}$ by more than $\frac{2^{2+(4i/5)}\epsilon k}{c} - \frac{2^{4i/5}\epsilon k}{c} - \frac{\epsilon k}{c} \geq \frac{2^{1+(4i/5)}\epsilon k}{c}$, which causes the algorithm to reject, and the claim follows. ∎

Now, for each $i \in [\ell]$, let us denote the set of the aforementioned deviating vertices by B_i; that is,

$$B_i \stackrel{\text{def}}{=} \{v \in [k] : |d_G(v) - d| > 2^{2+(4i/5)}\epsilon/c \cdot k\}.$$

Recall that $|B_i| \leq 2^{-i} \cdot k$. (Also, let $B_0 = [k]$, and note that $[k] \setminus B_\ell = \cup_{i\in[\ell]}(B_{i-1} \setminus B_i)$.)[15] Hence,

$$\sum_{v\in[k]\setminus B_\ell} |d_G(v) - d| = \sum_{i\in[\ell]} \sum_{v\in B_{i-1}\setminus B_i} |d_G(v) - d|$$

$$\leq \sum_{i\in[\ell]} |B_{i-1}| \cdot \max_{v\in[k]\setminus B_i} \{|d_G(v) - d|\}$$

$$\leq \sum_{i\in[\ell]} 2^{-(i-1)} \cdot 2^{2+(4i/5)}\epsilon k^2/c$$

$$= \sum_{i\in[\ell]} 2^{-0.2i} \cdot 8\epsilon k^2/c,$$

which is smaller than $0.04\epsilon k^2$ by a suitable choice of c. Furthermore, under such a choice, $|B_\ell| \leq 2^{-\ell} \cdot k = (\epsilon/c) \cdot k$ is smaller than $0.01\epsilon k$. Hence, $\sum_{v\in B_\ell} |d_G(v) - d| < 0.01\epsilon k^2$, and so $\sum_{v\in[k]} |d_G(v) - d| < 0.05\epsilon k^2$. Applying

---

[15] Indeed, the definition of B_0 is fictitious; it is made in order to have $[k] \setminus B_\ell = \cup_{i\in[\ell]}(B_{i-1} \setminus B_i)$ hold. The alternative would have been to treat the case of $i = 1$ separately; that is, write $[k] \setminus B_\ell = ([k] \setminus B_1) \cup \cup_{i=2}^{\ell}(B_{i-1} \setminus B_i)$. Note that, either way, we treat B_ℓ separately.

Claim 8.5.1, it follows that G is 0.3ϵ-close to being regular, and the theorem follows. ∎

8.2.4. Digest: Levin's Economical Work Investment Strategy

The strategy underlying Algorithm 8.5.2 can be traced to Levin's work on one-way functions and pseudorandom generators [199]. An attempt to abstract this strategy follows.

The strategy refers to situations in which one can sample a huge space that contains elements of different quality such that elements of lower quality require more work to utilize. The aim is to utilize some element, but the work required for utilizing the various elements is not known *a priori*, and it becomes known only after the entire amount of required work is invested. Only a lower bound on the expected quality of elements is known, and it is also known how the amount of required work relates to the quality of the element (see specific cases below). Note that it may be that most of the elements are of very poor quality, and so it is not a good idea to select a single (random) element and invest as much work as is needed to utilize it. Instead, one may want to select many random elements and invest in each of them a limited amount of work (which may be viewed as probing the required amount of work).

To be more concrete, let us denote the (unknown to us) quality of a sample point $\omega \in \Omega$ by $q(\omega) \in (0, 1]$, and suppose that the amount of work that needs to be invested in a sample point ω is $O(1/q(\omega)^c)$, where in the setting of Algorithm 8.5.2 it holds that $c = 2$. Indeed, $c = 1$ and $c = 2$ are the common cases, where $O(1/q(\omega))$ corresponds to the number of trials that is required to succeed in an experiment (which depends on ω) that succeeds with probability $q(\omega)$, and $O(1/q(\omega)^2)$ corresponds to the number of trials that is required for detecting that two experiments (which depend on ω) have different success probabilities when these probabilities differ by $q(\omega)$.

Recall that we only know a lower bound, denoted ϵ, on the average quality of an element (i.e., $\mathbb{E}_{\omega \in \Omega}[q(\omega)] > \epsilon$), and we wish to minimize the total amount of work invested in utilizing some element.

One natural strategy that comes to mind is to sample $O(1/\epsilon)$ points and invest $O(1/\epsilon^c)$ work in each of these points. In this case we succeed with constant probability, while investing $O(1/\epsilon^{c+1})$ work. The analysis is based on the fact that $\mathbb{E}_\omega[q(\omega)] > \epsilon$ implies that $\mathbf{Pr}_\omega[q(\omega) > \epsilon/2] > \epsilon/2$. This corresponds to the strategy that underlies the simple tester (of query complexity $\tilde{O}(1/\epsilon^3)$) presented upfront. In contrast, the strategy underlying Algorithm 8.5.2 is based on the fact that there exists $i \in [\log_2(O(1)/\epsilon)]$ such that $\mathbf{Pr}_\omega[q(\omega) > 2^{4i/5} \cdot \epsilon] = \Omega(2^{-i})$. In this case (when $c = 2$), for every i, we selected $O(2^i)$ points and invested $O(1/2^{4i/5}\epsilon)^2$ work in each of them. Hence, we achieved the goal while investing $(1/\epsilon^2)$ work.

> **Teaching Note:** In the following general analysis, we shall use a setting of parameters that is different from the one used above. This is done in order to better serve the case of $c = 1$. In addition, we believe that a different variation on the very same idea will serve the reader better.

In general, for any $c \geq 1$ and $\ell = \lceil \log_2(2/\epsilon) \rceil$, we may use the fact that there exists $i \in [\ell]$ such that $\mathbf{Pr}_\omega[q(\omega) > 2^i \cdot \epsilon] > 2^{-i}/(i+3)^2$. (The analysis is analogous to the one performed at the end of the proof of Theorem 8.5, although the quantity analyzed here is different (and so are some parameters).)[16] Hence, selecting $O(i^2 \cdot 2^i)$ points (for each $i \in [\ell]$), and investing $O(1/2^i \epsilon)^c$ work in each of them, we achieved the goal while investing a total amount of work that equals

$$\sum_{i \in [\ell]} O(i^2 \cdot 2^i/(2^i \epsilon)^c) = O(1/\epsilon^c) \cdot \sum_{i \in [\ell]} i^2 \cdot 2^{-(c-1) \cdot i},$$

which equals $O(1/\epsilon^c)$ if $c > 1$ and $\widetilde{O}(1/\epsilon)$ if $c = 1$. (For $c > 1$ we use $\sum_{i \in [\ell]} \text{poly}(i) \cdot 2^{-\Omega(i)} = O(1)$, whereas for $c = 1$ we use $\sum_{i \in [\ell]} i^2 = O(\ell^3)$.) See Exercise 8.3 for a couple of generalizations and Exercise 8.4 for a minor improvement (for the case of $c = 1$).

8.3. Graph Partition Problems

In this section we present a natural class of graph properties, called general graph partition properties, which contains properties such as k-Colorability (for any $k \geq 2$) and properties that refer to the density of the max-clique and to the density of the max-cut in a graph. The main result of this section is that each of these properties has a tester of query complexity that is polynomial in the reciprocal of the proximity parameter.

Loosely speaking, a graph partition problem calls for partitioning the graph into a specified number of parts such that the sizes of the parts fit the specified bounds and ditto with respect to the number of edges between parts. More specifically, each graph partition problem (resp., property) is specified by a number $t \in \mathbb{N}$ and a sequence of intervals (which serve as parameters of the problem). A graph $G = ([k], E)$ is a YES-instance of this problem (resp., has the corresponding property) if there exists a t-partition, $(V_1, \dots, V_t)$, of $[k]$ such that

1. For each $i \in [t]$, the density of V_i fits the corresponding interval (specified in the sequence of parameters).
2. For each $i, j \in [t]$ (including the case $i = j$), the density of edges between V_i and V_j fits the corresponding interval.

A formal definition of this framework is deferred to Section 8.3.2; here we only clarify the framework by considering a few appealing examples that refer to the case of $t \leq 2$.

We start by considering the case of $t = 1$, which is a bit of an abuse of the term "partition." Two natural properties that can be casted in that case are the property of being a clique and the property of having at least $\rho \cdot k^2$ edges, for any $\rho \in (0, 0.5)$. The first property can be ϵ-tested by uniformly selecting $O(1/\epsilon)$ vertex-pairs and checking if each

---

[16] Let $B_i = \{\omega \in \Omega : q(\omega) > 2^i \epsilon\}$ and $B_0 = \Omega$, and note that $B_\ell = \emptyset$. Suppose, toward the contradiction, that $|B_i| \leq 2^{-i} |\Omega|/(i+3)^2$ for every $i \in [\ell]$. Then,

$$\sum_{\omega \in \Omega} q(\omega) = \sum_{i \in [\ell]} \sum_{\omega \in B_{i-1} \setminus B_i} q(\omega)$$

$$\leq \sum_{i \in [\ell]} |B_{i-1}| \cdot 2^i \epsilon$$

$$\leq \sum_{i \in [\ell]} \frac{2^{-(i-1)} \cdot |\Omega|}{((i-1)+3)^2} \cdot 2^i \epsilon$$

$$< \epsilon \cdot |\Omega|,$$

where the last inequality uses $\sum_{i \geq 1} \frac{1}{(i+t)^2} < \sum_{i \geq 1} \frac{1}{(i+t)(i+t-1)}$, which equals $\sum_{i \geq 1} \left(\frac{1}{i+t-1} - \frac{1}{i+t} \right) = 1/t$.

of these pairs is connected by an edge of the graph. The second property can be ϵ-tested by estimating the fraction of edges in the graph, up to an additive deviation of $\epsilon/2$, which can be done using a random sample of $O(1/\epsilon^2)$ vertex-pairs. Turning to the case of $t = 2$, we consider the following natural properties.

Biclique: A graph $G = ([k], E)$ is a biclique (a.k.a. a complete bipartite graph) if its vertices can be 2-partitioned into two parts, denoted V_1 and V_2, such that each part is an independent set and all pairs in $V_1 \times V_2$ are connected in the graph (i.e., $E = \{\{u, v\} : (u, v) \in V_1 \times V_2\}$).

Bipartiteness: A graph $G = ([k], E)$ is bipartite (or 2-colorable) if its vertices can be 2-partitioned into two parts, V_1 and V_2, such that each part is an independent set (i.e., $E \subseteq \{\{u, v\} : (u, v) \in V_1 \times V_2\}$).

Max-Cut: For $\rho \in (0, 0.25]$, a graph $G = ([k], E)$ has a ρ-cut if its vertices can be 2-partitioned into two parts, V_1 and V_2, such that the number of edges between V_1 and V_2 is at least $\rho \cdot k^2$ (i.e., $|E \cap \{\{u, v\} : (u, v) \in V_1 \times V_2\}| \geq \rho \cdot k^2$).

Min-Bisection: For $\rho \in (0, 0.25]$, a graph $G = ([k], E)$ has a ρ-bisection if its vertices can be 2-partitioned into two equal-sized parts, V_1 and V_2, such that the number of edges between V_1 and V_2 is at most $\rho \cdot k^2$ (i.e., $|V_1| = |V_2|$ and $|E \cap \{\{u, v\} : (u, v) \in V_1 \times V_2\}| \leq \rho \cdot k^2$).

Max-Clique: For $\rho \in (0, 1]$, a graph $G = ([k], E)$ has a ρ-clique if its vertices can be 2-partitioned into two parts, V_1 and V_2, such that $|V_1| = \lceil \rho \cdot k \rceil$ and the subgraph induced by V_1 is a clique (i.e., for every distinct $u, v \in V_1$ it holds that $\{u, v\} \in E$).

Indeed, with the exception of Max-Clique, all the foregoing properties generalized naturally to the case of $t > 2$. As stated in the beginning of this section, each of these properties is ϵ-testable using poly$(1/\epsilon)$ queries (for details see Sections 8.3.1 and 8.3.2). For starters, we consider the case of Biclique.

Proposition 8.6 (Testing whether a graph is a biclique (in the dense graph model)): *The property* Biclique *has a (one-sided error) proximity-oblivious tester that makes three queries and has linear rejection probability. That is, a graph that is ϵ-far from being a biclique is rejected with probability at least $\Omega(\epsilon)$, whereas a biclique is accepted with probability 1.*

We stress that the empty graph $G = ([k], \emptyset)$ is considered a biclique (by virtue of a trivial 2-partition $([k], \emptyset)$). Note that ϵ-testing that a graph is not empty can be done by $O(1/\epsilon)$ queries (see Proposition 8.3).

Proof: The tester selects uniformly three random vertices and accepts if and only if the induced subgraph is a biclique (i.e., contains either two edges or no edges).[17] We stress that while the selected vertices are uniformly and independently distributed in $[k]$, the queried pairs are dependent (although each query is uniformly distributed in $[k] \times [k]$).

If $G = ([k], E)$ is a biclique, then it is accepted with probability 1, since the subgraph induced by the selected vertices is a 3-vertex biclique. Specifically, if all

---

[17] This description ignores the possibility that the selected vertices are not distinct. In such a case, we just accept without making any queries. Alternatively, we can select uniformly a 3-subset of $[k]$.

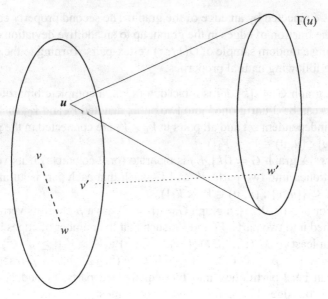

Figure 8.1: The 2-partition imposed by u. The dashed line represents a violating pair connected by an edge, whereas the dotted line represents a violating pair that lacks an edge.

three vertices were selected in the same independent set of the k-vertex biclique, then the induced subgraph is a 3-vertex independent set (which is a biclique), and otherwise (i.e., when one selected vertex resides in one independent set and the other two vertices reside in the other set) the induced subgraph is a 3-vertex biclique with two edges.

Assuming that G is ϵ-far from being a biclique, fix the first vertex u that is selected by the tester. Then, u defines a 2-partition of the vertices of G such that the neighbors of u are on one side and the other vertices are on the other; that is, the 2-partition is $(\Gamma(u), [k] \setminus \Gamma(u))$, where $\Gamma(u) = \{v \in [k] : \{u, v\} \in E\} \not\ni u$. (Note that if G had been a biclique, then this 2-partition would have been its unique partition to two independent sets with a complete bipartite graph between them.) Since G is ϵ-far from being a biclique, there are at least ϵk^2 vertex pairs[18] that *violate* this 2-partition, where a pair (v, w) is said to violate the 2-partition $(\Gamma(u), [k] \setminus \Gamma(u))$ if the subgraph induced by $\{u, v, w\}$ is not a biclique. (That is, a violating pair represents either an edge that is missing between the two parts (i.e., between $\Gamma(u)$ and $[k] \setminus \Gamma(u)$) or an edge that is present inside one of these parts (i.e., internal to either $\Gamma(u)$ or $[k] \setminus \Gamma(u)$); see Figure 8.1.) Hence, the probability that the tester selects a violating pair is at least $\frac{\epsilon k^2}{k^2}$, and the claim follows (since in this case the tester rejects). ∎

Digest. The analysis of the foregoing tester reveals that we can actually select the first vertex arbitrarily, and only select the two other vertices at random. More importantly, the foregoing proof illustrated a technique that is quite popular in the area (see, e.g.,

---

[18] Note that here we count ordered pairs of vertices, rather than unordered pairs. Indeed, in some cases it is more convenient to count in one way, and in other cases the other way is preferred. We did not try to be consistent regarding this matter, because we believe that when low-level details are concerned, local convenience should have precedence over global consistency.

Section 8.3.1). Specifically, in the current case, the first vertex "induces" (or forces) auxiliary conditions on the graph (i.e., the existence of edges between its neighbors and its nonneighbors and the nonexistence of other edges), and these conditions are checked by the random pair of vertices selected next. In general, in the "force and check" technique, the tester designates one part of its sample to force conditions on the object, and these conditions are checked by the second part of the sample. Note that the forcing can be implicit (like the partition of $[k]$ according to neighbors versus nonneighbors of u), whereas the checking actually tests these conditions via queries (e.g., the three queries of the foregoing tester are defined and performed only once the other two vertices are selected).

> **Teaching Note:** The following four paragraphs may be used as a motivation toward the tester for Bipartiteness (of Section 8.3.1), but some readers may find this discussion a bit too abstract.

Focusing again on the specific tester presented in the proof of Proposition 8.6, recall that the vertex u induced a 2-partition of $[k]$ and that the placement of each vertex v with respect to that partition can be determined by a single query to G. In other words, we have implemented an oracle $\chi : [k] \to \{1, 2\}$ such that $\chi(v) = 1$ if and only if $v \in \Gamma(u)$ (or equivalently, if and only if $\{v, u\} \in E$), and observed that G is a biclique if and only if χ is a 2-partition that witnesses this claim (i.e., $E = \{\{v, w\} : \chi(v) \neq \chi(w)\}$). We then checked if G is a biclique by selecting a random vertex-pair (v, w) and accepted if and only if $\{v, w\} \in E \iff \chi(v) \neq \chi(w)$.

As a motivation toward the presentation of the tester for Bipartiteness, suppose that one provides an implementation of T oracles $\chi_1, \ldots, \chi_T : [k] \to \{1, 2\}$ and shows that G *is a bipartite if and only if at least one of these χ_i's is a 2-partition that witnesses this claim* (i.e., $E \subseteq \{\{v, w\} : \chi_i(v) \neq \chi_i(w)\}$). Then, we can test whether G is bipartite or ϵ-far from being bipartite by selecting $m = O(\epsilon^{-1} \log T)$ random pairs $(v_1, w_1), \ldots, (v_m, w_m)$ and accepting if and only if there exists an $i \in [T]$ such that for every $j \in [m]$ it holds that $\{v_j, w_j\} \in E \implies \chi_i(v_j) \neq \chi_i(w_j)$.[19] Furthermore, if we can answer all these $T \cdot 2m$ queries (to the χ_i's) by making a total number of $q(\epsilon) - m$ queries to the graph G, then we would get an ϵ-tester of query complexity $q(\epsilon)$. As shown next, this would follow even if we can answer these queries (to the χ_i's) only for vertices in a ("good") set V, provided that all but at most $0.1\epsilon k^2$ of the edges have both their endpoints in V.

The tester operates as outlined above, except that whenever it gets no answer to $\chi_i(v)$ (i.e., $v \notin V$), it just sets $\chi_i(v)$ so to avoid rejection (whenever possible). This provision guarantees that the tester always accepts a bipartite graph, since for the suitable χ_i there exists a setting of $\chi_i(v)$ (for every $v \in [k] \setminus V$) that avoids rejection. On the other hand, if G is ϵ-far from being bipartite, then for every $\chi : [k] \to \{1, 2\}$ there exist at least ϵk^2 vertex pairs (v, w) such that $\{v, w\} \in E$ and $\chi(v) = \chi(w)$. In particular, this holds for each of the foregoing χ_i's, whereas only $0.2\epsilon k^2$ of these pairs may be "invisible" to the tester (i.e., the tester cannot determine χ_i for both elements of the pair).[20] Hence, each χ_i is detected as bad with probability at least $1 - (1 - 0.8\epsilon)^m = 1 - (1/3T)$, where the equality is due to the setting of m.

---

[19] See analysis at the end of the next paragraph.

[20] Recall that the number of edges that have at least one endpoint that is not in V is at most $0.1\epsilon k^2$.

The crucial details that were avoided so far are the specification of the T partitions χ_i's and their implementation via queries to the graph. We leave these crucial details to the proof of Lemma 8.8, since it makes little sense to give these details without proving that they actually work.[21]

8.3.1. Testing Bipartiteness

We first note that, in contrast to `Biclique`, the set of bipartite graphs has no proximity-oblivious tester that makes a constant number of queries (and has rejection probability that depends only on the distance of the graph from being bipartite).[22] This can be shown by considering graphs that have an "odd-girth" that is larger than the potential query complexity (see Exercise 8.5). Nevertheless, testing `Bipartitenss` is quite simple: It amounts to selecting a small random set of vertices, and checking whether the induced subgraph is bipartite. Specifically, the size of the sample is polynomial in the reciprocal of the proximity parameter.

Algorithm 8.7 (Testing `Bipartiteness` in the dense graph model): *On input k, ϵ and oracle access to an adjacency predicate of a k-vertex graph, $G = ([k], E)$, the tester proceeds as follows:*

1. *Uniformly select a subset of $\widetilde{O}(1/\epsilon^2)$ vertices of G.*
2. *Accept if and only if the subgraph induced by this subset is bipartite.*

Step (2) amounts to querying the adjacency predicate on all pairs of vertices that belong to the subset selected at Step (1), and testing whether the induced subgraph is bipartite (e.g., by running BFS).[23] As will become clear from the analysis, it actually suffices to query only $\widetilde{O}(1/\epsilon^3)$ of these pairs. Since being bipartite is "closed under taking subgraphs" (i.e., if G is bipartite then every subgraph of G is bipartite), Algorithm 8.7 always accepts bipartite graphs. On the other hand, in case of rejection, the algorithm sees a small subgraph that is not bipartite, and it can output a witness of (bit-)length $\mathrm{poly}(1/\epsilon) \cdot \log k$ that certifies that the graph is not bipartite.[24] The analysis of Algorithm 8.7 is completed by the following lemma.

Lemma 8.8 (The detection probability of Algorithm 8.7): *If $G = ([k], E)$ is ϵ-far from being bipartite, then Algorithm 8.7 rejects it with probability at least $2/3$, when invoked with the proximity parameter ϵ.*

---

[21] **Advanced comment:** Still, if one insists to know, then the answer is essentially as follows. For a random set U of size $t = \widetilde{O}(1/\epsilon)$, we consider all 2-partitions of U, and, for each such 2-partition (U_1, U_2), we define the 2-partition $\chi_{U_1, U_2} : [k] \to \{1, 2\}$ such that $\chi_{U_1, U_2}(v) = i$ if and only if v is a neighbor of some vertex in U_{3-i}. Note that this definition may be contradictory (when v neighbors both U_1 and U_2) and partial (if v neighbors no vertex in U). Both issues will be handled in the proof of Lemma 8.8.

[22] Recall that the definition of proximity-oblivious tester used in this text requires that the rejection probability depends only on the distance of the input from the property.

[23] This relies on the fact that, for any vertex v in a connected graph, it holds that the graph is bipartite if and only if there is no edge between a pair of vertices that are at equal distance from v. (Indeed, the existence of such an edge implies the existence of an odd cycle, and otherwise we can (legally) 2-color the vertices according to the parity of their distance from v.)

[24] Indeed, in this case, the witness may consist of an odd-length cycle of $\widetilde{O}(1/\epsilon^2)$ vertices.

It follows that Algorithm 8.7 is a tester of one-sided error for `Bipartiteness` (in the dense graph model).

Proof: Denoting by R the random $\widetilde{O}(1/\epsilon^2)$-subset of $[k]$ selected in Step (1), we shall show that, with probability at least $2/3$, the subgraph of G induced by R is not bipartite. That is, assuming that G is ϵ-far from bipartite, we prove that with high probability G_R is not bipartite, where G_R is the subgraph of G induced by R.

We view R as a union of two disjoint sets U and S such that S is $O(1/\epsilon)$ times larger than U; specifically, we use $t \stackrel{\text{def}}{=} |U| = O(\epsilon^{-1} \cdot \log(1/\epsilon))$ and $m \stackrel{\text{def}}{=} |S| = O(t/\epsilon)$. We will consider all possible 2-partitions of U, and associate a partial 2-partition of $[k]$ with each such 2-partition of U. Specifically, the partial 2-partition of $[k]$ that is associated with a specific 2-partition (of U), denoted (U_1, U_2), places all neighbors of U_1 (respectively, U_2) opposite to U_1 (respectively, U_2).[25] The point is that *such a placement of vertices is forced upon any 2-partition that is consistent with the 2-partition* (U_1, U_2) in the sense that if v neighbors U_i and the subgraph induced by $U \cup \{v\}$ is bipartite with a 2-partition that places U_1 on one side and U_2 on the other, then v must be on the side opposite to U_i.

The idea is that since G is ϵ-far from being bipartite, any 2-partition of its vertices (and, in particular, one associated with the 2-partition of U) must have at least $\epsilon k^2/2$ edges that have both their endpoints in the same side of the said 2-partition of $[k]$, and (with high probability) the sample S will hit some of these edges. There are a couple of problems with this idea. First, we do not know the 2-partition of U, but as hinted in the previous paragraph we shall consider all of them. (Indeed, there are only 2^t possibilities, whereas the size of S is selected such that the probability of not detecting a problem with any fixed 2-partition is smaller than $2^{-t}/10$.) Second, the 2-partition of U only forces the placement of vertices that neighbor U, while we do not know the placement of the other vertices (and so cannot detect problems with edges incident to them).

The second problem is solved by showing that, with high probability over the choice of U, almost all high-degree vertices in $[k]$ do neighbor U, and so are forced by each of its possible 2-partitions. Since there are relatively few edges incident at vertices that do not neighbor U, it follows that, with very high probability over the choice of S, each such 2-partition of U is detected as illegal by $G_{U \cup S}$. Details will follow, but before we proceed let us stress the key observation: *It suffices to rule out relatively few* (partial) *2-partitions of* $[k]$ (i.e., those induced by 2-partitions of U), rather than all possible 2-partitions of $[k]$.

We use the notations $\Gamma(v) \stackrel{\text{def}}{=} \{u : \{u, v\} \in E\}$ and $\Gamma(X) \stackrel{\text{def}}{=} \cup_{v \in X} \Gamma(v)$. Given a 2-partition (U_1, U_2) of U, we define a (possibly partial) 2-partition of $[k]$, denoted (V_1, V_2), such that $V_1 \stackrel{\text{def}}{=} \Gamma(U_2)$ and $V_2 \stackrel{\text{def}}{=} \Gamma(U_1)$, where we assume, for simplicity, that $V_1 \cap V_2$ is indeed empty (otherwise things are easier).[26] As suggested above, if one claims that G can be "legally bipartitioned" with U_1 and U_2 on different sides,

---

[25] Indeed, the placement of vertices that do not neighbor U remains undetermined (or is arbitrary). This is the reason that we referred to the associated partition as partial. On the other hand, it is unclear how to handle vertices that neighbor both U_1 and U_2, but such vertices are actually more beneficial to us. (Formally, we may just place them opposite to U_1.)

[26] In this case the 2-partition (U_1, U_2) is ruled out by $G_{U \cap \{v\}}$ for every $v \in V_1 \cap V_2$. In the rest of the analysis, we shall not use this fact. The reader may redefine $V_2 = \Gamma(U_1) \setminus V_1$.

then $V_1 = \Gamma(U_2)$ must be on the opposite side to U_2 (and $\Gamma(U_1)$ opposite to U_1).[27] Note that the 2-partition of U places no restriction on vertices that have no neighbor in U. Thus, we first ensure that *almost all* "influential" (i.e., "high-degree") vertices in $[k]$ have a neighbor in U.

Definition 8.8.1 (High-degree vertices and good sets): *We say that a vertex v is of high degree if it has degree at least $\epsilon k/6$. We call U good if all but at most $\epsilon k/6$ of the high-degree vertices have a neighbor in U.*

As will be shown in the proof of Claim 8.8.4, *if U is a good set, then all but at most $\epsilon k^2/3$ of the edges have both their endpoints in vertices that neighbor U.* We comment that NOT insisting that a good set U neighbors *all* high-degree vertices allows us to show that, with high probability, a random U of size $\widetilde{O}(1/\epsilon)$ is good, where the point is that this size is unrelated to the size of the graph. (In contrast, if we were to insist that a good U neighbors *all* high-degree vertices, then we would have had to use $|U| = \Omega(\epsilon^{-1} \log k)$.)

Claim 8.8.2 (Random t-sets are good): *With probability at least $5/6$, a uniformly chosen set U of size t is good.*

Proof: For any high-degree vertex v, the probability that v does not have any neighbor in a uniformly chosen U is at most $(1 - (\epsilon/6))^t < \epsilon/36$, since $t = \Omega(\epsilon^{-1} \log(1/\epsilon))$. Hence, the expected number of high-degree vertices that do not have a neighbor in a random set U is less than $\epsilon k/36$, and the claim follows by Markov's Inequality. ∎

Definition 8.8.3 (Disturbing a 2-partition of U): *We say that an edge disturbs the 2-partition (U_1, U_2) of U if both its endpoints are in the same set $\Gamma(U_i)$, for some $i \in \{1, 2\}$.*

Claim 8.8.4 (Lower bound on the number of disturbing edges): *For any good set U and any 2-partition of U, at least $\epsilon k^2/6$ edges disturb this 2-partition.*

Proof: Since G is ϵ-far from being bipartite, each 2-partition of $[k]$ has at least $\epsilon k^2/2$ *violating edges* (i.e., edges with both endpoints on the same side). In particular, this holds for the 2-partition (V_1, V_2) defined by letting $V_1 = \Gamma(U_2)$ and $V_2 = [k] \setminus V_1$, where (U_1, U_2) is the given 2-partition of U. We *upper-bound* the number of edges with both sides in the same V_i that are *not disturbing*. Actually, we upper-bound the number of edges that have an endpoint that is not in $\Gamma(U)$.

- The number of edges incident at high-degree vertices that do not neighbor the good set U is upper-bounded by $(\epsilon k/6) \cdot k$, since there are at most $\epsilon k/6$ such vertices.
- The number of edges incident at vertices that are not of high degree is upper-bounded by $k \cdot \epsilon k/6$, since each such vertex has at most $\epsilon k/6$ incident edges.

Hence, that are at most $\epsilon k^2/3$ edges that do not have both endpoints in $\Gamma(U)$. This leaves us with at least $\epsilon k^2/6$ violating edges with both endpoints in $\Gamma(U)$,

---

[27] Formally, we observe that if $\chi : [k] \to \{1, 2\}$ is a 2-coloring of G (i.e., a mapping χ such that $\chi(u) \neq \chi(v)$ for every $\{u, v\} \in E$) and $\chi(u) = i$ for every $u \in U_i$ and $i \in \{1, 2\}$, then $\chi(v) \neq i$ for every $v \in \Gamma(U_i)$.

whereas these edges disturb the 2-partition (U_1, U_2) (since $V_1 \cap \Gamma(U) = \Gamma(U_2)$ and $V_2 \cap \Gamma(U) \subseteq \Gamma(U_1)$). $\blacksquare$

The lemma follows by observing that G_R is bipartite only if either (1) the set U is not good; or (2) the set U is good but there exists a 2-partition of U such that none of the edges disturbing it appears in G_R. Using Claim 8.8.2 the probability of Event (1) is upper-bounded by $1/6$, whereas the probability of Event (2) is upper-bounded by the probability that there exists a 2-partition of U such that none of the corresponding disturbing edges has both endpoints in the (second) sample S. By Claim 8.8.4, each 2-partition of U has at least $\epsilon k^2/6$ disturbing edges, and (as shown next) the probability that none of them has both endpoints in S is at most $(1 - (\epsilon/3))^{m/2}$. Actually, we pair the m vertices of S, and consider the probability that none of these $m/2$ pairs constitutes a disturbing edge for some partition of U (i.e., there exists a 2-partition (U_1, U_2) such that none of these $m/2$ pairs is disturbing for (U_1, U_2)). Using a union bound over all 2-partitions of $U \equiv [t]$, we upper-bound the probability of Event (2) by

$$2^t \cdot \left(1 - \frac{\epsilon k^2/6}{k^2/2}\right)^{m/2} < \frac{1}{6},$$

where the inequality holds since $m = \Omega(t/\epsilon)$. The lemma follows. $\blacksquare$

Approximate 2-Coloring Procedures That Arises from the Proof of Lemma 8.8. By an approximate 2-coloring of a graph $G = ([k], E)$, we mean a 2-partition $\chi : [k] \to \{1, 2\}$ with relatively few edges having endpoints that are assigned the same color (e.g., $|\{\{u, v\} \in E : \chi(v) = \chi(w)\}| = o(|E|)$). The partitioning rule employed in the proof of Lemma 8.8 (i.e., $\chi(v) = 1$ if and only if $v \in \Gamma(U_2)$ for an adequate 2-partition (U_1, U_2) of U) yields a randomized poly$(1/\epsilon) \cdot k$-time algorithm for approximately 2-coloring a k-vertex bipartite graph such that (with high probability) at most ϵk^2 edges have endpoints that are assigned the same color. This randomized algorithm invokes the foregoing tester, determining a 2-partition (U_1, U_2) of U that is consistent with some 2-coloring of the subgraph induced by $R = U \cup S$, and 2-partitioning $[k]$ as done in the proof (with vertices that do not neighbor U, or neighbor both U_1 and U_2, placed arbitrarily). Thus, once the 2-partition (U_1, U_2) is determined, the placement (or coloring) of each vertex is determined by inspecting at most $\widetilde{O}(1/\epsilon)$ entries of the adjacency matrix. Hence, the aforementioned 2-partition of U constitutes a succinct representation of the 2-partition of the entire graph. (We mention that these facts are a typical consequence of using the "force-and-check" paradigm in the analysis of the tester.)

On the Complexity of Testing `Bipartiteness` (Advanced Comment). We comment that a more complex analysis, due to Alon and Krivelevich [13], implies that Algorithm 8.7 is an ϵ-tester for `Bipartiteness` even if one selects only $\widetilde{O}(1/\epsilon)$ vertices (rather than $\widetilde{O}(1/\epsilon^2)$ vertices) in Step (1). That is, *if G is ϵ-far from being bipartite, then, with high probability, the subgraph induced by a random set of $\widetilde{O}(1/\epsilon)$ vertices of G is not bipartite.* We mention that inspecting the subgraph induced by $o(1/\epsilon)$ random vertices will not do (see Exercise 8.6). Furthermore, while the result of Alon and Krivelevich [13] implies that `Bipartiteness` can be ϵ-tested using $\widetilde{O}(1/\epsilon^2)$ *nonadaptive* queries, Bogdanov and Trevisan [62] showed that $\Omega(1/\epsilon^2)$ queries are required by any *nonadaptive* ϵ-tester. For general (adaptive) testers, a lower bound of $\Omega(1/\epsilon^{3/2})$ queries is known [62], even if the input (k-vertex) graph has max-degree at most $O(\epsilon k)$, and this lower bound is almost tight for that case [162]. These facts beg the following question.

Open Problem 8.9 (What is the query complexity of testing Bipartiteness?): *Can* Bipartiteness *be ϵ-tested using $\widetilde{O}(1/\epsilon^c)$ queries for some $c < 2$? How about $c = 1.5$?*

We mention that Bogdanov and Li [60] showed that *the answer to the first question is positive, provided that the following conjecture holds.*

Conjecture 8.10 (A random induced subgraph preserves the distance from being bipartite): *If G is ϵ-far from being bipartite, then, with probability at least $2/3$, the subgraph induced by a random set of $\widetilde{O}(1/\epsilon)$ vertices of G is $\Omega(\epsilon)$-far from being bipartite.*

Recall that Alon and Krivelevich [13] showed that, with high probability, such a subgraph is not bipartite; but the conjecture postulates that this subgraph is far from being bipartite. Note that the proof of Lemma 8.8 implies that (with high probability) the subgraph induced by a random set of $\widetilde{O}(1/\epsilon^2)$ vertices of G is $\Omega(\epsilon)$-far from being bipartite (see Exercise 8.7).

8.3.2. The Actual Definition and the General Result

It is time to provide the actual definition of the class of *general graph partition problems*. Recall that a graph partition problem calls for partitioning the vertices of the graph into a predetermined number of parts such that the sizes of the parts fit predetermined bounds and ditto with respect to the number of edges between parts. Hence, each problem (or property) in this class is defined in terms of a sequence of parameters. The main parameter, denoted t, represents the number of sets (of vertices) in the partition. In addition, we have, (1) for each $i \in [t]$, a pair of corresponding upper and lower bounds on the density of the ith set, and (2) for each $(i, j) \in [t]^2$, two pairs of corresponding upper and lower bounds on the "absolute" and "relative" density of the edges between the ith and j^{th} sets, where by absolute (resp., relative) density we mean the number of edges normalized by k^2 (resp., by the maximum number possible, given the actual sizes of the ith and j^{th} sets).

In the following definition, for a graph $G = (V, E)$ and two sets $V', V'' \subseteq V$, we denote by $E(V', V'')$ the set of edges having one endpoint in V' and another endpoint in V''. (Indeed, if $V' = V''$, then $E(V', V'')$ denotes the set of edges with both endpoints in $V' = V''$.) Note that, for $V' \cap V'' = \emptyset$, it holds that $|E(V', V'')| \leq |V'| \cdot |V''|$, whereas $|E(V', V')| \leq \binom{|V'|}{2}$. For that reason (and for it only), Conditions 3 and 4 are separated.[28]

Definition 8.11 (General partition problem (or property)): *A graph partition problem (or property) is parameterized by a sequence $(t, (L_i, H_i)_{i \in [t]}, (L_{i,j}^{\text{abs}}, H_{i,j}^{\text{abs}})_{i,j \in [t]}, (L_{i,j}^{\text{rel}}, H_{i,j}^{\text{rel}})_{i,j \in [t]})$, where $t \in \mathbb{N}$, and consists of all graphs $G = (V, E)$ such that there exists a t-partition of V, denoted $(V_1, \ldots, V_t)$, that satisfies the following conditions:*

---

[28] Indeed, Condition 4 could have been integrated in Condition 3 if we had fictitiously defined $E(V', V')$ to include self-loops and two copies of each edge. Note that Conditions 2 and 3 are stated in a redundant manner since $E(V_i, V_j) = E(V_j, V_i)$; indeed, it suffices to consider the case $i \leq j$.

1. For every $i \in [t]$,

$$L_i \leq \frac{|V_i|}{|V|} \leq H_i.$$

2. For every $i, j \in [t]$,

$$L_{i,j}^{\text{abs}} \leq \frac{|E(V_i, V_j)|}{|V|^2} \leq H_{i,j}^{\text{abs}}.$$

3. For every $i, j \in [t]$ such that $i \neq j$,

$$L_{i,j}^{\text{rel}} \leq \frac{|E(V_i, V_j)|}{|V_i| \cdot |V_j|} \leq H_{i,j}^{\text{rel}}.$$

4. For every $i \in [t]$,

$$L_{i,i}^{\text{rel}} \leq \frac{|E(V_i, V_i)|}{\binom{|V_i|}{2}} \leq H_{i,i}^{\text{rel}}.$$

Definition 8.11 extends the definition used in [140, Sec. 9], which contained only Conditions 1 and 2. We believe that the added conditions (nos. 3 and 4) increase flexibility and avoid some annoying technicalities. Using Definition 8.11, we can easily formulate the natural partition problems that were stated at the beginning of Section 8.3, where in all cases we use $t = 2$.

Biclique: Here we use $L_{1,2}^{\text{rel}} = 1$ and $H_{1,1}^{\text{abs}} = H_{2,2}^{\text{abs}} = 0$.
    That is, we mandate maximal edge density between the two parts (i.e., no edges may be missing) and minimal edge density within each part (i.e., no edges may be present there).
    All other parameters are trivial, which means that the lower bounds (e.g., L_i's) are all set to 0, while the upper bounds (e.g., H_i's) are all set to 1.
Bipartiteness: Here we use $H_{1,1}^{\text{abs}} = H_{2,2}^{\text{abs}} = 0$. Again, all other parameters are trivial.
Max-Cut (for $\rho \in (0, 0.25]$): Here we use $L_{1,2}^{\text{abs}} = \rho$ (and again all other parameters are trivial).
Min-Bisection (for $\rho \in (0, 0.25]$): Here we use $H_{1,2}^{\text{abs}} = \rho$ and $L_1 = L_2 = H_1 = H_2 = 1/2$.
Max-Clique (for $\rho \in (0, 1]$): Here we use $L_1 = \rho$ and $L_{1,1}^{\text{rel}} = 1$.

The following result follows from the techniques used in the proof of [140, Thm. 9.1].[29]

Theorem 8.12 (Testing general partition properties (in the dense graph model)):
Every graph partition property can be ϵ-tested within query complexity $\text{poly}(t/\epsilon)^{t^2}$, where the polynomial does not depend on the parameters of the property and t is the

---

[29] We mention that [140, Thm. 9.1] states a query complexity bound of $O(t^2/\epsilon)^{2t+8+o(1)}$, but it only refers to the case in which all the relative bounds (i.e., the $L_{i,j}^{\text{rel}}$'s and $H_{i,j}^{\text{rel}}$'s) are trivial, since such bounds were not included in the definition used in [140, Sec. 9]. Nevertheless, the proof seems to extend in a straightforward manner, if one can use such an expression when referring to such a complex proof. Alternatively, as noted by Yonatan Nakar and Dana Ron (priv. comm.), the general case can be reduced to the special case treated in [140, Thm. 9.1] by approximating each general property by a union of $O(1/\epsilon)^{t^2}$ properties of the special case. To be on the safe side, we stated the result that follows from their transformation.

first parameter of the property (cf., Definition 8.11). *The computational complexity of the tester is exponential in its query complexity.*

The tester operates by selecting a sample of $\text{poly}(t/\epsilon)^t$ vertices and checking whether the induced subgraph satisfies the same graph partition property, possibly up to a small relaxation in the density parameters.[30] The latter checking is done by merely going over all possible t-partitions of the induced graph and checking if any of them satisfies the corresponding property. This explains the exponential time bound, which seems unavoidable in general, because a time bound of $T(1/\epsilon)$ for ϵ-testing properties such as Max-Cut or 3-coloring would have implied a $T(k^2)$-time algorithm for these problems (by setting $\epsilon = 1/k^2$).

Finding Approximately Good Partitions. As in the case of Bipartiteness, the tester for each graph partition problem can be modified into an algorithm that finds an (succinct representation of an) approximately adequate partition whenever it exists. That is, if the k-vertex graph has the desired (t-partition) property, then the testing algorithm may actually output auxiliary information that allows reconstructing, in $\text{poly}(1/\epsilon) \cdot k$-time, a t-partition that approximately obeys the property. (For example, for ρ-Cut, we can construct a 2-partition with at least $(\rho - \epsilon) \cdot k^2$ crossing edges.) Furthermore, the location of each vertex with respect to that t-partition can be determined in $\text{poly}(t/\epsilon)$-time. Hence, the auxiliary information output by the modified tester, which has length $\text{poly}(t/e)^t$, is a succinct representation of such a t-partition. We comment that this notion of a succinct representation of a structure that corresponds to an (approximate) NP-witness may be relevant for other sets in $\mathcal{NP}$ (i.e., not only to graph partition problems).[31]

The Case of t-Colorability. We mention that better bounds are known for some specific properties that fall into the framework of Definition 8.11. Most notably, t-Colorability (i.e., $H_{i,i}^{\text{abs}} = 0$ for all $i \in [t]$) can be ϵ-tested using $\text{poly}(t/\epsilon)$ queries. In this case, the tester selects a random sample of $\widetilde{O}(t/\epsilon^2)$ vertices and accepts if and only if the induced subgraph is t-colorable. Recall that for 2-Colorability (i.e., Bipartiteness), a random sample of $\widetilde{O}(1/\epsilon)$ vertices suffices. Let us state these results in combinatorial terms.

Theorem 8.13 (Testing t-Colorability (in the dense graph model)):[32] *For every $t \geq 2$, if a graph G is ϵ-far from being t-colorable, then, with high probability, the*

---

[30] **Advanced comment:** The analysis of the tester uses the force-and-check technique (which was outlined immediately after the proof of Proposition 8.6). In particular, we consider all possible t-partitions of the first part of the sample, denoted U, as well as all possible (approximate) values for a sequence of some auxiliary parameters. Each such pair of choices induces a t-partition of $[k]$, and $\exp(\text{poly}(1/\epsilon)^t)$ many choices are considered. It is shown that if the input graph satisfies the property, then one of these t-partitions of $[k]$ witnesses this fact, and that it is possible to determine the location of every vertex that is adjacent to U with respect each of these partitions based on its adjacency relation with U (and the auxiliary parameters), where all but at most $0.1\epsilon k^2$ of the edges are incident at vertices in $\Gamma(U)$. One crucial detail is the use of a sequence of auxiliary parameters that correspond to a finer (and somewhat less natural) notion of a partition problem than the one captured by Definition 8.11 (e.g., having conditions that refer to the statistics of vertex degrees in each part).

[31] **Advanced comment:** Indeed, an interesting algorithmic application was presented in [115], where an implicit partition of an imaginary hypergraph is used in order to efficiently construct a regular partition (with almost optimal parameters) of a given graph.

[32] Note that the problem of 1-coloring is almost trivial, since it asks whether the graph is empty.

subgraph of G induced by a random set of $\widetilde{O}(t/\epsilon^{c_t})$ vertices is not t-colorable, where $c_2 = 1$ and $c_t = 2$ for $t \geq 3$.

Indeed, this yields a one-sided error tester of query complexity $\widetilde{O}(t/\epsilon^{c_t})^2$.

Reflection: Why Are General Partition Properties Easily Testable? Indeed, such a question may arise with respect any other testing result seen in prior sections or chapters, but it seems to be acute here in light of the fact that the testers operate by inspecting the subgraph induced by a random set of poly($1/\epsilon$) vertices. As indicated by Theorem 8.25, the fact that testing is performed in this manner is an artifact of the dense graph model; that is, any graph property that can be tested within query complexity q, can be tested by inspecting the subgraph induced by a random set of $O(q)$ vertices. So the actual question is why does a sample of poly($1/\epsilon$) vertices suffice here. A good indication for the non-triviality of this question is provided by the fact that a sample of poly($1/\epsilon$) vertices does not suffice for testing triangle-freeness (see Corollary 8.19, Part 3). So why are general partition properties easier to test than triangle-freeness?

These are all good questions, but we do not have a truly good answer. We could have answered with an abstract overview of the proof of Theorem 8.12, which would have amounted to further detailing the vague outline presented in footnote 30, but this would not have been very satisfying. Instead, we believe that some intuition may be obtained by showing that *whenever a graph has the specified t-partition property, an approximately good t-partition can be succinctly described.* The reason that such succinct descriptions exist is that vertices that have approximately the same number of neighbors in each of the t parts are interchangeable (with respect to partition problems), and so we need only specify how many of these vertices should be placed in each part. Unfortunately, this description is circular, since the partition should be fixed in order to determine the number of neighbors that a vertex has in each part. This circularity is resolved by proceeding in $O(1/\epsilon)$ iterations such that we assign $\Theta(\epsilon k)$ vertices in each iteration, where the assignment is based on the number of neighbors that these vertices have among the vertices assigned in prior iterations.[33]

8.4. Connection to Szemerédi's Regularity Lemma

The problem of testing graph properties (in the dense graph model) is related to a celebrated combinatorial result, called Szemerédi's Regularity Lemma [258]. This relation is most tight when focusing on the question of *which graph properties are testable within query complexity that depends only on the proximity parameter.*

We stress the fact that the foregoing question ignores the specific dependence (of the query complexity on the proximity parameter). It rather stresses the independence of the query complexity from the size of the graph, and it seems adequate to say that such properties have size-oblivious testers, although this term is a bit misleading (since the tester must use the size parameter in order to operate).[34]

---

[33] **Advanced comment:** The auxiliary parameters mentioned in footnote 30 correspond to these quantities.

[34] For starters, even selecting a uniformly distributed vertex requires knowing the number of vertices. In addition, as pointed out by Alon and Shapira [21], the final decision of the tester may also depend on the number of vertices. A trivial example refers to the graph property that requires having an odd number of vertices. In any case, the term

8.4.1. The Regularity Lemma

Recall that for a graph $G = (V, E)$ and two disjoint sets $A, B \subseteq V$, we denote by $E(A, B)$ the set of edges having one endpoint in A and another endpoint in B. Using this notation, a pair (A, B) is call regular if $\frac{|E(A', B')|}{|A'| \cdot |B'|} \approx \frac{|E(A, B)|}{|A| \cdot |B|}$ for all sufficiently large $A' \subseteq A$ and $B' \subseteq B$.

Definition 8.14 (Edge density and regular pairs): *Let $G = (V, E)$ be a graph and $A, B \subseteq V$ be disjoint and nonempty sets of vertices.*

- *The edge density of the pair (A, B) is defined as $d(A, B) \stackrel{\text{def}}{=} \frac{|E(A, B)|}{|A| \cdot |B|}$.*
- *The pair (A, B) is said to be γ-regular if for every $A' \subseteq A$ and $B' \subseteq B$ such that $|A'| \geq \gamma \cdot |A|$ and $|B'| \geq \gamma \cdot |B|$ it holds that $|d(A', B') - d(A, B)| \leq \gamma$.*

In many ways, a regular pair in a graph "looks like" a random bipartite graph of the same edge density; that is, one may think of and analyze a regular pair as if it was such a random bipartite graph, and the conclusion reached in such an analysis would typically hold for the regular pair.[35] Indeed, for sufficiently large A and B, a random bipartite graph between A and B is regular with very high probability (see Exercise 8.9).

The Regularity Lemma asserts that, for every $\ell \in \mathbb{N}$ and $\gamma > 0$, every sufficiently large graph can be partitioned into (at least ℓ) almost equal sets such that all but at most a γ fraction of the set pairs are γ-regular, where the number of sets is upper-bounded by a function of ℓ and γ. That is:

Theorem 8.15 (Szemerédi's Regularity Lemma [258]):[36] *For every $\ell \in \mathbb{N}$ and $\gamma > 0$ there exists a $T = T(\ell, \gamma)$ such that every sufficiently large graph $G = (V, E)$ there exists a $t \in [\ell, T]$ and a t-partition of V, denoted $(V_1, \ldots, V_t)$ that satisfies the following two conditions:*

1. Equipartition: *For every $i \in [t]$, it holds that $\lfloor |V|/t \rfloor \leq |V_i| \leq \lceil |V|/t \rceil$.*
2. Regularity: *For all but at most a γ fraction of the pairs $\{i, j\} \in \binom{[t]}{2}$, it holds that (V_i, V_j) is γ-regular.*

Intuitively, Theorem 8.15 means that every graph can be equipartitioned into a constant number of parts such that almost all pairs of parts looks like a random bipartite graph of some edge density. The aforementioned constant depends on the parameters ℓ and γ, alas the upper bound on this quantity (i.e., $T(\ell, \gamma)$) is a tower of poly$(1/\gamma)$ exponents; that is, $T(\ell, \gamma) = \mathrm{T}(\text{poly}(1/\gamma))$, where T is defined inductively by $\mathrm{T}(m) = \exp(\mathrm{T}(m-1))$ with $\mathrm{T}(1) = 2$. It turns out that this huge upper bound cannot be improved significantly, since $T(\ell, \gamma) = \mathrm{T}((1/\gamma)^{\Omega(1)})$ is a lower bound on the number of

---

"size-oblivious testability" seems much better than the term "testability" that is often used when referring to the independence of the query complexity from the size of the graph.

[35] Of course, the word "typically" is crucial here, and it refers to natural assertions that one may want to make on graphs. For example, if the regular pair (A, B) has edge density ρ, then almost all vertices in A have degree that is approximately $\rho \cdot |B|$, and almost all pairs of vertices in A have approximately $\rho^2 \cdot |B|$ common neighbors in B. See Exercise 8.8.

[36] An alternative (popular) formulation requires all sets to be of equal size, but allows an exceptional set of size at most $\gamma \cdot |V|$.

required sets [164]. (A proof of Theorem 8.15 can be found in many sources; see, e.g., [22, Sec. 9.4].)[37]

8.4.2. Subgraph Freeness

The relevance of the Regularity Lemma to property testing can be illustrated by considering the problem of testing H-*freeness*, for a fixed graph H (say the triangle).

Definition 8.16 (Subgraph freeness): *Let H be a fixed graph. A graph $G = (V, E)$ is H-free if G contains no subgraph that is isomorphic to H.*[38]

(For example, if H contains a single edge, then H-freeness means having no edges.)[39] We stress that Definition 8.16 requires that G contains no copy of H as a subgraph, and this is a more strict requirement than requiring that G contains no *induced subgraph* that is isomorphic to H. (The difference between these two notion arises when H is not a clique.)

Suppose that H is a t-vertex graph. Then, a natural (one-sided error) proximity-oblivious tester for H-freeness consists of selecting t random vertices in the tested graph, and checking whether the induced subgraph contains a copy of H. The question is what is the rejection probability of this (one-sided error) tester. In other words, we pose the following question (for which only partial answers, reviewed next, are known).[40]

Open Problem 8.17 (On the number of copies of H in graphs that are ϵ-far from H-free): *Let H be a connected t-vertex graph and let $\#_H(\epsilon, k)$ denote the minimal number of copies of H in a k-vertex graph that is ϵ-far from being H-free. Provide relatively tight lower and upper bounds on $\#_H(\epsilon, k)$.*

A lower bound of $\#_H(\epsilon, k) \geq \epsilon \cdot \binom{k}{2}/\binom{t}{2}$ follows by omitting all edges in all copies of H (see Exercise 8.11), but this lower bound is proportional to the total number of t-tuples (i.e., $\binom{k}{t}$) only when $t = 2$. Indeed, for $t \geq 3$, it is not *a priori* clear whether $\#_H(\epsilon, k)$ can

---

[37] **Advanced comment:** The basic idea is to start with an arbitrary ℓ-equipartition and "refine" it in iteration till the current partition satisfies the regularity condition. If the current t-partition violates the regularity condition, then the $\gamma \cdot \binom{t}{2}$ nonregular pairs give rise to a 2^t-partition of each of the current parts such that some potential function, which ranges in $[0, 1]$, increases by at least $\mathrm{poly}(\gamma)$. This yields a refinement of the current t-partition, which yields a $\exp(O(t))$-equipartition (by further refinement, which never decreases the potential). Hence, we have $\mathrm{poly}(1/\gamma)$ many refinement steps, where in each step the number of parts grows exponentially. Finally, we mention that the potential function used assigns the partition $(V_1, \ldots, V_t)$ of $[k]$, the value $\sum_{i<j} \frac{|V_i| \cdot |V_j|}{k^2} \cdot d(V_i, V_j)^2$. The verification of the aforementioned features of this potential function is left to Exercise 8.10.

[38] That is, if $H = ([t], F)$, then G is H-free if and only if for every one-to-one mapping $\phi : [t] \to V$ there exists an edge $\{i, j\} \in F$ such that $\{\phi(i), \phi(j)\} \notin E$. Equivalently, G is *not* H-free if and only if there exists a one-to-one mapping $\phi : [t] \to V$ such that $\{\{\pi(i), \pi(j)\} : \{i, j\} \in F\} \subseteq E$.

[39] Hence, our focus is on graphs H that have at least two edges, which means that they have at least three vertices.

[40] We focus on the case of connected t-vertex graphs H, while noting that the general case is reducible to it. Specifically, if G is ϵ-far from being H-free and H' is a connected component of H, then G is ϵ-far from being H'-free (since if G' is H'-free then it is H-free). Hence, if for every connected t'-vertex graph H' it holds that $\#_{H'}(\epsilon, k) \geq \rho_{H'}(\epsilon) \cdot \binom{k}{t'}$ for some function $\rho_{H'} : (0, 1] \to \mathbb{N}$, then approximately the same holds for unconnected graphs H, because the number of intersections between copies of different connected components of H is at least one order of magnitude smaller: Specifically, the number of copies of H' that intersect copies of a t''-vertex H'' is at most $t' t'' \cdot \binom{k}{t'+t''-1} < k^{t'+t''-1}$, whereas the number of $(t' + t'')$-vertex sets that contain copies of both H' and H'' is at least $\rho_{H'}(\epsilon) \cdot \binom{k}{t'} \cdot \rho_{H''}(\epsilon) \cdot \binom{k}{t''} = \Omega_{\epsilon,t}(k^t)$, where the notation $\Omega_{\epsilon,t}(\cdot)$ hides arbitrary dependencies on ϵ and t.

be lower-bounded by $\rho_H(\epsilon) \cdot \binom{k}{t}$ for any function $\rho_H : (0, 1] \to \mathbb{N}$. Such a lower bound was established using the Regularity Lemma, and for a decade no other proof of it was known when H is *not* bipartite.[41] Furthermore, for any nonbipartite t-vertex graph H, the known (lower and upper) bounds on the function ρ_H are far apart. Interestingly, in this case it is known that $\rho_H(\epsilon) \ll \text{poly}(\epsilon)$. For example, if G is ϵ-far from triangle-free, then it does *not* follow that G has at least $\text{poly}(\epsilon) \cdot \binom{k}{3}$ triangles. These striking facts are summarized in the following theorem.

Theorem 8.18 (Upper and lower bounds on $\#_H(\epsilon, k)$): *Let H and $\#_H(\epsilon, k)$ be as in Problem 8.17. Then, it holds that*

1. *$\#_H(\epsilon, k) \geq \rho_H(\epsilon) \cdot \binom{k}{t}$ for $\rho_H(\epsilon) = \frac{(0.1\epsilon)^{t^2}}{T((0.1\epsilon)^{t-2}/t)^t}$, where $T(\gamma)$ is a tower of $\text{poly}(1/\gamma)$ exponents.*
2. *If H is bipartite, then $\#_H(\epsilon, k) \geq \rho_H(\epsilon) \cdot \binom{k}{t}$ for $\rho_H(\epsilon) = \Omega(\epsilon^{t^2/4})$.*
3. *If H is not bipartite, then for every positive polynomial p it holds that $\#_H(\epsilon, k) < p(\epsilon) \cdot \binom{k}{t}$. In fact, $\#_H(\epsilon, k) < \exp(-\Omega(\log(1/\epsilon))^2) \cdot \binom{k}{t}$.*

(Recall that t denotes the number of vertices in H.)

Theorem 8.18 summarizes the state of knowledge with respect to Problem 8.17, and indeed it leaves much to be understood (i.e., note the huge gap between Parts 1 and 3).[42] Nevertheless, Theorem 8.18 suffices for establishing the existence of (one-sided error) proximity-oblivious tester for all subgraph-freeness properties. Specifically, H-freeness has a proximity-oblivious tester with detection probability function ρ_H as asserted in Parts 1 and 2, but for nonbipartite H this detection probability is *not* polynomial in the distance from the corresponding property. Furthermore, when H is not bipartite, H-freeness has no ϵ-tester of $\text{poly}(1/\epsilon)$ query complexity, even when allowing two-sided error [17].[43] Here we shall only prove Part 1; the proofs of Parts 2 and 3 can be found in [6].[44]

Proof of Part 1: Fixing any k-vertex graph $G = ([k], E)$ that is ϵ-far from being H-free, we set $\gamma = (0.1\epsilon)^{t-2}$ and $\ell = 10/\epsilon$, and apply the Regularity Lemma to G. Denoting the partition provided by the Regularity Lemma, by $(V_1, \ldots, V_T)$, where T is upper-bounded by a tower of $\text{poly}(1/\gamma)$ exponents, we modify G as follows:

1. We omit all edges that are internal to any of the V_i's.
   In total, we omitted at most $T \cdot \binom{\lceil k/T \rceil}{2} < k^2/T \leq k^2/\ell = 0.1\epsilon k^2$ edges.

---

[41] A somewhat better lower bound (for $\rho_H(\epsilon)$) was subsequently proved by Fox [119]: It replaces the tower of $\text{poly}(1/\epsilon)$ exponents by a tower of $O(\log(1/\epsilon))$ exponents.

[42] In contrast, the result of Part 2 is tight (see Exercise 8.13).

[43] **Advanced comment:** For induced subgraph freeness, this lower bound holds for any graph H that has at least five vertices, regardless if it is bipartite or not [20].

[44] **Advanced comment:** A partial proof of Part 3 can be found in [242, Sec. 9.1]. The proof of Part 2 reduces to the fact that *if a k-vertex graph has at least ϵk^2 edges, then it contains at least $\Omega((2\epsilon)^{t_1 t_2}) \cdot k^{t_1+t_2}$ copies of K_{t_1,t_2}* (i.e., the biclique with t_1 vertices on one side and t_2 vertices on the other side). (This fact is proved in [6, Lem. 2.1]; see also Exercise 8.12.) Hence, if the k-vertex graph G is ϵ-far from being H-free, then G must be ϵ-far from the empty graph, and hence contain at least $\Omega(\epsilon^{t' \cdot (t-t')}) \cdot k^t$ copies of $K_{t',t-t'}$ for every $t' \in [t-1]$. (Thus, if H is a subgraph of $K_{t',t-t'}$, then G contains at least $\Omega(\epsilon^{t' \cdot (t-t')}) \cdot k^t$ copies of H.) We also mention that a two-sided error ϵ-tester of query complexity $O(1/\epsilon)$ (for H-freeness) can just estimate the number of edges in the tested graph, and reject if and only if it is safe to say that the graph has more than $0.4\epsilon k^2$ edges (cf., Proposition 8.4).

2. We omit all edges between pairs of sets that are not γ-regular.
   Here, we omitted at most $\gamma \cdot \binom{T}{2} \cdot \lceil k/T \rceil^2 < \gamma \cdot k^2 \le 0.1 \epsilon k^2$ edges.
3. We omit all edges between pairs of sets that have edge density below 0.2ϵ; that is, we omit all edges between V_i and V_j if and only if $d(V_i, V_j) \le 0.2\epsilon$.
   Here, we omitted at most $\binom{T}{2} \cdot 0.2\epsilon \cdot \lceil k/T \rceil^2 < 0.1\epsilon \cdot k^2$ edges.

Hence, the resulting graph, denoted $G' = ([k], E')$, is a subgraph of G that is *not* H-free.[45] Furthermore, by Steps 2 and 3, every pair (V_i, V_j) is γ-regular in G' and has edge density that is either at least 0.2ϵ or equals zero (i.e., there are no edges between V_i and V_j in G'). Lastly, by Step 1, the graph G' contains no edges that are internal to any V_i.

Given that G' contains some copies of H, we shall lower-bound the number of copies of H in G'. At this point we invoke the intuition, provided right after Definition 8.14, by which regular pairs behave like random bipartite graphs of similar edge density. Considering the guaranteed copy of $H = ([t], F)$ in $G' = ([k], E')$, we observe that its edges reside in regular pairs that have edge density at least 0.2ϵ. If these regular pairs would behave like random bipartite graphs of similar density, then we should expect to have at least $(0.2\epsilon)^{|F|} \cdot (k/T)^t$ copies of H in G', due merely to the t sets in which this copy of H reside, and Part 1 would follow (since $(0.2\epsilon)^{|F|} \cdot (k/T)^t = \Omega(\epsilon)^{t^2} \cdot T^{-t} \cdot \binom{k}{t}$). The actual proof amounts to materializing this observation in the real setting in which the regular pairs are fixed bipartite graphs rather than being random bipartite graphs of similar densities.

Turning to the actual proof and considering the guaranteed copy of H in G', we make the following initial observations. We first observe that if H is a clique, then this copy (of H) contains at most one vertex in each of the V_i's, since each pair of vertices in the copy of H must be connected in G' (whereas vertices in the same V_i are not connected in G'). Turning to the general case (i.e., a general t-vertex graph H), we admit that a copy of H may contain several vertices in the same V_i. But, in such a case, we can partition each V_i into t equal parts, while noting that the regularity condition is preserved, except that the regularity parameter is now t times bigger.[46] Hence, we should actually invoke the Regularity Lemma with $\gamma = (0.1\epsilon)^{t-2}/t$ (rather than with $\gamma = (0.1\epsilon)^{t-2}$). We shall assume, without loss of generality, that the ith vertex of the foregoing copy of H resides in V_i. Furthermore, we observe that if V_i and V_j contain vertices of this copy (of H) that are connected in H, then (by Steps 2 and 3) the pair (V_i, V_j) is γ-regular and has edge density at least 0.2ϵ. Let us summarize:

> **Starting point**: The graph G' contains a copy of H such that the ith vertex of the foregoing copy of H resides in V_i, and if i and j are connected in H then the pair (V_i, V_j) has edge density at least 0.2ϵ (and is γ-regular).

We now consider an auxiliary graph $A = ([T], E_A)$ such that $\{i, j\} \in E_A$ if and only if there is an edge in G' between some vertex of V_i and some vertex of V_j (i.e., there exists $u \in V_i$ and $v \in V_j$ such that $\{u, v\} \in E'$). The key observation is that, according to Step 3, the existence of a single edge (in G') between V_i and V_j implies the existence of at least

---

[45] Indeed, although we can show that G' is $(\epsilon - 3 \cdot 0.2\epsilon)$-far from being H-free, we only use the fact that G' is not H-free.

[46] Since every (V_i, V_j) is γ-regular, each of the t^2 resulting pairs is $t\gamma$-regular (see Exercise 8.14). Also, since there are no edges between vertices of V_i there will be no edges between its t parts.

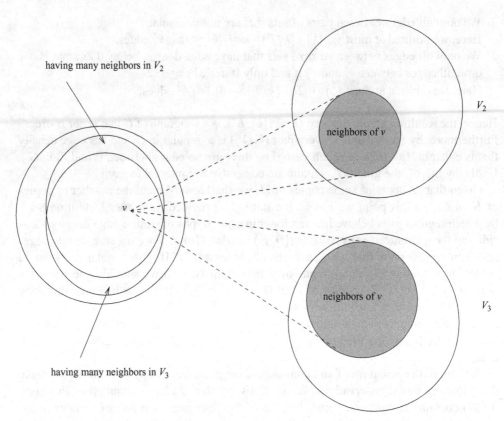

having many neighbors in V_2

V_2

neighbors of v

v

neighbors of v

V_3

having many neighbors in V_3

Figure 8.2: The triangles that contain a typical vertex $v \in V_1$, which has many neighbors in both V_2 and V_3. Note that each edge between $\Gamma_2(v)$ and $\Gamma_3(v)$ forms a triangle that contains v.

$0.2\epsilon \cdot \lfloor k/T \rfloor^2$ such edges. Furthermore, by Steps 2 and 3, if $\{i, j_1\}, \{i, j_2\} \in F$ (equivalently, if there are edges (in G') between V_i and both V_{j_1} and V_{j_2}), then there are many vertices in V_i that have many edges to both V_{j_1} and V_{j_2} (in G'). A more elaborate argument, which is presented next, shows that the existence of any t-vertex subgraph in A, implies that this subgraph appears in "abundance" in G'. This fact, combined with the fact that A must contain a copy of H (since G' is not H-free), implies that G' (and so also G) contains many copies of H. Let us first detail the argument for the case that H is the (three-vertex) triangle.

The case in which H is a triangle. Since the graph G' is not triangle-free, it follows that the graph A contains a triangle (which, w.l.o.g., consists of the vertices 1, 2, and 3). Turning back to G', for each vertex $v \in V_1$, we consider its neighbors in V_2 and V_3, and denote the corresponding sets by $\Gamma_2(v)$ and $\Gamma_3(v)$, respectively; that is, $\Gamma_i(v) = \{u \in V_i : \{u, v\} \in E'\}$. We make the following two observations (depicted in Figure 8.2):

Observation 1: If $|\Gamma_i(v)| \geq 0.1\epsilon \cdot |V_i|$ for both $i \in \{2, 3\}$, then the number of triangles that involve v is at least $(0.1\epsilon)^3 \cdot \lfloor k/T \rfloor^2$.

This follows since for such a vertex v, each pair $(w_2, w_3) \in \Gamma_2(v) \times \Gamma_3(v)$ such that $\{w_2, w_3\} \in E'$ yields a triangle, whereas the density of such edges (i.e., edges between $\Gamma_2(v)$ and $\Gamma_3(v)$) is approximately the density of edges between V_2 and V_3. Specifically, letting $d_{G'}(A, B)$ denote the density of edges between A and B in

G', we have

$$d_{G'}(\Gamma_2(v), \Gamma_3(v)) \cdot |\Gamma_2(v)| \cdot |\Gamma_3(v)| \geq (d_{G'}(V_2, V_3) - \gamma) \cdot |\Gamma_2(v)| \cdot |\Gamma_3(v)|$$
$$\geq 0.1\epsilon \cdot (0.1\epsilon \cdot \lfloor k/T \rfloor)^2,$$

where the first inequality uses the fact that (V_2, V_3) is a γ-regular pair (and $|\Gamma_i(v)| \geq 0.1\epsilon \cdot |V_i| \geq \gamma \cdot |V_i|$ for both $i \in \{2, 3\}$), whereas the second inequality uses the fact that (V_2, V_3) has edge density at least 0.2ϵ (and $\gamma \leq 0.1\epsilon$).

Observation 2: Most of the vertices $v \in V_1$ satisfy $|\Gamma_i(v)| \geq 0.1\epsilon \cdot |V_i|$ for both $i \in \{2, 3\}$. In fact, for every $i \in \{2, 3\}$, at least a $1 - \gamma$ fraction of the vertices $v \in V_1$ satisfy $|\Gamma_i(v)| \geq 0.1\epsilon \cdot |V_i|$.

To see this, let $V_1' \stackrel{\text{def}}{=} \{v \in V_1 : |\Gamma_i(v)| < 0.1\epsilon \cdot |V_i|\}$, and assume toward the contradiction that $|V_1'| > \gamma \cdot |V_1|$. Now, since the pair (V_1, V_i) is γ-regular (and $|V_1'| \geq \gamma \cdot |V_1|$), we have

$$d_{G'}(V_1', V_i) \cdot |V_1'| \cdot |V_i| \geq (d_{G'}(V_1, V_i) - \gamma) \cdot |V_1'| \cdot |V_i|$$
$$\geq 0.1\epsilon \cdot |V_1'| \cdot |V_i|,$$

but this contradicts the definition of V_1', which asserts that each $v \in V_1'$ has less than $0.1\epsilon \cdot |V_i|$ neighbors in V_i.

Combining the two observations, we conclude that there are at least $0.5|V_1| \cdot (0.1\epsilon)^3 \cdot \lfloor k/T \rfloor^2 > 0.4 \cdot (0.1\epsilon/T)^3 \cdot k^3$ triangles in G'. Recalling that T is upper-bounded by a tower of poly$(1/(0.1\epsilon))$ exponents, Part 1 follows in this case (in which H is a triangle).

The General Case: Arbitrary H. We now turn to the general case in which H is an arbitrary t-vertex graph. Recall that, by our hypothesis, G' contains a copy of H with a single vertex in V_i for every $i \in [t]$. It follows that the auxiliary graph A contains a copy of H, and that this copy resides on the vertices $1, 2, \ldots, t$. In this case we proceed in $t - 2$ iterations, starting with $H^{(0)} = H$ and $V_j^{()} = V_j$ for every $j \in [t]$, where $()$ denotes an empty sequence. In general, we let $H^{(i)}$ denote the subgraph of $H^{(i-1)}$ (equiv., of H) induced by $\{i + 1, \ldots, t\}$. We shall enter the ith iteration after having determined a choice of $i - 1$ vertices, denoted $v_1, \ldots, v_{i-1}$, such that for every $j \in [i - 1]$ the vertex v_j resides in $V_j^{(v_1, \ldots, v_{j-1})}$.

In the ith iteration, we identify a set, denoted $U_i^{(v_1, \ldots, v_{i-1})}$, of vertices in $V_i^{(v_1, \ldots, v_{i-1})}$ that have at least $0.1\epsilon \cdot |V_j^{(v_1, \ldots, v_{i-1})}|$ neighbors in each $V_j^{(v_1, \ldots, v_{i-1})}$ such that $j > i$ is a neighbor of i in $H^{(i-1)}$. We observe that $|U_i^{(v_1, \ldots, v_{i-1})}| > 0.5 \cdot |V_i^{(v_1, \ldots, v_{i-1})}|$, by using an argument analogous to Observation 2, while relying on $|V_i^{(v_1, \ldots, v_{i-1})}| \geq \gamma \cdot |V_i|$ (which will be established for the next i in the following Item 2). The ith iteration is completed by selecting an arbitrary $v_i \in U_i^{(v_1, \ldots, v_{i-1})}$, and defining, for every $j \in \{i + 1, \ldots, t\}$,

$$V_j^{(v_1, \ldots, v_{i-1}, v_i)} = \begin{cases} \{w \in V_j^{(v_1, \ldots, v_{i-1})} : \{w, v_i\} \in E'\} & \text{if } j \text{ neighbors } i \text{ in } H^{(i-1)} \\ V_j^{(v_1, \ldots, v_{i-1})} & \text{otherwise.} \end{cases}$$

Extending the foregoing definition to any $v \in V_i$, we note the following two facts:

1. For every $v \in V_i$, the number of copies of $H^{(i-1)}$ in G' that involve v as well as a single vertex from each $V_j^{(v_1, \ldots, v_{i-1})}$ for $j \in \{i + 1, \ldots, t\}$ is lower-bounded by the number

of copies of $H^{(i)}$ in G' that contain a single vertex from each $V_j^{(v_1,\dots,v_{i-1},v)}$ for $j \in \{i+1,\dots,t\}$.

(Recall that $H^{(i)}$ denotes the subgraph of $H^{(i-1)}$ induced by $\{i+1,\dots,t\}$.)

2. For every $v \in U_i^{(v_1,\dots,v_{i-1})}$ and $j \in \{i+1,\dots,t\}$, it holds that

$$\left|V_j^{(v_1,\dots,v_{i-1},v)}\right| \geq 0.1\epsilon \cdot \left|V_j^{(v_1,\dots,v_{i-1})}\right| \geq (0.1\epsilon)^i \cdot |V_j|. \tag{8.2}$$

Hence, for every $i \in [t-2]$ and $j \in \{i+1,\dots,t\}$, it holds that $\left|V_j^{(v_1,\dots,v_{i-1},v)}\right| \geq \gamma \cdot |V_j|$ (since $\gamma = (0.1\epsilon)^{t-2}$). (In particular, $\left|V_{i+1}^{(v_1,\dots,v_{i-1},v)}\right| \geq \gamma \cdot |V_{i+1}|$.)

Lastly, we show that the number of copies of $H^{(t-2)}$ in G' that involve a single vertex from each $V_j^{(v_1,\dots,v_{t-2})}$ for $j \in \{t-1,t\}$ is at least $0.1\epsilon \cdot \left|V_{t-1}^{(v_1,\dots,v_{t-2})}\right| \cdot \left|V_t^{(v_1,\dots,v_{t-2})}\right|$, which is at least $0.1\epsilon \cdot ((0.1\epsilon)^{t-2} \cdot \lfloor k/T \rfloor)^2$. This claim (which is nontrivial only if $H^{(t-2)}$ consists of an edge) is analogous to Observation 1, and is proved in the same manner (while relying on $\left|V_j^{(v_1,\dots,v_{t-2})}\right| \geq \gamma |V_j|$ for both $j \in \{t-1,t\}$).[47] Hence, the number of copies of H in G' is at least

$$\sum_{v_1 \in U_1^{(0)}} \sum_{v_2 \in U_2^{(v_1)}} \cdots \sum_{v_{t-2} \in U_{t-2}^{(v_1,\dots,v_{t-3})}} 0.1\epsilon \cdot \left((0.1\epsilon)^{t-2} \cdot \lfloor k/T \rfloor\right)^2$$

$$\geq \left(\prod_{i=1}^{t-2}(0.5 \cdot (0.1\epsilon)^{i-1} \cdot |V_i|)\right) \cdot 0.1\epsilon \cdot \left((0.1\epsilon)^{t-2} \cdot \lfloor k/T \rfloor\right)^2$$

$$> \left(0.5 \cdot (0.1\epsilon)^{t-3} \cdot \lfloor k/T \rfloor\right)^{t-2} \cdot (0.1\epsilon)^{2t-3} \cdot \lfloor k/T \rfloor^2$$

$$> \frac{(0.1\epsilon)^{t^2}}{T^t} \cdot k^t,$$

where the first inequality is due to $\left|U_i^{(v_1,\dots,v_{i-1})}\right| > 0.5 \cdot \left|V_i^{(v_1,\dots,v_{i-1})}\right| \geq 0.5 \cdot (0.1\epsilon)^{i-1} \cdot |V_i|$ (which uses Eq. (8.2)). This completes the proof. ∎

Digest: On an Apparent Waste in the Proof. The reader may wonder why we did not use the fact that G' is actually 0.4ϵ-far from being H-free (rather than only using the fact that G' is not H-free). Using this stronger fact, we can indeed infer that the auxiliary graph A is 0.4ϵ-far from being H-free. But we cannot capitalize on the latter fact, since we do not have a good lower bound on the number of copies of H in A. Indeed, getting such a lower bound is the contents of Part 1 of Theorem 8.18, but the result established there is meaningless for graphs of size T (such as A). We can only use the obvious lower bound with respect to A, which asserts that (the T-vertex graph) A has at least $\Omega(\epsilon T^2/t)$ different t-vertex subsets that contain a copy of H (see Exercise 8.11). But, at best, this would only allow us to assert that $\#_H(\epsilon, k) \geq \Omega(\epsilon T^2) \cdot (k/T)^t = \Omega(\epsilon/T^{t-2}) \cdot \binom{k}{t}$, which is not significantly better than the bound $\#_H(\epsilon, k) \geq ((0.1\epsilon)^t/T)^t \cdot \binom{k}{t}$ that we just proved (i.e., both bounds have the form $\text{poly}(\epsilon/T) \cdot \binom{k}{t}$).

---

[47] Alternatively, we can use yet another iteration, while setting $\gamma = (0.1\epsilon)^{t-1}$ (rather than $\gamma = (0.1\epsilon)^{t-2}$), and use the corresponding claim regarding $H^{(t-1)}$, which is trivial.

Summary. For the sake of good order, we spell out the results regarding testing subgraph freeness that are implied by Theorem 8.18 (and by the discussion that followed it (including footnote 44)).

Corollary 8.19 (On the complexity of testing subgraph freeness (in the dense graph model)): *Let H be a t-vertex graph. Then:*

1. *There exists a one-sided error proximity-oblivious tester that makes $\binom{t}{2}$ queries and has detection probability $\varrho_H(\delta) = 1/T(1/\text{poly}(\delta^t/t))^t$, where T is the tower-of-exponents function (i.e., $T(m) = \exp(T(m-1))$ and $T(1) = 2$).*
2. *If H is bipartite, then there exists a one-sided error proximity-oblivious tester that makes $\binom{t}{2}$ queries and has detection probability $\varrho_H(\delta) = \Omega(\delta^{t^2/4})$. In this case, H-freeness also has a two-sided error ϵ-tester of query complexity $O(1/\epsilon)$.[48]*
3. *If H is not bipartite, then H-freeness has no ϵ-tester of $\text{poly}(1/\epsilon)$ query complexity, even when allowing two-sided error.[49]*

Recall that a proximity-oblivious tester is said to have detection probability ϱ if it rejects graphs that are at distance δ from the property with probability at least $\varrho(\delta)$.

We mention that the corresponding properties that refer to *induced subgraphs freeness* also have constant-query (one-sided error) proximity-oblivious testers, but their detection probability is even worse (i.e., it is a tower of tower function [20]).[50] Furthermore, this result extends to the case that the property postulates freeness for a family of graphs; that is, for a fixed family of (forbidden) graphs $\mathcal{H}$, a graph G is induced $\mathcal{H}$-free if G contains no induced subgraph that is isomorphic to a graph in $\mathcal{H}$. (Note that here we focus on induced subgraph freeness, since noninduced subgraph freeness with respect to a finite set of graphs $\mathcal{H}$, can be captured by induced subgraph freeness with respect to a finite set of graphs $\mathcal{H}'$.)[51]

Actually, the foregoing result (i.e., that every induced subgraph freeness property has a constant-query proximity-oblivious tester) is, in some sense, the strongest possible. Loosely speaking, *a graph property has a constant-query* (one-sided error) *proximity-oblivious tester if and only if it expressible as an induced subgraph freeness property.* Recall that a proximity-oblivious tester (POT) is required to have detection probability that depends only on the distance of the tested object from the property. The actual result, stated next, allows the family of forbidden subgraphs to depend on the number of vertices in the tested graph, as long as the number of vertices in each graph in the family is uniformly bounded.

---

[48] See footnote 44.

[49] Indeed, this result (of Alon and Shapira [17]) is stronger than the corresponding part of Theorem 8.18: It refers to general testers (rather than to one-sided error testers that arise from repeating a $\binom{t}{2}$-query proximity-oblivious tester for a predetermined number of times).

[50] Recall that a graph G is H-free if G contains no subgraph that is isomorphic to H. In contrast, G is induced H-free if G contains no *induced* subgraph that is isomorphic to H.

[51] Specifically, suppose that $\mathcal{H}$ contains graphs with at most t vertices. Then, $\mathcal{H}'$ is the set of all t-vertex graphs that contain a subgraph that is in $\mathcal{H}$. Note that G contains a (general) subgraph that is isomorphic to a graph in $\mathcal{H}$ if and only if G contains an induced subgraph that is isomorphic to a graph in $\mathcal{H}'$.

Theorem 8.20 (Characterization of graph properties having a POT (in the dense graph model)): *Let* $\Pi = \bigcup_{k \in \mathbb{N}} \Pi_k$ *be a graph property such that each* Π_k *consists of all k-vertex graphs that satisfy* Π. *Then,* Π *has a constant-query* (one-sided error) *proximity-oblivious tester if and only if there exist a constant c and an infinite sequence* $\overline{\mathcal{H}} = (\mathcal{H}_k)_{k \in \mathbb{N}}$ *of sets of graphs such that*

1. *each* $\mathcal{H}_k$ *contains graphs of size at most c;*
2. Π_k *equals the set of k-vertex graphs that are induced* $\mathcal{H}_k$-*free.*

(Note that the number of possible $\mathcal{H}_k$'s is upper bounded by a function of c; indeed, it is at most double-exponential in c^2.)[52] The existence of POTs for properties that satisfy the (induced subgraph) condition follows from [20], whereas the opposite direction is based on a variant of Theorem 8.25 (which is presented in Section 8.5).

8.4.3. The Structure of Properties That Have Size-Oblivious Testers

The relevance of the Regularity Lemma to property testing is not confined to proving the existence of proximity-oblivious testers for any graph property that is expressible as an induced subgraph freeness property. It turns out that every graph property that can be tested using a number of queries that is independent of the size of the graph can be expressed in terms of properties having a regular partition that fits a predetermined sequence of edge densities. The exact meaning of the latter phrase is defined next, where t denotes the number of parts is the partition, γ denotes the regularity parameter, C denotes the set of regular pairs, and the $d_{i,j}$'s denote the prescribed densities.

Definition 8.21 (Regularity properties):[53] *A regularity property is parameterized by a sequence*

$$(\gamma, t, C, (d_{i,j})_{\{i,j\} \in C}) \tag{8.3}$$

such that $\gamma \in (0, 1]$ *and* $C \subseteq \binom{[t]}{2}$ *has size at least* $\lceil (1 - \gamma) \cdot \binom{t}{2} \rceil$. *This property consists of all graphs* $G = (V, E)$ *such that there exists a t-equipartition of V, denoted* $(V_1, \ldots, V_t)$, *and for every* $\{i, j\} \in C$ *the pair* (V_i, V_j) *is* γ-*regular and* $|E(V_i, V_j)| = \lfloor d_{i,j} \cdot |V_i| \cdot |V_j| \rfloor$. *We call* $\max(\gamma, 1/t)$ *the* fineness *of the property.*

We shall consider properties that can be expressed as the union of a finite number of regularity properties of a bounded fineness. In fact, we shall refer to properties that are approximated by the latter, where the notion of approximation is as in Definition 6.5.

Definition 8.22 (Approximation of a property, Definition 6.5 restated): *The property* Π *is* δ-*approximated by the property* Π' *if each object in* Π *is* δ-*close to some object in* Π', *and vice versa.*

---

[52] This fact is important toward applying the result of [20], which relates to the case that $\mathcal{H}_k$ is independent of k. Note that a property Π that satisfies the "$\overline{\mathcal{H}}$-freeness" condition is a union of a finite number of (trivially modified) induced freeness properties (as in [20]). Actually, the latter properties are each parameterized by a set of forbidden graphs $\mathcal{H}$ and a set $K \subseteq \mathbb{N}$ such that a k-vertex graph G has the property if $k \in K$ and G is $\mathcal{H}$-free.

[53] It seems that Theorem 8.23 holds also if the current definition is restricted by mandating that $C = \binom{[t]}{2}$, but the current version is more evocative of the Regularity Lemma.

We are finally ready to state the result alluded to above. It asserts that every graph property that can be tested using a number of queries that is independent of the size of the graph can be approximated by the union of regularity properties (where the fineness of these properties is lower-bounded in terms of the approximation parameter). Actually, the converse holds as well.

Theorem 8.23 (Characterization of properties that have size-oblivious testers (in the dense graph model)): *Let $\Pi = \bigcup_{k \in \mathbb{N}} \Pi_k$ be a graph property such that each Π_k consists of all k-vertex graphs that satisfy Π. Then, the following two conditions are equivalent.*

1. *There exists a function $q : (0, 1] \to \mathbb{N}$ such that the property Π has a tester of query complexity $q(\epsilon)$.*
2. *There exists a function $T : (0, 1] \to \mathbb{N}$ such that for every $\epsilon > 0$ and $k \in \mathbb{N}$, the property Π_k is ϵ-approximated by a union of at most $T(\epsilon)$ regularity properties of fineness $1/T(\epsilon)$.*

8.5. A Taxonomy of the Known Results

The current section is a kind of digest of the material presented in Sections 8.2–8.4, organized according to the query complexity of the various property testing problems. In addition, it presents two results: A query complexity hierarchy (Theorem 8.24) and a result asserting that nonadaptive testers can achieve query complexity that is at most quadratic in the query complexity of an arbitrary tester (Theorem 8.25). Actually, the tester derived in Theorem 8.25 is even more restricted: it merely inspects the subgraph induced by a random sample of vertices.

Testers of Query Complexity That Depends on the Size of the Graph. We first mention that graph properties of arbitrary query complexity are known (cf. [144]): Specifically, graph properties may have query complexity ranging from $O(1/\epsilon)$ to $\Omega(k^2)$, where k denotes the number of vertices, and the same holds also for *monotone graph properties*.[54] Furthermore, the computational complexity of these properties is bounded (i.e., they are in $\mathcal{P}$ and $\mathcal{NP}$, respectively). One of these hierarchy theorems is stated next.

Theorem 8.24 (Query hierarchy for testing graph properties in the dense graph model): *For every $q : \mathbb{N} \to \mathbb{N}$ that is at most quadratic such that $k \mapsto \lfloor \sqrt{q(k)} \rfloor$ is onto, there exists a graph property Π and a constant $\epsilon > 0$ such that ϵ-testing Π on k-vertex graphs has query complexity $\Theta(q(k))$. Furthermore, if $k \mapsto q(k)$ is computable in $\mathrm{poly}(k)$-time, then Π is in $\mathcal{P}$, and if $k \mapsto q(k)$ is computable in $\mathrm{poly}(\log k)$-time, then the tester is relatively efficient in the sense that its running time is polynomial in its query complexity.*[55]

---

[54] A graph property Π is called monotone if, for every $G \in \Pi$, the graph obtained from G by adding any edge to G is also in Π. The same result holds for anti-monotone properties (where omitting edges preserves the property). We warn that the term "monotone graph properties" is sometimes defined as closure under the removal of edges and vertices (see, e.g.,[18]).

[55] **Advanced comment:** The efficiency of the tester (combined with the fact that its query complexity is $\mathrm{poly}(1/\epsilon) \cdot q(k)$) implies that Π is in $\mathcal{BPP}$ (but not necessarily in $\mathcal{P}$). We mention that a hierarchy theorem for

We mention that the testers used toward establishing the upper bound have query complexity $\text{poly}(1/\epsilon) \cdot q(k)$.

Theorem 8.24 is established in [144] by using unnatural graph properties, starting from the $\Omega(k^2)$ lower bound of [140], which also uses an unnatural graph property.[56] In contrast, the $\Omega(k)$ lower bound established in [114] (following [8]) refers to the natural property of testing whether a k-vertex graph consists of two isomorphic copies of some $k/2$-vertex graph.

Testers of Query Complexity That Is Independent of the Size of the Graph. Our main focus is on properties that can be tested within *query complexity that only depends on the proximity parameter* (i.e., ϵ); that is, *the query complexity does not depend on the size of the graph being tested*. As we have seen, there is much to say about this class of properties. For $q : (0, 1] \to \mathbb{N}$, let $\mathcal{C}(q)$ denote the class of graph properties that can be tested within query complexity q. We shall focus on three classes of properties.

1. *The case of arbitrary q such that $q(\epsilon) \gg \text{poly}(1/\epsilon)$.* By Corollary 8.18, triangle-freeness is in the class $\mathcal{C}(q)$, for some function q (i.e., $q(\epsilon)$ is a tower-of-exponents in $O(\log(1/\epsilon))$), but is not in the class $\mathcal{C}(\text{poly}(1/\epsilon))$. The same holds for H-freeness for any nonbipartite H. See further discussion in Section 8.5.1.

2. *The case of $q(\epsilon) = \text{poly}(1/\epsilon)$.* By Theorem 8.12, every graph partition property is in the class $\mathcal{C}(\text{poly}(1/\epsilon))$. In particular, t-Colorability is in $\mathcal{C}(q_t)$ such that $q_2(\epsilon) \in [\Omega(\epsilon^{-3/2}), \widetilde{O}(\epsilon^{-2})]$ and $q_t(\epsilon) = \widetilde{O}(\epsilon^{-4})$ for any $t \geq 3$ (see Theorem 8.13 and Problem 8.9). See further discussion in Section 8.5.2.

3. *The case of $q(\epsilon) = \widetilde{O}(1/\epsilon)$.* By Proposition 8.6, Biclique is in $\mathcal{C}(O(1/\epsilon))$. As mentioned in footnote 44, the same bound holds for H-freeness for any bipartite H. Additional properties in this class are reviewed in Section 8.5.3.

Before further discussing the foregoing classes, we mention that, when disregarding a possible quadratic blow-up in the query complexity, we may assume that the tester is nonadaptive. Furthermore, it is actually canonical in the following sense.

Theorem 8.25 (Canonical testers [158, Thm 2]):[57] *Let Π be any graph property. If there exists a tester of query complexity q for Π, then there exists a tester for Π that uniformly selects at random a set of $O(q)$ vertices and accepts if and only if the induced subgraph has property Π', where Π' is a graph property that depends on Π and may also depend on the number of vertices in the tested graph (i.e., k). Furthermore, if the original tester has one-sided error, then so does the new tester, and a sample of $2q$ vertices suffices*

Indeed, the resulting tester is called canonical. In particular, *the tester decided based on an inspection of the subgraph induced by a random sample of vertices* (and, thus, is, in

---

one-sided error testers is also presented in [144] and it holds for properties in $\mathcal{P}$, but the testers used to establish the upper bound are not relatively efficient in the foregoing sense.

[56] This is a common phenomenon in hierarchy theorems; cf. [131, Chap. 4].

[57] As pointed out in [21], the statement of [158, Thm 2] should be corrected such that the auxiliary property Π' may depend on k and not only on Π. Thus, on input k and ϵ (and oracle access to a k-vertex graph G), the canonical tester checks whether a random induced subgraph of size $s = O(q(k, \epsilon))$ has the property Π', where Π' itself (or rather its intersection with the set of s-vertex graphs) may depend on k. In other words, the tester's decision depends only on the induced subgraph that it sees and on the size parameter k.

particular, nonadaptive). We warn that Π' need not equal Π (let alone that Π' may depend on k). Still, in many natural cases, $\Pi' = \Pi$ (e.g., t-Colorability). We also warn that, in addition to the (possible) quadratic blow-up in the query complexity of the tester, the time complexity of the canonical tester may be significantly larger than the time complexity of the original tester.

8.5.1. Testability in $q(\epsilon)$ Queries, for any Function q

Recall that Theorem 8.18 (Part 1) implies that *all subgraph freeness properties have constant-query* (one-sided error) *proximity-oblivious testers*. This yields a natural class of graph properties that are testable within query complexity that depends only on the proximity parameter. (Also recall that, for any fixed nonbipartite graph H, the query complexity of ϵ-testing H-freeness is superpolynomial in $1/\epsilon$.) Furthermore, Theorem 8.23 provides a combinatorial characterization of the class of properties that can be tested within query complexity that depends only on the proximity parameter.

The downside of the algorithms that emerge from the aforementioned results is that their query complexity is related to the proximity parameter via a function that grows tremendously fast. Specifically, in the general case, the query complexity is upper-bounded only by a tower of a tower of exponents (in a monotonically growing function of $1/\epsilon$, which in turn depends on the property at hand). Furthermore, it is known that a superpolynomial dependence on the proximity parameter is inherent to the foregoing result. Actually, as shown by Alon [6], such a dependence is essential even for testing *triangle freeness*.

The latter fact provides a nice demonstration of the nontriviality of testing graph properties. *One might have guessed that $O(1/\epsilon)$ or $O(1/\epsilon^3)$ queries would have sufficed to detect a triangle in any graph that is ϵ-far from being triangle-free, but Alon's result asserts that this guess is wrong and that* $\text{poly}(1/\epsilon)$ *queries do not suffice.* We mention that the best upper bound known for the query complexity of testing triangle freeness is $\text{T}(O(\log(1/\epsilon)))$, where T is the tower function defined inductively by $\text{T}(m) = \exp(\text{T}(m-1))$ with $\text{T}(1) = 2$ (cf. [119]).

Perspective: Is It All about Combinatorics? Theorem 8.25 seems to suggest that the study of testing graph properties (in this model) reduces to combinatorics, since it asserts that *testing reduces to inspecting a random induced subgraph* (of the corresponding size). This lesson is made more concrete by the characterization of "size-oblivious" testable graph properties provided by Theorem 8.23, which refers to the notion of a *regularity property*, where regularity is in the sense of Szemerédi's Regularity Lemma [258].[58] Recall that this result essentially asserts that a graph property can be tested in query complexity that depends only on ϵ if and only if it can be characterized in terms of a constant number of regularity properties. Hence, when ignoring the specific dependency on ϵ, *testing graph properties in query complexity that depends only on ϵ reduces to testing the edge densities of pairs in a regular partition.* However, as noted already and further discussed next, *this lesson ignores both the running time of the tester and the exact value of the query complexity.*

---

[58] Recall that the Regularity Lemma was also used in the proof of (Part 1 of) Theorem 8.18.

Perspective: The Exact Query Complexity Does Matter. It is indeed an amazing fact that many properties can be tested within (query) complexity that depends only on the proximity parameter (rather than also on the size of the object being tested). This amazing statement seems to put in shadow the question of the form of the aforementioned dependence, and blurs the difference between a reasonable dependence (e.g., a polynomial relation) and a prohibiting one (e.g., a tower-function relation). We beg to disagree with this sentiment and claim that, as in the context of standard approximation problems (cf. [172]), *the dependence of the complexity on the approximation* (or proximity) *parameter is a key issue.*

We wish to stress that we do value the impressive results of [8, 17, 18, 19, 116] (let alone [9]), which refer to graph property testers having query complexity that is independent of the graph size but depends prohibitively on the proximity parameter. We view such results as an impressive first step, which called for further investigation directed at determining the actual dependency of the query complexity on the proximity parameter.

Between $T(\log(1/\epsilon))$ **and** $\mathrm{poly}(1/\epsilon)$**.** While it is most likely that there exist (natural) graph properties that can be tested in less than $T(\log(1/\epsilon))$ queries but not in $\mathrm{poly}(1/\epsilon)$ queries, we are not aware of such a property. In particular, it is conceivable that there exist (natural) graph properties that can be tested in $\exp(1/\epsilon)$ queries but not in $\mathrm{poly}(1/\epsilon)$ queries. (Needless to say, demonstrating the existence of such (natural) properties is an interesting open problem.) Hence, currently, we (are forced to) move directly from complexities of the form $T(\log(1/\epsilon))$ (and larger) to complexities of the form $\mathrm{poly}(1/\epsilon)$.

8.5.2. Testability in $\mathrm{poly}(1/\epsilon)$ Queries

Testers of query complexity $\mathrm{poly}(1/\epsilon)$ are known for several natural graph properties, which fall under the general framework of *graph partition problems* (presented and studied in Section 8.3). We briefly recall some of these properties, while reminding the reader that by Theorem 8.12, every *graph partition problem* is testable in $\mathrm{poly}(1/\epsilon)$ queries.

- t-Colorability, for any fixed $t \geq 2$.
  Recall that by Theorem 8.13, t-Colorability has a one-sided error tester of query complexity $\widetilde{O}(t^2/\epsilon^4)$ for any $t > 2$. For $t = 2$ this tester has query-complexity (and running-time) $\widetilde{O}(1/\epsilon^2)$.
- ρ-Clique, for any fixed $\rho > 0$, where ρ-Clique is the set of graphs that have a clique of density ρ (i.e., k-vertex graphs having a clique of size ρk).
- ρ-Cut, for any fixed $\rho > 0$, where ρ-Cut is the set of graphs that have a cut of density at least ρ (i.e., k-vertex graphs having a cut with at least ρk^2 edges).
- ρ-Bisection, for any fixed $\rho > 0$, where ρ-Bisection is the set of graphs that have a bisection of density at most ρ (i.e., a k-vertex graph is in ρ-Bisection if its vertex set can be partitioned into two equal parts with at most ρk^2 edges going between them).

Except for t-Colorability, all the other testers have two-sided error, and this is unavoidable for any tester of $o(k)$ query complexity for any of these properties.

Beyond Graph Partition Problems. Although many natural graph properties can be formulated as partition problems, many other properties that can be tested with $\mathrm{poly}(1/\epsilon)$ queries cannot be formulated as such problems. The list includes the set of regular graphs, connected graphs, planar graphs, and more. We identify three classes of such natural properties:

1. Properties that depends only on the vertex degree distribution (e.g., degree regularity and bounds on the average degree). For example, for any fixed $\rho > 0$, the set of k-vertex graphs having ρk^2 edges can be tested using $O(1/\epsilon^2)$ queries, which is the best result possible.[59] The same holds with respect to testing degree regularity (see Theorem 8.5 and Exercise 8.1).
2. Properties that are satisfied only by sparse graphs (e.g., k-vertex graphs having $O(k)$ edges) such as Cycle-freeness and Planarity. See Proposition 8.4 for a more general statement.
3. Properties that are almost trivial in the sense that, for some constant $c > 0$ and every $\epsilon > k^{-c}$, all k-vertex graphs are ϵ-close to the property (see Proposition 8.3). For example, every k-vertex graph is k^{-1}-close to being connected (or being Hamiltonian or Eulerian).

In view of the foregoing, we believe that characterizing the class of graph properties that can be tested in poly$(1/\epsilon)$ queries may be far too challenging. Still, we cannot refrain from posing it as an explicit open problem.

Open Problem 8.26 (Characterization of graph properties that are testable in poly$(1/\epsilon)$ queries): *Characterize the class of graph properties that can be tested, in the dense graph model, within query complexity that is polynomial in the reciprocal of the proximity parameter.*

We mention that a dichotomy between properties having poly$(1/\epsilon)$-query testers and properties having $F(1/\epsilon)$-query testers only for some superpolynomial function F is known within some natural classes of graph properties. Specifically, such a dichotomy is known for the class of subgraph freeness properties (see Theorem 8.18), is almost known for induced subgraph freeness properties [20], and is partially known for the case of families of forbidden subgraphs [125].[60] It will be interesting to find other natural classes of graph properties that exhibit such a dichotomy.

8.5.3. Testability in $\widetilde{O}(1/\epsilon)$ Queries

While Theorem 8.25 may be interpreted as suggesting that testing in the dense graph model leaves no room for algorithmic design, this conclusion is valid only if one ignores a possible quadratic blow-up in the query complexity (and also disregards the time complexity). As advocated in [151], a finer examination of the model, which takes into account the exact query complexity (i.e., cares about a quadratic blow-up), reveals the role of algorithmic design. In particular, the results in [151] distinguish adaptive testers

---

[59] Both the upper and lower bounds can be proved by reduction to the problem of estimating the average value of Boolean functions (cf. [66]).

[60] The "almost known" dichotomy of [20, 10] leaves out one unclassified property, whereas the "partially known" dichotomy of [125] leaves a gap between the necessary and the sufficient conditions.

from nonadaptive ones, and distinguish the latter from canonical testers. These results refer to testability in $\widetilde{O}(1/\epsilon)$ queries. In particular, it is known that:[61]

- Testing every "nontrivial for testing" graph property requires $\Omega(1/\epsilon)$ queries, even when adaptive testers are allowed. Furthermore, any canonical tester for such a property requires $\Omega(1/\epsilon^2)$ queries, since it must inspect a subgraph that is induced by $\Omega(1/\epsilon)$ vertices.
- There exist an infinite class of natural graph properties that can be tested by $\widetilde{O}(1/\epsilon)$ *nonadaptive* queries. Specifically, this class contains all properties obtained by an (uneven) blow-up of some fixed graph.[62]
- There exists a natural graph property that can be tested by $\widetilde{O}(1/\epsilon)$ adaptive queries, requires $\Omega(\epsilon^{-4/3})$ nonadaptive queries, and is actually testable by $O(\epsilon^{-4/3})$ nonadaptive queries. The property for which this is shown is called `Clique Collection`, and contains all graphs that consist of a collection of isolated cliques. That is, *the problem of testing* `Clique Collection` *has* (general) *query complexity* $\widetilde{\Theta}(\epsilon^{-1})$ *and nonadaptive query complexity* $\Theta(\epsilon^{-4/3})$.
- There exists a natural graph property that can be tested by $\widetilde{O}(1/\epsilon)$ adaptive queries but requires $\Omega(\epsilon^{-3/2})$ nonadaptive queries. The property for which this is shown is called `Biclique Collection`, and contains all graphs that consist of a collection of isolated bicliques.

All the foregoing testers have one-sided error probability and are efficient, whereas the lower bounds hold also for two-sided error testers (regardless of efficiency).

The foregoing results seem to indicate that even at this low complexity level (i.e., testing in $\widetilde{O}(1/\epsilon)$ adaptive queries) there is a lot of structure and much to be understood. In particular, it is conjectured in [151] that, *for every $t \geq 4$, there exist graph properties that can be tested by $\widetilde{O}(1/\epsilon)$ adaptive queries and have nonadaptive query complexity* $\Theta(\epsilon^{-2+\frac{2}{t}})$. Partial progress toward establishing this conjecture is presented in [151].

8.5.4. Additional Issues

Let us highlight some issues that arise from the foregoing exposition.

Adaptive Testers versus Nonadaptive Ones. Recall that Theorem 8.25 asserts that canonical testers (which are, in particular, nonadaptive) have query complexity that is at most quadratic in the query complexity of general (possibly adaptive) testers. The results surveyed in Section 8.5.3 indicate that a polynomial gap does exist in some cases: In particular, there is a (natural) property that can be ϵ-tested by $\widetilde{O}(\epsilon^{-1})$ adaptive queries, but requires $\Omega(\epsilon^{-3/2})$ nonadaptive queries. We mention that it was conjectured (in [151]) that *for every integer $t \geq 2$, there exist graph properties that can be tested by $\widetilde{O}(1/\epsilon)$*

---

[61] With the exception of the result regarding testability by $\widetilde{O}(1/\epsilon)$ nonadaptive queries, all other results are due to [151]. The exceptional result was proved in a subsequent work of [27], which extended a corresponding result of [151], which in turn referred to the special case in which the fixed graph H is a t-clique.

[62] That is, for any fixed graph $H = ([t], F)$, a k-vertex blow-up of H is a k-vertex graph obtained by replacing each vertex of H by an independent set (of arbitrary size), called a cloud, and connecting the vertices of the ith and j^{th} clouds by a biclique if and only if $\{i, j\} \in F$.

adaptive queries and have nonadaptive query complexity $\Theta((1/\epsilon)^{2(t-1)/t})$.[63] Here we propose a possibly easier goal:

Open Problem 8.27 (Establishing a maximal gap between adaptive and nonadaptive queries): *Show that, for every constant $c < 2$, there exist graph properties that can be tested by $q(\epsilon)$ adaptive queries but requires $\Omega(q(\epsilon)^c)$ nonadaptive queries, where $q(\epsilon) = \Omega(1/\epsilon)$. For starters, establish this claim for some $c > 3/2$.*

A different question, raised by Michael Krivelevich, is whether these (adaptive versus nonadaptive complexity) gaps exist also for properties having query complexity that is significantly larger than $\widetilde{O}(1/\epsilon)$; that is, does there exists a graph property that, for some $c > 1$ and $q(\epsilon) \geq (1/\epsilon)^c$, has adaptive query complexity $q(\epsilon)$ and nonadaptive query complexity $\Omega(q(\epsilon)^c)$? A plausible candidate is Bipartiteness (see Problem 8.9): Recall that ϵ-testing Bipartiteness has *nonadaptive query complexity* $\widetilde{\Theta}(\epsilon^{-2})$ [13, 62][64] *and requires* $\Omega(\epsilon^{-3/2})$ *adaptive queries* [62], but it *may be testable in* $\epsilon^{-(2-\Omega(1))}$ *adaptive queries* (cf. [60]).

One-sided versus Two-sided Error Probability. As noted in Section 8.5.2, for many natural properties there is a significant gap between the complexity of one-sided and two-sided error testers. For example, ρ-Cut has a two-sided error tester of query complexity $\text{poly}(1/\epsilon)$, but no one-sided error tester of query complexity $o(k^2)$ where k is the number of vertices in the tested graph. In general, the interested reader may contrast the characterization of two-sided error testers in [9] with the results in [19].

Proximity-Oblivious Testers. Some of the positive results regarding property testing were obtained by presenting (one-sided error) proximity-oblivious testers (of constant-query complexity and detection probability that depends only on the distance of the tested graph from the property). Furthermore, Theorem 8.20 provided a simple characterization of properties having such testers. It follows that constant-query proximity-oblivious testers do not exist for many easily testable properties (e.g., Bipartiteness (see Exercise 8.5)). Furthermore, even when proximity-oblivious testers exist, repeating them does not necessarily yield the best standard testers for the corresponding property (see, e.g., the case of Clique Collection [152]).

Tolerant Testing. Recall that property testing calls for distinguishing objects having a predetermined property from object that are far from any objects that has this property (i.e., are far from the property). A more "tolerant" notion requires distinguishing objects that are close to having the property from objects that are far from this property. Such a distinguisher is called a tolerant tester, and is a special case of a distance approximator that given any object is required to approximate its distance to the property. The general study of these related notions (which are applicable to all three models discussed in

---

[63] Recall that this is known for $t \in \{2, 3\}$, and that there are promise problems that satisfy the conjecture. (For $t = 4$, only the $\Omega(\epsilon^{-3/2})$ lower bound was established.) On the other hand, it may be that the nonadaptive and adaptive complexities can be related only by a power of $2(t-1)/t$ for $t \in \mathbb{N}$. For starters, one may try to show that the said power cannot be irrational.

[64] The $\widetilde{O}(\epsilon^{-2})$ upper bound is due to [13], improving over [140], whereas the $\Omega(\epsilon^{-2})$ lower bound is due to [62].

Section 8.1) was initiated by Parnas, Ron, and Rubinfeld [225] (and is further discussed in Section 12.1).

A simple observation is that any tester that makes uniformly distributed queries offers some level of tolerance. Specifically, if a tester makes $q(\epsilon)$ queries and each query is uniformly distributed, then this tester distinguishes between objects that are ϵ-far from the property and objects that are $(\epsilon/10q(\epsilon))$-close to the property. Needless to say, the challenge is to provide stronger relations between property testing and distance approximators. Such a result was provided by Fischer and Newman [116]: They showed that *any graph property that can be tested in a number of queries that depends only on the proximity parameter, has a distance approximator of query complexity that depends only on the proximity parameter.*[65]

Directed Graphs. Our discussion was confined to undirected graphs. Nevertheless, the three models discussed in Section 8.1 extend naturally to the case of directed graphs. In particular, in the dense graph model, a directed graph is represented by its adjacency matrix, which is possibly asymmetric; that is, the $(i, j)^{\text{th}}$ entry in the matrix is 1 if and only if there is a directed edge from the ith vertex to the jth vertex. The study of testing properties of directed graphs was initiated by Bender and Ron [40]. In particular, in the dense graph model, they showed a $\text{poly}(1/\epsilon)$-query tester for Acyclicity (i.e., the set of directed graphs that contain no directed cycles). Testing directed graphs in the dense graph model was further studied in [17], which focuses on testing subgraph-freeness.

8.6. Chapter Notes

It should not come as a surprise that this relatively long chapter has relatively long chapter notes. Following the usual historical notes and before the usual exercises, we insert a discussion that relates property testing to other forms of approximation (Section 8.6.2) as well as contrasts it with the classical notion of recognizing graph properties (Section 8.6.3).

8.6.1. Historical Perspective and Credits

The study of property testing in the dense graph model was initiated by Goldreich, Goldwasser, and Ron [140], as a concrete and yet general framework for the study of property testing at large. From that perspective, it was most natural to represent graphs as Boolean functions, and the adjacency matrix representation was the obvious choice. This perspective dictated the choice of the type of queries as well as the distance measure, leading to the definition of the dense graph model.

Testing graph properties in the dense graph model has attracted a lot of attention. Among the directions explored are the study of the complexity of specific natural properties [140, 13, 62, 162, 114], attempts to explore general classes of easily testable properties [140, 8, 6], and characterizations of classes of properties that are testable under various restrictions (e.g., [6, 17, 158, 18, 19, 20, 116, 9, 64]). In addition, many studies of property testing at large have devoted special attention to testing graph properties in

---

[65] This result is implied by Theorem 8.23, but it was proved in [116] before the latter theorem was proved in [9]. In fact, the ideas in [116] paved the road to [9].

the dense graph model [144, 152, 156, 153]. Some of the aforementioned works as well as some that were not listed will be further discussed below.

Before proceeding, we comment on the relation between the dense graph model and the other two models that were briefly presented in Section 8.1 and will be the topic of the two subsequent chapters. In retrospect, the dense graph model seems most natural when graphs are viewed as representing generic (symmetric) binary relations. But, in many other setting, the other two models are more natural. Needless to say, the general graph model is the most general one, and it is indeed closest to actual algorithmic applications. In other words, this model is relevant for most applications, since these seem to refer to general graphs (which model various natural and artificial objects). In contrast, the dense graph model is relevant to applications that refer to (dense) binary relations over finite sets, whereas the bounded-degree graph model is relevant only to applications in which the vertex degree is bounded. The study of testing graph properties in the bounded-degree graph model was initiated by Goldreich and Ron [147], whereas the study of the general model was initiated by Parnas and Ron [222] and generalized to its current form by Kaufman, Krivelevich, and Ron [180].[66]

Simple Properties: Trivial, Sparse, and Degree-Regularity. The results presented in Sections 8.2.2 and 8.2.3 are taken from [140], with the exception of the improved bound stated in Theorem 8.5. The latter improvement (over [140, Prop. 10.2.1.3]) appeared in [133, Apdx A.1], but the proof of Claim 8.5.1 is reproduced from [156, Apdx A.1].

The strategy underlying Algorithm 8.5.2 can be traced to the last paragraph of Levin's work on one-way functions and pseudorandom generators [199, Sec. 9], and is stated explicitly in [145, Lem. 3] (see [128, Clm. 2.5.4.1] for an alternative presentation). Within the context of property testing, this strategy was first used in [147] (see Lemma 3.3 in the proceeding version and Lemma 3.6 in the journal version).

Testing General Partition Problems. The framework of general graph partition problems was introduced by Goldreich, Goldwasser, and Ron [140], and the testers for all properties in it (as summarized by Theorem 8.12) constitute the main results in their paper. We chose to present only the analysis of the Bipartiteness tester (i.e., Lemma 8.8, which is taken from [140]). The improved testers for t-Colorability (captured by Theorem 8.13) are due to Alon and Krivelevich [13].

Using Szemerédi's Regularity Lemma. In retrospect, it turns out that testers for k-Colorability were implicit in the works of Bollobas *et al.* [63] and Rodl and Duke [240], referring to $k = 2$ and $k > 2$, respectively. These works, which predate the definition of property testing, use the Regularity Lemma, and obtain testers of correspondingly huge query complexity (i.e., a tower of poly($1/\epsilon$) exponents). Testers for subgraph freeness, which are also based on the Regularity Lemma, were presented by Alon *et al.* [8]; the corresponding result is stated in Part 1 of Theorem 8.18. Several subsequent works also used the Regularity Lemma (or new extensions of it), culminating with the work of Alon *et al.* [9], to be reviewed next. A notable exception is provided

---

[66] Parnas and Ron [222] only allowed incidence queries (like in the bounded-degree graph model), and Kaufman, Krivelevich, and Ron [180] also allowed adjacency queries (as in the dense graph model).

by Fox's work [119], which asserts that H-freeness has a POT of detection probability $\varrho_H(\delta) = \Omega(1/T(O(\log(1/\delta)))$ (rather than $\varrho_H(\delta) = \Omega(1/T(\text{poly}(1/\delta))$, where T is the tower-of-exponents function).

Characterizations. The celebrated result of Alon, Fischer, Newman, and Shapira [9] provides a combinatorial characterization of the class of properties that can be tested within query complexity that depends only on the proximity parameter (see Theorem 8.23). We view this result more as a structural result regarding properties that can be tested within such a complexity (than as a characterization). It asserts that these properties can be approximated by finite unions of "regularity properties" (where each regular property is a set of graphs that has a regular partition with certain edge densities).[67] A result of a similar flavor was proved independently by Borgs *et al.* [64], while referring to "graph limits."

The characterization of graph properties that have constant-query (one-sided error) proximity-oblivious testers (i.e., Theorem 8.20) is due to Goldreich and Ron [152], which build on [20] for constructing testers and on [158] for inferring that such testers exist only for induced subgraph freeness properties.

Recall that the testers asserted in aforementioned characterizations (as well as all testers obtained by using the Regularity Lemma) have a prohibiting large query complexity. Furthermore, the class of graph properties that can be tested within query complexity that depends only on the proximity parameter ϵ, contains natural properties that are not testable in query complexity $\text{poly}(1/\epsilon)$; see [6]. (Providing better bounds on the query complexity of testing such properties is reflected in Problem 8.17, whereas characterizing the class of graph properties that are testable in $\text{poly}(1/\epsilon)$ queries is posed as Problem 8.26.)

Canonical Testers and the Power of Adaptivity. The notion of canonical testers and Theorem 8.25 are due to Goldreich and Trevisan [158]. Theorem 8.25 explains that the fact that almost all prior testers, in the dense graph model, work by inspecting a random induced subgraph is no coincidence, since the query complexity of such testers is at most quadratic in the query complexity of the best possible testers. Complexity gaps between canonical testers and general nonadaptive testers, and between the latter and general adaptive testers were shown by Goldreich and Ron [151]. While the demonstrated gap for the first case it optimal (i.e., it matches the quadratic upper bound), the gap shown in the second case is not optimal (see Problem 8.27).

8.6.2. Testing versus Other Forms of Approximation

We shortly discuss the relation of the notion of approximation underlying the definition of testing graph properties (in the dense graph model) to more traditional notions of approximation. (Analogous relations hold also in the other two models of testing graph properties, and also outside the domain of graph properties.) Throughout this section, we refer to randomized algorithms that have a small error probability, which we ignore for simplicity.

---

[67] These are regular partitions in the sense of Szemeredi's Regularity Lemma [258], and the specified edge densities may be different for each regular pair.

Application to the Standard Notion of Approximation. The relation of testing graph properties to standard notions of approximation is best illustrated in the case of Max-CUT. Any tester for ρ-Cut, working in time $T(\epsilon, k)$, yields an algorithm for approximating the size of the maximum cut in a k-vertex graph, up to additive error ϵk^2, in time $\widetilde{O}(\log(1/\epsilon)) \cdot T(\epsilon, k)$.[68] Thus, for any constant $\epsilon > 0$, using the tester of Theorem 8.12, we can approximate the size of the max-cut to within ϵk^2 in constant time. This yields a *constant-time approximation scheme* (i.e., to within any constant relative error) for dense graphs. Finding an approximate max-cut does not seem to follow from the mere existence of a tester for ρ-cut; yet, the tester of Theorem 8.12 can be used to find such a cut in time that is linear in k (see discussion following that theorem).

Relation to "Dual Approximation" (cf. [172, Chap. 3]). To illustrate this relation, we consider the tester for ρ-Clique. The traditional notion of approximating Max-Clique corresponds to distinguishing the case in which the given k-vertex graph has a clique of size ρk from, say, the case in which the graph has no clique of size $\rho k/2$. On the other hand, when we talk of testing ρ-Clique, the task is to distinguish the case in which a k-vertex graph has a clique of size ρk from the case in which it is ϵ-far from the class of k-vertex graphs having a clique of size ρk. This is equivalent to the "dual approximation" task of distinguishing the case in which a k-vertex graph has a clique of size ρk from the case in which any ρk-subset of the vertices misses at least ϵk^2 edges. To demonstrate that these two tasks are vastly different, we mention that whereas the former task is NP-Hard for any constant $\rho \in (0, 1/4)$ (see [37, 170]), the latter task can be solved in constant time, for any constant $\rho, \epsilon > 0$. We believe that there is no absolute sense in which one of these approximation tasks is more important than the other: Each of these tasks may be relevant in some applications and irrelevant in others.

8.6.3. A Contrast with Recognizing Graph Properties

The notion of testing a graph property Π is a *relaxation* of the classical notion of *recognizing the graph property* Π, which has received much attention since the early 1970s (cf. [200]). In the classical (recognition) problem there are no margins of error; that is, one is required to accept all graphs having property Π and reject all graphs that lack property Π. In 1975, Rivest and Vuillemin resolved the Aanderaa–Rosenberg Conjecture, showing that any deterministic procedure for deciding any nontrivial monotone k-vertex graph property must examine $\Omega(k^2)$ entries in the adjacency matrix representing the graph. The query complexity of randomized decision procedures was conjectured by Yao to be $\Omega(k^2)$, and the currently best lower bound is $\Omega(k^{4/3})$.

This stands in striking contrast to the aforementioned results regarding testing graph properties that establish that many natural (nontrivial) monotone graph properties can be *tested* by examining a constant number of locations in the matrix (where this constant depends on the constant value of the proximity parameter).

---

[68] Note that if a graph G is ϵ-close to having a ρ-cut, then it must have a cut of size at least $(\rho - 0.5\epsilon) \cdot k^2$. (This is since G is ϵ-close to a graph G' that has a ρ-cut, and this very cut only misses $\epsilon k^2/2$ edges in G.) Hence, if the tester accepts G with probability at least $2/3$, then G must have a $(\rho - 0.5\epsilon)$-cut. The $\widetilde{O}(\log(1/\epsilon))$ factor accounts for a binary search (for the highest value of $\rho \in \{\epsilon, 2\epsilon, \ldots, \lfloor 1/\epsilon \rfloor \cdot \epsilon\}$ for which G has a ρ-cut) as well as for error reduction needed for invoking the tester $\log(1/\epsilon)$ times.

8.6.4. Exercises

The following exercises seem more interesting than most exercises in prior chapters. The topics covered include testing degree regularity (Exercises 8.1 and 8.2), Levin's economical work investment strategy (Exercises 8.3 and 8.4), testing Bipartiteness (Exercises 8.5–8.7), the Regularity Lemma (Exercises 8.8–8.14), and supercanonical testers (Exercise 8.15).

Exercise 8.1 (Query complexity lower bound for testing degree regularity): Prove that ϵ-testing degree regularity requires $\Omega(1/\epsilon^2)$ queries.

> **Guideline:** Show that distinguishing the following two sets of graphs requires $\Omega(1/\epsilon^2)$ queries. The first set consists of k-vertex graphs that consist of two equal-sized connected components such that each component is $0.25k$-regular. The second set is similar except that one connected components is $(0.25 + \epsilon) \cdot k$-regular and the other is $(0.25 - \epsilon) \cdot k$-regular. Reduce from the problem of estimating the average of a Boolean function defined on a large set (see [66]). Specifically, first reduce the problem of distinguishing functions $f : [k] \to \{0, 1\}$ that have average value 0.5 from functions $f : [k] \to \{0, 1\}$ that have average value $0.5 + \epsilon$ to the problem of distinguishing pairs of functions $f_1, f_2 : [k] \to \{0, 1\}$ that have equal average value (of 0.5) from pairs of functions that have an average that differs by at least 2ϵ.[69] Next, reduce the latter problem to the one about graphs.[70]

Exercise 8.2 (Testing d-regularity): For any fixed $\rho > 0$, prove that ϵ-testing if a k-vertex graph is $\lfloor \rho k \rfloor$-regular can be done by $O(1/\epsilon^2)$ nonadaptive queries.

> **Guideline:** Use an adaptation of the proof of Theorem 8.5.

Exercise 8.3 (On Levin's economical work investment strategy): In continuation of Section 8.2.4, establish the following claims for any $c \geq 1$:

1. If the work invested in element ω is $\widetilde{O}(1/q(\omega)^c)$, then the goal *(as defined in Section 8.2.4)* can be achieved by investing $O(1/\epsilon^c)$ work.
2. The treatment in Section 8.2.4 *(as well as the foregoing claim)* hold also when the said investment of work in ω only yield the desired outcome with high constant probability.

> **Guideline:** For Claim 1, suppose that the work invested in ω is $((\log(1/q(\omega))^d / q(\omega)^c)$. Then, selecting $O(i^2 \cdot 2^i)$ points (for each $i \in [\ell]$), and investing $O(\ell^d)/(2^i \epsilon)^c$ work in each of them, will do. For Claim 2, for each $i \in [\ell]$ and each selected point, we repeat our attempt for $O(i)$ times so that to guaranteed that (with probability at least $2^{-i-O(1)}$) the information provided in iteration i is not misleading.

Exercise 8.4 (On Levin's economical work investment strategy, a logarithmic improvement for the case of $c = 1$):[71] In continuation of Section 8.2.4, show that if the work

---

[69] For example, map f to the pair $(f, f \oplus 1)$.

[70] For each $\sigma \in \{1, 2\}$, consider the $2k$-vertex bipartite graph G_σ described by adjacency predicate $g_\sigma : [2k]^2 \to \{0, 1\}$ such that for every $i, j \in [k]$ it holds that $g_\sigma(i, k + j) = g_\sigma(k + i, j) = f_\sigma((i + j \bmod k) + 1)$ and $g_\sigma(i, j) = g_\sigma(k + i, k + j) = 0$. Note that each vertex in G_σ has degree $\sum_{i \in [k]} f_\sigma(i)$. Finally, consider the graph consisting of G_1 and G_2 (i.e., the graph represented by the adjacency predicate $g : [4k]^2 \to \{0, 1\}$ such that for every $i, j \in [2k]$ and $\sigma \in \{1, 2\}$ it holds that $g((\sigma - 1) \cdot 2k + i, (\sigma - 1) \cdot 2k + j) = g_\sigma(i, j)$ and $g_\sigma(i, 2k + j) = g(2k + i, j) = 0$).

[71] Based on [50, Sec. 2.2]. Note that the bound on the total work in Section 8.2.4 can be easily improved to $O(\epsilon^{-1} \log^2(1/\epsilon))$ by selecting $O(\ell \cdot 2^i)$ (rather than $O(i^2 \cdot 2^i)$) points (for each $i \in [\ell]$).

invested in ω is $O(1/q(\omega))$, then the goal can be achieved by investing $O(\epsilon^{-1} \log(1/\epsilon))$ work.

Guideline: Letting $S_i = \{\omega \in \Omega : q(\omega) \in (2^{-i}, 2^{-(i-1)}]\}$ and $\ell = \lceil \log_2(2/\epsilon) \rceil$, prove that $\sum_{i \in [\ell]} \frac{|S_i|}{2^i} \geq \frac{\epsilon}{4} \cdot |\Omega|$ (by using $\sum_{i > \ell} \frac{|S_i|}{2^i} \leq 2^{-(\ell+1)} \cdot |\Omega|$ and $\sum_{i > 0} |S_i| \cdot 2^{-(i-1)} \geq \sum_{\omega \in \Omega} q(\omega)$). Observe that selecting $m_i = 8\epsilon^{-1}/2^i$ points, for each $i \in [\ell]$, and investing work 2^i work in each of them, yields success probability of at least

$$1 - \prod_{i \in [\ell]} \mathbf{Pr}_{\omega \in \Omega}[\omega \notin S_i]^{m_i} \geq 1 - \prod_{i \in [\ell]} \left(1 - \frac{|S_i|}{|\Omega|}\right)^{m_i}$$

$$\geq 1 - e^{-\sum_{i \in [\ell]} \frac{|S_i| \cdot 8\epsilon^{-1}/2^i}{|\Omega|}},$$

which is at least $1 - \exp(-8\epsilon^{-1} \cdot \epsilon/4) > 5/6$.

Exercise 8.5 (Bipartiteness has no proximity-oblivious tester):[72] Prove that Bipartiteness has no proximity-oblivious tester that makes a constant number of queries.

Guideline: See (Part 2 of) Exercise 1.10.

Exercise 8.6 (Testers for Bipartiteness must inspect $\Omega(1/\epsilon)$ vertices):[73] Bipartiteness can not be ϵ-tested by an algorithm whose queries touch $o(1/\epsilon)$ vertices. (Equivalently, if an ϵ-tester for Bipartiteness inspects the subgraph induced by $s(\epsilon)$ vertices, then $s(\epsilon) = \Omega(1/\epsilon)$.)

Guideline: Consider the following two distributions on k-vertex graphs. In both distributions, one selects uniformly a 3-partition (V_0, V_1, V_2) such that $|V_0| = 3\epsilon k$ and $|V_1| = |V_2| = (1 - 3\epsilon)k/2$. In the first distribution, each pair of parts is connected by a biclique, whereas in the second distribution only V_1 and V_2 are connected (by a biclique). Then, each graph in the first distribution is ϵ-far from being bipartite (because there are $3\epsilon k \cdot ((1 - 3\epsilon)k/2)^2$ triangles, whereas each edge participates in less than $k/2$ triangles). Yet, an algorithm that "inspects" $o(1/\epsilon)$ vertices is unlikely to distinguish the two distributions (since it is unlikely to inspect any vertex of V_0).

Exercise 8.7 (A random induced subgraph preserves the distance of a graph from being bipartite): Prove that if $G = ([k], E)$ is ϵ-far from being bipartite, then, with probability at least $2/3$, the subgraph induced by a random set of $\widetilde{O}(1/\epsilon^2)$ vertices of G is $\Omega(\epsilon)$-far from being bipartite.

Guideline: Following the proof of Lemma 8.8, show that, for every partition (U_1, U_2) of U, the set S approximates the number of disturbing edges. That is, while the current proof only shows that S hits some disturbing edges, one can actually show that the subgraph induced by S contains $\Omega(\epsilon \cdot |S|^2)$ disturbing edges. Specifically, consider a partition of $\binom{S}{2}$ into $|S| - 1$ disjoint perfect matchings, and show that (with high probability) each perfect matching contains $\Omega(\epsilon \cdot |S|)$ disturbing edges.

Exercise 8.8 (Some pseudorandom features of regular pairs): Let (A, B) be a γ-regular pair of edge density ρ, and let $\Gamma_B(v) = \{u \in B : \{u, v\}\}$ denote the neighbors of vertex $v \in A$ in the set B. Prove the following claims.

---

[72] Based on a result in [152].
[73] Based on a result in [13].

1. At least a $1 - 2\gamma$ fraction of the vertices $v \in A$ satisfy $(\rho - \gamma) \cdot |B| \leq |\Gamma_B(v)| \leq (\rho + \gamma) \cdot |B|$.
2. If $\rho \geq 2\gamma$, then at least a $(1 - 2\gamma)^2$ fraction of the vertex pairs $v_1, v_2 \in A$ satisfy $(\rho^2 - 2\gamma) \cdot |B| \leq |\Gamma_B(v_1) \cap \Gamma_B(v_2)| \leq (\rho^2 + 2\gamma) \cdot |B|$.

Guideline: For Item 1, consider the set of vertices v that violate the degree bound, and focus on the majority that violate the bound in the same direction (i.e., let A' be the latter set and $B' = B$, and consider $d(A', B')$). For Item 2, fix any vertex v_1 that satisfies Item 1 and consider the set $B' = \Gamma_B(v_1)$ along with the set of vertices v_2 such that (v_1, v_2) violate the bound.

Exercise 8.9 (Regular pairs in a random graph): Let A and B be disjoint sets of size N. Prove that a random bipartite graph between A and B is γ-regular with probability at least $1 - \exp(-\gamma^4 \cdot N^2 + 2N)$.

Guideline: Fixing any $A' \subseteq A$ and $B' \subseteq B$, the probability that $|d(A', B') - d(A, B)| > \gamma$ is exponentially vanishing in $\gamma^2 \cdot |A'| \cdot |B'|$.

Exercise 8.10 (On the proof of the Regularity Lemma): In continuation of footnote 37, consider the potential function that assigns the partition $(V_1, \ldots, V_t)$, of $[k]$, the value $k^{-2} \cdot \sum_{i<j} f(V_i, V_j)$, where $f(A, B) = |A| \cdot |B| \cdot d(A, B)^2$.

1. Prove that this function does not decrease under a refinement of the partition.
2. Prove that if (V_i, V_j) is not γ-regular, then V_i and V_j can be 2-partitioned, into $(V_{i,1}, V_{i,2})$ and $(V_{j,1}, V_{j,2})$, respectively, such that $\sum_{\sigma, \tau \in \{1,2\}} f(V_{i,\sigma}, V_{i,\tau}) \geq f(V_i, V_j) + \gamma^4 \cdot |V_i| \cdot |V_j|$.

(In each iteration of the proof, if the current partition violates the regularity condition, then Part 2 is applied to each of the nonregular pairs, which means that the number of parts grows exponentially in each iteration.)

Guideline: For Part 1, consider an arbitrary 2-partition of V_i, denoted (V_i', V_i''), and show that $f(V_i', V_j) + f(V_i'', V_j) \geq f(V_i, V_j)$. Specifically, consider a random variable Z that is assigned $d(V_i', V_j)$ with probability $|V_i'|/|V_i|$ and $d(V_i'', V_j)$ otherwise; observe that $\mathbb{E}[Z] = d(V_i, V_j) = \sqrt{\frac{f(V_i, V_j)}{|V_i| \cdot |V_j|}}$ whereas $\mathbb{E}[Z^2] = \frac{f(V_i', V_j) + f(V_i'', V_j)}{|V_i| \cdot |V_j|}$; and conclude by using $\mathbb{E}[Z]^2 \leq \mathbb{E}[Z^2]$. For Part 2, use the subsets $V_i' \subset V_i$ and $V_j' \subset V_j$ that witness the violation of the regularity condition (i.e., satisfy $|d(V_i', V_j') - d(V_i, V_j)| > \gamma$), and consider an analogous random variable Z (which selects one of the four relevant pairs).[74]

Exercise 8.11 (An obvious lower bound on $\#_H(\epsilon, k)$): Let H and $\#_H(\epsilon, k)$ be as in Problem 8.17. Show that $\#_H(\epsilon, k) \geq \epsilon \cdot \binom{k}{2}/(t - 1)$.

Guideline: Let G be ϵ-far from H-free, and suppose toward the contradiction that G has less than $\epsilon \cdot \binom{k}{2}/(t - 1)$ copies of H. The, using the hypothesis that H is connected, contradiction is reached by picking a single vertex in each copy of H and omitting all edges of this copy that are incident at this vertex.

---

[74] See, for example, [22, Sec. 9.4].

Exercise 8.12 (The number of copies of K_{t_1,t_2} in a dense graph):[75] Prove that if a k-vertex graph has at least ϵk^2 edges, then it contains at least $\Omega((2\epsilon)^{t_1 t_2}) \cdot k^{t_1+t_2}$ copies of K_{t_1,t_2} (i.e., the biclique with t_1 vertices on one side and t_2 vertices on the other side).

> **Guideline:** Let $G = ([k], E)$ have degree sequence $d_1, \ldots, d_k$. Then, $\mathbf{Pr}_{v,u_1,\ldots,u_t \in [k]}[(\forall i \in [t]) \{v, u_i\} \in E]$ equals $\frac{1}{k} \cdot \sum_{v \in [k]} (d_v/k)^t \geq (\frac{1}{k} \cdot \sum_{v \in [k]} d_v/k)^t = (2|E|/k^2)^t$. Define an auxiliary bipartite graph in which the t-subset U is connected to $v \notin U$ if for every $u \in U$ it holds that $\{v, u\} \in E$. Then, the average degree of t-subsets is at least $p \stackrel{\text{def}}{=} (2|E|/k^2)^t - \binom{t+1}{2}/k$, where the second term accounts for $\mathbf{Pr}_{v,u_1,\ldots,u_t \in [k]}[|\{v, u_1, \ldots, u_t\}| < t + 1]$. Show that the probability that a random U is connected to t' random v_i's is at least $p^{t'}$.

Exercise 8.13 (Testing H-freeness when H is bipartite): Let H be a fixed subgraph of K_{t_1,t_2}.

1. Using Exercise 8.12, present a $t_1 t_2$-query one-sided error POT of detection probability $\varrho(\delta) = \Omega(\delta^{t_1 t_2})$ for H-freeness.
2. Using Exercise 8.12, present a two-sided error ϵ-tester of query complexity $O(1/\epsilon)$ for H-freeness.
3. Prove that any one-sided error ϵ-tester for H-freeness must have query complexity $\Omega((1/\epsilon)^{d/2})$, where d is the average degree of H.
4. *Advanced:* Present a one-sided error ϵ-tester of query complexity $O((1/\epsilon)^{2t_1 t_2/(t_1+t_2)})$ for H-freeness.

> **Guideline:** For Part 3, consider a random graph of edge density 2ϵ, and lower-bound the number of vertices, denoted s, that must be inspected by a one-sided error canonical tester (cf. Theorem 8.25). Specifically, note that the probability that the subgraph induced by s vertices contains a copy of H is upper-bounded by $s^{t_1+t_2} \cdot (2\epsilon)^m$, where m denotes the number of edges in H. Recall that a one-sided error tester for H-freeness may reject a graph only when seeing a copy of H in it. (Note that this also implies that any constant-query POT (of one-sided error) for H-freeness has detection probability $\varrho(\delta) = O(\delta^m)$.)
>
> Turning to Part 4, for any graph G that is ϵ-far from being H-free, using Exercise 8.12, lower-bound the expected number of copies of H that appear in a subgraph of G that is induced by s random vertices. Note that you should show that such an induced subgraph contains a copy of H with high probability. This can be proved using the fact that the various $(t_1 + t_2)$-subsets of $[s]$ correspond to random variables that are almost pairwise independent (cf. proof of Claim 9.21.3).

Exercise 8.14 (Subsets of regular pairs): Let (A, B) be a γ-regular pair, and $A' \subseteq A$ and $B' \subseteq B$. Prove that (A', B') is a $t \cdot \gamma$-regular pair for $t = \max(2, |A|/|A'|, |B|/|B'|)$.

> **Guideline:** Note that the regularity parameter accounts both for the density of the subsets and for the deviation in the edge density.

Exercise 8.15 (Supercanonical testers): Let Π be any graph property. We say that a tester for Π is supercanonical if it selects at random a set of vertices and accepts if and only if the induced subgraph has property Π', where Π' is a graph property that depends only on Π. (That is, unlike in Theorem 8.25, the property Π' does not depend on the number of vertices in the tested graph.) Suppose that there exist a function $F : (0, 1] \to \mathbb{N}$,

---

[75] Based on a result in [6].

a graph property Ψ, and a constant $c > 0$ such that for every $\epsilon > 0$ and any graph G the following holds:

1. If $G \in \Pi$, then, with probability at least 0.9, the subgraph of G induced by a random set of $F(\epsilon)$ vertices is in Ψ.
2. If G is ϵ-far from Π, then, with probability at least 0.9, the subgraph of G induced by a random set of $F(c)$ vertices is $(c \cdot \epsilon)$-far from Ψ.

(Indeed, $\Psi = \Pi$ is a natural special case.) Assuming that $q : (0, 1] \to \mathbb{N}$ is monotonically nonincreasing, show that if Ψ has a tester of query complexity $q(\epsilon) = o(\sqrt{F(\epsilon/c)})$, then Π has a supercanonical tester that inspects $O(q(c \cdot \epsilon))$ vertices. Furthermore, if $\Psi = \Pi$ is closed under taking induced subgraphs, and if the original tester has one-sided error, then so does the new tester, and a sample of $2q(c \cdot \epsilon)$ vertices suffices.

> **Guideline:** The key observation is that selecting a random set of $F(\epsilon)$ vertices, denoted R, and then selecting a random $O(q(c\epsilon))$-subset of R yields a distribution that is very close to the uniform distribution over all $O(q(c\epsilon))$-vertex sets, since $q(c\epsilon)^2 = o(F(\epsilon))$. The supercanonical tester applies the canonical tester guaranteed by Theorem 8.25, while using the auxiliary property Π' that depends on Ψ and F. The crucial point is that, for $k' = O(q(c\epsilon))$, the set of k'-vertex graphs in Π' (i.e., $\Pi'_{k'}$) depends on $F(\epsilon)$, but not on the number of vertices in the tested graph, whereas k' effectively determines ϵ (as well as $F(\epsilon)$).[76]

Exercise 8.16 (Graph properties are not random self-reducible): Show that, except for a few trivial cases, graph properties of k-vertex graphs in the adjacency predicate representation are not random self-reducible by $o(k)$ queries.[77] The exceptional cases are the four subsets of $\{K_k, I_k\}$, where K_k is the k-vertex clique and I_k is the empty k-vertex graph.

> **Guideline:** Use Exercise 5.4, while showing that all other graph properties of k-vertex graphs have relative distance $O(1/k)$. Specifically, show that if $G = ([k], E)$ is neither the v-vertex clique nor the empty graph, then there exist $u, v \in [k]$ such that $\Gamma_G(u) \setminus \{v\} \neq \Gamma_G(v) \setminus \{u\}$, where $\Gamma_G(x) = \{w : \{x, w\}\}$.[78] Observe that in this case there exists an isomorphic copy of G, denoted $G' = ([k], E')$, such that $E' \neq E$ and the symmetric difference between E' and E has size at most k.

---

[76] The point is that the canonical tester rules according to the membership of the induced k'-vertex subgraph in Π', whereas k' determines the minimial ϵ such that $O(q(c\epsilon)) = k'$.

[77] See Definition 5.9.

[78] If there exists w such that $|\Gamma_G(w)| \in [k - 2]$, then pick $u \in \Gamma_G(w)$ and $v \in [k] \setminus (\Gamma_G(w) \cup \{w\})$.

CHAPTER NINE

Testing Graph Properties in the Bounded-Degree Graph Model

Summary: This chapter is devoted to testing graph properties in the bounded-degree graph model, where graphs are represented by their incidence lists (lumped together in an incidence function). The highlights of this chapter include

1. Presenting upper and lower bounds on the complexity of testing Bipartiteness; specifically, we present a poly$(1/\epsilon) \cdot \widetilde{O}(\sqrt{k})$-time tester, and an $\Omega\sqrt{k})$ lower bound on the query complexity of any tester for Bipartiteness.
2. Presenting a quasi-poly$(1/\epsilon)$-time tester for Planarity. The result extends to testing any minor-closed property (i.e., a graph property that is preserved under the omission of edges and vertices and under edge contraction).

We conclude this chapter with a taxonomy of known testers, organized according to their query complexity.

The current chapter is based on many sources; see Section 9.7.1 for details.

Organization. Following a general introduction to the bounded-degree graph model (Section 9.1), we study the problem of testing various graph properties in this model. The presentation of the various testers is organized by the algorithmic techniques that they utilize. These include local searches (see Section 9.2), random walks (see Section 9.4), and the implementation and utilization of partition oracles (see Section 9.5). In addition, the current chapter includes a section on (query complexity) lower bounds (Section 9.3), which justifies the fact that the testers presented in Section 9.4 have significantly higher complexity than those presented in Section 9.2.

Preliminaries. We assume that the reader is familiar with basic graph algorithmic techniques such as BFS and DFS (see, e.g., [104]). This will be important especially in Section 9.2.

Teaching Note: Much of this chapter (e.g., Sections 9.6 and 9.7) is intended for optional independent reading. We recommend basing the actual teaching on Section 9.1 and a selection from Sections 9.2–9.4. A very minimalistic choice includes Sections 9.2.3, 9.3.1, and 9.4.1. If time permits, we would also recommend including Section 9.2.4 (with a focus on Algorithm 9.10 and its analysis). Another recommendation consists of Sections 9.2.5 and 9.4.2 (along with Theorem 9.17 (which appears in Section 9.3.2)). We do share the temptation to cover also Section 9.5 in class, but think that teaching the material presented in prior sections should get higher priority.

9.1. The Bounded-Degree Model: Definitions and Issues

The study of property testing in the bounded-degree graph model is aimed at allowing the consideration of sparse graphs, which appear in numerous applications. The point is that the dense graph model, studied in the previous chapter, seems irrelevant to sparse graphs, both because the distance measure that underlies it deems all sparse graphs as close to one another, and because adjacency queries seems unsuitable for sparse graphs. Sticking to the paradigm of representing graphs as functions, where both the distance measure and the type of queries are determined by the representation, the following representation seemed the most natural choice. (Indeed, a conscious decision is made here not to capture, at this point (and in this model), sparse graphs that do not have constant (or low) maximum degree.)

The bounded-degree graph model refers to a fixed degree bound, denoted $d \geq 2$. An k-vertex graph $G = ([k], E)$, of maximum degree d, is represented in this model by a function $g : [k] \times [d] \to \{0, 1, \ldots, k\}$ such that $g(v, i) = u \in [k]$ if u is the ith neighbor of v and $g(v, i) = 0$ if v has less than i neighbors. Hence, it is also adequate to refer to this model as the incidence function model. For simplicity, we assume here that the neighbors of vertex v appear in an arbitrary order in the sequence $g(v, 1), \ldots, g(v, \deg(v))$, where $\deg(v) \overset{\text{def}}{=} |\{i : g(v, i) \neq 0\}|$ is the degree of v. Also, we shall always assume that if $g(v, i) = u \in [k]$, then there exists $j \in [d]$ such that $g(u, j) = v$.

Distance between graphs is measured in terms of their aforementioned representation (i.e., as the fraction of (the number of) different array entries (over $n = d \cdot k$)), but occasionally we shall use the equivalent and more intuitive notion of the fraction of (the number of) edges over $dk/2$.

Recall that we are interested in *graph properties*, which are sets of graphs that are closed under isomorphism; that is, Π is a graph property if for every graph $G = ([k], E)$ and every permutation π of $[k]$ it holds that $G \in \Pi$ if and only if $\pi(G) \in \Pi$, where $\pi(G) \overset{\text{def}}{=} ([k], \{\{\pi(u), \pi(v)\} : \{u, v\} \in E\})$. We now spell out the meaning of property testing in this model.

Definition 9.1 (Testing graph properties in the bounded-degree graph model):[1] *For a fixed d, a* tester *for a graph property* Π *is a probabilistic oracle machine that, on input parameters k and ϵ, and access to (the incidence function of) an k-vertex graph $G = ([k], E)$ of maximum degree d, outputs a binary verdict that satisfies the following two conditions.*

---

[1] As in the dense graph model, we provide the tester with the number of vertices, denoted k, rather than with the size of the representation, denoted $n = d \cdot k$. The definition of a tester can be made even more uniform by providing the degree bound, denoted d, as an auxiliary parameter.

1. *If $G \in \Pi$, then the tester accepts with probability at least 2/3.*
2. *If G is ϵ-far from Π, then the tester accepts with probability at most 1/3, where G is ϵ-far from Π if for every k-vertex graph $G' = ([k], E') \in \Pi$ of maximum degree d it holds that the symmetric difference between E and E' has cardinality that is greater than $\epsilon \cdot dk/2$. (Equivalently, we may say that G is ϵ-far from G' if for every $g : [k] \times [d] \rightarrow \{0, 1, \ldots, k\}$ and $g' : [k] \times [d] \rightarrow \{0, 1, \ldots, k\}$ that represent G and G', respectively, it holds that $|\{(v, i) : g(v, i) \neq g'(v, i)\}| > \epsilon \cdot dk$.)*

If the tester accepts every graph in Π with probability 1, then we say that it has one-sided error; *otherwise, we say that it has* two-sided error. *A tester is called* nonadaptive *if it determines all its queries based solely on its internal coin tosses (and the parameters k and ϵ); otherwise, it is called* adaptive.

The query complexity of a tester is the number of queries it makes to any k-vertex graph, as a function of the parameters k and ϵ.[2] We say that a tester is efficient if it runs in time that is linear in its query complexity, where basic operations on elements of $[k]$ (and in particular, uniformly selecting an element in $[k]$) are counted at unit cost. Unless explicitly stated otherwise, the testers presented in this chapter are efficient.

On the Degree Bound d. As stated in footnote 1, the degree bound, denoted d, may be viewed as an auxiliary parameter, and complexity bounds may be stated as a function of it too. Note that this parameter has two opposite effects. On the one hand, if our algorithm explores all neighbors of a given vertex, then its complexities increase linearly with d. On the other hand, (relative) distances are normalized by dk, which means that they decrease linearly with d, which in turn relaxes the requirements from a tester.

Degree Queries. The model can be augmented by allowing also degree queries (i.e., query $v \in [k]$ is answered with the degree of v in the tested graph). Degree queries can be emulated by $\lceil \log(d + 1) \rceil$ incidence queries, by performing a binary search (see Exercise 9.1).

Variants (which may be skipped). Recall that we are using the convention by which the neighbors of v appear in an arbitrary order in the sequence $g(v, 1), \ldots, g(v, \deg(v))$, where $\deg(v)$ denotes the degree of v. In contrast to this convention, one may consider the following three variants on the model.

1. Sorted incidence functions: In this case for each $v \in [k]$, the sequence $g(v, 1), \ldots, g(v, \deg(v))$ is sorted; that is, for every $i \in [\deg(v) - 1]$, it holds that $g(v, i) < g(v, i + 1)$.

   This variant decreases the complexity of the task of finding whether two vertices are adjacent (by conducting a binary search on the incidence list of one vertex). Unfortunately, the two definitions of distance given in Definition 9.1 are no longer equivalent (since the Hamming distance between d-long sequences is not preserved when the sequences are sorted).[3]

---

[2] As in footnote 1, we deviated from the convention of presenting the query complexity as a function of $n = dk$ and ϵ.

[3] Consider the sequences (3, 5, 7, 11) and (13, 5, 7, 11).

2. Unaligned incidence functions: In this case it is no longer guaranteed that the $\deg(v)$ neighbors of v appear in the $\deg(v)$-long prefix of the sequence $g(v, 1), \ldots, g(v, d)$. This variant increases the complexity of tasks such as finding a neighbor of a given vertex or determining the degree of a given vertex.

3. Incidence-set functions: Here we represent the (degree d) graph $G = ([k], E)$, by $g : [k] \rightarrow \cup_{i=0}^{d} \binom{[k]}{i}$ such that $g(v)$ is the set of neighbors of vertex v.
   This variant decreases the complexity of tasks such as finding all neighbors of a given vertex (and less so w.r.t. determining the degree of a given vertex). On the other hand, the two definitions of distance given in Definition 9.1 are no longer equivalent (since under this representation modifying the neighbor set costs one unit regardless of how much the set is modified).

We mention that none of the above variants is popular, and the first two variants seem a bit unnatural. Nevertheless, one may imagine applications in which these variants are adequate. In any case, it is legitimate to use these variants to facilitate the exposition, while recalling the cost of translation to the main model.[4]

The Role of Adaptivity. We mention that the ability to make adaptive queries is very important in the bounded-degree graph model; in particular, adaptive queries are far more important in the bounded-degree graph model than in the dense graph model: Recall that in the dense graph model, adaptive queries could be replaced by nonadaptive queries at a moderate cost of squaring the number of queries. In contrast, in the bounded-degree graph model, there is a huge gap between the adaptive and nonadaptive query complexities of testing many natural graph properties. Specifically, as shown in Section 9.2, properties such as subgraph freeness, connectivity, and cycle-freeness can all be tested by using $\mathrm{poly}(d/\epsilon)$ adaptive queries, but (as shown next) each of these testing tasks requires $\Omega(\sqrt{k})$ nonadaptive queries.

This lower bound follows as a special case of a result that asserts that testing any property that "is not determined by the vertex degree distribution" requires such complexity. We say that a property Π is not determined by the vertex degree distribution if there exists $\epsilon > 0$ such that for infinitely many $k \in \mathbb{N}$ there exists $(d_1, \ldots, d_k) \in \{0, 1, \ldots, d\}^k$ and two k-vertex graphs, one in Π and the other ϵ-far from Π, such that the degree of the ith vertex in each of these k-vertex graphs equals d_i. (If this is not the case, then we say that the property is determined by the vertex degree distribution.)[5]

Theorem 9.2 (Limitation of nonadaptive queries (in the bounded-degree graph model)): *For any function* $q' : (0, 1] \rightarrow \mathbb{N}$, *if a graph property* Π *can be tested in* $q(k, \epsilon) = o(\sqrt{k} \cdot q'(\epsilon))$ *nonadaptive queries, then* Π *is determined by the vertex degree distribution.*

This result is quite tight, since triangle-freeness can be tested by $O(\sqrt{d^2 k / \epsilon})$ nonadaptive queries (see Exercise 9.2).

---

[4] The unaligned version arises naturally in the proof of Theorem 9.28. At some point we considered using the incidence-set variant in the proof of Theorem 9.2, but eventually ended up not doing so. We mention that the incidence-set variant is used in [143].

[5] In that case, for every $\epsilon > 0$ and all but finitely many $k \in \mathbb{N}$, if two graphs have the same vertex degree distribution and one is in Π, then the other is ϵ-close to Π.

Proof Sketch: Fix an $\epsilon > 0$ such that there exist an infinite sequence of pairs of graphs (G_1, G_0) that have the same number of vertices (denoted k) and the same degree sequence, although $G_1 \in \Pi$ and G_0 is ϵ-far from Π. We shall show that an algorithm of query complexity $o(\sqrt{k})$ cannot distinguish random isomorphic copies of these two k-vertex graphs.

We call a pair of queries (u, i) and (v, j) bad (for a graph) if either v or the jth neighbor of v is the answer to the query (u, i) (i.e., if the answer to the query (u, i) either equals v or equals the answer to (v, j), assuming that the latter is not 0). The key observation is that if we take a random isomorphic copy of any of the two graphs, then the probability that q nonadaptive queries contain a bad pair of queries is at most $4 \cdot \binom{q}{2}/(k-1) < 2q^2/k$, since the probability that a specific pair of queries is bad is at most $4/(k-1)$. (To verify the latter claim, observe that these two queries (i.e., (u, i) and (v, j)) can be viewed as answered by a process that selects at random (without repetitions) two degrees $\deg(u)$ and $\deg(v)$ in the multiset $\{d_1, \ldots, d_k\}$, and answers the query (u, i) (resp., (v, j)) with a random $w \in [k] \setminus \{u\}$ (resp., $w' \in [k] \setminus \{v\}$) if $i \le \deg(u)$ (resp., $j \le \deg(v)$) and by 0 otherwise.) Note that, conditioned on having no bad pair of queries, the distribution of answers in the (two random isomorphic copies of the) two graphs is identical. (The answers obtained under this conditioning are distributed identically to those obtained by a process that first assigns random degrees (without repetitions) to all vertices, and then answers each query (v, i) such that $i \le \deg(v)$ with a different random vertex in $[k] \setminus \{v\}$.)[6] Hence, the distinguishing gap (w.r.t. these random copies) of a nonadaptive algorithm that makes q queries is smaller than $2q^2/k$, and the theorem follows. ∎

Nonadaptivity versus Label-Obliviousness. We note that a nonadaptive algorithm of $o(\sqrt{k})$ complexity cannot perform a local search on a k-vertex graph, since it cannot find a neighbor of a neighbor of a given vertex. We wish to stress that a BFS from a given vertex to a given distance cannot be performed by a nonadaptive algorithm, although such a search is oblivious of the vertex labels. That is, obliviousness of the labels of vertices is fundamentally different from nonadaptivity; for example, the jth neighbor of the ith neighbor of v is a *label-oblivious* formulation, although it refers to the adaptive query $(g(v, i), j)$. Indeed, all "normal" graph algorithms as well as testers of graph properties are oblivious of vertex labels, and in a sense this feature makes them "graph algorithms" (i.e., their operation is invariant under any relabeling of the graph's vertices).

On the Difference in Complexities between the Two Graph Testing Models. Another issue to notice is the difference between the query complexity of testing graph properties in the bounded-degree graph model as compared to the complexity of testing the same properties in the dense graph model. A few examples follow.

- Whereas Bipartiteness has a poly$(1/\epsilon)$-time tester in the dense graph model, it has no $o(\sqrt{k})$-query tester in the bounded-degree graph model. Furthermore, for $t \ge 3$,

---

[6] In other words, the process selects uniformly a permutation $\pi : [k] \to [k]$ and a function $\phi : [k] \times [d] \to [k]$ such that $|\{v, \phi(v, 1), \ldots \phi(v, d)\}| = d + 1$ for every v, and answers the query (v, i) with $\phi(v, i)$ if $i \le d_{\pi(v)}$ and with 0 otherwise.

the dense graph model has a poly($1/\epsilon$)-query tester for t-Colorability, but this property has no $o(k)$-query tester in the bounded-degree graph model.

- Whereas triangle-freeness has no poly($1/\epsilon$)-query tester in the dense graph model, it has a $O(1/\epsilon)$-query tester in the bounded-degree graph model.
- Whereas Connectivity (and even "t-connectivity") is trivial in the dense graph model, it is far from being so in the bounded-degree graph model (although poly($1/\epsilon$)-query testers do exist here too).

These examples and more will be discussed in the subsequent sections.

9.2. Testing by a Local Search

In this section we present relatively simple testers for subgraph freeness, degree regularity, connectivity, and cycle-freeness, where the latter tester has two-sided error. These poly($1/\epsilon$)-query testers (as well as the testers for higher levels of connectivity) are based on conducting a small number of *very local* searches, but the parameters of these searchers and their goals vary from one case to another.

9.2.1. Testing Subgraph Freeness

Testing subgraph freeness (e.g., triangle-freeness), when the subgraph is not bipartite, is quite a challenge in the dense graph model. Recall that even testing triangle-freeness (in that model) involves the invocation of the Regularity Lemma. In contrast, we will present a relatively simple tester for the same properties in the current model (i.e., the bounded-degree graph model). Let us first recall the definition that we refer to.

Definition 9.3 (Subgraph freeness): *Let H be a fixed graph. A graph $G = (V, E)$ is H-free if G contains no subgraph that is isomorphic to H.*

We shall focus on the case that H is connected, although the general case can be handled similarly (yielding similar, but not identical results).[7] Let $\mathrm{rd}(H)$ denote the radius of H; that is, $\mathrm{rd}(H)$ is the smallest integer r such that there exists a vertex v in H such that all vertices in H are at distance at most r from v. Such a vertex v is called a center of H, and indeed H may have several centers (e.g., consider the case that H is a clique).

Theorem 9.4 (Testing subgraph freeness (in the bounded-degree graph model)): *Let $H = ([t], F)$ be a fixed (connected) graph of radius $r = \mathrm{rd}(H)$. Then, H-freeness has a (one-sided error) proximity-oblivious tester of query complexity $2d^{r+1}$ and linear detection probability. Furthermore, the time complexity of this tester is at most $(2d)^{rt}$.*

Proof: We consider the following natural algorithm.

Algorithm 9.4.1 (Testing H-freeness): *On input parameters d and k and oracle access to the incidence function of a k-vertex graph $G = ([k], E)$, which has maximum degree d, the algorithm proceeds as follows.*

---

[7] If H is composed of the connected components $H_1, \ldots, H_m$, then Algorithm 9.4.1 can be modified so to select uniformly $v_1, \ldots, v_m \in [k]$ and start a BFS from each of them. See Exercise 9.3.

1. Uniformly selects a vertex $v \in [k]$.

2. Conducts a BFS of depth at most r starting from v.

3. Accept if and only if the explored subgraph is H-free.

Step 2 is implemented by querying the incidence function, and so the query complexity of this algorithm is upper-bounded by $\sum_{i=0}^{r} d^i \cdot d < 2d^{r+1}$. Step 3 can be implemented by checking all possible mappings of H to the explored graph, and so the time complexity of Algorithm 9.4.1 is upper-bounded by $\binom{2d^r}{t} \cdot (t!) < (2d)^{rt}$.

Algorithm 9.4.1 never rejects a graph that is H-free, since H-freeness is preserved by subgraphs of the original graph. (Algorithm 9.4.1 can be modified to check induced subgraph freeness, while noting that this property is preserved by induced subgraphs of the original graph.) It is left to analyze the detection probability of Algorithm 9.4.1.

Claim 9.4.2 (The detection probability of Algorithm 9.4.1): *If $G = ([k], E)$ is at distance δ from being H-free, then Algorithm 9.4.1 rejects it with probability at least $\delta/2$.*

Proof: A vertex $v \in [k]$ is called detecting if it is a center of a copy of H that resides in G. Then, G must have at least $\delta k/2$ detecting vertices, since omitting all edges that are incident at detecting vertices makes the graph H-free. The claim follows. ∎

This completes the proof of the theorem. ∎

9.2.2. Testing Degree Regularity

Testing degree regularity is somewhat easier in the bounded-degree graph model (as compared to the dense graph model), since determining the degree of a vertex is easier in this model. On the other hand, there is a minor issue that arises here: In the bounded-degree graph model, unlike in the dense graph model, a graph with an odd number of vertices in which almost all vertices are of the same odd degree is not closed to being regular. Hence, if k is odd and we observe some vertex of odd degree, then we better reject (as done in Step 4 of the following algorithm).

Algorithm 9.5 (Testing degree regularity (in the bounded-degree graph model)): *On input parameters d, k and ϵ and oracle access to the incidence function of a k-vertex graph $G = ([k], E)$, which has maximum degree d, the algorithm proceeds as follows.*

1. Uniformly selects a set of $O(1/\epsilon)$ vertices.

2. Determines the degree of each of the selected vertices.

3. If these degrees are not all the same, then the algorithm rejects.

4. If this same degree is odd and k is odd, then the algorithm rejects.

Otherwise, the algorithm accepts.

Step 2 is implemented by a binary search on the incidence list of each selected vertex, and so the query (and time) complexity of this algorithm is $O(\epsilon^{-1} \log d)$.[8] Evidently, Algorithm 9.4.1 never rejects a regular graph (where nonrejection in Step 4 is justified by noting that if a k-vertex graph is d'-regular, then $d'k$ is even).[9] The analysis of Algorithm 9.4.1 is based on the local versus global claim that was proved in the analysis of the degree-regularity tester for the dense graph model. This claim is restated next.

> **Claim 9.5.1** (Local versus global distance to degree regularity, Claim 8.5.1 restated): *Let $d' < k$ and $d'k/2$ be natural numbers, and let $d_G(v)$ denote the degree of vertex v in the graph $G = ([k], E)$. If $\sum_{v \in [k]} |d_G(v) - d'| \leq \epsilon' \cdot B$, then there exists a d'-regular k-vertex graph $G' = ([k], E')$ such that the symmetric difference between E and E' is at most $3\epsilon' B$.*

In Chapter 8, Claim 8.5.1 was stated with $B = k^2$ and the bound on the symmetric difference was stated in terms of distance in the dense graph model (i.e., in units of $k^2/2$). Nevertheless, since Claim 8.5.1 was stated for any $\epsilon' > 0$, it immediately yields Claim 9.5.1. Using Claim 9.5.1, we establish the following.

> **Claim 9.5.2** (Analysis of Algorithm 9.5): *If $G = ([k], E)$ is ϵ-far from being* (degree) *regular, then Algorithm 9.4.1 rejects with probability at least $2/3$.*

Proof: Let d' denote the degree of the first vertex selected in Step 1 of the algorithm. (Indeed, we may modify the algorithm so that the first vertex is selected arbitrarily.) If $d'k$ is odd, then the algorithm always rejects (in Step 4, if it reaches Step 4 at all), and so we may assume that $d'k$ is even. Combining the claim's hypothesis with Claim 9.5.1, we infer that $\sum_{v \in [k]} |d_G(v) - d'| > \epsilon \cdot dk/6$. (This is the case since the symmetric difference between E and the edge set of any d'-regular k-vertex graph is greater than $\epsilon dk/2$.)[10] It follows that $|\{v \in [k] : d_G(v) \neq d'\}| > \epsilon k/6$, and the claim follows (since at least one of the vertices having degree different than d' is selected, w.h.p., and in this case Step 3 rejects). ∎

The proof of Claim 9.5.2, reveals that selecting two vertices (one arbitrarily and the other at random) and determining their degrees will do for obtaining a proximity-oblivious tester. Hence, we get.

> **Theorem 9.6** (Testing degree regularity (in the bounded-degree graph model)): *Degree regularity has a* (one-sided error) *proximity-oblivious tester of* (query and) *time complexity $2\lceil \log(d+1) \rceil$ and linear detection probability.*

Proof: The tester is a version of Algorithm 9.4.1 that selects only two vertices in Step 1. As noted in the proof of Claim 9.5.2, if G is at distance δ from being regular and d' is the degree of the first vertex, then either $d'k$ is odd (in which case Step 4

---

[8] Actually, we can reduce the complexity to $O(\epsilon^{-1} + \log d)$ by only determining the degree of the first vertex and checking whether each of the other vertices has the same degree. If the degree of the first vertex is i, then we need only query the latter vertices for their i^{th} and $(i+1)^{\text{st}}$ neighbors.

[9] Recall that, in every graph, the sum of vertex degrees is even.

[10] Hence, using $B = dk/2$ and $\epsilon' = \epsilon/3$, we infer that $\sum_{v \in [k]} |d_G(v) - d'| \leq \epsilon' \cdot B$ is impossible, because it would yield a symmetric difference of at most $3\epsilon' B = \epsilon dk/2$ (in contradiction to the hypothesis that G is ϵ-far from being regular).

guarantees rejection) or at least $\delta k/6$ vertices have degree different from d'. Hence, this algorithm will reject G with probability at least $\delta/6$. ∎

Testing Whether a Graph Is Eulerian. Recall that a graph is called Eulerian if all its vertices have even degree. (Note that we do not require here that the graph be connected.) We can easily test if a graph is Eulerian by sampling a random vertex and determining its degree, but again the analysis is not trivial because we need to preserve the degree bound (and the simplicity) of the graph. That is, we need to show that if few vertices of a graph of maximum degree d have odd degree, then this graph is close to a (simple) Eulerian graph *of maximum degree d*. This is not trivial since the degree bound may prevent us from connecting pairs of vertices that have odd degree (whereas arbitrarily omitting edges incident at vertices of currently odd degree is a bad idea).[11] Nevertheless, Exercise 9.4 shows that if a graph $G = ([k], E)$ has maximum degree d, and k' of its vertices have odd degree, then there exists a k-vertex Eulerian graph $G' = ([k], E')$ of maximum degree d such that the symmetric difference between E and E' is at most $3k'/2$.

9.2.3. Testing Connectivity

The tester for Connectivity is based on the following observation.

Proposition 9.7 (Distance from connectivity versus number of connected components): *Let $G = ([k], E)$ be a graph of maximum degree $d \geq 2$ that has m connected components. Then, there exists a connected graph $G' = ([k], E')$ of maximum degree d such that the symmetric difference between E and E' is at most $2m - 1$.*

(The nontrivial aspect of this proposition is the preservation of the degree bound. Omitting this restriction allows to present a connected graph $G'' = ([k], E'')$ such that the symmetric difference between E and E'' equals $m - 1$, which is optimal.)

Proof: We would like to add $m - 1$ edges between the m connected components so that the resulting graph is connected, but this may not be possible because of the degree bound. Specifically, we say that a k'-vertex connected component is saturated if the sum of its vertex degrees is at least $k' \cdot d - 1$ (i.e., the sum is $k'd$ if $k'd$ is even and is $k'd - 1$ otherwise), and call it unsaturated otherwise. Note that each saturated connected component can be made unsaturated by omitting a single edge, while preserving its connectivity. This can be seen by noting that such a connected component has a spanning tree (which consists of $k' - 1$ edges), implying that it has at least $(k'd - 1) - (k' - 1) > 0$ nontree edges that can all be omitted without harming the connectivity.

Hence, by omitting at most m edges, we make all m connected components unsaturated, and now we can connect them by adding $m - 1$ edges (while preserving the degree bound). Specifically, we connect these components by ordering them arbitrarily, and connecting each pair of consecutive components by a single edge (using vertices of degree lower than d). Hence, we increase the sum of the vertex degrees

---

[11] Since the other endpoint of the edge may have even degree, and such a sequence of omissions may result in too many modifications (see the case of a long path).

in each component by at most two units, and we can afford to do so because the components are (now) unsaturated. ∎

Toward a Tester. Proposition 9.7 implies that a graph that is ϵ-far from being connected has more than $\epsilon dk/4$ connected components. The next observation, which is pivotal to the tester, is that many of these connected components are small. Specifically, if there are k' connected components of size (i.e., number of vertices) at most s, then $k' + (k/s) > \epsilon dk/4$. For example, there must be at least $\epsilon dk/8$ connected components of size at most $8/(d\epsilon)$. Hence, selecting at random $O(1/\epsilon d)$ vertices and conducting a "truncated BFS" from each of them so that the BFS is suspended once more than $8/(d\epsilon)$ vertices are encountered yields a tester for Connectivity. The time (and query) complexity this tester is $O(1/\epsilon d) \cdot O(d/d\epsilon) = O(1/d\epsilon^2)$. But using Levin's economical work investment strategy (see Section 8.2.4), we can do better.[12]

Theorem 9.8 (Testing connectivity (in the bounded-degree graph model)): Connectivity *has a* (one-sided error) *tester of time* (and query) *complexity* $\widetilde{O}(1/\epsilon)$.

***Proof*:** For the sake of self-containment, we provide a full analysis of application of Levin's economical work investment strategy to this context. Fixing a graph $G = ([k], E)$ that is ϵ-far from being connected, for every $i = 0, \ldots, \ell \stackrel{\text{def}}{=} \log(9/d\epsilon)$, we denote by B'_i the set of vertices that reside in connected components of size at most $\lfloor 8/(2^i d\epsilon) \rfloor$ and at least $\lfloor 8/(2^{i+1} d\epsilon) \rfloor + 1$.[13]

Recall that G must have more that $\epsilon dk/4$ connected components, whereas there are at most $k/(8/d\epsilon)$ connected components of size larger than $8/d\epsilon$. Furthermore, all other vertices of G (i.e., those residing in connected components of size at most $8/d\epsilon$) are in $\cup_{i=0}^{\ell} B'_i$, since there are no connected components of size at most $8/(2^\ell d\epsilon) < 1$. On the other hand, the number of connected components that contain vertices of B'_i is at most $\frac{|B'_i|}{8/(2^{i+1}d\epsilon)}$, since each of these connected components has size that is larger than $8/(2^{i+1} d\epsilon)$. Combining these facts, we get

$$\sum_{i=0}^{\ell} \frac{|B'_i|}{8/(2^{i+1} d\epsilon)} > \frac{\epsilon dk}{4} - \frac{\epsilon dk}{8} \tag{9.1}$$

since the l.h.s. of Eq. (9.1) represents an upper bound on the number of connected components of size at most $8/d\epsilon$, whereas the r.h.s. represents a lower bound on that number. Noting that Eq. (9.1) simplifies to $\sum_{i=0}^{\ell} 2^{i+1} |B'_i| > k$, it follows that there exists $i \in \{0, 1, \ldots, \ell\}$ such that $|B'_i| = \Omega(2^{-i}k/\ell)$, whereas every corresponding connected component can be explored in time $d \cdot (8/(2^i d\epsilon))$, since each of these connected components has size that is at most $8/(2^i d\epsilon)$. This leads to the following tester, where we assume that $8/(d\epsilon) < k$ (since otherwise we can retrieve the entire graph in time $dk = O(1/\epsilon)$).

---

[12] We get an improvement only when $\epsilon = o(1/d)$, whereas when $\epsilon = \omega(1/d)$ we are actually worse. But, the case of $\epsilon > 4/d$ is trivial, since (in the current context of the bounded-degree graph model) every graph is $4/d$-close to being connected.

[13] In terms of Section 8.2.4, we may view such vertices as having quality in $[2^{i-3}d\epsilon, 2^{i-2}d\epsilon)$, and as requiring work investment $\Theta(1/2^i \epsilon)$.

The actual tester. For $i = 0, 1, \ldots, \ell$, perform the following steps.

1. Select at random $O(2^i \ell)$ vertices.
2. For each of these vertices, denoted v, perform a (BFS or DFS) search starting at v, suspending the execution if more than $8/(2^i d \epsilon)$ vertices were encountered in this search (or if the search scanned the entire connected component).
   Note that this search can be implemented in time $8/(2^i \epsilon)$.
3. If any of these searches detected a connected component of size at most $8/(2^i d \epsilon)$, then the tester rejects. (Here we rely on $8/(d \epsilon) < k$.)

If none of these searches detected a connected component that is smaller than k, then the tester accepts. Note that any linear-time search can be used in Step 2, and in such a case the overall time complexity of the tester is $\sum_{i=0}^{\ell} O(2^i \ell) \cdot 8/(2^i \epsilon) = O(\ell^2/\epsilon)$.

By its construction, this tester always accepts a connected graph, whereas a graph that is ϵ-far from being connected is rejected with high probability, because there exists an $i \in \{0, 1, \ldots, \ell\}$ such that $|B_i'| = \Omega(2^{-i}k/\ell)$, which implies that a vertex residing in a connected component of size at most $8/(2^i d \epsilon)$ is selected, w.h.p., in Step 1 (of iteration i), fully explored in Step 2, and causing rejection in Step 3. ∎

Testing Whether a Graph Is Connected and Eulerian. Testing whether a graph is connected and Eulerian reduces to testing that it has both properties. This reduction relies on the fact that if G is ϵ-close to both properties, then it is $O(\epsilon)$-close to their intersection (see Exercise 9.5).

9.2.4. Testing t-Connectivity (Overview and One Detail)

There are two different natural notions that generalize the notion of connectivity.

> t-**edge connectivity**: A graph is t-edge–connected if there are t *edge-disjoint* paths between every pair of vertices.
> t-**vertex connectivity**: A graph is t-vertex–connected if there are t *vertex-disjoint* paths between every pair of vertices.[14]

Clearly, t-vertex connectivity implies t-edge connectivity, and for $t = 1$ both notions coincide with the notion of connectivity. The connectivity level of a graph cannot exceed the (minimum) degree of its vertices, which means that we shall focus on $t \le d$. All these t-connectivity properties can be tested in poly$(1/\epsilon)$-time, where the polynomial may depend on t.

Theorem 9.9 (Testing t-connectivity, in the bounded-degree graph model):

- *For every* $t \ge 2$, *testing* t-edge connectivity *can be performed in time* $\widetilde{O}(t^3/\epsilon^{c_t})$, *where* $c_t = \min(3, t - 1)$.
- *For every* $t \ge 2$, *testing* t-vertex connectivity *can be performed in time* $\widetilde{O}((t/d\epsilon)^t)$.

---

[14] Needless to say, the notion of vertex-disjoint paths excludes the endpoints of these paths.

The testers of t-connectivity generalize two ideas that appear in the tester for Connectivity: One main idea, which was conspicuous in the base case (of $t = 1$), is that distance from t-connectivity implies the existence of many small t-connected components. Furthermore, one can establish the existence of many small t-connected components that can be disconnected *from the rest of the graph* by omitting less than t edges (resp., vertices). This strengthening is important, because such small (and "isolatable") components seem easier to detect (than generic small components). The second idea, which was obvious and transparent in the base case (of $t = 1$), is that these small t-connected components can be easily detected.

Detailing the first idea, in the current context (of $t > 1$), requires getting into the structure of (the connections among the t-connected components of) graphs that are not t-connected, which we wish to avoid. As for the second idea, we focus on the case of edge connectivity, since the case of vertex-connectivity is more involved. We use the known fact that *a graph is t-edge–connected if and only if it contains no cut of less than t edges* (i.e., for every nontrivial 2-partition of its vertex set, there are at least t edges having one endpoint in each part). Now, suppose that you are given a vertex v that resides in a set S of size at most s such that the subgraph of $G = ([k], E)$ induced by S is t-connected and the cut $(S, [k] \setminus S)$ contains less than t edges.[15] *Can you find S within complexity that is related to s and unrelated to k?*

The rest of this section is devoted to the study of the foregoing problem, which is of independent interest. Recall that the task is easy for $t = 1$; that is, when given v, the connected component containing the vertex v can be found in time that is linearly related to its size (by invoking a BFS or a DFS at vertex v). In the case of $t > 1$, things are less obvious. Still, we may proceed (recursively) as follows.

1. Invoke a DFS at the vertex v and suspend its execution as soon as more than s vertices are encountered.
2. If the DFS detected a connected component of size at most s, then return this connected component. (In this case, the corresponding cut contains no edges.)
3. Otherwise, for each edge e in the DFS-tree constructed in Step 1, invoke the procedure on the graph $G' = ([k], E \setminus \{e\})$ with the same start vertex v but *with connectivity parameter $t - 1$*. If any of these (recursive) invocations returns a set that has less than $t - 1$ edges to the rest of the graph, then return this set. (In this case, the corresponding cut contains less than t edges in $G = ([k], E)$.)

The reader may verify that this recursive procedure finds the desired set in time $O(s^{t-1} \cdot ds) = O(ds^t)$, where the key observation is that in each iteration the guaranteed cut $(S, [k] \setminus S)$ either contains no edges in the current graph or contains an edge of the current DFS tree. Another good exercise (see Exercise 9.6) is handling the case of $t = 2$ in time $O(ds)$, which yields an upper bound of $O(ds^{t-1})$ for $t \geq 3$. Using randomization yields an improvement on the foregoing bound.

Algorithm 9.10 (Finding small t-edge–connected components): *On input parameters t, d, k and s; a vertex $v \in [k]$; and oracle access to $G = ([k], E)$, the algorithm*

---

[15] The edge $\{u, w\}$ is said to reside in the cut $(S, [k] \setminus S)$ if $(u, w) \in (S, [k] \setminus S)$. We shall often associate edges of the cut (i.e., the edges contained in the cut) with the corresponding ordered pairs $\{(u, w) \in (S, [k] \setminus S) : \{u, w\} \in E\}$.

proceeds in iterations, starting with $S' = \{v\}$. In each iteration the algorithm performs the following steps.

1. *If the cut $C' = (S', [k] \setminus S')$ contains at most $t - 1$ edges, then output S'.*
2. *Otherwise, assign uniformly distributed random weights in $[0, 1]$ to every edge in the cut C' that was not assigned a weight before.*
3. *Select an edge $(u, w) \in C'$ of minimum weight, and add w to S' (i.e., $S' \leftarrow S' \cup \{w\}$).*
4. *If $|S'| > s$, then halt with no output. (Otherwise, proceed to the next iteration.)*

Whenever Algorithm 9.10 outputs a set S', it is the case that $|S'| \le s$ and the cut $(S', [k] \setminus S')$ has less than t edges. It is also apparent that Algorithm 9.10 makes at most ds queries (and runs in $\widetilde{O}(ds)$ time), but the question is what is the probability that it outputs a set at all. While a naive guess may be that the answer is $\Theta(t/ds)^{t-1}$, the correct answer is much better.[16]

Theorem 9.11 (Analysis of Algorithm 9.10): *Suppose that v resides in a set S of size at most s such that the subgraph of $G = ([k], E)$ induced by S is t-connected and the cut $(S, [k] \setminus S)$ contains less than t edges. Then, Algorithm 9.10 outputs S with probability at least $\Omega(s^{-2(t-1)/t}/t)$.*

Hence, we obtain a randomized algorithm that succeeds with probability at least $2/3$ by invoking Algorithm 9.10 for $O(s^{2(t-1)/t} \cdot t) = o(s^2)$ times, which means that the total running time of the resulting algorithm is $o(ds^3)$.

Proof Sketch: As a mental experiment, we assume that weights are assigned (at random) to all edges of the graph, and we consider the weight of edges in the cut $C = (S, [k] \setminus S)$ as well as the weight of edges in the lightest spanning tree of the subgraph of G induced by S, denoted G_S. (One may assume that all weights are distinct, since we use infinite precision in this mental experiment.)[17] Using induction on the construction of the set S', one can prove the following (see Exercise 9.7).

Claim 9.11.1 (A sufficient condition for success): *If the weight of the each edge in the cut C is larger than the weight of each edge in the lightest spanning tree of G_S, then Algorithm 9.10 outputs S.*

The complementary claim asserts that this sufficient condition is satisfied with probability at least $\Omega(s^{-2(t-1)/t}/t)$.

Claim 9.11.2 (The main claim): *For natural numbers $t' < t < |S|$, suppose that the cut C has t' edges (and recall that G_S is t-edge–connected). Then, with probability at least $\Omega(s^{-2t'/t}/t)$, the weight of each edge in the cut C is larger than the weight of each edge in the lightest spanning tree of G_S.*

---

[16] The naive guess is based on considering the probability that the $t - 1$ edges of the cut are assigned the heaviest weights among all edges that are incident at S. It turns out that this sufficient condition (for the success of Algorithm 9.10) is *not* a necessary one: see Claim 9.11.1.

[17] In the actual algorithm, weights may be chosen in multiples of $1/(ds)^4$, adding an error term of $1/(ds)^2$ (for the case of a possible collision).

Toward proving Claim 9.11.2, it is instructive to consider an auxiliary graph $G' = (S \cup \{x\}, E')$, in which $[k] \setminus S$ is contracted into a single vertex, denoted x. In this graph, x has degree t', whereas all other vertices have degree at least t (since otherwise G_S cannot be t-edge–connected). The proof of Claim 9.11.2 can be reduced to the analysis of Karger's edge-contraction algorithm [178], when this algorithm is applied to G'. The edge-contraction algorithm proceeds in iterations, until the multigraph (which may contain parallel edges) contains exactly two vertices, and it refers to random edge-weights as assigned in our mental experiment. In each iteration, the algorithm chooses the edge $e = \{u, w\}$ of minimum weight, and contracts it, which means that it merges its endpoints into a single vertex that "takes over" the edges of both these endpoints (but not the edges between them).[18] That is, every edge that was incident at either u or w (but not incident at both) becomes incident to the "contracted vertex" (which may cause the appearance of multiple edges, but not of self-loops).

The proof of Claim 9.11.2 is reduced to the analysis of Karger's edge-contraction algorithm by observing that *if Karger's algorithm does not contract an edge incident at the vertex x, then G_S contains a spanning tree with edges that are each lighter than any edge in the cut C.*[19] Hence, Claim 9.11.2 follows by lower-bounding the probability that none of the iterations of Karger's algorithm (applied to G') contacts an edge incident at x. This event occurs if and only if, at each iteration, the current graph contains an edge that is lighter than any edge in C.

The key observation is that the probability that an edge incident at x is contacted in the ith iteration (conditioned on no such edge being contracted in prior iterations) is at most

$$\frac{t'}{((|S| - i + 1) \cdot t + t')/2}.$$

This observation is proved as follows.

- At the beginning of the ith iteration (assuming that no edge incident at x was contracted in prior iterations), the graph consists of $|S| - (i - 1)$ vertices of degree at least t and a single vertex (i.e., x) of degree t'. The former claim follows from the fact that each vertex corresponds to a subset of S, and by the hypothesis the cut between this subset and the rest of S has at least t edges.
  Hence, the number of edges in the current graph is at least $m \stackrel{\text{def}}{=} ((|S| - i + 1) \cdot t + t')/2$.
- The conditioning that *no edge incident at x was contracted in prior iterations* can be interpreted as saying that all edges in the current graph have weights that are larger than the weight of the edges contracted in prior iterations. But if the weight of the edge contracted in the last iteration is ω, then we can think of the weights of the current edges as being uniformly distributed in $[\omega, 1]$. Indeed,

---

[18] Note that, in advanced iterations, there may be edges that are parallel to the edge e.

[19] Indeed, the set of edges contracted by Karger's algorithm (together with the lightest remaining edge) form a spanning tree of the graph G'. Furthermore, if the last edge is incident at x, then the contracted edges form a spanning tree of G_S such that each edge in that tree is lighter than any edge incident at x. Recall that this spanning tree is actually the lightest one (e.g., it is found in a process that corresponds to Kruskal's algorithm for finding a minimum-weight spanning tree).

we may think that the weights of all current edges are re-selected uniformly at random in the interval $[\omega, 1]$.

Hence, the probability that an edge incident at x has minimum weight is at most t'/m.

Hence, the probability that we never contracted an edge incident at x is at least

$$\prod_{i=1}^{|S|}\left(1 - \frac{t'}{(t' + (|S| - i + 1) \cdot t)/2}\right) = \prod_{i=1}^{|S|} \frac{(|S| - (i-1)) \cdot t - t'}{(|S| - (i-1)) \cdot t + t'}$$

$$= \prod_{j=1}^{|S|} \frac{j - (t'/t)}{j + (t'/t)}.$$

Hence, it suffices to lower-bound $\prod_{j=1}^{s} \frac{j-\alpha}{j+\alpha}$, where $\alpha \in [0, 1)$. For starters (or as a motivation), note that $\prod_{j=2}^{s} \frac{j-\alpha}{j+\alpha}$ is lower-bounded by $\prod_{j=2}^{s} \frac{j-1}{j+1} = \frac{2}{s \cdot (s+1)}$. In general, using $\prod_{j=2}^{s} \frac{j-\alpha}{j+\alpha} = \Omega(s^{-2\alpha})$, the claim follows (since $\prod_{j=1}^{s} \frac{j-\alpha}{j+\alpha} = \Omega((1-\alpha) \cdot s^{-2\alpha})$), and so does the theorem. [20] ∎

9.2.5. Testing Cycle-Freeness (with Two-Sided Error)

The tester for `Cycle-freeness` is based on the following well-known observation, which generalizes the even more well-known fact by which a connected k-vertex graph is cycle-free if and only if it has $k-1$ edges.

Proposition 9.12 (The number of connected components in a cycle-free graph): *Let $G = ([k], E)$ be a graph with m connected components. Then, G is cycle-free if and only if it has $k - m$ edges.*

This proposition follows immediately by considering the number of edges in each connected component of G. Specifically, letting k_i denote the number of vertices in the ith

---

[20] For our purpose, it suffices to establish the claim for rational α, since here $\alpha = t'/t$. Indeed, we lower-bound $\prod_{j=2}^{s} \frac{j-(t'/t)}{j+(t'/t)}$ by using

$$\left(\prod_{j=2}^{s} \frac{j - (t'/t)}{j + (t'/t)}\right)^t = \prod_{j=2}^{s}\left(\frac{jt - t'}{jt + t'}\right)^t$$

$$> \prod_{j=2}^{s}\prod_{i=1}^{t} \frac{(j-1)t + i - t'}{(j-1)t + i + t'}$$

$$= \prod_{i=1}^{st-t} \frac{t - t' + i}{t + t' + i}$$

$$= \frac{\prod_{i=1}^{2t'}(t - t' + i)}{\prod_{i=1}^{2t'}(st - t' + i)}$$

$$> \frac{(2t'/3)^{2t'}}{(st + t')^{2t'}}.$$

Hence, $\prod_{j=2}^{s} \frac{j-(t'/t)}{j+(t'/t)} = \Omega(t'/st)^{2t'/t} = \Omega(1/s)^{2t'/t}$, and the claim follows.

connected component, we observe that G is cycle-free if for every $i \in [m]$ the ith connected component has exactly $k_i - 1$ edges.

Proposition 9.12 suggests that cycle-freeness can be tested by comparing the number of edges in the graph to the number of connected components in it. Estimating the number of edges is quite straightforward, but how can we estimate the number of connected components? The key idea is that it suffices to estimate the number of small connected components, whereas the number of large connected components is small and therefore can be ignored.

The number of small connected components is estimated by repeating the following experiment for an adequate number of times: Select uniformly a random vertex $v \in [k]$, perform a truncated search starting at v and suspending the search if too many vertices are encountered, and use k/s as the estimator if s is the size of the (small) connected component that was fully visited in this search. (Indeed, zero is used as the estimator in case the search was suspended before the component was fully visited.) Hence, if a small connected component has size s, then its contribution to the expected value of this experiment is $\frac{s}{k} \cdot \frac{k}{s}$, where the first factor represents the probability that a vertex residing in this component was selected and the second factor represents its contribution in such a case. Repeating the experiment for a sufficient number of times (and normalizing the count accordingly), we obtain the following algorithm.

Algorithm 9.13 (Two-sided error tester for cycle-freeness (in the bounded-degree graph model)): *On input parameters d, k, and ϵ and oracle access to the incidence function of a k-vertex graph $G = ([k], E)$, which has maximum degree d, the algorithm proceeds as follows.*

1. *Using $O(1/\epsilon^2)$ random queries (in $[k] \times [d]$), the algorithm estimates the number of edges up to $\pm 0.05 \epsilon dk$. Let $\widetilde{e}$ denote this estimate.[21]*
2. *The algorithm estimates the number of connected components up to $\pm 0.05 \epsilon dk$ by selecting at random $t = O(1/d\epsilon)^2$ start vertices, $v_1, \ldots, v_t$, and incrementing the counter by k/s_i if the search started at v_i encountered $s_i < \ell \overset{\text{def}}{=} 8/(d\epsilon)$ vertices (and by zero otherwise). That is, for each $i \in [t]$, the algorithm proceeds as follows:*
   (a) *Performs a linear-time (e.g., BFS or DFS) search starting at v_i, while suspending the search if more than ℓ vertices are encountered in it.*
      Hence, this search involves $O(\ell \cdot d) = O(1/\epsilon)$ queries.
   (b) *If the entire connected component is scanned and its size is s_i, then the counter is incremented by k/s_i.*
   Divide the accumulated sum by t, and denote the result by $\widetilde{m}$.
3. *If $\widetilde{e} \geq k - \widetilde{m} + \epsilon dk/4$, then reject. Otherwise, accept.*

The query complexity of Algorithm 9.13 is $O(1/\epsilon^2) + t \cdot O(1/\epsilon) = O(1/\epsilon^2) + O(1/d^2\epsilon^3)$. The algorithm may err (with small probability) both in the case that the graph

---

[21] **Advanced comment:** One can reduce the number of queries used in this step to $O(\max(1/d\epsilon^2, 1/\epsilon))$ by assuming that $|E| \leq m \overset{\text{def}}{=} \max(2k, \epsilon dk/2)$, since in this case we seek a multiplicative approximation factor of $1 \pm \frac{0.05\epsilon dk}{m}$ for an event that occurs with probability smaller than $2m/dk$, and a random sample of $O((2m/dk)^{-1} \cdot (\epsilon dk/m)^{-2}) = O(m/(dk\epsilon^2))$ pairs will do. The foregoing assumption can be justified by augmenting the algorithm with a step that checks this condition (and rejects if $|E| \leq \max(2k, \epsilon dk/2)$ seems not to hold, since this indicates that $|E| > k$). Such a check can be implemented using $O(1/\epsilon)$ queries (see Exercise 9.8).

is cycle-free and in the case it is far from being cycle-free, where the source of the error probability lies in the estimates that are performed in Steps 1 and 2.

Note that only connected components of size at most $\ell = 8/d\epsilon$ contribute to the estimate $\tilde{m}$, whereas $\tilde{m}$ is supposed to estimate the number of all connected components. However, since the number of the larger (than $8/d\epsilon$) connected components is at most $(d\epsilon/8) \cdot k$, we can ignore their contribution. Details follow.

Claim 9.14 (Analysis of Algorithm 9.13): *Algorithm 9.13 is a* (two-sided error) *tester for* Cycle-freeness.

Proof Sketch: The following analysis presumes that the samples used in Steps 1 and 2 provides the stated estimates, with high probability. This fact is easy to establish using an additive Chernoff Bound, while noting that the desired estimates are, respectively, an $\Omega(\epsilon)$ and an $\Omega(d\epsilon)$ fraction of the range of the corresponding random variables.[22] Specifically, when analyzing Step 2, let $m' \geq m - \epsilon dk/8$ denote the number of small connected components, and prove that (w.h.p.) $|\tilde{m} - m'| \leq 0.05\epsilon dk$.

If $G = ([k], E)$ is cycle-free and has m connected components, then $|E| = k - m$. In this case, with high probability it holds that $\tilde{e} \leq |E| + 0.05\epsilon dk = k - m + 0.05\epsilon dk$, whereas $\tilde{m} \leq m' + 0.05\epsilon dk \leq m + 0.05\epsilon dk$ (since $m' \leq m$ by definition). Hence, $\tilde{e} + \tilde{m} \leq (k - m + 0.05\epsilon dk) + (m + 0.05\epsilon dk) < k + \epsilon dk/4$, and Algorithm 9.13 accepts.

On the other hand, if $G = ([k], E)$ has m connected and is ϵ-far from being cycle-free, then $|E| \geq k - m + \epsilon dk/2$ (since otherwise G can be made cycle-free by omitting at most $\epsilon dk/2$ edges). Now, with high probability, it holds that $\tilde{e} \geq |E| - 0.05\epsilon dk \geq k - m + 0.45\epsilon dk$, whereas $\tilde{m} \geq m' - 0.05\epsilon dk > m - 0.18\epsilon dk$ (since $m' > m - 0.13\epsilon dk$, because $m - m' \leq \epsilon dk/8$ represents the number of large (i.e., larger than $8/d\epsilon$) connected components). In this case, $\tilde{e} + \tilde{m} > (k - m + 0.45\epsilon dk) + (m - 0.18\epsilon dk) > k + \epsilon dk/4$, and Algorithm 9.13 rejects. ∎

Improving over Algorithm 9.13. Recall that Step 2(a) of Algorithm 9.13 performs a search aimed at detecting small connected components toward estimating their number, where a connected component is defined as small if it has size at most $\ell = 8/d\epsilon$. But when upper-bounding the cost of such a search, we used $\ell \cdot d$ as a bound. This fails to capitalize on the fact that *if we encountered more edges than vertices in the current search, then we found a cycle in the current connected component.* Hence, it is begging to suspend the search in such a case, and reject. Note that the modified algorithm has complexity $O(1/\epsilon^2) + O(t \cdot \ell) = O(1/\epsilon^2) + O(1/d\epsilon)^3$, whereas its verdicts are at least as reliable as those of the original algorithm: On the one hand, graphs that are cycle-free are accepted by the modified algorithm with the same probability as they are accepted by Algorithm 9.13, since the modification has no effect in this case. On the other hand, graphs that are not cycle-free are rejected by the modified algorithm with probability that

---

[22] In Step 1, each random query, which is effectively answered with a value in $\{0, 1\}$, is an unbiased estimator of $|\{(v, i) \in [k] \times [d] : g(v, i) \neq 0\}|/dk$, and we consider the probability that the average of $O(1/\epsilon^2)$ such estimators deviates from the correct value by more than 0.05ϵ. In Step 2, each search returns a value in $[0, k]$ that is an unbiased estimator of the number of small connected components, and we consider the probability that the average of $O(1/d\epsilon)^2$ such estimators deviates from the correct value by more than $0.05\epsilon dk$.

is lower bounded by the probability that they are rejected by Algorithm 9.13, since the modification can only increase the rejection probability. Hence, we get:

Theorem 9.15 (An alternative two-sided error tester for cycle-freeness): *Testing* Cycle-freeness *(in the bounded-degree graph model) can be performed in time* $O(\epsilon^{-2} + d^{-3} \cdot \epsilon^{-3})$.

Recall that the tester establishing Theorem 9.15 has two-sided error probability. As we shall see in the next section, two-sided error probability is unavoidable for a tester for Cycle-freeness that has query complexity poly$(1/\epsilon)$. Actually, two-sided error probability is unavoidable even for query complexity $f(\epsilon) \cdot o(\sqrt{k})$, for any function $f : (0, 1] \to \mathbb{N}$ (see Theorem 9.17).

9.3. Lower Bounds

In this section we present lower bounds on the query complexity of testing a few natural properties, including Bipartiteness and 3-Colorability. These lower bounds justify our inablity to present significantly better testers for these properties (cf. Section 9.4, where we present testers that essentially match these bounds).

We focus on the case that $d \geq 3$, since otherwise (i.e., $d \leq 2$) any graph property of interest is either trivial or easy to test. (Note that when $d \leq 2$ the graph consists of a collection of isolated paths and cycles; actually, if $d = 1$, then the graph consists of a collection of isolated edges and isolated vertices.)

Teaching Note: This section relies on a technique for proving lower bounds that is presented in Section 7.2, and is called the method of indistinguishable distributions. This technique is simple enough to pick-up on the fly, but it may be better to study Section 7.2 first.

9.3.1. Bipartiteness

In contrast to the situation in the dense graph model, in the bounded degree graph model there exists no Bipartite tester of complexity that is independent of the graph's size. This fact reflects the fact that being far from Bipartiteness does not require having constant-size cycles of odd length. Actually, graphs that are far from being bipartite may lack odd-length cycles of sublogarithmic length (see Exercise 9.9), and so testing Bipartiteness (at least with one-sided error probability) cannot be performed in sublogarithmic (in k) query complexity. The stronger lower bound presented next goes beyond these existential considerations.

Theorem 9.16 (Lower bound on the complexity of testing Bipartiteness (in the bounded-degree graph model)): *For proximity parameter* $\epsilon = 0.01$ *and any degree bound* $d \geq 3$, *testing* Bipartiteness *requires* $\Omega(\sqrt{k})$ *queries.*

Note that graphs that are 0.01-far from being bipartite do have odd-length cycles of logarithmic length (see Exercise 9.10).[23]

---

[23] A weaker bound (i.e., odd-length cycles of polylogarithmic length) follows directly from Theorem 9.21.

Proof Sketch: We shall focus on the case of $d = 3$, and prove the lower bound using 3-regular graphs. For any (even) k, we consider the following two families of k-vertex graphs:

1. The first family, denoted $\mathcal{G}_1$, consists of all 3-regular graphs that are composed of the union of a Hamiltonian cycle and a perfect matching (which does not match vertices that are adjacent on the cycle). That is, there are k edges forming a simple k-vertex cycle, and the other $k/2$ edges are a perfect matching.
2. The second family, denoted $\mathcal{G}_2$, is the same as the first *except* that the choice of perfect matching is restricted such that the distance on the cycle between every two vertices that are connected by a perfect matching edge must be odd. Equivalently, labeling the vertices according to their location on the cycle (so that the ith vertex is adjacent to the $i + 1^{\text{st}}$ vertex, for every $i \in [k]$),[24] we require that if $\{i, j\}$ is a perfect matching edge, then $i \not\equiv j \pmod 2$.

Clearly, all graphs in $\mathcal{G}_2$ are bipartite. It can be shown (see Claim 9.16.1) that *almost all graphs in $\mathcal{G}_1$ are far from being bipartite*. On the other hand, one can prove (see Claim 9.16.2) that *an algorithm that performs $o(\sqrt{k})$ queries cannot distinguish between a graph chosen randomly from $\mathcal{G}_2$ (which is always bipartite) and a graph chosen randomly from $\mathcal{G}_1$ (which with high probability is far from bipartite)*. Loosely speaking, this is the case since in both situations the algorithm is unlikely to encounter a cycle (among the vertices that it has inspected).

Claim 9.16.1 (Almost all graphs in $\mathcal{G}_1$ are far from being bipartite): *All but an exponentially vanishing fraction of the graphs in $\mathcal{G}_1$ are 0.01-far from being bipartite.*

Proof: We consider a uniformly distributed graph in $\mathcal{G}_1$, and upper-bound the probability that it can be made bipartite by omitting $0.01 \cdot dk/2 = 0.015k$ of its edges. We shall actually consider an omission of $0.015k$ of its (Hamiltonian) cycle edges and $0.015k$ of the matching edges. For each of the possible $\binom{k}{0.015k} < 2^{0.12k}$ choices of $0.015k$ cycle edges, we consider all $2^{0.015k}$ legal 2-colorings of the resulting collection of $0.015k$ paths. For each such set of paths and 2-colorings, we upper-bound the probability that the random perfect matching does not have more than $0.015k$ edges that violate this fixed 2-coloring. This is done by selecting the $k/2$ matching edges in iterations, while noting that in the $i + 1^{\text{st}}$ iteration a violating edge is selected with probability at least

$$\min_{j \in \{0,\dots,k-2i\}} \left\{ \frac{\binom{j}{2} + \binom{k-2i-j}{2}}{\binom{k-2i}{2}} \right\} \geq \frac{2 \cdot \binom{(k-2i)/2}{2}}{\binom{k-2i}{2}} \approx \frac{1}{2}$$

where j represents the number of currently unmatched vertices that are colored with the first color and the approximation holds for any $i \leq (k/2) - \omega(1)$. Hence, the probability that we end up with at most $0.015k$ violating edges is less than $e^{-(0.5-o(1)-0.015)^2 \cdot ((k/2)-\omega(1))} = e^{-(0.485-o(1))^2 \cdot k/2}$. Using a union bound, the claim follows. ∎

---

[24] Indeed, we identify the $k + 1^{\text{st}}$ vertex with the first one.

Claim 9.16.2 (Indistinguishability by $o(\sqrt{k})$-query algorithms): *An algorithm that performs q queries can distinguish between a graph chosen randomly from $\mathcal{G}_1$ and a graph chosen randomly from $\mathcal{G}_2$ with gap of at most q^2/k.*

Proof: We shall assume, to the benefit of the algorithm, that the incidence function g is "nice" in the sense that for every vertex v it holds that $g(v, 1)$ is successor of v on the (Hamiltonian) cycle, whereas $g(v, 2)$ is the predecessor of v on that cycle (which means that $g(v, 3)$ is the vertex matched to v by the perfect matching). We assume, without loss of generality, that the algorithm does not make queries for which it knows the answers (e.g., after making the query $g(v, 1)$, it does not make the query $g(g(v, 1), 2)$). Recall that we use $d = 3$ and 3-regular graphs; hence, the queries of the algorithm correspond to edges (i.e., the query (v, i) corresponds to the edge $\{v, g(v, i)\}$). These conventions merely facilitate the verification of the key observation that appears next.

We consider an iterative process of generating a randomly distributed graph in $\mathcal{G}_1$ (resp., in $\mathcal{G}_2$) by answering queries of the algorithm, while keeping track of the "knowledge graph" of the algorithm (at each point), where the knowledge graph is defined as the subgraph consisting of the edges that correspond to the algorithm's queries so far. The key distinction is between vertices that are in the knowledge graph (i.e., vertices that have appeared either in a previous query of the algorithm or as a previous answer provided to it) and those that are not in this graph. The *key observation* is that *as long as the knowledge graph of the algorithm is cycle-free and contains relatively few edges, both generation processes* (i.e., the one constructing a random element of $\mathcal{G}_1$ and the one constructing a random element of $\mathcal{G}_2$) *behave in a very similar manner.* Actually, each of these processes answers the $i + 1^{st}$ query with an old vertex (i.e., a vertex in the knowledge graph) with probability at most $\frac{2i}{k-1}$, and otherwise the answer is uniformly distributed among the labels that do not appear in the current knowledge graph. Hence, the distinguishing gap of the algorithm is upper-bounded by the probability that at least one of the q queries is answered with an old vertex, and the claim follows. ∎

This completes the proof of the theorem. ∎

9.3.2. Applications to Other Properties

The proof of Theorem 9.16 can be adapted to yield hardness results for two natural testing problems, which seem unrelated to testing Bipartiteness.

Application to Testing Cycle-Freeness. Recall that, in Section 9.2.5, we presented *two-sided error* testers of query complexity poly($1/\epsilon$) for Cycle-freeness. We now show that the two-sided error was inherent to these testers, since Cycle-freeness does not have a *one-sided error* tester of complexity that depends on the proximity parameter only.

Theorem 9.17 (Lower bound on the query complexity of one-sided error testers for Cycle-freeness): *For any degree bound $d \geq 3$, every one-sided error $(1/d)$-tester for Cycle-freeness has query complexity $\Omega(\sqrt{k})$.*

Proof: We use any of the two families of graphs presented in the proof of Theorem 9.16, while noting that each of these graphs is $1/3$-far from being cycle-free (since it has $0.5k + 1$ superfluous edges). Hence, any $1/3$-tester for Cycle-freeness is required to reject each of these graphs with probability at least $2/3$. On the other hand, the proof of Claim 9.16.2 actually establishes that a q-query machine sees a cycle in a random graph (drawn from any of these families), with probability at most q^2/k. Hence, a cycle-freeness tester of query complexity $\sqrt{k/2}$ must, with probability at least $\frac{2}{3} - \frac{1}{2} > 0$, reject some graph without seeing a cycle in the subgraph that it has explored, which means that this tester cannot have one-sided error. ∎

Teaching Note: The rest of Section 9.3 is intended for optional independent reading. In the rest of Section 9.3.2 we present a lower bound on the query complexity of testing expansion. Section 9.3.3 reviews a linear lower bound on the query complexity of testing 3-Colorability.

Application to Testing Expansion. Fixing a constant $c > 0$, we say that the graph $G = ([k], E)$ is c-expanding if, for every set $S \subset [k]$ of cardinality at most $k/2$, it holds that $|\Gamma^+(S)| \geq c \cdot |S|$, where

$$\Gamma^+(S) \stackrel{\text{def}}{=} \{u \in ([k] \setminus S) : \exists v \in S \text{ s.t. } \{u, v\} \in E\} \tag{9.2}$$

denotes the set of vertices that are not in S but neighbor some vertices in S. One can show that, for sufficiently small constant $c > 0$ and all sufficiently large k, with high probability, a random 3-regular k-vertex graph is c-expanding.

Theorem 9.18 (Lower bound on the query complexity testing c-expansion): *For sufficiently small constant $c > 0$ and any degree bound $d \geq 3$, every (c/d)-tester for* c-expansion *has query complexity $\Omega(\sqrt{k})$. Furthermore, an algorithm of query complexity $o(\sqrt{k})$ cannot distinguish between k-vertex graphs that are c-expanding and graphs that consist of two ($k/2$-vertex) connected components.*

Proof Sketch: We start with the family $\mathcal{G}_1$ presented in the proof of Theorem 9.16, and show (see Claim 9.18.1) that, with high probability, a uniformly distributed (in $\mathcal{G}_1$) graph is c-expanding. We then show that a $o(\sqrt{k})$-query algorithm cannot distinguish a uniformly distributed k-vertex graph (drawn from $\mathcal{G}_1$) from a k-vertex graph that consists of two isolated $k/2$-vertex graphs drawn from (the $k/2$-vertex version of) $\mathcal{G}_1$. The theorem follows by noting that the latter graphs are far from being expanding (in any reasonable sense of that term), since the vertices of the first $k/2$-vertex graph neighbor no vertex in the second $k/2$-vertex graph.

Claim 9.18.1 (Almost all graphs in $\mathcal{G}_1$ are expanding): *For sufficiently small constant $c > 0$, with high probability, a uniformly distributed (in $\mathcal{G}_1$) graph is c-expanding.*

Proof Sketch: Using a (carefully executed) union bound, we upper-bound the probability that there exists a set S of size at most $k/2$ such that $|\Gamma^+(S)| < c \cdot |S|$.

Specifically, for every set $S \subseteq [k]$, we consider the random variable X_S that represents the size of $\Gamma^+(S)$ in a graph drawn at random (from $\mathcal{G}_1$). The union bound is based on a partition of the possible sets S to two classes.

1. Sets S such that the subgraph induced by S on the graph consisting only of the edges of the Hamiltonian cycle has at least $c \cdot |S|$ connected components.
   In this case, $\mathbf{Pr}[X_S \geq c \cdot |S|] = 1$, merely by virtue of the cycle edges.[25] Hence, sets of this type contribute nothing to the probability that there exists a set S of size at most $k/2$ such that $|\Gamma^+(S)| < c \cdot |S|$.
2. Sets S that have less than $c \cdot |S|$ such connected components.
   We first upper-bound the number of such sets. Specifically, observe that the number of such sets of size $s \leq k/2$ is at most $2 \cdot \sum_{i \in [cs]} \binom{k}{2i}$, since each choice of $2i$ vertices determine two possible i-long sequences of disjoint sectors of the cycle. Note that $2 \cdot \sum_{i \in [cs]} \binom{k}{2i} = \exp(H_2(2cs/k) \cdot k)$, where H_2 is the binary entropy function.[26] Next, for each such set S, we upper-bound the probability that $X_S < c \cdot |S|$ by observing that this event implies that there exists a set S' of $s - cs$ vertices in S such that each vertex in S' is matched to a vertex in S (by the perfect matching). Hence,

$$\mathbf{Pr}[X_S < c \cdot |S|] \leq \binom{s}{s - cs} \prod_{i \in [(1-c)s/2]} \frac{s - 2(i-1)}{k - 2(i-1)} = 2^{H_2(c) \cdot s} \cdot (s/k)^{\Omega(s)},$$

where the inequality is proved by considering, for each possible set $S' \subset S$ of size $s - cs$, an iterative process of matching vertices in S' at random.[27] Taking a union bound over all relevant sets S, we obtain the probability bound $\exp(H_2(2cs/k) \cdot k + H_2(c) \cdot s - \Omega(s \log(k/s)))$, which equals $\exp(-\Omega(s))$ when $c > 0$ is sufficiently small.

The claim follows. (Indeed, in the first case expansion was proved based on the edges of the fixed Hamiltonian cycle, whereas in the second case expansion was proved based on the edges of the random perfect matching.) ∎

Claim 9.18.2 (Indistinguishability by $o(\sqrt{k})$-query algorithms): *Let $\mathcal{G}'_1$ denote the set of k-vertex graphs that consist of two isolated $k/2$-vertex graphs taken from the $k/2$-vertex version of $\mathcal{G}_1$. Then, a q-query can distinguish between a graph chosen uniformly at random in $\mathcal{G}_1$ and a graph chosen uniformly in $\mathcal{G}'_1$ with gap of at most q^2/k.*

Claim 9.18.2 follows by noting that the argument used in the proof of Claim 9.16.2 extends to $\mathcal{G}'_1$; that is, a q-query algorithm revisited an old vertex (i.e., obtain an answer that is already in its knowledge graph) when inspecting a random graph drawn uniformly from $\mathcal{G}'_1$, with probability at most q^2/k. Note that as long as

---

[25] Note that, when "going around the cycle," the last vertex in each of the aforementioned connected components neighbors a distinct vertex not in S.

[26] That is, $H_2 : [0, 1] \rightarrow [0, 1]$ such that $H_2(p) = p \log(1/p) + (1 - p) \log(1/(1 - p))$.

[27] In the ith iteration of this process, we pick an unmatched vertex in S' and match it at random to an unmatched vertex, calling this choice successful if the latter vertex is in S. Observe that at the beginning of the ith iteration exactly $2(i - 1)$ vertices are matched, and if all prior iterations were successful then these matched vertices are all in S. We upper-bound the probability of success in the first $(s - cs)/2$ steps, although the process continues till all vertices in S' are matched.

no old vertex is revisited, the two distributions of answers are identical. Using Claim 9.18.1, the theorem follows. ∎

9.3.3. Linear Lower Bounds

While the $\Omega(\sqrt{k})$ lower bounds capitalize on the difficulty of detecting a cycle in the graph (or, equivalently, on the difficulty of reaching the same vertex in two nontrivially different ways), this strategy is unlikely to work for obtaining larger lower bounds. Indeed, different methods are used for obtaining results of the following type.

Theorem 9.19 (Lower bound on the complexity of testing 3-Colorability (in the bounded-degree graph model)): *For some proximity parameter $\epsilon > 0$ and a degree bound d, testing* 3-Colorability *requires* $\Omega(k)$ *queries.*

The proof of Theorem 9.19 can be found in [61]. Here we only sketch an alternative proof, also due to [61], that applies only to the one-sided error case. We note that this proof exhibits a general trade-off between $\epsilon \in (0, 1/3)$ and $d \geq 3$ (and the constant that is hidden in the Ω-notation). We note that $1/3$-testing 3-Colorability is trivial, since every graph is $1/3$-close to being 3-colorable.[28]

Proof Outline for the One-Sided Error Case: Let $\epsilon : \mathbb{N} \to (0, 1/3)$ and $\rho : \mathbb{N} \to (0, 1)$. The basic idea is that, for every $d \geq 3$, there exist d-regular k-vertex graphs that, one the one hand, are $\epsilon(d)$-far from being 3-colorable but, on the other hand, all their $\rho(d) \cdot k$-vertex induced subgraphs are 3-colorable. Such a graph must be rejected with probability at least $2/3$ by any $\epsilon(d)$-tester, but if this tester rejects without seeing a subgraph that is not 3-colorable, then it is not of the one-sided error type (because it would reject with positive probability a graph that consists of that subgraph and $k - \rho(d) \cdot k$ isolated vertices). Hence, all that is left is to show the existence of graphs with the aforementioned property.

We shall show that such graphs exist, by showing that a random d-regular graph satisfies the aforementioned property, with very high probability. Actually, it will be instructive to consider a random d-regular multigraph (which may contain parallel edges), and note that if it satisfies the property, then so does the graph obtained from it by omitting parallel edges (which are extremely few in number).

Claim 9.19.1 (A random d-regular graph is far from being 3-colorable): *Suppose that $G = ([k], E)$ is generated by taking the union of d random perfect matching of the elements of $[k]$. If $d = \Omega(((1/3) - \epsilon)^{-2})$, then, with probability at least $1 - \exp(-\Omega(k))$, the graph G is ϵ-far from 3-colorable.*

The proof of Claim 9.19.1 is rather technical and can be found in [61]. It uses a union bound over all 3^k possible 3-partitions of $[k]$, denoted (V_1, V_2, V_3), and upper-bounds (for each such 3-partition) the probability that at most $\epsilon dk/2$ of the edges have endpoints in the same V_i. Analyzing the latter event would have been easy if the $dk/2$ edges were selected independent of one another. In such a case, we would have had $dk/2$ independent events, each succeeding with probability $\sum_{i \in [3]} \binom{|V_i|}{2}/\binom{k}{2} > (1/3) - o(1)$,

---

[28] Note that a random assignment of three colors to the vertices of the graph $G = ([k], E)$ is expected to have exactly $|E|/3$ monochromatic edges.

and (by a Chernoff Bound) the probability of having at most $\epsilon dk/2$ successes is $\exp(-\Omega(((1/3) - o(1) - \epsilon)^2 dk))$.

Claim 9.19.2 (A random d-regular graph has large 3-colorable subgraphs): *Let G be as in Claim 9.19.1. For $\rho = \text{poly}(1/d)$, with probability at least $1 - \exp(-\Omega(\rho \cdot k))$, the subgraph of G induced by any set of ρk vertices is 3-colorable.*

The proof of Claim 9.19.2 reduces to showing that for any set S of at most ρk vertices, the subgraph induced by S, denoted G_S, contains a vertex of degree less than 3. Again, the actual proof is technical (see [61]).[29] The claim follows by considering a minimal set S of size at most ρk such that G_S is not 3-colorable, and reaching a contradiction by using the fact that this set contains a vertex v of degree at most two in G_S (since, by minimality, $G_{S\setminus\{v\}}$ is 3-colorable, but then contradiction is reached by extending this 3-coloring to G_S). ∎

9.4. Testing by Random Walks

The testers presented in this section are based on taking "random walks on the input graph" (defined momentarily). The intuition is that such walks may provide information that extends beyond what can be deduced based on local searches. It is not *a priori* clear whether this additional information may be beneficial to our (testing) goals, but for sure taking a random walk is a natural thing to try if one wants to get beyond local searches and still maintain sublinear complexity.

By a random walk of length ℓ on a graph $G = ([k], E)$ we mean a path $(v_0, \ldots, v_\ell)$ in G selected at random such that v_0 is uniformly distributed in $[k]$ and v_i is uniformly distributed among the neighbors of v_{i-1}.

As noted at the beginning of Section 9.3, we focus on the case of $d \geq 3$, since when $d \leq 2$ the graph consists of a collection of isolated paths and cycles, and any graph property of interest is either trivial or easy to test in that case.

9.4.1. Testing Bipartiteness

The executive summary is that the lower bound of Theorem 9.16 is essentially tight; that is, for every constant $\epsilon > 0$, Bipartiteness can be ϵ-tested in $\tilde{O}(\sqrt{k})$ queries. Furthermore, the following algorithm constitutes a Bipartite tester of running time $\text{poly}((\log k)/\epsilon) \cdot \sqrt{k}$. Essentially, the algorithm selects a random start vertex, takes $\tilde{O}(\sqrt{k})$ random walks from it, each of $\text{poly}(\epsilon^{-1} \log k)$-length, and accepts if and only if the subgraph explored in these walks is bipartite.

---

[29] **Advanced comment:** We upper-bound the probability that a subgraph induced by a set of $s = \rho k$ vertices has no vertex of degree lower than 3. We actually upper-bound the probability that such a set has at least $m = 3s/2$ edges, by using a union bound on all $\binom{k}{s} = O(k/s)^s$ possible choices of this set of vertices. For each such choice of s vertices, we upper-bound the probability that the induced subgraph has m edges by $\binom{\binom{s}{2}}{m} \cdot \prod_{i=0}^{m-1}(d/(k-2i))$, which is upper-bounded by $O(s^2/m)^m \cdot (2d/k)^m = O(s^2 d/mk)^m$. Hence, the union bound gives

$$O(k/s)^s \cdot O(s^2 d/mk)^m = O(k/s)^s \cdot O(s^2 d/sk)^{1.5s}$$

$$= O(sd^3/k)^{0.5s},$$

and the claim follows.

The natural question is why does this algorithm reject graphs that are far from being bipartite? The intuitive answer is as follows. Fixing a start vertex s, if many vertices are reached by an odd-length random walk from s with about the same probability as by an even-length random walk from s, then (with high probability) an odd-length cycle will be formed in the explored subgraph, and the algorithm will reject. Otherwise, we can color each vertex according to the more frequent parity of the random walk in which the vertex is reached, and infer that there are relatively few monochromatic edges. Hence, if the graph is far from being bipartite, then the algorithm will reject with high probability. This intuition will be implemented in Claims 9.21.3 and 9.21.2, respectively. But before doing so, let us spell out the algorithm.

Algorithm 9.20 (Testing Bipartiteness (in the bounded-degree graph model)): *On input d, k, ϵ and oracle access to an incidence function of an k-vertex graph, $G = ([k], E)$, of degree bound d, repeat the following steps $t \stackrel{\text{def}}{=} \Theta(\frac{1}{\epsilon})$ times:*

1. *Uniformly select s in $[k]$.*
2. *(Try to find an odd-length cycle through vertex s):*
   (a) *Perform $m \stackrel{\text{def}}{=} \text{poly}((\log k)/\epsilon) \cdot \sqrt{k}$ random walks starting from s, each of length $\ell \stackrel{\text{def}}{=} \text{poly}((\log k)/\epsilon)$.*
   (b) *Let R_0 (respectively, R_1) denote the set of vertices reached from s in an even (respectively, odd) number of steps in any of these walks. That is, assuming that ℓ is even, for every such walk $(s = v_0, v_1, \ldots, v_\ell)$, place $v_0, v_2, \ldots, v_\ell$ in R_0 and place $v_1, v_3, \ldots, v_{\ell-1}$ in R_1.*
   (c) *If $R_0 \cap R_1$ is not empty, then reject.*

If the algorithm did not reject in any of the foregoing t iterations, then it accepts.

The time (and query) complexity of Algorithm 9.20 is $t \cdot m \cdot \ell \cdot \log d = \text{poly}(1/\epsilon) \cdot \widetilde{O}(\sqrt{k})$, where the $\log d$ factor is due to determining the degree of each vertex encountered in the random walk (before selecting one of its neighbors at random). It is evident that the algorithm always accepts a bipartite graph. Furthermore, Algorithm 9.20 can be easily modified so that in case of rejection it outputs an odd-length cycle of length $\text{poly}((\log k)/\epsilon)$, which constitutes a "witness" that the graph is not bipartite. The difficult part of the analysis is proving the following.

Theorem 9.21 (Algorithm 9.20 is a Bipartiteness tester (for the bounded-degree graph model)): *If the input graph is ϵ-far from being bipartite, then Algorithm 9.20 rejects with probability at least $2/3$.*

The proof of Theorem 9.21 is quite involved. We shall provide only a proof of the "rapid mixing" case, and hint at the ideas used toward extending this proof to the general case.

The Special Case of Rapid Mixing Graphs. We consider the special case in which the input graph has a "rapid mixing" feature (defined next). Toward the analysis, it is convenient to modify the random walks so that at each step each neighbor is selected with probability $1/2d$, and otherwise (with probability at least $1/2$) the walk remains in the present vertex. Such a modified random walk is often called a lazy random walk. Indeed, using a lazy random walk, the next vertex on a walk can be selected at unit cost (rather than at $\log d$ cost, which is required for determining the degree of the current vertex).

We will consider a single execution of Step 2, starting from an arbitrary vertex, s, which is fixed for the rest of the discussion. (Indeed, in this special case it suffices to execute Step 2 once and the start vertex s may be arbitrary (i.e., it need not be selected at random).) The rapid mixing feature that we assume here is that, for every vertex v, a lazy random walk of length ℓ starting at s reaches v with probability approximately $1/k$ (say, up to a factor of 2).

Definition 9.21.1 (The rapid mixing feature): *Let $(v_1, \ldots, v_\ell) \leftarrow \mathcal{RW}_\ell$ be an ℓ-step lazy random walk (on $G = ([k], E)$) starting at $v_0 \stackrel{\text{def}}{=} s$; that is, for every $\{u, v\} \in E$ and every $i \in [\ell]$, it holds that*

$$\mathbf{Pr}_{(v_1,\ldots,v_\ell)\leftarrow\mathcal{RW}_\ell}[v_i = v | v_{i-1} = u] = \frac{1}{2d} \tag{9.3}$$

$$\mathbf{Pr}_{(v_1,\ldots,v_\ell)\leftarrow\mathcal{RW}_\ell}[v_i = u | v_{i-1} = u] = 1 - \frac{d_G(u)}{2d}, \tag{9.4}$$

where $d_G(u)$ denotes the degree of u in G. Then, the graph G is said to be rapidly mixing *if, for every $v_0, v \in [k]$, it holds that*

$$\frac{1}{2k} < \mathbf{Pr}_{(v_1,\ldots,v_\ell)\leftarrow\mathcal{RW}_\ell}[v_\ell = v] < \frac{2}{k}. \tag{9.5}$$

Indeed, Eq. (9.3) refers to moving to a neighbor of the current vertex, whereas Eq. (9.4) refers to staying at the current vertex. Note that if the graph is an expander, then it is rapidly mixing (since $\ell = \omega(\log k)$).

The key quantities in the analysis are the following probabilities that refer to the parity *of the length of a path obtained from the lazy random walk by omitting the self-loops* (transitions that remain at the current vertex). Let $p_0(v)$ (respectively, $p_1(v)$) denote the probability that a *lazy random walk of length ℓ, starting at s, reaches v while making an even* (respectively, *odd) number of real* (i.e., non–self-loop) *steps*. That is, for every $\sigma \in \{0, 1\}$ and $v \in [k]$,

$$p_\sigma(v) \stackrel{\text{def}}{=} \mathbf{Pr}_{(v_1,\ldots,v_\ell)\leftarrow\mathcal{RW}_\ell}[v_\ell = v \wedge |\{i \in [\ell] : v_i \neq v_{i-1}\}| \equiv \sigma \pmod 2]. \tag{9.6}$$

The path-parity of the walk $(v_1, \ldots, v_\ell)$ is defined as $|\{i \in [\ell] : v_i \neq v_{i-1}\}| \bmod 2$.

By the rapid mixing assumption (for every $v \in [k]$), it holds that

$$\frac{1}{2k} < p_0(v) + p_1(v) < \frac{2}{k}. \tag{9.7}$$

We consider two cases regarding the sum $\sum_{v\in[k]} p_0(v)p_1(v)$: If the sum is (relatively) "small," then we show that $[k]$ can be 2-partitioned so that there are relatively few edges between vertices that are placed in the same side, which implies that G is close to being bipartite. Otherwise (i.e., when the sum is not "small"), we show that, with high probability, when Step 2 is started at vertex s, it is completed by rejecting G. These two cases are analyzed in the following two (corresponding) claims.

Claim 9.21.2 (A small sum implies closeness to being bipartite): *Suppose that $\sum_{v\in[k]} p_0(v)p_1(v) \leq 0.01\epsilon/k$. Let $V_1 \stackrel{\text{def}}{=} \{v \in [k] : p_0(v) < p_1(v)\}$ and $V_2 = [k] \setminus V_1$. Then, the number of edges with both endpoints in the same V_σ is bounded above by $\epsilon dk/2$, which implies that G is ϵ-close to being bipartite.*

Proof Sketch: Consider an edge $\{u, v\}$ such that both u and v are in the same V_σ, and assume, without loss of generality, that $\sigma = 1$. Then, by the (lower bound of the) *rapid mixing hypothesis*, both $p_1(v)$ and $p_1(u)$ are greater than $\frac{1}{2} \cdot \frac{1}{2k}$. Using the hypothesis that u and v are connected in G, we infer that $p_0(v) > \frac{1}{3d} \cdot p_1(u)$. Intuitively, this is the case because (1) if an $(\ell - 1)$-step walk reaches u, then, with probability exactly $1/2d$, it continues to v in the next step; and (2) for our purposes, an $(\ell - 1)$-step random walk behaves like an ℓ-step random walk. Indeed, using the following two observations, we infer that $p_0(v) > \frac{1}{3d} \cdot p_1(u)$:

1. If an $(\ell - 1)$-step walk reaches u, then, with probability exactly $1/2d$, it continues to v in the next step. Hence, $p_0(v) \geq p_1'(u)/2d$, where $p_1'(u)$ denotes the probability that an $(\ell - 1)$-step lazy random walk (starting at s) reaches v while making an odd number of real (i.e., non–self-loop) steps.
2. An $(\ell - 1)$-step random walk of path-parity 1 ending at u is almost as likely as an ℓ-step random walk of path-parity 1 ending at u; that is, it holds that $p_1'(u) \approx p_1(u)$, where $p_1'(u)$ is as in Observation 1.
   This can be shown by noting that if we take a random $(\ell - 1)$-step walk of the type measured in $p_1'(u)$ and insert a "staying in place" step at a random location in it, then we obtain a distribution that is very close to the one measured in $p_1(u)$: see Exercise 9.11 for details.

Thus, the edge $\{u, v\}$ contributes at least $\frac{p_1(u)}{3d} \cdot p_1(v) \geq \frac{(1/4k)^2}{3d}$ to the sum $\sum_{w \in [k]} p_0(w) p_1(w)$. More formally, we have

$$\sum_{v \in [k]} p_0(v) p_1(v) = \sum_{\sigma \in \{0,1\}} \sum_{v \in V_\sigma} p_{1-\sigma}(v) p_\sigma(v)$$

$$\geq \sum_{\sigma \in \{0,1\}} \sum_{v \in V_\sigma} \sum_{u \in V_\sigma : \{u,v\} \in E} \frac{p_\sigma'(u)}{2d} \cdot p_\sigma(v)$$

$$> \sum_{\sigma \in \{0,1\}} \sum_{v \in V_\sigma} \sum_{u \in V_\sigma : \{u,v\} \in E} \frac{p_\sigma(u)}{3d} \cdot p_\sigma(v)$$

$$\geq \sum_{\sigma \in \{0,1\}} |\{\{u, v\} \in E : u, v \in V_\sigma\}| \cdot \frac{(1/4k)^2}{3d} ,$$

where the first inequality is due to Observation 1, the second inequality is due to Observation 2, and the third inequality is due to the rapid mixing hypothesis. Using the claim's hypothesis, it follows that we can have at most $\frac{0.01\epsilon/k}{1/(48dk^2)} < \epsilon dk/2$ such edges (i.e., edges with both endpoints in same V_σ), and the claim follows. ∎

Claim 9.21.3 (A large sum implies high rejection probability): *Suppose that* $\sum_{v \in [k]} p_0(v) p_1(v) \geq 0.01\epsilon/k$, *and that Step 2 is executed with start vertex s. Then, for $m \geq 25\sqrt{k/\epsilon}$, with probability at least 2/3, the set $R_0 \cap R_1$ is not empty (and rejection follows).*

Proof: Consider the probability space defined by an execution of Step 2 (with start vertex s). For every $i \neq j$ such that $i, j \in [m]$, we define an indicator random variable $\zeta_{i,j}$ representing *the event that the vertex encountered in the ℓth step of the ith walk equals the vertex encountered in the ℓth step of the jth walk, and that the ith walk has* an even path-parity whereas the jth walk has an odd path-parity. (That is, $\zeta_{i,j} = 1$ if the foregoing event holds, and $\zeta_{i,j} = 0$ otherwise.) Recalling the definition of the $p_\sigma(v)$'s, observe that $\mathbf{Pr}[\zeta_{i,j} = 1] = \sum_{v \in [k]} p_0(v)p_1(v)$. Hence,

$$\sum_{i \neq j} \mathbb{E}[\zeta_{i,j}] = m(m-1) \cdot \sum_{v \in [k]} p_0(v)p_1(v)$$

$$> \frac{600k}{\epsilon} \cdot \sum_{v \in [k]} p_0(v)p_1(v)$$

$$\geq 6,$$

where the first inequality is due to the setting of m, and the second inequality is due to the claim's hypothesis. On the other hand, note that $\mathbf{Pr}[|R_0 \cap R_1| > 0] \geq \mathbf{Pr}[\sum_{i \neq j} \zeta_{i,j} > 0]$, since whenever the event captured by $\zeta_{i,j}$ holds it is the case that the endpoints of the ith and j^{th} paths are equal and this common vertex is in $R_0 \cap R_1$.

Intuitively, the sum of the $\zeta_{i,j}$'s should be positive with high probability, since the expected value of the sum is large enough and the $\zeta_{i,j}$'s are "sufficiently independent" (almost all pairs of $\zeta_{i,j}$'s are independent). The intuition is indeed correct, but proving it is less straightforward than it seems, since the $\zeta_{i,j}$'s are not pairwise independent.[30] Yet, since the sum of the covariances of the dependent $\zeta_{i,j}$'s is quite small, Chebyshev's Inequality is still very useful (cf. [22, Sec. 4.3]). Specifically, letting $\mu \overset{\text{def}}{=} \mathbb{E}[\zeta_{i,j}] = \sum_{v \in [k]} p_0(v)p_1(v)$, and $\overline{\zeta}_{i,j} \overset{\text{def}}{=} \zeta_{i,j} - \mu$, we get:

$$\mathbf{Pr}\left[\sum_{i \neq j} \zeta_{i,j} = 0\right] < \frac{\mathbb{V}\left[\sum_{i \neq j} \zeta_{i,j}\right]}{(m(m-1) \cdot \mu)^2}$$

$$= \frac{1}{m^2(m-1)^2 \mu^2} \cdot \sum_{i_1 \neq j_1, i_2 \neq j_2} \mathbb{E}\left[\overline{\zeta}_{i_1,j_1} \overline{\zeta}_{i_2,j_2}\right].$$

We partition the terms in the last sum according to the number of distinct indices appearing in each term such that, for $t \in \{2,3,4\}$, we let $(i_1, j_1, i_2, j_2) \in S_t \subseteq [m]^4$ if and only if $|\{i_1, j_1, i_2, j_2\}| = t$ (and $i_1 \neq j_1 \wedge i_2 \neq j_2$). Hence,

$$\mathbf{Pr}\left[\sum_{i \neq j} \zeta_{i,j} = 0\right] < \frac{1}{m^2(m-1)^2 \mu^2} \cdot \sum_{t \in \{2,3,4\}} \sum_{(i_1,j_1,i_2,j_2) \in S_t} \mathbb{E}\left[\overline{\zeta}_{i_1,j_1} \overline{\zeta}_{i_2,j_2}\right]. \tag{9.8}$$

Now, note that if $i_1 = j_2$ (resp., $i_2 = j_1$), then $\mathbb{E}[\overline{\zeta}_{i_1,j_1} \overline{\zeta}_{i_2,j_2}] \leq \mathbb{E}[\zeta_{i_1,j_1} \zeta_{i_2,j_2}] = 0$, where the equality is due to the fact that in this case $\zeta_{i_1,j_1} = 1$ and $\zeta_{i_2,j_2} = 1$ make conflicting requirements of the path-parity of walk number $i_1 = j_2$ (resp., $i_2 = j_1$).[31] Hence, rather than summing over the S_t's, we can sum over the corresponding subsets S'_t's that contain only tuples $(i_1, j_1, i_2, j_2) \in S_t$ such that $i_1 \neq j_2 \wedge i_2 \neq j_1$. Furthermore,

---

[30] Indeed, if the $\zeta_{i,j}$'s were pairwise independent, then a straightforward application of Chebyshev's Inequality would do.

[31] Recall that $\zeta_{i_1,j_1} = 1$ requires that the i_1^{th} walk has even path-parity, whereas $\zeta_{i_2,j_2} = 1$ requires that the j_2^{th} walk has odd path-parity, and these requirements conflict when $i_1 = j_2$. Ditto for the i_2^{th} and j_1^{th} walks when $i_2 = j_1$. We also used the inequality $\mathbb{E}[(X - \mathbb{E}[X]) \cdot (Y - \mathbb{E}[Y])] \leq \mathbb{E}[XY]$, which holds for any nonnegative random variables X and Y, and the equality $\mathbb{E}[XY] = \mathbf{Pr}[X = Y = 1]$, which holds for any 0-1 random variables.

the contribution of each element in $S'_4 = S_4$ to the sum is zero, since the four walks are independent and so $\mathbb{E}[\overline{\zeta}_{i_1,j_1}\overline{\zeta}_{i_2,j_2}] = \mathbb{E}[\overline{\zeta}_{i_1,j_1}] \cdot \mathbb{E}[\overline{\zeta}_{i_2,j_2}] = 0$. Plugging all of this into Eq. (9.8), we get

$$\mathbf{Pr}\left[\sum_{i \neq j} \zeta_{i,j} = 0\right] < \frac{1}{m^2(m-1)^2\mu^2} \cdot \sum_{t \in \{2,3\}} \sum_{(i_1,j_1,i_2,j_2) \in S'_t} \mathbb{E}\left[\overline{\zeta}_{i_1,j_1}\overline{\zeta}_{i_2,j_2}\right]$$

$$= \frac{1}{m^2(m-1)^2\mu^2}$$

$$\cdot \left(\sum_{i \neq j} \mathbb{E}\left[\overline{\zeta}^2_{i,j}\right] + \sum_{i_1,i_2,i_3:|\{i_1,i_2,i_3\}|=3} \left(\mathbb{E}\left[\overline{\zeta}_{i_1,i_2}\overline{\zeta}_{i_1,i_3}\right] + \mathbb{E}\left[\overline{\zeta}_{i_1,i_2}\overline{\zeta}_{i_3,i_2}\right]\right)\right)$$

$$< \frac{m(m-1) \cdot \mu + m(m-1)(m-2) \cdot (\mathbb{E}[\zeta_{1,2}\zeta_{1,3}] + \mathbb{E}[\zeta_{1,2}\zeta_{3,2}])}{m^2(m-1)^2\mu^2}$$

$$< \frac{1}{(m-1)^2\mu} + \frac{1}{(m-1)\mu^2} \cdot (\mathbb{E}[\zeta_{1,2}\zeta_{1,3}] + \mathbb{E}[\zeta_{1,2}\zeta_{3,2}]),$$

where in the second inequality we use $\mathbb{E}[\overline{\zeta}^2_{i,j}] \leq \mathbb{E}[\zeta^2_{i,j}] = \mu$ and $\mathbb{E}[\overline{\zeta}_{i_1,j_1}\overline{\zeta}_{i_2,j_2}] \leq \mathbb{E}[\zeta_{i_1,j_1}\zeta_{i_2,j_2}]$. For the second term, we observe that $\mathbb{E}[\zeta_{1,2}\zeta_{1,3}] = \mathbf{Pr}[\zeta_{1,2} = \zeta_{1,3} = 1]$ is upper-bounded by $\mathbf{Pr}[\zeta_{1,2} = 1] = \mu$ times the probability that the ℓth vertex of the third walk appears as the ℓth vertex of the first path, since $\zeta_{1,3} = 1$ mandates the latter event. Using the (upper bound of the) *rapid mixing hypothesis*, we upper-bound the latter probability by $2/k$, and obtain $\mathbb{E}[\zeta_{1,2}\zeta_{2,3}] \leq \mu \cdot 2/k$. (Ditto for $\mathbb{E}[\zeta_{1,2}\zeta_{3,2}]$.) Hence,

$$\mathbf{Pr}[|R_0 \cap R_1| = 0] < \frac{1}{(m-1)^2\mu} + \frac{2}{(m-1)\mu^2} \cdot \frac{2\mu}{k}$$

$$= \frac{1}{(m-1)^2\mu} + \frac{4}{(m-1)\mu k}$$

$$< \frac{1}{3},$$

where the last inequality uses $\mu \geq 0.01\epsilon/k$ and $(m-1)^2 \geq 600k/\epsilon$ (along with $m > 2400/\epsilon$). The claim follows. ∎

Beyond Rapid Mixing Graphs (an Overview). For starters, suppose that the graph consists of several connected components, each having the rapid mixing property. Then, we can apply the foregoing argument to each connected component separately. Note that, already in this case, it is important that we select a start vertex at random, since some of the connected components may be bipartite (e.g., it may be that only an $O(\epsilon)$ fraction of the vertices reside in connected components that are $\Omega(1)$-far from being bipartite). But otherwise, the extension is straightforward. We define a sum of the foregoing type (i.e., $\sum_v p_0(v)p_1(v)$) for each connected components, and argue as in Claims 9.21.2 and 9.21.3.

Intuitively, the same strategy should work also if these "strongly connected components" (which each have the rapid mixing property) are actually connected by relatively few edges; however, things are less straightforward in this case. For starters, a random walk can exit such a component (and enter a different component that is connected to it), and the definition of $p_\sigma(v)$ should be adapted accordingly. More importantly, we cannot assume that the graph has such a structure, but should rather impose an adequate structure on it. Indeed, this is the complicated part of the analysis.

Teaching Note: The following three paragraphs provide additional hints regarding the ideas used toward extending the proof from the special case of rapid mixing to the general case. These paragraphs are terse and abstract and may be hard to follow. An illustration of the basic strategy appears in the guidelines of Exercise 9.10, which addresses a much weaker claim.

The proof in [148] refers to a more general sum of products; that is, $\sum_{u \in U} p_{\text{odd}}(u) p_{\text{even}}(u)$, where $U \subseteq [k]$ is an appropriate set of vertices, and $p_{\text{odd}}(v)$ (respectively, $p_{\text{even}}(v)$) is essentially the probability that an ℓ-step random walk (starting at s) passes through v after more than $\ell/2$ steps and the corresponding path to v has odd (respectively, even) parity. Note that these probabilities refer to the vertices visited in the last $\ell/2$ steps of the walk rather than to the very last vertex visited in it, and this change is done in order to account for walks that leave U (and possibly return to it at a later stage).

Much of the analysis in [148] goes into selecting the appropriate U (and an appropriate starting vertex s), and pasting together many such U's to cover all of $[k]$. Loosely speaking, U and s are selected so that there are few edges from U to the rest of the graph, and $p_{\text{odd}}(u) + p_{\text{even}}(u) \approx 1/\sqrt{k \cdot |U|}$, for every $u \in U$. The selection is based on the "combinatorial treatment of expansion" of Mihail [208]. Specifically, it uses the contrapositive of the standard analysis, which asserts that rapid mixing occurs when all cuts are relatively large, to assert that the failure of rapid mixing yields small cuts that partition the graph so that vertices reached with relatively high probability (in a short random walk) are on one side and the rest of the graph is on the other side. The first set corresponds to the aforementioned U, and the cut is relatively small with respect to the size of U. A start vertex s for which the corresponding sum is big is shown to cause Step 2 to reject (when started with this s), whereas a small corresponding sum enables to 2-partition U while having few violating edges among the vertices in each part of U.

The actual argument of [148] proceeds in iterations. In each iteration a vertex s for which Step 2 accepts with high probability is fixed, and an appropriate set of remaining vertices, U, is found. The set U is then 2-partitioned so that there are few violating edges inside U. Since we want to paste all these partitions together, U may not contain vertices treated in previous iterations. This complicates the analysis, since the analysis must refer to the part of G, denoted H, not treated in previous iterations. We consider walks over an (imaginary) Markov Chain representing the H-part of the walks performed by the algorithm on G. Statements about rapid mixing are made with respect to this Markov Chain, and are related to what happens in random walks performed on G. In particular, a subset U of H is determined so that the vertices in U are reached with probability $\approx 1/\sqrt{k \cdot |U|}$ (in the chain) and the cut between U and the rest of H is small. Relating the sum of products defined for the chain to the actual walks performed by the algorithm, we infer that U may be partitioned with few violating edges inside it. Edges to previously treated parts of the graphs are charged to these parts, and edges to the rest of $H \setminus U$ are accounted for by using the fact that this cut is small (relative to the size of U). A simplified version of this argument appears in the guideline for Exercise 9.10.

9.4.2. One-Sided Error Tester for Cycle-Freeness

Recall that, by Theorem 9.17, a one-sided error tester for Cycle-freeness requires $\Omega(\sqrt{k})$ queries. Here, we show that this lower bound can be almost met.

Theorem 9.22 (One-sided error tester for Cycle-freeness, in the bounded-degree graph model): Cycle-freeness *has a one-sided error tester of time* (and query) *complexity* $\mathrm{poly}(d/\epsilon) \cdot \widetilde{O}(\sqrt{k})$.

As in the case of the tester for Bipartiteness, the asserted tester can be modified so that in case of rejection it outputs a cycle of length $\mathrm{poly}((d \log k)/\epsilon)$. Hence, this one-sided error tester yields an algorithm for finding (relatively short cycles) in graphs that are ϵ-far from being cycle-free. See further discussion following the proof (i.e., right after Problem 9.23).

Proof: The proof is by a randomized (local) reduction of testing Cycle-freeness to testing Bipartiteness, where the notion of such a reduction was presented in Section 7.4 and will be reviewed (and modified) below. But before doing so, let us provide some intuition.

Given a graph $G = ([k], E)$, which we wish to test for cycle-freeness, we shall map it at random to a graph $G' = (V', E')$ such that cycle-free graphs are mapped to bipartite graphs, whereas graphs that are far from being cycle-free are mapped (with high probability) to graphs that are far from being bipartite. Specifically, we shall map $G = ([k], E)$ at random to a graph $G' = (V', E')$ by making, for each edge of G, a random choice on whether to keep this edge in G' or to replace it by a 2-path (with a new auxiliary vertex). That is, with probability $1/2$, the edge $e = \{u, v\}$ is kept as is, and otherwise it is replaced by the edges $\{u, a_e\}$ and $\{a_e, v\}$, where a_e is an auxiliary vertex that is connected (only) to u and v. Note that if G is cycle-free then so is G', which implies that G' is bipartite. On the other hand, with probability $1/2$, each cycle in G is mapped to an odd-length cycle in G'. We shall show that, with high probability, the random transformation maps graphs that are far from being cycle-free to graphs that are far from being bipartite.

Formally, for any function $\tau : E \to \{1, 2\}$, we denote by G_τ the graph obtained from G by replacing each edge $e \in E$ such that $\tau(e) = 2$ by a 2-edge path (with an auxiliary intermediate vertex), and keeping the edge in G_τ otherwise (i.e., if $\tau(e) = 1$). That is, the graph $G_\tau = (V_\tau, E_\tau)$ is defined as follows:

$$V_\tau \overset{\mathrm{def}}{=} [k] \cup \{a_e : e \in E \wedge \tau(e) = 2\}$$

$$E_\tau \overset{\mathrm{def}}{=} \{e : e \in E \wedge \tau(e) = 1\} \cup \{\{u, a_e\}, \{a_e, v\} : e = \{u, v\} \in E \wedge \tau(e) = 2\}.$$

Hence, G' is obtained by selecting $\tau : E \to \{1, 2\}$ uniformly at random, and letting $G' = G_\tau$.

Suppose that G is cycle-free. Then, for any choice of τ (i.e., with probability 1 over all possible choices of τ), the resulting graph G_τ is also cycle-free, which implies that G_τ is bipartite. On the other hand, if G is not cycle-free, then, *each of its cycles is mapped to an odd-length cycle* (in G_τ) *with probability* $1/2$. Hence, with probability at least $1/2$, the graph G_τ is not bipartite. However, we need to prove more than that in order to reduce testing Cycle-freeness to testing Bipartiteness. Indeed, we shall show that if G is ϵ-far from Cycle-freeness, then, with high probability, the graph G_τ is $\Omega(\epsilon)$-far from Bipartiteness.

Lemma 9.22.1 (Analysis of the foregoing reduction): *Suppose that G is ϵ-far from* Cycle-freeness. *Then, with positive constant probability over the choice of τ, the graph G_τ is $\Omega(\epsilon/d)$-far from* Bipartiteness.

The error probability can be made arbitrary small by invoking the reduction sufficiently many times, and considering a single graph composed of the graphs obtained in the various invocations. (This may reduce the constant hidden in the Ω-notation by a factor related to the constant success probability that is asserted in the Lemma 9.22.1.)

Proof Sketch: Let $\Delta \geq |E| - (k-1)$ denote the actual number of edges that should be omitted from G in order to obtain a cycle-free graph. We shall show that, with probability $1 - \exp(-\Omega(\Delta))$ over the choice of τ, the number of edges that should be omitted from G_τ in order to obtain a bipartite graph is $\Omega(\Delta)$.

The basic intuition is that the interesting case is when all vertices of G are of degree at least 3, in which case $\Delta > k/2$. This is so because vertices of degree 1 and 2 (in G) do not really matter: Vertices of degree 1 do not participate in any cycle, and their removal from the graph does not change Δ, while it reduces $|E|$ and k (by a similar amount). Vertices of degree 2 are intermediate vertices on paths or cycles, and these paths or cycles act as a single edge, where in the analysis (which is a mental experiment) we allow also multiple edges and self-loops. (See more details at the end of the proof.)

The benefit of focusing on the case of $\Delta > k/2$ is that in this case we can afford to perform a union bound on all possible 2-partitions of the vertex-set of $G = ([k], E)$. Specifically, for each such partition, we show that, with probability at least $1 - 2^{-k-\Omega(\Delta)}$ over the choice of τ, there exist more than $m \stackrel{\text{def}}{=} \Omega(\Delta)$ edges that are inconsistent with that partition (under τ), where an edge $e = \{u, v\}$ is inconsistent with the partition (V_1, V_2) under τ *if either $u, v \in V_i$ and $\tau(e) = 1$ or $(u, v) \in V_1 \times V_2$ and $\tau(e) = 2$*. Applying a union bound, it follows that, with probability at least $1 - 2^{-\Omega(\Delta)}$, more than m edges should be omitted from G_τ in order to obtain a bipartite graph. Details follow.

We focus on the case that G is connected, where $\Delta = |E| - (k-1)$, leaving the general case to the reader (see Exercise 9.12). Fixing any partition (V_1, V_2) of $[k]$, observe that *the probability, over a random choice of τ, that s specific edges are all consistent with (V_1, V_2) under τ equals 2^{-s}*, since for each edge e the value of $\tau(e)$ that is consistent with (V_1, V_2) is uniquely determined (i.e., if $\{u, v\}$ is consistent with (V_1, V_2) under τ, then $\tau(\{u, v\}) = 2$ if u and v are in the same V_i, and $\tau(\{u, v\}) = 1$ otherwise). Using a union bound (on all sets of m edges) it follows that the probability, over a random choice of τ, that at most m edges of $G = ([k], E)$ are inconsistent with (V_1, V_2) under τ is at most

$$\binom{|E|}{m} \cdot 2^{-(|E|-m)}, \tag{9.9}$$

Using $|E| = k + \Delta - 1$ and $m = c \cdot \Delta$, Eq. (9.9) yields

$$\binom{k + \Delta - 1}{c \cdot \Delta} \cdot 2^{c \cdot \Delta - k - \Delta + 1} = 2^{-k+1} \cdot \binom{k + \Delta - 1}{c \cdot \Delta} \cdot 2^{-(1-c) \cdot \Delta}$$

$$< 2^{-k+1} \cdot \binom{3\Delta}{c \cdot \Delta} \cdot 2^{-(1-c) \cdot \Delta}$$

$$\approx 2^{-k+1} \cdot 2^{H_2(c/3) \cdot 3\Delta} \cdot 2^{-(1-c) \cdot \Delta},$$

where the inequality is due to $\Delta > k/2$. Hence, any choice of $c > 0$ that satisfies $3H_2(c/3) + c < 1$ will do. (The foregoing argument assumes a sufficiently large k, but otherwise we can just use the fact that with probability at least $1/2$ the graph G_r is not bipartite.)

It is left to justify the focus on graphs G in which all vertices are of degree at least 3. Formally, we show that graphs G that do not satisfy this condition can be transformed into graphs that do satisfy this condition, while preserving Δ as well as (the distribution of) the number of edges that have to be removed from G_τ to make it bipartite. As hinted at the beginning of this proof, vertices of degree 1 are irrelevant and can be removed from the graph G (along with the edges that connects them to the rest of G). As for vertices of degree 2, we contract paths (and cycles) that contain only *intermediate* vertices of degree 2 to a single edge, while noting that the resulting graph may have parallel edges and self-loops. We note, however, that the foregoing argument is oblivious to this fact (i.e., it applies also to such nonsimple graphs). The key observation is that the effect of applying the reduction to a t-path (resp., t-cycle) is identical to applying it to the resulting edge: In both cases, the reduction yields a path (resp., cycle) that has odd length with probability exactly half. The lemma follows. ∎

On the Locality of the Reduction. Lemma 9.22.1 asserts that the foregoing reduction preserves distances in the sense that instances that are far from one property are mapped (with high probability) to instances that are far from the second property. (We also noted that instances that have the first property are mapped to instances that have the second property.) But this does not suffice for a reduction between the corresponding testing problems: Towards that end, we have to show that the reduction preserves the query complexity. Typically, this is done by showing that each query of the tester of the second property can be answered by few queries to the instance of the first problem.

All these conditions are summarized in the definition of randomized reductions that was presented in Section 7.4. Here, we reproduce this definition (i.e., Definition 7.17) while adapting it to the current context.

Definition 9.22.2 (Randomized local reductions, specialized): *Let Π_n and Π'_n be sets of functions that represent graph properties in the bounded-degree model as in Definition 9.1; that is, the function $g : D_n \rightarrow R_n$, where $D_n = [n/d] \times [d]$ and $R_n = \{0, 1, \ldots, n/d\}$, represents an n/d-vertex graph of degree bound d. A distribution of mappings $\mathcal{F}_n$ from the set of functions $\{f : D_n \rightarrow R_n\}$ to the set of functions $\{f' : D_{n'} \rightarrow R'_{n'}\}$ is called a* randomized q-local (ϵ, ϵ')-reduction *of Π_n to $\Pi'_{n'}$ if for every $f : D_n \rightarrow R_n$ the following conditions hold with probability at least $5/6$ when the mapping F_n is selected according to the distribution $\mathcal{F}_n$.*

1. Locality (local reconstruction): *There exist randomized algorithms $Q_n : D_{n'} \to (D_n)^q$ and $V_n : D_{n'} \times R_n^q \to R_{n'}'$, which may depend on F_n, such that for every $e \in D_{n'}$ it holds that*

$$\mathbf{Pr}_{(e_1,\ldots,e_q) \leftarrow Q_n(e)}[V_n(e, f(e_1), \ldots, f(e_q)) = (F_n(f))(e)] \geq 2/3. \qquad (9.10)$$

2. Preservation of the properties: *If $f \in \Pi_n$, then $F_n(f) \in \Pi_{n'}'$.*
3. Partial preservation of distance to the properties: *If f is ϵ-far from Π_n, then $F_n(f)$ is ϵ'-far from $\Pi_{n'}'$.*

If Condition 2 holds for all F_n's and Eq. (9.10) holds with probability 1, then the reduction is said to have one-sided error.

Hence, if $f \in \Pi_n$ (resp., if f is ϵ-far from Π_n), then, with probability at least $5/6$, over the choice of F_n, Conditions 1 and 2 both hold (resp., Conditions 1 and 3 both hold).

As hinted in the foregoing, Lemma 9.22.1 asserts that the randomized mapping from `Cycle-freeness` to `Bipartiteness` satisfies Conditions 2 and 3 of Definition 9.22.2. Furthermore, the reduction has one-sided error (since Condition 2 holds for all F_n's), and so employing it preserves the one-sided error of the tester for `Bipartiteness`. Unfortunately, this randomized mapping does not seem to satisfy Condition 1. For starters, when applying the reduction to $G = ([k], E)$, the number of vertices in the reduced graph, $G_\tau = (V_\tau, E_\tau)$, is not a fixed function of k (but is rather a random variable that varies with τ). In addition, there is no simple mapping between V_τ and $[|V_\tau|]$. This means that, formally speaking, the representation of G_τ does not fit Definition 9.1. Nevertheless, we overcome this difficulty by directly emulating the tester for `Bipartiteness` that was presented in Section 9.4.1, while capitalizing on some of its features.

Specifically, we observe that the tester for `Bipartiteness` that was presented in Section 9.4.1 does not make arbitrary queries. It rather performs two types of operations: (1) it selects uniformly a vertex in the graph, and (2) given a vertex name, it selects uniformly one of its neighbors. Hence, it suffices to locally implement both these operations. First, we select uniformly $\tau : \binom{[k]}{2} \to \{1, 2\}$ (and use it rather than $\tau : E \to \{1, 2\}$ used in our description). Next, we note that it is easy to determine the ith neighbor of a vertex in G_τ by making the corresponding query to G (i.e., query its incidence function g); specifically, for $v \in [k]$ and $i \in [d]$, we have $g_\tau(v, i) = g(v, i)$ if either $g(v, i) = 0$ or $\tau(\{v, g(v, i)\}) = 1$, and $g_\tau(v, i) = a_{\{v, g(v,i)\}}$ otherwise (i.e., if $w = g(v, i) \in [k]$ and $\tau(\{v, w\}) = 2$), whereas for $e = \{u, w\} \in E$ such that $\tau(e) = 2$ it holds that $\{g_\tau(a_e, 1), g_\tau(a_e, 2)\} = \{u, w\}$. (Indeed, g_τ denotes the incidence function of G_τ.)[32] Now, to select a random neighbor of $v \in V_\tau$ with uniform probability distribution, we just retrieve all its neighbors (and select one of them at random).[33] Selecting at random a vertex in V_τ (with uniform probability

---

[32] Hence, if $w \in [k]$ is the ith neighbor of v in G (i.e., $w = g(v, i)$), then the ith neighbor of $v \in [k]$ in G_τ is w if $\tau(\{v, w\}) = 1$ and $a_{\{v,w\}}$ otherwise, whereas for $e = \{u, w\} \in E$ such that $\tau(e) = 2$ the neighbors of a_e in G_τ are u and w. Here we assume that u and v are explicit in the name of $a_{\{u,v\}}$, and so retrieving them requires no queries to g.

[33] Alternatively (and in fact less wastefully), we can first determine the number of its neighbors, denoted d_v, and then select uniformly $i \in [d_v]$ (and answer with the ith neighbor of v). Yet another alternative is to just use, in the algorithm, the version of a random walk that was used in the analysis (i.e., just select uniformly $i \in [2d]$, use the ith neighbor of v if such exists, and stay in place otherwise).

distribution) is slightly more complex, and is done as follows (using the "repeated sampling" paradigm):

1. First, we select uniformly at random an identifier $w \in [k] \cup ([k] \times [d])$ of a potential vertex in V_τ. If $w \in [k]$, then we just output it (and are done).
2. Otherwise (i.e., $w \in ([k] \times [d])$), we let $w = (v, i)$ and query G for the ith neighbor of v (i.e., we query its incidence function g).
   (a) If v has less than i neighbors (i.e., $g(v, i) = 0$), then we stop with no output.
   (b) Otherwise, letting $u = g(v, i)$ be the ith neighbor of v, we check whether $u < v$ and $\tau(\{u, v\}) = 2$. If both conditions are satisfied, we output the vertex $a_{\{u,v\}}$, and otherwise we halt with no output.

Note that each vertex in V_τ is output with probability $1/(k + dk)$: A vertex $w \in [k]$ is output if and only if it was selected in Step 1, whereas a vertex $a_{\{u,v\}}$ is output in Step 2 if and only if $w = (v, i)$ was selected in Step 1 and it holds that $g(v, i) = u < v$ and $\tau(\{u, v\}) = 2$. (In particular, $a_{\{u,v\}}$ is output only if $\tau(\{u, v\}) = 2$, and in that case it is output if and only if (v, i) was chosen in Step 1, where $v > u$ and $g(v, i) = u$.) Indeed, with probability $1 - \frac{|V_\tau|}{k+dk} \leq 1 - \frac{1}{d+1}$, there is no output, but in such a case we just try again. We can stop trying after $(d + 1) \cdot \log k$ attempts, which will just add an error probability of q/k to the error probability of the q-query tester that we emulate. (In order to obtain a one-sided error tester, we should accept in case we suspend the execution.) ∎

Digest. We have presented a *randomized* reduction of Cycle-freeness to Bipartiteness that satisfies a *relaxed locality* condition. The relaxation that we used allows the vertex-set of the reduced graph to be arbitrary (rather than equal $[k']$ for some k' that is determined by k), but required an efficient way of sampling this vertex-set (and answering incidence queries with respect to it). This raises a couple of questions.

Open Problem 9.23 (Cleaner local reductions of Cycle-freeness to Bipartiteness): *In both items, we refer to $q = \mathrm{poly}(d \log k)$ and seek reductions that have one-sided error probability.*

1. *Does there exist a* nonrelaxed *(randomized) q-local reduction of Cycle-freeness to Bipartiteness? That is, a reduction satisfying Definition 9.22.2.*
2. *Does there exist a (relaxed) deterministic q-local reduction of Cycle-freeness to Bipartiteness?*

In fact, $q = \mathrm{poly}((d/\epsilon) \log k)$ will be interesting too.

Perspective: Finding Substructures and One-Sided Error Testers. As stated in the beginning of this section, the one-sided error tester for Cycle-freeness yields a sublinear time algorithm that finds (relatively small) cycles in a (bounded-degree) graph that is far from being cycle-free. Likewise, the one-sided error tester for Bipartiteness yields a sublinear time algorithm that finds (relatively small) odd-length cycles in a (bounded-degree) graph that is far from being bipartite (i.e., far from lacking odd-length cycles). The correspondence between *one-sided error* testers and sublinear time algorithms that find certain substructures in the input arises whenever the property can be characterized as the set of objects that lack this type of substructure. This fact provides additional motivation for the interest in one-sided error (rather than general) testers, a motivation that goes beyond the natural desire to avoid error probability in the case that the object is perfectly fine (i.e., the object has the property).[34]

In light of the foregoing perspective, we mention a few additional results regarding finding substructures in bounded-degree graphs.

Theorem 9.24 (Finding cycles and trees in graphs (in the bounded-degree graph model)):

1. *For every $\ell \geq 3$, there exists a $\mathrm{poly}(d^\ell/\epsilon) \cdot \tilde{O}(\sqrt{k})$-time algorithm that finds simple cycles of length at least ℓ in k-vertex graphs that are ϵ-far from lacking such cycles.*
2. *For every $\ell \geq 3$, there exists an $O(\ell^3/\epsilon)$-time algorithm that finds trees that have at least ℓ leaves in k-vertex graphs that are ϵ-far from lacking such trees.*

Indeed, Part 1 generalizes Theorem 9.22, which refers to the case $\ell = 3$, whereas Part 2 extends the trivial algorithm that finds edges in a graph that has many edges (and corresponds to the case of $\ell = 2$). Theorem 9.24 is proved in [81], which contains additional results of similar flavor.

9.5. Testing by Implementing and Utilizing Partition Oracles

The testers presented in this section are based on implementing and utilizing certain "partition oracles" to be defined shortly (see Definition 9.27). We demonstrate this method by deriving testers for any minor-free property, a notion we defined next.

The graph H is a minor of the graph G if H can be obtained from G by a sequence of edge removal, vertex removal, and edge contraction operations, where contracting the edge $\{u, v\}$ means that u and v (as well as the edge $\{u, v\}$) are replaced by a single vertex that is incident to all vertices that were incident to either u or v. We say that G is H-minor free if H is not a minor of G. In particular, a graph is cycle-free if and only if it is K_3-minor free, where K_t denotes the t-vertex clique.[35]

The notion of minor freeness extends to sets of graphs; that is, for a set of graphs $\mathcal{H}$, the graph G is $\mathcal{H}$-minor free if no element of $\mathcal{H}$ is a minor of G. Recall that a graph G is planar if and only if it is $\{K_5, K_{3,3}\}$-free, where $K_{3,3}$ denotes the biclique having three vertices on each side.

A graph property is minor-closed if it is closed under removal of edges, removal of vertices, and edge contraction. Clearly, for every finite set of graphs $\mathcal{H}$, the property of being $\mathcal{H}$-minor free is minor closed. On the other hand, the celebrated theorem of Robertson and Seymour (see [239]) asserts that any minor-close property equals the set of $\mathcal{H}$-minor free graphs, for some finite set of graphs $\mathcal{H}$. With these preliminaries in place, we can state the main result presented in this section.

---

[34] **Advanced comment:** Note the analogy to the notion of "perfect completeness" in the setting of probabilistic proof systems [131, Chap. 9].

[35] Recall that a graph is cycle-free if and only if it contains no simple cycle (of length at least 3).

Theorem 9.25 (Testing minor-close graph properties (in the bounded-degree graph model)):[36] *Any minor-closed property can be tested in query* (and time) *complexity that is quasi-polynomial in* $1/\epsilon$ (i.e., $\exp(\text{poly}(\log(1/\epsilon)))$). *Actually, the time bound is* $(d/\epsilon)^{O(\log(1/\epsilon))}$.

We mention that this tester has two-sided error, which is unavoidable for any tester of query complexity $o(\sqrt{k})$, except in the case that the forbidden minors are all cycle-free. Before turning to the proof of Theorem 9.25, we state the begging question of whether the bound in Theorem 9.25 can be improved to a polynomial.

Open Problem 9.26 (Improving the upper bound of Theorem 9.25): *Can any minor-closed property be tested in query* (and time) *complexity that is polynomial in* d/ϵ? *What about the special case of* Planarity?

The proof of Theorem 9.25 (as well as several related studies in this area) evolves around the local construction and utilization of a *partition oracle*. Loosely speaking, such an oracle provides a partition of the input graph $G = ([k], E)$ into *small connected components with few edges connecting different components*. Specifically, for given parameters $\epsilon > 0$ and $t \in \mathbb{N}$, such a partition oracle of a graph $G = ([k], E)$ is a function $P : [k] \to \cup_{i \in [t]} \binom{[k]}{i}$ such that (1) vertex v resides in $P(v)$ (which has size at most t); (2) the $P(v)$'s form a partition of $[k]$; (3) the subgraph of G induced by each $P(v)$ is connected; and (4) the total number of edges among different $P(v)$'s is at most ϵk.

Definition 9.27 (Partition oracles): *We say that* $P : [k] \to 2^{[k]}$ *is an* (ϵ, t)-partition *of the graph* $G = ([k], E)$ *if the following conditions hold.*

1. *For every* $v \in [k]$, *vertex* v *is in the set* $P(v)$, *and* $|P(v)| \leq t$.
2. *The sets* $P(v)$'s *form a partition of* $[k]$; *that is, for every* $v, u \in [k]$, *the sets* $P(v)$ *and* $P(u)$ *are either identical or disjoint.*[37]
3. *For every* $v \in [k]$, *the subgraph of* G *induced by* $P(v)$ *is connected.*
4. *The number of edges among the different* $P(v)$'s *is at most* ϵk; *that is,* $|\{\{u, w\} \in E : P(u) \neq P(w)\}| \leq \epsilon k$.

Note that the trivial partition (i.e., $P(v) = \{v\}$ for every $v \in [k]$) is a $(0.5d, 1)$-partition of any graph of maximum degree d, since Condition 4 holds vacuously when the error parameter is at least half the maximum degree. We mention that Conditions 1–3 are quite local (i.e., they refer to individual $P(v)$'s or to pairs of $P(v)$'s), whereas Condition 4 is global.

As shown next, if we are given access to a partition oracle P for a graph G, then we can test whether G has a predetermined minor-close property. Of course, in the standard model, we are given oracle access only to the (incidence representation of the) graph G; so the next item on the agenda will be to implement a partition oracle for G when given oracle access only to G. But let us first show the testing consequence.

---

[36] This result is due to [197], improving over [169], which improved on [41]: The improvements are in the query complexity. Specifically, the query complexity obtained in [41] is triple-exponential in $1/\epsilon$, and in [169] it is exponential in $\text{poly}(1/\epsilon)$.

[37] The fact that $\cup_{v \in [k]} P(v) = [k]$ follows from Condition 1.

Theorem 9.28 (Testing minor-close graph properties by using a partition oracle):
*Let Π be a minor-closed property and suppose that we are given oracle access
to a graph $G = ([k], E)$, represented by its incidence function $g : [k] \times [d] \rightarrow
\{0, 1, \ldots, k\}$, as well as to an $(d\epsilon/4, t)$-partition oracle $P : [k] \rightarrow 2^{[k]}$ of G. Then,
using $O(td/\epsilon)$ queries to g and to P, we can distinguish (in $\mathrm{poly}(td/\epsilon)$-time) the
case that $G \in \Pi$ from the case that G is ϵ-far from Π. Actually, we accept each
graph in Π with probability at least 0.9, and reject with probability at least 0.9 any
graph that is ϵ-far from Π. Furthermore, a graph that is ϵ-far from Π is rejected
with probability at least 0.9 even if $P : [k] \rightarrow 2^{[k]}$ only satisfies Conditions 1–3 of
Definition 9.27.*

The furthermore clause is important because our implementation of the partition oracle
is guaranteed to satisfy Condition 4 (with high probability) only when the input graph is
in Π. Hence, it is important that the foregoing decision procedure rejects graphs that are
far from Π also when the partition oracle does not satisfy Condition 4. We mention that
our implementation of the partition oracle always satisfies Conditions 1–3.

Proof: Let $G' = ([k], E')$ be the graph obtained from $G = ([k], E)$ by omitting
all edges that have endpoints in different $P(i)$'s; that is, $E' \stackrel{\text{def}}{=} \{\{u, v\} \in E : P(u) =
P(v)\}$. On the one hand, if $G \in \Pi$, then $G' \in \Pi$ (since Π is closed under omission
of edges) and $|E \setminus E'| \leq \epsilon dk/4$ (by Condition 4). On the other hand, if G is ϵ-far
from Π, then either $|E \setminus E'| \geq \epsilon dk/4$ (i.e., G' is $\epsilon/2$-far from G) or G' is $\epsilon/2$-far
from Π. Hence, it suffices to estimate the size of $E \setminus E'$ and to test whether G' is
in Π.

The key observation is that when given oracle access to P and G, it is easy
to emulate oracle access to G'. Specifically, letting $g'(v, i) = g(v, i)$ if $P(v) =
P(g(v, i))$ and $g'(v, i) = 0$ otherwise (where $P(0) = \emptyset$), we obtain an "unaligned"
incidence function of G' (see variants at the beginning of Section 9.1). Hence, the
neighbors of v in G' can be found by making at most d queries to g and $d + 1$
queries to P.

The next observation is that testing whether G' has property Π reduces to checking whether a random connected component of G' has this property. Specifically,
selecting $O(1/\epsilon)$ random vertices, and exploring the connected component in which
they reside, will do (see details below). Since each $P(v)$ has size at most t, each
exploration is performed by making at most td queries, and so the query complexity is as claimed. (Deciding whether the explored subgraph is in Π can be done in
time that is polynomial of the subgraph's size [238].)

Lastly, we turn to the task of estimating the size of $E \setminus E' = \{\{u, v\} \in E : P(u) \neq
P(v)\}$; that is, estimating the probability that $\{v, g(v, i)\} \in E \setminus E'$ when (v, i) is uni-
formly distributed in $[k] \times [d]$. Selecting $O(1/\epsilon)$ random pairs $(v, i) \in [k] \times [d]$,
allows to distinguish the case that $|E \setminus E'| \leq \epsilon dk/6$ from the case that $|E \setminus E'| >
\epsilon dk/3$. Hence, our actual algorithm proceeds as follows, where we assume for sim-
plicity that, for some set of *connected* graphs $\mathcal{H}$, the set Π equals the set of $\mathcal{H}$-minor
free graphs.[38]

---

[38] The general case, where $\mathcal{H}$ may contain graphs that are not connected is left as an exercise. In that case, the tester
employed in Step 2 should check for minors that are distributed among several connected components. Likewise, the
analysis should refer to tuples of connected components that contain parts of a minor in $\mathcal{H}$ (cf. Exercise 9.3).

1. Using $O(1/\epsilon)$ random pairs $(v, i) \in [k] \times [d]$, the algorithm estimates $|E \setminus E'|$ up to an additive deviation of $\epsilon dk/12$. If the estimate is greater than $\epsilon dk/4$, then the algorithm rejects. Otherwise, it continues to the next step.
2. The algorithm tests whether G' is in Π or is $\epsilon/3$-far from it. This is done by selecting $O(1/\epsilon)$ random vertices, exploring the connected component in which each of these vertices resides, and rejecting if any of the explored subgraphs contains a minor in $\mathcal{H}$. If all explored subgraphs are $\mathcal{H}$-minor free, then the algorithm accepts.

The queries to G' that are made by this algorithm are answered by emulating G' as outlined in the penultimate paragraph (i.e., by using oracle calls to G and P).

Now, if $G \in \Pi$ and P is an $(\epsilon d/4, t)$-partition oracle of it, then with high probability the algorithm continues to Step 2, and in that case it always accepts. On the other hand, if G is ϵ-far from Π, then there are two cases to consider. The first case is that the partition defined by P yields a graph $G' = ([k], E')$ such that $|E \setminus E'| > \epsilon dk/3$. In this case, with high probability, Step 1 rejects. The second case is that $|E \setminus E'| \leq \epsilon dk/3$ (i.e., G' is $(2\epsilon/3)$-close to G), which implies that G' is $\epsilon/3$-far from Π. In this case, with high probability, Step 2 rejects because at least $\epsilon k/6$ vertices must reside in connected components that are not in Π (since otherwise G' can be placed in Π by omitting all edges that are incident at these vertices).[39]

We stress that the analysis of the case in which G is ϵ-far from Π does not refer to Condition 4 (and it holds also if P satisfies Conditions 1–3 only). The claim follows. ∎

Implementing a Partition Oracle. In light of Theorem 9.28, we now focus on the task of implementing (or rather emulating) partition oracles. Since the implementations that we use are randomized, it is crucial that the same randomness (denoted ω) is used in all invocations of the machine emulating the oracle. In other words, each choice of internal coin tosses for this machine yields a function $f : [k] \to 2^{[k]}$, and, with high probability (over these choices), this function is a good partition oracle (i.e., it satisfies Definition 9.27). Specifically, f satisfies Condition 4 (with high probability) if the input graph has a predetermined property Π (which in our application is the property being tested), whereas f always satisfies Conditions 1–3 (even if the graph does not have the property Π).

Definition 9.29 (Implementing a partition oracle): *We say that the oracle machine M emulates an (ϵ, t)-partition oracle for graphs having property Π if the following two conditions hold.*

1. *For any possible outcome ω of M's internal coin tosses, when given oracle access to any bounded-degree graph $G = ([k], E)$, the answers provided by M to all possible inputs $v \in [k]$ correspond to a function $P(v) \stackrel{\text{def}}{=} M^G(k, \omega; v)$ that satisfies Conditions 1–3 of Definition 9.27.*
2. *For any graph $G = ([k], E)$ in Π, with probability at least 0.9 over all possible choices of ω, the function $P(v) \stackrel{\text{def}}{=} M^G(k, \omega; v)$ is an (ϵ, t)-partition; that is, it also satisfies Condition 4 of Definition 9.27.*

---

[39] This is the case because a graph is $\mathcal{H}$-minor free if and only if all its connected components are $\mathcal{H}$-minor free.

Typically, t is a function of ϵ. Actually, any graph G that satisfies a minor-close property has $(\epsilon, O(d/\epsilon)^2)$-partitions (for every $\epsilon > 0$);[40] the problem is finding such partitions "locally" or rather implementing corresponding partition oracles. A crucial aspect of such implementations is the number of queries that they make to their own oracle (i.e., the number of queries that M makes to G, per each query that M answers). In particular, the overhead created by utilizing such an implementation in Theorem 9.28 (i.e., using such an implementation instead of the hypothetic oracle P) is linear in the query (resp., time) complexity of the implementation. Typically, like t, the query complexity of the implementation is a function of ϵ only (i.e., independent of the size of the graph), but it will be larger than t. In these cases, the query complexity of the implementation will dominate the complexity of the tester that is derived from Theorem 9.28.

We shall present two implementations of a partition oracle for any minor-free property Π. The first (and simpler) implementation has query complexity that is exponential in poly$(1/\epsilon)$, whereas the second implementation (which builds on the first) has quasi-polynomial (in $1/\epsilon$) complexity.

9.5.1. The Simpler Implementation

We first present the implementation as a linear-time algorithm that gets the entire graph as input and generates an (ϵ, t)-partition of it, but the reader may notice that all operations are relatively local. This means that it will be relatively easy to convert this algorithm into an oracle machine that on input $v \in [k]$ makes relatively few queries to $G = ([k], E)$ and returns $P(v)$, where P is an (ϵ, t)-partition of G. In the following description, we shall assume that the graph G is H-minor free, for some fixed graph H. (This assumption will be removed when using Theorem 9.28.)

The algorithm proceeds in iterations, starting with the trivial partition P_0 in which each vertex is in a part of its own (i.e., $P_0(v) = \{v\}$ for every $v \in [k]$). In each iteration, we "coarsen" the partition (i.e., each set of the new partition is a union of sets in the prior partition). Note that P_0 satisfies Conditions 1–3 of Definition 9.27, but violates Condition 4 (unless G is very sparse). Our goal, in each iteration, is to reduce the number of edges between different parts of the current partition, while preserving Conditions 1–3, where the nontrivial issue is preserving Condition 3 (i.e., the subgraph of G induced by $P(v)$ is connected).

The natural way of preserving Condition 3 is using *edge contractions*, which means replacing two adjacent vertices u and v by a new vertex, denoted $a_{u,v}$, and connecting the edges incident at u and v to $a_{u,v}$ (while omitting the edge $\{u, v\}$).[41] Note that we should do so without violating Condition 1 (i.e., each $P(v)$ has size at most t). (Indeed, we shall keep track both of the original graph and of the currently contracted graph, where vertices of the contracted graph correspond to sets of the current partition of the original graph.)

Of course, a key question is which edges to contract (in each iteration). This is a nontrivial question because there is a tension between the number of inter-parts edges that are removed by contraction and the size of the parts (which also effects the locality of the procedure). Note that contracting an edge between u and v removes all the parallel edges between these two vertices, where parallel edges are created by the contraction process (e.g., if both u and v are connected to w, then the contraction of the edge $\{u, v\}$

---

[40] See Alon *et al.* [16], as detailed in [197, Cor. 2].

[41] We stress that if there are parallel edges between u and v, then all are omitted (when contracting any of them).

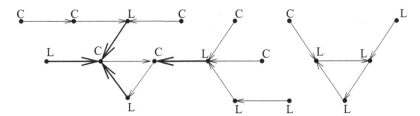

Figure 9.1: A directed graph of heaviest edges and a random choice of values for the vertices. The edges are directed from each vertex to its heaviest neighbor, and the edges that will be contracted are shown by wider arrows.

will form two parallel edges between the resulting vertex and w). Hence, it is a good idea to contract an edge that has many parallel edges (which can be represented as a single edge of corresponding weight). On the other hand, we should avoid contracting a set of edges that span a large subgraph. Looking ahead to a local implementation, it is natural that each vertex will contract an edge incident at it that has the largest number of parallel edges, but we should avoid a long path of contractions (by some "symmetry breaking" mechanism).[42]

It will be instructive to consider both the current partition (to be denoted P_i) of the original graph G and the currently contracted graph (to be denoted G_i). Starting with $G_0 \equiv G$, in the ith iteration we shall contract some edges of G_{i-1} obtaining a graph G_i and a corresponding partition P_i such that each set in P_i corresponds to a vertex in G_i (i.e., the vertex set of G_i equals the set $\{P_i(v) : v \in [k]\}$).[43] Actually, we shall represent parallel edges by a single edge of corresponding weight (which represents the number of parallel edges). Hence, the graph G_i will have weighted edges, whereas all edges in G_0 have weight 1. The weight of edges in G_i will equal the number of edges in G that connect the corresponding parts (i.e., the weight of $\{U, V\}$ in G_i equals the number of edges in G that connect vertices in U and vertices in V). Finally, we get to the contraction rule itself: *Each vertex in G_{i-1} selects uniformly at random a value in $\{L, C\}$, and the edge $\{U, V\}$ is contracted if and only if vertex U selected L, vertex V selected C, and $\{U, V\}$ is the heaviest edge incident at U, where ties are broken arbitrarily.*[44]

That is, for every vertex U in G_{i-1}, which corresponds to a set in P_{i-1} (which is a set of vertices in G), we denote by $h_i(U)$ the neighbor of U in G_{i-1} such that the edge $\{U, h_i(U)\}$ is heaviest among all the edges incident at U (in G_{i-1}). (In other words, the number of edges in G between U and $h_i(U)$ is the largest among the number of edges (in G) between $U = P_{i-1}(u)$ and any other $P_{i-1}(v)$.) Letting $r_i(U)$ denote the random choice of U, *we contract the edge $\{U, h_i(U)\}$ if and only if $r_i(U) = $ L and $r_i(h_i(U)) = $ C (see Figure 9.1, which depicts edges as directed from U to $h_i(U)$).

---

[42] The term "symmetry breaking" is used because we may have a long path of vertices such that the local view of each of them is identical (when ignoring vertex labels). In what follows, these potential symmetries are broken by assigning random binary values to the vertices and using a nonsymmetric contraction rule that refers to these random values.

[43] Thus, G_0 has the vertex set $\{\{v\} : v \in [k]\} \equiv [k]$, and its edges are pairs of singletons of the form $\{\{u\}, \{v\}\}$ such that $\{u, v\}$ is an edge of G.

[44] The symbol C (resp., L) stands for "center" (resp., "leaf"), and the justification for this term will be spelled out shortly. The foregoing description presumes that U is not an isolated vertex in G_{i-1}, and this assumption will be made throughout the rest of this section. Formally, if U is an isolated vertex, then we may fictitiously define $h_i(U) = U$ (and note that no contraction involving U takes place).

Note that the set of heaviest edges incident at the various vertices defines a directed graph in which there is a single edge directed from each vertex of G_{i-1} to its heaviest neighbor. Hence, each vertex in this directed graph has out-degree 1. Among these directed edges, only edges directed from a vertex that chose L (for leaf) to a vertex that chose C (for center) are contracted. Thus, the set of contracted edges corresponds to a collection of inward-directed stars (see Figure 9.1), where the center of each star is a vertex that chose C and the star's other vertices chose L. (Hence, the random values were used in order to "break" the directed graph, which may have directed paths of unbounded length, into components of very small diameter.)

The vertices of G_i are the sets obtained by the contraction of all the stars (or rather all the star edges) as well as all vertices of G_{i-1} that did not participate in any contraction. Hence, the weight of each edge $\{P_i(u), P_i(v)\}$ of G_i is the sum of the weight of the corresponding edges in G_{i-1} (i.e., the weight of the edges between the vertices of G_{i-1} that were contracted into $P_i(v)$ and $P_i(u)$, resp.), which equals the number of edges in G between $P_i(v)$ and $P_i(u)$. Note that the weight of contracted edges (of G_{i-1}) disappears from G_i, since they represent edges of G with both endpoints in the same part of P_i. Hence, we are interested in the rate at which the weight of the edges in the graphs G_i's decreases during the iterations (see Item 2 of Lemma 9.30). We also spell out the dependence of P_i on P_{i-1} (and h_i, r_i).

Lemma 9.30 (The effect of an iteration): *Let $G = ([k], E)$ be a graph of maximum degree d, and consider the foregoing iterative process. Then, for every $i \geq 1$ the following holds.*

1. *For every $v \in [k]$, let $\Gamma_{i-1}(v)$ denote the set of all vertices $u \in [k]$ such that some vertex of $P_{i-1}(u)$ neighbors some vertex of $P_{i-1}(v)$ in G; that is, $\Gamma_{i-1}(v)$ consists of all vertices of G that reside in some vertex $U \in 2^{[k]}$ of G_{i-1} that neighbors vertex $P_{i-1}(v)$ in G_{i-1}. Then:*
   (a) If $r_i(P_{i-1}(v)) = C$, then

$$P_i(v) = P_{i-1}(v) \cup \{u \in \Gamma_{i-1}(v) : h_i(P_{i-1}(u)) = P_{i-1}(v) \text{ and } r_i(P_{i-1}(u)) = L\}.$$

(9.11)

   (b) Otherwise (i.e., $r_i(P_{i-1}(v)) = L$), letting u be an arbitrary vertex in $h_i(P_{i-1}(v))$, we have $P_i(v) = P_i(u)$ if $r_i(h_i(P_{i-1}(v))) = C$ and $P_i(v) = P_{i-1}(v)$ otherwise.
   Hence, $\max_{v \in [k]}\{|P_i(v)|\} \leq (d+1) \cdot \max_{w \in [k]}\{|P_{i-1}(w)|^2\}$.
2. *Supposed that for some fixed graph H, the graph G is H-minor free. Then, with constant probability, the total weight of the edges in G_i is a constant factor smaller than the total weight of the edges in G_{i-1}. This holds even if the values of r_i on the various parts are selected in a pairwise independent manner.*

We stress that Item 1 holds for any graph $G = ([k], E)$ of maximum degree d.

Proof Sketch: The main part of Item 1 is proved by noting that the edge $\{P_{i-1}(v), h_i(P_{i-1}(v))\}$ is contracted only if exactly one of its endpoint is assigned the value C (i.e., $r_i(P_{i-1}(v)) \neq r_i(h_i(P_{i-1}(v)))$). Assuming that $r_i(P_{i-1}(v)) = C$, we note that the claim (i.e., Eq. (9.11)) holds (since $P_i(v)$ contains both $P_{i-1}(v)$ and all $P_{i-1}(u)$'s such that $h_i(P_{i-1}(u)) = P_{i-1}(v)$ and $r_i(P_{i-1}(u)) = \mathsf{L}$). In this case, $P_i(v) \subseteq P_{i-1}(v) \cup \bigcup_{u \in \Gamma_{i-1}(v)} P_{i-1}(u)$, and the conclusion follows since $|\Gamma_{i-1}(v)| \leq |P_{i-1}(v)| \cdot d$.

Item 2 relies on the hypothesis that the graph G is H-minor free, for some fixed graph H, and the unspecified constants depend on H. Specifically, we shall rely on the fact that, for every H, *there exists a constant d_H such that every H-minor free graph has a vertex of degree at most d_H* (see [197] and the references therein).[45] Using this fact, it can be shown (see Exercise 9.15) that the set of heaviest edges in G_{i-1} has total weight that is at least a $1/2d_H$ fraction of the total weight of the edges of G_{i-1}.

Focusing on the set of heaviest edges, note that if the values of r_i (at the various parts) are pairwise independent and uniformly distributed in $\{\mathsf{L}, \mathsf{C}\}$, then each heavy edge is contracted with probability $1/4$. Hence, the expected total weight of the edges contracted in iteration i is at least a $1/8d_H$ fraction of the total weight of the edges in G_{i-1}, and the claim follows (by Markov inequality). ∎

Local Implementation. We next show how to emulate oracle access to P_i, when given oracle access to P_{i-1} and to G as well as to r_i. (Note that we do not emulate oracle access to G_i, nor do we use oracle access to G_{i-1}, although this could be done too; the graphs G_i's are used only in the analysis.)

Algorithm 9.31 (Emulating P_i based on P_{i-1}): *Let $\Gamma(v) = \{u : \{u, v\} \in E\}$ denote the set of neighbors of v in G. On input $v \in [k]$, we find $P_i(v)$ as follows.*

1. *Using an oracle call to P_{i-1}, we obtain $V \leftarrow P_{i-1}(v)$.*
2. *Using $d \cdot |V|$ oracle calls to G, we obtain $U \leftarrow \bigcup_{v \in V} \Gamma(v) \setminus V$. Along the way, we also obtain all edges between V and U.*
3. *Using $|U| \leq d \cdot |V|$ oracle calls to P_{i-1}, we obtain the collection of sets $\{P_{i-1}(u) : u \in U\}$, which is part of the partition P_{i-1}. We denote these sets by $U_1, \ldots, U_m$, where $m \leq |U|$.*
   Using the information gathered in Step 2, we compute, for each $j \in [m]$, the weight of the edge $\{V, U_j\}$, which is an edge of G_{i-1}; indeed, this weight equals $\sum_{v' \in V} |\Gamma(v') \cap U_j|$. This determines $h_i(V)$.
4. *Using $m + 1$ oracle call to r_i, we obtain $r_i(V)$ and $r_i(U_1), \ldots, r_i(U_m)$. Next, we determine whether or not the edge $\{V, h_i(V)\}$ is contracted such that $h_i(V)$ serves as the center of a contracted star. Specifically:*
   (a) *If $r_i(V) = r_i(h_i(V)) = \mathsf{L}$, then we return V.*
   (b) *If $r_i(V) = \mathsf{L}$ and $r_i(h_i(V)) = \mathsf{C}$, then we return $P_i(u) \supseteq V \cup P_{i-1}(u)$, where u is an arbitrary vertex in $h_i(V)$.*
   (We stress that invoking the procedure in order to obtain the value of $P_i(u)$ for $u \in h_i(V)$ does not open a vicious cycle, because in that case $r_i(P_{i-1}(u)) = \mathsf{C}$, which means that this invocation will not try to obtain the value of $P_i(w)$ for some $w \in h_i(P_{i-1}(u))$.)[46]

---

[45] Specifically, by [197, Fact 1] the edges of each such graph can be partitioned into d_H forests. Noting that each forest has average degree smaller than 1, the claim follows.

[46] Alternatively, we can augment Step 6 so to allow determining $h_i(W_{j'})$ for every $j' \in [m']$. This can be done by finding $X = \bigcup_{j' \in [m']} \bigcup_{w \in W_{j'}} \Gamma(w)$, and determining $P_{i-1}(x)$ for each $x \in X$. Doing so allows to determine whether or not $h_i(W_{j'}) = h_i(V)$ (for each $j' \in [m']$), and so determine $P_i(u)$ for $u \in h_i(V)$, which in turn determines $P_i(v)$.

Otherwise (i.e., $r_i(V) = C$), *we continue.* (In this case, V serves as the center of a contracted star, which consists of V and an arbitrary subset of the U_i's.)

5. *Using* $d \cdot \sum_{j \in [m]} |U_j|$ *oracle calls to G, we obtain* $W \leftarrow \bigcup_{j \in [m]} \bigcup_{u \in U_j} \Gamma(u) \setminus (V \cup \bigcup_{j \in [m]} U_j)$. *Along the way, we also obtain all edges between each U_j and W.*

6. *Using* $|W| \leq d \cdot \sum_{j \in [m]} |U_j|$ *oracle calls to P_{i-1}, we obtain the collection of sets* $\{W_1, \ldots, W_{m'}\} \leftarrow \{P_{i-1}(w) : w \in W\}$.

   Using the information gathered in Step 5, we compute, for each $j \in [m]$ and $j' \in [m']$, the weight of the edge $\{U_j, W_{j'}\}$, which is an edge of G_{i-1}; indeed, this weight equals $\sum_{u \in U_j} |\Gamma(u) \cap W_{j'}|$. *This determines $h_i(U_j)$ for all $j \in [m]$.*

The foregoing information determines $P_i(v)$; that is, we return $P_i(v) = V \cup \bigcup_{j \in J} U_j$ such that $J = \{j \in [m] : h_i(U_j) = V \wedge r_i(U_j) = L\}$.

Hence, Algorithm 9.31 makes $\mathrm{poly}(d \cdot N_{i-1})$ oracle calls to P_{i-1} and G, where $N_{i-1} = \max_{w \in [k]}\{|P_{i-1}(w)|\}$. The oracle calls to $r_i : 2^{[k]} \to \{L, C\}$ can be implemented by oracle calls to a random function $s_i : [k] \to \{L, C\}$ that assigns pairwise independent (and uniformly distributed) values to elements of $[k]$, which in turn can be implemented using $2 \log_2 k$ random bits.[47] (The latter comment matters only for bounding the time complexity of Algorithm 9.31.)

We now consider what happens when Algorithm 9.31 is iterated $\ell \stackrel{\text{def}}{=} O(\log(d/\epsilon))$ times, where in the ith iteration we use this algorithm to emulate P_i when using oracle access to P_{i-1} (as well as to G and r_i). Letting $N_i \stackrel{\text{def}}{=} \max_{v \in [k]}\{|P_i(v)|\}$, recall that by Item 1 of Lemma 9.30 it holds that $N_i \leq (d + 1) \cdot N_{i-1}^2$, and $N_i \leq (d + 1)^{2^i - 1}$ follows. Hence, each query to P_i can be implemented at the cost of making $\prod_{j \in [i]} \mathrm{poly}(d \cdot N_{i-j}) = \prod_{j \in [i]} \mathrm{poly}(d^{2^{i-j}}) = \mathrm{poly}(d)^{2^i}$ queries to G, since $\prod_{j \in [i]} \mathrm{poly}(d \cdot N_{i-j})$ upper-bounds the size of the tree that describes the recursive calls made by Algorithm 9.31. On the other hand, by Item 2 of Lemma 9.30, with very high probability, after ℓ iterations, the resulting graph has less than $(1 - \Omega(1))^{\Omega(\ell)} \cdot dk = \epsilon \cdot k$ edges, provided that G is H-minor free.[48] This means that, in this case, we can use P_ℓ as the desired partition, since in this case, with high probability, P_ℓ is an (ϵ, t)-partition for $t = \mathrm{poly}(d)^{2^\ell} = \mathrm{poly}(d)^{\mathrm{poly}(d/\epsilon)}$. Recall that for any graph G of maximum degree d, the partition P_ℓ can be emulated using $\mathrm{poly}(d)^{2^\ell} = d^{\mathrm{poly}(d/\epsilon)}$ queries.[49]

Reducing the Size of Sets. The size of the partitions generated by the foregoing iterations can be reduced considerably, while essentially maintaining the query complexity. This can be done by employing a partitioning algorithm to each set in the aforementioned partition.

---

[47] Specifically, let $r_i(X)$ equal $s_i(x)$ such that $x \in [k]$ is the smallest element in $X \subseteq [k]$. Hence, *if the values that s_i assigns to elements of $[k]$ are pairwise independent and uniformly distributed in $\{L, C\}$, then so are the values assigned by r_i to sets in any fixed partition of $[k]$.* Note that a k-long pairwise independent sequence over $\{0, 1\}$ can be generated by letting $s_i(x)$ be the least significant bit of $s' + xs''$, where s' and s'' are uniformly distributed in $\mathbb{Z}_{2^\ell}$ and $\ell = \lceil \log_2 k \rceil$. (Indeed, here we associated $[k]$ with $\mathbb{Z}_{2^\ell}$.)

[48] Indeed, $(1 - \Omega(1))^{\Omega(\ell)} = \exp(-\Omega(\ell)) < \epsilon/d$.

[49] Also recall that, when seeking an ϵ-tester, Theorem 9.28 is invoked with a purported $(\epsilon d/4, t)$-partition oracle. Hence, the resulting tester has query complexity $d^{\mathrm{poly}(1/\epsilon)}$.

Theorem 9.32 (Finding good partitions in polynomial time):[50] *For every fixed graph H, there exists a polynomial-time algorithm that, for every $\epsilon > 0$, finds a $(\epsilon, O(d/\epsilon)^2)$-partition in any given H-minor free graph. Furthermore, if the input graph is not H-minor free, then the algorithm outputs a $(d, O(d/\epsilon)^2)$-partition of it.*[51]

Hence, for any $\epsilon > 0$ and $t \in \mathbb{N}$, when given an (ϵ, t)-partition oracle $P : [k] \rightarrow 2^{[k]}$ of an H-minor free graph $G = ([k], E)$, we can emulate an $O(2\epsilon, O(d/\epsilon)^2)$-partition oracle as follows. On input $v \in [k]$, we first retrieve the set $P(v)$, next we retrieve the subgraph of G induced by $P(v)$, and finally we invoke the (deterministic) partitioning algorithm of Theorem 9.32 on this subgraph (and answer with the set containing v).

9.5.2. The Better Implementation

Invoking the algorithm of Theorem 9.32 *on the final partition* generated by ($\ell = O(\log(d/\epsilon))$ iterations of) Algorithm 9.31 does reduce the size of the final sets in the partition, but it does not (and cannot) improve the complexity of generating the partition. The key to improving the said complexity is invoking the algorithm of Theorem 9.32 *after each iteration of Algorithm 9.31*.

This means that, in each iteration, we first decrease the number of edges between the sets of the current partition by a constant factor (by employing Algorithm 9.31), and then increase it by an additive term of $\epsilon'k$ (for an adequate constant $\epsilon' > 0$, by employing the algorithm of Theorem 9.32). (This is slightly inaccurate since the decrease occurs only with constant probability, but this is good enough.) So we lose a little in terms of the progress made in each iteration, but we gain in maintaining the sets relatively small (i.e., we enter each iteration with a partition having sets of size poly(d/ϵ)). In particular, while in Section 9.5.1 the size of the sets in the partition was squared in each iteration, here these sets remain smaller than some fixed quantity (i.e., poly(d/ϵ)). It follows that the query complexity of implementing the final partition is only poly(d/ϵ)$^{O(\log(d/\epsilon))}$. Details follow.

Algorithm 9.33 (Emulating P_i based on P_{i-1}, revised): *On input $v \in [k]$, we find $P_i(v)$ as follows.*

1. *Invoking Algorithm 9.31, denoted A, we obtain the part in which v reside, which we denote $P_i'(v)$; that is, $P_i'(v) \leftarrow A^{P_{i-1},G,r_i}(v)$. Recall that invoking Algorithm 9.31 requires providing it with oracle access to P_{i-1}, G and r_i.*
2. *Using oracle access to G, we first construct the subgraph induced by $P_i'(v)$.*[52] *Next, invoking the algorithm of Theorem 9.32, with an error parameter $\epsilon' = \Theta(\epsilon)$, we obtain an $(\epsilon', O(d/\epsilon')^2)$-partition of this induced subgraph, and let $P_i(v)$ be the part containing v.*
   (Note that the algorithm of Theorem 9.32 is invoked on a graph that we hold in hand, so no queries are needed in this step.)

---

[50] This result is based on a separator theorem of Alon *et al.* [16]; see [197, Cor. 2] for details.

[51] For example, it may use a trivial partition that places each vertex in a part of its own. In this case, the resulting partition satisfies Conditions 1–3 of Definition 9.27, since Condition 4 of Definition 9.27 holds vacuously when the error parameter is at least $d/2$.

[52] Actually, this subgraph is implicit in the information gathered by Algorithm 9.31.

Hence, Algorithm 9.33 makes $\mathrm{poly}(d \cdot |P_{i-1}(v)|)$ oracle calls to P_{i-1} and G, and the oracle calls to r_i are implemented as in Section 9.5.1. The point is that $|P_i(v)| = O(d/\epsilon)^2$ for all $i \in [\ell]$ (and $v \in [k]$), and so the complexity of emulating the final partition is merely $\mathrm{poly}(d/\epsilon)^\ell$, since this is an upper bound on the size of the recursion tree.

It is left to analyze the quality of the final partition, when assuming that the input graph G is H-minor free. Let us denote by Z_i the number of edges in G_i, which is the graph that corresponds to the partition P_i; that is, Z_i is a random variable that depends on $r_1, \ldots, r_i$. Letting Z_i' denote the number of edges in the graph that corresponds to the partition P_i', note that the proof of Lemma 9.30 actually establishes that $\mathbb{E}[Z_i'|Z_{i-1} = z] \leq c_H \cdot z$, where $c_H = (1 - (1/8d_H))$ is a constant that depends on H. Hence, $\mathbb{E}[Z_i] \leq c_H \cdot \mathbb{E}[Z_{i-1}] + \epsilon'k$, which implies $\mathbb{E}[Z_\ell] < c_H^\ell \cdot dk + (1 - c_H)^{-1} \cdot \epsilon'k$.[53] Letting $\ell = O(\log(d/\epsilon))$ such that $c_H^\ell < \epsilon/20d$, and $\epsilon' = (1 - c_H) \cdot \epsilon/20$, we have $\mathbb{E}[Z_\ell] < \epsilon k/10$. It follows that $\mathbf{Pr}[Z_\ell \geq \epsilon k] < 1/10$. Hence, we obtain:

Theorem 9.34 (Implementing a partition oracle for a H-minor free graph): *For every fixed H, there exists an efficient mapping from $\epsilon > 0$ to M_ϵ such that M_ϵ is an $\exp(O(\log(d/\epsilon))^2)$-time oracle machine that emulates an $(\epsilon, O(d/\epsilon)^2)$-partition oracle for H-minor free graphs of maximum degree d.*

Recall that the notion of emulating a partition oracle for a property (as stated in Definition 9.29) mandates that, given oracle access to any graph of maximum degree d, (1) machine M_ϵ always implements a function that satisfies Conditions 1–3 of Definition 9.27, and that (2) when the graph has the property then, with probability at least 0.9, machine M_ϵ emulates an $(\epsilon, O(d/\epsilon)^2)$-partition oracle for it. Combining Theorems 9.28 and 9.34, we finally establish Theorem 9.25.

Proof of Theorem 9.25. For every fixed set of graphs $\mathcal{H}$, we are required to present a tester for $\mathcal{H}$-minor freeness. Fixing an arbitrary $H \in \mathcal{H}$ (and given proximity parameter ϵ), we invoke Theorem 9.34, while setting the approximation parameter to $\epsilon d/4$. This yields an implementation of a $(d\epsilon/4, O(1/\epsilon^2))$-partition oracle of query (and time) complexity $\exp(O(\log(1/\epsilon))^2)$ for H-minor freeness (and hence also for $\mathcal{H}$-minor freeness).[54] Invoking the algorithm guaranteed by Theorem 9.28, while providing it with this implementation, we obtain an ϵ-tester of query complexity $\mathrm{poly}(1/\epsilon)^{O(\log(1/\epsilon))} \cdot d$ for $\mathcal{H}$-minor freeness.[55]

---

[53] Here we use $\sum_{i=0}^{\ell-1} c_H^i < \sum_{i \geq 0} c_H^i = 1/(1 - c_H)$.

[54] Alternatively, we can invoke Theorem 9.28 (w.r.t. H-minor freeness), obtain a tester for H-minor freeness, and use the fact that the $\mathcal{H}$-minor freeness property equals the intersection over all $H \in \mathcal{H}$ of the H-minor freeness properties. Indeed, we use the fact that the testability of monotone properties is preserved under intersection (see Theorem 1.13), while noting that minor-freeness properties are monotone (in the sense of being closed under removal of edges).

[55] Note that $\mathcal{H}$-minor free graphs are accepted with probability at least 0.9^2, whereas graphs that are ϵ-far from being $\mathcal{H}$-minor free are rejected with probability at least 0.9. The error bound in the first case accounts both for the probability that M_ϵ fails to satisfy Condition 4 and for the probability that the invoked algorithm (of Theorem 9.28) errs. Hence, it is important that Theorem 9.28 asserts error probability that is strictly smaller than $1/3$ and ditto regarding the implementation error in Theorem 9.34. In the second case (i.e., graphs that are far from the property), we only suffer the error of the invoked algorithm, since in this case Condition 4 is not relied upon.

9.6. A Taxonomy of the Known Results

We first mention that, also in the current model, graph properties of arbitrary query complexity are known: Specifically, in this model, *graph properties* (in $\mathcal{NP}$) *may have query complexity ranging from* $O(1/\epsilon)$ *to* $\Omega(k)$, and furthermore such properties are monotone and natural (cf. [144], which builds on [61]). In particular, testing 3-Colorability requires $\Omega(k)$ queries, whereas testing 2-Colorability (i.e., Bipartiteness) requires $\Omega(\sqrt{k})$ queries [147] and can be done using $\widetilde{O}(\sqrt{k}) \cdot \text{poly}(1/\epsilon)$ queries [148]. We also mention that many natural properties are testable in query complexity that depends only on the proximity parameter (i.e., ϵ). A partial list includes t-edge connectivity, for every fixed t, and Planarity. Details follow.

9.6.1. Testability in $q(\epsilon)$ Queries, for Any Function q

Recall that, with the exception of properties that depend only on the degree distribution, adaptive testers are essential for obtaining query complexity that depends only on ϵ (see Theorem 9.2, which is due to [233]). Still, as observed in [152], at the cost of an exponential blow-up in the query complexity, we may assume that the tester's adaptivity is confined to performing searches of *predetermined depth* from several randomly selected vertices. However, the best testing results are typically obtained by testers that perform "more adaptive" searches such as performing searches till a *predetermined number of vertices* is visited. In all these cases, the predetermined number is a function of the proximity parameter, denoted ϵ, and the degree bound, denoted d.

Testability in $\widetilde{O}(1/\epsilon)$ Queries. As shown in Section 9.2.3, Graph Connectivity can be tested in $\widetilde{O}(1/\epsilon)$ time. Essentially, the tester starts a search (e.g., a BFS) from a few randomly selected vertices, and each such search is terminated after a predetermined number of vertices is encountered (rather than after visiting all vertices that are at a predetermined distance from the start vertex). Specifically, as per Levin's economical work investment strategy (see Section 8.2.4), for every $i \in [\log(1/\epsilon)]$, we select $O(2^i \log(1/\epsilon))$ random start vertices, and conduct searches from each of them, while suspending each search once $O(2^{-i}/d\epsilon)$ vertices are encountered (which guarantees that each of these searches has complexity $O(2^{-i}/\epsilon)$). This tester rejects if and only if it detects a small connected component, and thus it has one-sided error.

Testability in $O(F(d)/\epsilon)$ Queries. The testers of degree regularity and Eulerian have $O(1/\epsilon)$ query complexity when provided with a degree oracle (see Section 9.2.2), which can be implemented at the cost of $\log d$ incidence queries. Hence, when using only incidence queries, the complexity grows moderately as a function of d. In contrast, the dependence on d is much larger in the testers of subgraph freeness: Specifically, these testers have query complexity $O(F(d)/\epsilon)$, where F is a polynomial of degree that is linearly related to the radius of the fixed subgraph that determines the property (see Section 9.2.1).

Testability in $\text{poly}(1/\epsilon)$ Queries. As mentioned in Section 9.2.4, for every fixed $t > 1$, the property t-edge connectivity can be tested in $\widetilde{O}(t^3/\epsilon^c)$ time, where $c = \min(t - 1, 3)$. For t-vertex connectivity the known upper bound is $\widetilde{O}(t/d\epsilon)^t$; see [275].

Cycle-freeness can be tested in $O(\epsilon^{-3})$ time, by a tester having two-sided error probability (see Section 9.2.5). Essentially, the tester compares the number of edges to the number of connected components, while exploring any small connected components that it happens to visit. The two-sided error probability is unavoidable for any Cycle-freeness tester that has query complexity $o(\sqrt{k})$ (see Section 9.3.2).[56]

Testability in More Than $\text{poly}(d/\epsilon)$ **Queries.** Viewing cycle-free graphs as graphs that have no K_3-minor leads us to the following general result of [41], which refers to graph minors (see Section 9.5). While their original result asserted that any minor-close property can be tested in query complexity that is triple-exponential in $O(d/\epsilon)$, the currently known upper bound is quasi-polynomial in d/ϵ; see [197], which builds on [169]. (These testers have two-sided error probability.)[57] It is indeed a begging open problem whether the bound can be improved to a polynomial in d/ϵ (see Problem 9.26).

We mention that properties in a broader class, which consists of sets of *hyperfinite graphs*, are each testable in complexity $\exp(d^{\text{poly}(1/\epsilon)})$. A graph is called (ϵ, t)-hyperfinite if it is $(2\epsilon/d)$-close to a graph that consists of connected components that are each of size at most t (i.e., removing ϵk edges yields the latter graph). A set of graphs is hyperfinite if there exists a function $T : (0, 1] \to \mathbb{N}$ such that, for every $\epsilon > 0$, every graph in the set is $(\epsilon, T(\epsilon))$-hyperfinite. (Minor-closed properties are hyperfinite [16].)[58] The result of Hassidim *et al.* [169] implies that any monotone property of hyperfinite graphs is testable in $\exp(d^{O(T(\text{poly}(1/\epsilon)))})$-time, where T is the foregoing function and a property is called monotone if it is preserved under omission of edges.[59]

9.6.2. Testability in $\widetilde{O}(k^{1/2}) \cdot \text{poly}(1/\epsilon)$ Queries

The query complexity of testing Bipartiteness is $\widetilde{\Theta}(k^{1/2}) \cdot \text{poly}(1/\epsilon)$, and the time complexity has the same form. Furthermore, the Bipartiteness tester has one-sided error, and whenever it rejects it may also output a short proof that the graph is not bipartite (i.e., an odd cycle of length $\text{poly}(\epsilon^{-1} \log k)$). A similar upper bound holds for testing Expansion, except that there the bound refers to a "gap problem" (i.e., distinguishing graphs that are c-expanding from graphs that are ϵ-far from being $\text{poly}(c/d)$-expanding (where d is the degree bound)) and has the form $O(k^\alpha/\epsilon)$ for any constant $\alpha > 1/2$.

In both cases, the algorithm is based on taking many *random walks* from a few randomly selected vertices, where each walk has length $\text{poly}(\epsilon^{-1} \log k)$. This algorithmic approach originates in [148], where it was applied to testing Bipartiteness; for further details see Section 9.4.1. (Indeed, this approach is even more natural for testing

---

[56] A one-sided error tester of query complexity $\text{poly}(d/\epsilon) \cdot \widetilde{O}(\sqrt{k})$ for Cycle-freeness is presented in Section 9.4.2.

[57] This is unavoidable in light of the lower bound on the query complexity of one-sided error testers for cycle-freeness (presented in Section 9.3.2). Furthermore, by [81], for any H that is not cycle-free, one-sided error testing H-minor freeness requires $\Omega(\sqrt{k})$ queries.

[58] See [197, Cor. 2] for details.

[59] We warn that the term "monotone graph properties" is sometimes defined as closure under the removal of edges and vertices (see, e.g.,[18]). We also mention that a graph property is called hereditary if it is preserved under omission of vertices (and their incident edges); that is, hereditary graph properties are preserved by induced subgraphs.

Expansion, but the analysis was blocked by a combinatorial difficulty [149], which was resolved later in [175, 214].)[60]

The $\Omega(k^{1/2})$ lower bounds on the query complexity of testing each of the aforementioned properties were proved in [147]; for details see Section 9.3. We note that the lower bound for testing Bipartiteness stands in sharp contrast to the situation in the dense graph model, where this testing problem can be solved in poly($1/\epsilon$)-time. This discrepancy is due to the difference between the notions of relative distance employed in the two models.

9.6.3. Additional Issues

Let us highlight some issues that arise from the foregoing exposition.

Adaptive Testers versus Nonadaptive Ones. As stated at the very beginning of this chapter (see Theorem 9.2), nonadaptive testers are significantly handicapped in the current model: Unless they use $\Omega(\sqrt{k})$ queries, such testers cannot do more than gather statistics regarding the degrees of vertices in a k-vertex graph. In contrast, adaptive testers of constant query complexity can explore local neighborhood in the graph, which allows for deducing numerous global properties such as connectivity and planarity (see Sections 9.2 and 9.5).

One-Sided versus Two-Sided Error Probability. The problem of testing Cycle-freeness provides a dramatic illustration of the gap between one-sided error and two-sided error. Recall that Theorem 9.17 asserts that one-sided error testers for Cycle-freeness require $\Omega(\sqrt{k})$ queries,[61] whereas two-sided error ϵ-testing of Cycle-freeness is possible within query complexity poly($1/\epsilon$) (see Section 9.2.5).

Proximity-Oblivious Testers. The testers for subgraph freeness and degree regularity (see Sections 9.2.1 and 9.2.2, respectively) were obtained by presenting (one-sided error) proximity-oblivious testers (of constant-query complexity and detection probability that depends only on the distance of the tested graph from the property). A partial characterization of properties that have such testers appears in [152], where one of the directions relies on a natural combinatorial conjecture.

An Application to the Study of the Dense Graph Model. As noted several times, the bounded-degree graph model differs fundamentally from the dense graph model. In light of this fact, it is interesting to note that the Bipartiteness tester for the *bounded-degree graph model* was used in order to derive an alternative Bipartiteness tester for the *dense graph model* [162]. For any $\alpha \geq 0$, assuming that almost all vertices in the k-vertex graph have degree $O(\epsilon^{1-\alpha}k)$, this tester has query complexity $\widetilde{O}(\epsilon^{-(1.5+O(\alpha))})$, which (for small $\alpha > 0$) improves over the testers presented in [140, 13]. Essentially, this *dense-graph model tester* invokes the foregoing *bounded-degree model tester* on the

---

[60] **Advanced comment:** As stated at the beginning of Section 9.4.1, it is not *a priori* clear that taking many short random walks (from a random start vertex) is a good strategy toward testing Bipartiteness. In contrast, it is apparent that the collision probability of random walks of logarithmic length is related to the graph's expansion, provided that we consider random walks that start at the *worst* possible vertex. Unfortunately, the tester only approximates the collision probability of random walks that start at *typical* vertices, and relating this measure to the distance of the graph from being an expander is more evasive.

[61] Recall that this lower bound is relatively tight (see Section 9.4.2).

subgraph induced by a sample S of $\widetilde{O}(\epsilon^{-1})$ random vertices, while emulating neighbor queries regarding a vertex $v \in S$ by making adjacency queries of the form (v, w) for every $w \in S$.

Relations to Other Areas of Algorithmic Research. The fact that the bounded-degree graph model is closer (than the dense graph model) to standard algorithmic research offers greater opportunities for interaction at the technical level. Indeed, techniques such as local search and random walks are quite basic in both domains, and the relationship will become even tighter when we move to the general graph model (in the next chapter). A few concrete examples in which such interaction has occurred are stated next.

- Karger's randomized algorithm for finding minimum-cuts [178] inspired the algorithm for finding small t-connected components (i.e., Algorithm 9.10) and is used in its analysis (see proof of Theorem 9.11).
- Distributed network algorithms with few communication rounds were used to obtain property testers, superfast parameter estimators, and local computation algorithms (see [223] followed by [218]). Implications in the opposite direction were foreseen by Onak [218] and materialized in [103].
- The idea underlying the Cycle-freeness tester (presented in Section 9.2.5) was employed to the design of an algorithm for approximating the weight of a minimum spanning tree in sublinear time [74].
- The one-sided error testers for cycle-freeness and other minor-free properties yield sublinear time algorithms for finding natural substructures in graphs (see Theorem 9.24 and the discussion preceding it).[62]

9.7. Chapter Notes

9.7.1. Historical Perspective and Credits

The study of property testing in the bounded-degree graph model was initiated by Goldreich and Ron [147], with the aim of allowing the consideration of sparse graphs, which appear in numerous applications. The point was that the dense graph model, introduced earlier in [140], seems irrelevant to sparse graphs, both because the distance measure that underlies it deems all sparse graphs as close to one another, and because adjacency queries seems unsuitable for sparse graphs. Sticking to the paradigm of representing graphs as functions, where both the distance measure and the type of queries are determined by the representation, the bounded-degree incidence function representation seemed the most natural choice. Indeed, a conscious decision was (and is) made not to capture, at this point (and in this model), sparse graphs that do not have constant (or low) maximum degree.

Most testers presented in Section 9.2 (which operate via "local searches") are taken from the work of Goldreich and Ron [147]. This includes the (one-sided error) testers for subgraph-freeness and connectivity, and the two-sided error tester for cycle-freeness.[63] (The one-sided error tester for cycle-freeness (presented in Section 9.4.2) is due to [81], and the tester of degree-regularity (presented in Section 9.2.2) is adapted from the one

---

[62] **Advanced comment:** For further discussion and results of this nature, the interested reader is referred to [81].

[63] Actually, the two-sided error tester for cycle-freeness is a variant on the tester presented in [147], and the complexity improvement (captured in Theorem 9.15) has not appeared before.

used for the dense graph model.) The tester for t-Edge Connectivity is due to [147], and Algorithm 9.10 was inspired by Karger's work [178].[64] The tester for t-Vertex Connectivity is due to Yoshida and Ito [275], while only the case of $t \leq 3$ was handled in (the conference version) of [147].

The $\Omega(\sqrt{k})$ lower bounds on the query complexity of Bipartiteness (presented in Section 9.3.1) and its applications to testing cycle-freeness and expansion (presented in Section 9.3.2) are also due to Goldreich and Ron [147]. The linear lower bound on the query complexity of 3-Colorability is due to Bogdanov, Obata, and Trevisan [61].

The (random-walk based) tester for Bipartiteness was presented by Goldreich and Ron [148], and the one-sided error tester for Cycle-freeness was presented in [81]. Using random walks is most natural in the context of testing Expansion [149], but the analysis of such testers was successfully completed only in later works [175, 214]. We mention that the reduction of testing the uniformity of a distribution to estimating its collision probability, which underlies the Expansion tester, has become quite pivotal to the study of testing distributions, which emerged with [35].

Testing minor-free properties was first considered by Benjamini, Schramm, and Shapira [41], who presented testers of query complexity that is triple-exponential in $1/\epsilon$. (These testers as well as all subsequent ones have two-sided error probability.) The bound was improved to a single exponential by Hassidim, Kelner, Nguyen, and Onak [169], who also provided testers for any hyperfinite properties (with complexity that is double-exponential in $1/\epsilon$). The quasi-polynomial (in $1/\epsilon$) time-bound for testing minor-free properties (Theorem 9.25) is due to Levi and Ron [197]. The technique of constructing and using partition oracles was presented explicitly in [169, 218], where two different approaches for constructing such oracles are outlined (see [218, Sec. 2.5.1] and [218, Sec. 2.5.2], respectively).[65] In Section 9.5, we followed the approach described in Onak [218, Sec. 2.5.2], and its improvement by Levi and Ron [197], which led to the aforementioned quasi-polynomial bound.

9.7.2. Directed Graphs

Our exposition of the bounded-degree model was confined to undirected graphs. Nevertheless, as noted in the prior chapter, the model extends naturally to the case of directed graphs. Actually, when considering incidence queries, four natural submodels emerge:[66]

1. The first two models refer to graphs in which both the out-degree and the in-degree are bounded by d. In the first submodel the tester may query only for edges in the forward direction, whereas in the second submodel both forward and backward directions are allowed:

   (a) In the first submodel, the directed k-vertex graph $G = ([k], E)$ is represented by a function $g_{\text{out}} : [k] \times [d] \to \{0, 1, \ldots, k\}$ such that $g_{\text{out}}(v, i) = u$ if the ith outgoing edge of v leads to u, and $g_{\text{out}}(v, i) = 0$ if v have less than i out-going edges.

---

[64] Indeed, the proof of Claim 9.11.2 is essentially due to [178].

[65] The first approach is applicable to any hyperfinite graph, whereas the second approach is applicable only to minor-free graphs.

[66] Actually, two additional models can be presented by considering in-coming edges only. These models are analogous to the two submodels that consider out-going edges only. We believe that the forward direction is more natural.

(b) In the second submodel, the directed graph $G = ([k], E)$ is represented by two functions, g_{out} and g_{in}, where g_{out} is as in the first submodel and $g_{in} : [k] \times [d] \to \{0, 1, \dots, k\}$ is defined analogously with respect to in-coming edges (i.e., $g_{in}(v, i) = u$ if the ith in-coming edge of v arrives from u).

These models were introduced and studied in [40].

2. The other two models refers to graphs in which the out-degree is bounded by d, but there is no bound on the in-degree. Again, in the first submodel the tester may query only for edges in the forward direction, whereas in the second submodel both forward and backward directions are allowed. That is, in the first submodel the graph is represented by a function $g_{out} : [k] \times [d] \to \{0, 1, \dots, k\}$ as in Model 1a, whereas in the second submodel the tester is also provided with oracle access to a function $g_{in} : [k] \times [k-1] \to \{0, 1, \dots, k\}$ that represents the in-coming edges (as in Model 1b, except that here $k-1$ is used as an upper bound on the in-degree).

To the best of our knowledge, these models were not considered so far.

The four different models can be justified by different settings, and they differ vastly in their power. Needless to say, graphs of bounded out-degree and unbounded in-degree are not captured by the first couple of models. The gap between the two query models (in the case that both the out-degree and the in-degree are bounded) was demonstrated by Bender and Ron, who initiated the study of testing properties of directed graphs [40]. In particular, they showed that Strong Connectivity can be tested (with one-sided error) by $\widetilde{O}(1/\epsilon)$ forward and backward queries [40, Sec. 5.1], but when only forward queries are allowed the query complexity of testing Strong Connectivity is $\Omega(\sqrt{k})$ (even when allowing two-sided error [40, Sec. 5.2]).[67] A recent study of the gap between these two models shows that if a property can be tested with a constant number of queries in the bi-directional query model, then it can be tested in a sublinear number of queries in the unidirectional query model [83].[68]

Another task studied in [40] is testing whether a given directed graph is acyclic (i.e., has no directed cycles). The authors presented an Acyclicity tester of $poly(1/\epsilon)$ complexity in the adjacency predicate model, and showed that in the incidence list model no Acyclicity tester has query complexity $o(k^{1/3})$ (even when both forward and backward queries are allowed). The question of whether Acyclicity can be tested with $o(k)$ queries (in the bounded-degree digraph model) remains open. In general, it seems that the study of the foregoing models deserves more attention than it has received so far.

9.7.3. Exercises

In addition to exercises that are directly related to property testing problems (e.g., Exercises 9.2–9.6), we suggest a few exercises of a graph theoretic nature (e.g., Exercises 9.9 and 9.10), and highlight the repeated sampling paradigm (Exercise 9.13).

---

[67] The lower bound can be strengthened to $\Omega(k)$ when considering only one-sided error testers. In the case of two-sided error, sublinear complexity is possible also in the unidirectional model (i.e., for every constant $\epsilon > 0$, strong connectivity is ϵ-testable by $k^{1-\Omega(1)}$ forward queries) [133, Apdx. A.3].

[68] The transformation does *not* preserve one-sided error probability, and this is inherent, since there are properties that have a constant-query one-sided error tester in the bidirectional model but no sublinear-query one-sided error tester in the unidirectional model.

Exercise 9.1 (Determining the degree of a vertex): Given a k-vertex graph G of maximal degree d, represented by $g : [k] \times [d] \to \{0, 1, \ldots, k\}$, prove the following claims.

1. The degree of a given vertex can be determined using $\lceil \log(d + 1) \rceil$ incidence queries.
2. Determining the degree of a given vertex requires at least $\lceil \log(d + 1) \rceil$ incidence queries.
3. Show that a randomized algorithm (which errs with probability at most $1/3$) may use one query less, and this is optimal up to one query.

Indeed, the first two claims refer to deterministic algorithms.

> **Guideline:** The pivot of this exercise is reducing a question regarding a sequence over $[k]$ to a question regarding a binary sequence. This suggestion is quite straightforward with respect to the upper bounds, but requires some care when applied to the derivation of lower bounds. Specifically, regarding Claim 1, given vertex v, reduce the problem of determining its degree to the problem of determining the largest $i \in \{0, 1, \ldots, d\}$ such that $f(i) = 1$, where $f : \{0, 1, \ldots, d\} \to \{0, 1\}$ is defined such that $f(j) = 1$ if and only if $g(v, j) \in [k]$ (with $g(v, 0) = 1$).
>
> Turning to Claim 2 (and assuming $d < k$), we consider k-vertex graphs such that, for each $i \in [d] \cup \{0\}$, the graph G_i consists of a single i-vertex star centered at vertex k. Specifically, for each $i \in \{0, 1, \ldots, d\}$, it holds that $G_i = ([k], \{\{j, k\} : j \in [i]\})$ and the corresponding incidence function $g_i : [k] \times [d] \to \{0, 1, \ldots, k\}$ satisfies $g_i(k, j) = j$ and $g_i(j, 1) = k$ for every $j \in [i]$, and $g_i(v, j) = 0$ for all other (v, j)'s. The key observation is that for some fixed function $f : [k] \times [d] \to [k]$, which does not depend on i, it holds that $g_i(v, j) \in \{0, f(v, j)\}$ for all i and v, j, and so each query has at most two possible answers. Note that any q-query algorithm that determines i (which equals the degree of vertex k), when given access to an unknown function g_i, yields a depth q *binary* decision tree that queries the unknown g_i and has at least $d + 1$ leaves (which are labeled by the different possible outputs $i \in \{0, 1, \ldots, d\}$).
>
> For the positive part of Claim 3, consider an algorithm that discards a random $\lfloor d/3 \rfloor$-subset of $[d]$ when applying the reduction of Claim 1. (That is, for a selected subset I of size $\lfloor d/3 \rfloor$, we consider the function $f' : (\{0, 1, \ldots, d + 1\} \setminus I) \to \{0, 1\}$ such that $f'(j) = 1$ if and only if $g(v, j) \in [k]$, and seek to find the largest $i \in \{0, 1, \ldots, d\} \setminus I$ such that $f'(i) = 1$.) For the negative part, consider a choice of internal coin tosses for which the residual deterministic algorithm errs on at most $\lfloor (d + 1)/3 \rfloor$ of the possible i's (considered in Claim 2).

Exercise 9.2 (Nonadaptive tester of triangle-freeness):[69] Show that triangle-freeness has a non-adaptive tester of query complexity $O(d\sqrt{k/\epsilon})$.

> **Guideline:** First observe that a graph that is ϵ-far from being triangle-free must have more than $\epsilon dk/2$ different triangles, since each triangle can be removed by omitting a single edge. Hence, at least $\epsilon k/2$ different vertex pairs participate in some triangle, which means that a random vertex-pair participates in a triangle with probability at least $\Omega(\epsilon/k)$. The nonadaptive tester selects a random sample S of $O(\sqrt{k/\epsilon})$ vertices, and queries the graph at all the vertex-index pairs $S \times [d]$. The claim is proved by considering the vertex-pairs $S \times S$, while using the fact that $S \times S$ constitutes an *almost pairwise independent sample* of all vertex-pairs (cf. proof of Claim 9.21.3).

---

[69] Based on a result in [133, Apdx. A.2].

Exercise 9.3 (Testing subgraph freeness for an unconnected subgraph): Let H be a fixed graph that consists of the connected components $H_1, \ldots, H_m$, having radii $r_1, \ldots, r_m$, respectively. Let $r = \max_{i \in [m]} \{r_i\}$. Show that H-freeness has a (one-sided error) proximity-oblivious tester of query complexity $O(m \cdot d^{r+1})$ and polynomial detection probability. Furthermore, show that H-freeness has a (one-sided error) tester of query complexity $\widetilde{O}(m) \cdot d^{r+1}/\epsilon$.

> **Guideline:** A vertex $v \in [k]$ is called i-detecting if it is a center of a copy of H_i that resides in G. Prove that if G is at distance δ from H-free, then, for every $i \in [m]$, the graph G must have at least $\delta k/2$ vertices that are i-detecting. The proximity-oblivious tester selects m random vertices, performs an r-deep BFS from each, and rejects if and only if (vertex disjoint) copies of all the H_i's were found in these m searches. The ϵ-tester selects $m' = O(m \log m)/\epsilon$ random vertices, performs an r-deep BFS from each, and rejects if and only if (vertex disjoint) copies of all the H_i's were found in these m' searches.

Exercise 9.4 (On testing whether a graph is Eulerian): Suppose that $G = ([k], E)$ has maximum degree d, and k' of its vertices have odd degree. Prove that there exists a k-vertex Eulerian graph $G' = ([k], E')$ of maximum degree d such that the symmetric difference between E and E' is at most $3k'/2$. Present a (one-sided error) proximity-oblivious tester based on this observation, and determine its query complexity and detection probability.

> **Guideline:** If d is even, then vertices of odd degree have degree smaller than d. In this case, we just proceed in iterations such that at each iteration we choose a pair of vertices of (current) odd degree and change their adjacency relation (i.e., if they were adjacent, then we omit the edge between them, and otherwise we insert an edge between them). Hence, we are done in $k'/2$ iterations, while modifying a single edge in each iteration. If d is odd, then we first omit a single edge from each vertex that has degree d, while observing that this does not increase the number of vertices of odd degree. Once this stage is completed, we proceed as before, while observing that (from this point on) vertices of odd degree have degree at most $d - 2$.

Exercise 9.5 (On testing whether a graph is connected and Eulerian): We stress that all graphs here are of maximal degree d, and distances between them are as in Definition 9.1.

1. Prove that if $G = ([k], E)$ is ϵ_1-close to being connected and ϵ_2-close to being Eulerian, then it is $O(\epsilon_1 + \epsilon_2)$-close to a graph that is both connected and Eulerian.
2. Using Item 1, present and analyze a tester for the property of being a connected Eulerian graph.

> **Guideline:** Let $G' = ([k], E')$ be an Eulerian graph that is ϵ_2-close to G. Observe that G' is $(\epsilon_1 + \epsilon_2)$-close to being connected, and hence it has at most $(\epsilon_1 + \epsilon_2) \cdot (dk/2) + 1$ connected components. On the other hand, assuming that G' has k' connected components, turn it into a connected graph while preserving the degrees of all vertices and making exactly $2k'$ modifications.[70]

---

[70] Using the fact that each of the connected components is Eulerian, omit a single edge $\{u_i, v_i\}$ from the ith connected component, and add the edges $\{v_i, u_{i+1}\}$ for $i = 1, \ldots, k'$, where the index $k' + 1$ is viewed as 1.

Exercise 9.6 (Finding small 2-edge–connected components):[71] Given a vertex v that resides in a set S of size at most s such that the subgraph of $G = ([k], E)$ induced by S is 2-edge–connected and the cut $(S, [k] \setminus S)$ contains at most one edge, prove that the following algorithm finds S in time $O(ds)$.

1. Invoke a DFS at the vertex v and suspend its execution as soon as more than s vertices are encountered.
2. If the DFS detected a connected component of size at most s, then output it. Otherwise, consider a *directed* graph, denoted $\vec{G}$, that is obtained from G as follows. If $\{u, v\}$ is an edge of the DFS-tree that was first traversed (during the DFS) from u to v, then only the edge directed from v to u is placed in $\vec{G}$ (i.e., we do not include edges in the direction used by the DFS in discovering a new vertex). Any edge $\{u, v\}$ that is not an edge of the DFS-tree is replaced by a pair of antiparallel edges (i.e., we include both (u, v) and (v, u), where (x, y) denotes the edge directed from x to y).
3. Invoke a directed search, starting at vertex v, on the directed graph $\vec{G}$, and output the set of vertices visited in this search. The directed search (e.g., a directed BFS or DFS) traverses directed edges only in the forward direction.

   Guideline: Suppose that $(S, [k] \setminus S)$ contains a single edge. Then, in Step 2, this edge must be traversed by the DFS in the direction from S to $[k] \setminus S$, and it follows that Step 3 outputs a subset of S. Prove that the output cannot be a strict subset of S, by relying on the hypothesis that S is 2-edge connected.

Exercise 9.7 (Proof of Claim 9.11.1):[72] Prove Claim 9.11.1 by showing that at each iteration of Algorithm 9.10 the current set S' satisfies $S' \subseteq S$.

   Guideline: Note that when $S' = S$ the algorithm halts in Step 1 (and outputs S). Otherwise (i.e., when $S' \subset S$), the algorithm does not halt in Step 1 (since G_S is t-connected). But in that case, the cut $C' = (S', [k] \setminus S')$ must contain an edge of the lightest spanning tree of G_S, whereas all edges of this tree are lighter than any edge of C. Hence, in Step 3, the algorithm chooses an edge of $C' \setminus C$, which implies that S' is extended by a vertex in $S \setminus S'$.

Exercise 9.8 (Obtaining a rough estimation for the number of edges): Show that by using $O(1/\epsilon)$ queries, one can distinguish the case that a k-vertex graph of maximum degree d has more than $m \stackrel{\text{def}}{=} \max(2k, \epsilon dk/2)$ edges from the case that it has less than $m/2$ edges.

   Guideline: Show that such an approximation can be obtained by taking a sample of $O(dk/m)$ pairs, and note that $O(dk/\max(2k, \epsilon dk/2)) = O(\min(d, \epsilon^{-1})) = O(1/\epsilon)$.

Exercise 9.9 (Graphs that are far from being bipartite may lack odd cycles of sublogarithmic length):[73] Show that there exist (bounded degree) k-vertex graphs that are $\Omega(1)$-far from being bipartite but have no odd-cycle of length $o(\log k)$.

   Guideline: Using Theorem 9.16 infer that it cannot be the case that each k-vertex graph that is $\Omega(1)$-far from being bipartite has $\Omega(k)$ vertices that reside on odd-cycles

---

[71] Proved in [147].

[72] Proved in [147].

[73] We mention that such graphs can be constructed: The explicit expander graphs in [201] are far from being bipartite.

of length at most $L = o(\log k)$. (This is the case by virtue of a potential tester that selects a random start vertex and explores all vertices at distance $\lceil L/2 \rceil$ from it.) Next, show that if every k-vertex graph that is ϵ-far from being bipartite has an odd cycle of length at most L, then every k-vertex graph that is $(\epsilon + 2\rho)$-far from being bipartite has at least $\rho \cdot k$ vertices that reside on odd-cycles of length at most L.

Exercise 9.10 (Graphs that are far from being bipartite have odd cycles of logarithmic length):[74] Prove that if a (bounded degree) k-vertex graph is ϵ-far from being bipartite, then it has an odd cycle of length at most $L = O(\epsilon^{-1} \log k)$.

Guideline: For starters, note that if all vertices of the graph are at distance at most $(L-1)/2$ from some vertex v, then the claim follows by considering a BFS that starts at v. (Note that some layer of this BFS must contain an edge, which yields an odd cycle of length at most $1 + (L-1)$, since otherwise the graph is bipartite.) In the general case, we apply an iterative process. In each iteration, we pick an arbitrary vertex in the residual graph and perform a truncated BFS that is suspended when the next layer of the BFS grows by less than an $\epsilon/2$ factor; that is, denoting by k' the number of vertices visited so far by the current BFS, we stop (at the current layer) if the next layer has less than $\epsilon k'/2$ vertices. Hence, the BFS is suspended after at most $\log_{1+0.5\epsilon} k$ iterations, and if some layer of this BFS contains an edge, then we are done (as in the simple case). Otherwise, we discard the explored k'-vertex portion of the graph and omit all edges that connect it to the rest of the graph, which means that we omitted less than $\epsilon k' d/2$ edges. Note that this iterative process must find an edge in some layer of some BFS, because otherwise the graph can be made bipartite by omitting $\epsilon dk/2$ edges.

Exercise 9.11 (A detail for the proof of Claim 9.21.2): Let $p_1(u)$ and $p'_1(u)$ be as in Claim 9.21.2 (and in its proof sketch). Prove that $p'_1(u) \in [0.9 \cdot p_1(u), 1.1 \cdot p_1(u)]$.

Guideline: It is instructive to view the ℓ-step walks (starting at vertex s) as ℓ-long sequences over $[2d]$ such that the ith symbol in the sequence $(\alpha_1, \ldots, \alpha_\ell)$ is interpreted as moving to the α_i^{th} neighbor of the current vertex if that vertex has at least α_i neighbors, and staying in place otherwise. Hence, symbols in $[d+1, 2d]$ always represent staying in place, since the degree of the current vertex is always at most d. Now, define $S_{\ell,\ell'}$ as the set of ℓ-long sequences with exactly ℓ' symbols in $[d+1, 2d]$ that correspond to walks of odd path-parity that end at u. Lastly, for every $\gamma \in [d]^{\ell-\ell'}$, let $S^\gamma_{\ell,\ell'}$ denote the set of sequences in $S_{\ell,\ell'}$ whose $[d]$-symbols match γ; that is,

$$S^\gamma_{\ell,\ell'} \stackrel{\text{def}}{=} \bigcup_{I \in \binom{[\ell]}{\ell'}} \{\alpha \in S_{\ell,\ell'} : \alpha_I \in [d+1, 2d]^{\ell'} \wedge \alpha_{[\ell]\setminus I} = \gamma\}.$$

The sets $S_{\ell-1,\ell'-1}$ and $S^\gamma_{\ell-1,\ell'-1}$ are defined analogously. Prove the following claims:

1. $\mathbf{Pr}_{\alpha \in [2d]^\ell}[\alpha \notin \cup_{\ell' \in [0.49\ell, 0.51\ell]} S_{\ell,\ell'}] = \exp(-\Omega(\ell)) < 0.01/k$.
2. For every $\ell' \in [\ell]$ and $\gamma \in [d]^{\ell-\ell'}$, it holds that $\ell' \cdot |S^\gamma_{\ell,\ell'}| = d \cdot \ell \cdot |S^\gamma_{\ell-1,\ell'-1}|$.
   Hence, $\mathbf{Pr}_{\alpha \in [2d]^\ell}[\alpha \in S_{\ell,\ell'}] = \frac{d\ell}{2d \cdot \ell'} \cdot \mathbf{Pr}_{\beta \in [2d]^{\ell-1}}[\beta \in S_{\ell-1,\ell'-1}]$.

Finally, combine the two claims.

---

[74] Proved in [148]. The proof is analogous to the proof of the widely known upper bound on the girth of graphs with certain edge density, where the girth of a graph is the length of its shortest simple cycle. Specifically, the latter claim asserts that if a k-vertex graph has at least $(1 + \epsilon) \cdot k$ edges (which means that, in the context of the bounded-degree model, it is viewed as $\Omega(\epsilon)$-far from being cycle-free), then it has a cycle of length at most $O(\epsilon^{-1} \log k)$.

Exercise 9.12 (A detail for the proof of Lemma 9.22.1): Recall that the proof provided in the text assumed that G is connected. Extend the proof to the general case.

> **Guideline:** Focus on the case of $\Delta > k/2$, while observing that the reduction of the general case to the case of $\Delta > k/2$ made no reference to connectivity. Considering a graph with m connected components, having sizes $k_1, \ldots, k_m$, use the fact that with probability at least $\max(0.5, 1 - \exp(-\Omega(k_i)))$, the ith connected component is $\Omega(1)$-far from being bipartite.

Exercise 9.13 (The repeated sampling paradigm): Let A be a randomized algorithm that, for every $i \in [n]$, outputs i with probability p_i, and halts without output with probability $1 - \sum_{i \in [n]} p_i > 0$. Present an algorithm that generates a distribution that is 2^{-t}-close to the distribution in which $j \in [n]$ appears with probability $p_j / \sum_{i \in [n]} p_i$, by invoking A for $O(t / \sum_{i \in [n]} p_i)$ times.

> **Guideline:** Output the result of the first invocation that produces any output, and output 0 if no invocation produced an output.

Exercise 9.14 (Correcting a given sampler): Suppose that you are given independently drawn samples from a distribution X over $[n]$, but you wish to produce a distribution in which i occurs with probability $\rho(i) \cdot \mathbf{Pr}[X = i]$, where you have oracle access to $\rho : [n] \to [0, O(1)]$. Solve this problem by using a constant number of samples and a constant number of queries to ρ, in expectation.

> **Guideline:** Using the repeated sampling paradigm (see Exercise 9.13), focus on producing an output with a constant probability by using a single sample of X. Specifically, when given a sample i, output it with probability $\rho(i)/c$, where $c = O(1)$ is the guaranteed upper bound on ρ.

Exercise 9.15 (A detail for the proof of Lemma 9.30): Suppose that $G' = ([k'], E')$ is an H-minor–free graph with weights on its edges and let $h(v)$ denote the other endpoint of the heaviest edge incident at vertex v (of G'). Show that the set of directed edges $\{(v, h(v)) : v \in [k']\}$ has total weight that is at least a $1/d_H$ fraction of the total weight of the edges of G', where d_H is a constant such that every H-minor–free graph has a vertex of degree at most d_H. (Consequently, the set of undirected edges $\{\{v, h(v)\} : v \in [k']\}$ has total weight that is at least a $1/2d_H$ fraction of the total weight of the edges of G'.)[75]

> **Guideline:** Consider an iterative process of selecting a vertex of smallest degree in G', and omitting it and its edges from G'. Note that each of the resulting graphs is H-minor free, and thus has a vertex of degree at most d_H. It follows that the heaviest (directed) edge of this vertex, which may not be present at the current graph, has weight that is at least a $1/d_H$ fraction of the weight of the edges omitted at this step. That is, if at the current iteration we omitted the vertex v and all edges incident at it, then the weight of the directed edge $(v, h(v))$ is at least a $1/d_H$ fraction of the total weight of the undirected edges that are incident to v at the beginning of the current iteration.

---

[75] Indeed, an edge $\{u, v\}$ of E' may be the heaviest edge of both u and v; that is, it is possible that $h(v) = u$ and $h(u) = v$.

Exercise 9.16 (Graph properties are not random self-reducible): Show that, except for a few trivial cases, graph properties of k-vertex graphs in the incidence function representation are not random self-reducible by $o(k)$ queries.[76]

    Guideline: See Exercise 8.16.

CHAPTER TEN

Testing Graph Properties in the General Graph Model

Summary: This chapter is devoted to testing graph properties in the general graph model, where graphs are inspected via incidence and adjacency queries, and distances between graphs are normalized by their actual size (i.e., actual number of edges). The highlights of this chapter include

1. Demonstrating the derivation of testers for this model from testers for the bounded-degree graph model
2. Studying the tasks of estimating the number of edges in a graph and sampling edges uniformly at random

We conclude this chapter with some reflections regarding the three models of testing graph properties.

The current chapter is based on several sources; see Section 10.5.2 for details.

Teaching Note: Although it is possible to study the current chapter without first studying Chapter 9, we strongly recommend not doing so. Basic familiarity with the bounded-degree graph model (see Section 9.1) seems necessary for a good perspective on the general graph model. In addition, familiarity with some of the results and ideas of Chapter 9 will greatly facilitate the study of the current chapter. Specifically, it will be most beneficial to be familiar with the connectivity tester and the bipartiteness tester (presented in Sections 9.2.3 and 9.4.1, respectively).

Organization. Following an introduction to the general graph model (Section 10.1), we study the issues that arise when trying to extend testers for the bounded-degree graph model to testers for the current model (Section 10.2). Next, in Section 10.3, we study the related problems of estimating the average degree in a general graph and selecting random edges in it, presenting two different algorithmic approaches toward solving these problems (see Sections 10.3.2.1 and 10.3.2.2, respectively). As illustrated in Section 10.2.2, these problems are pivotal for the design of some testers. Lastly, in Section 10.4, we illustrate the possible benefits of using both incidence and gadjacency queries.

> **Teaching Note:** We recommend covering only part of the contents of this chapter in class, and leaving the rest for optional independent reading. Aside from Section 10.1, which seems a must, the choice of what to teach and what to leave out is less clear. If pressed for our own choice, then the fact is that we chose to cover Sections 10.2.2 and 10.3.2.1 in class.

10.1. The General Graph Model: Definitions and Issues

The general graph model is intended to capture arbitrary graphs, which may be neither dense nor of bounded degree. Such graphs occur most naturally in many settings, but they are not captured (or not captured well) by the models presented in the previous two chapters (i.e., the dense graph model and the bounded-degree graph model).

Recall that both in the dense graph model and in the bounded-degree graph model, the query types (i.e., ways of probing the tested graph) and the distance measure (i.e., distance between graphs) were linked to the representation of graphs as functions. In contrast to these two models, in the general graph model the representation is blurred, and the query types and distance measure are decoupled.

Giving up on the representation as a yardstick (for the relative distance between graphs) leaves us with no absolute point of reference. Instead, we just define the relative distance between graphs in relation to the actual number of edges in these graphs; specifically, the relative distance between the graphs $G = ([k], E)$ and $G' = ([k], E')$ may be defined as $\frac{|E \triangle E'|}{\max(|E|,|E'|)}$, where $E \triangle E' = (E \setminus E') \cup (E' \setminus E)$ denotes the symmetric difference between E and E'. Indeed, the normalization by $\max(|E|, |E'|)$ is somewhat arbitrary, and alternatives that seem as natural include $|E| + |E'|$, $|E \cup E'|$ and $(|E| + |E'|)/2$; yet, all these alternatives are within a factor of 2 from one another (and the slackness is even smaller in the typical case where $|E \cup E'| \approx |E \cap E'|$).

Turning to the question of query types, we again need to make a choice, which is now free from representational considerations. The most natural choice is to allow both *incidence queries* and *adjacency queries*; that is, we allow the two types of queries that were each allowed in one of the two previous models. Hence, the graph $G = ([k], E)$ is (redundantly) represented by (or rather accessed via) two functions:

1. An incidence function $g_1 : [k] \times [k-1] \to \{0, 1, \ldots, k\}$ such that $g_1(u, i) = 0$ if u has less than i neighbors and $g_1(u, i) = v$ if v is the ith neighbor of u. That is, if $d_G(u)$ denotes the degree of u in G, then $\{g_1(u, i) : i \in [d_G(u)]\} = \{v : \{u, v\} \in E\}$.
   Indeed, here $k - 1$ serves as a (trivial) degree bound. (Recall that the bounded-degree graph model relied on an explicit degree bound, which was denoted d.)
2. An adjacency predicate $g_2 : [k] \times [k] \to \{0, 1\}$ such that $g_2(u, v) = 1$ if and only if $\{u, v\} \in E$.

Typically, adjacency queries are more useful when the graph is more dense, whereas incidence queries (a.k.a. neighbor queries) are more useful when the graph is more sparse (cf. [42]). Nevertheless, both types of queries are allowed in the current model, and at times both are useful (see, e.g., Algorithm 10.13).

10.1.1. Perspective: Comparison to the Two Previous Models

Recall that in the bounded-degree graph model we have implicitly assumed that the degree bound, denoted d, is of the same order of magnitude as the actual average degree (i.e., $d = O(|E|/k)$, or, equivalently, $|E| = \Omega(dk)$). This assumption is immaterial in case the parameter d is viewed as a constant, but the meaningfulness of the model for the case of a variable d relies on the assumption that the average degree is $\Omega(d)$ or so. When this assumption holds, the difference between the measure of relative distance used here (i.e., in the general graph model) and the measure used in the bounded-degree graph model is not significant.

Likewise, in the dense graph model we have implicitly assumed that the density of edges is a constant (i.e., $|E| = \Omega(k^2)$). Whenever this assumption holds, the difference between the measure of relative distance used here (i.e., in the general graph model) and the measure used in the dense graph model is not significant.

We also note that in each of the two previous models, when the corresponding implicit assumption holds, it was easy to approximate the number of edges in the graph and to sample an edge uniformly at random: In the bounded-degree graph model, if $|E| = \Omega(dk)$, then we can approximate $|E|$ (resp., select an edge at random) by uniformly selecting $(u, i) \in [k] \times [d]$ at random, and checking whether $g_1(u, i) \in [k]$ (resp., output $\{u, g_1(u, i)\}$ if and only if $g_1(u, i) \in [k]$). Hence, we obtain a $1 \pm \epsilon$ factor approximation by repeating this experiment for $O(1/\epsilon^2)$ times (resp., obtain a random edge after $O(1)$ trials).[1] Likewise, in the dense graph model, if $|E| = \Omega(k^2)$, then we can approximate $|E|$ (resp., select an edge at random) by uniformly selecting $(u, v) \in [k] \times [k]$ at random, and checking whether $g_2(u, v) = 1$ (resp., output $\{u, v\}$ if and only if $g(u, v) = 1$). Hence, we obtain a $1 \pm \epsilon$ factor approximation by repeating this experiment for $O(1/\epsilon^2)$ times (resp., obtain a random edge after $O(1)$ trials).[2]

10.1.2. The Actual Definition

For the sake of good order, we explicitly present the definition of testing graph properties in the general graph model.

Definition 10.1 (Testing graph properties in the general graph model): *A* tester *for a graph property Π is a probabilistic oracle machine that, on input parameters k and ϵ and access to functions answering incidence queries and adjacency queries regarding an k-vertex graph $G = ([k], E)$, outputs a binary verdict that satisfies the following two conditions.*

1. *If $G \in \Pi$, then the tester accepts with probability at least $2/3$.*
2. *If G is ϵ-far from Π, then the tester accepts with probability at most $1/3$, where G is ϵ-far from Π if for every k-vertex graph $G' = ([k], E') \in \Pi$ it holds that the symmetric difference between E and E' has cardinality that is greater than $\epsilon \cdot \max(|E|, |E'|)$.*

If the tester accepts every graph in Π with probability 1, then we say that it has one-sided error; *otherwise, we say that it has* two-sided error. *A tester is called* nonadaptive *if it determines all its queries based solely on its internal coin tosses (and the parameters k and ϵ); otherwise, it is called* adaptive.

---

[1] In both cases, the O-notation hides a factor of $dk/|E|$.
[2] In both cases, the O-notation hides a factor of $k^2/|E|$.

The query complexity of a tester is the total number of queries it makes to any graph $G = ([k], E)$, as a function of the graph's parameters (i.e., k and $|E|$) and the proximity parameter ϵ. We stress that we count both the incidence queries and the adjacency queries, and each of these queries is counted as one unit.

As stated earlier, the motivation for the model captured by Definition 10.1 is to allow the consideration of arbitrary graphs (which may be neither dense nor of bounded degree). In doing so, this model strengthens the relation between property testing and standard algorithmic studies. On the other hand, forsaking the paradigm of representing graphs as functions means that the connection to the rest of property testing is a bit weakened (or at least becomes more cumbersome).

On Extremely Sparse Graphs. Extremely sparse graphs, in which the number of edges is significantly smaller than the number of vertices, raise conceptual questions regarding the testing model captured by Definition 10.1. Conceptually, defining the relative distance between graphs as a fraction of the number of edges in these graphs represents the feeling that the number of edges in a graph represent its size. This is indeed the case in the typical cases in which the graph is not extremely sparse (i.e., the number of edges in the graph is at least of the same order of magnitude as the number of vertices). But in the pathological case of extremely sparse graphs, it seems that the number of vertices represents its size better. Hence, in general, it seems that $k + |E|$ represents the size of the graph $G = ([k], E)$ better than either $|E|$ or k. This leads to the following revision of the testing model (where the difference is at the very end of the definition).

Definition 10.2 (Testing graph properties in the general graph model, revised): *A tester in the revised model is defined as in Definition 10.1, except that the definition of distance to the graph property Π is modified so that the graph $G = ([k], E)$ is said to be ϵ-far from Π if for every k-vertex graph $G' = ([k], E') \in \Pi$ it holds that the symmetric difference between E and E' has cardinality that is greater than $\epsilon \cdot (k + \max(|E|, |E'|))$.*

Definitions 10.1 and 10.2 differ only in the definition of (relative) distance between graphs: In Definition 10.1 the symmetric difference is divided by $\max(|E|, |E'|)$, whereas in in Definition 10.2 the symmetric difference is divided by $k + \max(|E|, |E'|)$. This difference is insignificant whenever $|E| = \Omega(k)$; that is, for $|E| = \Omega(k)$, the definitions of (relative) distance underlying Definitions 10.1 and 10.2 coincide up to a constant factor, which we can ignore just as we ignored the difference between $|E| + |E'|$, $|E \cup E'|$, $\max(|E|, |E'|)$ and $(|E| + |E'|)/2$. Furthermore, the definitions collide (up to a constant factor) also in case the property contains only k-vertex graphs with $\Omega(k)$ edges (e.g., Connectivity).

We note that the two definitions do differ when applied to properties that contain the empty graph (or any other extremely sparse graphs). Consider, for example, the case of Bipartiteness. In this case, the k-vertex graph that consists of a single triangle and $k - 3$ isolated vertices is deemed 0.33-far from Bipartiteness by Definition 10.1, whereas Definition 10.2 views it as $1/k$-close to Bipartiteness. Hence, $\Omega(1)$-testing Bipartiteness under Definition 10.1 requires $\Omega(k)$ queries, merely due to the need to find a tiny portion of the graph that violates the property. But this need stands in contrast to the entire mindset of property testing that postulates that small parts of the object that violate the property can be ignored. The source of trouble is that Definition 10.1 may view such small portions as a large fraction of the object. We believe that the foregoing illustrates our opinion that Definition 10.1 does not account properly for the "size" of the tested object (when the tested object is an extremely sparse graph).

In light of the preceding, we believe that Definition 10.2 should be preferred over Definition 10.1. Hence, whenever there is a significant difference between these two definitions, we shall use Definition 10.2.

10.2. On Obtaining Testers for the Current Model

The general graph model is closer in spirit to the bounded-degree graph model than to the dense graph model, since the focus of the two former models is on sparse (or at least nondense) graphs. The main difference between the general graph model and the bounded-degree model is that the former deals with graphs in which *vertex degree may vary in an extreme manner*. An additional issue is that the dependence of the complexity on the average vertex degree is viewed as more important. (We shall elaborate on these two issues shortly.)

Since a tester in the general graph model must definitely work also in the bounded-degree graph model and since designing testers in the general graph model is typically more difficulty, it makes sense to try first to design a tester for the bounded-degree graph model. (One may object the foregoing assertion by claiming that the general graph model endows the tester with additional power (i.e., it allows adjacency queries), but this power is irrelevant in the case that the graph has bounded degree.)[3]

In light of the foregoing, designing testers for the general graph model may be viewed as adapting and/or extending testers designed for the bounded-degree graph model to the general graph model. Such an adaptation and/or extension faces the two aforementioned difficulties (or issues).

1. *The dependence of the original tester on the degree bound*: In the bounded-degree graph model, one tends to ignore the dependence of the complexity of testing on the degree bound, denoted d, which is often viewed as a constant. Note that this parameter has two opposite effects. On the one hand, when d increases, the relative distances decrease, and so testing may become easier. On the other hand, the complexity of some operations (e.g., scanning all neighbors of a given vertex) may grow with d. So the first challenge is figuring out the exact effect of d on the complexity of the original tester.

   For example, the tester for Bipartiteness, presented in [148], was originally analyzed assuming that the degree bound is a constant, which led to ignoring the dependence of its complexity on the degree bound. Fortunately, a closer look at the analysis, taken in [180], revealed that the complexity does not grow with the degree bound (since the two opposite effects cancel out).[4] Note that this is the case also with the tester for connectivity (see Section 9.2.3).

2. *The effect of drastically varying vertex degrees*: A more acute problem with the bounded-degree graph model is that it tends to blur the difference between the average degree of the graph and its maximal degree. But in the general graph model these two

---

[3] Formally, adjacency queries can be emulated by d incidence queries, when d is the maximum degree in the graph. Hence, when d is a constant, we gain very little by using adjacency queries.

[4] This can be seen in the special case of rapid-mixing, which was analyzed in Section 9.4.1.

quantities play different roles. The average degree is used to normalize the relative distance of the input graph to the property (since this distance is normalized by the input's average degree), whereas the query complexity may depend on the maximal degree. (In contrast, in the bounded-degree graph model, the relative distance is also normalized by the maximum degree.)

Hence, when these two quantities are significantly different, the aforementioned cancelling effect does not apply, and typically we cannot use the tester for the bounded-degree graph model as is. Instead, we should adapt the tester so that its operation is better tailored to the varying degrees of the vertices of the input graph. There are two ways of doing so.

(a) An explicit adaption: Changing the original tester, by possibly generalizing an idea that underlies the original design.

(b) A reduction: The original tester remains intact; however, it is not applied to the input graph but rather to a graph that is derived from it by a local reduction. Needless to say, in this case, the reduced graph will have a maximum degree that is of the same order of magnitude as its average degree.

We shall demonstrate both ways next.

Before turning to the actual demonstrations, let us comment that the second approach (i.e., using a reduction) *seems* to require estimating the average degree of the graph (as well as selecting edges uniformly at random in the input graph). But as will be shown in Section 10.3.1, estimating the average degree of a k-vertex graph requires query complexity $\Omega(\sqrt{k})$, at least in case that it has $O(k)$ edges, and so this route is to be avoided when seeking lower complexity.

Teaching Note: In Sections 10.2.1 and 10.2.2 we demonstrate the two routes outlined in Items 2 and 2, respectively, while referring to the specific testers for Connectivity and Bipartiteness. Since our focus is on demonstrating the general principles, we do not provide detailed analyses of the two resulting testers, but rather confine ourselves to overviews.

10.2.1. An Explicit Adaptation: The Case of Connectivity

The tester for Connectivity in the bounded-degree graph model, presented in Section 9.2.3, can be easily adapted to the current context. We first recall that *if a graph has m connected components, then it can be made connected by adding $m - 1$ edges.* In our context, this means that the k-vertex graph is m/k-close to being connected; specifically, if $G = ([k], E)$ has m connected components, then it is ϵ-close to being connected for $\epsilon = \frac{m-1}{|E|+m-1} \leq \frac{m-1}{k-1} \leq \frac{m}{k}$ (since $|E| + m - 1 \geq k - 1$ and $k \geq m$).[5]

Recall that the tester for Connectivity (in the bounded-degree graph model), presented in the proof of Theorem 9.8, consisted of conducting truncated BFSes that are suspended once a specified number of vertices, denoted s, is encountered. In the context of the bounded-degree graph model, the complexity of such a search was $d \cdot s$, where d was the degree bound. But in the current setting, there is no degree bound; still, the

---

[5] Recall that the bound used in Section 9.2.3 was $\frac{2m-1}{dk/2}$, where d was the degree bound (and the factor of 2 was due to the need to preserve the degree bound).

complexity of the search is smaller than s^2, since the subgraph induced by these s vertices has at most $\binom{s}{2}$ edges. Hence, the complexity of the tester is $\widetilde{O}(1/\epsilon^2)$ rather than $\widetilde{O}(1/\epsilon)$.

A minor improvement over the foregoing upper bound can be obtained by a different setting of the parameters in Levin's economical work investment strategy. Specifically, for $i = 0, 1, \ldots, \ell \stackrel{\text{def}}{=} \log(1/\epsilon)$, we select at random $O(i^2 \cdot 2^i)$ start vertices, and conduct a truncated BFS from each of them such that the search is suspended once $O(2^{-i}/\epsilon)$ vertices are encountered. Using an analysis as in Section 8.2.4, we obtain:

Theorem 10.3 (Testing connectivity (in the general graph model)):[6] *Connectivity has a (one-sided error) tester of time (and query) complexity $O(1/\epsilon^2)$.*

10.2.2. Using a Reduction: The Case of Bipartiteness

Our aim here is to present an extension of the testing result for Bipartiteness from the bounded-degree graph model to the general graph model.

Theorem 10.4 (Testing Bipartiteness (in the general graph model)):[7] *Bipartiteness has a (one-sided error) tester of time (and query) complexity* $\text{poly}(1/\epsilon) \cdot \widetilde{O}(\sqrt{k})$.

This result will be established by a *reduction from testing in the general graph model to testing in the bounded-degree graph model*. That is, we shall transform the input graph, which may have vertices of significantly varying degrees, into a graph that fits the bounded-degree graph model, and apply the original tester on the resulting graph. But first, we observe that the performance of the original tester (for Bipartiteness in the bounded-degree graph model) does not deteriorate when the degree bound d increases. Furthermore, its analysis continues to hold also if the input graph is not simple (i.e., has parallel edges). The reader can easily verify both claims for the special case of rapid-mixing, presented in Section 9.4.1. Hence, we focus on handling the case that the degree in the input graph $G = ([k], E)$ vary significantly; that is, the average degree $\overline{d} \stackrel{\text{def}}{=} 2|E|/k$ may be much smaller than the maximal degree $d_{\max} \stackrel{\text{def}}{=} \max_{v \in [k]}\{d_G(v)\}$, where $d_G(v) \stackrel{\text{def}}{=} |\{u : \{u, v\} \in E\}|$. For sake of simplicity, we assume that $\overline{d} \geq 1$ is an integer (which is definitely the case if G contains no isolated vertices).

We obtain a tester for Bipartiteness in the general graph model by invoking the original tester on an imaginary graph that is obtained by replacing vertices of high degree (in the input graph $G = ([k], E)$) with adequate *gadgets*, and distributing the edges incident at the original high-degree vertices among the vertices of these gadgets. Specifically, a vertex v having degree $d_G(v)$ is replaced by a $O(\lceil d_G(v)/\overline{d} \rceil)$-vertex graph G_v of maximal degree $\overline{d}$, while connecting the original neighbors of v to vertices of the gadget G_v such that each vertex of the gadget has at most $\overline{d}$ *external edges* (which lead to other gadgets, which replace the neighbors of v).[8]

---

[6] This result holds under both testing models presented in Section 10.1 (cf. Definitions 10.1 and 10.2).

[7] We stress that this result refers to the testing model captured by Definition 10.2.

[8] Indeed, it unecessary to apply this replacement to vertices of degree at most $\overline{d}$, but it is simpler to apply it also to these vertices. In this case (i.e., when $d_G(v) \leq \overline{d}$), the graph G_v consists of a single pair of vertices that are connected by $\overline{d}$ parallel edges, which means that v remains connected to its original neighbors, but also gets connected to a new auxiliary neighbor.

Needless to say, this intended replacement of vertices by gadgets should preserve the distance of the original graph from being bipartite (up to a constant factor). That is, if G is bipartite, then the resulting graph G' should be bipartite, and if G is ϵ-far from being bipartite, then G' should be $\Omega(\epsilon)$-far from being bipartite. In such a case, we obtain a (local) reduction of testing Bipartiteness in the general graph model to testing Bipartiteness in the bounded-degree graph model.

The choice of adequate gadgets is, of course, crucial. For starters, these gadgets should be bipartite graphs, since otherwise bipartiteness is not preserved by the replacement. Furthermore, for connections to other gadgets, we should use vertices of only one side of the bipartite graph, called its external side. However, preserving the distance to Bipartiteness requires more than that (i.e., more than preserving the distance in case it is zero). We want it to be the case that if the original graph G is far from being bipartite, then so is the resulting graph G'; equivalently, if G' is close to being bipartite, then so is G. This will be the case if for every 2-partition of G' that has few violating edges (i.e., edges with both endpoints on the same side), the gadgets "force" placing all the external vertices of each gadget on the same side of the 2-partition. In such a case, the 2-partition of G' (with few violating edges) induces a 2-partition of G with a few violating edges.

(The reader may observe that the foregoing feature is satisfied by random $\bar{d}$-regular bipartite graphs (see Exercise 10.1), and may assume at this point that this is what we use, although we shall actually use $\bar{d}$-regular bipartite graphs that are expanders in a sense to be defined in the sequel.)

The actual transformation (i.e., the gadgets). In general, a vertex v having degree $d_G(v)$ is replaced by a $\bar{d}$-regular bipartite graph G_v with $t_v = \lceil d_G(v)/\bar{d} \rceil$ vertices on each side, while connecting the original neighbors of v (or rather the gadgets that replace them) to vertices on the external side of the gadget G_v. That is, at most $\bar{d}$ edges that are incident at v are connected to each vertex on the external side of the bipartite gadget G_v, whereas the vertices on the "internal" side of G_v are connected only to the "external" vertices of G_v (see Figure 10.1).[9]

Hence, each vertex in the resulting graph, denoted G', has degree between $\bar{d}$ and $2\bar{d}$. Note that the number of vertices in G' is

$$\sum_{v \in [k]} 2 \cdot \lceil d_G(v)/\bar{d} \rceil < 2 \cdot \sum_{v \in [k]} ((d_G(v)/\bar{d}) + 1) = 2k + 2k. \tag{10.1}$$

Recall that in such a case (i.e., when the average degree and the maximal degree are of the same order of magnitude), the definition of relative distance in the general graph model fits the definition of relative distance in the bounded-degree graph model (up to a constant factor). We stress that the bipartite gadget graphs (i.e., the G_v's) are not necessarily simple graphs (i.e., they may have parallel edges),[10] and consequently the graph G' is not necessarily a simple graph.

Having described the transformation of G into G', we need to address two key questions: Does this transformation preserve the distance from Bipartiteness? and is this transformation local? In other words, we need to address the conditions of the definition of a local reduction, as defined in Section 7.4 and adapted in Section 9.4.2.

---

[9] Denoting the bipartite graph by $G_v = ((X_v, I_v), E_v)$ such that $|X_v| = |I_v| = t_v$ and $E_v \subseteq X_v \times I_v$, we connect the neighbors of v to vertices in X_v, where X stands for external and I for internal. Indeed, the vertices in I_v are connected only to vertices in X_v.

[10] This will definitely happen when $\lceil d_G(v)/\bar{d} \rceil < \bar{d}$.

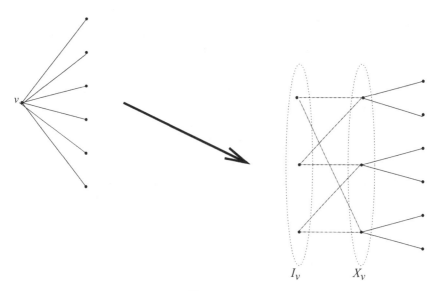

Figure 10.1: The gadget G_v for the case of $\overline{d} = 2$ and $t_v = 3$. The vertex v is replaced by a bipartite graph with sides X_v and I_v, where X stands for external and I for internal.

Preservation of the Distance from `Bipartiteness`. Starting with the first question, we first note that if G is bipartite, then so is the reduced graph G'. In order to guarantee that if G is ϵ-far from bipartite, then G' is $\Omega(\epsilon)$-far from bipartite, we use $\overline{d}$-regular bipartite gadgets that have an expansion feature that is postulated below (in Definition 10.4.1). To motivate this definition, suppose that G is far from being bipartite, and consider an arbitrary 2-partition of G'. In such a case, if the vertices of each gadget are 2-partitioned in the natural way (i.e., all external vertices of each gadget are assigned the same side), then the 2-partition of G' induces a 2-partition of G, which implies that the *fraction* of edges in G' with both endpoints on the same side is large (since the edges that connect different gadgets constitute a constant fraction of the edges in G').[11] We stress that, in this case, the *number* of violating edges with respect to a natural 2-partition of G' equals the *number* of violating edges in the corresponding 2-partition of G, where an edge is called violating with respect to a 2-partition if its two endpoints are assigned to the same side.

The problem is that a general 2-partition of G' may split some of the external vertices of some gadgets, and in this case it does not yield a 2-partition of G. The expansion feature (defined next) penalizes such a 2-partition in a way that makes it violate at least a constant fraction of the number of edges that are violated by the best natural 2-partition of G'. This happens because such a 2-partition has many violating edges that are internal to the gadgets. In particular, placing $t' \le t/2$ out of the t external vertices of a gadget on the "wrong" side of a 2-partition may allow to avoid $t'\overline{d}$ violating edges that connect this gadget to other gadgets, but it causes $\Omega(t'\overline{d})$ violations inside the gadget. This feature is exactly what the following definition provides.

Definition 10.4.1 (Bipartite expanders): *A (not necessarily simple) d-regular bipartite graph with vertex partition (X, Y) is c-edge expanding if for every $S \subset X$*

---

[11] Recall that the number of edges that connect different gadgets is $|E| = \overline{d}k/2$, whereas the number of edges in G' is at most $2\overline{d} \cdot 4k/2$.

of size at most $|X|/2$ it holds that

$$\sum_{y \in Y} \min(|\Gamma(y) \cap S|, |\Gamma(y) \setminus S|) \geq c \cdot d \cdot |S|,$$

where $\Gamma(y) \subseteq X$ denotes the multiset of neighbors of y. For $c > 0$, we say that a family of (not necessarily simple) regular bipartite graphs $\{B_{d,t} : d, t \in \mathbb{N}\}$ is c-edge expanding if, for all sufficiently large $d, t \in \mathbb{N}$, the bipartite graph $B_{d,t}$ is d-regular, contains t vertices on each side, and is c-edge expanding.

The definition mandates that typical vertices in Y have many neighbors in both S and $X \setminus S$, where "many" is related to the density of S in X; that is, Definition 10.4.1 asserts that the average "edge mixture" (the ratio $|\Gamma(y) \cap S|/|\Gamma(y)|$ for a random $y \in Y$) is related to $|S|/|X|$. This is a slightly nonstandard definition of expansion in that it refers to bipartite graphs and to edge expansion, but it follows from the standard definition of expander graphs.[12] Using c-edge expanding $\overline{d}$-regular bipartite graphs as gadgets in the transformation of G into G', we observe that if G is ϵ-far from bipartite, then G' is $(c \cdot \epsilon/8)$-far from bipartite (see Exercise 10.3).

On the Locality of the Transformation. We now turn to the question of the locality of the transformation of G into G'. Intuitively, the transformation, which is based on local gadgets, seems very local. However, as in Section 9.4.2, the transformation is not local enough to fit the definition presented in Section 7.4. Specifically, the set of vertices of G' is not easily put in correspondence with a set of the form $[n']$. Furthermore, unlike in Section 9.4.2, it is not clear how to emulate incidence queries to G' by using incidence queries to G: The problem is that an incidence query (v, i) to G is answered with a vertex u that is the ith neighbor of v, but the answer does not reveal an index j such that v is the jth neighbor of u. Consequently, it is not clear to which of the external vertices of the gadget that replace u we should connect the (corresponding external vertex of the) gadget of v. Nevertheless, as will be outlined below, the transformation does fit a relaxed notion of a local reduction.

We first note that vertices in G' can be represented by tuples of the form $\langle v, i, \sigma \rangle$ such that $v \in [k]$, $i \in [t_v]$ and $\sigma \in \{0, 1\}$ (where $\sigma = 1$ corresponds to an external vertex associated with v and $\sigma = 0$ corresponds to an internal vertex). Note, however, that determining $t_v = \lceil d_G(v)/\overline{d} \rceil$ requires determining $\overline{d}$; actually, using a reasonable approximation of $\overline{d}$ rather than its exact value does suffice for the reduction we describe here. Now, assuming we know $\overline{d}$ (or an approximation of it), given $\langle v, i, \sigma \rangle$ and $j \in [2\overline{d}]$, we can tell whether $\langle v, i, \sigma \rangle$ is a vertex of G' and in the case of an internal vertex (i.e., $\sigma = 0$) we can also determine who is its jth neighbor. In the case of an external vertex $\langle v, i, 1 \rangle$, its neighbors in the same gadget are determined as for internal vertices, whereas its neighbors in other gadgets are determined on-the-fly as follows. (Indeed, the issue is handling queries that correspond to inter-gadget edges of G', which correspond to edges of G.)

---

[12] The standard definition refers to families of nonbipartite (regular) graphs of constant degree and to vertex expansion. It asserts that, for some constants $d \in \mathbb{N}$ and $c > 1$, and for each $n \in \mathbb{N}$, the family contain a d-regular n-vertex graph G_n such that any set S of at most $n/2$ vertices in G_n has at least $c \cdot |S|$ neighbors. A bipartite graph B_t as in Definition 10.4.1 is obtained by considering a "double cover" of G_t (i.e., replacing each vertex v in G_t by two vertices, denoted v' and v'', and connecting v' and w'' if and only if $\{v, w\}$ is an edge in G_t). Note that since d is a constant, the edge expansion of B_t follows from its vertex expansion feature (see Exercise 10.2, which shows that B_t is $((c-1)/d)$-edge expanding). To obtain a bipartite graph of larger (and possibly nonconstant) degree D, one can just duplicate each edge for D/d times.

Throughout our emulation of G', we maintain the list of inter-gadget edges (equiv., edges of G) seen so far. For each such edge, we maintain the pair of ports that it uses, where the jth edge incident at $\langle v, i, 1 \rangle$ is said to use the $(i, j)^{th}$ port of v. We also maintain the list of all queries we made to G along with the answers provided for these queries. When a new query to G' is made, we first check whether it corresponds to an edge that is already on the list (possibly due to a query made at its other endpoint). If the edge is on the list, then it is answered accordingly, and otherwise we proceed as follows.

On query $(\langle v, i, 1 \rangle, j)$, which refers to a possible inter-gadget edge (i.e., incident at the $(i, j)^{th}$ port of v), we first determine the degree of v in G, and answer with 0 if $(i - 1) \cdot \overline{d} + j > d_G(v)$. Otherwise, we select a *new random neighbor of v in G*, denoted u, and select a *random vacant port of u*, denoted (i', j'). The query is answered with $\langle u, i', 1 \rangle$, and the edge $\{u, v\}$ is placed on the list of assigned edges along with the port indices (i, j) and (i', j'), which means that the (possible future) query $(\langle u, i', 1 \rangle, j')$ will be answered with $\langle v, i, 1 \rangle$. A new random neighbor of v (in G) is selected by selecting uniformly an index r in $[d_G(v)] \setminus S_v$ and querying (the incidence function of) G at (v, r), where S_v is the set of indices that correspond to neighbors of v that were selected before. Note that, when selecting a neighbor of v, we may select u although v was already selected as a neighbor of u (i.e., the index of v is in S_u although the index of u is not in S_v), which means that the edge $\{u, v\}$ is on the list of assigned edges. In this case, we update S_v and try again.[13]

Lastly, selecting a vertex in G' uniformly at random reduces to selecting at random $v \in [k]$ with probability that is proportional to t_v. Using a few sampling tricks,[14] the latter task is reducible to selecting $v \in [k]$ with probability that is proportional to $d_G(v)$, which is equivalent to uniformly selecting an edge of the graph G (see Exercise 10.4).

Hence, emulating the execution of the Bipartiteness tester (presented in Section 9.4.1) on G' amounts to approximating $\overline{d}$ and sampling $O(1/\epsilon)$ edges of G with probability that is sufficiently close to the uniform distribution. These tasks will be addressed in the next section. (Actually, we can avoid the task of approximating $\overline{d}$ by just trying all powers of two, and relying on the fact that the tester has one-sided error.)[15]

10.3. Estimating the Average Degree and Selecting Random Edges

We focus on estimating the average degree (equiv., the number of edges) in a graph, while noting that similar considerations apply to selecting an edge uniformly at random (equiv., selecting a vertex with probability proportional to its degree),[16] and detailing the required adaptations whenever they are not straightforward (i.e., in Section 10.3.2). To justify the relatively high complexity of these tasks, we first present lower bounds (see

---

[13] Hence, each edge $\{u, v\}$ may cause at most one failure, which involves one useless query to G, which can be charged to the useful query made before (in the opposite direction). Alternatively, we may update both S_u and S_v when adding the edge $\{u, v\}$ to the list of assigned edges.

[14] Specifically, with probability 1/2 select $v \in [k]$ uniformly at random, and otherwise we select v with probability proportional to $d_G(v)$. Hence, v is selected with probability $\frac{1}{2} \cdot \frac{1}{k} + \frac{1}{2} \cdot \frac{d_G(v)}{k \cdot \overline{d}} = \frac{t'_v}{2k}$, where $t'_v = \frac{d_G(v)}{\overline{d}} + 1 > t_v$. Finally, we output v with probability t_v/t'_v, and repeat the selection process otherwise.

[15] The point is that using a very bad approximation of $\overline{d}$ will *not* lead the tester to reject a bipartite graph (but may only affect the number of vertices in G' (e.g., increasing the number in case of underestimation)). Hence, the desired tester is obtained by invoking the original tester with all possible approximate values of $\overline{d}$ and accepting if and only if all invocations accepted. Specifically, we may invoke the original tester $\log k$ times such that in the ith invocation we use 2^i as an approximation of $\overline{d}$.

[16] See Exercise 10.4.

Section 10.3.1). Specifically, we show that these tasks require $\Omega(\sqrt{k})$ queries, and we shall indeed meet these lower bound in the algorithms that are presented in Section 10.3.2. We stress that we confine ourselves to simple graphs, because for graph with parallel edges no meaningful approximation can be obtained in sublinear (in k) complexity (see Exercise 10.5).

10.3.1. Lower Bounds

For perspective, we first consider the analogous problem for functions; that is, given oracle access to a function $f : [k] \rightarrow \{0, 1, \ldots, k-1\}$, we wish to obtain an approximation to $\sum_{i \in [k]} f(i)$. In this case, any constant factor approximation requires $\Omega(k)$ queries to f. To see this, consider the set of functions $\{f_i : i \in [k]\}$ such that $f_i(j) = k-1$ if $j = i$ and $f_i(j) = 0$ otherwise (i.e., $j \in [k] \setminus \{i\}$). Then, an algorithm that makes $o(k)$ queries cannot distinguish a random f_i from the all-zero function.[17]

Estimating the Average Degree via Degree Queries. In contrast to the situation with generic functions, as will be shown in Section 10.3.2, when $f : [k] \rightarrow \{0, 1, \ldots, k-1\}$ describes the vertex degrees of a simple k-vertex graph, for any $c > 2$, a factor c approximation can be obtained in time $O(\sqrt{k})$. This is obtained by an algorithm that uses only degree queries, and we next observe that such an algorithm cannot obtain a better approximation factor.

> **Proposition 10.5** (Limitations on approximating the average degree with degree queries): *Suppose that, algorithm A approximating the average degree of a simple graph $G = ([k], E)$ by making only degree queries such that*
>
> $$\mathbf{Pr}\left[\frac{|E|}{k} \leq A^G(k) \leq \frac{2|E|}{k} \right] \geq 2/3. \tag{10.2}$$
>
> *Then, A makes $\Omega(k)$ queries, even if it is guaranteed that $|E| = \Theta(k)$.*

Indeed, Eq. (10.2) refers to an approximation factor of $\frac{2|E|/k}{|E|/k} = 2$.

Proof Sketch: We show that an algorithm that makes $o(k)$ degree queries cannot distinguish the following two distributions.

1. The uniform distribution on the set of $(k-1)$-stars; that is, k-vertex graphs consisting of $k-1$ edges that are all incident at a single vertex (i.e., the graphs $G_i = ([k], \{\{i, j\} : j \in [k] \setminus \{i\}\})$, where $i \in [k]$).
2. The uniform distribution on the set of k-vertex graphs consisting of a matching of size $(k-2)/2$ and two isolated vertices; that is, k-vertex graphs containing $k-2$ vertices of degree 1 and four vertices of degree 0.

---

[17] In light of the discussion at the end of Section 10.1, one may ask what happens if we confine ourselves to functions of average value at least 1. In this case, one can trivially obtain a factor $k-1$ approximation, but, for any $t < k/2$, obtaining a factor t approximation requires $\Omega(k/t)$ queries. This can be shown by considering, for every t-subset $I \subset [k]$, the function $f_I(j) = k-1$ if $j \in I$ and $f_I(j) = 1$ otherwise. Note that each f_I has average value $t + 1 - (2t/k) > t$, but an algorithm that makes $o(k/t)$ queries cannot distinguish a random function f_I from the all-one function.

When using only degree queries, these two distributions can be distinguished only by querying one of the vertices that have degree different from 1, whereas there is only one such vertex in the first distribution and only four such vertices in the second distribution. But, when given access to a $(k-1)$-star, algorithm A is required to output a value that is at least $(k-1)/k$, whereas when given access to a matching of size $(k-2)/2$ it is required to output a value that is at most $(k-2)/k$. $\blacksquare$

Estimating the Average Degree via Incidence and Adjacency Queries. The complexity of approximating the average degree in a graph is also lower-bounded when we consider algorithms that also use incidence and adjacency queries. But here the complexity bound is $\Omega(\sqrt{k})$ (rather than $\Omega(k)$, as in the case of Proposition 10.5, where only degree queries were allowed but the approximation factor was required to be 2).

Proposition 10.6 (On the complexity of approximating the average degree): *Any constant-factor approximation algorithm for the average degree of a simple graph $G = ([k], E)$ must make $\Omega(\sqrt{k})$ queries, even when allowed degree, incidence, and adjacency queries, and even if it is guaranteed that $|E| = \Theta(k)$.*

Proof Sketch: For any constant $\gamma > 0$, we show that an algorithm that makes $o(\sqrt{k})$ queries cannot distinguish the following two distributions.

1. The uniform distribution on k-vertex graphs consisting of a clique of size $k' = \sqrt{\gamma k}$ and an isolated matching of size $(k - k')/2$.
2. The uniform distribution on a k-vertex graphs consisting of a single perfect matching.

These two distributions can be distinguished only by making a query that refers to a vertex that belongs to the k'-clique, since any other query is answered in the same manner by both distributions (e.g., degree queries are answered with 1).[18] But, the average degree of vertices in the first distribution is $\frac{k-k'}{k} \cdot 1 + \frac{k'}{k} \cdot (k'-1) \approx 1 + \gamma$, whereas the average degree of vertices in the second distribution is 1. $\blacksquare$

10.3.2. Algorithms

We show that, for every constant $\alpha > 1$, a 2α-factor approximation of the average degree can be obtained by using $\tilde{O}(\sqrt{k})$ degree queries, and that a α-factor approximations can be obtained by using $\tilde{O}(\sqrt{k})$ incidence queries. These results refer to the case that the average degree is $\Omega(1)$, and a more general statement holds: Denoting the average degree by $\overline{d}$, one can obtain an arbitrary good constant factor approximation of $\overline{d}$ in *expected* time $\tilde{O}(\sqrt{k/\overline{d}})$, which is the best possible (see Exercise 10.6, which extends Proposition 10.6). That is, when $\overline{d} \gg 1$ we actually obtain algorithms of complexity $o(\sqrt{k})$, but when $\overline{d} \ll 1$ the complexity may be $\omega(\sqrt{k})$.

---

[18] When referring to the second distribution, it is instructive to designate k' vertices as "corresponding to the k'-clique" (although there is no clique in this case). Incidence queries involving a vertex not in the k'-clique are answered with the matched neighbor if the query refers to the first neighbor and by zero otherwise. Adjacency queries regarding a pair of vertices not in the clique are answered by 1 if and only if these vertices are matched.

> **Teaching Note:** Actually, we shall show two algorithmic approaches that obtain the stated result. The first approach (presented in Section 10.3.2.1) seems more intuitive, but the second approach (presented in Section 10.3.2.2) seems more insightful. We believe that both approaches have educational benefits.

10.3.2.1. Bucketing Vertices According to Their Degree

The basic idea is to partition the vertices to "buckets" according to their approximate degree, and distinguish large buckets from small buckets, where "large" means having size at least $\sqrt{k}$. The key observation is that the size of large buckets can be approximated at reasonable cost, yielding an approximation to the number of edges that are incident at vertices that belong to large buckets, whereas there are few edges with *both* endpoints in a small bucket. Hence, *giving up on small buckets means that there are only relatively few edges that are not counted at all*. In addition, edges with a single endpoint in a small bucket are counted once, whereas edges with no endpoint in a small bucket are counted twice. This discrepancy is the reason that when using only degree queries we obtain an approximation factor of 2 (or rather arbitrary close to 2).

Note that we can determine to which bucket a vertex belongs (by determining its degree), and estimate the size of buckets by sampling enough vertices (where for large buckets we obtain a good approximation of their size and for small buckets we only obtain an indication that they are small). Hence, by using $\widetilde{O}(\sqrt{k})$ degree queries, we obtain good estimates of the sizes of large buckets, which yields good estimates the number of edges that are incident at large buckets, which in turn provides a 2-factor approximation to the total number of edges. (More generally, if we are willing to tolerate an additive error term of $\binom{s}{2}$, then we can let s be the threshold below which a bucket is considered small, and make only $O(k/s)$ degree queries.)

To get a better approximation factor, we also use incidence queries. Specifically, we estimate, for each large bucket, the fraction of edges that have one endpoint in this bucket and the other endpoint in a small bucket. This estimation is obtained by picking random vertices in the bucket, selecting a random neighbor of each of them (by using incidence queries), and determining whether this vertex reside in a small bucket.

The resulting algorithm is described next, while referring to a size parameter, denoted s (which governs the definition of a "small bucket"),[19] and to an approximation parameter, denoted $\beta > 1$. The algorithm outputs approximations to the foregoing quantities (i.e., to the sizes of buckets and to the number of edges going from each large bucket to small buckets), which yield an approximation to the average degree of the input graph. Specifically, fixing an input graph $G = ([k], E)$, and letting $d_G(v)$ denote the degree of vertex v in G, for $i = 0, 1, \ldots, \ell \stackrel{\text{def}}{=} \log_\beta k$ (so $\ell = O((\beta - 1)^{-1} \log k)$), the ith bucket is defined as $B_i = \{v \in [k] : \beta^{i-1} \leq d_G(v) < \beta^i\}$. Note that

$$\sum_{i=0}^{\ell} |B_i| \cdot \beta^{i-1} \leq \sum_{v \in [k]} d_G(v) < \sum_{i=0}^{\ell} |B_i| \cdot \beta^i. \tag{10.3}$$

Hence, a β-factor approximations to the sizes of *all* the buckets yield a β^2-factor approximation to the average degree of G. Recall, however, that we shall obtain such good approximations only for large buckets (i.e., buckets of size at least s).

---

[19] The reader may think of $s = \sqrt{k}$, but we shall consider other settings too.

Algorithm 10.7 (A basic algorithmic scheme for estimating the average degree): *On input a graph $G = ([k], E)$, parameters $\beta > 1$ and $s \in \mathbb{N}$, and while referring to buckets B_i's such that $B_i = \{v \in [k] : \beta^{i-1} \le d_G(v) < \beta^i\}$, proceed as follows.*

1. Estimate the sizes of the various buckets: *Take a sample of $m = \widetilde{O}(k)/s$ vertices, determine the degree of each of them, and let ρ_i denote the fraction of sampled vertices that reside in B_i. If $\rho_i < s/k$, then call B_i small; otherwise, estimate $|B_i|$ as $\rho_i k$.*

2. Estimate the number of edges to small buckets: *For each vertex v selected in Step 1, select uniformly at random a neighbor u of v, by selecting uniformly $j \in [d_G(v)]$ and taking the jth neighbor of v. Let $\rho_i' \le \rho_i$ denote the fraction of sampled vertices v that reside in B_i such that their neighbor u resides in a small bucket. That is, denoting by $v_1, \ldots, v_m$ the sample of vertices selected in Step 1 and by $u_1, \ldots, u_m$ their random neighbors as selected in the current step, we let ρ_i' denote the fraction of $j \in [m]$ such that $v_j \in B_i$ and $u_j \in \cup_{i':\rho_{i'}<s/k}B_{i'}$.*

Output $\rho_0, \ldots, \rho_\ell$ as well as $\rho_0', \ldots, \rho_\ell'$.

Note that, with probability at least 0.9, for every i it holds that B_i is declared small only if $|B_i| < (1 + o(1)) \cdot s$, and otherwise $\rho_i k \in (1 \pm o(1)) \cdot |B_i|$. Recall that the contribution of an edge to $\sum_{i:\rho_i \ge s/k} \sum_{v \in B_i} d_G(v)$ depends on the number of endpoints it has in large buckets (i.e., buckets deemed not small): If both endpoints are in large buckets the edge contributes two units, if a single endpoint is in a large bucket the edge contributes one unit, and otherwise (i.e., no endpoint is in a large bucket) the edge contributes nothing. Hence, in this case (i.e., with high probability), we have

$$\sum_{i:\rho_i \ge s/k} \beta^{i-1} \cdot (1 - o(1)) \cdot \rho_i k \le \sum_{v \in [k]} d_G(v) < (1 + o(1)) \cdot (\ell s)^2$$

$$+ 2 \cdot \sum_{i:\rho_i \ge s/k} \beta^i \cdot (1 + o(1)) \cdot \rho_i k, \quad (10.4)$$

where $2 \cdot \binom{(1+o(1))\ell s}{2} < (1 + o(1)) \cdot (\ell s)^2$ is an upper bound on the contribution to $\sum_{v \in [k]} d_G(v)$ of edges with both endpoints in small buckets, whereas each other edge contribute either one or two units to $\sum_{i:\rho_i \ge s/k} \sum_{v \in B_i} d_G(v)$ (and so the lower bound uses one unit and the upper bound uses two).[20] Hence, if $(\ell s)^2 = o(1) \cdot \sum_{v \in [k]} d_G(v)$, then Eq. (10.4) yields a $2 \cdot (\beta + o(1))$-factor approximation to the average degree of G. Note that this approximation is obtained based on Step 1 only, which uses only degree queries. But using the quantities estimated in Step 2, we can do better.

Specifically, recall that $\beta^{i-1} \cdot (1 - o(1)) \cdot \rho_i k$ was used in Eq. (10.4) as a lower bound on the contribution of vertices in (a large) B_i to $\sum_{v \in [k]} d_G(v)$ whereas $2 \cdot \beta^i \cdot (1 + o(1)) \cdot \rho_i k$ was used as an upper bound. But assuming that ρ_i'/ρ_i

---

[20] Furthermore, for every i such that $\rho_i \ge s/k$, we use

$$\beta^{i-1} \cdot (1 - o(1)) \cdot \rho_i k \le \sum_{v \in B_i} d_G(v) < \beta^i \cdot (1 + o(1)) \cdot \rho_i k,$$

which relies on $\rho_i k \in (1 \pm o(1)) \cdot |B_i|$.

estimates the average over $v \in B_i$ of the fraction of neighbors of v that reside in small buckets, we get much tighter bounds: The contribution of vertices in a large B_i to $\sum_{v \in [k]} d_G(v)$ is at least $(1 - o(1)) \cdot (\rho_i + \rho_i') \cdot \beta^{i-1}k$ and at most $(1 + o(1)) \cdot (\rho_i + \rho_i') \cdot \beta^i k$, since ρ_i' represents the "lost" contribution of edges with one endpoint in B_i and one endpoint in a small bucket. This argument is captured in the following claim and further detailed in its proof.

Claim 10.8 (The core of the analysis of Algorithm 10.7): *Suppose that for every i it holds that if $\rho_i < s/k$, then $|B_i| < (1 + o(1)) \cdot s$, and otherwise $\rho_i k \in (1 \pm o(1)) \cdot |B_i|$. Further suppose that if $\rho_i \geq s/k$, then*

$$\rho_i' = (1 \pm o(1)) \cdot \frac{1}{k} \cdot \sum_{v \in B_i} \frac{d_G'(v)}{d_G(v)},$$

where $d_G'(v)$ denotes the number of neighbors of v in $S = \cup_{i':\rho_{i'} <s/k} B_{i'}$. Then,

$$(1 - o(1)) \cdot \sum_{i:\rho_i \geq s/k} (\rho_i + \rho_i') \cdot \beta^{i-1}k < \sum_{v \in [k]} d_G(v) < (1 + o(1)) \cdot (\ell s)^2$$

$$+ (1 + o(1)) \cdot \sum_{i:\rho_i \geq s/k} (\rho_i + \rho_i') \cdot \beta^i k.$$

Proof: The claim reduces to proving that

$$\sum_{v \in [k]} d_G(v) = 2 \cdot |E(S, S)| + \sum_{i:\rho_i \geq s/k} \sum_{v \in B_i} (d_G(v) + d_G'(v)), \tag{10.5}$$

where $E(S, S)$ denotes the set of edges with both endpoints in S. To prove Eq. (10.5), we consider the contribution of each edge $\{v, u\}$ to each of its sides. First note that each edge contributes exactly two units to the l.h.s. of Eq. (10.5). Now, we consider its contribution to the r.h.s. of Eq. (10.5), by distinguishing three cases.

1. If both endpoints of $\{u, v\}$ are in S, then $\{u, v\}$ contributes two units to $2 \cdot |E(S, S)|$ and nothing to the sum.
2. If exactly one endpoint of $\{u, v\}$ is in S, then $\{u, v\}$ contributes nothing to $2 \cdot |E(S, S)|$ and contributes two units to the sum, since it contributes one unit to $d_G(v)$ and one unit to $d_G'(v)$, where we assume (w.l.o.g.) that $u \in S$.
3. If no endpoint of $\{u, v\}$ is in S, then $\{u, v\}$ contributes nothing to $2 \cdot |E(S, S)|$ and contributes two units to the sum, since it contributes one unit to $d_G(v)$ and one unit to $d_G(u)$, while contributing nothing to $d_G'(v) + d_G'(u)$.

Hence, in all cases, the edge $\{u, v\}$ contributes two units to the r.h.s. of Eq. (10.5). In fact, the argument can be summarized by writing

$$\sum_{v \in [k]} d_G(v) = 2 \cdot |E(S, S)| + \sum_{v \in [k] \setminus S} d_G(v) + \sum_{v \in [k] \setminus S} d_G'(v), \tag{10.6}$$

but Eq. (10.5) is more instructive toward finishing the proof. Indeed, the claim follows since $2 \cdot |E(S, S)| < |S|^2$, whereas for $i \in [k]$ such that $\rho_i \geq s/k$ it holds that $\sum_{v \in B_i} d_G(v) \approx |B_i| \cdot \beta^i \approx \rho_i k \cdot \beta^i$ and $\sum_{v \in B_i} d_G'(v) \approx \rho_i' k \cdot \beta^i$ (since $d_G(v) \approx \beta^i$ for every $v \in B_i$). ∎

Digest. The idea underlying Algorithm 10.7 is that all vertices in the same bucket have approximately the same contribution to $\sum_{v \in [k]} d_G(v)$ (i.e., each vertex in B_i contributes approximately β^i). Hence, approximating all $|B_i|$'s yields an approximation to the said sum. The problem is that we cannot afford to approximate all $|B_i|$'s well enough, since some B_i may be too small. Fortunately, as shown in the foregoing discussion, a good approximation of the sizes of the large B_i's (which we can afford) suffices for a factor 2 approximation of the sum, since there are very few edges that have both endpoints in small buckets. Getting a better approximation requires approximating the fraction of edges that have a single endpoint in a large bucket, and this can actually be done without attributing these edges to specific large buckets (although Algorithm 10.7 did use such an attribution). The last assertion hints that the bucketing is actually not so important; what is important is the handling the case that a small set of vertices (i.e., the set of vertices in small buckets) has many incident edges (especially, edges to the rest of the graph).[21] This observation will become more explicit in Section 10.3.2.2.

Teaching Note: The rest of Section 10.3.2.1 is a bit tedious, and can be skipped if under time pressure. In such a case, we recommend leaving it for independent reading, since it does make two important points. The first point is that we can set the threshold s "adaptively" rather than rely on its being given to us from the outside. The technique used here is quite generic and good to know (see also Exercises 10.7 and 10.8). The second point is using the output provided by Algorithm 10.7 in order to sample random edges in the graph.

Setting the Parameters. As apparent in Claim 10.8, the parameter $\beta > 1$ determines the quality of the approximation, and it can be set to a constant that is arbitrarily close to 1. This means that $\ell = \log_\beta k = O(\epsilon^{-1} \log k)$, where $\epsilon \stackrel{\text{def}}{=} \beta - 1 > 0$ is a positive constant. Hence, for constant $\beta > 1$, we have $\ell = O(\log k)$.

The setting of the parameter s is less obvious. On the one hand, we should set s such that $(\ell s)^2 < \epsilon \cdot |E|$, which guarantees that the omission of edges with both endpoints in small buckets has little effect on the quality of the approximation of $|E|$. On the other hand, we should set s as large as possible (subject to $(\ell s)^2 < \epsilon \cdot |E|$), since the complexity of Algorithm 10.7 is inversely proportional to s. Specifically, recall that the time complexity of Algorithm 10.7 is $\widetilde{O}(k)/s$, so under an optimal setting (i.e., $s = \Omega(\sqrt{\epsilon \cdot |E|}/\ell)$) we get a complexity bound of $\widetilde{O}(k)/\sqrt{\epsilon \cdot |E|}$, which equals $\widetilde{O}(\sqrt{k})/\sqrt{\bar{d}}$, since $\epsilon > 0$ is a constant and $\bar{d} = 2|E|/k$.

Note that if we know that $|E| = \Omega(k)$, then we can use $s = \Omega(\sqrt{k}/\log k)$ and get a complexity bound of $\widetilde{O}(\sqrt{k})$. However, if we know a higher lower bound on $|E|$, then we get a better complexity bound. In general, if we know that $|E| \geq L$, then we can set s accordingly (i.e., $s = \Theta(\sqrt{L}/\log k)$), and obtain a good estimate of $|E|$ in time $\widetilde{O}(k)/\sqrt{L}$.

Actually, we can avoid the use of an *a priori* lower bound on $|E|$, and obtain an algorithm with a complexity bound that depends on the actual value of $|E|$. This is done by iteratively invoking Algorithm 10.7 using guesses for $|E|$ that are cut by half in each iteration, and producing an output as soon as we obtain an estimate that exceeds the current guess. The analysis relies on the fact that, with high probability, Algorithm 10.7 does not overestimate the value of $|E|$ (beyond a possible $1 + o(1)$ factor), *regardless of the value*

---

[21] For example, consider the case of a $(k-1)$-star versus the case of a k-vertex graph in which all vertices have degree 1 (see the proof of Proposition 10.5).

of s that is used; that is, the bound $(1 - o(1)) \cdot \sum_{i:\rho_i \geq s/k}(\rho_i + \rho_i') \cdot \beta^{i-1}k < \sum_{v \in [k]} d_G(v)$ holds regardless of the value of the parameter s (see Claim 10.8). Let us spell out the result obtained.

Theorem 10.9 (Approximating the average degree with incidence queries): *For every constant $\alpha > 1$, there exists an algorithm that approximates the average degree, $\overline{d}$, in a given k-vertex graph to within a factor of α in expected time $\widetilde{O}(\sqrt{k/\overline{d}})$.*

Note that the time bound provided in Theorem 10.9 refers to the expectation, while admitting that much longer executions are possible (typically when some approximations fail, which happens with small probability).

Proof Sketch: We shall only prove a weaker bound of $\widetilde{O}(\sqrt{k})/\sqrt{\overline{d}}$, while noting that obtaining the better bound is possible by a small modification of Algorithm 10.7.[22] On input $G = ([k], E)$, we proceed in iterations such that in the ith iteration, guessing that $\overline{d} \approx k/2^{i-1}$, we invoke Algorithm 10.7 while using $s = \sqrt{k^2/2^i}/O(\ell) = k/O(2^{i/2}\ell)$. (We also apply error reduction so that the probability the algorithm provides an overestimate of $|E|$ in any iteration is at most $1/3$.)[23] Actually, in the ith iteration we use the hypothesis that $\overline{d} \geq k/2^{i-1}$, while noting that if this hypothesis is correct then (w.h.p.) we obtain a good estimate of $\overline{d}$, and in any case (w.h.p.) we do not get an overestimate of $\overline{d}$ (beyond a possible $1 + o(1)$ factor). If the ith iteration outputs an estimate (for $\overline{d}$) that is larger than $k/2^{i-1}$, then we output it and halt, since (w.h.p.) the algorithm does not overestimate $\overline{d}$, which implies that our current hypothesis $\overline{d} \geq k/2^{i-1}$ was correct and so (w.h.p.) the output is a good estimate of $\overline{d}$. Otherwise, we proceed to the next iteration.

Hence, with high constant probability, we halt by iteration $i = \log(2k/\overline{d})$, which has complexity $\widetilde{O}(k)/(k/2^{i/2}) = \widetilde{O}(\sqrt{k})/\sqrt{\overline{d}}$. The claim about the expected running time follows by observing that invoking Algorithm 10.7 with smaller than the required value of s (where the required value is $\Theta\left(\sqrt{k\overline{d}}\right)/\ell$) yields error probability that is exponentially decreasing in $\sqrt{k\overline{d}}/s$. Alternatively, see Exercise 10.8. ∎

Sampling. In order to sample uniformly at random an edge in the graph $G = ([k], E)$, we first approximate the number of edges as described in the proof of Theorem 10.9. Recall that this approximation procedure also provides us with the identity of the large buckets and their approximate sizes, denoted by a_i's (i.e., $a_i = \rho_i \cdot k$). Note that within the very same complexity bound, we can sample vertices uniformly at random from each of the large buckets. Hence, we can sample vertices in the large buckets at random according to their degree, by first selecting a bucket B_i with probability proportional to $a_i \cdot \beta^i$, and then

---

[22] **Advanced comment:** Basically, the source of trouble is that the analysis of the algorithm referred to $\ell = \log_\beta k$ buckets and to the setting of $s = \sqrt{k\overline{d}}/\ell$, whereas it suffices to consider the $\ell' \overset{\text{def}}{=} \log_\beta(k/\overline{d}) + O((\beta - 1)^{-1})$ buckets that contain vertices of degree at least $(\beta - 1) \cdot \overline{d}$ and to use $s = \sqrt{k\overline{d}}/\ell'$. Alternatively, one can prove the better bound by using the approach presented in Section 10.3.2.2.

[23] Since there are only $2 \log k$ iterations, the cost of such an error reduction is rather small. Furthermore, we can apply nonidentical levels of error reduction in the various iterations so that in the ith iteration the error probability is at most $1/(i + 3)^2$. Doing so allows to have a smaller overhead in the first iterations, which have lower complexity.

select a vertex $v \in B_i$. Lastly, with probability one half we output v, and with probability one half we select uniformly a neighbor of v, denoted u, and output u if and only if u resides in a small bucket (i.e., we output nothing if the neighbor u resides in a large bucket). This description is to be understood within the *repeated sampling paradigm*, where in case no output is generated the procedure is repeated. Letting L denote the set of large buckets and $M = \sum_{i \in L} a_i \cdot \beta^i$, observe that (in each iteration of this sampling procedure) each vertex v that resides in a large bucket B_i is output with probability

$$\mathbf{Pr}[i \text{ chosen}] \cdot \mathbf{Pr}[v \text{ chosen in } B_i] \cdot \mathbf{Pr}[v \text{ is output}] = \frac{a_i \cdot \beta^i}{M} \cdot \frac{1}{|B_i|} \cdot \frac{1}{2}$$

$$\approx \frac{d_G(v)}{M} \cdot \frac{1}{2}$$

$$= \frac{|E|}{M} \cdot \frac{d_G(v)}{2|E|}$$

where the approximation is due to $a_i \approx |B_i|$ and $\beta^i \approx d_G(v)$. Similarly, the probability that such an iteration outputs a vertex u that resides in a small bucket equals

$$\mathbf{Pr}[\text{a neighbor of } u \text{ is chosen in a large bucket}] \cdot \mathbf{Pr}[u \text{ is output}]$$

$$= \sum_{i \in L} \sum_{v \in \Gamma(u) \cap B_i} \mathbf{Pr}[v \text{ is chosen}] \cdot \mathbf{Pr}[u \text{ is output}]$$

$$= \sum_{i \in L} \sum_{v \in \Gamma(u) \cap B_i} \left(\frac{a_i \cdot \beta^i}{M} \cdot \frac{1}{|B_i|} \right) \cdot \left(\frac{1}{2} \cdot \frac{1}{d_G(v)} \right)$$

$$\approx \sum_{i \in L} \sum_{v \in \Gamma(u) \cap B_i} \frac{1}{2M}$$

$$= \frac{|E|}{M} \cdot \frac{d_G''(u)}{2|E|}$$

where $\Gamma(u)$ denotes the set of u's neighbors and $d_G''(u) = |\Gamma(u) \setminus S| \leq d_G(u)$ denotes the number of neighbors of u that reside in large buckets (while recalling that S denotes the set of vertices that reside in small buckets). Recall that $\sum_{u \in S}(d_G(u) - d_G''(u)) = 2 \cdot |E(S, S)| \ll |E|$, which means that $\frac{1}{k} \cdot \sum_{u \in S} d_G(u) = \frac{1}{k} \cdot \sum_{u \in S} d_G''(u) \pm o(\bar{d})$. Hence, a single iteration produces an output with probability approximately $|E|/M \geq 0.5 - o(1)$, and the output distribution is close to the distribution of vertices selected in proportion to their degree.

10.3.2.2. Sorting Vertices According to Their Degree

The bottom line of the digest provided after the proof of Claim 10.8 is that, when approximating the average degree of a graph, the main issue is handling the case that a small set of vertices has many incident edges. The observation that fuels the current approach is that these vertices are necessarily those of the highest degree. Hence, rather that setting aside buckets of size at most s, we set aside the s vertices that have highest degree (breaking ties arbitrarily).

To see what is gained by setting aside these high-degree vertices, let us consider a naive approach to approximating $\bar{d}$ (i.e., $\sum_{v \in [k]} d_G(v)/k$). This approach consists of selecting m random vertices and using their average degree as an estimator to $\bar{d}$. Now, let the random variable ζ_i denote the result of the ith experiment; that is, $\zeta_i = d_G(v_i)$, where

v_i is uniformly distributed in $[k]$. Then, $\mathbb{E}[\zeta_i] = \overline{d}$ obviously holds, but the problem is that $\mathbb{V}[\zeta_i]$ can be upper-bounded only by $k \cdot \overline{d}$ (whereas in some cases a lower bound of $\Omega(k \cdot \overline{d})$ does hold).[24] The point is that, when using a law of large numbers (e.g., Chernoff Bound), we need to set $m = \Omega(\frac{\mathbb{V}[\zeta_i]}{\mathbb{E}[\zeta_i]^2}) = \Omega(k/\overline{d})$. In particular, if $\overline{d} = \Theta(1)$, then we get $m = \Omega(k)$, which is useless.

Denoting the set of s vertices of highest degree by H, let us now see what happens when we approximate $\overline{d}$ by $\sum_{v \in [k] \setminus H} d_G(v)/k$, where the latter term is approximated by sampling.[25] Specifically, suppose that we select m random vertices and use as our estimate the average contribution to the foregoing sum. Let ζ_i' denote the result of the ith experiment; that is, $\zeta_i' = d_G(v_i)$ if $v_i \in [k] \setminus H$ and $\zeta_i' = 0$ otherwise, where v_i is uniformly distributed in $[k]$. Note that $\mathbb{E}[\zeta_i'] \leq \overline{d}$ and $\mathbb{E}[\zeta_i'] \geq (|E| - s^2)/k = 0.5\overline{d} - (s^2/k) \approx 0.5\overline{d}$, provided that $s = \sqrt{k\overline{d}}/O(1)$. The good news are that $\mathbb{V}[\zeta_i']$ can be upper-bounded by $\max_{v \in [k] \setminus H}\{d_G(v)\} \cdot \overline{d} \leq k \cdot \overline{d}^2/s$, since $\max_{v \in [k] \setminus H}\{d_G(v)\} \leq \min_{v \in H}\{d_G(v)\} \leq k \cdot \overline{d}/s$ (which holds because $\sum_{v \in H} d_G(v) \leq k \cdot \overline{d}$ and $|H| = s$). Hence, when using a law of large numbers, we can set $m = O(\frac{\mathbb{V}[\zeta_i']}{\mathbb{E}[\zeta_i']^2}) = O(\frac{k \cdot \overline{d}^2/s}{\overline{d}^2}) = O(k/s)$, provided that $\mathbb{E}[\zeta_i'] > \overline{d}/3$, which holds when $s^2 < \overline{d}k/3$. In particular, if we pick $s = \sqrt{k\overline{d}}/O(1)$, then we get a constant (larger than two) factor approximation using $m = O(\sqrt{k/\overline{d}})$.

Note that the foregoing procedure assumes that we can tell whether or not a sampled vertex is in H (i.e., is among the s vertices of highest degree). While it is not clear how to determine the exact ranking of vertices according to this order, we can approximate their rank based on the degrees of the sampled vertices, and such an approximation will suffice. However, this issue will disappear in the modification presented next, which is aimed at reducing the approximation factor from (a constant arbitrary close to) 2 to a constant arbitrary close to 1. Recall that the source of problem is that we only have the following bounds

$$|E| - 2 \cdot |E(H, H)| \leq \sum_{v \in [k] \setminus H} d_G(v) \leq 2 \cdot |E|, \tag{10.7}$$

where the additive loss of $2 \cdot |E(H, H)|$ is due to edges with both endpoints in H and the loss of a factor of 2 is due to edges with exactly one endpoint in H, which are counted (only) at the endpoint that resides in $[k] \setminus H$. The new idea is to count edges only at the endpoint that has lower degree (while breaking ties arbitrarily). Specifically, let $\vec{d}_G(v)$ denote the number of neighbors of v that have rank higher than v (i.e., $\vec{d}_G(v) = |\{u \in \Gamma(v) : (d_G(u), u) > (d_G(v), v)\}|$).[26] Then, $\sum_{v \in [k]} \vec{d}_G(v) = |E|$ and

$$|E| - |E(H, H)| \leq \sum_{v \in [k] \setminus H} \vec{d}_G(v) \leq |E|. \tag{10.8}$$

---

[24] Here (and in the rest of this exposition), we use the fact that, for any random variable $Z \in [0, B]$, it holds that $\mathbb{V}[Z] \leq \mathbb{E}[Z^2] \leq B \cdot \mathbb{E}[Z]$. In general, this inequality is tight (e.g., when $\mathbf{Pr}[Z = B] = p \leq 1/2$ and $\mathbf{Pr}[Z = 0] = 1 - p$, we get $\mathbb{E}[Z] = pB$ and $\mathbb{V}[Z] = p \cdot B^2 - (p \cdot B)^2 \geq B \cdot \mathbb{E}[Z]/2$). This inequality is tight also when Z represents the degree distribution in a graph. For example, generalizing the proof of Proposition 10.5, consider the graph $K_{t,k-t}$. Then, letting ζ_i be as above, we have $\overline{d} < 2t$ and $\mathbb{V}[\zeta_i] > \frac{t}{k} \cdot (k - t - \overline{d})^2 > t \cdot (k - 3t)^2/k$, which is $\Omega(tk)$ when $t < k/4$.

[25] Obtaining such an approximation is *not* obvious (and will be discussed later).

[26] Note that the definition of $\vec{d}_G(v)$ breaks ties (in the ranking according to degrees) by using a lexicographic order on pairs consisting of the vertex's degree and its label.

(This observation holds for any way of assigning edges to one of their endpoints.) The key observation is that $\vec{d}_G(v) \leq \sqrt{2|E|}$ holds for every $v \in [k]$. In particular, if G is sparse, then $\vec{d}_G(v) \ll k$ for every v.

Claim 10.10 (Bounding $\vec{d}_G(v)$): *For every vertex v in the graph $G = ([k], E)$, it holds that $\vec{d}_G(v) \leq \sqrt{2|E|}$.*

Proof: If v is one of the first $\sqrt{2|E|}$ vertices according to the foregoing order, then the claim holds since $\vec{d}_G(v)$ only counts edges that go to the higher ranked vertices. But otherwise (i.e., at least $\sqrt{2|E|}$ vertices have higher ranking than v), it must hold that $\vec{d}_G(v) \leq d_G(v) \leq \sqrt{2|E|}$, since (by the hypothesis) the number of higher ranked vertices is at least $\sqrt{2|E|}$, whereas the degree of each of them is at least $\vec{d}_G(v)$, which implies $\sqrt{2|E|} \cdot \vec{d}_G(v) \leq 2|E|$. ∎

In light of the foregoing, for any $\epsilon > 0$, we can obtain a factor $(1 + \epsilon)$ approximation of $|E|$ by selecting a sample of $m = O(\sqrt{2|E|}/\epsilon^2 \bar{d})$ vertices, denoted S, and using $Z \stackrel{\text{def}}{=} \sum_{v \in S} \vec{d}_G(v)/m$ as our estimate. Letting ζ_i'' denote the result of the ith experiment (i.e., $\zeta_i'' = \vec{d}_G(v_i)$ for a uniformly distributed $v_i \in [k]$), we have $\mathbb{E}[Z] = \mathbb{E}[\zeta_i''] = \frac{1}{k} \cdot \sum_{v \in [k]} \vec{d}_G(v) = \bar{d}/2$ and $\mathbb{V}[Z] = \mathbb{V}[\zeta_i'']/m \leq \sqrt{2|E|} \cdot \mathbb{E}[\zeta_i'']/m$ (where we use $\mathbb{V}[\zeta_i''] \leq \mathbb{E}[(\zeta_i'')^2] \leq \max_{v \in [k]}\{\vec{d}_G(v)\} \cdot \mathbb{E}[\zeta_i'']$). Hence,

$$\Pr[|Z - 0.5\bar{d}| \geq 0.5\epsilon \cdot \bar{d}] \leq \frac{\mathbb{V}[Z]}{(0.5\epsilon\bar{d})^2} \tag{10.9}$$

$$\leq \frac{\sqrt{2|E|} \cdot 0.5\bar{d}/m}{(0.5\epsilon\bar{d})^2}$$

$$= \frac{\sqrt{8|E|}}{\epsilon^2 \bar{d} \cdot m} \tag{10.10}$$

which can be made an arbitrary small positive constant by setting $m = O(\sqrt{|E|}/\epsilon^2 \bar{d})$ appropriately. The "only" problem is that it is not clear how to compute $\vec{d}_G$. Fortunately, we can approximate $\sum_{v \in S} \vec{d}_G(v)$ by computing $\sum_{v \in S} d_G(v)$ and approximating $\rho \stackrel{\text{def}}{=} \frac{\sum_{v \in S} \vec{d}_G(v)}{\sum_{v \in S} d_G(v)}$, since $\sum_{v \in S} \vec{d}_G(v) = \rho \cdot \sum_{v \in S} d_G(v)$. Specifically, we approximate ρ by sampling pairs (v, u) such that $v \in S$ and $\{v, u\} \in E$, and computing the fraction of pairs such that $(d_G(v), v) < (d_G(u), u)$. This works well, provided that the foregoing fraction (i.e., $\rho = \frac{\sum_{v \in S} \vec{d}_G(v)}{\sum_{v \in S} d_G(v)}$) is not too small, which can be guaranteed by lower-bounding the numerator and upper-bounding the denominator. As noted in Eqs. (10.9) and (10.10), the numerator is "well concentrated" around its mean, but dealing with expression in the denominator is what we were trying to avoid. Still a very weak upper bound, of the type that is provided by Markov's inequality, will suffice here (i.e., the value of $\sum_{v \in S} d_G(v)$ cannot be *much larger* than its expectation). Details follow.

Starting with the actual algorithm, we let m' denote a generic parameter; the reader may think of the case that m' equals $\Theta(\sqrt{|E|}/\bar{d}) = \Theta(\sqrt{k/\bar{d}})$.

Algorithm 10.11 (An alternative algorithmic scheme for estimating the average degree): *On input a graph $G = ([k], E)$ and parameters m' and ϵ, proceed as follows.*

— **291** —

1. Take a primary sample (of uniformly distributed vertices): *Select uniformly at random $m = O(m'/\epsilon^2)$ vertices, and let $\{v_1, \ldots, v_m\}$ denote the resulting multiset. Using degree queries, compute $D \leftarrow \sum_{i \in [m]} d_G(v)$.*

2. Take a secondary sample of edges: *For $j = 1, \ldots, t \overset{\text{def}}{=} O(1/\epsilon^2)$, select $i_j \in [m]$ such that $\mathbf{Pr}[i_j = i] = d_G(v_i)/D$, and select u_{i_j} uniformly at random among the neighbours of v_{i_j}. Let J denote the set of $j \in [t]$ such that $(d_G(v_{i_j}), v_{i_j}) < (d_G(u_{i_j}), u_{i_j})$.*

The value of $\frac{|J|}{t} \cdot \frac{D}{m}$ can be output as an estimate of $|E|/k$, and a uniformly chosen edge in $\{\{v_{i_j}, u_{i_j}\} : j \in J\}$ can be output as an almost uniformly distributed edge of the graph.

As shown in the foregoing motivating discussion, if $m' \geq \sqrt{8|E|/\bar{d}}$ and $m \geq c \cdot m'/\epsilon^2$, then $\frac{1}{m} \cdot \sum_{i \in [m]} \vec{d}_G(v_i) = (1 \pm \epsilon) \cdot \frac{|E|}{k}$ with probability at least $1 - (1/c)$, where we pick c to be a sufficiently large constant.[27] We next observe that the expected value of D is $m \cdot 2|E|/k$, and hence $\mathbf{Pr}[D > 2cm|E|/k] < 1/c$. Assuming that $D \leq 2cm|E|/k$, note that

$$\frac{\sum_{i \in [m]} \vec{d}_G(v_i)}{D} > \frac{(1-\epsilon) \cdot (m|E|)/k}{2cm|E|/k} = \frac{1-\epsilon}{2c} = \Omega(1).$$

Hence, sampling $O(\epsilon^{-2})$ pairs uniformly in $\{(v_i, u) : i \in [m] \wedge \{u, v_i\} \in E\}$ yields an $(1 + \epsilon)$-factor approximation of $\sum_{i \in [m]} \vec{d}_G(v_i)$ (w.h.p.). Specifically, with high probability,

$$\frac{|J|}{t} = (1 \pm \epsilon) \cdot \frac{\sum_{i \in [m]} \vec{d}_G(v_i)}{D}.$$

Recalling that $\frac{1}{m} \cdot \sum_{i \in [m]} \vec{d}_G(v_i) = (1 \pm \epsilon) \cdot \frac{|E|}{k}$ (w.h.p.), we conclude that

$$\frac{|J|}{t} \cdot \frac{D}{m} = (1 \pm \epsilon) \cdot \frac{\sum_{i \in [m]} \vec{d}_G(v_i)}{m} = (1 \pm \epsilon)^2 \cdot \frac{|E|}{k}.$$

Lastly, we turn to the analysis of the sampling feature provided by Algorithm 10.11 (when $m' \geq \sqrt{8|E|/\bar{d}}$ and $m = \Omega(m'/\epsilon^2)$). Letting $\vec{\Gamma}_G(v)$ denote the set of neighbors of v with rank higher than v (i.e., the vertices counted in $\vec{d}_G(v)$), we first observe that each edge $\{u, v\} \in E$ appears in the set $E' \overset{\text{def}}{=} \bigcup_{i \in [m]}\{\{v_i, u'\} : u' \in \vec{\Gamma}_G(v_i)\}$ with probability $1 - (1 - (1/k))^m \approx m/k$, since the edge appears in E' if and only if its lower ranked endpoint is selected in the primary sample $\{v_1, \ldots, v_m\}$. Next note that, conditioned on v appearing in the primary sample, the edge $\{u, v\} \in E'$ is selected (for output) with probability approximately $(t \cdot (d_G(v)/D)) \cdot (1/d_G(v)) \cdot (1/|J|)$, where the first factor is due to the probability that v is selected in the secondary sample, the second factor is due to the probability that u is included in J, and the third factor is due to u being actually selected. Recall that, with high probability, it holds that $|J|/t = (1 \pm \epsilon) \cdot |E'|/D$ and $|E'|/m = (1 \pm \epsilon) \cdot |E|/k$, since $|E'| = \sum_{i \in [m]} \vec{d}_G(v_i)$. In this case, $(t/D) \cdot (1/|J|) = (1 \pm \epsilon)/|E'|$, which implies that each edge appears as output with probability approximately $(m/k) \cdot (1 \pm \epsilon)/|E'| = (1 \pm \epsilon)^2/|E|$.

---

[27] This was essentially shown in the motivating discussion that preceded Algorithm 10.11 (see Eqs. (10.9) and (10.10)), where Z represented the average of the $\vec{d}_G(v_i)$'s and $0.5\bar{d}$ was used instead of $|E|/k$.

10.4. Using Adjacency Queries: The Case of Bipartiteness

Two natural questions arise regarding the tester for Bipartiteness asserted in Theorem 10.4: First, recall that in case the input graph is dense (i.e., $|E| = \Omega(k^2)$), testing Bipartiteness is possible within complexity that is independent of the size of the graph (see Section 8.3.1), but this is not reflected in Theorem 10.4. In other words, in light of the results regarding the dense graph model (let alone their contrast with the results for the bounded-degree graph model), one may suspect that the complexity of testing Bipartiteness in the general graph model may be related to the density of edges in the input graph, whereas Theorem 10.4 does not relate to the edge density. Second, we note that the algorithm used in the proof of Theorem 10.4 uses only incidence queries, whereas the model allows also adjacency queries.

The issues raised by these two questions are actually related. As shown in [180], for every k and $\rho = \rho(k) \in (\Omega(1/k), 1)$, a tester for Bipartiteness (of k-vertex graphs) that *only makes incidence queries* must have query complexity $\Omega(\sqrt{k})$ even when guaranteed that the edge density in the input graph is $\Theta(\rho)$. On the other hand, we observe that using adjacency queries (only), allows to emulate the tester for the dense graph model within complexity that depends only on the edge density. This is actually a generic result.

Theorem 10.12 (Emulating testers for the dense graph model (in the general graph model)): *Let T be a tester of the graph property* Π *in the dense graph model, and let* $q : \mathbb{N} \times [0, 1] \to \mathbb{N}$ *denote its query complexity. Then,* Π *can be tested in the general graph model such that the expected query complexity of ϵ-testing the input graph $G = ([k], E)$ is* $q(k, 0.9\rho \cdot \epsilon) + \widetilde{O}(1/\rho)$, *where* $\rho \stackrel{\text{def}}{=} 2|E|/k^2$. *Furthermore, the resulting tester preserves one-sided error and uses only adjacency queries.*

The fact that the complexity bound refers to the expectation is due to the need to approximate ρ (and this is also the source of the $\widetilde{O}(1/\rho)$ term). If we know a lower bound ρ' on ρ, then we can ϵ-test the input graph $G = ([k], E)$ using exactly $q(k, \rho' \cdot \epsilon)$ queries.

Proof Sketch: We first observe that using $\widetilde{O}(1/\rho)$ random adjacency queries, we can approximate ρ up to any desired constant factor (where the point is actually getting a good lower bound ρ' on ρ). This is done in iterations such that in the ith iteration we try to confirm the hypothesis $\rho \approx 2^{-i+0.5}$. Using $O(i \cdot 2^i)$ random queries in the ith iteration, we can upper-bound the error probability of iteration i by $0.1 \cdot 2^{-i}$.

Having obtained an approximation $\widetilde{\rho}$ to ρ, we invoke the tester T with proximity parameter $\widetilde{\rho} \cdot \epsilon$, where ϵ is the proximity parameter given to us and (w.l.o.g.) $\rho \geq \widetilde{\rho}$. The point is that a proximity-parameter value of ϵ in the general graph model, where we normalize by $|E| = \rho k^2/2$, corresponds to a proximity-parameter value of $\rho\epsilon$ in the dense graph model (where we normalize by $k^2/2$). ∎

Back to the Special Case of Bipartiteness. Applying Theorem 10.12 to the Bipartiteness tester (of the dense graph model), we derive a tester of (query and time) complexity $\widetilde{O}(1/\epsilon\rho)^2$ for the general graph model.[28] But this result is not optimal: An alternative approach, to be presented next, yields a tester of (query and time) complexity

---

[28] Recall that the best ϵ'-tester for the dense graph model has time complexity $\widetilde{O}(1/\epsilon')^2$ and that $\Omega(1/\epsilon')^{3/2}$ is a lower bound on the query complexity in this case.

poly$(\epsilon^{-1} \log k) \cdot \rho^{-1}$. (Note that the improvement is significant when $\rho = k^{-\Omega(1)}$; e.g., $\rho = k^{-1/3}$, let alone $\rho = k^{-2/3}$).

The following algorithm uses both adjacency and incidence queries. In light of the ideas presented in Section 10.2.2, we shall focus on *the case that the maximal degree of the input graph is of the same order of magnitude as its average degree*; that is, we assume that the maximal degree is $O(\overline{d})$, where $\overline{d}$ denotes the average degree of the input graph. Furthermore, we assume that the algorithm is given an upper bound, denoted d, on the maximal degree, and that $d = O(\overline{d})$. The following algorithm is a variant of the Bipartite tester presented in Section 9.4.1. It differs in the number of random walks that it takes from each vertex (as determined by m), and in what it does with the sets R_0 and R_1 (see Step 2c).

Algorithm 10.13 (An alternative algorithm for testing Bipartiteness (in the general graph model)): *On input d, k, ϵ and oracle access to incidence and adjacency functions of a k-vertex graph, $G = ([k], E)$, of degree bound d, repeat $t \overset{\text{def}}{=} \Theta(\frac{1}{\epsilon})$ times:*

1. *Uniformly select s in $[k]$.*
2. *(Try to find an odd-length cycle through vertex s):*
   (a) *Perform $m \overset{\text{def}}{=} $ poly$(\epsilon^{-1} \log k) \cdot \sqrt{k/d}$ random walks starting from s, each of length $\ell \overset{\text{def}}{=} $ poly$(\epsilon^{-1} \log k)$.[29]*
   (b) *Let R_0 (respectively, R_1) denote the set of vertices reached from s in an even (respectively, odd) number of steps in any of these walks. That is, assuming that ℓ is even, for every such walk $(s = v_0, v_1, \ldots, v_\ell)$, place $v_0, v_2, \ldots, v_\ell$ in R_0 and place $v_1, v_3, \ldots, v_{\ell-1}$ in R_1.*
   (c) *For every $\sigma \in \{0, 1\}$ and $u, v \in R_\sigma$, if $\{u, v\}$ is an edge in G, then* reject.

If the algorithm did not reject in any of the foregoing t iterations, then it accepts.

Note that Step 2a is implemented by using incidence queries, whereas Step 2 is implemented using adjacency queries. The time (and query) complexity of Algorithm 10.13 is $t \cdot (m \cdot \ell \cdot \log d + (m \cdot \ell)^2) = $ poly$(\epsilon^{-1} \log k) \cdot (k/d)$, where the $\log d$ factor is due to determining the degree of each vertex encountered in the random walk. It is evident that the algorithm always accepts a bipartite graph.

As in Section 9.4.1, the core of the analysis is proving that *if the input graph is ϵ-far from being bipartite and $\overline{d} = \Omega(d)$, then Algorithm 10.13 rejects with probability at least $2/3$*.[30] Again, we confine ourselves to the "rapid mixing" case, and consider a single execution of Step 2, starting from an arbitrary vertex s, and using lazy random walks instead of the natural random walks that are used in the algorithm. (For sake of self-containment, we reproduce the relevant definitions next.)

Definition 10.13.1 (Lazy random walks and the rapid mixing feature): *Let $(v_1, \ldots, v_\ell) \leftarrow \mathcal{RW}_\ell$ be an ℓ-step lazy random walk (on $G = ([k], E)$) starting at*

---

[29] Recall that a random walk of length ℓ starting at s is a path $(s = v_0, v_1, \ldots, v_\ell)$ in G selected at random such that v_i is uniformly distributed among the neighbors of v_{i-1}.

[30] The hypothesis $\overline{d} = \Omega(d)$ is used in Claim 10.13.3, where it is postulated that $m = \Omega(\sqrt{k/\overline{d}\epsilon})$.

$v_0 \stackrel{\text{def}}{=} s$; *that is, for every* $\{u, v\} \in E$ *and every* $i \in [\ell]$, *it holds that*

$$\mathbf{Pr}_{(v_1,\dots,v_\ell) \leftarrow \mathcal{RW}_\ell}[v_i = v | v_{i-1} = u] = \frac{1}{2d} \tag{10.11}$$

$$\mathbf{Pr}_{(v_1,\dots,v_\ell) \leftarrow \mathcal{RW}_\ell}[v_i = u | v_{i-1} = u] = 1 - \frac{d_G(u)}{2d} \tag{10.12}$$

where $d_G(u) \le d$ *denotes the degree of u in G. The graph G is said to be* rapidly mixing *if, for every* $v_0, v \in [k]$, *it holds that*

$$\frac{1}{2k} < \mathbf{Pr}_{(v_1,\dots,v_\ell) \leftarrow \mathcal{RW}_\ell}[v_\ell = v] < \frac{2}{k} \tag{10.13}$$

As in Section 9.4.1, the key quantities in the analysis are the following probabilities that refer to the parity *of the length of a path obtained from the lazy random walk by omitting the self-loops* (transitions that remain at the current vertex). Let $p_0(v)$ (respectively, $p_1(v)$) denote the probability that a *lazy random walk of length* ℓ, *starting at s, reaches v while making an even* (respectively, *odd*) *number of real* (i.e., non–self-loop) *steps*. That is, for every $\sigma \in \{0, 1\}$ and $v \in [k]$,

$$p_\sigma(v) \stackrel{\text{def}}{=} \mathbf{Pr}_{(v_1,\dots,v_\ell) \leftarrow \mathcal{RW}_\ell}[v_\ell = v \wedge |\{i \in [\ell] : v_i \ne v_{i-1}\}| \equiv \sigma \pmod 2] \tag{10.14}$$

The path-parity of the walk $(v_1, \dots, v_\ell)$ is defined as $|\{i \in [\ell] : v_i \ne v_{i-1}\}| \bmod 2$. By the rapid mixing assumption (for every $v \in [k]$), it holds that

At this point the analysis finally depart from the exposition of Section 9.4.1: Rather than considering the sum $\sum_{v \in [k]} p_0(v) p_1(v)$, we consider the sum $\sum_{\sigma \in \{0,1\}} \sum_{\{u,v\} \in E} p_\sigma(u) p_\sigma(v)$. If the sum is (relatively) "small," then we show that $[k]$ can be 2-partitioned so that there are relatively few edges between vertices that are placed in the same side, which implies that G is close to being bipartite. Otherwise (i.e., when the sum is not "small"), we show that with significant probability, when Step 2 is started at vertex s, it is completed by rejecting G. These two cases are analyzed in the following two (corresponding) claims.

Claim 10.13.2 (A small sum implies closeness to being bipartite): *Suppose that* $\sum_\sigma \sum_{\{u,v\} \in E} p_\sigma(u) p_\sigma(v) \le 0.01 \epsilon \bar{d}/k$, *where* $\bar{d}$ *is the average degree of* $G = ([k], E)$. *Let* $V_1 \stackrel{\text{def}}{=} \{v \in [k] : p_0(v) < p_1(v)\}$ *and* $V_2 = [k] \setminus V_1$. *Then, the number of edges with both endpoints in the same* V_σ *is less than* $\epsilon \bar{d} k / 2$.

Note that the proof of this claim is easier than the proof of Claim 9.21.2 (i.e., the corresponding claim in Section 9.4.1).

Proof Sketch: Consider an edge $\{u, v\}$ such that both u and v are in the same V_σ, and assume, without loss of generality, that $\sigma = 1$. Then, by the (lower bound of the) *rapid mixing hypothesis*, both $p_1(v)$ and $p_1(u)$ are greater than $\frac{1}{2} \cdot \frac{1}{2k}$. Hence, the edge $\{u, v\}$ contributes at least $(1/4k)^2$ to the sum, and it follows that we can have at most $\frac{0.01 \epsilon \bar{d}/k}{1/(16k^2)} < \epsilon \bar{d} k / 2$ such edges. The claim follows. ∎

Claim 10.13.3 (A large sum implies high rejection probability): *Suppose that* $\sum_\sigma \sum_{\{u,v\} \in E} p_\sigma(u) p_\sigma(v) \ge 0.01 \epsilon \bar{d}/k$, *where* $\bar{d}$ *is the average degree of* $G = ([k], E)$, *and that Step 2 is started with vertex s. Then, for* $m = \Omega(\sqrt{k/\bar{d}\epsilon})$, *with probability at least* $2/3$, *there exist an edge with both endpoints in the same* R_σ *(and rejection follows).*

The proof of this claim is very similar to the proof of Claim 9.21.3 (i.e., the corresponding claim in Section 9.4.1).[31]

The Final Result. Applying the reduction of Section 10.2.2, while approximating $\overline{d}$ and sampling edges by using adjacency queries (see Exercise 10.9), we obtain an alternative Bipartiteness tester, for the general graph model, that has expected time complexity $\mathrm{poly}(\epsilon^{-1}\log k) \cdot (k/\overline{d})$.[32] Combining the two algorithms (i.e., the algorithm of Theorem 10.4 and Algorithm 10.11), we obtain.

> **Theorem 10.14** (Testing Bipartiteness (in the general graph model), revised):[33] Bipartiteness *has a* (one-sided error) *tester of expected time* (and query) *complexity* $\mathrm{poly}(\epsilon^{-1}\log k) \cdot \min(\sqrt{k}, k/\overline{d})$, *where* $\overline{d}$ *denotes the average degree of the input graph.*

In other words, ignoring $\mathrm{poly}(\epsilon^{-1}\log k)$ factors, the time complexity of the tester is $O(\sqrt{k})$ if $\overline{d} \leq \sqrt{k}$ and $O(k/\overline{d})$ otherwise. We mention that the "nonsmooth" behavior of the complexity bound stated in Theorem 10.14 (i.e., the change of behavior at $\overline{d} \approx \sqrt{k}$) is not an artifact of its proof (which combines two different algorithms), but rather reflects the reality: *For every value of $d \in [k]$, any* Bipartiteness *tester in the general graph model must have query complexity* $\min(\sqrt{k}, k/d)$, *even when guaranteed that the input graph has average degree $d \pm 1$.*

10.5. Chapter Notes

10.5.1. Gaps between the General Graph Model and the Bounded-Degree Model

As argued at the beginning of Section 10.2, a good starting point for the design of testers for the general graph model is the design of testers for the bounded-degree graph model. In Section 10.2 we presented cases in which either an adaptation of the latter testers or a local reduction (from testing in the general graph model) to testing in the bounded-degree graph model works well. It is fair to indicate that there are cases in which such an adaptation inherently fails (and any reduction must have significant overhead). This is certainly the case when there are lower bounds on the complexity of testing graph properties in the general graph model that are significantly higher than the corresponding upper bounds that hold in the bounded-degree graph model. Examples include testing *cycle-freeness* and *subgraph freeness*. In both cases (as well as for *degree regularity*), testers of time complexity $\mathrm{poly}(1/\epsilon)$ are known for the bounded-degree graph model, but

---

[31] Here we define $\zeta_{i,j} = 1$ if there exists an edge $\{u, v\} \in E$ such that the ℓth step of the ith walk reaches u, the ℓth step of the jth walk reaches v, and both walks have the same path-parity. Note that $\mathbb{E}[\zeta_{i,j}]$ equals the sum in the claim, since the events referring to different edges $\{u, v\}$ are mutually exclusive. We use the hypothesis that lower-bounds the said sum by $0.01\epsilon \cdot \overline{d}/k$, and the hypothesis that lower-bounds the number of pairs of walks by $\Omega(\epsilon^{-1}k/\overline{d})$.

[32] We believe that the $\mathrm{poly}(\log k)$ factor can be eliminated when $\overline{d} \geq k^{\Omega(1)}$, since it is due to considerations related to the distribution of the endpoint of a random walk on regular k-vertex graphs. Recall that in the original context (of bounded-degree graphs), these graphs had constant degree, and so a random walk had to be of length $\Omega(\log k)$ in order to have its endpoint well distributed. But here we deal with $\overline{d}$-regular k-vertex graphs, where $\overline{d} > k^{\Omega(1)}$, and so it stands to reason that a constant length random walk will do.

[33] We stress that this result refers to the testing model captured by Definition 10.2.

it is easy to see that testing these properties in the general graph model requires $\Omega(\sqrt{k})$ queries (even when the average degree is a constant).

Theorem 10.15 (Lower bound on testing cycle-freeness and subgraph freeness): *Testing the following properties in the general graph model requires $\Omega(\sqrt{k})$ queries, when allowed both incidence and adjacency queries to a k-vertex graph.*

1. *Cycle-freeness;*
2. *H-freeness, for any fixed connected graph H that have more than a single edge;*
3. *Degree regularity.*

Furthermore, this holds even if it is guaranteed that the average degree of the tested graph is between 1 and 2 (and the maximum degree is $\sqrt{k}$).

The furthermore clause clarifies that the difficulty lies in the varying vertex degrees (equiv., the gap between the average degree and the maximal degree) rather than in the magnitude of the average degree. (Theorem 10.15 is implicit in the proof of Proposition 10.6; in fact, we use the very same proof strategy here.)

Proof Sketch: We show that an algorithm that makes $o(\sqrt{k})$ queries cannot distinguish the following two distributions.

1. The uniform distribution on k-vertex graphs that consist of $k/2$ isolated edges.
2. The uniform distribution on k-vertex graphs that consist of $(k - \sqrt{k})/2$ isolated edges and a clique of $\sqrt{k}$ vertices.

The point is that as long as the algorithm makes no query to a vertex in the clique, the two distributions are identical. However, graphs in the first distribution are cycle-free and H-free (and degree regular), whereas graphs in the second distribution are $\Omega(1)$-far from being cycle-free (resp., H-free and degree regular).[34] ∎

Another Lower Bound. Theorem 10.15 asserts the existence of graph properties that are ϵ-testable with poly$(1/\epsilon)$ queries in the bounded-degree graph model but requires $\Omega(\sqrt{k})$ queries for testing in the general graph model. Recall that the lower bound is established also under the guarantee that the average degree of the tested graph is $\Theta(1)$ and the maximum degree is $\sqrt{k}$, which represents a gap of $\Omega(\sqrt{k})$ between the average and maximal degrees. We mention that, in the general graph model, testing `triangle freeness` has query complexity $\Omega(k^{1/3})$ also when the average degree of the graph is $k^{1-o(1)}$, which represents a smaller gap between the average degree and the maximal degree [12].[35] Recalling that the query complexity of `triangle freeness` in the other

---

[34] To see that a $\sqrt{k}$-vertex clique is far from being H-free, observe that a k'-vertex graph of average degree at least $(1 - \epsilon) \cdot k'$ must have a clique of size $\Omega(1/\epsilon)$. For starters, note that the subgraph induced by *most* sets of $\sqrt{1/\epsilon}$ vertices in such a graph is a clique. To prove the stronger bound, observe that at least $k'/2$ vertices in such a k'-vertex graph have degree at least $(1 - 2\epsilon) \cdot k'$, and consider an $(0.25/\epsilon)$-step iterative process of selecting vertices of high degree that neighbor all previously selected vertices.

[35] Note that this does not contradict Theorem 10.12, since the query complexity of ϵ-testing `triangle freeness` in the dense graph model is greater than any polynomial in $1/\epsilon$. Recall that Theorem 10.12 implies that if ϵ-testing `triangle freeness` in the dense graph model has query complexity $q(\epsilon)$, then ϵ-testing `triangle freeness` in the general graph model has query complexity $q(\rho\epsilon)$, where $\rho \cdot k$ is the average degree of the tested graph.

two model is independent of the size of the graph, this shows that *the query complexity of testing the graph property* Π *in the general graph model cannot be upper-bounded by* $\mathrm{poly}(r(G), Q_{\mathrm{dns}}, Q_{\mathrm{bd}})$, *where* $r(G)$ *denotes the ratio between the maximal and average degrees in the tested graph* G, *and* Q_{dns} (resp., Q_{bd}) *denotes the query complexity of testing* Π *in the dense graph model* (resp., in the bounded-degree graph model).

10.5.2. History and Credits

The study of property testing in the general graph model was initiated by Parnas and Ron [222], who considered only incidence queries, and extended by Kaufman, Krivelevich, and Ron [180], who considered both types of queries.[36] Needless to say, the aim of these works was to address the limitations of the previous models for testing graph properties; that is, to allow the consideration of arbitrary graphs. (Recall that the dense graph model is suitable mostly for dense graphs and the bounded-degree model is applicable only to graph of bounded degree.) Allowing the consideration of arbitrary graphs also strengthen the relation between property testing and standard algorithmic studies. However, forsaking the paradigm of representing graphs as functions means that the connection to the rest of property testing is a bit weakened (or at least becomes more cumbersome).

Turning to the specific results, we mention that the adaptation of the connectivity tester to the current model is due to [222]. The results regarding testing Bipartiteness in the general graph model were obtained by Kaufman, Krivelevich, and Ron [180]. This refers both to the upper and lower bounds when only incidence queries are allowed, and to the upper and lower bounds in the full-fledged model (where also adjacency queries are allowed).

The lower and upper bounds on the complexity of degree estimation when only degree queries are allowed were proved by Feige [106], and the corresponding bounds for the case when also incidence (and adjacency) queries are allowed were proved by Goldreich and Ron [150]. The method presented in Section 10.3.2.1 is the one used in [150]; the alternative method presented in Section 10.3.2.2 was discovered recently by Eden, Ron, and Seshadhri [99].

10.5.3. Reflections

The bulk of algorithmic research regarding graphs refers to general graphs. Of special interest are graphs that are neither very dense nor have a bounded degree. In contrast, research in testing properties of graphs started (in [140]) with the study of dense graphs, proceeded to the study of bounded-degree graphs (in [147]), and reached general graphs only in [222, 180]. This evolution has historical reasons, which will be reviewed next.

Testing graph properties was initially conceived (by Goldreich, Goldwasser, and Ron [140]) as a special case of the framework of testing properties of functions. Thus, graphs had to be represented by functions, and two standard representations of graphs (indeed the ones used in Chapters 8 and 9) seemed most fitting in this context. In particular, in the dense graph model graphs are represented by their adjacency predicate, whereas in the bounded-degree (graph) model graphs are represented by their (bounded-degree)

---

[36] The suggested treatment of extremely sparse graphs as captured in Definition 10.2 did not appear before (as far as we know).

incidence functions. Hence, the representation of graphs by functions, which originated in the dense graph model, was maintained in the bounded-degree graph model, introduced by Goldreich and Ron [147], although the functions in this case were different. We stress that both models were formulated in a way that identifies the graphs with a specific functional representation, which in turn defines both the type of queries allowed to the tester and the notion of relative distance (which underlies the performance guarantee).

The identification of graphs with a specific functional representation was abandoned by Parnas and Ron [222], who developed a more general model by decoupling the type of queries allowed to the tester from the distance measure: Whatever is the mechanism of accessing the graph, the distance between graphs is defined as the number of edges in their symmetric difference (rather than the number of different entries with respect to some specific functional representation). Furthermore, the relative distance is defined as the size of the symmetric difference divided by the actual (total) number of edges in both graphs (rather than divided by some (possibly nontight) upper bound on the latter quantity). Also, as advocated by Kaufman *et al.* [180], it is reasonable to allow the tester to perform both adjacency and incidence queries (and indeed each type of query may be useful in a different range of edge densities). Needless to say, this model seems adequate for the study of testing properties of arbitrary graphs, and it strictly generalizes the positive aspects of the two prior models (i.e., the models based on the adjacency matrix and bounded-degree incidence list representations).

We wish to advocate further study of the general graph model. We believe that this model, which allows for a meaningful treatment of property testing of general graphs, is the one that is most relevant to computer science applications. Furthermore, it seems that designing testers in this model requires the development of algorithmic techniques that may be applicable also in other areas of algorithmic research. As an example, we mention that techniques in [180] underlie the average degree approximation of [150]. (Likewise techniques of [147] underlie the minimum spanning tree weight approximation of [74]; indeed, as noted next, the bounded-degree incidence list model is also more algorithmic oriented than the adjacency matrix model.)[37]

Let us focus on the algorithmic contents of property testing in the context of graphs. Recall that, when ignoring a quadratic blow-up in the query complexity, property testing in the adjacency matrix representation reduces to sheer combinatorics (as reflected in the notion of canonical testers, see Theorem 8.25). Indeed, as shown in [151], a finer look (which does not allow for ignoring quadratic blow-ups in complexity) reveals the role of algorithmic design also in this model. Still, property testing in the incidence list representation seems to require more sophisticated algorithms. Testers in the general graph models seem to require even more algorithmic ideas (cf. [180]).

To summarize, we advocate further study of the model of [222, 180] for two reasons. The first reason is that we believe in the greater relevance of this model to computer science applications. The second reason is that we believe in the greater potential of this model to have cross fertilization with other branches of algorithmic research. Nevertheless, this advocation is not meant to undermine the study of the dense graph and bounded-degree graph models. The latter models have their own merits and also offer a host of interesting open problems, which are of potential relevance to computer science at large.

---

[37] Here and in the rest of this section, we use the terms "bounded-degree incidence list model" and "adjacency matrix model" rather than the terms "bounded-degree graph model" and "dense graph model" (used so far).

10.5.4. Exercises

Exercises 10.7 and 10.8 present a general technique for converting approximation algorithms that rely on a rough estimate into ones that do not need such an estimate.

Exercise 10.1 (Random bipartite graphs are good gadgets for the proof of Theorem 10.4): Let $G = ((X, Y), E)$ be a random d-regular graph such that $|X| = |Y| = t$ and $E \subseteq \{\{x, y\} : x \in X \wedge y \in Y\}$.

1. Show that, with high probability, for every $S \subseteq X$ and $T \subseteq Y$ it holds that $|E(S, T)| = \Omega(d \cdot |S| \cdot |T|/t)$, where $E(S, T) = \{\{u, v\} \in E : x \in S \wedge y \in T\}$.
2. Using Part 1, show that, with high probability, for each 2-partition $(S, \overline{S})$ of the vertices of X such that $|S| \leq t/2$ and for every 2-partition $(T, \overline{T})$ of the vertices of Y it holds that $\min(|E(S, T)|, |E(\overline{S}, \overline{T})|) = \Omega(d \cdot |S|)$.
3. Using Part 2, infer that any 2-partition of G that places $t' \leq t/2$ vertices of X on one side, has at least $\Omega(t'd)$ violating edges (i.e., edges with both endpoints on the same side).

We mention that for a fixed set as in Part 3, a 2-partition of Y that has the least violating edges places each $y \in Y$ on opposite side to the majority of its neighbors.

> **Guideline:** For Part 1, fix any S and T, and note that for a random d-regular $G = ((X, Y), E)$ it holds that $|E(S, T)| = \sum_{u \in S, v \in T} \zeta_{u,v}$, where $\zeta_{u,v}$ is a random variable indicating whether $\{u, v\} \in E$ (which means that $\mathbb{E}[\zeta_{u,v}] = d/t$). As a warm-up, establish a variant of Part 1 that refers to the case that the $\zeta_{u,v}$'s are totally independent, then handle the case that each vertex in X is assigned d random neighbors (while assuming, w.l.o.g., that $|S| \geq |T|$), and finally handle random d-regular graphs. The other parts follow easily.[38]

Exercise 10.2 (Obtaining edge expanding bipartite graphs): For any constants $d \in \mathbb{N}$ and $c > 1$, let $\{G_n = ([n], E_n)\}_{n \in \mathbb{N}}$ be a family of d-regular n-vertex expanding graphs in the sense that every $S \subset [n]$ of size at most $n/2$ it holds that $|\Gamma_n(S)| \geq c \cdot |S|$, where $\Gamma_n(S) = \cup_{v \in S}\{u \in [n] : \{u, v\} \in E_n\}$. Consider a bipartite graph B_n with vertex-set $[2n]$ such that $\{i, n + j\}$ is an edge in B_n if and only if either $\{i, j\} \in E_n$ or $i = j$. Prove that for every $S \subset [n]$ of size at most $n/2$ it holds that

$$\sum_{y \in [n+1, 2n]} \min(|\Gamma(y) \cap S|, |\Gamma(y) \setminus S|) \geq (c - 1) \cdot |S|$$

where $\Gamma(y) \subseteq [n]$ denotes the set of neighbors of y.

> **Guideline:** Observe that $\sum_{y \in [n+1, 2n]} \min(|\Gamma(y) \cap S|, |\Gamma(y) \setminus S|)$ is lower-bounded by
>
> $$|\{y \in [n + 1, 2n] : \Gamma(y) \cap S \neq \emptyset \wedge \Gamma(y) \setminus S \neq \emptyset\}| = |\Gamma_n(S) \cap \Gamma_n([n] \setminus S)|$$
>
> which is at least $(c - 1) \cdot |S|$, since $|\Gamma_n(S)| \geq c \cdot |S|$ and $|\Gamma_n([n] \setminus S)| \geq |[n] \setminus S|$.

---

[38] In Part 2, observe that if $|T| \geq t/2$ (resp., $|\overline{T}| \geq t/2$), then $d \cdot |S| \cdot |T|/t = \Omega(d \cdot |S|)$ (resp., $d \cdot |\overline{S}| \cdot |\overline{T}|/t = \Omega(d \cdot |\overline{S}|)$). In Part 3, let S denote the aforementioned t'-subset of X, and let T denote the set of vertices being on the same side as S.

Exercise 10.3 (Distance preservation of the reduction presented in Section 10.2.2):[39] Referring to the transformation presented in Section 10.2.2, suppose that G is transformed to G' by replacing vertices with c-edge expanding $\overline{d}$-regular bipartite graphs. Show that if G is ϵ-far from bipartite, then G' is $(c \cdot \epsilon/8)$-far from bipartite.

> **Guideline:** Given a 2-coloring χ' of the vertices of G', consider a 2-coloring χ : $[k] \to \{1, 2\}$ of G obtained by coloring each $v \in [n]$ according to the majority color used by the external vertices associated with v; that is, $\chi(v) = 1$ if the majority of the vertices in X_v (the external vertices of the bipartite graph replacing v) are χ'-colored 1, and $\chi(v) = 0$ otherwise. Denoting the minority vertices in X_v by S_v, observe that the number of χ'-monochromatic edges in the bipartite graph replacing v is at least $c \cdot \overline{d} \cdot |S_v|$, since the number of monochromatic edges incident at an internal vertex y is at least $\min(|\Gamma(y) \cap S_v|, |\Gamma(y) \setminus S_v|)$. On the other hand, the number of edges between S_v and other bipartite graphs is at most $\overline{d} \cdot |S_v|$. Hence, extending χ to the vertices of G' increases the number of monochromatic edges by a factor of at most $1/c$ (in comparison to χ'). It follows that the number of χ-monochromatic edges in G is at most $1/c$ times the number of χ'-monochromatic edges in G'. Recalling that G' has at most $4k \cdot 2\overline{d}/2$ edges (whereas G has $k \cdot \overline{d}/2$ edges), infer that if G' is δ-close to being bipartite, then G is $(8\delta/c)$-close to being bipartite.

Exercise 10.4 (On sampling edges and vertices): Show that selecting an edge uniformly at random in a given graph and selecting a random vertex with probability proportional to its degree in the graph are locally reducible to one another, where one of the reductions utilizes logarithmically many queries mainly in order to determine the degree of the sampled vertex.

Exercise 10.5 (Estimating the average degree of graphs with parallel edges): Show that for any t (e.g., $t = \omega(k)$), a $((k + t - 2)/k)$-factor approximation to the number of edges in k-vertex graphs in which there are at most t parallel edges requires $\Omega(k)$ queries, even when allowed degree, incidence, and adjacency queries, and even when guaranteed that the graph has no isolated vertices.

> **Guideline:** Consider a random graph that consists of a perfect matching, and a graph in which one of these matching edges is duplicated t times.

Exercise 10.6 (Extending Proposition 10.6):[40] For every $\rho \in (0, 1)$, any constant-factor approximation algorithm for the average degree of a graph $G = ([k], E)$ must make $\Omega(k/\sqrt{|E|})$ queries to G, even when allowed degree, incidence, and adjacency queries, and even if it is guaranteed that $|E| = \Theta(\rho k^2)$.

> **Guideline:** For any $\rho = \rho(k) > 1/k$ and constant approximation factor $\gamma > 1$, proceed as in the proof of Proposition 10.6, while setting $k' = \sqrt{\gamma\rho} \cdot k$ (rather than $k' = \sqrt{\gamma k}$) and using $d \overset{\text{def}}{=} \lfloor \rho k \rfloor$ matchings (rather than one).[41] Note that the average degree in the second distribution is d, whereas the average degree in the first distribution is $\frac{k-k'}{k} \cdot d + \frac{k'}{k} \cdot (k' - 1) \approx (1 + \gamma - \sqrt{\gamma\rho}) \cdot d \geq (1 + \gamma - o(\sqrt{\gamma})) \cdot d$, where we assume that $\rho = o(1)$. (Note that $\Omega(k/k')$ queries are required to distinguish these two distributions, whereas $k' \approx \sqrt{\gamma \cdot dk}$.) For $\rho < 1/k$, we also use

---

[39] Based on a result in [180].
[40] Based on a result in [150].
[41] In the first distribution use d matchings of the remaining $k - k'$ vertices (rather than 1), and in the second distribution just use d perfect matchings (rather than 1).

$k' = \sqrt{\gamma\rho} \cdot k$ but only match ρk^2 of the remaining $k - k'$ vertices (rather than all of them).[42] Here, the average degree in the second distribution is $d \stackrel{\text{def}}{=} \rho k$, whereas the average degree in the first distribution is $d + \frac{k'}{k} \cdot (k' - 1) \approx (1 + \gamma) \cdot d$.

Exercise 10.7 (Getting rid of the need for a rough estimate – deterministic case): Let $v : \{0, 1\}^* \to (0, 1]$ be a value functions and suppose that A is a deterministic algorithm that approximates v when given a valid lower for it. Specifically, suppose that A satisfies the following conditions.

1. *A never overestimates v:* For every x and b, it holds that $A(x, b) \leq v(x)$.
2. *A performs well when given a valid lower bound on $v(x)$:* For some $\alpha \in (0, 1)$ and every (x, b), if $v(x) \geq b$, then $A(x, b) \geq \alpha \cdot v(x)$.
3. *The complexity of A grows with $1/b$:* The complexity of A on (x, b) is upper bounded by $Q_x(b)$, where $Q_x : (0, 1) \to \mathbb{N}$ is monotonically nonincreasing and $Q_x(b) = \Omega(1/b)$.

Then, $v(x)$ can be approximate to within a factor of $1/\alpha$ within complexity $\tilde{O}(Q_x(\alpha \cdot v(x)/2))$. Actually, an upper bound of $\sum_{i \in [\lceil \log_2(1/\alpha \cdot v(x)) \rceil]} Q_x(2^{-i})$ holds regardless of the growth rate of Q_x.

> **Guideline:** On input x, invoke A iteratively such that in the ith iteration A is invoked on input $(x, 2^{-i})$, and halt in iteration i if and only if the output is at least 2^{-i} (i.e., if $A(x, 2^{-i}) \geq 2^{-i}$).[43]

Exercise 10.8 (Getting rid of the need for a rough estimate – randomized case): In continuation to Exercise 10.7, suppose that A is randomized and that Conditions 1 and 2 hold only with probability $2/3$. Consider an algorithm as in the guidelines to Exercise 10.7, except that in the ith iteration it invokes $A(2^{-i}, x)$ for $\Theta(\log Q_x(2^{-(i+1)}))$ times and treats the median value as if it was the verdict of a deterministic algorithm. Analyze the probability that this algorithm outputs an $1/\alpha$-factor approximation of $v(x)$ as well as its expected complexity. Assuming that $Q_x(b/2) \leq \text{poly}(Q_x(b))$ and $Q_x(b) \geq b^{-\Omega(1)}$ for every $b \in (0, 1]$, upper-bound the expected complexity by $\tilde{O}(Q_x(\alpha \cdot v(x)/2))$.

> **Guideline:** Letting $t \stackrel{\text{def}}{=} \lceil \log_2(1/\alpha \cdot v(x)) \rceil$, observe that the probability that A fails to output an $1/\alpha$-factor approximation of $v(x)$ is at most
> $$\sum_{i \in [t]} \exp(-\Omega(\log Q_x(2^{-(i+1)}))) < \sum_{i \in [\lceil \log_2(1/\alpha \cdot v(x)) \rceil]} 2^{-2(i+1)} < \frac{1}{8}$$
> where the first inequality uses $Q_x(b) \geq b^{-\Omega(1)}$, and that its expected complexity is
> $$\sum_{i \in [t]} O(Q_x(2^{-i}) \log Q_x(2^{-(i+1)})) + \sum_{i > t} 2^{-2 \log Q_x(2^{-i})} \cdot O(Q_x(2^{-i}) \log Q_x(2^{-(i+1)})).$$
> Lastly, note that $Q_x(b/2) \leq \text{poly}(Q_x(b))$ implies that $\log Q_x(b/2) = O(\log Q_x(b))$.

Exercise 10.9 (Estimating average degree and sampling edges by using adjacency queries):

1. Show that the number of edges in a given graph $G = ([k], E)$ can be approximated to within any constant factor by making $O(k^2/|E|)$ adjacency queries, in expectation.

---

[42] In the second distribution, we only match ρk^2 of the k vertices (rather than all of them).
[43] Note that in this case $v(x) \geq 2^{-i}$ (by Condition 1), and so Condition 2 is applicable.

2. Show that given a graph $G = ([k], E)$, an edge can be sampled uniformly at random by making $O(k^2/|E|)$ adjacency queries, in expectation.

Guideline: The key observation is that a random pair of vertices constitutes an edge with probability $|E|/\binom{k}{2}$. In Part 1, for any desired constant factor $\alpha > 1$, sample pairs till $t \overset{\text{def}}{=} O((\alpha - 1)^{-2})$ edges are seen, and output the empirical frequency (i.e., t over the number of trials).[44] In Part 2, apply the paradigm of repeated sampling.

---

[44] In the analysis, letting $\rho \overset{\text{def}}{=} 2|E|/k^2$ and assuming that $\epsilon = \alpha - 1 \in (0, 1)$, consider the probability that at least t (resp., at most t) edges are seen in a sample of size $(1 - \epsilon) \cdot t/\rho$ (resp., $(1 + \epsilon) \cdot t/\rho$).

CHAPTER ELEVEN
Testing Properties of Distributions

Summary: We provide an introduction to the study of testing properties of distributions, where the tester obtains samples of an unknown distribution (resp., samples from several unknown distributions) and is required to determine whether the distribution (resp., the tuple of distributions) has some predetermined property. We focus on the problems of testing whether an unknown distribution equals a fixed distribution and of testing equality between two unknown distributions. Our presentation is based on reductions from the general cases to some seemingly easier special cases. In addition, we also provide a brief survey of general results.

The current chapter is based on many sources; see Section 11.5.1 for details.

Teaching Note: Unless one intends to devote several lectures to the current topic, one cannot hope to cover all the material that is presented in this chapter in class. Hence, we recommend focusing on Sections 11.1 and 11.2, while leaving Sections 11.3 and 11.4 for optional independent reading. Note that Section 11.3 is quite technical, whereas Section 11.4 is mostly an overview section.

Key Notations: We consider *discrete* probability distributions. Such distributions have a finite *support*, which we assume to be a subset of $[n]$, where the support of a distribution is the set of elements assigned positive probability mass. We represent such distributions either by random variables, like X, that are assigned values in $[n]$ (indicated by writing $X \in [n]$), or by probability mass functions like $p : [n] \to [0, 1]$ that satisfy $\sum_{i \in [n]} p(i) = 1$. These two representations are related via $p(i) = \mathbf{Pr}[X = i]$. At times, we also refer to distributions as such, and denote them by D. (Distributions over other finite sets can be treated analogously, but in such a case one should provide the tester with a description of the set; indeed, n serves as a concise description of $[n]$.)

11.1. The Model

The difference between property testing as discussed so far and testing distributions is quite substantial. So far, we have discussed the testing of objects that were viewed as

---

functions (equiv., as sequences over some alphabet), whereas distributions were mentioned only implicitly (when viewing the distance between functions as the probability that they differ on a uniformly distributed argument).[1] That is, the tested object was a function, and the tested property was a property of functions (equiv., a set of functions). Furthermore, the tester was given query access to the tested object, and the (uniform) distribution was used merely as a basis for defining distance between objects.[2]

In contrast, in the context of testing distributions, the tested object is a distribution, the tested property is a property of distributions (equiv., a set of distributions), and the tester (only) obtains samples drawn according to the tested distribution. For example, we may be given samples that are drawn from an arbitrary distribution over $[n]$, and be asked to "determine" whether the given distribution is uniform over $[n]$.

The foregoing formulation raises some concerns. We can never determine, not even with (nontrivial) error probability, whether samples that are given to us were taken from some fixed distribution. That is, given $s(n)$ (say $s(n) = 2^n$) samples from $X \in [n]$, we cannot determine whether or not X is the uniform distribution, since X may be such that $\mathbf{Pr}[X = i] = \frac{1}{n} - \frac{1}{2^n s(n)}$ if $i \in [n-1]$ and $\mathbf{Pr}[X = n] = \frac{1}{n} + \frac{n-1}{2^n s(n)}$ otherwise. Of course, what is missing is a relaxed interpretation of the term "determine" (akin to the interpretation we gave when defining approximate decision problems).

But before presenting this natural relaxation, we stress that here exact decision faces an impossibility result (i.e., any finite number of samples does not allow to solve the exact decision problem), whereas in the context of deciding properties of functions exact decision "only" required high complexity (i.e., it only ruled out decision procedures of sublinear query complexity).

The natural choice of a relaxation (for the aforementioned task) is to only require the rejection of distributions that are far from having the property, where the distance between distributions is defined as the total variation distance between them (a.k.a. the statistical difference). That is, X and Y are said to be ϵ-close if

$$\frac{1}{2} \cdot \sum_i |\mathbf{Pr}[X = i] - \mathbf{Pr}[Y = i]| \leq \epsilon, \tag{11.1}$$

and otherwise they are deemed ϵ-far. With this definition in place, we are ready to provide the definition of testing properties of distributions.

11.1.1. Testing Properties of Single Distributions

Having specified the objects (i.e., distributions), the view obtained by the tester (i.e., samples), and the distance between objects (i.e., Eq. (11.1)), we can apply the "testing" paradigm and obtain the following definition. (Let us just stress that, unlike in the context of testing properties of functions, the tester is not an oracle machine but is rather an ordinary algorithm that is given a predetermined number of samples.)[3]

---

[1] An extension of this study to testing properties of functions under arbitrary distributions on their domain was briefly mentioned in Section 1.3.2, but not discussed further. A different extension, pursued in Chapter 10, focused on testing properties of graphs that are accessible via various types of queries (without specifying their representation).

[2] Actually, we also mentioned (in Section 1.3.2) and used (in Section 6.2) the notion of testing functions based on random (labeled) examples.

[3] Indeed, such ordinary machines are also used in the case of sample-based testing, discussed in Section 1.3.2 and defined in Section 6.2. In both cases, the sample complexity is stated as part of the basic definition, rather than being introduced later (as a relevant complexity measure). (We deviate from this convention in Exercise 11.7.)

Definition 11.1 (Testing properties of distributions): *Let $\mathcal{D} = \{\mathcal{D}_n\}_{n \in \mathbb{N}}$ be a property of distributions such that $\mathcal{D}_n$ is a set of distributions over $[n]$, and $s : \mathbb{N} \times (0, 1] \to \mathbb{N}$. A* tester, *denoted T, of sample complexity s for the property $\mathcal{D}$ is a probabilistic machine that, on input parameters n and ϵ, and a sequence of $s(n, \epsilon)$ samples drawn from an unknown distribution $X \in [n]$, satisfies the following two conditions.*

1. The tester accepts distributions that belong to $\mathcal{D}$: *If X is in $\mathcal{D}_n$, then*

$$\mathbf{Pr}_{i_1,\ldots,i_s \sim X}[T(n, \epsilon; i_1, \ldots, i_s) = 1] \geq 2/3,$$

   where $s = s(n, \epsilon)$, and $i_1, \ldots, i_s$ are drawn independently from the distribution X.
2. The tester rejects distributions that are far from $\mathcal{D}$: *If X is ϵ-far from any distribution in $\mathcal{D}_n$ (i.e., X is ϵ-far from $\mathcal{D}$), then*

$$\mathbf{Pr}_{i_1,\ldots,i_s \sim X}[T(n, \epsilon; i_1, \ldots, i_s) = 0] \geq 2/3,$$

   where $s = s(n, \epsilon)$ and $i_1, \ldots, i_s$ are as in the previous item.

If the tester accepts every distribution in $\mathcal{D}$ with probability 1, then we say that it has one-sided error.

Indeed, the *error probability* of the tester is bounded by $1/3$. As in the case of testing properties of functions (cf. Definition 1.6), the error can be decreased by repeated application of the tester (while ruling by majority; see Exercise 11.1). Note that n fully specifies the set of distributions $\mathcal{D}_n$, and we do not consider the computational complexity of obtaining an explicit description of $\mathcal{D}_n$ from n (not even when $\mathcal{D}_n$ is a singleton). For the sake of simplicity, in the rest of this chapter, we will consider a generic n and present the relevant properties as properties of distributions over $[n]$.

We comment that testers of one-sided error are quite rare in the context of testing properties of distributions (unlike in the context of testing properties of functions). This phenomenon seems rooted in the fact that one-sided error testers exist only for a very restricted class of properties of distributions. Specifically, *a property of distributions, $\mathcal{D}$, has a one-sided error tester if and only if there exists a collection of sets $\mathcal{C} \subseteq 2^{[n]}$ such that $\mathcal{D}$ consists of all distributions that have a support that is a subset of some $S \in \mathcal{C}$.* We stress that the impossibility claim holds regardless of the sample complexity. To verify the impossibility claim, it is instructive to restate it as asserting that *if there exist distributions X and Y such that X is in $\mathcal{D}$ but Y is not in $\mathcal{D}$ and the support of Y is a subset of the support of X, then $\mathcal{D}$ has no one-sided error tester.*[4] On the other hand, whenever one-sided error testing is possible, it is possible using $O(n/\epsilon)$ samples (see Exercise 11.2).

Relation to Learning Distributions. As in the context of testing properties of functions, it is possible to reduce testing to learning; alas, in the context of testing properties

---

[4] The claim follows by noting that any possible sample of Y is also a possible sample of X, which implies that an algorithm that rejects Y with positive probability must also reject X with positive probability. Now, since, for some $\epsilon > 0$, the distribution Y is ϵ-far from $\mathcal{D}$, an ϵ-tester for $\mathcal{D}$ must reject Y with probability at least $2/3$, and so must reject X with positive probability, which implies that it is not a one-sided error tester for $\mathcal{D}$.

of distributions the cost of such a reduction is higher. Nevertheless, let us outline this reduction.

1. When using proximity parameter ϵ, the tester uses part of the sample in order to learn a distribution in $\mathcal{D}$ such that if the input distribution X is in $\mathcal{D}$ then, with high probability, the learning algorithm outputs a description of a distribution Y in $\mathcal{D}$ that is $\epsilon/2$-close to X.
2. The tester uses a different part of the sample in order to check whether X is $\epsilon/2$-close to Y or is ϵ-far from it.

The problem with this reduction is that, in general, Step 2 has almost linear complexity (i.e., it has complexity $\Omega(n/\log n)$). In contrast, recall that in the context of testing properties of functions, the analogous step has extremely low complexity.[5] Furthermore, in many natural cases (of distribution testing) the cost of Step 2 is significantly higher than the cost of Step 1 (e.g., Step 2 may require $\Omega(n/\log n)$ samples also when Step 1 is trivial, as in the case that $\mathcal{D}$ is the singleton containing the uniform distribution). Hence, like in the context of testing properties of functions, we shall seek to outperform this reduction; however, unlike in the case of testing functions, typically this will not be because learning (i.e.,., Step 1) is too expensive but rather because testing closeness (i.e., Step 2) is too expensive. Nevertheless, in some cases, this reduction or variants of it (cf., e.g., [263, 2]) are very useful. Finally, we note that Step 2 can always be performed by using $O(n/\epsilon^2)$ samples, and the same holds for Step 1 (see [87, Lem. 3]).[6]

Notations: In order to simplify some of the discussion, we refer to ϵ-testers derived by setting the proximity parameter to ϵ. Nevertheless, all testers discussed here are actually uniform with respect to the proximity parameter ϵ. This refers also to testers of properties of pairs of distributions, defined next.

11.1.2. Testing Properties of Pairs of Distributions

Definition 11.1 generalizes naturally to testing properties of m-tuples of distributions (i.e., sets of m-tuples of distributions), where the cases of $m = 1$ and $m = 2$ are most popular. When testing an m-tuple of distributions, we are given samples drawn from each of the m distributions being tested (where the samples are presented separately so that it is clear which samples belong to which of the tested distributions). For example, given samples from two distributions, one may be asked to test whether they are identical.

---

[5] Recall that $O(1/\epsilon)$ samples suffice in order to determine whether an unknown input function is $\epsilon/2$-close to a fixed function or is ϵ-far from it.

[6] It turns out that approximating an unknown distribution $X \in [n]$ by the "empirical distribution" of $O(n/\epsilon^2)$ samples will do (for both tasks). The analysis, presented in Exercise 11.4, is highly recommended. As a motivation, we point out that naive attempts at such an analysis do not yield the desired result. For example, one may seek to approximate each $p(i) = \mathbf{Pr}[X = i]$ up to an additive term of $\epsilon/4n$ (or so), but this will require $\Omega(n/\epsilon)^2$ samples. A less naive attempt is based on the observation that it suffices to have a $1 + 0.1\epsilon$ factor approximation of each $p(i) \geq 0.1\epsilon/n$ (as well as a list containing all i's such that $p(i) < 0.1\epsilon/n$). Such an approximation can be obtained, with high probability, using a sample of size $\widetilde{O}(n)/\epsilon^2$. That is, for each i, using a sample of such size, with probability at least $1/3n$, we either provide a $1 + 0.1\epsilon$ factor approximation of $p(i)$ or detect that $p(i) < 0.1\epsilon/n$. As stated previously, a better approach is presented in Exercise 11.4. Furthermore, as discussed in Section 11.4, relaxed forms of both tasks (i.e., learning and testing closeness), which suffice for many testing problems, can be performed using $O(\epsilon^{-2} \cdot n/\log n)$ samples (see [263, Thm. 1]).

Definition 11.2 (Testing properties of m-tuples of distributions):[7] *Let $\mathcal{D}$ be a property of m-tuples of distributions and $s : \mathbb{N} \times (0, 1] \to \mathbb{N}$. A tester, denoted T, of sample complexity s for the property $\mathcal{D}$ is a probabilistic machine that, on input parameters n and ϵ, and m sequences each consisting of $s(n, \epsilon)$ samples drawn from one of the m unknown distributions $X_1, \ldots, X_m \in [n]$, satisfies the following two conditions.*

1. *The tester accepts tuples that belong to $\mathcal{D}$: If $(X_1, \ldots, X_m)$ is in $\mathcal{D}$, then*

$$\mathbf{Pr}_{i_1^{(1)}, \ldots, i_s^{(1)} \sim X_1; \ldots; i_1^{(m)}, \ldots, i_s^{(m)} \sim X_m}[T(n, \epsilon; i_1^{(1)}, \ldots, i_s^{(1)}; \ldots; i_1^{(m)}, \ldots, i_s^{(m)}) = 1] \geq 2/3,$$

   where $s = s(n, \epsilon)$, and $i_1^{(j)}, \ldots, i_s^{(j)}$ are drawn independently from the distribution X_j.

2. *The tester rejects tuples that are far from $\mathcal{D}$: If $(X_1, \ldots, X_m)$ is ϵ-far from any tuple in $\mathcal{D}$ (i.e., for every $(Y_1, \ldots, Y_m)$ in $\mathcal{D}$ the average variation distance between X_j and Y_j, where $j \in [m]$, is greater than ϵ), then*

$$\mathbf{Pr}_{i_1^{(1)}, \ldots, i_s^{(1)} \sim X_1; \ldots; i_1^{(m)}, \ldots, i_s^{(m)} \sim X_m}[T(n, \epsilon; i_1^{(1)}, \ldots, i_s^{(1)}; \ldots; i_1^{(m)}, \ldots, i_s^{(m)}) = 0] \geq 2/3,$$

   where $s = s(n, \epsilon)$ and $i_1^{(j)}, \ldots, i_s^{(j)}$ are as in the previous item.

We stress that the property that consists of pairs of identical distributions (i.e., $\{(D_1, D_2) : D_1 = D_2\}$) is a property of pairs of distributions. In contrast, the property that consists of being identical to a fixed distribution D (i.e., the property $\{D\}$) is a property of (single) distributions. In the former case, the tester is given samples from two unknown distributions, whereas in the latter case the tester is given samples from one unknown distribution (whereas the fixed distribution D is a ("massive") parameter of the testing problem).

Note that, for any $m > 1$, testing m-tuples of distributions includes testing $(m - 1)$-tuples of distributions as a special case (e.g., by just ignoring the last distribution). On the other hand, testing m-tuples of distributions reduces to testing the single distribution that corresponds to the Cartesian product of the m distributions, but this (single distribution) testing task may be harder than the original testing task (for m-tuples), because the tester also has to deal with the case that the input distribution is not a product of m distributions. (In contrast, when testing an m-tuple of distributions, the tester is guaranteed that the samples provided for the various m distributions are independent.)[8]

11.1.3. Label-invariant Properties

A very natural class of properties of distributions consists of *label-invariant* properties: For a distribution $X \in [n]$ and a permutation $\pi : [n] \to [n]$, we let $Y = \pi(X)$ be the distribution obtained by sampling X and applying π to the outcome; that is,

---

[7] The current definition mandates that the same number of samples is given for each of the m distributions. A more flexible definition that allows a different sample size for each distribution is natural and has been used in several studies.

[8] Let $\mathcal{D}$ be a property of m-tuples of distributions. When testing whether the m-tuple of distributions $(X_1, \ldots, X_m)$ is in $\mathcal{D}$, we are given a sequence $(i_1^{(1)}, \ldots, i_s^{(1)}; \ldots; i_1^{(m)}, \ldots, i_s^{(m)})$ such that the $i_k^{(j)}$'s are drawn from X_j independently of all other $i_k^{(j')}$'s (for $j' \neq j$). But when testing whether the distribution $\overline{X} \in [n]^m$ is in $\overline{\mathcal{D}}$, where $\overline{\mathcal{D}} = \{\overline{D} \equiv D_1 \times \cdots \times D_m : (D_1, \ldots, D_m) \in \mathcal{D}\}$, we are given a sequence $\bar{i}_1, \ldots, \bar{i}_s$ such that each $\bar{i}_k$ is drawn independently from $\overline{X}$, but it is not necessarily the case that $\overline{X} \equiv X_1 \times \cdots \times X_m$ for some distributions $X_1, \ldots, X_m \in [n]$.

$\Pr[Y = \pi(i)] = \Pr[X = i]$. A property $\mathcal{D}$ of distributions (over $[n]$) is label invariant if for every distribution X in $\mathcal{D}$ and for every permutation $\pi : [n] \rightarrow [n]$ the distribution $\pi(X)$ is in $\mathcal{D}$. Likewise, a property $\mathcal{D}$ of m-tuples of distributions is label invariant if for every tuple $(X_1, \ldots, X_m)$ in $\mathcal{D}$ and for every permutation $\pi : [n] \rightarrow [n]$ the tuple $(\pi(X_1), \ldots, \pi(X_m))$ is in $\mathcal{D}$.

Note that the property that consists of the uniform distribution over $[n]$ and the property that consists of pairs of identical distributions are both label-invariant. On the other hand, the property that consists of a single distribution D that is not uniform over $[n]$ is not label-invariant. Other label-invariant properties include the set of distributions over $[n]$ having support that is smaller than some threshold, and the set of distributions having entropy greater than some threshold.

In general, properties of distributions that depend only on the histograms of the distributions are label-invariant, and vice versa. The histogram of a distribution D over $[n]$ is a multiset of all the probabilities in the distribution D; that is, the histogram of the distribution represented by the probability function $p : [n] \rightarrow [0, 1]$ is the multiset $\{p(i) : i \in [n]\}$. We stress that this multiset is presented in a fixed order (typically, as a sequence of n sorted values). Equivalently, the histogram of p is the set of pairs $\{(v, m) : m = |\{i \in [n] : p(i) = v\}| > 0\}$.

11.1.4. Organization

We focus on the problems of testing whether an unknown distribution equals a fixed distribution and of testing equality between two unknown distributions: Solutions to these problems are presented in Sections 11.2 and 11.3, respectively. The corresponding testers have complexity $\mathrm{poly}(1/\epsilon) \cdot n^{1/2}$ and $\mathrm{poly}(1/\epsilon) \cdot n^{2/3}$, respectively, which is the best possible.

In Section 11.4 we consider the general study of the complexity of testing properties of (single) distributions, and survey a few general results. On the positive side, it turns out that any label-invariant property of distributions can be tested in complexity $\mathrm{poly}(1/\epsilon) \cdot n/\log n$, which means cutting off a logarithmic factor in comparison to the result obtained via the generic learning algorithm (mentioned at the end of Section 11.1.1, see also Exercise 11.4). On the negative side, it turns out that, for many natural properties, this is the best possible.

11.2. Testing Equality to a Fixed Distribution

By testing equality to a fixed distribution D, we mean testing whether an unknown distribution over $[n]$ equals the distribution D. In other words, we refer to testing the property $\{D\}$, which is a property of single distributions. Recall that the analogous task is quite trivial in the context of testing properties of functions (i.e., testing whether an unknown function equals a fixed function can be performed by using $O(1/\epsilon)$ random samples). In contrast, ϵ-testing the property $\{D\}$ typically[9] requires $\Omega(\epsilon^{-2} \cdot \sqrt{n})$ samples, and this holds also in the case that D is uniform over $[n]$. It turns out that this bound can always be

---

[9] Pathological examples do exist. For example, if D is concentrated on few elements, then the complexity depends on this number rather than on n. A general study of the complexity of ϵ-testing the property $\{D\}$ as a function of D (and ϵ) was carried out by Valiant and Valiant [264]. As shown in subsequent work [55], the complexity depends on the "effective support" size of D.

achieved; that is, for every distribution over $[n]$, testing the property $\{D\}$ can be performed in time $O(\epsilon^{-2} \cdot \sqrt{n})$.

We start by considering the special case in which D is the uniform distribution over $[n]$, denoted U_n. Testing the property $\{U_n\}$ will be reduced (in Section 11.2.1) to estimating the collision probability of the tested distribution, where the collision probability of a distribution is the probability that two samples drawn independently from it collide (i.e., yield the same value). In Section 11.2.2 we shall reduce the task of testing the property $\{D\}$, for any D (over $[n]$), to the task of testing the property $\{U_n\}$.

11.2.1. The Collision Probability Tester and Its Analysis

The collision probability of a distribution X is the probability that two samples drawn according to X are equal; that is, the collision probability of X is $\mathbf{Pr}_{i,j\sim X}[i = j]$, which equals $\sum_{i\in[n]} \mathbf{Pr}[X = i]^2$. For example, the collision probability of U_n is $1/n$. Letting $p(i) = \mathbf{Pr}[X = i]$, observe that

$$\sum_{i\in[n]} p(i)^2 = \frac{1}{n} + \sum_{i\in[n]} \left(p(i) - n^{-1}\right)^2, \tag{11.2}$$

which means that the collision probability of X equals the sum of the collision probability of U_n and the square of the $\mathcal{L}_2$-norm of $X - U_n$ (viewed as a vector, i.e., $\|X - U_n\|_2^2 = \sum_{i\in[n]} |p(i) - u(i)|^2$, where $u(i) = \mathbf{Pr}[U_n = i] = 1/n$).

The key observation is that, while the collision probability of U_n equals $1/n$, *the collision probability of any distribution that is ϵ-far from U_n is greater than $\frac{1}{n} + \frac{4\epsilon^2}{n}$*. To see the latter claim, let p denote the corresponding probability function, and note that if $\sum_{i\in[n]} |p(i) - n^{-1}| > 2\epsilon$, then

$$\sum_{i\in[n]} \left(p(i) - n^{-1}\right)^2 \geq \frac{1}{n} \cdot \left(\sum_{i\in[n]} |p(i) - n^{-1}|\right)^2$$

$$> \frac{(2\epsilon)^2}{n},$$

where the first inequality is due to Cauchy–Schwarz inequality.[10] Indeed, using Eq. (11.2), we get $\sum_{i\in[n]} p(i)^2 > \frac{1}{n} + \frac{(2\epsilon)^2}{n}$. This yields the following test.

Algorithm 11.3 (The collision probability tester): *On input $(n, \epsilon; i_1, \ldots, i_s)$, where $s = O(\sqrt{n}/\epsilon^4)$, compute $c \leftarrow |\{j < k : i_j = i_k\}|$, and accept if and only if $\frac{c}{\binom{s}{2}} < \frac{1+2\epsilon^2}{n}$.*

Algorithm 11.3 approximates the collision probability of the distribution X from which the sample is drawn, and the issue at hand is the quality of this approximation. The key observation is that each pair of sample points provides an unbiased estimator[11] of the

---

[10] That is, use $\sum_{i\in[n]} |p(i) - n^{-1}| \cdot 1 \leq (\sum_{i\in[n]} |p(i) - n^{-1}|^2)^{1/2} \cdot (\sum_{i\in[n]} 1^2)^{1/2}$.

[11] A random variable X (resp., an algorithm) is called an unbiased estimator of a quantity v if $\mathbb{E}[X] = v$ (resp., the expected value of its output equals v). Needless to say, the key question with respect to the usefulness of such an estimator is the magnitude of its variance (and, specifically, the relation between its variance and the square of its

collision probability (i.e., for every $j < k$ it holds that $\mathbf{Pr}_{i_j,i_k \sim X}[i_j = i_k] = \sum_{i \in [n]} \mathbf{Pr}[X = i]^2$), and that these $\binom{s}{2}$ pairs are "almost pairwise independent" (in the same sense as in the proof of Claim 9.21.3). Recalling that the collision probability of $X \in [n]$ is at least $1/n$, it follows that a sample of size $O(\sqrt{n})$ (which "spans" $O(n)$ pairs) provides a good approximation of the collision probability of X.

Lemma 11.4 (Analysis of the collision probability estimation): *Suppose that $i_1, \ldots, i_s$ are drawn from a distribution X that has collision probability μ. Then,*

$$\mathbf{Pr}\left[\left|\frac{|\{j < k : i_j = i_k\}|}{\binom{s}{2}} - \mu\right| \geq \gamma \cdot \mu\right] < 1/3,$$

provided that $s = \Omega(\gamma^{-2} \cdot \mu^{-1/2})$.

Hence, if X is the uniform distribution (i.e., $\mu = 1/n$), then, with probability at least $2/3$, Algorithm 11.3 accepts (since $\mathbf{Pr}[c/\binom{s}{2} \geq (1 + \epsilon^2)/n] < 1/3$).[12] On the other hand, if $\mu > (1 + 4\epsilon^2)/n$, then (setting $\gamma = \epsilon^2$ again) it follows that $\mathbf{Pr}[c/\binom{s}{2} \leq (1 - \epsilon^2) \cdot \mu] < 1/3$, whereas $(1 - \epsilon^2) \cdot \mu > (1 - \epsilon^2) \cdot (1 + 4\epsilon^2)/n > (1 + 2\epsilon^2)/n$. Thus, in this case, with probability at least $2/3$, Algorithm 11.3 rejects. It follows that Algorithm 11.3 constitutes a tester for the property $\{U_n\}$.

Proof: [13] As noted before, each pair of samples provides an unbiased estimator of μ. If these pairs of samples would have been pairwise independent, then $O(\gamma^{-2}\mu^{-1})$ such pairs would have sufficed to obtain a $(1 + \gamma)$ factor approximation of μ. But the pairs are not pairwise independent, although they are close to being so (i.e., (i_j, i_k) and $(i_{j'}, i_{k'})$ are independent if and only if $|\{j, k, j', k'\}| = 4$). Hence, the desired bound is obtained by going inside the standard analysis of pairwise independent sampling, and analyzing the effect of the few pairs that are not independent. Specifically, we consider $m = \binom{s}{2}$ random variables $\zeta_{j,k}$ that represent the possible collision events; that is, for $j, k \in [s]$ such that $j < k$, let $\zeta_{j,k} = 1$ if the jth sample collides with the kth sample (i.e., $i_j = i_k$) and $\zeta_{j,k} = 0$ otherwise. Then, $\mathbb{E}[\zeta_{j,k}] = \sum_{i \in [n]} \mathbf{Pr}[i_j = i_k = i] = \mu$ and $\mathbb{V}[\zeta_{j,k}] \leq \mathbb{E}[\zeta_{j,k}^2] = \mu$. Letting $\overline{\zeta}_{i,j} \overset{\text{def}}{=} \zeta_{i,j} - \mu$ and using Chebyshev's Inequality (while recalling that $\mathbb{V}[Z] = \mathbb{E}[(Z - \mathbb{E}[Z])^2]$), we get

$$\mathbf{Pr}\left[\left|\sum_{j<k} \overline{\zeta}_{j,k}\right| > m \cdot \gamma\mu\right] < \frac{\mathbb{E}\left[\left(\sum_{j<k} \overline{\zeta}_{j,k}\right)^2\right]}{(m \cdot \gamma\mu)^2}$$

$$= \frac{1}{m^2\gamma^2\mu^2} \cdot \sum_{j_1 < k_1, j_2 < k_2} \mathbb{E}\left[\overline{\zeta}_{j_1,k_1}\overline{\zeta}_{j_2,k_2}\right].$$

expectation). For example, for any NP-witness relation $R \subseteq \bigcup_{n \in \mathbb{N}}(\{0, 1\}^n \times \{0, 1\}^{p(n)})$, the (trivial) algorithm that on input x selects at random $y \in \{0, 1\}^{p(|x|)}$ and outputs $2^{p(|x|)}$ if and only if $(x, y) \in R$, is an unbiased estimator of the number of witnesses for x, whereas counting the number of NP-witnesses is notoriously hard. The catch is, of course, that this estimation has a huge variance; letting $\rho(x) > 0$ denote the fraction of witnesses for x, this estimator has expected value $\rho(x) \cdot 2^{p(|x|)}$ whereas its variance is $(\rho(x) - \rho(x)^2) \cdot 2^{2 \cdot p(|x|)}$, which is typically much larger than the expectation squared (i.e., when $0 < \rho(x) \ll 1/\text{poly}(|x|)$).

[12] Indeed, here we use $\gamma = \epsilon^2$.

[13] The following proof is similar to the technical core of the proof of Claim 9.21.3.

We partition the terms in the last sum according to the number of distinct indices that occur in them such that, for $t \in \{2, 3, 4\}$, we let $(j_1, k_1, j_2, k_2) \in S_t \subseteq [s]^4$ if and only if $|\{j_1, k_1, j_2, k_2\}| = t$ (and $j_1 < k_1 \wedge j_2 < k_2$). Hence,

$$\mathbf{Pr}\left[\left|\sum_{j<k} \bar{\zeta}_{j,k}\right| > m \cdot \gamma \mu\right] < \frac{1}{m^2 \gamma^2 \mu^2} \cdot \sum_{t \in \{2,3,4\}} \sum_{(j_1,k_1,j_2,k_2) \in S_t} \mathbb{E}\left[\bar{\zeta}_{j_1,k_1} \bar{\zeta}_{j_2,k_2}\right]. \quad (11.3)$$

The contribution of each element in S_4 to the sum is zero, since the four samples are independent and so $\mathbb{E}[\bar{\zeta}_{j_1,k_1} \bar{\zeta}_{j_2,k_2}] = \mathbb{E}[\bar{\zeta}_{j_1,k_1}] \cdot \mathbb{E}[\bar{\zeta}_{j_2,k_2}] = 0$. Each element in S_2 (which necessarily satisfies $(j_1, k_1) = (j_2, k_2)$) contributes $\mathbb{E}[\bar{\zeta}_{j_1,k_1}^2] = \mathbb{V}[\zeta_{j_1,k_1}] \leq \mu$ to the sum, but there are only m such elements, and so their total contribution is at most $m \cdot \mu$. Turning to S_3, we note that each of its $O(ms)$ elements contributes

$$\mathbb{E}[\bar{\zeta}_{1,2} \bar{\zeta}_{2,3}] \leq \mathbb{E}[\zeta_{1,2} \zeta_{2,3}]$$

$$= \sum_{i \in [n]} \mathbf{Pr}[X = i]^3$$

$$\leq \mu^{3/2},$$

where the first inequality holds since the variables have nonnegative expectation, and the second inequality holds since $\mathbf{Pr}[X = i] \leq \sqrt{\mu}$ (for each i).[14] Hence, the total contribution of the elements of S_3 is $O(ms) \cdot \mu^{3/2} = O(m\mu)^{3/2}$. Plugging all of this into Eq. (11.3), we get an upper bound of $\frac{m\mu + O(m\mu)^{3/2}}{m^2 \mu^2 \gamma^2} = O((m\mu\gamma^4)^{-1/2})$. Recalling that $m = \binom{s}{2} = \Omega(\gamma^{-4}\mu^{-1})$, the claim follows. ∎

Reflection. When trying to test label-invariant properties of distributions, the only relevant information provided by the sample is the *collision statistics*, where the collision statistics of the sequence $(i_1, \ldots, i_s)$ is the sequence $(c_1, \ldots, c_t)$ such that c_j denotes the number of elements that occur j times in the sequence (i.e., $c_j = |\{i \in [n] : \#_i(i_1, \ldots, i_s) = j\}|$, where $\#_i(i_1, \ldots, i_s) = |\{k \in [s] : i_k = i\}|$). Indeed, by the label-invariance condition, the specific labels of the c_j elements that have each occurred j times do not matter for determining how likely it is that the sample was drawn from a distribution that has the property (or is at any given distance from the property). This is formally proved in Theorem 11.12. Intuitively, this is the case since, for every distribution $X \in [n]$ and every permutation $\pi : [n] \to [n]$, the sample $(i_1, \ldots, i_s)$ is as likely to be drawn from X as the sample $(\pi(i_1), \ldots, \pi(i_s))$ is to be drawn from $\pi(X)$.

The most basic type of information that can be deduced from the collision statistics is an estimate to the collision probability of the original distribution. Given a sequence of samples $(i_1, \ldots, i_s)$, this estimate is computed as $|\{j < k : i_j = i_k\}|/\binom{s}{2}$. (Letting $(c_1, \ldots, c_t)$ denote the collision statistics, this value equals $\sum_{j \geq 2} \binom{j}{2} \cdot c_j / \binom{s}{2}$.) In any case, this statistic is the basis of the test that is captured by Algorithm 11.3.

---

[14] Recall that X denotes the distribution from which the samples are drawn; hence, $\mathbb{E}[\zeta_{1,2}\zeta_{2,3}] = \sum_{i \in [n]} \mathbf{Pr}[i_1 = i_2 = i_3 = i]$ equals $\sum_{i \in [n]} \mathbf{Pr}[X = i]^3$. (Also, $\mathbf{Pr}[X = i]^2 \leq \mu$, for each i.) We mention that in the second inequality we used $\sum_{i \in [n]} \mathbf{Pr}[X = i]^3 \leq \sqrt{\mu} \cdot \sum_{i \in [n]} \mathbf{Pr}[X = i]^2$, and in the first inequality we used $\mathbb{E}[(Y - \mathbb{E}[Y]) \cdot (Z - \mathbb{E}[Z])] = \mathbb{E}[YZ] - \mathbb{E}[Y] \cdot \mathbb{E}[Z]$.

Testing uniformity. As stated right after Lemma 11.4, an immediate corollary of Lemma 11.4 is that the property of being the uniform distribution over $[n]$ can be tested in $poly(1/\epsilon) \cdot \sqrt{n}$ time.

Corollary 11.5 (An upper bound on the complexity of testing uniformity): *Let U_n denote the uniform distribution over $[n]$. Then, the property $\{U_n\}$ can be ϵ-tested in sample and time complexity $O(\epsilon^{-4}\sqrt{n})$.*

We comment that an alternative analysis of the collision probability tester (of Algorithm 11.3) as well as some closely related testers yield an upper bound of $O(\epsilon^{-2}\sqrt{n})$, which is optimal.[15]

Approximating the $\mathcal{L}_2$-norm. Lemma 11.4 implies more than a tester for the property $\{U_n\}$. It actually asserts that the collision probability of a distribution can be approximated up to any desired multiplicative factor by using a number of samples that is inversely proportional to the square root of the collision probability. Viewing the collision probability of a distribution as the square of the $\mathcal{L}_2$-norm (i.e., $\|\cdot\|_2$) of the distribution (viewed as a vector), we get

Corollary 11.6 (Approximating the $\mathcal{L}_2$-norm of a distribution):[16] *Given s samples from an unknown distribution p, Algorithm 11.3 yields an $(1 + \gamma)$-factor approximation of $\|p\|_2$ with probability $1 - O(1/(\gamma^2\|p\|_2 \cdot s))$. Furthermore, this estimate equals $\sqrt{c/\binom{s}{2}}$, where c is as computed by Algorithm 11.3.*

We mention that, in a model that allows the algorithm to obtain samples on demand, the $\mathcal{L}_2$-norm of a distribution can be approximated within expected sample complexity that is inversely related to its norm (see Exercise 11.5).

Proof: Indeed, Lemma 11.4 only asserts that $\mathbf{Pr}[|(c/\binom{s}{2})) - \|p\|_2^2| \geq \gamma \cdot \|p\|_2^2] < 1/3$, provided that $s = \Omega(\gamma^{-2} \cdot \|p\|_2^{-1})$, but its proof actually establishes

$$\mathbf{Pr}\left[\left|\frac{c}{\binom{s}{2}} - \|p\|_2^2\right| \geq \gamma \cdot \|p\|_2^2\right] = O(1/(\gamma^2\|p\|_2 \cdot s))$$

for any s. Hence, with probability $1 - O(1/(\gamma^2\|p\|_2 \cdot s))$, it holds that $c/\binom{s}{2}$ is $(1 \pm \gamma) \cdot \|p\|_2^2$, and the claim follows. ∎

11.2.2. The General Case (Treated by a Reduction to Testing Uniformity)

Recall that testing equality to a fixed distribution D means testing the property $\{D\}$; that is, testing whether an unknown distribution equals the fixed distribution D. For any

---

[15] Both this upper bound and the matching lower bound are due to [221]. Alternative proofs of these bounds can be found in [73] (see also [90, Apdx.]) and [89, Sec. 3.1.1], respectively. The fact that $O(\sqrt{n}/\epsilon^2)$ samples actually suffice for the collision probability test (of Algorithm 11.3) was recently established by Diakonikolas *et al.* [88] (see review on the book's web-page).

[16] Recall that $\|p\|_2 = \sqrt{\sum_{i\in[n]} p(i)^2}$, which is the square root of the collision probability of p.

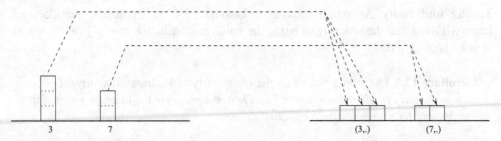

Figure 11.1: The grained-to-uniform filter corresponding to the 5-grained distribution q that satisfies $q(3) = 3/5$ and $q(7) = 2/5$.

distribution D over $[n]$, we present a reduction of the task of ϵ-testing $\{D\}$ to the task of $\epsilon/3$-testing the uniform distribution over $[O(n)]$.

We decouple the reduction into two steps. In the first step, we assume that the distribution D has a probability function q that ranges over multiples of $1/m$, for some parameter $m \in \mathbb{N}$; that is, $m \cdot q(i)$ is a nonnegative integer (for every i). We call such a distribution m-*grained*, and reduce testing equality to any fixed m-grained distribution to testing uniformity (over $[m]$). Since every distribution over $[n]$ is $\epsilon/4$-close to an $O(n/\epsilon)$-grained distribution, it stands to reason that the general case can be reduced to the grained case. This is indeed true, but the reduction is less obvious than the treatment of the grained case. (Actually, we shall use a different "graining" procedure, which yields a better result.)

> **Definition 11.7** (Grained distributions): *We say that a probability distribution over $[n]$ having a probability function $q : [n] \to [0, 1]$ is m-grained if q ranges over multiples of $1/m$; that is, if for every $i \in [n]$ there exists a non-negative integer m_i such that $q(i) = m_i/m$.*

Clearly, the uniform distribution over $[n]$ is n-grained. More generally, if a distribution D results from applying some function to the uniform distribution over $[m]$, then D is m-grained. On the other hand, any m-grained distribution must have support size at most m.

11.2.2.1. Testing Equality to a Fixed Grained Distribution

Fixing any m-grained distribution (represented by a probability function) $q : [n] \to \{j/m : j \in \mathbb{N} \cup \{0\}\}$, we consider a randomized transformation (or "filter"), denoted F_q, that maps the support of q to $S = \{\langle i, j \rangle : i \in [n] \wedge j \in [m_i]\}$, where $m_i = m \cdot q(i)$. Specifically, for every i in the support of q, we map i uniformly to $S_i = \{\langle i, j \rangle : j \in [m_i]\}$; that is, $F_q(i)$ is uniformly distributed over S_i. If i is outside the support of q (i.e., $q(i) = 0$), then we map it to $\langle i, 0 \rangle$. (An illustration of this filter is depicted in Figure 11.1.) We stress that invoking the filter several times on the same input yields independently and identically distributed outcomes.[17] Note that $|S| = \sum_{i \in [n]} m_i = \sum_{i \in [n]} m \cdot q(i) = m$. The key observations about this filter are:

---

[17] This convention is consistent with the standard convention regarding repeated applications of randomized algorithms (including property testers), but not with the definition of randomized local reductions (i.e., Definition 7.17, where a global random choice (i.e., the mapping F_n) was fixed and used in all invocations).

1. *The filter F_q maps q to a uniform distribution*: If Y is distributed according to q, then $F_q(Y)$ is distributed uniformly over S; that is, for every $\langle i, j \rangle \in S$, it holds that

$$\mathbf{Pr}[F_q(Y) = \langle i, j \rangle] = \mathbf{Pr}[Y = i] \cdot \mathbf{Pr}[F_q(i) = \langle i, j \rangle]$$

$$= q(i) \cdot \frac{1}{m_i}$$

$$= \frac{m_i}{m} \cdot \frac{1}{m_i},$$

which equals $1/m = 1/|S|$.

2. *The filter preserves the variation distance between distributions*: The total variation distance between $F_q(X)$ and $F_q(X')$ equals the total variation distance between X and X'. This holds since, for $S' = S \cup \{\langle i, 0 \rangle : i \in [n]\}$, we have

$$\sum_{\langle i,j \rangle \in S'} \left| \mathbf{Pr}[F_q(X) = \langle i, j \rangle] - \mathbf{Pr}[F_q(X') = \langle i, j \rangle] \right|$$

$$= \sum_{\langle i,j \rangle \in S'} \left| \mathbf{Pr}[X = i] \cdot \mathbf{Pr}[F_q(i) = \langle i, j \rangle] - \mathbf{Pr}[X' = i] \cdot \mathbf{Pr}[F_q(i) = \langle i, j \rangle] \right|$$

$$= \sum_{\langle i,j \rangle \in S'} \mathbf{Pr}[F_q(i) = \langle i, j \rangle] \cdot \left| \mathbf{Pr}[X = i] - \mathbf{Pr}[X' = i] \right|$$

$$= \sum_{i \in [n]} \left| \mathbf{Pr}[X = i] - \mathbf{Pr}[X' = i] \right|.$$

Indeed, this is a generic statement that applies to any filter that maps i to a pair $\langle i, Z_i \rangle$, where Z_i is an arbitrary distribution that depends only on i. (Equivalently, the statement holds for any filter that maps i to a random variable Z_i that depends only on i such that the supports of the different Z_i's are disjoint; see Exercise 11.6.)

Observing that a knowledge of q allows to implement F_q as well as to map S to $[m]$, yields the following reduction.

Algorithm 11.8 (Reducing testing equality to m-grained distributions to testing uniformity over $[m]$): *Let D be an m-grained distribution with probability function $q : [n] \to \{j/m : j \in \mathbb{N} \cup \{0\}\}$. On input $(n, \epsilon; i_1, \ldots, i_s)$, where $i_1, \ldots, i_s \in [n]$ are samples drawn according to an unknown distribution $p : [n] \to [0, 1]$, invoke an ϵ-tester for uniformity over $[m]$ by providing it with the input $(m, \epsilon; i'_1, \ldots, i'_s)$ such that for every $k \in [s]$ the sample i'_k is generated as follows:*

1. *Generate $\langle i_k, j_k \rangle \xleftarrow{} F_q(i_k)$.*
   Recall that if $m_{i_k} \overset{\text{def}}{=} m \cdot q(i_k) > 0$, then j_k is selected uniformly in $[m_{i_k}]$, and otherwise $j_k \leftarrow 0$. We stress that if F_q is invoked t times on the same i, then the t outcomes are (identically and) independently distributed. Hence, the s samples drawn independently from p are mapped to s samples drawn independently from p' such that $p'(\langle i, j \rangle) = p(i)/m_i$ if $j \in [m_i]$ and $p'(\langle i, 0 \rangle) = p(i)$ if $m_i = 0$. (If $j > m_i > 0$, then $p'(\langle i, j \rangle) = 0$, whereas by convention $[0] = \emptyset$.)

2. *If $j_k \in [m_{i_k}]$, then $\langle i_k, j_k \rangle \in S$ is mapped to its rank in S (according to a fixed order of S), where $S = \{\langle i, j \rangle : i \in [n] \wedge j \in [m_i]\}$, and otherwise $\langle i_k, j_k \rangle \notin S$ is mapped to $m + 1$.*

(Alternatively, the reduction may just reject if any of the j_k's equals 0.)[18]

The foregoing description presumes that the tester for the uniform distribution over $[m]$ also operates well when testing arbitrary distributions (which may have a support that is not a subset of $[m]$). However, any tester for uniformity can be easily extended to do so (see Exercise 11.7). Hence, *the sample complexity of testing equality to m-grained distributions equals the sample complexity of testing uniformity over $[m]$* (which is indeed a special case). Using any of the known uniformity (over $[n]$) testers that have sample complexity $O(\sqrt{n}/\epsilon^2)$,[19] we obtain –

Corollary 11.9 (Testing equality to m-grained distributions): *For any fixed m-grained distribution D, the property $\{D\}$ can be ϵ-tested in sample complexity $O(\sqrt{m}/\epsilon^2)$.*

Note that the complexity of the said tester depends on the level of grainedness of D, which may be smaller than the *a priori* bound on the size of the support of the tested distribution. Hence, the foregoing *tester for equality to grained distributions* is of independent interest, which extends beyond its usage toward testing equality to arbitrary distributions.

11.2.2.2. From Arbitrary Distributions to Grained Ones

We now turn to the problem of testing equality to an arbitrary known distribution, represented by $q : [n] \rightarrow [0, 1]$. The basic idea is to round all probabilities to multiples of γ/n, for an error parameter γ (which will be a small constant). Of course, this rounding should be performed so that the sum of the probabilities equals 1. For example, we may use a randomized filter that, on input i, outputs i with probability $\frac{m_i \cdot \gamma/n}{q(i)}$, where $m_i = \lfloor q(i) \cdot n/\gamma \rfloor$, and outputs $n + 1$ otherwise. Hence, if i is distributed according to $p : [n] \rightarrow [0, 1]$, then the output of this filter will be i with probability $\frac{\gamma m_i/n}{q(i)} \cdot p(i)$. This works well if $\gamma m_i/n \approx q(i)$, which is the case if $q(i) \gg \gamma/n$ (equiv., $m_i \gg 1$), but may run into trouble otherwise.

For starters, we note that if $q(i) = 0$, then we should replace $\frac{\gamma m_i/n}{q(i)}$ by γ/n, because otherwise we may not distinguish between distributions that differ significantly on i's on which $q(i) = 0$ (but are identical when conditioned on i's such that $q(i) > 0$).[20] Similar problems occur when $q(i) \in (0, \gamma/n)$: In this case $m_i = 0$ and so the proposed filter ignores the probability assigned by the distribution p on this i. Hence, we modify the basic idea such as to avoid these problems.

---

[18] The justification for this alternative is implicit in Exercise 11.7 (see footnote 55). Another alternative is presented in Exercise 11.8.

[19] Recall that the alternatives include the testers of [221] and [73] or the collision probability test (of Algorithm 11.3), per its improved analysis in [88].

[20] Consider for example the case that $q(i) = 2/n$ on every $i \in [n/2]$ and a distribution X that is uniform on $[n]$. Then, $\mathbf{Pr}[X = i | q(X) > 0] = q(i)$ for every $i \in [n/2]$, but $\mathbf{Pr}[X = i | q(X) = 0] = 2/n$ for every $i \in [(n/2) + 1, n]$. Hence, X and the uniform distribution on $[n/2]$ are very different, but are identical when conditioned on i's such that $q(i) > 0$.

Figure 11.2: The general-to-grained filter (as applied to part of the fixed distribution q that satisfies $q(3) = 3.2/6n$ and $q(7) = 2.8/6n$). The dotted lines indicate multiples of γ/n, for $\gamma = 1/6$.

Specifically, we first use a filter that averages the input distribution p with the uniform distribution, and so guarantees that all elements occur with probability at least $1/2n$, while preserving distances between different input distributions (up to a factor of 2). Only then do we apply the foregoing proposed filter (which outputs i with probability $\frac{m_i \cdot \gamma/n}{q(i)}$, where $m_i = \lfloor q(i) \cdot n/\gamma \rfloor$, and outputs $n + 1$ otherwise). Details follow.

1. We first use a filter F' that, on input $i \in [n]$, outputs i with probability $1/2$, and outputs the uniform distribution (on $[n]$) otherwise. Hence, if i is distributed according to the distribution p, then $F'(i)$ is distributed according to $p' = F' \circ p$ such that

$$p'(i) = \frac{1}{2} \cdot p(i) + \frac{1}{2} \cdot \frac{1}{n}. \tag{11.4}$$

(Indeed, we denote by $F' \circ p$ the probability function of the distribution obtained by selecting i according to the probability function p and outputting $F'(i)$.)

Let $q' = F' \circ q$; that is, $q'(i) = 0.5 \cdot q(i) + (1/2n) \geq 1/2n$ for every $i \in [n]$.

2. Next, we apply a filter $F''_{q'}$, which is related to the filter F_q used in Algorithm 11.8. Letting $m_i = \lfloor q'(i) \cdot n/\gamma \rfloor$, on input $i \in [n]$, the filter outputs i with probability $\frac{m_i \cdot \gamma/n}{q'(i)}$, and outputs $n + 1$ otherwise (i.e., with probability $1 - \frac{m_i \gamma/n}{q'(i)}$), where $\gamma > 0$ is a small constant (e.g., $\gamma = 1/6$ will do). (An application of this filter is depicted in Figure 11.2.) Note that $\frac{m_i \gamma/n}{q'(i)} \leq 1$, since $m_i \leq q'(i) \cdot n/\gamma$. On the other hand, observing that $m_i \cdot \gamma/n > ((q'(i) \cdot n/\gamma) - 1) \cdot \gamma/n = q'(i) - (\gamma/n)$, it follows that $\frac{m_i \gamma/n}{q'(i)} > \frac{q'(i) - (\gamma/n)}{q'(i)} \geq 1 - 2\gamma$, since $q'(i) \geq 1/2n$.

Now, if i is distributed according to the distribution p', then $F''_{q'}(i)$ is distributed according to $p'' : [n + 1] \rightarrow [0, 1]$ such that, for every $i \in [n]$, it holds that

$$p''(i) = p'(i) \cdot \frac{m_i \cdot \gamma/n}{q'(i)} \tag{11.5}$$

and $p''(n + 1) = 1 - \sum_{i \in [n]} p''(i)$.

Let q'' denote the probability function related to q'. Then, for every $i \in [n]$, it holds that $q''(i) = q'(i) \cdot \frac{m_i \gamma/n}{q'(i)} = m_i \cdot \gamma/n \in \{j \cdot \gamma/n : j \in \mathbb{N} \cup \{0\}\}$ and $q''(n + 1) = 1 - \sum_{i \in [n]} m_i \cdot \gamma/n < \gamma$, since $m \stackrel{\text{def}}{=} \sum_{i \in [n]} m_i > \sum_{i \in [n]} ((n/\gamma) \cdot q'(i) - 1) = (n/\gamma) - n$. We highlight the fact that *if n/γ is an integer, then q'' is (n/γ)-grained.*[21]

Combining these two filters, we obtain the desired reduction.

---

[21] We also mention that if $m = n/\gamma$, which happens if and only if q' is n/γ-grained (since $\sum_{i \in [n]} m_i = n/\gamma$ iff $m_i = q'(i) \cdot n/\gamma$ for every $i \in [n]$), then q'' has support $[n]$, and otherwise q'' has support $[n + 1]$.

Algorithm 11.10 (Reducing testing equality to a general distribution to testing equality to an $O(n)$-grained distribution): *Let D be an arbitrary distribution with probability function $q : [n] \to [0, 1]$, and T be an ϵ'-tester for m-grained distributions having sample complexity $s(m, \epsilon')$. On input $(n, \epsilon; i_1, \ldots, i_s)$, where $i_1, \ldots, i_s \in [n]$ are $s = s(O(n), \epsilon/3)$ samples drawn according to an unknown distribution $p : [n] \to [0, 1]$, the tester proceeds as follows:*

1. *It produces an s-long sequence $(i_1'', \ldots, i_s'')$ by applying $F_{F'\circ q}'' \circ F'$ to $(i_1, \ldots, i_s)$, where F' and $F_{q'}''$ are as in Eqs. (11.4) and (11.5); that is, for every $k \in [s]$, it produces $i_k' \leftarrow F'(i_k)$ and $i_k'' \leftarrow F_{F'\circ q}''(i_k')$.*
   (Recall that $F_{q'}''$ depends on a universal constant γ, which we shall set to $1/6$.)
2. *It invokes the $(\epsilon/3)$-tester T for the $O(n)$-grained distribution $q'' = F_{F'\circ q}'' \circ F' \circ q$ providing it with the sequence $(i_1'', \ldots, i_s'')$. Note that this is a sequence over $[n+1]$.*

We stress that if $F_{F'\circ q}'' \circ F'$ is invoked t times on the same i, then the t outcomes are (identically and) independently distributed. Hence, the s samples drawn independently from p are mapped to s samples drawn independently from p'' that satisfies Eqs. (11.4) and (11.5).

Using the notations of Eqs. (11.4) and (11.5), we first observe that the total variation distance between $p' = F' \circ p$ and $q' = F' \circ q$ is half the total variation distance between p and q (since $p'(i) = 0.5 \cdot p(i) + (1/2n)$ and ditto for q'). Next, we observe that the total variation distance between $p'' = F_{q'}'' \circ p'$ and $q'' = F_{q'}'' \circ q'$ is lower-bounded by a constant fraction of the total variation distance between p' and q'. To see this, let X and Y be distributed according to p' and q', respectively, and observe that

$$\sum_{i\in[n+1]} \left|\mathbf{Pr}[F_{q'}(X) = i] - \mathbf{Pr}[F_{q'}(Y) = i]\right| \geq \sum_{i\in[n]} \left|\mathbf{Pr}[F_{q'}(X) = i] - \mathbf{Pr}[F_{q'}(Y) = i]\right|$$

$$= \sum_{i\in[n]} \left|p'(i) \cdot \frac{m_i\gamma/n}{q'(i)} - q'(i) \cdot \frac{m_i\gamma/n}{q'(i)}\right|$$

$$= \sum_{i\in[n]} \frac{m_i\gamma/n}{q'(i)} \cdot \left|p'(i) - q'(i)\right|$$

$$\geq \min_{i\in[n]} \left\{\frac{m_i\gamma/n}{q'(i)}\right\} \cdot \sum_{i\in[n]} \cdot \left|p'(i) - q'(i)\right|.$$

As stated above, recalling that $q'(i) \geq 1/2n$ and $m_i = \lfloor (n/\gamma) \cdot q'(i) \rfloor > (n/\gamma) \cdot q'(i) - 1$, it follows that

$$\frac{m_i\gamma/n}{q'(i)} > \frac{((n/\gamma) \cdot q'(i) - 1) \cdot \gamma/n}{q'(i)} = 1 - \frac{\gamma/n}{q'(i)} \geq 1 - \frac{\gamma/n}{1/2n} = 1 - 2\gamma.$$

Hence, if p is ϵ-far from q, then p' is $\epsilon/2$-far from q', and p'' is $\epsilon/3$-far from q'', where we use $\gamma \leq 1/6$. On the other hand, if $p = q$, then $p'' = q''$. Recalling that q'' is an (n/γ)-grained distribution, provided that n/γ is an integer (as is the case for $\gamma = 1/6$), we complete the analysis of the reduction. Hence, *the sample complexity of ϵ-testing equality to arbitrary distributions over $[n]$ equals the sample complexity of $(\epsilon/3)$-testing equality to $O(n)$-grained distributions* (which is essentially a special case).

Digest. One difference between the filter underlying Algorithm 11.8 and the one underlying Algorithm 11.10 is that the former preserves the exact distance between distributions, whereas the later only preserves them up to a constant factor. The difference is rooted in the fact that the first filter maps the different i's to distributions of disjoint support, whereas the second filter (which is composed of the filters of Eqs. (11.4) and (11.5)) maps different i's to distributions of nondisjoint support. (Specifically, the filter of Eq. (11.4) maps every $i \in [n]$ to a distribution that assigns each $i' \in [n]$ probability at least $1/2n$, whereas the filter of Eq. (11.5) typically maps each $i \in [n]$ to a distribution having the support $\{i, n+1\}$.)

11.2.2.3. From Arbitrary Distributions to the Uniform One

Combining the reductions captured by Algorithms 11.10 and 11.8, we obtain:

> **Theorem 11.11** (Testing equality to any fixed distribution): *For any fixed distribution D over $[n]$, the property $\{D\}$ can be ϵ-tested in sample complexity $O(\sqrt{n}/\epsilon^2)$.*

Indeed, this generalizes Corollary 11.5. We mention that $\Omega(\epsilon^{-2}\sqrt{n})$ is a lower bound for testing $\{D\}$ for many fixed distributions D over $[n]$, including the uniform one. Nevertheless, as indicated by Corollary 11.9, in some (natural) cases testing the property $\{D\}$ has lower complexity. We mention that the complexity of ϵ-testing the property $\{D\}$ as a function of D (and ϵ) is roughly known [264]; as shown in subsequent work [55], the complexity depends on the "effective support" size of D (essentially, the size of a minimal set that is assigned almost all the probability mass of D).

> **Proof**: We first reduce the problem of ϵ-testing equality to D to the problem of $(\epsilon/3)$-testing equality to a $O(n)$-grained distribution (by using Algorithm 11.10), and then reduce the latter task to $(\epsilon/3)$-testing equality to the uniform distribution over $[O(n)]$ (by using Algorithm 11.8). Finally, we use any of the known uniformity testers that have sample complexity $O(\sqrt{n}/\epsilon^2)$.[22] ∎

11.2.3. A Lower Bound

We first establish the claim eluded to in the reflection that follows the proof of Lemma 11.4. We say that a distribution tester T is label-invariant if it ignores the labels of the samples and only considers their collision statistics. In other words, for every sequence $(i_1, \ldots, i_s)$ and every permutation $\pi : [n] \to [n]$, the verdict of T on input $(n, \epsilon; i_1, \ldots, i_s)$ is identical to its verdict on the input $(n, \epsilon; \pi(i_1), \ldots, \pi(i_s))$.

> **Theorem 11.12** (Label-invariant algorithms suffice for testing label-invariant properties): *Let $\mathcal{D}$ be a label-invariant property of distributions that is testable with sample complexity s. Then, $\mathcal{D}$ has a label-invariant tester of sample complexity s.*

A similar statement holds for testing label-invariant properties of m-tuples of distributions.

---

[22] Recall that the alternatives include the testers of [221] and [73] or the collision probability test (of Algorithm 11.3), per its improved analysis in [88].

Proof: Given a tester T of sample complexity s for $\mathcal{D}$, consider a tester T' that on input $(n, \epsilon; i_1, \ldots, i_s)$ selects uniformly a random permutation $\phi : [n] \to [n]$, invokes T on input $(n, \epsilon; \phi(i_1), \ldots, \phi(i_s))$, and rules accordingly. (Actually, it suffices to select random distinct values $\phi(i_j)$'s, for the distinct i_j's that appear in the sample.)

By construction, for every sequence $(i_1, \ldots, i_s)$ and every permutation $\pi : [n] \to [n]$, the verdict of T' on input $(n, \epsilon; i_1, \ldots, i_s)$ is identical to its verdict on the input $(n, \epsilon; \pi(i_1), \ldots, \pi(i_s))$. On the other hand, the verdict of T' on distribution X is identical to the verdict of T on the distribution Y obtained from X by selecting a random permutation ϕ and letting $Y \leftarrow \phi(X)$. Using the label-invariance feature of $\mathcal{D}$, it follows that T' is a valid tester (because, if X is in $\mathcal{D}$ then so is Y, and if X is ϵ-far from $\mathcal{D}$ then so is Y). ∎

Corollary 11.13 (Lower bound on the complexity of testing uniformity): *Let U_n denote the uniform distribution over $[n]$. Then, 0.99-testing the property $\{U_n\}$ requires $\Omega(\sqrt{n})$ samples.*

Note that this result does not say how the complexity of ϵ-testing the property $\{U_n\}$ depends on ϵ. Yet, the argument can be extended to show a lower bound of $\Omega(\min(n^{2/3}, \epsilon^{-2}\sqrt{n}))$ on the sample complexity of ϵ-testing $\{U_n\}$ (see Exercise 11.11). The latter lower bound is not tight either: Recall that it is known that ϵ-testing the property $\{U_n\}$ has sample (and time) complexity $\Theta(\epsilon^{-2}\sqrt{n})$ (cf. [221, 73]).

Proof: Using Theorem 11.12, it suffices to consider label-invariant testers. Note that, with probability at least $1 - (s^2/n)$, a sequence of s samples that are drawn from the uniform distribution on $[n]$ contains no collisions (i.e., the collision statistics is $c_1 = s$ and $c_j = 0$ for all $j > 1$).[23] Note that the same happens, with probability $1 - (s^2/(0.01n - 1))$, when the s samples are drawn from the uniform distribution on $[0.01n - 1]$, which is 0.99-far from U_n. Hence, in both cases, a sample of size $s = o(\sqrt{n})$ is likely to contain s different elements, and so the tester cannot distinguish the two cases. ∎

11.3. Testing Equality between Two Unknown Distributions

Here we consider the problem of testing the property $\{(D_1, D_2) : D_1 = D_2\}$, where (D_1, D_2) denotes a generic pair of distributions (over $[n]$). We stress that this is a property of pairs of distributions, and accordingly the tester obtains samples from each of the two unknown distributions (whose equality is being tested).

The pivot of our presentation is a rather natural algorithm for estimating the $\mathcal{L}_2$-distance between two distributions. This algorithm *takes s samples from each of the distributions, and outputs*

$$\frac{\sqrt{\sum_{i \in [n]} ((x_i - y_i)^2 - (x_i + y_i))}}{s}, \tag{11.6}$$

---

[23] Recall that c_j denotes the number of elements that occur j times in the sequence of samples $(i_1, \ldots, i_s)$; that is, $c_j = |\{i \in [n] : \#_i(i_1, \ldots, i_s) = j\}|$, where $\#_i(i_1, \ldots, i_s) = |\{k \in [s] : i_k = i\}|$.

where x_i (resp., y_i) denotes the number of occurrences of i in the sample taken from the first (resp., second) distribution.

To see why this makes sense, suppose first that the number of samples is huge (e.g., $s = \omega(n)$), which is not what we actually want (since we seek algorithms of sublinear complexity). Still, in this case x_i and y_i will reflect the actual probability of item i in each of the two distributions, and so $(\sum_{i \in [n]} (x_i - y_i)^2)^{1/2}/s$ is close to the $\mathcal{L}_2$-distance between the two distributions. Note that this is not exactly the quantity used in Eq. (11.6).

It turns out that Eq. (11.6) actually performs better. For starters, it ignores the contribution of items i that appears exactly once (i.e., $x_i + y_i = 1$). This is a good thing because, when $s = o(n)$, such a case indicates nothing and should not "count" towards asserting that the distance between the two distributions is large. In general, the statistic (x_i, y_i) contributes positively if $|x_i - y_i| > \sqrt{x_i + y_i}$, and contributes negatively if $|x_i - y_i| < \sqrt{x_i + y_i}$. This reflects the intuition that a deviation of less than a square root of the expectation actually indicates that i is as likely in both distributions. But the question, of course, is *how well does this algorithm approximate the $\mathcal{L}_2$-distance between two distributions?*

Answering this simple question (i.e., analyzing this simple algorithm) turns out to be quite challenging.[24] In particular, the analysis is simplified if the number of samples is not fixed (possibly as a function of other parameters), but is rather selected at random according to a Poisson distribution. Since this phenomenon is not unique to the current algorithm, but is rather very common within the study of testing properties of distributions, we start with a brief review of the Poisson distribution (and the reasons that it is useful in this study).

11.3.1. Detour: Poisson Distributions

When we take s samples from a distribution p, the number of occurrences of each value i behaves like a binomial distribution with parameters s and $p(i)$; that is, the probability that i occurs t times is $\binom{s}{t} \cdot p(i)^t \cdot (1 - p(i))^{s-t}$. But when we condition on the number of occurrences of $j \neq i$, this affects the distribution on the number of occurrences of i, and calculations that depend on the latter distribution become messy. In contrast, if we take a number of samples that is distributed as a Poisson distribution with parameter s (defined next), then the frequency of occurrence of i is independent of the frequency of occurrence of $j \neq i$. This fact is the reason for the popularity of taking a number of samples that is Poisson distributed rather than taking a fixed number of samples. The appeal of this practice is enhanced by the fact (shown in Proposition 11.15) that the number of samples under the Poisson distribution is well concentrated.

Definition 11.14 (Poisson distribution): *The* Poisson distribution *with parameter $\lambda > 0$, denoted $\Psi(\lambda)$, is a discrete distribution over nonnegative integers such that the number k occurs with probability*

$$\frac{\lambda^k \cdot e^{-\lambda}}{k!},\qquad\qquad (11.7)$$

---

[24] Recall that this phenomenon is quite common also in the context of testing properties of functions.

where e is the natural base and $0! = 1$. (It is also convenient to fictitiously define the "Poisson distribution" for the parameter 0 (i.e., $\Psi(0)$) as the distribution that is identically 0.)[25]

We first observe that $\sum_{k \geq 0} \frac{\lambda^k \cdot e^{-\lambda}}{k!} = 1$: This follows from the fact that the Taylor expansion of e^x at 0 equals $\sum_{k \geq 0} \frac{e^0}{k!} \cdot (x - 0)^k$, which implies that $e^\lambda = \sum_{k \geq 0} \frac{\lambda^k}{k!}$. We next establish the following facts regarding the Poisson distribution.

Proposition 11.15 (Basic facts about the Poisson distribution): *Let* $X \leftarrow \Phi(\lambda)$ *be a random variable describing a number drawn from the Poisson distribution with parameter* $\lambda > 0$. *Then:*

1. *The expectation of X equals* λ.
2. *The variance of X equals* λ.
   In general, for every $t \in \mathbb{N}$, *it holds that* $\mathbb{E}[X^t] = \sum_{i=1}^{t} S(t, i) \cdot \lambda^i$, *where* $S(t, i) = \frac{1}{i!} \cdot \sum_{j=0}^{i} (-1)^{i-j} \cdot \binom{i}{j} \cdot j^t$ *is the Stirling number of the second type.*[26]
3. *For every* $\Delta > 0$, *it holds that* $\mathbf{Pr}[|X - \lambda| > \Delta] = \exp(-\Omega(\Delta^2/(\lambda + \Delta)))$.

We note, for perspective, that $\mathbf{Pr}[X = \lambda] = \Theta(\lambda)^{-1/2}$ for any integer $\lambda > 0$.[27]

Teaching Note: The proof of Proposition 11.15 consists of straightforward manipulations of the probability function of the Poisson distribution (as defined in Eq. (11.7)). Hence, the proof may be skipped, but the claims are important and should be communicated. The same applies to Proposition 11.16.

Proof: We first present a recursive formula for $\mathbb{E}[X^t]$. For every $t \geq 1$, we have

$$\mathbb{E}[X^t] = \sum_{k \geq 0} \frac{\lambda^k \cdot e^{-\lambda}}{k!} \cdot k^t$$

$$= \lambda \cdot \sum_{k \geq 1} \frac{\lambda^{k-1} \cdot e^{-\lambda}}{(k-1)!} \cdot k^{t-1}$$

$$= \lambda \cdot \sum_{k \geq 1} \frac{\lambda^{k-1} \cdot e^{-\lambda}}{(k-1)!} \cdot \sum_{i=0}^{t-1} \binom{t-1}{i} \cdot (k-1)^i$$

$$= \lambda \cdot \sum_{i=0}^{t-1} \binom{t-1}{i} \cdot \sum_{k \geq 0} \frac{\lambda^k \cdot e^{-\lambda}}{k!} \cdot k^i.$$

---

[25] This is consistent with the common technical definitions of $0^0 = 0! = 1$.

[26] Recall that $S(t, i)$ is the number of i-partitions of $[t]$; that is, the number of ways to partition $[t]$ into i nonempty sets.

[27] This holds since

$$\mathbf{Pr}[X = \lambda] = \frac{\lambda^\lambda \cdot e^{-\lambda}}{\lambda!} = \frac{\lambda^\lambda \cdot e^{-\lambda}}{\Theta(\lambda^{1/2}) \cdot (\lambda/e)^\lambda} = \Theta(\lambda)^{-1/2}.$$

Hence, we get

$$E[X^t] = \lambda \cdot \sum_{i=0}^{t-1} \binom{t-1}{i} \cdot E[X^i]. \tag{11.8}$$

Fact 1 follows from Eq. (11.8) by using $t = 1$ and $E[X^0] = 1$. Fact 2 follows from Eq. (11.8) by using $t = 2$ and $V[X] = E[X^2] - E[X]^2 = \lambda \cdot (1 + \lambda) - \lambda^2$. The general formula for $E[X^t]$ follows by induction on t (and using $S(0, 0) = 1$ and $S(0, j) = S(j, 0) = 0$ for $j \geq 1$):

$$E[X^t] = \lambda \cdot \sum_{i=0}^{t-1} \binom{t-1}{i} \cdot E[X^i]$$

$$= \lambda \cdot \sum_{i=0}^{t-1} \binom{t-1}{i} \cdot \sum_{j=0}^{i} S(i, j) \cdot \lambda^j$$

$$= \sum_{j=0}^{t-1} \sum_{i=j}^{t-1} \binom{t-1}{i} \cdot S(i, j) \cdot \lambda^{j+1}$$

$$= \sum_{j=0}^{t-1} S(t, j+1) \cdot \lambda^{j+1},$$

where the last equality uses the combinatorial identity $S(t, j+1) = \sum_{i=j}^{t-1} \binom{t-1}{i} \cdot S(i, j)$.

Turning to Fact 3, for every integer $k \in (0, \lambda]$, we have

$$\frac{\mathbf{Pr}[X = \lambda - k]}{\mathbf{Pr}[X = \lambda]} = \frac{\lambda^{-k}}{(\lambda - k)!/(\lambda!)}$$

$$= \lambda^{-k} \cdot \prod_{i=0}^{k-1} (\lambda - i)$$

$$= \prod_{i=0}^{k-1} \left(1 - \frac{i}{\lambda}\right)$$

$$< \left(1 - \frac{(k/2) - 1}{\lambda}\right)^{k/2}$$

$$\approx \exp(-k^2/4\lambda),$$

where the approximation is up to constant factors. Similarly, for every integer $k > 0$, we have

$$\frac{\mathbf{Pr}[X = \lambda + k]}{\mathbf{Pr}[X = \lambda]} = \frac{\lambda^k}{(\lambda + k)!/(\lambda!)}$$

$$= \lambda^k \cdot \prod_{i=1}^{k} (\lambda + i)^{-1}$$

$$= \prod_{i=1}^{k} \left(1 - \frac{i}{\lambda + i} \right)$$

$$< \left(1 - \frac{k/2}{\lambda + (k/2)} \right)^{k/2}$$

$$\approx \exp(-k^2/(4\lambda + 2k)).$$

The claim follows (using $\mathbf{Pr}[X = \lambda] = \Theta(\lambda^{-1/2})$). ∎

The Relevance to the Study of Sampling Algorithms. We now turn back to our original motivation for reviewing the Poisson distribution. Recall that $\Psi(s)$ denotes the Poisson distribution with parameter s.

Proposition 11.16 (Poisson sampling): *Let $p : [n] \to [0, 1]$ be a distribution and suppose that we select m according to $\Psi(s)$, and then select m samples from the distribution p. Then, the numbers of occurrences of the various values $i \in [n]$ are independently distributed such that the number of occurrences of the value i is distributed as $\Psi(s \cdot p(i))$.*

(The implies that if X_i's are selected independently such that X_i is a Poisson distribution with parameter λ_i, then $\sum_i X_i$ is a Poisson distribution with parameter $\sum_i \lambda_i$.)

Proof Sketch: We prove the claim for $n = 2$, but the proof generalizes easily.[28] Let X denote the number of occurrences of the value 1, and Y denote the number of occurrences of the value 2. Then, for every k and ℓ, it holds that

$$\mathbf{Pr}[X = k \wedge Y = \ell] = \frac{s^{k+\ell} \cdot e^{-s}}{(k + \ell)!} \cdot \binom{k + \ell}{k} \cdot p(1)^k \cdot p(2)^\ell$$

$$= \frac{(s \cdot p(1))^k \cdot (s \cdot p(2))^\ell \cdot e^{-s \cdot p(1)} \cdot e^{-s \cdot p(2)}}{k! \cdot \ell!}$$

$$= \frac{(s \cdot p(1))^k \cdot e^{-s \cdot p(1)}}{k!} \cdot \frac{(s \cdot p(2))^\ell \cdot e^{-s \cdot p(2)}}{\ell!},$$

which equals $\mathbf{Pr}[X = k] \cdot \mathbf{Pr}[Y = \ell]$. ∎

11.3.2. The Actual Algorithm and Its Analysis

Having defined (and discussed) the Poisson distribution, we now present the actual algorithm that we shall analyze. This algorithm depends on a parameter s, which will determine the distribution of the number of samples obtained from two unknown distributions, denoted p and q.

Algorithm 11.17 (The basic $\mathcal{L}_2$-distance estimator): *On input parameters n and s, and access to $m' \leftarrow \Psi(s)$ samples from an unknown distribution $p : [n] \to [0, 1]$*

---

[28] Alternatively, the claim can be proved by induction on m.

and to $m'' \leftarrow \Psi(s)$ samples from an unknown distribution $q : [n] \rightarrow [0, 1]$, the algorithm proceeds as follows.

1. *For each $i \in [n]$, let x_i denote the number of occurrences of i in the sample taken from p, and y_i denote the number of occurrences of i in the sample taken from q.*
2. *Compute $z \leftarrow \sum_{i \in [n]}((x_i - y_i)^2 - (x_i + y_i))$.*
   If $z < 0$ output a special symbol, otherwise output $\sqrt{z}/s$.

Recall that by Item 3 of Proposition 11.15, it holds that $\mathbf{Pr}[|m - s| > s] = \exp(-\Omega(s))$. Hence, Algorithm 11.17 yields an algorithm that always uses $2s$ samples from each of the two distributions. This algorithm selects $m' \leftarrow \Psi(s)$ and $m'' \leftarrow \Psi(s)$, aborts in the highly rare case that $\max(m', m'') > 2s$, and otherwise invokes Algorithm 11.17 while providing it the first m' samples of p and the first m'' samples of q.

We now turn to the analysis of Algorithm 11.17. Let X_i (resp., Y_i) denote the number of occurrences of i when taking $\Psi(s)$ samples from distribution p (resp., q), and let $Z_i = (X_i - Y_i)^2 - (X_i + Y_i)$. By Proposition 11.16, X_i (resp., Y_i) is a Poisson distribution with parameter $s \cdot p(i)$ (resp., $s \cdot q(i)$). The next (key) lemma implies that $\mathbb{E}[Z_i] = (s \cdot p(i) - s \cdot q(i))^2$, whereas $\mathbb{V}[Z_i]$ can be bounded by a degree 3 polynomial in $s \cdot p(i)$ and $s \cdot q(i)$. Actually, it is important to assert that the degree 3 term has the form $O(s^3) \cdot (p(i) + q(i)) \cdot (p(i) - q(i))^2$.

Lemma 11.18 (The expectation and variance of the Z_i's): *Suppose that $X \leftarrow \Psi(a)$ and $Y \leftarrow \Psi(b)$ are independent Poisson distributions, and let $Z = (X - Y)^2 - (X + Y)$. Then, $\mathbb{E}[Z] = (a - b)^2$ and $\mathbb{V}[Z] \leq B(a, b)$ for some universal bivariate polynomial B of degree 3. Furthermore, $B(a, b) = O((a - b)^2 \cdot (a + b) + (a + b)^2)$.*

Proof Sketch: For the expectation of Z, using Proposition 11.15, we have

$$\mathbb{E}[(X - Y)^2 - (X + Y)] = \mathbb{E}[X^2 - 2XY + Y^2] - (a + b)$$
$$= \mathbb{E}[X^2] - 2 \cdot \mathbb{E}[X] \cdot \mathbb{E}[Y] + \mathbb{E}[Y^2] - (a + b)$$
$$= (a^2 + a) - 2ab + (b^2 + b) - (a + b),$$

which equals $(a - b)^2$, as asserted. Turning to the variance of Z, we provide only a proof of the main part. By Part 2 of Proposition 11.15, for every $t \in \mathbb{N}$, there exists a degree t polynomial P_t such that $\mathbb{E}[\Psi(\lambda)^t] = P_t(\lambda)$; furthermore, $P_t(z) = z^t + P'_{t-1}(z)$, where P'_{t-1} has degree $t - 1$ (and free term that equals zero). Using this fact, it follows that

$$\mathbb{V}[(X - Y)^2 - (X + Y)] = \mathbb{E}[((X - Y)^2 - (X + Y))^2] - \mathbb{E}[(X - Y)^2 - (X + Y)]^2$$
$$= \mathbb{E}[(X - Y)^4] - 2 \cdot \mathbb{E}[(X - Y)^2 \cdot (X + Y)]$$
$$+ \mathbb{E}[(X + Y)^2] - ((a - b)^2)^2,$$

which is a bivariate polynomial B of total degree 4 in a and b, since $\mathbb{E}[X^i Y^j] = \mathbb{E}[X^i] \cdot \mathbb{E}[Y^j] = P_i(a) \cdot P_j(b)$ for every $i, j \in \mathbb{N}$. Furthermore, using the aforementioned form of P_t (i.e., $P_t(z) = z^t + P'_{t-1}(z)$), it follows that B is of degree 3, since the degree 4 terms of $\mathbb{E}[(X - Y)^4]$ are cancelled by $(a - b)^4$. This establishes the main claim. A very tedious calculation shows that

$B(a, b) = 4 \cdot (a - b)^2 \cdot (a + b) + 2 \cdot (a + b)^2$. (Needless to say, an insightful or at least a nonpainful proof of the fact that $B(a, b) = O((a - b)^2 \cdot (a + b) + (a + b)^2)$ would be most welcome.) ∎

> **Teaching Note:** The proofs of the next four results are rather technical. In our applications (see Section 11.3.3), we shall use only Part 2 of Corollary 11.22, and the reader may just take this result on faith. The proof of Corollary 11.19 illustrates the benefit of Poisson sampling, by relying on the fact that the X_i's (resp., Y_i's) are independent. The proofs of Theorem 11.20 and Corollaries 11.21 and 11.22 are rather tedious, and reading them can serve as an exercise.

Corollary 11.19 (The expectation and variance of the square of the output of Algorithm 11.17): *Let X_i (resp., Y_i) denote the number of occurrences of i when taking $\Psi(s)$ samples from distribution $p : [n] \to [0, 1]$ (resp., $q : [n] \to [0, 1]$), and let $Z_i = (X_i - Y_i)^2 - (X_i + Y_i)$ and $Z = \sum_{i \in [n]} Z_i$. Then, $\mathbb{E}[Z] = s^2 \cdot \|p - q\|_2^2$ and $\mathbb{V}[Z] = O(s^3 \cdot \|p - q\|_2^2 \cdot \beta + s^2 \beta^2)$, where $\beta = \max(\|p\|_2, \|q\|_2) \geq 1/\sqrt{n}$.*

Hence, Z/s^2 is an unbiased estimator of $\mu \overset{\text{def}}{=} \|p - q\|_2^2$, whereas $\mathbb{V}[Z/s^2] = O(\mu \cdot \beta/s) + O(\beta^2/s^2)$. It follows that the probability that Z/s^2 deviates from μ by more than ϵ is

$$\frac{O(\mu\beta)}{s \cdot \epsilon^2} + \frac{O(\beta^2)}{s^2 \cdot \epsilon^2}. \tag{11.9}$$

For $\epsilon = \Omega(\mu)$, Eq. (11.9) simplifies to $O(\beta/s\epsilon) + O(\beta/s\epsilon)^2$, which means that setting $s = \Omega(\beta/\epsilon)$ will do. Before exploring this direction, let us prove Corollary 11.19.

Proof: We first note that, by construction, the sequence of X_i's is independent of the sequence of Y_i's, where the crucial fact is that the number of samples taken from p is selected independently of the number of samples taken from q (i.e., in Algorithm 11.17, the numbers m' and m'' are independently distributed (according to $\Psi(s)$)). Combining this fact with Proposition 11.16, it follows that Lemma 11.18 can be applied to each of the Z_i's. Hence, we have

$$\mathbb{E}[Z] = \sum_{i \in [n]} \mathbb{E}[Z_i]$$

$$= \sum_{i \in [n]} (s \cdot p(i) - s \cdot q(i))^2,$$

which equals $s^2 \cdot \|p - q\|_2^2$.

We now turn to the analysis of $\mathbb{V}[Z]$. The key fact here is that the Z_i's are (pairwise) independent, which follows by the independence of the X_i's (resp., Y_i's), which is guaranteed by Proposition 11.16. Now, invoking Lemma 11.18, we have

$$\mathbb{V}[Z] = \sum_{i \in [n]} \mathbb{V}[Z_i]$$

$$= \sum_{i \in [n]} B(s \cdot p(i), s \cdot q(i)),$$

where $B(a, b) = O((a - b)^2 \cdot (a + b) + (a + b)^2)$. Applying the Cauchy–Schwarz inequality, we obtain

$$\sum_{i\in[n]} (p(i) - q(i))^2 \cdot (p(i) + q(i)) \leq \left(\sum_{i\in[n]} (p(i) - q(i))^4\right)^{1/2} \cdot \left(\sum_{i\in[n]} (p(i) + q(i))^2\right)^{1/2}$$

$$= \|p - q\|_4^2 \cdot \|p + q\|_2$$

$$\leq \|p - q\|_2^2 \cdot \|p + q\|_2.$$

Finally, using

$$\sum_{i\in[n]} B(s \cdot p(i), s \cdot q(i)) = O(s^3) \cdot \sum_{i\in[n]} (p(i) - q(i))^2 \cdot (p(i) + q(i))$$

$$+ O(s^2) \cdot \sum_{i\in[n]} (p(i) + q(i))^2$$

$$\leq O(s^3) \cdot \|p - q\|_2^2 \cdot \|p + q\|_2 + O(s^2) \cdot \|p + q\|_2^2,$$

the claim follows. ∎

Algorithm 11.17 as an Approximator of $\mathcal{L}_2$ and $\mathcal{L}_1$ Distances. Recall that Algorithm 11.17 was presented as an approximator of the $\mathcal{L}_2$-distance between the distributions p and q. We now establish two forms of this feature, while referring to the $\mathcal{L}_2$-norm of the individual distributions.[29] (Part 1 provides a good multiplicative approximation of $\|p - q\|_2$ in the case that the sample is large enough, while Part 2 refers to smaller sample sizes. In both cases, no reference is made to the range of the distributions.)

Theorem 11.20 (Algorithm 11.17 as a $\mathcal{L}_2$-distance approximator): *Referring to the distributions p and q, suppose that* $\max(\|p\|_2, \|q\|_2) \leq \beta$.

1. (Multiplicative approximation of $\|p - q\|_2$): *Let* $\gamma \in (0, 0.1]$. *For* $\delta \stackrel{\text{def}}{=} \|p - q\|_2 > 0$, *if* $s = \Omega(\beta / \gamma^2 \delta^2)$, *then, with probability at least 2/3, Algorithm 11.17 outputs a value in* $(1 \pm \gamma) \cdot \delta$.
2. (Crude approximation of $\|p - q\|_2$): *Let* $\epsilon \in (0, 1)$. *If* $s = \Omega(\beta / \epsilon^2)$, *then, with probability at least 2/3, Algorithm 11.17 distinguishes between the case that* $\|p - q\|_2 \leq \epsilon / 2$ *and the case that* $\|p - q\|_2 \geq \epsilon$.

Note that Part 2 is meaningful only for $\epsilon \leq 2\beta$, since $\|p - q\|_2 \leq \|p\|_2 + \|q\|_2 \leq 2\beta$ always holds.

---

[29] Unfortunately, establishing this feature seems to require the sharper analysis of the variance of Z that is provided by the furthermore part of Lemma 11.18. Recall that this part of Lemma 11.18 establishes $\mathbb{V}[Z_i] \leq B(p(i), q(i))$, where $B(a, b) = O((a - b)^2 \cdot (a + b) + (a + b)^2)$, which implies $\mathbb{V}[Z] = O(s^3 \cdot \|p - q\|_2^2 \cdot \beta + s^2 \beta^2)$, where $\beta = \max(\|p\|_2, \|q\|_2)$ (see Corollary 11.19). As noted in the proof of Lemma 11.18, it seems easier to only prove that $\mathbb{V}[Z_i]$ is a degree 3 polynomial in $\max(p(i), q(i))$, and $\mathbb{V}[Z] = O(s^3 \beta^3 + s^2 \beta^2)$ will follow (but does not suffice for the following proof).

Proof: Recall that Corollary 11.19 means that $\mathbb{E}[Z/s^2] = \delta^2$ and $\mathbb{V}[Z/s^2] = O(\delta^2 \cdot (\beta/s) + (\beta/s)^2)$, where $\delta = \|p - q\|_2 > 0$. Starting with Part 1, we have

$$\mathbf{Pr}\left[\left|\frac{Z}{s^2} - \delta^2\right| > \gamma \cdot \delta^2\right] \leq \frac{\mathbb{V}[Z/s^2]}{(\gamma \delta^2)^2}$$

$$\leq \frac{O(\delta^2 \cdot \beta)}{s \cdot \gamma^2 \delta^4} + \frac{O(\beta^2)}{s^2 \cdot \gamma^2 \delta^4}$$

$$= \frac{O(\beta)}{s \cdot \gamma^2 \delta^2} + \gamma^2 \cdot \left(\frac{O(\beta)}{s \cdot \gamma^2 \delta^2}\right)^2.$$

Using $s = \Omega(\beta/\gamma^2 \delta^2)$ and $\gamma < 1$, we get $\mathbf{Pr}[Z/s^2 = (1 \pm \gamma) \cdot \delta^2] \geq 2/3$, and Part 1 follows (because $\mathbf{Pr}[\sqrt{Z}/s = (1 \pm \gamma)^{1/2} \cdot \delta] \geq 2/3$ and $(1 \pm \gamma)^{1/2} \approx 1 \pm (\gamma/2)$, since $\gamma \leq 1/10$.).

Turning to Part 2, we note that by Part 1 (using $\gamma = 0.1$), if $\|p - q\|_2 \geq \epsilon$ and $s = \Omega(\beta/\epsilon^2)$, then $\mathbf{Pr}[\sqrt{Z}/s < 0.9\epsilon] \leq 1/3$. On the other hand, if $\delta = \|p - q\|_2 \leq \epsilon/2$ and $s = \Omega(\beta/\epsilon^2)$, then (as shown next) $\mathbf{Pr}[\sqrt{Z}/s > 0.6\epsilon] \leq 1/3$. The point is that, in this case, $\mathbb{V}[Z/s^2] = O(\epsilon^2 \cdot (\beta/s) + (\beta/s)^2)$, and we can perform a calculation as in Part 1. Specifically, we get

$$\mathbf{Pr}\left[\frac{\sqrt{Z}}{s} > 0.6\epsilon\right] \leq \mathbf{Pr}\left[\left|\frac{Z}{s^2} - \delta^2\right| > (0.6^2 - 0.5^2) \cdot \epsilon^2\right]$$

$$\leq \frac{\mathbb{V}[Z/s^2]}{\Omega(\epsilon^4)}$$

$$\leq \frac{O(\epsilon^2 \cdot \beta)}{s \cdot \epsilon^4} + \frac{O(\beta^2)}{s^2 \cdot \epsilon^4}$$

$$= \frac{O(\beta)}{s \cdot \epsilon^2} + \left(\frac{O(\beta)}{s \cdot \epsilon^2}\right)^2,$$

where the first inequality is due to the fact that $x > v > u$ and $y \leq u$ implies $x^2 - y^2 > v^2 - u^2$. Recalling that $s = \Omega(\beta/\epsilon^2)$, we get $\mathbf{Pr}[\sqrt{Z}/s > 0.6\epsilon] \leq 1/3$, and Part 2 follows. ∎

Corollary 11.21 (Algorithm 11.17 as a very crude $\mathcal{L}_1$-distance approximator): *Let $p, q : [n] \to [0, 1]$ be distributions, and suppose that $\max(\|p\|_2, \|q\|_2) \leq \beta$. For $\epsilon \in (0, 1)$, if $s = \Omega(\beta n/\epsilon^2)$, then, with probability at least $2/3$, Algorithm 11.17 distinguishes between the case that $p = q$ and the case that $\|p - q\|_1 \geq \epsilon$.*

In other words, Algorithm 11.17 yields an ϵ-tester of sample complexity $O(\beta n/\epsilon^2)$ for equality between two given distributions (i.e., the property $\{(p, q) : p = q\}$), under the promise that both distributions have bounded $\mathcal{L}_2$-norm (i.e., $\max(\|p\|_2, \|q\|_2) \leq \beta$). In the case that $\beta = O(1/\sqrt{n})$, the claimed tester has sample complexity $O(\sqrt{n}/\epsilon^2)$, which is optimal, but for very large β (e.g., $\beta = \Omega(1)$) this tester is not optimal. Nevertheless, as shown in Section 11.3.3, Corollary 11.21 (or rather its revision provided as Corollary 11.22), can be used toward obtaining optimal testers for the general case (i.e., for arbitrary β).

Proof: Clearly, $p = q$ implies $\|p - q\|_2 = 0$. On the other hand, if $\|p - q\|_1 \geq \epsilon$, then

$$\|p - q\|_2 = \left(\sum_{i \in [n]} (p(i) - q(i))^2 \right)^{1/2}$$

$$\geq \sum_{i \in [n]} |p(i) - q(i)| \cdot 1/\sqrt{n}$$

$$\geq \epsilon/\sqrt{n},$$

where the first inequality is due to the Cauchy–Schwarz inequality.[30] By Part 2 of Theorem 11.20, if $s = \Omega(\beta/(\epsilon/\sqrt{n})^2) = \Omega(\beta n/\epsilon^2)$, then, with probability at least $2/3$, Algorithm 11.17 distinguishes between the case that $\|p - q\|_2 = 0$ and the case that $\|p - q\|_2 \geq \epsilon/\sqrt{n}$, and the claim follows. ∎

Moving from a Bound on $\max(\|p\|_2, \|q\|_2)$ to a Bound on $\min(\|p\|_2, \|q\|_2)$. Theorem 11.20 and Corollary 11.21 rely on an upper bound on the $\mathcal{L}_2$-norm of *both* distributions. It turns out that (in two of the three cases)[31] it suffices to upper bound the $\mathcal{L}_2$-norm of *one* of the two distributions. This is the case because $\|p - q\| \geq \|p\| - \|q\|$, for any norm $\| \cdot \|$, since $\|q + (p - q)\| \leq \|q\| + \|p - q\|$. Hence, we can first check whether $\|p\|_2 \approx \|q\|_2$, reject if the answer is negative and invoke the algorithm that refers to $\max(\|p\|_2, \|q\|_2)$ otherwise.

Corollary 11.22 (Part 2 of Theorem 11.20 and Corollary 11.21, revised): *Let $p, q :$ $[n] \to [0, 1]$ be distributions, and suppose that $\min(\|p\|_2, \|q\|_2) \leq \beta$.*

1. *(Approximation of $\|p - q\|_2$): If $s = \Omega(\beta/\epsilon^2)$ and $\epsilon \in (0, \beta]$, then there exists an algorithm that uses s samples and distinguishes between the case that $\|p - q\|_2 \leq \epsilon/2$ and the case that $\|p - q\|_2 \geq \epsilon$.*
2. *(Very crude approximation of $\|p - q\|_1$): If $s = \Omega(\beta n/\epsilon^2)$ and $\epsilon \in (0, 1)$, then there exists an algorithm that uses s samples and distinguishes between the case that $p = q$ and the case that $\|p - q\|_1 \geq \epsilon$.*

This result is nonvacuous only for $\beta \geq n^{-1/2}$, whereas when $\beta = O(n^{-1/2})$ we can use $s = O(\sqrt{n}/\epsilon^2)$ in Part 2.

Proof: We first approximate $\|p\|_2$ and $\|q\|_2$ by invoking the $\mathcal{L}_2$-approximation algorithm of Corollary 11.6 with $s = \Omega(1/\beta)$. This allows us to distinguish the case that $\|p\|_2 \leq 2\beta$ from the case that $\|p\|_2 \geq 3\beta$, and ditto for $\|q\|_2$. If one of the two distributions is judged to have norm greater than $2.5 \cdot \beta$ (whereas the other is smaller than β by the hypothesis), then we can safely announce that the distributions are far apart (hereafter referred to as an early verdict). Otherwise, we assume that $\max(\|p\|_2, \|q\|_2) \leq 3\beta$, in which case we can afford to invoke Algorithm 11.17, where in Part 1 we use $s = O(\beta/\epsilon^2)$ and in Part 2 we use $s = O(\beta n/\epsilon^2)$.

---

[30] That is, use $\sum_{i \in [n]} |p(i) - q(i)| \cdot 1 \leq (\sum_{i \in [n]} |p(i) - q(i)|^2)^{1/2} \cdot (\sum_{i \in [n]} 1^2)^{1/2}$.

[31] Specifically, for Part 2 of Theorem 11.20 and for Corollary 11.21.

In analyzing this algorithm we assume that the approximation provided by the algorithm of Corollary 11.6 is within a factor of 1 ± 0.1 of the true value. Hence, if $\max(\|p\|_2, \|q\|_2) > 3\beta$, then (with high probability) this is reflected by the early verdict, since in this case (w.h.p.) the approximate value of $\max(\|p\|_2, \|q\|_2)$ is greater than $2.5 \cdot \beta$. On the other hand, if $\max(\|p\|_2, \|q\|_2) \leq 2\beta$, then (with high probability) the approximate value of $\max(\|p\|_2, \|q\|_2)$ is smaller than $2.5 \cdot \beta$, and we invoke Algorithm 11.17. (In the latter case, the output of Algorithm 11.17 is as desired: For Part 1 we use Part 2 of Theorem 11.20, whereas for Part 2 we use Corollary 11.21.)

We now show that, when the early verdict is made, it is rarely wrong. That is, we assume that $\max(\|p\|_2, \|q\|_2) > 2\beta$, and show that in this case it is justified to assert that p and q are sufficiently far apart. For Part 1 this is justified because $\|p - q\|_2 \geq |\|p\|_2 - \|q\|_2| > 2\beta - \beta \geq \epsilon$, where we use the hypothesis $\epsilon \leq \beta$. In Part 2, we just observe that $\|p\|_2 \neq \|q\|_2$ implies $p \neq q$.

It is left to upper bound the sample complexity of the full algorithm. In Part 1 the overall sample complexity is $O(1/\beta) + O(\beta/\epsilon^2) \leq O(\beta/\epsilon^2)$, where the inequality is due to the hypothesis $\epsilon \leq \beta$. In Part 2 the overall sample complexity is $O(1/\beta) + O(\beta n/\epsilon^2) \leq O(\beta n/\epsilon^2)$, where the inequality is due to the fact $\beta \geq 1/\sqrt{n}$ (and the hypothesis $\epsilon \leq 1$). ∎

11.3.3. Applications: Reduction to the Case of Small Norms

As noted upfront, Corollary 11.21 (resp., Corollary 11.22) is interesting only when the probability distributions have very small $\mathcal{L}_2$-norm (resp., when at least one of the probability distributions has very small $\mathcal{L}_2$-norm). This deficiency is addressed by the following transformation that preserves $\mathcal{L}_1$-distances between distributions, while mapping a target distribution into one of small max-norm (and, hence, small $\mathcal{L}_2$-norm). In other words, the transformation *flattens* the target distribution (according to max-norm and thus also according to $\mathcal{L}_2$-norm), while preserving $\mathcal{L}_1$-distances between distributions. Hence, the transformation offers a unified way of deriving many testing results by a reduction to the case of small norms. We shall illustrate this phenomenon by presenting two reductions (in Sections 11.3.3.2 and 11.3.3.3, respectively).

11.3.3.1. Flattening Distributions

The core of the aforementioned reductions is a (randomized) filter, tailored for a given distribution $q : [n] \to [0, 1]$ and a parameter m. This filter maps q to a distribution $q' : [n + m] \to [0, 1]$ of max-norm at most $1/m$, which implies that $\|q'\|_2 \leq 1/\sqrt{m}$, while preserving the variation distances between distributions. Setting $m = n$, we obtain a distribution q' with extremely small $\mathcal{L}_2$-norm, since in this case $\|q'\|_2 = O(1/\sqrt{2n})$, where $1/\sqrt{2n}$ is the minimum $\mathcal{L}_2$-norm of any distribution over $[2n]$. But, as we shall see in Section 11.3.3.3, other settings of m are also beneficial. In any case, it seems fair to say that q' is *flat*, and view the filter as intended to flatten q.

The aforementioned filter is closely related to the filter underlying Algorithm 11.8. Specifically, for any probability function $q : [n] \to [0, 1]$ and a parameter m (e.g., $m = n$), we consider a randomized filter, denoted $F_{q,m}$, that maps $[n]$ to $S = \{\langle i, j \rangle : i \in [n] \land j \in [m_i]\}$, where $m_i = \lfloor m \cdot q(i) \rfloor + 1$, such that $F_{q,m}(i)$ is uniformly distributed in $\{\langle i, j \rangle : j \in [m_i]\}$. Hence, if i is distributed according to the probability function p, then each $\langle i, j \rangle \in S$

occurs as output with probability $p(i)/m_i$; that is, if X is distributed according to p, then

$$\mathbf{Pr}[F_{q,m}(X) = \langle i, j \rangle] = p(i) \cdot \frac{1}{m_i} \quad \text{(where } m_i = \lfloor m \cdot q(i) \rfloor + 1\text{)}. \tag{11.10}$$

The key observations about this filter are:

1. *The filter $F_{q,m}$ maps q to a distribution with small max-norm:* If Y is distributed according to q, then, for every $\langle i, j \rangle \in S$, it holds that

$$\mathbf{Pr}[F_{q,m}(Y) = \langle i, j \rangle] = q(i) \cdot \frac{1}{m_i}$$

$$= \frac{q(i)}{\lfloor m \cdot q(i) \rfloor + 1},$$

   which is upper-bounded by $1/m$. Hence, the $\mathcal{L}_2$-norm of $F_{q,m} \circ q$ is at most $\sqrt{m \cdot (1/m)^2} = \sqrt{1/m} < \frac{1+(n/m)}{\sqrt{|S|}}$, where the inequality is due to $|S| = \sum_{i \in [n]} m_i \leq \sum_{i \in [n]} (m \cdot q(i) + 1) = m + n$. In the case of $m = n$, we get $\|F_{q,m} \circ q\|_2 < 2/\sqrt{|S|}$.

2. *The filter preserves the variation distance between distributions:* The total variation distance between $F_{q,m}(X)$ and $F_{q,m}(X')$ equals the total variation distance between X and X'. Indeed, this is a generic statement that applies to any filter that maps i to a pair $\langle i, Z_i \rangle$, where Z_i is an arbitrary distribution that depends only on i, and it was already proved in the corresponding item of Section 11.2.2.1 (see also Exercise 11.6).

In short, the filter $F_{q,m}$ flattens q while preserving the total variation distance between q and any other distribution p. We also stress that knowledge of q (and m) allows to implement $F_{q,m}$ as well as to map S to $[m']$, where $m' = |S|$.

Note that the parameter m only governs the level of flatness obtained by the filter $F_{q,m}$ (when applied to q); larger values of m yield smaller max-norm (and $\mathcal{L}_2$-norm) of $F_{q,m} \circ q$, but this comes at the cost of a larger support (i.e., the support size of $F_{q,m} \circ q$ is at least m). The filter preserves the variation distance between distributions for any value of m, including $m = 0$ (which essentially corresponds to the identity transformation; i.e., $F_{q,0}(i) = \langle i, 1 \rangle$ for every i).

11.3.3.2. Testing Equality to a Fixed Distribution

The foregoing observations regarding the filter $F_{q,n}$ (when using the setting $m = n$), lead to the following reduction of the task of *testing equality to a fixed distribution D* to the task captured by Part 2 of Corollary 11.22. (Indeed, this yields an alternative proof of Theorem 11.11.)

Algorithm 11.23 (Reducing testing equality to an arbitrary distribution to testing equality between pairs of distributions such that at least one of them has a small $\mathcal{L}_2$-norm): *Let D be an arbitrary distribution with probability function $q : [n] \rightarrow [0, 1]$, and T be an ϵ'-tester of sample complexity $s(m', \beta, \epsilon')$ for equality between distribution pairs over $[m']$ such that at least one of the two distributions has $\mathcal{L}_2$-norm at most β. On input $(n, \epsilon; i_1, \ldots, i_s)$, where $i_1, \ldots, i_s \in [n]$ are $s = s(2n, n^{-1/2}, \epsilon)$ samples drawn according to an unknown distribution p, the tester proceeds as follows:*

1. It produces a s-long sequence $(i'_1, \ldots, i'_s)$ by sampling each i'_k from the known distribution D.

2. It produces a s-long sequence $(e'_1, \ldots, e'_s)$ by applying $F_{q,n}$ to $(i'_1, \ldots, i'_s)$, where $F_{q,n}$ is as in Eq. (11.10); that is, for every $k \in [s]$, it produces $e'_k \leftarrow F_{q,n}(i'_k)$. (Recall that each e'_k is in S, and that the $\mathcal{L}_2$-norm of $F_{q,n} \circ q$ is at most $\frac{1}{\sqrt{n}} \leq \frac{2}{\sqrt{|S|}}$.)

3. It produces a s-long sequence $(e_1, \ldots, e_s)$ by applying $F_{q,n}$ to $(i_1, \ldots, i_s)$; that is, for every $k \in [s]$, it produces $e_k \leftarrow F_{q,n}(i_k)$.

4. It invokes the ϵ-tester T for equality providing it with the sequence $(e_1, \ldots, e_s, e'_1, \ldots, e'_s)$. Note that this is a sequence over S, but it can be translated to a sequence over $[m']$ such that $m' = |S|$ (by mapping each element of S to its rank in S).

We stress that if $F_{q,n}$ is invoked t times on the same i, then the t outcomes are (identically and) independently distributed.

Hence, *the complexity of testing equality to a general distribution D over [n] is upper-bounded by the complexity of testing equality between two unknown distributions over [2n] such that one of them has $\mathcal{L}_2$-norm at most $1/\sqrt{n}$.* Using Part 2 of Corollary 11.22, we reestablish Theorem 11.11.[32]

Digest. We solved a testing task regarding a single unknown distribution by reducing it to a testing task regarding two unknown distributions. This was done (in Step 1 of Algorithm 11.23) by generating samples from the fixed distribution D, and presenting these samples as samples of a second (supposedly unknown) distribution. Obviously, there is nothing wrong with doing so (i.e., such a reduction is valid), except that it feels weird to reduce a seemingly easier problem to a seemingly harder one. Note, however, that the two problems are not really comparable, since the problem of testing two distributions refers to a special case in which one of these distributions is flat. Indeed, the core of the reduction is the use of the flattening filter, which mapped the fixed distribution to a flat one, and by doing so allows to apply the two-distribution tester (which requires one of the distributions to be flat).

In Section 11.3.3.3, we shall see a reduction that uses the flattening filter in order to reduce one testing problem regarding two distributions to another testing problem regarding two distributions (of which one is flat).

11.3.3.3. Testing Equality between Two Unknown Distributions

The filter $F_{q,m}$ captured in Eq. (11.10) can be applied also to testing properties of tuples of distributions. Actually, this is a more interesting application, since reducing a problem regarding a single unknown distribution to a problem regarding two unknown distributions seems an over-kill. On the other hand, the reader may wonder how one can apply this filter (i.e., the filter $F_{q,m}$) when the distribution (i.e., q) is not known. The answer is that we shall use one part of the sample of q in order to obtain some statistics of q, denoted $\tilde{q}$, and then use a filter tailored to this statistics (i.e., $F_{\tilde{q},\tilde{m}}$). Of course, the larger the sample we take of q, the better statistics $\tilde{q}$ we derive, which in turn offers lower norm

---

[32] Recall that by Part 2 of Corollary 11.22, the tester T, used in the foregoing reduction, can be implemented within complexity $O(\sqrt{n}/\epsilon^2)$.

of $F_{\tilde{q},\tilde{m}} \circ q$. This leads to the following reduction, where m is a parameter that governs the size of the aforementioned sample.

Algorithm 11.24 (Reducing testing equality between pairs of arbitrary distributions to testing equality between pairs of distributions such that at least one of them has a small $\mathcal{L}_2$-norm):[33] *Let T be an ϵ-tester of sample complexity $s(m', \beta, \epsilon)$ for equality between distribution pairs over $[m']$ such that at least one of the two distributions has $\mathcal{L}_2$-norm at most β. On input $(n, \epsilon; i_1, \ldots, i_s; i'_1, \ldots, i'_{s+2m})$, where $i_1, \ldots, i_s \in [n]$ are $s = s(n + 2m, O(m^{-1/2}), \epsilon)$ samples drawn according to an unknown distribution $p : [n] \to [0, 1]$ and $i'_1, \ldots, i'_{s+2m} \in [n]$ are $s + 2m$ samples drawn according to an unknown distribution $q : [n] \to [0, 1]$, the tester proceeds as follows:*

1. *Generates $\tilde{m} \leftarrow \Psi(m)$, and halts and accepts if $\tilde{m} > 2m$.*

   Let $\tilde{q} : [n] \to [0, 1]$ be the distribution function that corresponds to the sample $(i'_{s+1}, \ldots, i'_{s+\tilde{m}})$; that is, $\tilde{q}(i) = |\{k \in [\tilde{m}] : i'_{s+k} = i\}| / \tilde{m}$.

2. *Produces a s-long sequence $(e'_1, \ldots, e'_s)$ by applying $F_{\tilde{q},\tilde{m}}$ to $(i'_1, \ldots, i'_s)$, where $F_{\tilde{q},\tilde{m}}$ is as in Eq. (11.10); that is, for every $k \in [s]$, it produces $e'_k \leftarrow F_{\tilde{q},\tilde{m}}(i'_k)$.*

   (Recall that each e'_k is in $S = \{\langle i, j \rangle : i \in [n] \wedge j \in [m_i]\}$, where $m_i = \lfloor \tilde{m} \cdot \tilde{q}(i) \rfloor + 1 = \tilde{m} \cdot \tilde{q}(i) + 1$. Hence, $|S| = \tilde{m} + n \leq 2m + n$.)[34]

   (We shall show that, with high probability, the $\mathcal{L}_2$-norm of $F_{\tilde{q},\tilde{m}} \circ q$ is at most $O(m^{-1/2})$.)

3. *Produces a s-long sequence $(e_1, \ldots, e_s)$ by applying $F_{\tilde{q},\tilde{m}}$ to $(i_1, \ldots, i_s)$; that is, for every $k \in [s]$, it produces $e_k \leftarrow F_{\tilde{q},\tilde{m}}(i_k)$.*

4. *Invokes the tester T for equality providing it with the input $(n + 2m, \epsilon; e_1, \ldots, e_s; e'_1, \ldots, e'_s)$. Note that $(e_1, \ldots, e_s, e'_1, \ldots, e'_s)$ is a sequence over S, but it can be translated to a sequence over $[n + 2m]$ (by mapping each element of S to its rank in S).*

We stress that if $F_{\tilde{q},\tilde{m}}$ is invoked t times on the same i, then the t outcomes are (identically and) independently distributed.[35]

Recall that, for every $\tilde{q}$ (and $\tilde{m}$), the total variation distance between $F_{\tilde{q},\tilde{m}} \circ p$ and $F_{\tilde{q},\tilde{m}} \circ q$ equals the total variation distance between p and q. Hence, the analysis of Algorithm 11.24 reduces to proving that, with high probability, it holds that the $\mathcal{L}_2$-norm of $F_{\tilde{q},\tilde{m}} \circ q$ is at most $O(\sqrt{1/m})$.

Lemma 11.25 (The $\mathcal{L}_2$-norm of $F_{\tilde{q},\tilde{m}} \circ q$): *Let $\tilde{m}$ and $\tilde{q}$ be generated at random as in Algorithm 11.24. Then, for every t, the probability that $\|F_{\tilde{q},\tilde{m}} \circ q\|_2$ exceeds $t \cdot m^{-1/2}$ is lower than t^{-2}.*

---

[33] Note that the resulting tester takes s samples from p and $s + 2m$ samples of q. Needless to say, we can fit Definition 11.2 by taking $s + 2m$ samples from each distribution, and ignoring the $2m$ last samples of p.

[34] Note that $\lfloor \tilde{m} \cdot \tilde{q}(i) \rfloor = \tilde{m} \cdot \tilde{q}(i)$ holds since $\tilde{q}(i)$ is a multiple of $1/\tilde{m}$.

[35] **Advanced comment:** We mention that using the filter $F_{\tilde{q},\tilde{m}}$ is the most natural choice, although we could have used the filter $F_{\tilde{q},n'}$ for any $n' \in [\tilde{m}, O(n)]$. Note that for each i such that $q(i) = O(1/m)$, with positive constant probability $\tilde{q}(i) = 0$, and in that case $(F_{\tilde{q},n'} \circ q)(i) = q(i)$ for any n'. Hence, for q that is uniform over a set of size $\Theta(m)$, the $\mathcal{L}_2$-norm of $F_{\tilde{q},n'} \circ q$ is $\Theta(1/\sqrt{m})$ for any $n' \geq \tilde{m}$.

We stress that this lemma refers to a probability space that includes the event that $\widetilde{m} > 2m$, but this event occurs with probability $\exp(-m)$ and it can be ignored (in the analysis of Algorithm 11.24).

Proof: Before presenting the actual proof, we offer some intuition as to why the lemma holds. Suppose that $q(i) = \omega(1/m)$. Then, with high probability, $\widetilde{q}(i) = \Theta(q(i))$, and so $F_{\widetilde{q},\widetilde{m}} \circ q$ maps i to the uniform distribution over a set of s_i elements, where $s_i = \Theta(m \cdot q(i))$. Hence, the contribution of i to the square of the $\mathcal{L}_2$-norm of $F_{\widetilde{q},\widetilde{m}} \circ q$ is $q(i)^2/s_i = O(q(i)/m)$, and so the aggregated contribution of all such i's is $O(1/m)$. Furthermore, the contribution of each i is always at most $q(i)^2$, and for $q(i) = O(1/m)$ this bound is good enough (since $q(i)^2 = O(q(i)/m)$ holds).[36] Ignoring the low-probability events (for the case of $q(i) = \omega(1/m)$), we infer that the square of the $\mathcal{L}_2$-norm of $F_{\widetilde{q},\widetilde{m}} \circ q$ is $O(1/m)$.

Teaching Note: The actual proof is quite technical and can be skipped. It consists of various manipulations and utilizes features of the probability function of the Poisson distribution.

Turning to the actual proof, we first bound the expected square of the $\mathcal{L}_2$-norm of $F_{\widetilde{q},\widetilde{m}} \circ q$, where the expectation is taken over the sample of q that defines $\widetilde{q}$ (and over the choice of $\widetilde{m} \leftarrow \Psi(m)$). Let ζ_i be a random variable representing the distribution of m_i; that is, $\zeta_i - 1$ equals $|\{k \in [\widetilde{m}] : i_k = i\}|$, which indeed equals $\widetilde{m} \cdot \widetilde{q}(i)$. Then, for fixed $\widetilde{m}$ and $(i_{s+1}, \ldots, i_{s+2m})$, which determine $\widetilde{q}$ and S, the square of the $\mathcal{L}_2$-norm of $q' = F_{\widetilde{q},\widetilde{m}} \circ q$ equals

$$\sum_{\langle i, j \rangle \in S} q'(\langle i, j \rangle)^2 = \sum_{i \in [n]} \sum_{j \in [\zeta_i]} (q(i)/\zeta_i)^2 = \sum_{i \in [n]} q(i)^2/\zeta_i.$$

Hence, our first task is to upper-bound $\mathbb{E}[1/\zeta_i]$, while assuming $q(i) > 0$ (as otherwise $\zeta_i \equiv 1$). Recalling that (by Proposition 11.16) the random variable $\zeta_i' = \zeta_i - 1$ is distributed as $\Psi(m \cdot q(i))$, we have[37]

$$\mathbb{E}\left[\frac{1}{1 + \zeta_i'}\right] = \mathbb{E}\left[\int_0^1 x^{\zeta_i'} dx\right]$$

$$= \int_0^1 \mathbb{E}\left[x^{\zeta_i'}\right] dx$$

$$= \int_0^1 e^{(x-1) \cdot m \cdot q(i)} dx$$

$$= \frac{1 - e^{-m \cdot q(i)}}{m \cdot q(i)},$$

---

[36] We mention that, if $q(i) = o(1/m)$, then, with high probability, $\widetilde{q}(i) = 0$, and so $F_{\widetilde{q},\widetilde{m}} \circ q$ maps i to itself. Hence, the contribution of this i to the square of the $\mathcal{L}_2$-norm of $F_{\widetilde{q},\widetilde{m}} \circ q$ equals $q(i)^2 = o(q(i)/m)$.

[37] The first equality is due to the fact that for every $c \in \mathbb{N} \cup \{0\}$ it holds that $\int_0^1 x^c dx = (1-0)/(c+1)$. The third equality is due to the fact that for every $r \in [0, 1]$ it holds that $\mathbb{E}[r^{\Psi(\lambda)}] = e^{(r-1)\lambda}$, which can be proved by straightforward manipulations of the probability function of the Poisson distribution (as defined in Eq. (11.7)).

which is at most $1/(m \cdot q(i))$. Hence, the expected value of $\|F_{\widetilde{q},\widetilde{m}} \circ q\|_2^2$ equals

$$\mathbb{E}\left[\sum_{i \in [n]} q(i)^2/\zeta_i\right] = \sum_{i \in [n]} q(i)^2 \cdot \mathbb{E}[1/\zeta_i]$$

$$\leq \sum_{i \in [n]} \frac{q(i)^2}{m \cdot q(i)},$$

which equals $1/m$. Using Markov's inequality, we have $\mathbf{Pr}[\|F_{\widetilde{q},\widetilde{m}} \circ q\|_2^2 > t^2/m] < 1/t^2$. ∎

Setting the Parameter m. Algorithm 11.24 works under any choice of the parameter $m = \Omega(1)$. Combined with a tester T as provided by Part 2 of Corollary 11.22 (while setting $\beta = O(m^{-1/2})$), Algorithm 11.24 yields an ϵ-tester of sample complexity $O(m + (n + 2m) \cdot m^{-1/2}/\epsilon^2)$. (Indeed, with small constant probability, T is invoked on an input distribution that violates the promise, but this event is accounted for by the error probability of the resulting tester.) Using $m = \min(n^{2/3}/\epsilon^{4/3}, n)$, we get[38]

Theorem 11.26 (Testing equality of two unknown distributions): *The property consisting of pairs of identical distributions over $[n]$ (i.e., $\{(D, D) : D \in [n]\}$) can be ϵ-tested in sample and time complexity $O(\max(n^{2/3}/\epsilon^{4/3}, \sqrt{n}/\epsilon^2))$.*

We mention that this result is tight; that is, ϵ-testing equality of two unknown distributions over $[n]$ requires $\Omega(\max(n^{2/3}/\epsilon^{4/3}, \sqrt{n}/\epsilon^2))$ samples [266] (see also [73]).

11.4. On the Complexity of Testing Properties of Distributions

As noted at the end of Section 11.1.1, any distribution $p : [n] \to [0, 1]$ can be learned up to accuracy of ϵ by a $O(n/\epsilon^2)$-time algorithm (Exercise 11.4). Thus, our focus is on testers that outperform this bound. We have already seen such testers in Sections 11.2 and 11.3, but here we address the question of testing properties of distributions in full generality.

A very general positive answer is provided via "learning distributions up to relabeling" (where the notion of "relabeling" is implicit in Section 11.1.3). Specifically, we call the distribution $q : [n] \to [0, 1]$ a relabeling of the distribution $p : [n] \to [0, 1]$ if there exists a permutation $\pi : [n] \to [n]$ such that $q(i) = p(\pi(i))$ for every $i \in [n]$. Equivalently, we may consider the task of learning the histogram of an unknown distribution $p : [n] \to [0, 1]$, where the histogram of p is defined as the set of pairs $\{(v, m) : m = |\{i \in [n] : p(i) = v\}| > 0\}$.[39] The following result of Valiant and Valiant [263] asserts that *the histogram of an unknown distribution can be learned faster (and using less samples) than the distribution itself, where the saving is of a logarithmic factor.*

---

[38] Under this setting (which implies $m \leq n$), the complexity is $O(m + n \cdot m^{-1/2}/\epsilon^2)$, which can be bounded by considering the two cases (i.e., $m = n^{2/3}/\epsilon^{4/3}$ and $m = n \leq n^{2/3}/\epsilon^{4/3}$).

[39] Note that this is one of the two equivalent definitions of a histogram that were presented in Section 11.1.3. We prefer this definition here since it yields a more succinct representation.

Theorem 11.27 (Learning the histogram):[40] *There exists an $O(\epsilon^{-2} \cdot n/\log n)$ time algorithm that, on input n, ϵ and $O(\epsilon^{-2} \cdot n/\log n)$ samples drawn from an unknown distribution $p : [n] \to [0, 1]$, outputs, with probability $1 - \exp(-n^{\Omega(1)})$, a histogram of a distribution that is ϵ-close to p.*

(The error probability is stated here, since error reduction to such a (lower than usual) level would have increased the time and sample complexities by more than a $O(\log n)$ factor.) The implication of this result on testing any label-invariant property of distributions is immediate.

Corollary 11.28 (Testing label-invariant properties of single distributions): *Let $\mathcal{D}$ be a label-invariant property of distributions over $[n]$. Then, $\mathcal{D}$ has a tester of sample complexity $s(n, \epsilon) = O(\epsilon^{-2} \cdot n/\log n)$.*

The tester consists of employing the algorithm of Theorem 11.27 with proximity parameter $\epsilon/2$ and accepting if and only if the output fits a histogram of a distribution that is $\epsilon/2$-close to $\mathcal{D}$. Using the same idea, we get *algorithms for estimating the distance of an unknown distribution to any label-invariant property of distributions*. Actually, obtaining such an estimation may be viewed as a special case of Corollary 11.28, by considering, for any property $\mathcal{D}$ and any distance parameter $\delta > 0$, the set of all distributions that are δ-close to $\mathcal{D}$.

On the negative side, it turns out that, for many natural properties, the tester asserted in Corollary 11.28 is the best possible (up to a factor of $1/\epsilon$). Examples are presented in the sequel (see Corollaries 11.30 and 11.31), while relying on Theorem 11.29.

Theorem 11.29 (Optimality of Theorem 11.27):[41] *For every sufficiently small $\eta > 0$, there exist two distributions $p_1, p_2 : [n] \to [0, 1]$ that are indistinguishable by any label-invariant algorithm that takes $O(\eta n/\log n)$ samples, although p_1 is η-close to the uniform distribution over $[n]$ and p_2 is η-close to the uniform distribution over $[n/2]$.*[42]

Hence, learning the histograms of distributions in the sense stated in Theorem 11.27 (even with proximity parameter $\epsilon = 1/5$) requires $\Omega(n/\log n)$ samples.[43] As an immediate corollary, we infer that testing the property that consists of all relabelings of p_1

---

[40] Valiant and Valiant [263] stated this result for the "relative earthmover distance" (REMD) and commented that the total variation distance up to relabeling is upper-bounded by REMD. This claim appears as a special case of [265, Fact 1] (using $\tau = 0$), and a detailed proof appears in [154].

[41] Like in footnote 40, we note that Valiant and Valiant [263] stated this result for the "relative earthmover distance" (REMD) and commented that the total variation distance up to relabelling is upper-bounded by REMD. This claim appears as a special case of [265, Fact 1] (using $\tau = 0$), and a detailed proof appears in [154].

[42] Here indistinguishability means that the distinguishing gap of such potential algorithms is $o(1)$. Note that the statement is nontrivial only for $\eta < 1/4$, since the uniform distribution over $[n]$ is 0.5-close to the uniform distribution over $[n/2]$.

[43] This is the case because otherwise, given $o(n/\log n)$ samples of p_1 (resp., p_2), w.h.p., the algorithm outputs a histogram of a distribution that is ϵ-close to p_1 (resp., p_2), which in turn is η-close to the uniform distribution over $[n]$ (resp., over $[n/2]$). As in Theorem 11.12, we may assume, w.l.o.g., that this algorithm is label-invariant. But by Theorem 11.29 the output in these two cases is distributed almost identically, which implies that (w.h.p.) this output describes a distribution that is $(\epsilon + \eta)$-close both to the uniform distribution over $[n]$ and to the uniform distribution over $[n/2]$, which is impossible since these two distributions are at distance $1/2$ apart (whereas $\epsilon = 1/5$ and we can have $\eta < 1/20$).

requires $\Omega(n/\log n)$ samples, which means that Corollary 11.28 is, in general, optimal (up to a factor of $1/\epsilon$).[44]

Corollary 11.30 (Testing the set of relabelings of a fixed distribution may require $\Omega(n/\log n)$ samples): *Let p_1 be as in Theorem 11.29, and $\mathcal{D}_1$ be the set of all distributions that have the same histogram as p_1 (i.e., are relabelings of p_1). Then, testing $\mathcal{D}_1$ requires $\Omega(n/\log n)$ samples.*

We stress that the property $\mathcal{D}_1$ is label-invariant (by its very definition); hence, for fixed $\epsilon > 0$, the sample complexity of ϵ-testing $\mathcal{D}_1$ is $\Theta(n/\log n)$. In contrast, $\{p_1\}$ is ϵ-testable with $O(\sqrt{n})$ samples (see Theorem 11.11). Hence, testing equality to a fixed distribution may be easier than testing equality to any of its relabelings. (The two problems are trivially equivalent when the fixed distribution is uniform on the predetermined domain.)

Proof Sketch: The key observation is that p_2 is far from $\mathcal{D}_1$, since p_2 is close to the uniform distribution over $[n/2]$ whereas each distribution in $\mathcal{D}_1$ is close to the uniform distribution over $[n]$. Hence, any tester of $\mathcal{D}_1$ must reject p_2 with probability at least $2/3$. But such a tester (which, by Theorem 11.12, may be assumed to be label-invariant) must accept p_1 with probability at least $2/3$, whereas distinguishing these two distributions requires $\Omega(n/\log n)$ samples. ∎

More on the Optimality of Corollary 11.28. Additional cases in which Corollary 11.28 yields the best possible testers (up to a factor of $1/\epsilon$) are presented next. For any property of distributions $\mathcal{D}_0$ and $\delta > 0$, we may consider the set of distributions $\mathcal{D}$ that are δ-close to $\mathcal{D}_0$. Indeed, if $\mathcal{D}_0$ is label-invariant, then so is $\mathcal{D}$ (and Corollary 11.28 applies to it). Corollary 11.31 asserts that for some "base properties" $\mathcal{D}_0$ testing the corresponding property $\mathcal{D}$ requires $\Omega(n/\log n)$ samples. In general, as detailed in Claim 11.31.1, any label-invariant property that contains all distributions that are close to the uniform distribution over $[n]$ but contains only distributions that are far from the uniform distribution over $[n/2]$ cannot be tested by $o(n/\log n)$ samples. Ditto for any property that contains all distributions that are close to the uniform distribution over $[n/2]$ but contains only distributions that are far from the uniform distribution over $[n]$. In particular:

Corollary 11.31 (Optimality of Corollary 11.28 in some cases): *For all sufficiently small constant $\delta > 0$, testing each of the following (label-invariant) properties of distributions over $[n]$ requires $\Omega(n/\log n)$ samples.*

1. *The set of distributions that are δ-close to the uniform distribution over $[n]$.*
2. *The set of distributions that are δ-close to having support size (exactly or at most) $n/2$.*
3. *The set of distributions that are δ-close to being m-grained, for any integer $m \in [\Omega(n), O(n)]$.*

Here, testing means ϵ-testing for a sufficiently small constant $\epsilon > 0$. Furthermore, the bound holds for any $\delta \in (0, \Omega(\eta_0))$ and any $\epsilon \in (0, 0.5 - 2\delta)$, where

---

[44] Some indication to the possible nonoptimality of Corollary 11.28 with respect to the dependence on ϵ is provided in [271, 1].

$\eta_0 \in (0, 0.25)$ *is the constant implicit in Theorem 11.29* (i.e., in the phrase "for all sufficiently small $\eta > 0$").[45]

We stress that the lower bounds do not necessarily hold for the "base property" (i.e., the case of $\delta = 0$): This is definitely the case with respect to Item 1, since the uniform distribution over $[n]$ is testable by $O(\sqrt{n})$ samples (see Corollary 11.5). On the other hand, the $\Omega(n/\log n)$ lower bound holds also for the base case of Item 2 (i.e., testing the set of distributions over $[n]$ that have support size at most $n/2$ requires $\Omega(n/\log n)$ samples).[46] We also note that the restriction on m in Item 3 is inherent (for example, note that any distribution over $[n]$ is ϵ-close to being $\lceil n/\epsilon \rceil$-grained).

Proof: We first detail the general observation that underlies all results, while letting U_m denote the uniform distribution over $[m]$.

Claim 11.31.1 (The general observation): *Let $\eta \in (0, \eta_0]$ and suppose that $\mathcal{D}$ is a label-invariant property of distributions over $[n]$ such that all distributions that are η-close to U_n are in $\mathcal{D}$ and $U_{n/2}$ is $(\epsilon + \eta)$-far from $\mathcal{D}$. Then, ϵ-testing $\mathcal{D}$ requires $\Omega(n/\log n)$ samples. Ditto when all distributions that are η-close to $U_{n/2}$ are in $\mathcal{D}$ and U_n is $(\epsilon + \eta)$-far from $\mathcal{D}$.*

Proof: We focus on the primary claim. Invoking Theorem 11.29, observe that p_1 is in $\mathcal{D}$ (since p_1 is η-close to U_n), whereas p_2 is ϵ-far from $\mathcal{D}$ (since p_2 is η-close to $U_{n/2}$, which is $(\epsilon + \eta)$-far from $\mathcal{D}$). The situation is illustrated in Figure 11.3. The main claim follows since Theorem 11.29 asserts that p_1 and p_2 are indistinguishable by any label-invariant algorithm that takes $o(n/\log n)$ samples, whereas ϵ-testing $\mathcal{D}$ requires distinguishing them. Recall that, by Theorem 11.12, we may assume that the tester is label-invariant. The secondary claim follows by reversing the roles of p_1 and p_2 (i.e., noting that in this case p_2 is in $\mathcal{D}$ whereas p_1 is ϵ-far from $\mathcal{D}$). ∎

Using Claim 11.31.1, we establish the various items of the current corollary. Specifically, denoting by $\mathcal{D}_i$ the set of distributions defined in Item i, we proceed as follows. For $\epsilon + 2\delta < 1/2$, we recall that $\mathcal{D}_1$ equals the set of all distributions that are δ-close to U_n, and observe that $U_{n/2}$ is $(\epsilon + \delta)$-far from $\mathcal{D}_1$ (since otherwise $U_{n/2}$ is $((\epsilon + \delta) + \delta)$-close to U_n, which contradicts $\epsilon + 2\delta < 1/2$). Item 1 follows by applying the primary claim (with $\eta = \min(\delta, \eta_0)$).

Turning to Item 2, for $\epsilon + 2\delta < 1/2$, observe that $\mathcal{D}_2$ contains all distributions that are δ-close to $U_{n/2}$ whereas U_n is $(\epsilon + \delta)$-far from $\mathcal{D}_2$ (since otherwise U_n is $((\epsilon + \delta) + \delta)$-close to a distribution with support size $n/2$, which contradicts $\epsilon + 2\delta < 1/2$). Item 2 follows by applying the secondary claim (with $\eta = \min(\delta, \eta_0)$). The same holds for Item 3 when $m = n/2$, but we have to handle the other cases too. For $m < n/2$ we proceed as in the case of $m = n/2$, while resetting n to $2m$, which means that we consider distributions over $[n]$ with a support that is a subset

---

[45] The case of small $\delta > 0$, which may depend on ϵ, is typically called "tolerant testing" (for the "base property"); see Section 12.1.

[46] This follows from [261, Sec. 5.5] which implies that approximating the support size of n-grained distributions (up to an additive term of $n/8$) requires $\Omega(n/\log n)$ samples. Hence, there exists $i \in [17]$ such that testing the set of distributions over $[n]$ that have support size at most $i \cdot n/17$ requires $\Omega(n/\log n)$ samples. We do not know whether the lower bounds for Item 3 hold also for the "base property" (i.e., the case of $\delta = 0$); we consider this an interesting open problem.

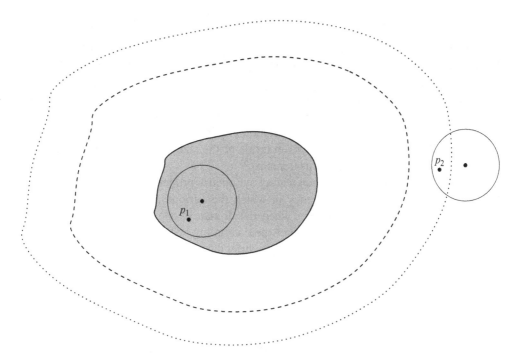

Figure 11.3: The proof of Claim 11.31.1. The shaded region represents $\mathcal{D}$, and the dashed (resp., dotted) line represents distance ϵ (resp., $\epsilon + \eta$) from $\mathcal{D}$. The left (resp., right) circle represents the set of distributions that are η-close to U_n (resp., to $U_{n/2}$), which contains p_1 (resp., p_2). In the figure, p_2 is depicted as being at distance $\delta \in (\epsilon, \epsilon + \eta]$ from $\mathcal{D}$, but it may be the case that p_2 is $(\epsilon + \eta)$-far from $\mathcal{D}$.

of $[2m]$. (So the lower bound is $\Omega(m/\log m) = \Omega(n/\log n)$, where the inequality uses $m = \Omega(n)$.) For $m > n/2$ (satisfying $m = O(n)$), we provide a lower bound by reducing the case of $m \in (0.25n, 0.5n]$ to the case of $m = O(n)$.

Claim 11.31.2 (A reduction for Item 3): *Let $\mathcal{G}_{n,m,\delta}$ denote the set of distributions over $[n]$ that are δ-close to being m-grained. Then, for every $\epsilon > 0$ and $t \in \mathbb{N}$, the task of ϵ-testing $\mathcal{G}_{n,m,\delta}$ is reducible to the task of ϵ/t-testing $\mathcal{G}_{n+1,tm,\delta/t}$, while preserving the number of samples.*

Proof Sketch: Consider a randomized filter, denoted $F_{n,t}$, that with probability $1/t$ maps $i \in [n]$ to itself, and otherwise maps it to $n + 1$. This filter maps m-grained distributions over $[n]$ to tm-grained distributions over $[n + 1]$. Furthermore, a distribution $p : [n] \to [0, 1]$ that is at distance γ from being m-grained is mapped by $F_{n,t}$ to a distribution that is at distance γ/t from being tm-grained. (This follows by observing that the distribution $p' = F_{n,t} \circ p$ satisfies $p'(i) = p(i)/t$ for every $i \in [n]$, and $p'(n + 1) = (t - 1)/t$.) ∎

Item 3 follows by using an adequate $t = O(1)$. Specifically, wishing to establish the claim for $m > n/2$, pick $t = \lceil 2m/n \rceil$ and reduce from ϵ-testing $\mathcal{G}_{n,\lfloor m/t \rfloor,\delta}$, which yields a lower bound for ϵ/t-testing $\mathcal{G}_{n,m',\delta/t}$ such that $m' = t \cdot \lfloor m/t \rfloor \in (m - t, m]$. (See Exercise 11.13 for a reduction to the case of $m' = m$.) ∎

11.5. Chapter Notes

As stated at the very beginning of this chapter, testing properties of distributions, also known as *distribution testing*, is fundamentally different from testing properties of functions (as discussed in the rest of this book). Nevertheless, as observed in [257, Sec. 2.1] and detailed in [153, Sec. 6.3], testing properties of distributions is closely related to testing *symmetric* properties of functions (i.e., properties that are invariant under all permutations of the domain). Articulating this relation requires stating the complexity of testers of (symmetric) properties of functions in terms of the size of the range of the function (rather than in terms of the size of its domain).[47]

The key observation is that, when testing symmetric properties of functions, we may confine our attention to the frequency in which the various range elements appear as values of the function. Furthermore, when the domain is significantly larger than the range, we can ignore the difference between sampling with repetitions and sampling without repetitions. In such a case, we may restrict the tester to obtaining the value of the function at uniformly distributed arguments, *while ignoring the identity of the argument.*[48] Hence, the function $f : S \to R$ is identified with the distribution generated by selecting uniformly at random $s \in S$ and outputting $f(s)$, and the testing tasks are related accordingly.

While the foregoing perspective attempts to link distribution testing (i.e., testing properties of distributions) to the rest of property testing, the following perspective, which advocates the study of distribution testing of linear or even superlinear (sample) complexity, goes in the opposite direction. Recall that any property of functions can be tested by querying all arguments of the function (i.e., locations in the object), and that the aim of property testing is to obtain sublinear time (or at least query) complexity. In contrast, distribution testing does not trivialize when one obtains $O(n)$ samples from a distribution over $[n]$. In particular, learning such a distribution up to a deviation of ϵ requires $\Omega(n/\epsilon^2)$ samples. So the question is whether one can do better than this yardstick. While the study of property testing typically focuses on the dependence of the complexity on n, as noted by Ilias Diakonikolas, in some settings of distribution testing, one may care more about the dependence on ϵ.

11.5.1. History and Credits

The study of testing properties of distributions was initiated by Batu, Fortnow, Rubinfeld, Smith, and White [35].[49] Their starting point was a test of uniformity, which was implicit in the work of Goldreich and Ron [149], where it is applied to test the distribution of the endpoint of a relatively short random walk on a bounded-degree graph. Generalizing this tester of uniformity, Batu *et al.* [35, 34] presented testers for the property consisting of pairs of identical distributions as well as for all properties consisting of any single

---

[47] Of course, one may use a statement that refers to the sizes of both the domain and the range.

[48] The hypothesis that the domain is sufficiently large justifies ignoring the probability that the same $s \in S$ was selected twice.

[49] Actually, testing properties of distributions was considered by Goldreich, Goldwasser, and Ron, who showed that testing may be harder than learning in that context [140, Sec. 3.4.3]. Being in the mindset that focused on complexity that is polylogarithmic in the size of the object (see discussion in Section 1.4), they interpreted their result as a strong negative result, and failed to note that it does not rule out sublinear time testers. Furthermore, they later forgot that the topic is mentioned at all in [140]. We thank Ronitt Rubinfeld for reminding us of that fact.

distribution.[50] Both results are presented in this text, but the presentation follows an approach proposed recently by Diakonikolas and Kane [89].

Actually, our presentation focused on these two classes of properties (of distributions): the class of single-distribution properties that are singletons (i.e., testing equality to a *known* distribution), and the class of pairs of distributions that are equal or close according to some norm.

We start with the tester for the property of being the uniform distribution over $[n]$, which is implicit in [149]. (As noted in the text, the analysis that we present yields optimal sample complexity in terms of n, but not in terms of ϵ; a recent result of Diakonikolas *et al.* [88] establishes the optimality of this tester over both n and ϵ.)[51] Next, we apply the approach that underlies [89] in order to reduce testing any property consisting of a single distribution (i.e., testing equality to a *known* distribution) to testing the uniform distribution; this reduction appeared in [137].

Turning to the task of testing equality between a pair of *unknown* distributions, we start with a (sample optimal) tester for the case that the distributions have small $\mathcal{L}_2$-norm, which is provided in [73], and then apply the reduction presented in [89].

The results surveyed in Section 11.4 are based on the work of Valiant and Valiant [263]. In particular, Theorems 11.27 and 11.29 are due to [263], but the corollaries were not explicitly stated there.[52] Theorem 11.27 was inspired by works of Orlitsky *et al.* [219, 220, 3], which are pivoted at finding a distribution that maximizes the likelihood of a given collision statistics.[53] Theorem 11.29 builds on [232], which presents two n-grained distributions with vastly different support sizes (i.e., $\Theta(n)$ versus $n^{1-o(1)} = o(n)$) that cannot be distinguished using less than $n^{1-o(1)}$ samples.

We stress that the current chapter covers only a few of the many distribution testing problems that were studied in computer science in the last two decades (see, e.g., [32, 261, 263, 266]). The interested reader is referred to Canonne's survey [68] (which also reviews alternative models such as the model of conditional sampling [70]).

Lastly, we mention the work of Daskalakis, Diakonikolas, and Servedio, which crucially uses testing as a tool for learning [84]. Indeed, the use of testing toward learning is in line with one of the generic motivations for testing, but this work demonstrates the potential in a very concrete manner.

11.5.2. Exercises

Some of the following exercises are quite educational. We call the reader's attention to Exercise 11.15, which was not referred to in the main text, that shows that distribution testers can be made deterministic at a minor cost.

---

[50] The original results obtained an optimal dependence on n but not on ϵ. Specifically, in these results the complexity is proportional to poly$(1/\epsilon)$ rather than to $O(1/\epsilon^2)$. Optimal results were obtained in [221, 73, 264].

[51] Recall that the optimal $O(\sqrt{n}/\epsilon^2)$ upper bound was first established by Paninski [221] (for $\epsilon = \Omega(n^{-1/4})$) and then extended in [73] for all $\epsilon > 0$, where both bounds are based on the analysis of a slightly different test. The optimality of this upper bound (i.e., a matching lower bound) was first established in [221] (see alternative proof in [89, Sec. 3.1.1]).

[52] Actually, Corollary 11.30 did not appear before, whereas Item 3 of Corollary 11.31 appeared only in [137].

[53] Note that, rather than finding a distribution that maximizes the likelihood of a given collision statistics, Valiant and Valiant [263] find a distribution that has a similar collision statistics in expectation. This yields $O(\epsilon^{-2}n/\log n)$ sample complexity estimators for various statistical measures (e.g., entropy and support size), which is optimal in terms of n but not necessarily in terms of ϵ (cf. [1]).

Exercise 11.1 (Error reduction for distribution testers): Show that the error probability of a distribution tester can be reduced to 2^{-t} at the cost of increasing its sample (and time) complexity by a factor of $O(t)$, and while preserving one-sided error.

Guideline: See Exercise 1.4.

Exercise 11.2 (One-sided testers for properties of distributions): Suppose that $\mathcal{D}$ is a property of distributions over $[n]$ such that for some collection of sets $\mathcal{C} \subseteq 2^{[n]}$ it holds that the distribution X is in $\mathcal{D}$ if and only if the support of X is a subset of some $S \in \mathcal{C}$. Prove that $\mathcal{D}$ has a one-sided error tester of sample complexity $O(n/\epsilon)$.

Guideline: The tester rejects a distribution Y if and only if the multiset of samples that it sees forms a set that is not a subset of a set in $\mathcal{C}$. Show that if Y is ϵ-far from having a support that is a subset of S, then a sample of $O(n/\epsilon)$ elements drawn from Y will hit a point outside of S with probability at least $1 - \exp(-n)$.

Exercise 11.3 (On the optimality of the sample complexity asserted in Exercise 11.2): Show that there exists a property of distributions $\mathcal{D}$ that satisfies the hypothesis of Exercise 11.2 such that the sample complexity of ϵ-testing $\mathcal{D}$ with one-sided error is $\Omega(n/\epsilon)$.

Guideline: Consider the set $\mathcal{D}$ of all distributions over $[n]$ such that each distribution in $\mathcal{D}$ has support of a size smaller than $n/2$. Note that a one-sided tester may reject a distribution only when it sees at least $n/2$ different elements of $[n]$ in the sample. On the other hand, the distribution p that satisfies $p(n) = 1 - 3\epsilon$ and $p(i) = 3\epsilon/(n-1)$ for all $i \in [n-1]$ is ϵ-far from $\mathcal{D}$.

Exercise 11.4 (Learning via the empirical distribution):[54] Let $p : [n] \to [0, 1]$ be a probability function. Consider an algorithm that on input $m = O(n/\epsilon^2)$ samples, $i_1, \ldots, i_m \in [n]$, that are drawn according to p, outputs the empirical distribution $\widetilde{p}$ defined by letting $\widetilde{p}(i) = |\{j \in [m] : i_j = i\}|/m$ for every $i \in [n]$; that is, $\widetilde{p}$ represents the relative frequency of each of the values $i \in [n]$ in the sample $i_1, \ldots, i_m$. Using the following steps, prove that, with high probability, $\widetilde{p}$ is ϵ-close to p.

1. For every $i \in [n]$, let X_i denote the distribution of the fraction of the number of occurrences of i in the sample. Then, $\mathbb{E}[X_i] = p(i)$ and $\mathbb{V}[X_i] \leq p(i)/m$.
2. Show that $\mathbb{E}[|X_i - p(i)|] \leq \mathbb{V}[X_i]^{1/2}$.
3. Show that $\mathbb{E}[\sum_{i\in[n]} |X_i - p(i)|] \leq \sqrt{n/m}$.

Setting $m = 9n/\epsilon^2$, we get $\mathbb{E}[\sum_{i\in[n]} |X_i - p(i)|] \leq \epsilon/3$, which implies that $\Pr[\sum_{i\in[n]} |X_i - p(i)| > \epsilon] < 1/3$.

Guideline: In Step 1, use $\mathbb{V}[m \cdot X_i] = m \cdot p(i) \cdot (1 - p(i))$, since $m \cdot X_i$ is the sum of m independent Bernoulli trials, each having success probability $p(i)$. In Step 2, use $\mathbb{E}[|X_i - p(i)|] \leq \mathbb{E}[|X_i - p(i)|^2]^{1/2} = \mathbb{V}[X_i]^{1/2}$, where the inequality is due to $\mathbb{V}[Y] = \mathbb{E}[Y^2] - \mathbb{E}[Y]^2 \geq 0$, and the equality uses $p(i) = \mathbb{E}[X_i]$. In Step 3, use

$$\mathbb{E}\left[\sum_{i\in[n]} |X_i - p(i)|\right] = \sum_{i\in[n]} \mathbb{E}[|X_i - p(i)|] \leq \sum_{i\in[n]} \sqrt{p(i)/m},$$

---

[54] This seems to be based on folklore, which was communicated to the author by Ilias Diakonikolas.

where the last inequality is due to Steps 1-2, and $\sum_{i \in [n]} \sqrt{p(i)/m} < \sqrt{n/m}$ can be justified by the Cauchy–Schwarz inequality.

Exercise 11.5 (Approximating the $\mathcal{L}_2$-norm of a distribution): Consider a model in which the algorithm obtains samples on demand; that is, the algorithm is initially presented only with the parameters n and ϵ, and it obtains an additional sample when asking for it. Hence, the number of samples used by such an algorithm is a random variable, and we consider the distribution of that random variable. Now, for any $\gamma > 0$, using Corollary 11.6, present an algorithm that when obtaining samples from an unknown distribution p, outputs, with probability at least 2/3, an $(1 + \gamma)$-factor approximation of $\|p\|_2$ while using at most $O(1/\gamma^2\|p\|_2)$ samples. Present an alternative algorithm that achieves the same goal while using $\tilde{O}(1/\gamma^2\|p\|_2)$ samples *in expectation*.

> **Guideline:** The basic idea is to proceed in iterations such that in the ith iteration we check the hypothesis that $\|p\|_2 \approx 2^{-i}$. Hence, in the ith iteration we apply Corollary 11.6, using $O(2^i/\gamma^2)$ samples, and note that (for every $t > 0$) the probability that we halt before iteration $\log_2(1/\|p\|_2) - t$ (resp., after iteration $\log_2(1/\|p\|_2) + t$) is 2^{-t-4}. Note that the expected number of samples used this algorithm can be bounded by suspending the execution after $0.5 \log_2 n$ iterations (relying on $\|p\|_2 \geq 1/\sqrt{n}$). The claimed bound on the expected number of samples can be obtained by using $O(i^2 \cdot 2^i/\gamma^2)$ samples in the ith iteration. An alternative solution is implied by Exercise 10.8.

Exercise 11.6 (Filters that perfectly preserve distances between distributions): Let $F : [n] \to S$ be a randomized process such that the supports of the different $F(i)$'s are disjoint. Prove that for every two distributions X and X' over $[n]$, the total variation distance between $F(X)$ and $F(X')$ equals the total variation distance between X and X'. Note that distances may not be preserved if the supports of some $F(i)$'s are not disjoint, and that the level of preservation is related to the relation between the distributions of the various $F(i)$'s.

> **Guideline:** Just use the definition of the total variation distance; that is, show that
> $$\sum_{j \in S} \left| \Pr[F(X) = j] - \Pr[F(X') = j] \right| = \sum_{i \in [n]} \left| \Pr[X = i] - \Pr[X' = i] \right|.$$

Exercise 11.7 (Testing the uniform distribution over $[n]$, extended): By definition, a tester for the uniform distribution over $[n]$ is supposed to satisfy the conditions of Definition 11.1 when given an arbitrary distribution over $[n]$; in particular, when given the parameters n and ϵ, the tester is required to reject any distribution over $[n]$ that is ϵ-far from U_n (the uniform distribution over $[n]$). Show that any such tester T can be easily adapted to satisfy the rejection requirement also when given an arbitrary distribution, which may have a support that is not a subset of $[n]$.

> **Guideline:** The adapted tester rejects if the sample contains any element not in $[n]$ and otherwise invokes T on the sample. Provide a rigorous analysis of this tester.[55]

---

[55] Denoting the tested distribution by $p : S \to [0, 1]$, we may assume that $q \stackrel{\text{def}}{=} \sum_{i \in [n]} p(i) > 0$, and let $i_0 \in [n]$ be such that $p(i_0) \geq p(i)$ for every $i \in [n]$. The key observation is that the rejection probability of the *adapted tester* can be related to the rejection probability of a *thought experiment* in which we map each sample-point not in $[n]$ to i_0 and invoke T on the resulting sample. Specifically, in the mental experiment, T is invoked on a distribution

Exercise 11.8 (Testing uniform distributions, yet another look): In continuation to Exercise 11.7, present a filter that maps U_m to U_{2m}, while mapping any distribution X that is ϵ-far from U_m to a distribution over $[2m]$ that is $\epsilon/2$-far from U_{2m}. We stress that X is not necessarily distributed over $[m]$ and remind the reader that U_n denotes the uniform distribution over $[n]$.

Guideline: The filter, denoted F, maps $i \in [m]$ uniformly at random to an element in $\{i, m+i\}$, while mapping any $i \notin [m]$ uniformly at random to an element in $[m]$. Observe that $F(U_m) \equiv U_{2m}$, while for every X it holds that

$$\sum_{i \in [m+1,2m]} |\mathbf{Pr}[F(X) = i] - \mathbf{Pr}[U_{2m} = i]| = \frac{1}{2} \cdot \sum_{i \in [m]} |\mathbf{Pr}[X = i] - \mathbf{Pr}[U_m = i]|$$

$$\sum_{i \in [m]} |\mathbf{Pr}[F(X) = i] - \mathbf{Pr}[U_{2m} = i]| \geq \mathbf{Pr}[F(X) \in [m]] - \mathbf{Pr}[U_{2m} \in [m]]$$

$$= \frac{1}{2} \cdot \mathbf{Pr}[X \in [m]] + \mathbf{Pr}[X \notin [m]] - \frac{1}{2}$$

$$= \frac{1}{2} \cdot \mathbf{Pr}[X \notin [m]]$$

$$= \frac{1}{2} \cdot \sum_{i \notin [m]} |\mathbf{Pr}[X = i] - \mathbf{Pr}[U_m = i]| .$$

Exercise 11.9 (Optimizing the reduction that underlies the proof of Theorem 11.11):[56] Optimize the choice of γ in Algorithm 11.10 so to obtain "optimal" sample complexity in that reduction. Note that the filter of Eq. (11.4) can also be generalized by using a suitable parameter, which can then be optimized. (Recall that n/γ must be an integer.)

Guideline: Start by generalizing the filter of Eq. (11.4) by introducing a parameter $\beta \in (0, 1)$ and letting $p'(i) = (1 - \beta) \cdot p(i) + \beta/n$. Present the complexity of the resulting tester as a function of β and $\gamma \in (0, \beta)$ (in addition to its dependence on n and ϵ), and minimize this function.

Exercise 11.10 (Another filter): For a fixed probability function $p : [n] \rightarrow [0, 1]$, consider the randomized process $F : [n] \rightarrow [n]$ that, on input $i \in [n]$, outputs i with probability $0.5 + 0.5 \cdot p(i)$, and outputs $j \in [n] \setminus \{i\}$ with probability $0.5 \cdot p(j)$.

1. Prove that for every two distributions X and X' over $[n]$, the total variation distance between $F(X)$ and $F(X')$ is at least half of the total variation distance between X and X'.

2. Prove that for every distribution X over $[n]$ and every $i \in [n]$, it holds that $\mathbf{Pr}[F(X) = i] \geq p(i)/2$.

$p' : [n] \rightarrow [0, 1]$ such that $p'(i_0) = p(i_0) + (1 - q)$ and $p'(i) = p(i)$ for every $i \in [n]$. Note that if $p'(i_0) \geq 1/n$, then $\sum_{i \in [n]} |p'(i) - u(i)| = \sum_{i \in S} |p(i) - u(i)|$, where $u(i) = 1/n$ for every $i \in [n]$ and $u(i) = 0$ otherwise, since $|p'(i_0) - u(i_0)| = (1 - q) + |p(i_0) - u(i_0)|$. Otherwise (i.e., $p'(i_0) < 1/n$), it holds that $\sum_{i \in S} |p(i) - u(i)| = 2 \cdot (1 - q)$, and $\sum_{i \in [n]} |p'(i) - u(i)| = 2 \cdot (1 - q) - 2 \cdot |p(i_0) - u(i_0)| \geq \frac{n-1}{n} \cdot \sum_{i \in S} |p(i) - u(i)|$, since $p(i_0) \geq q/n$. An alternative analysis starts with an arbitrary distribution X that is ϵ-far from U_n, and considers two cases regarding $q = \mathbf{Pr}[X \in [n]]$. If $1 - q \geq \epsilon/2$, then the adapted tester rejects with high probability (since its sample complexity is definitely $\Omega(1/\epsilon)$). Otherwise (i.e., $1 - q < \epsilon/2$), the distribution of X conditioned on $X \in [n]$ is $\epsilon/2$-far from U_n, and the tester T (which is invokes on it) rejects with probability at least $2/3$.

[56] We do not consider such an optimization important, but it may serve as a good exercise.

Exercise 11.11 (Extending the lower bound of Corollary 11.13): Show that ϵ-testing the property $\{U_n\}$ requires $\Omega(\min(n^{2/3}, \epsilon^{-2}\sqrt{n}))$ samples.

> **Guideline:** Note that, with probability $1 - (s^3/n^2)$, a sequence of s samples that are drawn from the uniform distribution on $[n]$ contains no three-way collisions (i.e., $c_j = 0$ for all $j > 2$).[57] This happens, with similar probability, also when the distribution assigns probability either $(1 - 2\epsilon)/n$ or $(1 + 2\epsilon)/n$ to each element. Hence, a tester that uses $o(n^{2/3})$ samples may rely only on the two-way collisions that it sees. Assuming that $\sqrt{n}/\epsilon^2 < n^{2/3}$ (and resetting ϵ such that $\sqrt{n}/\epsilon^2 = n^{2/3}$ otherwise), observe that $\Omega(\sqrt{n}/\epsilon^2)$ samples are required in order to tell the two distributions apart, since the collision probability of the second distribution equals $(1 + \Theta(\epsilon^2))/n$. (Hence we need to estimate the collision probability to within a factor of $1 + \Omega(\epsilon^2)$, and so the number of pairs of samples must be $\Omega((\epsilon^2)^{-2} \cdot (1/n)^{-1})$.)

Exercise 11.12 (Upper bounds on the length of approximate histograms): Recall that Theorem 11.27 implies that every distribution $p : [n] \to [0, 1]$ is ϵ-close to a distribution that has a histogram of length $O(\epsilon^{-2} \cdot n/\log n)$. Provide a direct proof of this fact by proving that p is actually ϵ-close to a distribution that has a histogram of length $O(\epsilon^{-1} \cdot \log(n/\epsilon))$.

> **Guideline:** First, modify p into p' such that $p'(i) = p(i)$ if $p(i) > \epsilon/2n$, and $p'(i_1) = p'(i_2)$ for every i_1, i_2 that satisfy $p(i_1), p(i_2) \le \epsilon/2n$. Next, partition the i's that satisfy $p'(i) > \epsilon/2n$ into $\log_{1+0.5\epsilon}(2n/\epsilon)$ buckets B_j's such that $B_j = \{i : (1 + 0.5\epsilon)^{j-1} \cdot \epsilon/2n < p'(i) \le (1 + 0.5\epsilon)^j \cdot \epsilon/2n\}$, and modify p' such that it is uniform on the i's in each B_j. Note that the resulting distribution is ϵ-close to p, and has a histograph of length at most $1 + \log_{1+0.5\epsilon}(2n/\epsilon)$.

Exercise 11.13 (Reduction among testing grained properties): For every $m_1 < m_2$, present a reduction of the task of estimating the distance to m_1-grained distributions over $[n]$ to estimating the distance to m_2-grained distributions over $[n]$. Specifically, present a filter that maps m_1-grained distributions to m_2-grained distributions such that the filter preserved the distance between distributions up to a fixed scaling (of m_1/m_2).

> **Guideline:** For starters, consider the filter F'_{m_1,m_2} that maps $i \in [n]$ to itself with probability m_1/m_2 and maps it to $n + 1$ otherwise. Then, consider the filter F_{m_1,m_2} that maps the excessive probability mass (of $(m_2 - m_1)/m_2$) to n (rather than to $n + 1$).

Exercise 11.14 (Testing whether two unknown distributions are identical up-to relabeling): Let $\mathcal{D}_2$ denote the set of pairs of distributions over $[n]$ that have equal histograms (i.e., are identical up to relabeling). Show that for every constant $\epsilon > 0$, the sample complexity of ϵ-testing $\mathcal{D}_2$ is $\Theta(n/\log n)$.

> **Guideline:** Use Theorem 11.27 for the upper bound, and Corollary 11.30 for the lower bound.

Exercise 11.15 (Distribution testers can be made deterministic at a minor cost): Let $\mathcal{D}$ be a property of distributions over $[n]$. Show that if $\mathcal{D}$ can be tested in sample complexity $s(n, \epsilon)$, then it can be tested by a deterministic machine of sample complexity $3 \cdot s(n, \epsilon) + O(\ell/\epsilon)$, where $\ell = \log s(n, \epsilon) + \log \log n$. (The factor of 3 increase in the

---

[57] Recall that c_j denotes the number of elements that occur j times in the sequence of samples $(i_1, \ldots, i_s)$; that is, $c_j = |\{i \in [n] : \#_i(i_1, \ldots, i_s) = j\}|$, where $\#_i(i_1, \ldots, i_s) = |\{k \in [s] : i_k = i\}|$.

sample complexity is due to the desire to maintain the same error bound, and it can be avoided if one is willing to increase the error probability from $1/3$ to, say, 0.35. Hence, the actual cost of the derandomization is captured by the relatively small additive term of $O(\ell/\epsilon)$.)

> **Guideline:** First reduce the randomness complexity of the randomized tester by using ideas as in Exercise 1.21, obtaining a tester of randomness complexity $\log s(n, \epsilon) + \log \log n + O(1)$ that has error probability at most 0.34 (rather than at most $1/3$). This is done by considering all n^s possible s-long sequences of samples, and picking a set of $O(s \cdot \log n)$ random pads that approximate the behavior of the tester (on all possible sample sequences). Next, present a deterministic tester that emulates the execution of a randomized tester that uses s samples and r random coins, by using $O(r/\epsilon)$ additional samples. The idea is to partition these additional samples into pairs and try to extract a random bit from each pair (x, y) such that the extracted bit is 1 (resp., 0) if $x < y$ (resp., if $x > y$), where in case $x = y$ no bit is extracted. Specifically, for some suitable constant c, we are given $c \cdot r/\epsilon$ samples from the tested distribution X, and we attempt to extract at least r bits by using the foregoing procedure. Consider the following three (somewhat overlapping) cases.
>
> 1. The typical case is that at least r random bits were extracted. In this case, we just emulate the randomized tester.
> 2. A pathological case, which arises when the tested distribution X is concentrated on one value $i \in [n]$ (i.e., $\mathbf{Pr}[X = i] > 1 - \epsilon/2$), is that a majority of the pairs equal (i, i) for some $i \in [n]$. In this case we accept if and only if the distribution that assigns all the probability mass to i is $\epsilon/2$-close to $\mathcal{D}$.
> 3. An extremely rare case is that less than r bits were extracted but no pair (i, i) appears in majority. This case is extremely unlikely, and it does not matter what we do when it occurs.
>
> The analysis refers to two overlapping cases regarding X. On the one hand, if the tested distribution X satisfies $\mathbf{Pr}[X = i] < 1 - \epsilon/4$ for all $i \in [n]$, then Case 1 occurs with very high probability. On the other hand, if there exists $i \in [n]$ such that $\mathbf{Pr}[X = i] > 1 - \epsilon/2$, then with very high probability either Case 1 or Case 2 occurs. In this case X is $\epsilon/2$-close to X' that assigns all the probability mass to i, and so if X is in $\mathcal{D}$ (resp., X is ϵ-far from $\mathcal{D}$), then X' is $\epsilon/2$-close to $\mathcal{D}$ (resp., $\epsilon/2$-far from $\mathcal{D}$).

Exercise 11.16 (On the algebra of distribution testing):[58] Let $\mathcal{D}'$ and $\mathcal{D}''$ be properties of distributions over $[n]$ that are each testable within sample complexity s.

1. Show that $\mathcal{D}' \cup \mathcal{D}''$ is testable within sample complexity $O(s)$.
2. Show that the sample-complexity of testing $\mathcal{D}' \cap \mathcal{D}''$ may be $\Omega(n/\log n)$ even if $s = \widetilde{O}(1/\epsilon)$ and each of the properties is label-invariant.

> **Guideline:** Part 1 can be proven as Theorem 1.10. To prove Part 2, start with any of the properties $\mathcal{D}$ of Corollary 11.31. Let $\mathcal{D}'$ (resp., $\mathcal{D}''$) consist of $\mathcal{D}$ as well as of all distributions that have a support of odd (resp., even) size. Then, each distribution over $[n]$ is $1/n$-close to $\mathcal{D}'$ (resp., $\mathcal{D}''$), whereas $\mathcal{D}' \cap \mathcal{D}'' = \mathcal{D}$. Lastly, for the sake of formal preciseness, present an ϵ-tester for the case of $\epsilon < 1/n$, while relying on the fact that $O(\epsilon^{-1} \log n) = \widetilde{O}(1/\epsilon)$ holds in this case.

---

[58] See analogous section on the algebra of testing properties of functions (i.e., Section 1.3.4).

Exercise 11.17 (Testing the union of many properties): Suppose that $\mathcal{D}^{(1)}, \ldots, \mathcal{D}^{(k)}$ are properties of distributions that are each testable within sample complexity s. Show that $\bigcup_{i \in [k]} \mathcal{D}^{(i)}$ is testable within sample complexity $O(\log k) \cdot s$. *(Note that only the case of $k = 2$ was treated in Exercise 11.16, and that an iterative application of it to the general case would yield sample complexity* $\mathrm{poly}(k) \cdot s$.*)*

> **Guideline:** First reduce the error probability to $1/3k$, by repeating each tester $O(\log k)$ times. Invoking all the resulting tests, while providing each tester with a different sample, would yield a tester of sample complexity $\widetilde{O}(k) \cdot s$. The key observation is that the same sample can be used for all testers.

CHAPTER TWELVE

Ramifications and Related Topics

In continuation to Section 1.3.2, we review a few ramifications of the notion of property testers as well as related topics. Some of these ramifications were briefly mentioned in Section 1.3.2, and others were not even mentioned there.

Summary: We briefly review a few ramifications of the notion of property testers as well as related topics. The list includes

1. Tolerant testing and distance approximation;
2. Testing under additional promises on the input;
3. Sample-based testers;
4. Testing with respect to other distance measures;
5. Local computation algorithms;
6. Noninteractive proofs of proximity (MAPs).

While some of these topics have received a fair amount of attention, others still beg for more attention.

The different sections of this chapter can be read independently of one another.

12.1. Tolerant Testing and Distance Approximation

In some settings, objects that are close to having the property may be almost as useful for these settings as objects that have the property (e.g., see some of the settings discussed in Section 1.1.2). But in such a case, when testing for the property, it may be desirable not to reject objects that are very close to having the property (or, put differently, "tolerate" a small deviation). This leads to a natural generalization of the testing task that calls for distinguishing between objects that are ϵ'-close to the property and objects that are ϵ-far from the property, for parameters $\epsilon' < \epsilon$. Indeed, standard property testing refers to the case of $\epsilon' = 0$, and tolerant testing may be viewed as "tolerating" a small deviation of the object from having the property, where typically ϵ' is a function of ϵ (and sometimes also of n).

Definition 12.1 (Tolerant testers): *Let $\Pi = \cup_{n \in \mathbb{N}} \Pi_n$ such that $\Pi_n \subseteq \{f : [n] \to R_n\}$, and $\epsilon' : \mathbb{N} \times (0, 1] \to (0, 1]$. An ϵ'-tolerant tester for Π is a probabilistic oracle machine, denoted T, that satisfies the following two conditions.*

1. *T accepts inputs that are ϵ'-close to Π: For every $n \in \mathbb{N}$ and $\epsilon > 0$, and for every $f : [n] \to R_n$ such that $\delta_{\Pi}(f) \leq \epsilon'(n, \epsilon)$, it holds that $\mathbf{Pr}[T^f(n, \epsilon) = 1] \geq 2/3$.*
2. *T rejects inputs that are ϵ-far from Π: For every $n \in \mathbb{N}$ and $\epsilon > 0$, and for every $f : [n] \to R_n$ such that $\delta_{\Pi}(f) > \epsilon$, it holds that $\mathbf{Pr}[T^f(n, \epsilon) = 0] \geq 2/3$.*

(Recall that $\delta_{\Pi}(f)$ denotes the distance of f from Π_n.)

We avoided defining a one-sided error probability version, because it is quite useless (see Exercise 12.1). Note that standard testers (as in Definition 1.6) may be viewed as 0-tolerant testers. On the other hand, tolerant testing is related to distance approximation, where no *proximity parameter* is given and the tester is required to output an approximation (up to a given approximation parameter) of the distance of the object to the property.

Definition 12.2 (Distance approximation for a property): *Let $\Pi = \cup_{n \in \mathbb{N}} \Pi_n$ and δ_{Π} be as in Definition 12.1. A* distance approximator *for Π is a probabilistic oracle machine, denoted M, that satisfies one of the following two conditions.*

Additive version: *For every $n \in \mathbb{N}$ and $f : [n] \to R_n$ and for every $\eta > 0$, it holds that*

$$\mathbf{Pr}\left[\left|M^f(n, \eta) - \delta_{\Pi}(f)\right| \leq \eta\right] \geq 2/3.$$

Multiplicative version[1]: *For every $\eta, \eta' > 0$, every $n \in \mathbb{N}$ and $f : [n] \to R_n$ that is η'-far from Π_n, it holds that*

$$\mathbf{Pr}\left[\left|M^f(n, \eta, \eta') - \delta_{\Pi}(f)\right| \leq \eta \cdot \delta_{\Pi}(f)\right] \geq 2/3.$$

Typically, the term "tolerant testing" is used when the parameter ϵ' is a fixed function of ϵ (e.g., $\epsilon' = \epsilon/2$ or $\epsilon' = \epsilon^2$), and "distance approximation" is used when one seeks an approximation scheme that is governed by an approximation parameter (which corresponds to $\epsilon - \epsilon'$ when the sought approximation is additive and to ϵ/ϵ' when it is multiplicative).

Note that *any property tester that makes queries that are each uniformly distributed in $[n]$ yields a mildly tolerant tester*. Specifically, if the tester has query complexity $q(n, \epsilon)$, then it accepts every function that is $(1/10q(n, \epsilon))$-close to the property with probability at least $2/3 - 0.1$, and using error reduction we can regain the original error bound of $2/3$ (see Exercise 12.2). Providing higher (i.e., higher than $1/q(n, \epsilon)$) levels of tolerance is typically harder than providing standard testers. Furthermore, in some cases the tolerant testers must have significantly higher complexity: In fact, a very dramatic gap may exist, in general, even for properties of Boolean functions [109]. Specifically, *there exists a property of functions $f : [n] \to \{0, 1\}$ that is testable in a number of queries that depends*

---

[1] We warn that, when defining multiplicative approximation, one should be careful in the case that the optimized value may be zero (as is the case here), since asking for a multiplicative approximation in such cases will force the approximator to distinguish the value zero from a value that is extremely close to zero. This problem is resolved by confining the approximation task to cases in which the value is above some minimal threshold (which is denoted here by η'). Indeed, the problem does not arise in cases where the optimized value is always inside an interval that is sufficiently far from zero (e.g., the interval $[1, 2]$). A good practice in other cases is to combine the use of both approximators; that is, first invoke an additive approximator with deviation parameter set to $0.1\eta'$, and invoke a multiplicative approximator with parameters (η, η') only if the first estimate is at least $1.1\eta'$. Thus, we obtain a $0.1\eta'$ additive approximation to values in $[0, \eta']$, a $1 \pm \eta$ multiplicative approximation to values above $1.2\eta'$, and one of these two approximations otherwise.

only on the proximity parameter, but tolerantly testing it requires $n^{\Omega(1)}$ *queries*. Neverthe-less, in some cases, good tolerant testers can be obtained. A few examples follow.

In the Context of Testing Graph Properties. We first consider testing graph properties in the dense graph model (of Chapter 8). Recall that ϵ-testing whether a graph is bipartite can be done by inspecting the subgraph induced by a random set of $\widetilde{O}(1/\epsilon)$ vertices. In contrast, an ϵ'-tolerant ϵ-tester of this property is known only when inspecting a polyno-mially larger induced subgraph. Specifically, such tolerant testing can be performed by invoking a tester for a generalized partition problem (see Exercise 12.3). A much more general result follows.

> **Theorem 12.3** (Tolerant testing in the dense graph model): *Let* Π *be a graph prop-erty that can be tested within query complexity that depends only on the proximity parameter. Then, for every constants* $\epsilon > \epsilon' > 0$, *the property* Π *has an* ϵ'-*tolerant* ϵ-*tester of query complexity that depends only on* ϵ *and* ϵ'.

We note that the query complexity of the tolerant tester provided by the known proof of Theorem 12.3 is significant higher than that of the corresponding standard tester. An interesting open problem is providing a functional relationship between the complexity of testing and the complexity of tolerant testing, even just for a natural subclass of graph properties. Specifically, consider the following version of this question.

> **Open Problem 12.4** (Tolerant testing in the dense graph model): *Let* C *be a natural class of graph properties. Present a function* $F : \mathbb{N} \to \mathbb{N}$ *such that, for every* $\Pi \in C$ *and every constant* $\epsilon > 0$, *it holds that if* Π *is* ϵ-*testable in query complexity* $q(n, \epsilon)$, *then* Π *has an* 0.5ϵ-*tolerant* ϵ-*tester of query complexity* $F(q(n, \epsilon))$. *Alternatively, show that no such function* F *may exist for* C.

The same question can be posed with respect to testing graph properties in the bounded-degree graph model. We mention that some of the testers presented in Section 9.2 are tolerant or can be easily modified to be tolerant (see Exercise 12.4).

In the Context of Testing Distributions. Tolerant testing and distance approximation have been studied extensively in the context of testing distributions (see Chapter 11). Recall that, in this context, the tester gets samples from the tested distribution (rather than oracle access to some function). Actually, Corollaries 11.28 and 11.31 are typically stated in terms of tolerant testing. We do so next, while referring to the notion of label-invariant properties of distributions (defined in Section 11.1.3).

> **Corollary 12.5** (Tolerantly testing label-invariant properties of single distribu-tions): *Let* $\mathcal{D}$ *be a label-invariant property of distributions over* $[n]$. *Then, for every* $\epsilon' : (0, 1] \to [0, 1]$, *the property* $\mathcal{D}$ *has an* ϵ'-*tolerant tester of sample complexity* $s(n, \epsilon) = O((\epsilon - \epsilon'(\epsilon))^{-2} \cdot n/\log n)$.

> **Corollary 12.6** (Optimality of Corollary 12.5): *For all sufficiently small constants* $\epsilon > \epsilon' > 0$, *any* ϵ'-*tolerant* ϵ-*tester for each of the following properties of distribu-tions over* $[n]$ *requires* $\Omega(n/\log n)$ *samples.*

1. *The uniform distribution over* $[n]$.
2. *The set of distributions that have support size* (exactly or at most) $n/2$.
3. *The set of distributions that are m-grained, for any integer* $m \in [\Omega(n), O(n)]$, *where a distribution is* m-grained *if each element appears in it with probability that is an integer multiple of* $1/m$.

Recall that these lower bounds do not necessarily hold for standard testing of the same properties (i.e., the case of $\epsilon' = 0$): Part 1 provides a striking example, since (as shown in Chapter 11) the uniform distribution over $[n]$ is ϵ-testable by $O(\epsilon^{-2} \cdot \sqrt{n})$ samples.

12.2. Additional Promises on the Input

As stated at the very beginning of this book, property testing refers to *promise problems* (cf. [105, 129] or [131, Sec. 2.4.1]) of a specific type. These problems consist of distinguishing inputs that have a predetermined property from inputs that are far from that property, where inputs that are neither in the property nor far from it are disregarded. (Tolerant testing follows this theme in distinguishing between inputs that are ϵ'-close to the property and inputs that are ϵ-far from it, where $\epsilon' < \epsilon$.)

We note that, as in all of computer science, some additional promises are typically made about the format in which the input is presented.[2] For example, when the tester is given the size parameter n, it is guaranteed that the oracle (which represents the main input) is a function over $[n]$. Most conspicuously, in the study of testing graph properties, we have made such an explicit assumption. Specifically, in the study of the dense graph model, we assumed that the adjacency predicate $g : [k] \times [k] \rightarrow \{0, 1\}$ is symmetric (i.e., $g(u, v) = g(v, u)$ for every $u, v \in [k]$). Likewise, when studying the bounded-degree graph model, we assumed that the incidence function $g : [k] \times [d] \rightarrow \{0, 1, \ldots, k\}$ is consistent in the sense that if $g(u, i) = v$ for some $u, v \in [k]$ and $i \in [d]$, then there exists $j \in [d]$ such that $g(v, j) = u$. These, however, are syntactic assumptions, which are easy to dispose of (or waive) by first testing whether the input oracle satisfies the corresponding syntactic condition.[3]

More essential promises refer to real properties of the objects, rather than to syntactic properties of their representation that mandate only that the representation is legal. Such promises are sometimes introduced for scholarly reasons, but in many cases they are justified by natural settings.[4] The point is that in many cases more efficient testers may be obtained under the promise. A few examples, all in the domain of graph properties, follow.

---

[2] For a wider perspective see discussions in [129] and [131, Sec. 2.4.1].

[3] In the dense graph model, one may just select $O(1/\epsilon)$ pairs $(u, v) \in [k] \times [k]$ at random and check whether $g(u, v) = g(v, u)$ holds. In addition, when answering queries of the original tester, we answer the query (u, v) with the conjunction of $g(u, v)$ and $g(v, u)$, which means that we effectively replace (or "self-correct") g by the $\epsilon/2$-close g' such that $g'(u, v) = g(u, v) \wedge g(v, u)$. In the bounded-degree graph model, for each random choice $(u, i) \in [k] \times [d]$, if $g(u, i) = v \in [k]$ then we may need to query $g(v, j)$ for all $j \in [d]$ (and apply a similar self-correction); see Exercise 12.5.

[4] A clear case where a promise is introduced for scholarly reasons appears in [151, Sec. 5.4], where a natural conjecture regarding complexity gaps between adaptive and nonadaptive testers is established in the context of promise problems. We mention that in some cases promise problems were introduced for scholarly reasons, but turned out to have good conceptual justifications.

- Assuming a *degree bound in the dense graph model*: For any constant $\eta > 0$, the promise is that each vertex in the input k-vertex graph has degree at most $\eta \cdot k$. Under this promise, ϵ-testing Bipartiteness has query complexity $\text{poly}(\lceil \eta/\epsilon \rceil) \cdot \widetilde{O}(\epsilon^{-3/2})$, whereas for general graphs only a bound of $\widetilde{O}(\epsilon^{-2})$ is known (see [162] and [13], respectively).

- Assuming *minor-freeness in the bounded-degree graph model*: For any constant graph H, the promise is that the input graph is H-minor free (and of bounded degree). Under this promise, ϵ-testing any graph property has query complexity that depends only on ϵ (see [217]). The result extends to any family of minor-closed graphs (and actually even to hyperfinite graphs).[5]

  In contrast, recall that testing 3-Colorability of general k-vertex (bounded-degree) graphs, in this model, requires $\Omega(k)$ queries.

- Assuming *planarity in the general graph model*: The promise is that the input graph is planar (or, more generally, belongs to a family of minor-closed graphs). Under this promise, ϵ-testing Bipartiteness has query complexity that only depends on ϵ (see [82]).

  In contrast, recall that testing Bipartiteness of general k-vertex graphs, in this model, requires $\Omega(\sqrt{k})$ queries (even when the input graph is promised to be of bounded-degree).

12.3. Sample-Based Testers

Throughout most of this book (i.e., with the exception of Chapter 11), we studied testers that may freely *query the functions* that they test. In contrast, here we consider testers that only obtain "labeled samples"; that is, when testing a function $f : [n] \to R_n$, the tester is given a sequence of f-labeled samples, $((i_1, f(i_1)), \ldots, (i_s, f(i_s)))$, where $i_1, \ldots, i_s$ are drawn *independently and uniformly* in $[n]$. Such a tester is called sample-based, and it was already introduced (as a tool) in Section 6.2. We reproduce its definition (i.e., Definition 6.2) next.

Definition 12.7 (Sample-based testers): *Let $\Pi = \cup_{n \in \mathbb{N}} \Pi_n$ such that $\Pi_n \subseteq \{f : [n] \to R_n\}$, and $s : \mathbb{N} \times (0, 1] \to \mathbb{N}$. A sample-based tester of (sample) complexity s for Π is a probabilistic machine, denoted T, that satisfies the following two conditions.*

1. *T accepts inputs in Π: For every $n \in \mathbb{N}$ and $\epsilon > 0$, and for every $f \in \Pi_n$, it holds that $\mathbf{Pr}[T(n, \epsilon; ((i_1, f(i_1)) \ldots, (i_s, f(i_s))) = 1] \geq 2/3$, where $s = s(n, \epsilon)$, and $i_1, \ldots, i_s$ are drawn independently and uniformly in $[n]$.*

2. *T rejects inputs that are ϵ-far from Π: For every $n \in \mathbb{N}$ and $\epsilon > 0$, and for every f with domain $[n]$ such that $\delta_\Pi(f) > \epsilon$, it holds that $\mathbf{Pr}[T(n, \epsilon; ((i_1, f(i_1)) \ldots, (i_s, f(i_s))) = 0] \geq 2/3$, where $i_1, \ldots, i_s$ are as in Item 1.*

If the first condition holds with probability 1, then we say that T has one-sided *error.*

We mention that any class $\Pi = \cup_{n \in \mathbb{N}} \Pi_n$ can be tested by using a sample of size $O(\epsilon^{-1} \log |\Pi_n|)$, via reducing (sample-based) testing to (sample-based) proper learning (see Section 1.3.5).

---

[5] See terminology in Sections 9.5 and 9.6.1.

As we have seen in prior chapters, the ability to make queries is very powerful: even when the queries are selected nonadaptively, they may be selected to depend on one another. In contrast, a sample-based tester is quite restricted (i.e., it cannot obtain related samples). Nevertheless, a sample-based tester is desirable in many applications where obtaining samples is far more feasible than obtaining answers to queries of one's choice. The question, of course, is what can such sample-based testers achieve. One general answer is that sample-based testers of sublinear complexity exist for any property that has a constant-query proximity-oblivious tester in which each query is uniformly distributed.[6]

Theorem 12.8 (From POTs to sample-based testers): *Let* $\Pi = \cup_{n \in \mathbb{N}} \Pi_n$ *such that* $\Pi_n \subseteq \{f : [n] \to R_n\}$, *and suppose that* Π *has a q-query POT with threshold probability* τ *and detection probability* ϱ.

1. *If each query made by this POT is uniformly distributed in the function's domain, then* Π *has a sample-based tester of sample complexity* $s(n, \epsilon) = \max(O(n^{(q-1)/q}/\varrho(\epsilon)^{b+(3/q)}), O(\varrho(\epsilon)^{-(3+b)}))$, *where* $b = 2$ *in the general case and* $b = 1$ *if the POT has one-sided error (i.e.,* $\tau = 1$). *Furthermore, if the POT has one-sided error, then so does the sample-based tester.*
2. *If the POT is nonadaptive and has one-sided error (i.e.,* $\tau = 1$), *then* Π *has a sample-based* ϵ-*tester that uses* $O(\log |R_n|) \cdot n^{\gamma}$ *samples, where* γ *depends on* q *and* $\varrho(\epsilon)$, *and ditto for the hidden constant in the O-notation. In the general case (i.e., adaptive POT with* $\tau < 1$), *the exponent* γ *may also depend on* $|R_n|$.

Both parts of Theorem 12.8 are actually more general, but some flavor of the conditions made in them is inherent (since there exists a property Π that has no sample-based tester of sublinear complexity although it does have a one-sided nonadaptive two-query POT [153, Prop. 3.3]).[7] Applying Part 1 of Theorem 12.8 to any of the known 2-query POTs for monotonicity, which were presented in Chapter 4, we obtain a sample-based tester of sample complexity $\widetilde{O}(\sqrt{n}) \cdot \text{poly}(1/\epsilon)$. It is actually easy to obtain such testers directly: Considering, for example, the "edge tester" presented in Section 4.2.1, we can emulate a selection of a random edge in the ℓ-dimensional hypercube by using a sample of $O(\sqrt{2^{\ell}/\ell})$ vertices.

12.4. Testing with Respect to Other Distance Measures

Recall that distance between functions (having the same domain $[n]$) was defined in Section 1.3.1 as the fraction of the domain on which the functions disagree, which can be interpreted as the probability that the functions disagree on a *uniformly distributed point in their domain*. A more general definition may refer to the disagreement with respect to an arbitrary distribution $\mathcal{D}_n$ over $[n]$; that is, we may have

$$\delta_{\mathcal{D}_n}(f, g) \stackrel{\text{def}}{=} \mathbf{Pr}_{i \sim \mathcal{D}_n}[f(i) \neq g(i)], \tag{12.1}$$

where $i \sim \mathcal{D}_n$ means that i is distributed according to $\mathcal{D}_n$. In such a case, for a "distribution ensemble" $\mathcal{D} = \{\mathcal{D}_n\}$, we let $\delta_{\Pi, \mathcal{D}}(f) \stackrel{\text{def}}{=} \min_{g \in \Pi_n}\{\delta_{\mathcal{D}_n}(f, g)\}$. This leads to a definition of

---

[6] We stress that different queries are allowed to depend on one another; we postulate only that each query, by itself, is uniformly distributed in the function's domain.

[7] The range of the corresponding functions is exponential in n.

testing with respect to an arbitrary distribution ensemble $\mathcal{D}$, viewing Definition 1.6 as a special case in which $\mathcal{D}_n$ is the uniform distribution over $[n]$.

One step further is to consider *distribution-free testers*. Such a tester should satisfy the foregoing requirement for *all* possible distributions $\mathcal{D}$, and it is typically equipped with a special device that provides it with samples drawn according to the distribution in question (i.e., the distribution $\mathcal{D}_n$ used in the definition of distance). That is, a distribution-free tester for Π is an oracle machine that can query the function $f : [n] \to R_n$ as well as obtain samples drawn from *any* distribution $\mathcal{D}_n$, and its performance should refer to $\delta_{\Pi,\mathcal{D}}(f)$ (i.e., the distance of f from Π_n as measured according to the distribution $\mathcal{D}_n$). We stress that $\mathcal{D}_n$ is *a priori* unknown to the tester, which may gain partial information about it from the samples.

> **Definition 12.9** (Distribution-free testing): *A distribution-free tester for Π is a probabilistic oracle machine, denoted T, such that for every $\epsilon > 0$ and $n \in \mathbb{N}$ and every distribution $\mathcal{D}_n$ over $[n]$, the following two conditions hold:*
>
> 1. *For every $f \in \Pi_n$, it holds that $\mathbf{Pr}[T^{f,\mathcal{D}_n}(n, \epsilon) = 1] \geq 2/3$.*
> 2. *For every $f : [n] \to R_n$ such that $\delta_{\Pi,\mathcal{D}}(f) > \epsilon$, it holds that $\mathbf{Pr}[T^{f,\mathcal{D}_n}(n, \epsilon) = 0] \geq 2/3$.*
>
> *In both items, $T^{f,\mathcal{D}_n}(n, \epsilon)$ denotes the output of T when given oracle access to $f : [n] \to R_n$ as well as samples that are drawn independently from $\mathcal{D}_n$ (and explicit inputs n and ϵ).*

Note that, unlike in Section 12.3, the tester has oracle access to the function f. It is provided with samples drawn according to $\mathcal{D}_n$, but there is no need to provide it with the corresponding f-labels (since it can obtain these by itself by querying f). In such a case, one may consider both the tester's query complexity and its sample complexity.[8]

In order to justify the foregoing definition, let us spell out the type of settings that it is supposed to capture. In such settings the function f represents some measurement (or numerical parameter) of possible situations, which are represented by f's domain. In other words, f represents an assignment of values to possible situations. The distribution $\mathcal{D}_n$ represents an (a priori) unknown distribution on the possible situations, and testing is defined with respect to this distribution because this is the distribution in which situations occur. But in such a case, it stands to reason that samples from this distribution are available to the tester.

Taking a more technical attitude, one may say that if the tester is being evaluated with respect to an arbitrary distribution, then it is fair to provide it with some information regarding this distribution. Failure to do so will deem the testing task infeasible; that is, for any nondegenerate property, a distribution-free tester that obtains no samples of the distribution will have to query all locations in the function's domain (since the distribution may be totally concentrated on any of them).

Few efficient distribution-free testers are known (see, e.g., [167, 97]); in general, it seems that distribution-free testing is quite hard (see, e.g., [126]). We wonder whether this gloomy picture may change if one restricts the class of distributions. For example, one may consider only distributions that have a minimal amount of min-entropy, where a

---

[8] In particular, one may also consider the case that the tester does not query the function on each sample obtained from $\mathcal{D}_n$; see [30].

distribution over $[n]$ is said to have min-entropy (at least) t if no element occurs with probability greater than 2^{-t} (e.g., the uniform distribution over $[n]$ has min-entropy $\log_2 n$). Indeed, a model of *lower-bounded randomness* (i.e., a lower bound on the min-entropy) seems reasonable here like in other cases in which one seeks a probabilistic model of a natural reality.

Beyond (Weighted) Hamming Distance. Almost all research in property testing focuses on the distance measure defined in Section 1.3.1, which corresponds to the relative Hamming distance between sequences. We already saw a deviation from this archetypical case in Eq. (12.1), but the measure defined in Eq. (12.1) is merely a weighted Hamming distance. That is, the distance between functions is defined in terms of the set of domain elements on which they disagree. In the archetypical definition (presented in Section 1.3.1) one just considers the density of this set in the domain, and in Eq. (12.1) one considers its weighted density. But measures of the set of points of disagreements do not exhaust the natural measures of distance between functions (or objects).

Different distance measures, which are natural in some settings, include the *edit distance* and the $\mathcal{L}_1$-*distance*. The edit distance is most natural when the object is viewed as a sequence. In such a case, *deleting* or *inserting* a symbol has unit cost, regardless of the position in which the operation takes place (whereas the Hamming distance may charge such an operation according to the length of the corresponding suffix, which is being shifted by the operation).[9] As in the case of Hamming distance, a relative notion of edit distance is obtained by dividing the absolute distance (or edit cost) by the total length of the sequences (which may be of different length). Variants of "edit distance" vary with the set of operations that are counted at unit cost (e.g., in addition to symbol deletion and insertion, one sometimes includes also operations on substrings such as the cut-and-paste operation).

We stress that the Hamming distance (and also the edit distance) counts each disagreement alike (i.e., for every two values σ and τ, it only distinguishes $\sigma = \tau$ from $\sigma \neq \tau$). But when the function's values are nonbinary and its range is equipped with a natural notion of distance, it makes sense to "charge" disagreements according to their magnitude. This is particularly appealing for function that range over the reals. Specifically, for $f, g : [n] \to [0, 1]$, it makes sense to consider the norm of the function $f - g$, and the $\mathcal{L}_1$-norm is indeed most appealing. In contrast, Hamming distance corresponds to the "$\mathcal{L}_0$-norm" (i.e., $\|h\|_0 = \sum_{i \in [n]} h(i)^0$, where $0^0 = 0$). The reader may easily conceive of situations in which a tiny $\mathcal{L}_1$-distance is insignificant (e.g., it may be due to "measurement error"), and in such cases considering the Hamming distance is inappropriate.

12.5. Local Computation Algorithms

Recall that property testing is a *decision problem* (of the promise type); that is, the desired output is a bit, which indicates whether the (huge) object has the tested property or is far from having it. Distance approximation (see Definition 12.2) generalizes property testing in the sense that the desired output is supposed to approximate a quantity in $[0, 1]$. More generally, we can consider superfast algorithms that approximate other parameters of the (huge) object such as the average degree of a graph, its girth, its diameter, its expansion

---

[9] For example, the string $(01)^t$ is at Hamming distance $2t$ from the string $(10)^t$, but the edit distance between them is only two, since $(10)^t = 1(01)^{t-1}0$.

coefficient, etc (where we confined ourselves to the domain of graphs). In all cases, we refer to a relatively short output that approximates a numerical parameter of the huge object.

A more general task refers to *solving search problems* concerning these huge objects, where the desired output is also a huge object. Clearly, we cannot expect a superfast algorithm to output an object that is larger than its running time. Hence, the notion of outputting an object is to be modified. The algorithm will not explicitly output the desired object, but will rather provide oracle access to it; that is, the algorithm will answer queries regarding the output by making queries to its own input oracle.

12.5.1. Definitions

The following definition generalizes the definition of a local (deterministic) reduction, presented in the context of lower bound techniques (i.e., Definition 7.13). Actually, we extend the definition by allowing the algorithm to be adaptive and make a nonconstant number of queries. Furthermore, we consider any search problem $S_{\bar{\epsilon}}$ that is parameterized by a tuple[10] of approximation parameters $\bar{\epsilon} > 0$; that is, on input f, the task is to find a (solution) f' such that $(f, f') \in S_{\bar{\epsilon}}$. We denote the set of solutions (for f) by $S_{\bar{\epsilon}}(f) = \{f' : (f, f') \in S_{\bar{\epsilon}}\}$.

> **Definition 12.10** (Local computation algorithms, deterministic version): *For every $\bar{\epsilon} > 0$, let $S_{\bar{\epsilon}}$ be a binary relation containing pairs of finite functions, and let $q :$ $\mathbb{N} \times (0, 1]^* \to \mathbb{N}$. A deterministic oracle machine M is said to q-locally solve the search problem $\{S_{\bar{\epsilon}}\}_{\bar{\epsilon}>0}$ if for every $n \in \mathbb{N}$ there exists $n' \in \mathbb{N}$ such that for every $\bar{\epsilon} > 0$ and for every function f over $[n]$ there exists a function f' over $[n']$ such that the following conditions hold.*
>
> *1. Locality (Emulating oracle access to f'): On input $n, \bar{\epsilon}$ and $i \in [n']$, and oracle access to f, the machine M outputs $f'(i)$ after making at most $q(n, \bar{\epsilon})$ queries.*
> *2. Validity (i.e., f' is a valid solution to f): If $S_{\bar{\epsilon}}(f) \neq \emptyset$, then the pair (f, f') is in $S_{\bar{\epsilon}}$.*
>
> *In addition, we require that n' be computable based on n.*

Note that for functions f such that $S_{\bar{\epsilon}}(f) = \emptyset$, it is only required that the machine answers consistently with some function f'. Indeed, Definition 7.13 (a local (ϵ, ϵ')-reduction of Π to Π') is a special case of Definition 12.10: It corresponds to the case that the local computation algorithm defines a mapping of functions over $[n]$ to functions over $[n']$ such that any $f \in \Pi_n$ is mapped to $f' \in \Pi'_{n'}$ and any f that is ϵ-far from Π_n is mapped to f' that is ϵ'-far from $\Pi'_{n'}$; that is, $(f, f') \in S_{\epsilon, \epsilon'}$ if either $f \in \Pi_n$ and $f' \in \Pi'_{n'}$ or f is ϵ-far from Π_n and f' is ϵ'-far from $\Pi'_{n'}$.

Definition 12.10 is restricted to deterministic computation, whereas we may gain more applications by allowing also randomized machines (let alone that our entire mindset in this book views randomized algorithms as the norm). It is crucial, however, that all invocations of the local computation algorithm refer to the same function f'. Towards this end, we provide the machine M with global randomness, denoted ω, which should be

---

[10] A tuple of approximation parameters (rather than a single parameter) is used for greater expressibility. In fact, this is essential in some cases (e.g., for capturing the notion of a local (ϵ, ϵ')-reduction presented in Definition 7.13).

used in all invocations. In addition, the machine may use auxiliary ("local") randomness, which is implicit in our notation. We distinguish the global randomness from the local randomness, because we wish to use different error probability parameters with respect to each of them (see further discussion following Definition 12.11). The following definition generalizes the definition of a randomized local reduction (i.e., Definition 7.17, although the presentation here is different).[11]

Definition 12.11 (Local computation algorithms, randomized version): *Let q and $\{S_{\bar{\epsilon}}\}_{\bar{\epsilon}>0}$ be as in Definition 12.10, and let $r : \mathbb{N} \times (0, 1]^* \to \mathbb{N}$ and $\eta : \mathbb{N} \to [0, 1]$. A randomized oracle machine M is said to q-locally solve the search problem $\{S_{\bar{\epsilon}}\}_{\bar{\epsilon}>0}$ with error probability η if for every $n \in \mathbb{N}$ there exists $n' \in \mathbb{N}$ such that for every $\bar{\epsilon} > 0$ and for every function f over $[n]$ the following conditions hold.*

1. *Locality (Emulating oracle access to f'_ω):* For every $\omega \in \{0, 1\}^{r(n,\bar{\epsilon})}$ there exists a function f'_ω over $[n']$ such that, on input $n, \bar{\epsilon}, \omega$ and $i \in [n']$, and oracle access to f, with probability at least $2/3$, the machine M outputs $f'_\omega(i)$ after making at most $q(n, \bar{\epsilon})$ queries. In other words, M always makes at most $q(n, \bar{\epsilon})$ queries and $\mathbf{Pr}[M^f(n, \bar{\epsilon}, \omega; i) = f'_\omega(i)] \geq 2/3$, where the probability is over the internal coin tosses of M (whereas ω is fixed).

2. *Validity (i.e., f'_ω is a valid solution to f):* If $S_{\bar{\epsilon}}(f) \neq \emptyset$, then, with probability at least $1 - \eta(n)$ over the choice of ω, the pair (f, f'_ω) is in $S_{\bar{\epsilon}}$, where f'_ω is as in the locality condition. That is,

$$\mathbf{Pr}_{\omega \in \{0,1\}^{r(n,\bar{\epsilon})}}[(f, f'_\omega) \in S_{\bar{\epsilon}}] \geq 1 - \eta(n).$$

In addition, we require that n' be computable based on n. The string ω is called the global randomness, *and the internal coin tosses of M are called the* local randomness.

Note that $\omega \in \{0, 1\}^{r(n,\bar{\epsilon})}$ constitutes a succinct representation of a function f'_ω, which is an alleged solution for the function f. Hence, the length of ω is of major interest, whereas the length of the local randomness is less important. We stress that Definition 12.11 refers to two types of error probability. The first type is the probability that the choice of the global randomness ω yields an invalid solution f'_ω. Note that this error probability cannot be generically reduced by repetitions, since different ω's may yield different functions f'_ω (whereas it is not necessarily easy to determine whether or not f'_ω is in $S_{\bar{\epsilon}}(f)$).[12] This is a general phenomenon that refers to any randomized algorithms for solving search problems, and it is the reason that we introduced an explicit parameter, denoted η, for bounding this error probability. In contrast, the second type of error probability, which refers to the (implicit) local randomness of M, can be reduced by repetitions (and therefore we felt no need to introduce a parameter that governs it, but rather set this error probability to $1/3$).[13]

---

[11] Specifically, as in Definition 12.10, we explicitly refer to the (possibly adaptive) computing machine. In addition, here we explicitly refer to the global randomness and to the error probability.

[12] Indeed, if the property $S_{\bar{\epsilon}}(f)$ has an efficient property tester, then error reduction is possible.

[13] This difference provides an additional motivation for distinguishing the local randomness from the global randomness. In contrast, incorporating the local randomness in the global randomness would have set the error probability for each computation of f'_ω to η, whereas the current formalism allows greater flexibility (which is particularly important in the case that the expected number of local computations is larger than $1/\eta(n)$).

A Richer Formalism. In Definition 12.11, the oracle machine M is provided with the global randomness ω. A richer formalism allows to provide it (or rather its query-serving module) with arbitrary information that is computed based on ω and the oracle f during a *preprocessing stage*. In such a case, the query complexity of the preprocessing stage (or rather module) is stated separately. Needless to say, an oracle machine as in Definition 12.11 can be obtained by invoking the preprocessing module each time a query (to f'_{ω}) needs to be served, but this is wasteful (especially since typically the preprocessing module has higher complexity than the query-serving module). This motivates the following definition, where the output of the preprocessing module, denoted z, may (but need not) explicitly contain the global randomness ω.

Definition 12.12 (Local computation algorithms, two-stage version): *Let r, η and $\{S_{\overline{\epsilon}}\}_{\overline{\epsilon}>0}$ be as in Definition 12.11, and $q_1, q_2 : \mathbb{N} \times (0, 1]^* \to \mathbb{N}$. A pair of oracle machines, (M_1, M_2), is said to (q_1, q_2)-locally solve the search problem $\{S_{\overline{\epsilon}}\}_{\overline{\epsilon}>0}$ with error probability η if for every $n \in \mathbb{N}$ there exists $n' \in \mathbb{N}$ such that for every $\overline{\epsilon} > 0$ and for every function f over $[n]$ the following conditions hold.*

1. *Preprocessing: The oracle machine M_1 is deterministic, and for every $\omega \in \{0, 1\}^{r(n,\overline{\epsilon})}$, on input $(n, \overline{\epsilon})$ and ω, it makes at most $q_1(n, \overline{\epsilon})$ queries.*
2. *Locality (Emulating oracle access to f'_z): For every $z \in \{0, 1\}^*$ there exists a function f'_z over $[n']$ such that, on input $n, \overline{\epsilon}, z$ and $i \in [n']$, and oracle access to f, with probability at least $2/3$, the machine M_2 outputs $f'_z(i)$ after making at most $q_2(n, \overline{\epsilon})$ queries. In other words, M_2 always makes at most $q_2(n, \overline{\epsilon})$ queries and $\mathbf{Pr}[M_2^f(n, \overline{\epsilon}, z; i) = f'_z(i)] \geq 2/3$, where the probability is over the internal coin tosses of M_2.*
3. *Validity (i.e., f'_z is a valid solution to f): If $S_{\overline{\epsilon}}(f) \neq \emptyset$, then, with probability at least $1 - \eta(n)$ over the choice of $\omega \in \{0, 1\}^{r(n,\overline{\epsilon})}$, the pair (f, f'_z) is in $S_{\overline{\epsilon}}$, where $z \leftarrow M_1^f(n, \overline{\epsilon}, \omega)$ and f'_z is as in the locality condition.*

Again, we require that n' be computable based on n. The string ω is called the global randomness, *and the internal coin tosses of M_2 are called the* local randomness.

Without loss of generality, z may consist of ω and the sequence of answers provided to M_1 in the execution $M_1^f(n, \overline{\epsilon}, \omega)$. As noted previously, every (q_1, q_2)-local solver yields a $(q_1 + q_2)$-local solver, but it is beneficial to use the former formulation when $q_1 \gg q_2$. (On the other hand, any q-local solver yields a $(0, q)$-local solver, where the fictitious preprocessing just maps ω to itself, but this trivial fact is quite useless.)

We comment that locally decodable codes (briefly discussed in Section 13.4.4) can be viewed within the current framework. Specifically, given oracle access to a slightly corrupted codeword, the task is to recover the original message (locally); that is, a q-local decodable code $C : \{0, 1\}^k \to \{0, 1\}^n$, is equipped with a q-local algorithm for the search problem that consists of all pairs $(w, x) \in \{0, 1\}^n \times \{0, 1\}^k$ such that w that is close to the codeword $C(x)$.

12.5.2. Finding Huge Structures

As mentioned in Section 8.3, local computations of huge structures are implicit in the testers for the various graph partition problems (in the dense graph model). For concreteness, we consider the case of Bipartiteness. In this case, we seek a local computation algorithm that finds a 2-partition of the vertices of a given bipartite graph such that there are relatively few edges with both endpoints in the same part. Such a local computation algorithm is implicit in the corresponding tester.

Proposition 12.13 (Finding approximate 2-colorings in bipartite graphs, in the dense graph model): *There exists a* $(\text{poly}(1/\epsilon) \cdot \log(1/\eta), \widetilde{O}(1/\epsilon))$-*local algorithm that, on input k, ϵ, η and oracle access to an adjacency predicate of a k-vertex Bipartite graph, $G = ([k], E)$, finds, with probability at least $1 - \eta$, a 2-partition $\chi : [k] \to \{1, 2\}$ such that $|\{\{u, v\} \in E : \chi(u) = \chi(v)\}| < \epsilon k^2/2$.*

In other words, the algorithm solve the search problem S_ϵ with error probability η, where S_ϵ contains all pairs (G, χ) such that $G = ([k], E)$ is a bipartite graph and $|\{\{u, v\} \in E : \chi(u) = \chi(v)\}| < \epsilon k^2/2$, where $k^2/2$ is used as an approximation to the total number of pairs over $[k]$ (see discussion in Section 8.2).

Proof Sketch: Our starting point is the analysis of Algorithm 8.7, which views the sample of $\widetilde{O}(1/\epsilon^2)$ vertices selected by the algorithm as consisting of two parts, U and S, such that $|U| = \widetilde{O}(1/\epsilon)$ and $|S| = \widetilde{O}(1/\epsilon^2)$. The analysis establishes that for 5/6 of the possible U's, there exists a 2-partition of U, denoted (U_1, U_2), such that *letting $\chi(v) = 1$ if and only if v has no neighbor in U_1* yields a 2-partition $\chi : [k] \to \{1, 2\}$ as desired (i.e., $|\{\{u, v\} \in E : \chi(u) = \chi(v)\}| < \epsilon k^2/2$). The set S is used to (implicitly) estimate the suitability of each of the 2-partitions of U. Specifically, if χ has at least $\epsilon k^2/4$ monochromatic (w.r.t. χ) edges, then, with probability at least $1 - \exp(-\Omega(\epsilon \cdot |S|)) = 1 - 2^{-|U|-3}$, the subgraph induced by S will contain a monochromatic edge.[14] Hence, we can find, in a preprocessing stage, a partition of U that determines a suitable χ.

Let us spell out the local computation algorithm that emerges. The preprocessing stage of this algorithm uses the global randomness in order to select random sets of vertices U and S such that $|U| = \widetilde{O}(1/\epsilon)$ and $|S| = \widetilde{O}(1/\epsilon^2)$. It then determines a 2-partition of U, denoted (U_1, U_2), such that, with high probability (over the choice of U and S), the corresponding 2-partition χ is a good solution (where $\chi(v) = 1$ if and only if v has no neighbor in U_1). *The 2-partition of U is determined by finding a legal 2-coloring of the subgraph of G that is induced by $U \cup S$, and using the 2-partition that it induces on U.* The query-serving stage is deterministic: It answers the query v by querying the graph G on the pairs $\{v, u\}$ for all $u \in U_1$, and answers accordingly. (Hence, this algorithm uses no local randomness.)

As shown in the proof of Lemma 8.8, with high probability, the set U neighbors both endpoints of almost all edges in G (i.e., all but at most $\epsilon k^2/4$ of the edges). Whenever this event occurs, a 2-partition of U that yields a bad solution $\chi : [k] \to \{1, 2\}$ will be detected as bad (by S), with overwhelmingly high probability. Hence, with high probability, the 2-partition of U selected in the preprocessing stage is good. Finally, in order to obtain error probability of η, we perform the foregoing procedure using $\ell = O(\log(1/\eta))$ candidate sets U and a set S that is ℓ times larger.[15] ∎

---

[14] Actually, letting $S = \{s_1, \ldots, s_m\}$, it suffices to check the pairs (s_{2i-1}, s_{2i}) for $i = 1, \ldots, m/2$.

[15] That is, in the preprocessing stage, we select ℓ random sets $U^{(1)}, \ldots, U^{(\ell)}$, each of size $\widetilde{O}(1/\epsilon)$ and a single set S of size $\ell \cdot \widetilde{O}(1/\epsilon^2)$, find an i such that $U^{(i)}$ is good (per Definition 8.8.1), determine the 2-partition of $U^{(i)}$ by

Finding Other Huge Structures. In general, in the context of graphs, two notable types of desired output are (1) a partition of the vertices of the (input) graph that satisfies some properties, and (2) a subgraph (of the input graph) that satisfies some properties. We briefly review these types of problems next.

As mentioned in the beginning of this section, in the dense graph model, for any fixed t and any sequence of desired vertex and edge densities, a t-partition of the vertices that approximately satisfies these densities can be found by a poly$(1/\epsilon)$-local algorithm (with error probability poly(ϵ), whenever the exact t-partition exists), where ϵ is the proximity parameter. This follows from the methods used to construct testers for the corresponding graph partition problems (discussed in Section 8.3).

Turning to the bounded-degree graph model, we mention that Section 9.5 evolves around the local construction and utilization of *partition oracles*. Recall that for given parameters $\epsilon > 0$ and $t \in \mathbb{N}$, such a partition oracle of a graph $G = ([k], E)$ is a function $P : [k] \to \cup_{i \in [t]} \binom{[k]}{i}$ such that (1) for every vertex $v \in [k]$ it holds that $v \in P(v)$; (2) the subgraph of G induced by $P(v)$ is connected (and has at most t vertices); and (3) different $P(v)$'s are disjoint and the total number of edges among them is at most ϵk.

The problem of *finding huge subgraphs* that satisfy various properties was also considered in several works. In particular, the related problems of finding a *maximal matching* and *approximate maximum matching* in bounded-degree graphs were considered in several works (see [103] and the references therein).[16] The problem of finding a *sparse spanning subgraph* was studied in [198].

12.5.3. Local Reconstruction

A natural computational problem, which falls within the framework of local computation, is designing a "filter" that returns the input function if this function has a designed property and returns an arbitrary function having the property otherwise. In other words, the filter must always return an output in Π, but if the input f is in Π then the filter must return f itself. That is, for a property of functions Π, we consider the search problem S such that for every f it holds that $\emptyset \neq S(f) \subseteq \Pi$, and $S(f) = \{f\}$ if $f \in \Pi$. A more smooth definition requires that, for some monotonically nondecreasing function $\rho : [0, 1] \to [0, 1]$ such that $\rho(0) = 0$, it holds that *if f is δ-close to Π, then $S(f) \subseteq \Pi$ contains only functions that are $\rho(\delta)$-close to f* (and, as before, $S(f) \neq \emptyset$ for any f).[17] Needless to say, the aim is to solve this search problem by a local computation algorithm; that is, the filter is required to implement an oracle access to some $f' \in S(f)$ by making few queries to f.

Such filters, also called *local reconstructors*, are extremely beneficial in settings that are complementary to ones that motivate tolerant testers. Specifically, here we envision a gap between the usefulness of functions having a certain property and functions lacking it. Testing the function for the property eliminates the danger of functions that are far

---

considering the subgraph of G that is induced by $U^{(i)} \cup S$, and output this 2-partition (for use by the query-serving module). Recall that a set is good if it neighbors all but at most $\epsilon k/6$ of the vertices that have degree at least $\epsilon k/6$, and note that we can use S (or an auxiliary set of $\ell \cdot \tilde{O}(1/\epsilon^2)$ random vertices) in order to test this condition. Hence, the verdict regarding the goodness of each $U^{(i)}$ is correct with probability $1 - \exp(-\ell)$, and with the same probability at least one of the $U^{(i)}$'s is good. Lastly, since $|S| = \Omega(\ell \cdot |U^{(i)}|/\epsilon)$, with probability $1 - \exp(-\ell)$, the 2-coloring of the subgraph induced by $U^{(i)} \cup S$ yields a valid 2-partition of $[k]$.

[16] These works also study finding *d-coloring* in graphs of maximal degree d.

[17] Indeed, it follows that $S(f) = \{f\}$ for any $f \in \Pi$, since in this case $S(f)$ contains only functions that are 0-close to f.

from the property. The foregoing filters guarantee that also functions that are close to the property will not cause problems; they will be transformed into functions that have the property and are close to the original functions (and so they may preserve other features of the original functions).

A concrete case where this issue arises is the one of mechanisms that preserve the "privacy" of the data when answering questions that correspond to functions of the data, provided that these functions satisfy certain properties (e.g., Lipschitz properties, cf. [173]). The point is that the security guarantee (i.e., "privacy") may be compromised even if the function deviates only a little from the property, but the utility of the function does not change by much if the function is slightly modified.

In any case, properties that consist of functions that are randomly self-reducible by few queries (see Definition 5.9) have trivial local reconstruction algorithms, which use no global randomness (but do use local randomness). Recall, however, that such properties must have distance (i.e., every two distinct functions in the property are far apart). Hence, the focus of the study of local reconstruction algorithms is on properties that have no distance, like monotonicity (and Lipschitz) properties.

12.6. Noninteractive Proofs of Proximity (MAPs)

The $\mathcal{P} \neq \mathcal{NP}$ conjecture means that, in general, *verifying the validity of a proof for a given assertion is easier than deciding the validity of the given assertion, when it is not accompanied by a proof.* A natural question is whether the same holds also with respect to approximate decisions; that is, can short proofs assist property testers, which in this case may be called property verifiers.

This question leads to the following model of probabilistic proof systems, which is a hybrid of MA ("randomized NP") and property testing. These proof systems, called MAPs (for Merlin–Arthur proofs of proximity), consist of a (relatively short) proof given to a verifier that has (randomized) query access to the main (tested) object. We stress that the verifier has free access to the alleged proof, and that our focus is on short proofs (i.e., proofs that are significantly shorter than the input).[18] Insisting on short proofs is natural in the current context, since our final goal is to obtain superfast algorithms; recall that, in general, property testing is concerned with sublinear complexity (i.e., sublinear in input length).

The choice of considering a randomized proof system, rather than a deterministic one, also fits the context of property testing, since property testers are inherently randomized.[19] Hence, we view the MAP model as the natural "NP analogue" of property testing.

The following definition augments the property testing framework by providing the tester, which may be called a *verifier*, with free access to a short proof (denoted π), in addition to its oracle access to the input (denoted f). The guarantee is that, for any input that has the property, there exists a proof that makes the verifier accept (with high probability), whereas for any input that is far from the property the verifier will reject any alleged proof (with high probability).

---

[18] Jumping ahead, we mention that any property can be ϵ-verified by making $O(1/\epsilon)$ queries, when given access to a proof of linear length (see Exercise 12.6). On the other hand, if the proof is shorter than the query complexity, then having free access (rather than query access) to it is immaterial; however, this is not necessarily the case.

[19] Indeed, deterministic MAPs are quite restricted; see Exercise 12.7.

Definition 12.14 (Noninteractive proofs of proximity (MAPs)): *Let* $\Pi = \cup_{n \in \mathbb{N}} \Pi_n$ *such that* $\Pi_n \subseteq \{f : [n] \to R_n\}$. *A system of* noninteractive proofs of proximity (MAP) *for* Π *is a probabilistic oracle machine, called a* verifier *and denoted* V, *that satisfies the following two conditions, for every* $n \in \mathbb{N}$ *and* $\epsilon > 0$.

1. Completeness: V accepts inputs in Π when given an adequate proof. *Specifically, for every* $f \in \Pi_n$ *there exists* $\pi \in \{0, 1\}^*$ *such that* $\mathbf{Pr}[V^f(n, \epsilon, \pi) = 1] \geq 2/3$. *If* $\mathbf{Pr}[V^f(n, \epsilon, \pi) = 1] = 1$, *then we say that* V *has* perfect completeness.
2. Soundness: V rejects inputs that are far from Π. *Specifically, for every* $f : [n] \to R_n$ *that is* ϵ*-far from* Π_n *and every* $\pi \in \{0, 1\}^*$ *it holds that* $\mathbf{Pr}[V^f(n, \epsilon, \pi) = 0] \geq 2/3$.

We say that V *has* proof complexity $p : \mathbb{N} \to \mathbb{N}$ *if the completeness condition holds with a proof* π *of length at most* $p(n)$. *We say that* V *has* query complexity $q : \mathbb{N} \times (0, 1] \to \mathbb{N}$ *if, on input* n, ϵ, π *and oracle access to any* $f : [n] \to R_n$, *the verifier makes at most* $q(n, \epsilon)$ *queries.*[20]

In addition, one may limit the computational complexity of the verifier; for example, require that its running time is sublinear in the length of the input (or almost linear in its proof and query complexities). We note that property testers may be viewed as MAPs of proof complexity zero, and in that case perfect completeness corresponds to one-sided error probability.

As mentioned upfront, our focus is on MAPs of sublinear proof complexity; indeed, any property has a "trivial" MAP with linear proof complexity and query complexity $O(1/\epsilon)$ (see Exercise 12.6). Interestingly, even very short proofs can reduce the query complexity in a significant fashion: For example, $\Pi = \{uuvv : u, v \in \{0, 1\}^*\}$ has a MAP of logarithmic proof complexity and query complexity $O(1/\epsilon)$, whereas testing Π requires $\Omega(\sqrt{n})$ queries (see Exercise 12.9).

General results. A few of the known results regarding MAPs include

- *MAPs versus property testers.* There exists a property Π that has a MAP of logarithmic proof complexity and query complexity poly$(1/\epsilon)$, whereas testing Π requires $\Omega(n^{0.999})$ queries (see [141], building on [166]). Indeed, 0.999 stands for any constant smaller than 1.
- *Proof length versus query complexity trade-off in MAPs.* There exists a property Π such that, for every $p \geq 1$, the property Π has a MAP of proof complexity p and query complexity poly$(1/\epsilon) \cdot n/p$, whereas every MAP of proof complexity p for Π requires $\Omega(n^{0.999}/p)$ queries [166].
- *Two-sided versus one-sided error MAPs.* Any MAP can be transformed into a MAP with perfect completeness at the cost of increasing its proof and query complexities by at most a polylogarithmic (in n) factor [166].
- *Properties that are extremely hard for MAPs.* There exists a property Π such that every MAP of proof complexity $n/100$ for Π requires $\Omega(n)$ queries [166].

---

[20] Indeed, as in the definition of property testers, the query complexity of the verifier depends on ϵ. A conscious decision is made here not to allow the proof complexity to depend on ϵ (and not to allow the query complexity to depend on π), since this choice seems more natural.

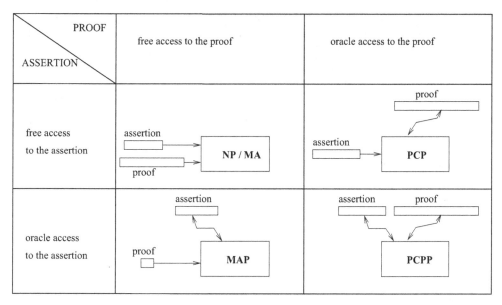

Figure 12.1: A taxonomy of four types of noninteractive proof systems.

In addition, we mention that, for every $p < n$, every context-free language has a MAP of proof complexity p and query complexity $\epsilon^{-1} \cdot \tilde{O}(n)/p$; the same holds for sets recognized by read-once branching programs of polynomial size [142].

Relation to Other Forms of Noninteractive Proof Systems. MAPs are a type of noninteractive and probabilistic proof systems, and as such they are related to but different from three other types of such proof systems. The other proof systems that we refer to are PCPPs (PCPs of Proximity), PCPs, and "randomized NP" proof systems (captured by the complexity class $\mathcal{MA}$).[21] These four types of noninteractive proof systems differ in the way they refer to the (purported) assertion and to the (alleged) proof. In MAPs and PCPPs, the verifier gets only oracle access to the assertion, its queries are accounted for (in the query complexity), but the soundness condition refers only to inputs that are far from the set of valid assertions. In contrast, in (randomized) NP-proof systems and in PCPs the verifier gets free access to the assertion (and the soundness condition refers to all invalid assertions). Turning to the alleged proof, in (randomized) NP-proofs and in MAPs, the verifier gets free access to it, whereas in PCPs and PCPPs the verifier gets only oracle access to the alleged proof. A crucial difference between MAPs and all the other three types of proof systems is that in MAPs the focus is on short proofs (whereas in NP, as well as in PCPs and PCPPs, the proof is typically longer than the assertion).[22] The taxonomy that arises is captured in Figure 12.1.

To summarize: In MAPs, the input is presented via an oracle (like in PCPP and in property testers), whereas the proof is presented explicitly (like in NP/MA). Hence, as stated previously, MAPs are an NP version of property testers.

---

[21] PCPs and PCPPs are discussed in Chapter 13; see, in particular, Sections 13.2.2 and 13.2.3.3. For a wider perspective on probabilistic proof systems, the interested reader is referred to [131, Chap. 9].

[22] **Advanced comment:** The focus on short proofs is reminiscent of the study of *laconic interactive proof systems*, but that study focused on systems in which at least two messages are sent [159].

Relation to Interactive Proofs of Proximity. The MAP model can be viewed as a special case of the more general model of *interactive proofs of proximity* (IPP), which is an interactive proof (IP) version of property testing. In an IPP, the prover and verifier exchange messages, but the verifier can only access the main input via oracle queries. In this case the verifier V is an interactive strategy, which also has oracle access to the main input (denoted f). In addition, we also consider interactive strategies for the prover. For a pair of interactive strategies, (A, B), we denote by $\langle A, B^f \rangle(z)$ the output of strategy B after interacting with A on explicit input z, while having oracle access to f.[23]

> **Definition 12.15** (Interactive proofs of proximity (IPPs): *Let* $\Pi = \cup_{n \in \mathbb{N}} \Pi_n$ *such that* $\Pi_n \subseteq \{f : [n] \to R_n\}$. *A system of* interactive proofs of proximity (IPP) *for* Π *is a probabilistic and interactive strategy, called a* verifier *and denoted* V, *that satisfies the following two conditions, for every* $n \in \mathbb{N}$ *and* $\epsilon > 0$.
>
> 1. Completeness: V *accepts inputs in* Π *when interacting with an adequate prover. Specifically, for every* $f \in \Pi_n$ *there exists a prover strategy* P *such that* $\mathbf{Pr}[\langle P, V^f \rangle(n, \epsilon) = 1] \geq 2/3$.
> 2. Soundness: V *rejects inputs that are far from* Π. *Specifically, for every* $f : [n] \to R_n$ *that is* ϵ-*far from* Π_n *and every strategy* $\widetilde{P}$ *it holds that* $\mathbf{Pr}[\langle \widetilde{P}, V^f \rangle(n, \epsilon) = 0] \geq 2/3$.
>
> *We say that* V *has* query complexity $q : \mathbb{N} \times (0, 1] \to \mathbb{N}$ *if, on input* n, ϵ *and oracle access to any* $f : [n] \to R_n$, *the verifier makes at most* $q(n, \epsilon)$ *queries. The* communication complexity *of the IPP is defined as the total length of messages sent by the prover to the verifier.*

As with MAPs, the focus is on IPPs of sublinear query and communication complexities. In addition, we may also bound the length of the messages sent by the verifier, and the total number of messages exchanges (a.k.a the number of communication rounds). And, again, we may also limit the computational complexity of the verifier.

Indeed, MAPs may be viewed as IPPs with unidirectional communication going from the prover to the verifier, and in this case the prover may just send a single message. We mention that IPPs are more powerful than MAPs: *there exists a property* Π *that has an IPP of polylogarithmic communication and query complexities such that every MAP of proof complexity* $n^{0.499}$ *for* Π *requires more than* $n^{0.499}$ *queries* [166]. We also mention that IPPs of sublinear complexity are known for natural complexity classes such as $\mathcal{NC}$ and $\mathcal{SC}$. Specifically:

1. Every set that has log-space uniform circuits of polynomial-size and $n^{o(1)}$ depth, has an IPP in which the verifier total running time is $n^{0.5+o(1)}$ [244].
2. For every constant $\gamma > 0$, every set that can be decided in polynomial-time and n^γ space, has an IPP of constant round complexity in which the verifier total running time is $n^{0.5+O(\gamma)}$ [236].

A Complexity Theoretic Perspective. The foregoing separation results illustrate complexity gaps between property testing, noninteractive proofs of proximity, and interactive

---

[23] In the following definition the first strategy (i.e., A) may depend arbitrarily on f, and so there is no point in providing it with oracle access to f.

proofs of proximity. Tentatively denoting by $\mathcal{PT}^{\mathrm{pl}}$, $\mathcal{MAP}^{\mathrm{pl}}$, and $\mathcal{IPP}^{\mathrm{pl}}$ the classes of properties that admit testers and verifiers of polylogarithmic query and communication complexity,[24] we get a separation between these classes; that is, $\mathcal{PT}^{\mathrm{pl}} \subset \mathcal{MAP}^{\mathrm{pl}} \subset \mathcal{IPP}^{\mathrm{pl}}$. In some sense, this means that (very natural) approximate decision versions of the complexity classes $\mathcal{BPP}$, $\mathcal{MA}$ and $\mathcal{IP}$ are separated.

12.7. Chapter Notes

12.7.1. Historical Notes

Property testing with respect to general distributions as well as distribution-free testing, sample-based testing, and tolerant testing were all mentioned in [140, Sec. 2]. However, the focus of [140] as well as of almost all subsequent works was on the basic framework of Definition 1.6 (i.e., using queries in testing w.r.t. the uniform distribution). An explicit study of the various ramifications started (later) in [167, 153, 225], respectively.

The study of *tolerant testing* of properties (and distance approximation for them) was initiated by Parnas, Ron, and Rubinfeld [225]. Theorem 12.3 was proved by Fischer and Newman [116]. Distance approximation in the context of bounded-degree and general graphs was first studied in [203].

An extensive study of *sample-based testers* was initiated by Goldreich and Ron [153]. Part 1 of Theorem 12.8 is due to [153], whereas Part 2 is due to [112]. A characterization of properties that have sample-based testers of constant complexity has recently appeared in [57].

The study of *distribution-free testers* was effectively initiated by Halevy and Kushilevitz [167], and a few works followed. We mention the work of Glasner and Servedio, which proves that distribution-free testing is significantly harder than standard testing even for very basic properties of Boolean functions [126].

The study of property testing *with respect to the edit distance* was initiated by Batu *et al.* [33], and a study of testing *with respect to the $\mathcal{L}_p$-distance* was initiated by Berman, Raskhodnikova, and Yaroslavtsev [50].

Local computation algorithms were defined, in full generality, by Rubinfeld *et al.* [247]. This notion generalizes the notion of finding huge structures, which is implicit in [140], and the notion of *local reconstruction* proposed by Ailon *et al.* [5] (and pursued in [248, 173]). An analogue of the notion of local reconstruction for the context in which the object is a distribution, called *sampling correctors*, was recently proposed in [69].

The notion of *noninteractive proofs of proximity* (MAPs) was introduced and studied by Gur and Rothblum [166], subsequent to the introduction and study of *interactive proofs of proximity* (IPPs) by Rothblum, Vadhan, and Wigderson [244].[25] We mention that IPPs are a special case of a general framework suggested before by Ergün, Kumar, and Rubinfeld [102]. We also mention that the notion of MAPs is implicit in the work of Fischer, Goldhirsh, and Lachish [110], who (concurrently and independently of [166]) referred to the existence of MAPs as an obstacle to proving lower bounds on a robust notion of testing (which they call "partial tests").

---

[24] More generally, we may denote by $\mathcal{PT}[q]$ the class of properties that admit testers of query complexity q, and by $\mathcal{MAP}[p, q]$ (resp., $\mathcal{IPP}[c, q]$) the class of properties that admit verifiers of query complexity q and proof complexity p (resp., communication complexity c). The foregoing results assert that $\mathcal{PT}[n^{0.999}]$ does not contain $\mathcal{MA}[O(\log n), \text{poly}(1/\epsilon)]$, and that $\mathcal{MA}[n^{0.499}, n^{0.499}]$ does not contain $\mathcal{IPP}[\text{poly}(\log n), \text{poly}(\epsilon^{-1} \log n)]$.

[25] We mention that Rothblum in [166] is different from Rothblum in [244].

12.7.2. Massively Parameterized Properties

Before concluding this chapter, we briefly discuss the notion of testing massively parameterized properties. Strictly speaking, this notion falls within the framework of property testing, but conceptually it does represent a certain deviation from that mind-frame.

Recall that throughout this book, we focused on properties of the form $\Pi = \cup_{n \in \mathbb{N}} \Pi_n$ such that Π_n is a set of functions over the domain $[n]$. Thus, the (size) parameter n, which was given to the tester, specifies a set of functions over $[n]$. A generalization of this setting consists of considering properties that are arbitrarily parameterized such that the parameter determines the size of the tested object but is not confined to that role. Specifically, we consider properties of the form $\Pi = \cup_{z \in \{0,1\}^*} \Pi_z$ such that Π_z is a set of functions over $[n(z)]$, where $n : \{0, 1\}^* \to \mathbb{N}$. In this case, the tester is given the parameter z (rather than $n(z)$) as an explicit input, and its running-time is at least linear in $|z|$ (although its query complexity may be much lower).

The term *massively parameterized properties* refers to the case that $|z| \geq n(z)^{\Omega(1)}$ (or even $|z| = \Omega(n(z))$), which means that the size of the tested object is at most polynomial (or at most linear) in the length of the parameter z (i.e., $n(z) = \text{poly}(|z|)$, or even $n(z) = O(|z|)$). This stands in contrast to the standard case in which the length of the size-parameter n is logarithmic in the size of the object (i.e., $n = \exp(|n|)$). In particular, when $n(z) = O(|z|)$, the running-time of the tester is at least linear in the size of the tested object (although, again, its query complexity may be sublinear in $n(z)$). In this case, property testing no longer offers sublinear time algorithms, although it may still offer sublinear query complexity, which is valuable in settings in which accessing the input is more expensive than computing time.

For example, as briefly mentioned in Section 6.4, the massive parameter may be a Boolean formula $\phi : \{0, 1\}^n \to \{0, 1\}$, and the property may consist of the set of (n-bit long) assignments that satisfy this formula (cf. [47]). In this case, the input assignment is typically shorter than the description of the formula (i.e., $n < |\phi|$); still, the tester is given the formula "for free" and is charged only for queries to the assignment. Another example is the *graph orientation model*, where the massive parameter is a graph $G = ([k], E)$, and the property consists of a set of orientations of the edges (e.g., all orientations that yield a directed Eulerian graph). Again, the input orientation $\xi : E \to \{\pm 1\}$ is shorter than the description of the parameter (graph).

We comment that the framework of massively parameterized properties has often been used implicitly. For example, the problem of testing equality to a fixed target distribution (studied in Section 11.2) is massively parameterized (by the target distribution). Likewise, the property of being isomorphic to a fixed target graph, studied in [114], is massively parameterized (by the target graph).[26] For a survey of studies of testing massively parameterized properties, the reader is referred to [216].

12.7.3. Exercises

Exercise 12.1 (Tolerant testers with one-sided error probability):[27] We say that a tolerant tester (as in Definition 12.1) has one-sided error if Condition 1 holds with probability 1 (i.e., T accepts with probability 1 any $f : [n] \to R_n$ that is ϵ'-close to Π). Show that

---

[26] Interestingly, this paper also studies the problem of testing isomorphism between two unknown input graphs.
[27] Based on [260].

if for some $\epsilon > 0$ and $n \in \mathbb{N}$ it holds that Π_n is nontrivial w.r.t. ϵ-testing (i.e., $\Pi_n \neq \emptyset$ and there exists a function that is ϵ-far from Π), then any ϵ'-tolerant ϵ-tester for Π_n makes more than $\epsilon'n$ queries, for any $\epsilon' \in (0, \epsilon)$.

> **Guideline:** Suppose that an ϵ'-tolerant ϵ-tester T makes q queries, and consider its execution when given access $f : [n] \to R_n$ that is ϵ-far from Π. Then, with positive probability, T rejects. Fix such a rejecting sequence of coins for T, and consider the set of locations Q that were queried. Finally, for an arbitrary $g \in \Pi_n$, consider a hybrid, denoted h, of g and f such that $h(j) = f(j)$ if $j \in Q$ and $h(j) = g(j)$ otherwise. Since, h is rejected with positive probability, it must hold that h is ϵ'-far from $g \in \Pi_n$, which implies $|Q| > \epsilon'n$.

Exercise 12.2 (Generic derivation of a weak tolerant tester): Show that any ϵ-tester for Π that makes q queries that are each uniformly distributed,[28] yields and $(1/10q)$-tolerant ϵ-tester for Π of query complexity $O(q)$.

> **Guideline:** Observe that such a tester accepts any function that is ϵ'-close to Π with probability at least $2/3 - q \cdot \epsilon'$. Use error reduction to regain the original error bound of $2/3$.

Exercise 12.3 (Tolerant tester for t-colorability in the dense graph model): For any $t \geq 2$, present an ϵ'-tolerant ϵ-tester for t-Colorability by using a reduction to several graph partition problems. Specifically, referring to the framework presented in Definition 8.11, use t-partition problems in which the absolute upper bounds on the edge density inside parts (i.e., the $H_{i,i}^{\mathrm{abs}}$'s) sum-up to ϵ', and test these properties with a proximity parameter set to $(\epsilon - \epsilon')/2$ or so.

> **Guideline:** In case of $t = 2$, let $\epsilon'' = (\epsilon - \epsilon')/4$, and, for every $i \in [\lceil 1/\epsilon'' \rceil]$, consider the property associated with the nontrivial bounds $H_{1,1}^{\mathrm{abs}} = i \cdot \epsilon''$ and $H_{2,2}^{\mathrm{abs}} = \epsilon' - (i - 1) \cdot \epsilon''$. Essentially, run each of the m corresponding testers with proximity parameter ϵ'', and accept if and only if at least one of them accepts.

Exercise 12.4 (Tolerant testers in the bounded-degree graph model): Present tolerant testers for degree regularity, connectivity, and cycle-freeness. Specifically, present ϵ'-tolerant ϵ-testers of query complexity $\mathrm{poly}(1/\epsilon')$ for some $\epsilon' = \Omega(\epsilon)$.

> **Guideline:** Use Claim 9.5.1, Proposition 9.7, and Proposition 9.12, respectively. Note that algorithmic steps that reject based on the mere *existence* of evidence for violation of the property should be replaces by steps that reject based only on *sufficient amount* of such evidence.

Exercise 12.5 (Disposing of a promise underlying the bounded-degree graph model): Recall that, in the bounded-degree graph model, the tester is given oracle access to a purported incidence function $g : [k] \times [d] \to \{0, 1, \ldots, k\}$ of a k-vertex graph of maximal degree d such that if $g(u, i) = v$ for some $u, v \in [k]$ and $i \in [d]$, then there exists $j \in [d]$ such that $g(v, j) = u$. Show that we can waive the latter assumption by increasing the query complexity of the tester by a factor of d and an additive term of $O(d/\epsilon)$.

---

[28] We stress that different queries are allowed to depend on one another; we only postulate that each query, by itself, is uniformly distributed in the function's domain.

Guideline: First, test the condition by selecting $O(1/\epsilon)$ random pairs $(u, i) \in [k] \times [d]$. Assuming that this test passed, invoke the original tester while answering its queries according to the function $g' : [k] \times [d] \to \{0, 1, \ldots, k\}$ such that $g'(u, i) = v$ if $g(u, i) = v \in [k]$ and $u \in \{g(v, j) : j \in [d]\}$ (and set $g'(u, i) = 0$ otherwise). Provide a detailed analysis of the performance of this tester.

Exercise 12.6 (MAPs with linear length proofs): Show that every property Π has a MAP of linear proof complexity and query complexity $O(1/\epsilon)$.

> **Guideline:** The proof π consists of a copy of the input function f; the verifier checks whether $\pi \in \Pi$, and then checks that $\pi = f$ by querying f at $O(1/\epsilon)$ random locations.

Exercise 12.7 (A lower bound on the randomness complexity of MAPs):[29] Consider a promise problem $(\Pi_{\text{YES}}, \Pi_{\text{NO}})$ regarding functions from $[n]$ to R, and say that Π is strongly ρ-evasive if there exists a function $f_1 : [n] \to R$ in Π_{YES} such that for every $Q \subset [n]$ of density ρ, there exists $f_0 \in \Pi_{\text{NO}}$ such that for every $x \in Q$ it holds that $f_1(x) = f_0(x)$. Suppose that $(\Pi_{\text{YES}}, \Pi_{\text{NO}})$ is strongly ρ-evasive and that membership in Π_{YES} can be verified *(say, with error probability $1/3$)* by an oracle machine M that makes q queries, while getting a proof of arbitrary length, and being guaranteed that the input is in $\Pi_{\text{YES}} \cup \Pi_{\text{NO}}$. Show that M must toss at least $\log_2(\rho n/q)$ coins. Note that this means that if $(\Pi, \{f : \delta_\Pi(f) > \epsilon\})$ is strongly ρ-evasive, then an ϵ-MAP for Π *(i.e., a MAP that works when the proximity parameter is set to ϵ)* must toss at least $\log_2(\rho n/q)$ coins.[30]

> **Guideline:** Suppose that M tosses r coins, and let f_1 be a function as in the strong ρ-evasive condition, and π be a suitable proof for f_1. Consider all 2^r possible executions of $M^{f_1}(\pi)$, and let Q denote the set of queries made in these executions. Then, $|Q| \leq 2^r \cdot q$. On the other hand, $|Q| > \rho \cdot n$, since otherwise these executions cannot distinguish f_1 from the corresponding function f_0 that is guaranteed by the strong ρ-evasive condition.

Exercise 12.8 (Upper bound on the randomness complexity of MAPs):[31] Let $\Pi = \cup_n \Pi_n$, where Π_n is a subset of $\{f : [n] \to R_n\}$. Suppose that Π has a MAP of error probability $1/4$, query complexity q, and proof complexity p such that $p(n) = O(n)$. Show that Π has a MAP of query complexity q, proof complexity p, and randomness complexity at most $\log n + \log \log |R_n| + O(1)$ coins. Note that the randomness-efficient verifier derived here is not necessarily computationally efficient.

> **Guideline:** Suppose that the MAP V tosses $r = r(n)$ coins, and observe that the number of possible functions that V is required to rule about is at most $|R_n|^n$, whereas each such function has $2^{p(n)}$ possible proofs. Using the probabilistic method, show that

---

[29] This exercise is related to Exercise 1.22, which refers to the case of deciding rather than verifying. In Exercise 1.22, ρ-evasive meant that there exists a function $f : [n] \to R$ such that for every $Q \subset [n]$ of density ρ, there exist $f_1 \in \Pi_{\text{YES}}$ and $f_0 \in \Pi_{\text{NO}}$ such that for every $x \in Q$ it holds that $f_1(x) = f_0(x) = f(x)$. Here, we also mandate that $f = f_1$.

[30] Note that for many natural properties and for sufficiently small constant $\epsilon > 0$, the problem of ϵ-testing the property is strongly $\Omega(1)$-evasive. A partial list includes sets of low-degree polynomials, any code of linear distance, monotonicity, juntas, and various graph properties.

[31] Based on [155, 166]. This exercise extends Exercise 1.21, which refers to the case of deciding rather than verifying.

there exists a set $S \subseteq \{0, 1\}^r$ of size $O(\log(|R_n|^n \cdot 2^{p(n)}))$ such that for every function $f : [n] \to R$ and every $\pi \in \{0, 1\}^{p(n)}$ it holds that

$$|\mathbf{Pr}_{\omega \in S}[M^f(\omega; \pi) = 1] - \mathbf{Pr}_{\omega \in \{0,1\}^r}[M^f(\omega; \pi) = 1]| < 1/12.$$

Then, a randomness-efficient machine may select ω uniformly in S, and emulate M while providing it with ω (as the outcome of the internal coin tosses used by M).

Exercise 12.9 (MAPs are stronger than property testers):[32] Show that the property $\Pi = \{uuvv : u, v \in \{0, 1\}^*\}$ has a MAP of logarithmic proof complexity and query complexity $O(1/\epsilon)$, whereas it is not testable with $o(\sqrt{n})$ queries.

> **Guideline:** Regarding the MAP, for $uuvv \in \Pi$, consider the proof $\pi = |u| \in [n] \equiv \{0, 1\}^{\log_2 |uuvv|}$. As for the lower bound, consider the uniform distribution over $\Pi_n = \Pi \cap \{0, 1\}^n$ versus the uniform distribution over all n-bit long strings. Actually, consider a minor variation on the first distribution obtained by picking $i \in [n/2]$ uniformly at random and selecting $u \in \{0, 1\}^i$ and $v \in \{0, 1\}^{0.5n-i}$ uniformly at random. Note that a machine that makes $o(\sqrt{n})$ queries cannot distinguish these two distributions, since in the first distribution only locations that are at distance either i or $0.5n - i$ apart are correlated.

---

[32] Based on [14, 110]: The lower bound is based on [14], which actually considered the context-free language $\{uu^R vv^R : u, v \in \{0, 1\}^*\}$, where $u^R = u_m \cdots u_1$ is the "reverse" of $u = u_1 \cdots u_m$. The upper bound was first mentioned in [110].

CHAPTER THIRTEEN

Locally Testable Codes and Proofs

Summary: We survey known results regarding locally testable codes
and locally testable proofs (known as PCPs). Local testability refers to
approximately testing large objects based on a very small number of
probes, each retrieving a single bit in the representation of the object.
This yields superfast approximate testing of the corresponding property
(i.e., being a codeword or a valid proof).

In terms of property testing, locally testable codes are error-
correcting codes such that the property of being a codeword can be
tested within low query complexity. As for locally testable proofs
(PCPs), these can be viewed as massively parameterized properties that
are testable within low query complexity such that the parameterized
property is nonempty if and only if the corresponding parameter is in a
predetermined set (of "valid statements").

Our first priority is minimizing the number of probes, and we focus
on the case that this number is a constant. In this case (of a constant
number of probes), we aim at minimizing the length of the constructs.
That is, we seek locally testable codes and proofs of short length.

We stress a fundamental difference between the study of locally testable codes and the
study of property testing. Locally testable codes are artificially *designed* with the aim of
making codeword testing easy. (The same holds with respect to locally testable proofs.)
In contrast, property testing envisions natural objects and properties that are *prescribed*
by an external application.

This chapter has been adapted from our survey [130, 132], which was intended for
readers who have general background in the theory of computation but may lack familiarity with property testing. We chose to maintain this feature of the original text and keep
this chapter self-contained. Hence, the property testing perspective is mentioned but is not
extensively relied upon. In particular, the fact that locally testable codes correspond to a
special case of property testing is not pivotal to the presentation, although it is spelled out.
Viewing PCPs in terms of property testing is less natural, yet this perspective is offered
too (even in the foregoing summary); but again it is not pivotal to the presentation.

This chapter also differs from the other chapters in its style: It only provides *overviews*
of results and proofs, rather than detailed proofs. Furthermore, the footnotes provide additional details that may be more essential than in other chapters.

13.1. Introduction

Codes (i.e., error-correcting codes) and proofs (i.e., automatically verifiable proofs) are fundamental to computer science as well as to related disciplines such as mathematics and computer engineering. Redundancy is inherent to error-correcting codes, whereas testing validity is inherent to proofs. In this survey we also consider less traditional combinations such as testing validity of codewords and the use of proofs that contain redundancy. The reader may wonder why we explore these nontraditional possibilities, and the answer is that they offer various advantages (as will be elaborated next).

Testing the validity of codewords is natural in settings in which one may want to take an action in case the codeword is corrupted. For example, when storing data in an error-correcting format, we may want to recover the data and re-encode it whenever we find that the current encoding is corrupted. Doing so may allow to maintain the data integrity over eternity, although the encoded bits may all get corrupted in the course of time. Of course, we can use the error-correcting decoding procedure associated with the code in order to check whether the current encoding is corrupted, but the question is whether we can check (or just approximately check) this property *much faster*.

Loosely speaking, locally testable codes are error-correcting codes that allow for a superfast probabilistic testing of whether a given string is a valid codeword or is far from any such codeword. In particular, the tester works in sublinear time and reads very few bits of the tested object. Needless to say, the answer provided by such a tester can be only approximately correct (i.e., distinguish, with high probability, between valid codewords and strings that are far from the code), but this may suffice in many applications (including the one outlined in the previous paragraph).

Similarly, locally testable proofs are proofs that allow for a superfast probabilistic verification. Again, the tester works in sublinear time and reads very few bits of the tested object (i.e., the alleged proof). The tester's (a.k.a. verifier's) verdict is correct only with high probability, but this may suffice for many applications, where the assertion is rather mundane but of great practical importance. In particular, it suffices in applications in which proofs are used for establishing the correctness of *specific* computations of practical interest. Lastly, we comment that such *locally testable proofs must be redundant* (or else there would be no chance for verifying them based on inspecting only a small portion of them).

Our first priority is on minimizing the number of bits of the tested object that the tester reads, and we focus on the case that this number is a constant. In this case (of a constant number of probes), we aim at minimizing the length of these constructs (i.e., codes or proofs). An opposite regime, studied in [191, 192], refers to codes of linear length and seeks to minimize the number of bits read. We shall briefly review this alternative regime in Section 13.4.3.

Our interest in relatively *short* locally testable codes and proofs is not surprising in view of the fact that *we envision such objects as actually being used in practice*. Of course, we do not suggest that one may actually use (in practice) any of the constructions surveyed here (especially not the ones that provide the stronger bounds). We rather argue that this direction of research may find applications in practice. Furthermore, it may even be the case that some of the current concepts and techniques may lead to such applications.

Organization: In Section 13.2 we provide a quite comprehensive definitional treatment of locally testable codes and proofs, while relating them to PCPs, PCPs of Proximity, and property testing. In Section 13.3, we survey the main results regarding locally testable codes and proofs as well as many of the underlying ideas.

13.2. Definitions

Local testability is formulated by considering oracle machines. That is, the tester is an oracle machine, and the object that it tests is viewed as an oracle. When talking about oracle access to a string $w \in \{0, 1\}^n$ we viewed w as a function $w : \{1, \ldots, n\} \to \{0, 1\}$. For simplicity, we confine ourselves to *nonadaptive* probabilistic oracle machines; that is, machines that determine their queries based on their explicit input (which in case of codes is merely a length parameter) and their internal coin tosses (but not depending on previous oracle answers). Most importantly, this simplifies the composition of testers (see Section 13.3.2.1), and it comes at no real cost (since almost all known testers are actually nonadaptive).[1] Similarly, we focus on testers with one-sided error probability. Here, the main reason is aesthetic (since one-sided error is especially appealing in case of proof testers), and again almost all known testers are actually of this type.[2]

13.2.1. Codeword Testers

We consider codes mapping sequences of k (input) bits into sequences of $n \geq k$ (output) bits. Such a generic code is denoted by $C : \{0, 1\}^k \to \{0, 1\}^n$, and the elements of $\{C(x) : x \in \{0, 1\}^k\} \subseteq \{0, 1\}^n$ are called codewords (of C).[3]

The distance of a code $C : \{0, 1\}^k \to \{0, 1\}^n$ is the minimum (Hamming) distance between its codewords; that is, $\min_{x \neq y}\{\Delta(C(x), C(y))\}$, where $\Delta(u, v)$ denotes the number of bit-locations on which u and v differ. Throughout this work, *we focus on codes of linear distance*; that is, codes $C : \{0, 1\}^k \to \{0, 1\}^n$ of distance $\Omega(n)$.

The distance of $w \in \{0, 1\}^n$ from a code $C : \{0, 1\}^k \to \{0, 1\}^n$, denoted $\Delta_C(w)$, is the minimum distance between w and the codewords of C; that is, $\Delta_C(w) \stackrel{\text{def}}{=} \min_x\{\Delta(w, C(x))\}$. For $\delta \in [0, 1]$, the n-bit long strings u and v are said to be δ-far (resp., δ-close) if $\Delta(u, v) > \delta \cdot n$ (resp., $\Delta(u, v) \leq \delta \cdot n$). Similarly, w is δ-far from C (resp., δ-close to C) if $\Delta_C(w) > \delta \cdot n$ (resp., $\Delta_C(w) \leq \delta \cdot n$).

Loosely speaking, a codeword tester (or a tester for the code C) is a tester for the property of being a codeword; that is, such a tester should accept any valid codeword, and reject (with high probability) any string that is far from being a codeword. In the following (basic) version of this notion, we fix the proximity parameter ϵ (which determines which words are considered "far" from the code) as well as the query complexity, denoted q. (Furthermore, since we consider a one-sided error version, we fix the rejection probability to $1/2$ (rather than to $1/3$).)[4]

---

[1] In particular, all testers that we shall present are nonadaptive. Furthermore, any oracle machine that makes a constant number of queries (to a binary oracle) can be emulated by a nonadaptive machine that makes a constant number of queries to the same oracle, albeit the second constant is exponential in the first one. Finally, we mention that if the code is linear, then adaptivity is of no advantage [47].

[2] In the context of proof testing (or verification), one-sided error probability is referred to as *perfect completeness*. We mention that in the context of linear codes, one-sided error testing comes with no extra cost [47].

[3] Indeed, we use C to denote both the encoding function (i.e., the mapping from k-bit strings to n-bit codewords) and the set of codewords.

[4] This is done in order to streamline this definition with the standard definition of PCP. As usual, the error probability can be decreased by repeated invocations of the tester.

Definition 13.1 (Codeword tests, basic version): *Let* $C : \{0, 1\}^k \to \{0, 1\}^n$ *be a code (of distance d), and let $q \in \mathbb{N}$ and $\epsilon \in (0, 1)$. A q-local (codeword) ϵ-tester for C is a (nonadaptive) probabilistic oracle machine M that makes at most q queries and satisfies the following two conditions:[5]*

Accepting codewords (a.k.a. completeness): *For any $x \in \{0, 1\}^k$, given oracle access to $C(x)$, machine M accepts with probability 1. That is, $\mathbf{Pr}[M^{C(x)}(1^k) = 1] = 1$, for any $x \in \{0, 1\}^k$.*

Rejection of non-codeword (a.k.a. soundness): *For any $w \in \{0, 1\}^n$ that is ϵ-far from C, given oracle access to w, machine M rejects with probability at least $1/2$. That is, $\mathbf{Pr}[M^w(1^k) = 1] \leq 1/2$, for any $w \in \{0, 1\}^n$ that is ϵ-far from C.*

We call q the query complexity *of M, and ϵ the* proximity parameter.

The foregoing definition is interesting only in case ϵn is smaller than the covering radius of C (i.e., the smallest r such that for every $w \in \{0, 1\}^n$ it holds that $\Delta_C(w) \leq r$).[6] Actually, we shall focus on the case that $\epsilon < d/2n \leq r/n$, while noting that the case $\epsilon > 1.01d/n$ is of limited interest (see Exercise 13.1).[7] On the other hand, observe that $q = \Omega(1/\epsilon)$ must hold, which means that we focus on the case that $d = \Omega(n/q)$.

We next consider families of codes $C = \{C_k : \{0, 1\}^k \to \{0, 1\}^{n(k)}\}_{k \in K}$, where $n, d : \mathbb{N} \to \mathbb{N}$ and $K \subseteq \mathbb{N}$, such that C_k has distance $d(k)$. While we do not mandate $K = \mathbb{N}$, we do wish K to be a "dense" subset of $\mathbb{N}$ (or rather have "relatively small gaps" in K).[8] In accordance with the above, our main interest is in the case that $\epsilon(k) < d(k)/2n(k)$. Furthermore, seeking constant query complexity, we focus on the case $d = \Omega(n)$.

Definition 13.2 (Codeword tests, asymptotic version): *For functions $n, d : \mathbb{N} \to \mathbb{N}$, let $C = \{C_k : \{0, 1\}^k \to \{0, 1\}^{n(k)}\}_{k \in K}$ be such that C_k is a code of distance $d(k)$. For functions $q : \mathbb{N} \to \mathbb{N}$ and $\epsilon : \mathbb{N} \to (0, 1)$, we say that a machine M is a q-local (codeword) ϵ-tester for $C = \{C_k\}_{k \in K}$ if, for every $k \in K$, machine M is a $q(k)$-local $\epsilon(k)$-tester for C_k. Again, q is called the* query complexity *of M, and ϵ the* proximity parameter.

Recall that being particularly interested in constant query complexity (and recalling that $d(k)/n(k) \geq 2\epsilon(k) = \Omega(1/q(k))$), we focus on the case that $d = \Omega(n)$ and ϵ is a constant smaller than $d/2n$. In this case, we may consider a stronger definition (which mandates local testability for all $\epsilon > 0$ rather than for a specific value of $\epsilon > 0$).

---

[5] In order to streamline this definition with the definition of PCP, we provide the tester with 1^k (rather than with n) as an explicit input. Since $n = n(k)$ can be determined based on k, the tester can determine the length of its oracle (before making any query to it). Recall that providing the tester with the length of its oracle is the standard convention in property testing.

[6] Note that $\lfloor d/2 \rfloor \leq r \leq n - \lceil d/2 \rceil$. The lower bound on r follows by considering a string that resides in the middle of the shortest path between two distinct codewords, and the upper bound follows by considering the distance of any string to an arbitrary set of two codewords. Codes satisfying $r = \lfloor d/2 \rfloor$ do exist but are quite pathologic (e.g., the code $\{0^t, 1^t\}$). The typical case is of $r \approx d$ (see, e.g., Hadamard codes and the guideline to Exercise 13.1).

[7] This observation was suggested to us by Zeev Dvir. Recall that the case of $\epsilon \geq r/n$, which implies $\epsilon \geq d/2n$, is always trivial.

[8] Note that a local testable code $C = \{C_k\}_{k \in K}$ does not yield a local testable code for lengths in $K - 1$ (e.g., the code $C'_{k-1}(x) = C_k(0x)$ does not necessarily have a local codeword tester).

Definition 13.3 (Locally testable codes (LTCs)): *Let n, d, and C be as in Definition 13.2 and suppose that $d = \Omega(n)$. We say that C is* locally testable *if for every constant $\epsilon > 0$ there exist a constant q and a probabilistic polynomial-time oracle machine M such that M is a q-local ϵ-tester for C.*

We will be concerned with the growth rate of n as a function of k, for locally testable codes $C = \{C_k : \{0, 1\}^k \to \{0, 1\}^{n(k)}\}_{k \in K}$ of distance $d = \Omega(n)$. In other words, our main focus is on the case in which $\epsilon > 0$ and q are fixed constants; that is, we consider the mapping $k \mapsto n(k)$ that supports q-local ϵ-tesability for every $\epsilon > 0$, when $q = q(\epsilon)$ and $k \in K$ is sufficiently large.[9]

13.2.2. Proof Testers

We start by recalling the standard definition of PCP.[10] Here, the verifier is explicitly given a main input, denoted x, and is provided with oracle access to an alleged proof, denoted π; that is, the verifier can read x for free, but its access to π is via queries and the number of queries made by the verifier is the most important complexity measure. Another key complexity measure is the length of the alleged proof (as a function of $|x|$).

Definition 13.4 (PCP, standard definition): *A* probabilistically checkable proof (PCP) *system for a set S is a* (nonadaptive) *probabilistic polynomial-time oracle machine* (called a verifier), *denoted V, satisfying*

Completeness: *For every $x \in S$, there exists a string π_x such that, on input x and oracle access to π_x, machine V always accepts x; that is, $\mathbf{Pr}[V^{\pi_x}(x) = 1] = 1$.*

Soundness: *For every $x \notin S$ and every string π, on input x and oracle access to π, machine V rejects x with probability at least $\frac{1}{2}$; that is, $\mathbf{Pr}[V^{\pi}(x) = 1] \leq 1/2$,*

Let $Q_x(\omega)$ denote the set of oracle positions inspected by V on input x and random-tape $\omega \in \{0, 1\}^*$. The query complexity *of V is defined as $q(n) \stackrel{\text{def}}{=} \max_{x \in \{0,1\}^n, \omega \in \{0,1\}^*} \{|Q_x(\omega)|\}$. The* proof complexity *of V is defined as $p(n) \stackrel{\text{def}}{=} \max_{x \in \{0,1\}^n} \{|\bigcup_{\omega \in \{0,1\}^*} Q_x(\omega)|\}$.*

Note that the proof complexity (i.e. p) of V is upper-bounded by $2^r \cdot q$, where r and q are the *randomness complexity* and the query complexity of the verifier, respectively. On the other hand, all known PCP constructions have randomness complexity that is at most logarithmic in their proof complexity (and in some sense this upper bound always holds [37, Prop. 11.2]). Thus, the proof complexity of a PCP is typically captured by its randomness complexity, and the latter is prefered since using it is more convenient when composing proof systems (cf. Section 13.3.2.2).

Recall that the proof complexity of V is defined as the number of bits in the proof that are inspected by V; that is, it is the "effective length" of the proof. Typically, this effective length equals the actual length; that is, all known PCP constructions can be easily

---

[9] **Advanced comment:** More generally, for $d = \Omega(n)$, one may consider the trade-off between n, the proximity parameter ϵ, and the query complexity q; that is, $n = n(k)$ may depend on ϵ and q.

[10] For a more paced introduction to the subject as well as a wider perspective, see [131, Chap. 9].

modified such that the oracle locations accessed by V constitute a prefix of the oracle (i.e., $\bigcup_{\omega \in \{0,1\}^*} Q_x(\omega) = \{1, \ldots, p(|x|)\}$ holds, for every x). (For simplicity, the reader may assume that this is the case throughout the rest of this exposition.) More importantly, all known PCP constructions can be easily modified to satisfy the following definition, which is closer in spirit to the definition of locally testable codes.

Definition 13.5 (PCP, augmented): *For functions $q : \mathbb{N} \to \mathbb{N}$ and $\epsilon : \mathbb{N} \to (0, 1)$, we say that a PCP system V for a set S is a q-locally ϵ-testable proof system if it has query complexity q and satisfies the following condition, which augments the standard soundness condition.*[11]

Rejecting invalid proofs: For every $x \in \{0, 1\}^*$ and every string π that is ϵ-far from $\Pi_x \overset{\text{def}}{=} \{w : \mathbf{Pr}[V^w(x) = 1] = 1\}$, on input x and oracle access to π, machine V rejects x with probability at least $\frac{1}{2}$, where $\Pi_x \neq \emptyset$ if and only if $x \in S$.

The proof complexity of V is defined as in Definition 13.4.

At this point it is natural to refer to the verifier V as a *proof tester*. Note that Definition 13.5 uses the tester V itself in order to define the set (denoted Π_x) of valid proofs (for $x \in S$). That is, V is used both to define the set of valid proofs and to test for the proximity of a given oracle to this set. A more general definition (presented next) refers to an arbitrary proof system, and lets Π_x equal the set of valid proofs (in that system) for $x \in S$. Obviously, it must hold that $\Pi_x \neq \emptyset$ if and only if $x \in S$. (The reader is encouraged to think of Π_x as of a set of (redundant) proofs for an NP-proof system, although this is only the most appealing case.) Typically, one also requires the existence of a polynomial-time procedure that, on input a pair (x, π), determines whether or not $\pi \in \Pi_x$.[12] For simplicity we assume that, for some function $p : \mathbb{N} \to \mathbb{N}$ and every $x \in \{0, 1\}^*$, it holds that $\Pi_x \subseteq \{0, 1\}^{p(|x|)}$. The resulting definition follows.

Definition 13.6 (Locally testable proofs): *Suppose that, for some function $p : \mathbb{N} \to \mathbb{N}$ and every $x \in \{0, 1\}^*$, it holds that $\Pi_x \subseteq \{0, 1\}^{p(|x|)}$. For functions $q : \mathbb{N} \to \mathbb{N}$ and $\epsilon : \mathbb{N} \to (0, 1)$, we say that a (nonadaptive) probabilistic polynomial-time oracle machine V is a q-locally ϵ-tester for proofs in $\Pi = \{\Pi_x\}_{x \in \{0,1\}^*}$ if V has query complexity q and satisfies the following conditions:*

Accepting valid proofs:[13] *For every $x \in \{0, 1\}^*$ and every $\pi \in \Pi_x$, on input x and oracle access to π, machine V accepts x with probability 1.*

---

[11] Definition 13.5 relies on two natural conventions:

1. All strings in Π_x are of the same length, which equals $|\bigcup_{\omega \in \{0,1\}^*} Q_x(\omega)|$, where $Q_x(\omega)$ is as in Definition 13.4. Furthermore, we consider only π's of this length.

2. If $\Pi_x = \emptyset$ (which happens if and only if $x \notin S$), then every π is considered ϵ-far from Π_x.

These conventions will also be used in Definition 13.6.

[12] Recall that in the case that the verifier V uses a logarithmic number of coin tosses, its proof complexity is of polynomial length (and so the "effective length" of the strings in Π_x must be polynomial in $|x|$). Furthermore, if in addition it holds that $\Pi_x = \{w : \mathbf{Pr}[V^w(x) = 1] = 1\}$, then (scanning all possible coin tosses of) V yields a polynomial-time procedure for determining whether a given pair (x, π) satisfies $\pi \in \Pi_x$.

[13] Note that the definition does not mention the set of inputs having valid proofs (i.e., the set $\{x : \Pi_x \neq \emptyset\}$).

Rejecting invalid proofs:[14] *For every $x \in \{0, 1\}^*$ and every $\pi \in \{0, 1\}^{p(|x|)}$ that is $\epsilon(|x|)$-far from Π_x, on input x and oracle access to π, machine V rejects x with probability at least $\frac{1}{2}$.*

The proof complexity *of V is defined as p, and ϵ is called the* proximity parameter. *In such a case, we say that $\Pi = \{\Pi_x\}_{x \in \{0,1\}^*}$ is q-locally ϵ-testable, and that $S = \{x \in \{0, 1\}^* : \Pi_x \neq \emptyset\}$ has q-locally ϵ-testable proofs of length p.*

We say that Π is locally testable *if for every constant $\epsilon > 0$ there exists a constant q such that Π is q-locally ϵ-testable. In such a case, we say that S has* locally testable proofs of length p.

This notion of locally testable proofs is closely related to the notion of probabilistically checkable proofs (i.e., PCPs). The difference is that in the definition of locally testable proofs (i.e., Definition 13.6) we required rejection of strings that are far from any valid proof also in the case that valid proofs exists (i.e., $\Pi_x \neq \emptyset$, which means that x is a valid assertion). In contrast, the standard rejection criterion of PCPs (see Definition 13.4) refers only to false assertions (i.e., x's such that $\Pi_x = \emptyset$). Still, all known PCP constructions actually satisfy the stronger definition.[15]

Needless to say, the term "locally testable proof" was introduced to match the term "locally testable codes." In retrospect, "locally testable proofs" seems a more fitting term than "probabilistically checkable proofs," because it stresses the positive aspect (of locality) rather than the negative aspect (of being probabilistic). The latter perspective has been frequently advocated by Leonid Levin.

13.2.3. Ramifications and Relation to Property Testing

We first comment about a few definitional choices made in the preceding text. First, we chose to focus on one-sided error testers; that is, we only consider testers that always accept valid objects (i.e., accept valid codewords (resp., valid proofs) with probability 1). In the current context, this is more appealing than allowing two-sided error probability, but the latter weaker notion is meaningful too. A second choice, which is a standard one, was to fix the error probability (i.e., the probability of accepting objects that are far from valid), rather than introducing yet another parameter. Needless to say, the error probability can be reduced by sequential invocations of the tester.

In the rest of this section, we consider an array of definitional issues. First, we consider two natural strengthenings of the definition of local testability (cf. Section 13.2.3.1). Next, we discuss the relation of local testability to property testing (cf. Section 13.2.3.2) and to PCPs of Proximity (cf. Section 13.2.3.3), while reviewing the latter notion. In Section 13.2.3.4, we discuss the motivation for the study of *short* local testable codes and proofs. Finally (in Section 13.2.3.5), we mention a relaxed (nonmonotone) definition, which seems natural only in the context of codes.

---

[14] Recall that if $\Pi_x = \emptyset$, then all strings are far from it. Also, since the length of the valid proofs for x is predetermined to be $p(|x|)$, there is no point to consider alleged proofs of different lengths. Finally, note that the current definition of the proof complexity of V is lower-bounded by the definition used in Definition 13.4.

[15] **Advanced comment:** In some cases this holds only under a weighted version of the Hamming distance, rather than under the standard Hamming distance. Alternatively, these constructions can be easily modified to work under the standard Hamming distance.

13.2.3.1. Stronger Definitions

The definitions of testers presented so far, allow for the construction of a different tester for each relevant value of the proximity parameter. However, whenever such testers are actually constructed, they tend to be "uniform" over all relevant values of the proximity parameter ϵ. Thus, it is natural to present a single tester for all relevant values of the proximity parameter, provide this tester with the said parameter, allow it to behave accordingly, and measure its query complexity as a function of that parameter. For example, we may strengthen Definition 13.3, by requiring the existence of a function $q : (0, 1) \to \mathbb{N}$ and an oracle machine M such that, for every constant $\epsilon > 0$, all (sufficiently large) k and all $w \in \{0, 1\}^{n(k)}$, the following conditions hold:

1. On input $(1^k, \epsilon)$, machine M makes $q(\epsilon)$ queries.
2. If w is a codeword of $\mathcal{C}$, then $\mathbf{Pr}[M^w(1^k, \epsilon) = 1] = 1$.
3. If w is ϵ-far from $\{\mathcal{C}(x) : x \in \{0, 1\}^k\}$, then $\mathbf{Pr}[M^w(1^k, \epsilon) = 1] \leq 1/2$.

An analogous strengthening applies to Definition 13.6. A special case of interest is when $q(\epsilon) = O(1/\epsilon)$. In this case, it makes sense to ask whether or not an even stronger "uniformity" condition may hold. Like in Definitions 13.1 and 13.2 (resp., Definitions 13.5 and 13.6), the tester M will not be given the proximity parameter (and so its query complexity cannot depend on it), but we shall require it to reject only with probability that is proportional to the distance of the oracle from the relevant set. For example, we may strengthen Definition 13.3, by requiring the existence of an oracle machine M and a *constant* q such that for every (sufficiently large) k and $w \in \{0, 1\}^{n(k)}$, the following conditions hold:

1. On input 1^k, machine M makes q queries.
2. If w is a codeword of $\mathcal{C}$, then $\mathbf{Pr}[M^w(1^k) = 1] = 1$.
3. If w is δ-far from $\{\mathcal{C}(x) : x \in \{0, 1\}^k\}$, then $\mathbf{Pr}[M^w(1^k) = 1] < 1 - \Omega(\delta)$.

More generally, we may require the existence of a monotonically nondecreasing function ϱ such that inputs that are δ-far from the code are rejected with probability at least $\varrho(\delta)$ (rather than with probability at least $\Omega(\delta)$).

13.2.3.2. Relation to Property Testing

Locally testable codes (and their corresponding testers) are essentially special cases of property testing algorithms (i.e., property testers), as studied throughout this book. Specifically, the property being tested is membership in a predetermined code. The only difference between the definitions presented in Section 13.2.1 and the formulation that is standard in the property testing literature is that in the latter the tester is given the proximity parameter as input and determines its behavior (and in particular the number of queries) accordingly. This difference is eliminated in the first strengthening outlined in Section 13.2.3.1, while the second strengthening outlined in Section 13.2.3.1 is related to the notion of proximity-oblivious testing (cf. [152]). Specifically, using the language of property testing (cf., Definitions 1.6 and 1.7), we have

Definition 13.7 (Locally testable codes, property testing formulations): *Let n, d, and $\mathcal{C} = \{\mathcal{C}_k : \{0, 1\}^k \to \{0, 1\}^{n(k)}\}_{k \in K}$ be as in Definition 13.2, and suppose that $d = \Omega(n)$.*

1. Weak version:[16] *For $q : (0, 1] \to \mathbb{N}$, we say that C is* uniformly q-locally testable *if there exists a nonadaptive tester of query complexity q and one-sided error for the property C.* (We stress that, here, the query complexity q depends only on the proximity parameter ϵ.)

2. Strong version:[17] *For a a monotonically nondecreasing function $\varrho : (0, 1] \to (0, 1]$, we say that C is* locally testable in a ϱ-strong sense *if there exists a* (nonadaptive) *proximity-oblivious tester of constant query complexity, detection probability ϱ, and one-sided error for the property C.*

Although locally testable codes emerge as a special case of property testing, we stress that most of the property testing literature is concerned with "natural" objects (e.g., graphs, sets of points, functions) presented in a "natural" form rather than with objects designed artificially to withstand noise (i.e., codewords of error-correcting codes).

Our general formulation of proof testing (i.e., Definition 13.6) can also be viewed within the framework of property testing. Specifically, we view the set Π_x as a set of objects having a certain x-dependent property (rather than as a set of valid proofs for some property of x). In other words, Definition 13.6 allows to consider properties that are parameterized by auxiliary information (i.e., x), which falls into the framework of testing massively parameterized properties (cf. [216] or Section 12.7.2). Note that $\Pi_x \subseteq \{0, 1\}^{p(|x|)}$, where p is typically a polynomial (which means that the length of the tested object is polynomial in the length of the parameter). In contrast, most property testing research refers to the case that the length of the tested object is exponential in the length of the parameter (i.e., $\Pi_n \subseteq \{0, 1\}^n = \{0, 1\}^{\exp(|n|)}$).[18] Hence, using the language of property testing, we can reformulate Definition 13.6, as follows.

Definition 13.8 (Locally testable proofs as property testers):[19] *Suppose that, for some function $p : \mathbb{N} \to \mathbb{N}$ and every $x \in \{0, 1\}^*$, it holds that $\Pi_x \subseteq \{0, 1\}^{p(|x|)}$, and let $q : \{0, 1\}^* \times (0, 1] \to \mathbb{N}$. We say that a* (nonadaptive) *probabilistic polynomial-time oracle machine V is a q-locally tester for proofs in $\{\Pi_x\}_{x \in \{0,1\}^*}$ if V has query complexity q and constitutes a tester for the parameterized property $\{\Pi_x\}_{x \in \{0,1\}^*}$, where such a tester gets x and ϵ as input parameters and ϵ-tests membership in Π_x using $q(x, \epsilon)$ queries.*

A special case of interest is when $q(x, \epsilon) = q'(\epsilon)$ for some function $q' : (0, 1] \to \mathbb{N}$.

---

[16] Indeed, this version corresponds to the first strengthening outlined in Section 13.2.3.1. Recall that the formulation in Section 13.2.3.1 required testability only for any constant $\epsilon > 0$ and sufficiently large k (which is formulated by saying that "for every $\epsilon > 0$, there exists k_ϵ such that for all $k \geq k_\epsilon$ ..."). Nevertheless, as shown in Exercise 13.2, this implies the current version. We warn, however, that the effectiveness of the derived query complexity bound depends on the rate in which k_ϵ grows as an (inverse) function of ϵ. Likewise the computational complexity of the derived tester depends on the complexity of the mapping $\epsilon \mapsto k_\epsilon$.

[17] Indeed, this version corresponds to the second strengthening outlined in Section 13.2.3.1. Recall that the restricted version of this definition referred to the case that ϱ is linear (i.e., $\varrho(\delta) = \Omega(\delta)$). When ϱ is not specified one often means that it is linear.

[18] Indeed, in the context of property testing, the length of the oracle must always be given to the tester (although some sources neglect to account for this fact).

[19] Here, we allow the query complexity to depends (also) on the parameter x, rather than merely on its length (which also determines the length $p(|x|)$ of the tested object). This seems more natural in the context of testing massively parameterized properties.

13.2.3.3. Relation to PCPs of Proximity

We start by reviewing the definition of a PCP of Proximity, which may be viewed as a "PCP version" of a property tester (or a "property testing analogue" of PCP).[20] In the following definition, the tester (or verifier) is given oracle access both to its main input, denoted x, and to an alleged proof, denoted π, and the query complexity accounts for its access to both oracles (which can be viewed as a single oracle, (x, π)). That is, in contrast to the definition of PCP and like in the definition of property testing, the main input is presented as an oracle and the verifier is charged for accessing it. In addition, like in the definition of PCP (and unlike in the definition of property testing), the verifier gets oracle access to an alleged proof.

> **Definition 13.9** (PCPs of Proximity):[21] *A* PCP of Proximity *for a set S with proximity parameter ϵ and* proof complexity $p : \mathbb{N} \to \mathbb{N}$ *is a* (nonadaptive) *probabilistic polynomial-time oracle machine, denoted V, satisfying*
>
> Completeness: *For every $x \in S$ there exists a string $\pi_x \in \{0, 1\}^{p(|x|)}$ such that V always accepts when given access to the oracle (x, π_x); that is, $\mathbf{Pr}[V^{x,\pi_x}(1^{|x|}) = 1] = 1$.*
>
> Soundness: *For every x that is ϵ-far from $S \cap \{0, 1\}^{|x|}$ and for every string π, machine V rejects with probability at least $\frac{1}{2}$ when given access to the oracle (x, π); that is, $\mathbf{Pr}[M^{x,\pi}(1^{|x|}) = 1] \leq 1/2$.*
>
> *The* query complexity *of V is defined as in case of PCP, but here also queries to the x-part are counted.*

The definition of a property tester (i.e., an ϵ-tester for S) is obtained as a special case by requiring that the proof complexity (or length) equals zero. As shown in Exercise 13.3, for any (efficiently computable) code C of constant relative distance, a PCP for a set S can be obtained from a PCP of Proximity for $\{C(x) : x \in S\}$, where the complexity of the PCP is related to the complexity of the PCP of Proximity via the rate of the code (since the complexities of these proof testers are measured in terms of the length of their main input).

Relation to Locally Testable Proofs (a Bit Contrived). The definition of a PCP of Proximity is related to but different from the definition of a locally testable proof: Definition 13.9 refers to the distance of the input-oracle x from S, whereas locally testable proofs (see Definition 13.6) refer to the distance of the proof-oracle from the set Π_x of valid proofs of membership of $x \in S$. Still, PCPs of Proximity can be viewed within the framework of locally testable proofs, by considering an artificial set of proofs for membership in a generic set. Specifically, given a PCP of Proximity verifier V of proof complexity p and proximity parameter ϵ for a set S (such that $S \cap \{0, 1\}^n \neq \emptyset$ for all sufficiently

---

[20] An "NP version" (or rather an "MA version") of a property tester was presented by Gur and Rothblum [166] (and is discussed in Section 12.6). In their model, called MAP, the verifier has oracle access to the main input x, but gets free access to an alleged proof π.

[21] Note that this definition builds on Definition 13.4 (rather than on Definition 13.6), except that the proof complexity is defined as in Definition 13.6. (We mention that PCPs of Proximity, introduced by Ben-Sasson *et al.* [44], are almost identical to Assignment Testers, introduced independently by Dinur and Reingold [94]. Both notions are (important) special cases of the general definition of a "PCP spot-checker" formulated before by Ergün *et al.* [102].)

large n), we consider the set of proofs (for membership of 1^n in the generic set $\{1\}^*$)

$$\Pi'_{1^n} \stackrel{\text{def}}{=} \left\{ x^t \pi : x \in (S \cap \{0, 1\}^n), \pi \in \Pi_x, t = \frac{p(n)}{\epsilon n} \right\} \tag{13.1}$$

$$\text{where } \Pi_x \stackrel{\text{def}}{=} \{\pi \in \{0, 1\}^{p(|x|)} : \mathbf{Pr}[V^{x,\pi}(1^n) = 1]\} \tag{13.2}$$

so that $|\pi| = \epsilon \cdot |x^t|$. A 3ϵ-tester for proofs in $\Pi' = \{\Pi'_{1^n}\}_{n \in \mathbb{N}}$ can be obtained by emulating the execution of V and checking that the t copies in the tn-bit long prefix of the oracle are indeed identical.[22] On the other hand, any ϵ-tester for proofs in Π' yields a PCP of Proximity verifier of proof complexity p and proximity parameter $\epsilon + \epsilon^2$ for a set S, since if x is $(\epsilon + \epsilon^2)$-far from S then $x^t \pi$ is ϵ-far from Π' for every $\pi \in \{0, 1\}^{p(|x|)}$.

Digest: The Use of Repetitions. The problem we faced in the construction of Π' is that the proof-part (i.e., π) is essential for verification, but we wish the distance to be dominated by the input-part (i.e., x). The solution was to repeat x multiple times so that these repetitions dominate the length of the oracle. The new tester can still access the alleged proof π, but we are guaranteed that if $x^t \pi$ is 3ϵ-far from Π', then x is 2ϵ-far from S. The repetition test is used in order to handle the possibility that the oracle does not have the form $x^t \pi$ but is rather ϵ-far from any string having this form.

PCPs of Proximity Yield Locally Testable Codes. We mention that PCPs of Proximity (of constant query complexity) yield a simple way of obtaining locally testable codes. More generally, we can combine any code C_0 with any PCP of Proximity V, and obtain a q-locally testable code with distance essentially determined by C_0 and rate essentially determined by the proof complexity of V, where q is the query complexity of V. Specifically, x will be encoded by appending $c = C_0(x)$ with a proof that c is a codeword of C_0, and distances will be determined by the *weighted Hamming distance* that assigns all weight (uniformly) to the first part of the new code. As in the previous paragraph, these weights can be (approximately) "emulated" by making suitable repetitions. Specifically, the new codeword, denoted $C(x)$, equals $C_0(x)^t \pi(x)$, where $\pi(x) \in \{0, 1\}^{p(|x|)}$ is the foregoing proof and $t = \omega(|\pi(x)|)/|C_0(x)|$. We stress that $\pi(x)$ is a unique designated proof for $x \in S$. Turning to the codeword tester, on input $w \in \{0, 1\}^{t \cdot n + p(n)}$, it checks that the tn-bit long prefix of w consists of t repetitions of some n-bit long string, and invokes the PCP of Proximity, while providing it with access to the n-bit prefix of w (as main input) and to the $p(n)$-bit long suffix of w (as an alleged proof). As before, the analysis is based on the observation that a string that is $3/t$-far from a codeword (of C) must have a tn-bit long prefix that is far from being a repetition of a codeword of C_0. For details, see Exercise 13.4.

We stress that the foregoing construction only yields a weak locally testable code (as in Definition 13.3 or in the weak version of Definition 13.7), since nothing is guaranteed

---

[22] That is, on input $x^{(1)} \cdots x^{(t)} \pi$, the verifier invokes $V^{x^{(1)}, \pi}(1^n)$ as well as performs checks to verify that $x^{(1)} = x^{(i)}$ for every $i \in [t]$. The latter test is conducted by selecting uniformly several $i \in [t]$ and several $j \in [n]$ per each i, and comparing $x_j^{(1)}$ to $x_j^{(i)}$. The key observation is that if $x^{(1)} \cdots x^{(t)} \pi$ is 3ϵ-far from Π'_{1^n}, then either $x^{(1)} \cdots x^{(t)}$ is ϵ-far from $(x^{(1)})^t$ or $x^{(1)}$ is ϵ-far from $S = \{x : \Pi_x \neq \emptyset\}$, since $|\pi| < \epsilon \cdot |x^{(1)} \cdots x^{(t)} \pi|$. See related Exercise 13.4.

for non-codewords (of C) that consist of repetitions of some $C_0(x)$ and an undesignated (resp., false) proof (i.e., $\tilde{\pi} \neq \pi(x)$).[23] Obtaining a strong locally testable code using this method is possible when the PCP of Proximity is stronger in a sense that is analogous to Definition 13.6, but with a single valid proof (called *canonical*) per each $x \in S$ (i.e., $|\Pi_x| = 1$ for every $x \in S$). Such strong PCPs of Proximity were introduced in [157]; see also [141].

13.2.3.4. Motivation for the Study of Short Locally Testable Codes and Proofs

Local testability offers an extremely strong notion of efficient testing: The tester makes only a constant number of bit probes, and determining the probed locations (as well as the final decision) can often be done in time that is polylogarithmic in the length of the probed object. Recall that the tested object is supposed to be related to some primal object; in the case of codes, the probed object is supposed to encode the primal object, whereas in the case of proofs the probed object is supposed to help verify some property of the primal object. In both cases, the length of the secondary (probed) object is of natural concern, and this length is stated in terms of the length of the primary object.

The length of codewords in an error-correcting code is widely recognized as one of the two most fundamental parameters of the code (the second one being the code's distance). In particular, the length of the code is of major importance in applications, because it determines the overhead involved in encoding information.

As argued in Section 13.1, the same considerations apply also to proofs. Unfortunately, in the case of proofs, this obvious point has been blurred by the (unexpected and) highly influential applications of PCPs to establishing hardness results regarding the complexity of natural approximation problems. In our view, the significance of locally testable proofs (or PCPs) extends far beyond their applicability to deriving non-approximability results. The mere fact that proofs can be transformed into a format that supports superfast probabilistic verification is remarkable. From this perspective, the question of how much redundancy is introduced by such a transformation is a fundamental one. Furthermore, locally testable proofs (i.e., PCPs) have been used not only to derive non-approximability results but also for obtaining positive results (e.g., CS-proofs [190, 207] and their applications [31, 67]), and the length of the PCP affects the complexity of those applications.

Turning back to the celebrated application of PCP to the study of the complexity of natural approximation problems, we note that the length of PCPs is relevant also to these non-approximability results; specifically, the length of PCPs affects the *tightness with respect to the running time* of the non-approximability results derived from these PCPs. For example, suppose that (exact) SAT has complexity $2^{\Omega(n)}$. Then, while the original PCP Theorem [25, 24] only implies that approximating MaxSAT requires time $2^{n^{\alpha}}$, for some (small constant) $\alpha > 0$, the results of [48, 92] yield a lower bound of $2^{n/\text{poly}(\log n)}$. We mention that the result of [210] (cf. [93]) allows to achieve a time lower bound of $2^{n^{1-o(1)}}$ simultaneously with optimal non-approximability ratios, but this is currently unknown for the better lower bound of $2^{n/\text{poly}(\log n)}$. (A lower bound of $2^{\Omega(n)}$ is also unknown for any constant approximation ratio (see Problem 13.12).)

---

[23] Note that a standard PCP of Proximity is not required to reject (with positive probability) proof-oracles that are different from the designated proof oracle for $x \in S$ (i.e., $\tilde{\pi} \neq \pi(x)$), let alone that it is not required to do so with probability that is related to the distance of these proof-oracles from the designated proof oracle.

13.2.3.5. A Relaxed (Nonmonotone) Definition

One of the concrete motivations for locally testable codes refers to settings in which one may want to re-encode the information when discovering that the codeword is corrupted. In such a case, assuming that re-encoding is based solely on the corrupted codeword, one may assume (or rather needs to assume) that the corrupted codeword is not too far from the code. Thus, the following version of Definition 13.1 may suffice for various applications.

Definition 13.10 (Relaxed nonmonotone codeword tests): *Let $C : \{0, 1\}^k \to \{0, 1\}^n$ be a code of distance d, and let $q \in \mathbb{N}$ and $\epsilon_1, \epsilon_2 \in (0, 1)$ be such that $\epsilon_1 < \epsilon_2$. A q-local (codeword) (ϵ_1, ϵ_2)-tester for C is a (nonadaptive) probabilistic oracle machine M that makes at most q queries, accepts any codeword with probability 1, and rejects (w.h.p.) non-codewords that are both ϵ_1-far and ϵ_2-close to C. That is, the rejection condition of Definition 13.1 is modified as follows.*

Rejection of non-codeword (relaxed nonmonotone version): *For any $w \in \{0, 1\}^n$ such that $\Delta_C(w) \in [\epsilon_1 n, \epsilon_2 n]$, given oracle access to w, machine M rejects with probability at least $1/2$.*

Needless to say, there is something highly nonintuitive in this definition: It requires rejection of non-codewords that are somewhat far from the code, but not the rejection of codewords that are very far from the code. In other words, the rejection probability of this tester may be nonmonotone in the distance of the tested string from the code. Still, such nonmonotone codeword testers may suffice in some applications. Interestingly, nonmonotone codeword testers seem easier to construct than standard locally testable codes; they even achieve linear length (cf. [255, Chap. 5]), whereas this is not known for the standard notion (see Problem 13.12). We mention that the nonmonotonicity of the rejection probability of testers has been observed before; the most famous example being linearity testing (see Section 13.3.1.1).

13.2.4. On Relating Locally Testable Codes and Proofs

This section offers an advanced discussion, which is intended mainly for PCP enthusiasts. We discuss the common beliefs that locally testable codes and proofs are closely related, and point out that the relation is less clear than one may think.

Locally testable codes can be thought of as the combinatorial counterparts of the complexity theoretic notion of locally testable proofs (PCPs). In particular, as detailed below, the use of codes with features related to local testability is implicit in known PCP constructions. This perspective raises the question of whether one of these notions implies the other, or at least is useful toward the understanding of the other.

13.2.4.1. Do PCPs Imply Locally Testable Codes?

As started previously, the use of codes with features related to local testability is implicit in known PCP constructions. Furthermore, each of the the known constructions of PCPs (and locally testable proofs) provides a transformation of *standard proofs* (for say SAT) to *locally testable proofs* (i.e., PCP-oracles) such that transformed strings are accepted with probability one by the PCP verifier. Specifically, denoting by S_x the set of standard proofs (i.e., NP-witnesses) that establish the validity of an assertion x, there exists a polynomial-time mapping f_x of S_x to $R_x \stackrel{\text{def}}{=} \{f_x(y) : y \in S_x\}$ such that for every $\pi \in R_x$ it holds that $\mathbf{Pr}[V^\pi(x) = 1] = 1$, where V is the PCP verifier. Moreover, starting from different standard proofs, one obtains locally testable proofs that are far apart, and hence constitute a good code (i.e., for every x and every $y \neq y' \in S_x$, it holds that $\Delta(f_x(y), f_x(y')) \geq \Omega(|f_x(y)|)$). It is tempting to think that the corresponding PCP verifier yields a codeword tester, but this is not really the case.

For starters, we stress that Definition 13.4 refers only to the case of false assertions, in which case all strings are far from any valid proof (since the latter does not exist). Indeed, this deficiency is addressed by Definition 13.5 that requires rejection of strings that are far from any valid proof (i.e., any string far from Π_x), and the known PCP constructions do satisfy this augmented requirement. However, Definition 13.5 does not mandate that the only valid proofs (w.r.t. V) are those in R_x (i.e., the proofs obtained by the transformation f_x of standard proofs (in S_x) to locally testable ones). In fact, the standard PCP constructions accept also valid proofs that are not in the range of the corresponding transformation (i.e., f_x); that is, Π_x as in Definition 13.5 is a strict superset of R_x (rather than satisfying $\Pi_x = R_x$). Nevertheless, many known PCP constructions can be modified to satisfy $\Pi_x = R_x$, and so to yield a locally testable code, but these modifications are far from being trivial. The interested reader is referred to [157, Sec. 5.2] for a discussion of typical problems that arise when trying this way. In any case, this is not necessarily the best way to obtain locally testable codes from PCPs; an alternative way is outlined in Section 13.2.3.3.

13.2.4.2. Do Locally Testable Codes Imply PCPs?

Saying that locally testable codes are the combinatorial counterparts of locally testable proofs (PCPs) raises the expectation (or hope) that it would be easier to construct locally testable codes than to construct PCPs. The reason is that combinatorial objects (e.g., codes) should be easier to understand than complexity theoretic ones (e.g., PCPs). Indeed, this feeling was among the main motivations of Goldreich and Sudan, and their first result (cf. [157, Sec. 3]) was along this vein: They showed a relatively simple construction (i.e., simple in comparison to PCP constructions) of a locally testable code of length $\ell(k) = k^c$ for any constant $c > 1$. Unfortunately, their stronger result, providing a locally testable code of even shorter length (i.e., length $\ell(k) = k^{1+o(1)}$) is obtained by constructing (cf. [157, Sec. 4]) and using (cf. [157, Sec. 5]) a corresponding locally testable proof (i.e., PCP).

Most subsequent works (e.g., [44, 92]) have followed this route (i.e., of going from a PCP to a code), but there are notable exceptions. Most importantly, we mention that Meir's work [204] provides a combinatorial construction of a locally testable code that does not seem to yield a corresponding locally testable proof. The prior work of Ben-Sasson and Sudan [48] may be viewed as reversing the course to the "right one": They first construct locally testable codes, and next use them towards the construction of proofs, but their set of valid codewords is an NP-complete set. Still, conceptually they go from codes to proofs (rather than the other way around).

13.3. Results and Ideas

We review some of the known constructions of locally testable codes and proofs, starting from codes and proofs of exponential length and concluding with codes and proofs of nearly linear length. In all cases, we refer to testers of constant query complexity.[24] Before embarking on this journey, we mention that random linear codes (of linear length) require any codeword tester to read a linear number of bits of the codeword (see Exercises 1.12–1.14). Furthermore, good codes that correspond to random "low-density parity check" matrices are also as hard to test [47]. These facts provide a strong indication to the nontriviality of local testability.

Teaching Note: Recall that this section only provides overviews of the constructions and their analysis. The intention is merely to offer a taste of the ideas used. The interested reader should look for detailed descriptions in other sources, which are indicated in the text.

13.3.1. The Mere Existence of Locally Testable Codes and Proofs

The mere existence of locally testable codes and proofs, regardless of their length, is nonobvious. Thus, we start by reviewing the simplest constructions known.

13.3.1.1. The Hadamard Code Is Locally Testable

The simplest example of a locally testable code (of constant relative distance) is the Hadamard code. This code, denoted C_{Had}, maps $x \in \{0, 1\}^k$ to a string (of length $n = 2^k$) that provides the evaluation of all GF(2)-linear functions at x; that is, the coordinates of the codeword are associated with linear functions of the form $\ell(z) = \sum_{i=1}^{k} \ell_i z_i$ and so $C_{Had}(x)_\ell = \ell(x) = \sum_{i=1}^{k} \ell_i x_i$. Testing whether a string $w \in \{0, 1\}^{2^k}$ is a codeword amounts to linearity testing. This is the case because w is a codeword of C_{Had} if and only if, when viewed as a function $w : GF(2)^k \to GF(2)$, it is linear (i.e., $w(z) = \sum_{i=1}^{k} c_i z_i$ for some c_i's, or equivalently $w(y + z) = w(y) + w(z)$ for all y, z). Hence, local testability of C_{Had} is achieved by invoking the linearity tester of Blum, Luby, and Rubinfeld [59], which amounts to uniformly selecting $y, z \in GF(2)^k$ and checking whether $w(y + z) = w(y) + w(z)$.

This natural tester always accepts linear functions, and (as shown in Chapter 2) it rejects any function that is δ-far from being linear with probability at least $\min(\delta/2, 1/6)$. Surprisingly, the exact behavior of this tester is unknown; that is, denoting by $\varrho(\delta)$ the minimum rejection probability of a string that is at (relative) distance δ from C_{Had}, we know lower and upper bounds on ϱ that are tight only in the interval $[0, 5/16]$ (and at the point 0.5). Specifically, it is known that $\varrho(\delta) \geq \Gamma(\delta)$, where the function $\Gamma : [0, 0.5] \to [0, 1]$ is defined as follows:

$$\Gamma(x) \overset{\text{def}}{=} \begin{cases} 3x - 6x^2 & 0 \leq x \leq 5/16 \\ 45/128 & 5/16 \leq x \leq \tau_2 \quad \text{where } \tau_2 \approx 44.9962/128 \\ x + \eta(x) & \tau_2 \leq x \leq 1/2, \quad \text{where } \eta(x) \overset{\text{def}}{=} 1376 \cdot x^3 \cdot (1 - 2x)^{12} \geq 0. \end{cases} \quad (13.3)$$

The lower bound Γ is composed of three different bounds with "phase transitions" at $x = \frac{5}{16}$ and at $x = \tau_2$, where $\tau_2 \approx \frac{44.9962}{128}$ is the solution to $x + \eta(x) = 45/128$ (see

---

[24] The opposite regime, in which the focus is on linear length codes and the aim is to minimize the query complexity, is briefly reviewed in Section 13.4.3.

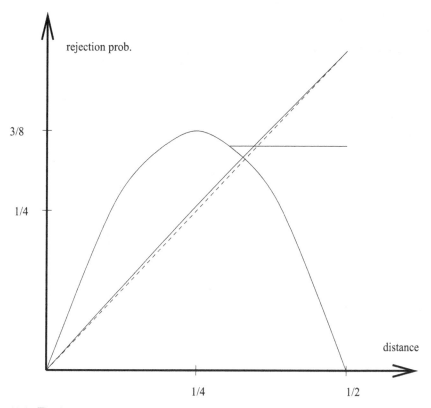

Figure 13.1: The lower bounds that underlie the function Γ. The dashed diagonal line represents the bound $\varrho(x) \geq x$, which is slightly improved by the bound $\varrho(x) \geq x + \eta(x)$.

Figure 13.1).[25] It was shown in [36] that the first segment of Γ (i.e., for $x \in [0, 5/16]$) is the best bound possible, and that the first "phase transitions" (i.e., at $x = \frac{5}{16}$) is indeed a reality; in other words, $\varrho = \Gamma$ in the interval $[0, 5/16]$.[26] We highlight the nontrivial behavior of the detection probability of the aforementioned test, and specifically the fact that the detection probability does not increase monotonically with the distance of the tested string from the code (i.e., Γ decreases in the interval $[1/4, 5/16]$, while being equal to ϱ in this interval).

Other codes. We mention that Reed–Muller Codes of constant order are also locally testable [11]. These codes have subexponential length, but are quite popular in practice. The Long Code is also locally testable [37], but this code has double-exponential length (and was introduced merely for the design of PCPs).[27]

---

[25] The third segment is due to [181], which improves over the prior bound of [36] that asserted $\varrho(x) \geq \max(45/128, x)$ for every $x \in [5/16, 1/2]$.

[26] In contrast, the lower bound provided by the other two segments (i.e., for $x \in [5/16, 1/2]$) is unlikely to be tight, and in particular it is unlikely that the "phase transition" at $x = \tau_2$ represents the behavior of ϱ itself. We also note that $\eta(x) \geq 59 \cdot (1 - 2x)^{12} > 0$ for every $x \in [\tau_2, 0.5)$, but $\eta(x) < 0.0001$ for every $x \in [\tau_2, 0.5)$. Lastly, recall that $\varrho(0.5) = \Gamma(0.5) = 0.5$.

[27] We also mention that some of the best PCP results are obtained by using a *relaxed* notion of local testability [170, 171]. Loosely speaking, this relaxed notion requires that *if the tester accepts a strong w with some noticeable probability $\alpha > 0$, then this event may be attributed* (or charged) *to* poly$(1/\alpha)$ *codewords* (which are not necessarily close to w).

13.3.1.2. The Hadamard-Based PCP of ALMSS

The simplest example of a locally testable proof (for arbitrary sets in $\mathcal{NP}$)[28] is the "inner verifier" of the PCP construction of Arora, Lund, Motwani, Sudan and Szegedy [24], which in turn is based on the Hadamard code. Specifically, proofs of the satisfiability of a given system of quadratic equations over GF(2), which is an NP-complete problem (see Exercise 13.6), are presented by providing a Hadamard encoding of the outer product of a satisfying assignment with itself (i.e., a satisfying assignment $\alpha \in \{0, 1\}^n$ is presented by $C_{\text{Had}}(\beta)$, where $\beta = (\beta_{i,j})_{i,j \in [n]}$ and $\beta_{i,j} = \alpha_i \alpha_j$). Hence, the alleged proofs are of length 2^{n^2}, and locations in these proofs correspond to n^2-bit long strings (or, equivalently, to n-by-n Boolean matrices).

Given an alleged proof $\pi \in \{0, 1\}^{2^{n^2}}$, viewed as a Boolean function $\pi : \text{GF}(2)^{n^2} \to \text{GF}(2)$, the proof tester (or verifier) proceeds as follows:[29]

1. Tests that π is indeed a codeword of the Hadamard Code (i.e., that it is a linear function from $\text{GF}(2)^{n^2}$ to $\text{GF}(2)$). If this test passes (with high probability), then π is close to some codeword $C_{\text{Had}}(\beta)$, for an arbitrary $\beta = (\beta_{i,j})_{i,j \in [n]}$; that is, for (say) 99% of the Boolean matrices $C = (c_{i,j})_{i,j \in [n]}$, it holds that $\pi(C) = \sum_{i,j \in [n]} c_{i,j} \beta_{i,j}$.
2. Tests that the aforementioned β is indeed an outer product of some $\alpha \in \{0, 1\}^n$ with itself. This means that for every $C = (c_{i,j})_{i,j \in [n]}$ (or actually for 99% of them), it holds that $\pi(C) = \sum_{i,j \in [n]} c_{i,j} \alpha_i \alpha_j$. That is, we wish to test whether $(\beta_{i,j})_{i,j \in [n]}$ equals $(\alpha_i \alpha_j)_{i,j \in [n]}$ (i.e., the equality of two Boolean matrices).

Teaching Note: Some readers may prefer to skip the description of how the current step is implemented, proceed to Step 3, and return to the current step later.

Note that the Hadamard encoding of α is supposed to be part of the Hadamard encoding of β (because $\sum_{i=1}^{n} c_i \alpha_i = \sum_{i=1}^{n} c_i \alpha_i^2$ is supposed to equal $\sum_{i=1}^{n} c_i \beta_{i,i}$).[30] So we would like to test that the latter codeword matches the former one. (Recall that this means testing whether the matrix $(\beta_{i,j})_{i,j \in [n]}$ equals the matrix $(\alpha_i \alpha_j)_{i,j \in [n]}$.) This test can be performed by uniformly selecting $(r_1, \ldots, r_n), (s_1, \ldots, s_n) \in \text{GF}(2)^n$, and comparing $\sum_{i,j} r_i s_j \beta_{i,j}$ and $\sum_{i,j} r_i s_j \alpha_i \alpha_j = (\sum_i r_i \alpha_i) \cdot (\sum_j s_j \alpha_j)$, where the value $\sum_{i,j} r_i s_j \beta_{i,j}$ is supposed to reside in the location that corresponds to the outer-product of $(r_1, \ldots, r_n)$ and $(s_1, \ldots, s_n)$. The key observation here is that for n-by-n matrices $A \neq B$, when $r, s \in \{0, 1\}^n$ are uniformly selected (vectors), it holds that $\mathbf{Pr}_s[As = Bs] = 2^{-\text{rank}(A-B)}$ and it follows that $\mathbf{Pr}_{r,s}[rAs = rBs] \leq 3/4$ (see Exercise 13.7). The foregoing suggestion would have been fine if $\pi = C_{\text{Had}}(\beta)$, but we know only that π is close to $C_{\text{Had}}(\beta)$. The Hadamard encoding of α is a tiny part of the latter, and so we should not try to retrieve the latter directly (because this tiny part may be

---

[28] A simpler example for a set not known to be in $\mathcal{BPP}$ is provided by the interactive proof for graph non-isomorphism [146]. Note that any interactive proof system in which the prover sends a constant number of bits yields a PCP system (see Exercise 13.5).

[29] See [131, Sec. 9.3.2.1] for a more detailed description.

[30] Note that, for every $(c_1, \ldots, c_n) \in \{0, 1\}^n$, it holds that $\sum_{i \in [n]} c_i \beta_{i,i} = \sum_{i,j \in [n]} c_{i,j} \beta_{i,j}$, where $c_{i,j} = c_i$ if $i = j$ and $c_{i,j} = 0$ otherwise. Hence, the value of location $(c_1, \ldots, c_n)$ in $C_{\text{Had}}(\alpha)$ appears at location $(c_{i,j})_{i,j \in [n]}$ in $C_{\text{Had}}(\beta)$.

totally corrupted).[31] Instead, we use the paradigm of self-correction (cf. Section 5.2.3): In general, for any fixed $c = (c_{i,j})_{i,j\in[n]}$, whenever we wish to retrieve $\sum_{i,j\in[n]} c_{i,j}\beta_{i,j}$, we uniformly select $\omega = (\omega_{i,j})_{i,j\in[n]}$ and retrieve both $\pi(\omega)$ and $\pi(\omega+c)$. Thus, we obtain a self-corrected value of $\pi(c)$; that is, if π is δ-close to $C_{\text{Had}}(\beta)$ then $\pi(\omega + c) - \pi(\omega) = \sum_{i,j\in[n]} c_{i,j}\beta_{i,j}$ with probability at least $1 - 2\delta$ (over the choice of ω). Using self-correction, we indirectly obtain bits in $C_{\text{Had}}(\alpha)$, for $\alpha = (\alpha_i)_{i\in[n]} = (\beta_{i,i})_{i\in[n]}$. Similarly, we can obtain any other desired bit in $C_{\text{Had}}(\beta)$, which in turn allows us to test whether $(\beta_{i,j})_{i,j\in[n]} = (\alpha_i\alpha_j)_{i,j\in[n]}$. In fact, we are checking whether $(\beta_{i,j})_{i,j\in[n]} = (\beta_{i,i}\beta_{j,j})_{i,j\in[n]}$, by comparing $\sum_{i,j} r_i s_j \beta_{i,j}$ and $(\sum_i r_i \beta_{i,i}) \cdot (\sum_j s_j \beta_{j,j})$, for randomly selected $(r_1, \ldots, r_n), (s_1, \ldots, s_n) \in GF(2)^n$.

3. Finally, we get to the purpose of all of the foregoing, which is checking whether the aforementioned α satisfies the given system of quadratic equations. Towards this end, the tester uniformly selects a linear combination of the equations, and checks whether α satisfies the (single) resulting equation. Note that the value of the corresponding quadratic expression (which is a linear combination of quadratic (and linear) forms) appears as a bit of the Hadamard encoding of β, but again we retrieve it from π by using self-correction.

The foregoing description presumes that each step performs a constant number of checks such that if the corresponding condition fails then this step rejects with high (constant) probability.[32] In the analysis, one shows that if π is 0.01-far from a valid Hadamard codeword, then Step 1 rejects with high probability. Otherwise, if π is 0.01-close to $C_{\text{Had}}(\beta)$ for $\beta = (\beta_{i,j})_{i,j\in[n]}$ that is *not* an outer-product of some $\alpha = (\alpha_i)_{i\in[n]}$ with itself (i.e., $(\beta_{i,j})_{i,j\in[n]} \neq (\alpha_i\alpha_j)_{i,j\in[n]}$), then Step 2 rejects with high probability. Lastly, if π is 0.01-close to $C_{\text{Had}}(\beta)$ such that $\beta_{i,j} = \alpha_i\alpha_j$ for some α (and all $i, j \in [n]$) but α does not satisfy the given system of quadratic equations, then Step 3 rejects with high probability.

13.3.2. Locally Testable Codes and Proofs of Polynomial Length

The constructions presented in Section 13.3.1 have exponential length in terms of the relevant parameter (i.e., the amount of information being encoded in the code or the length of the assertion being proved). Achieving local testability by codes and proofs that have polynomial length turns out to be much more challenging.

13.3.2.1. Locally Testable Codes of Almost Quadratic Length

A rather natural interpretation of *low-degree tests* (cf. [29, 28, 124, 246, 120]) yields a locally testable code of almost quadratic length over a *sufficiently large alphabet*. Similar (and actually better) results for *binary* codes required additional ideas, and have appeared only later (cf. [157]). We sketch both constructions below, starting with locally testable codes over very large alphabets (which are defined analogously to the binary case).

---

[31] Likewise, the values at the locations that correspond the outer product of $(r_1, \ldots, r_n)$ and $(s_1, \ldots, s_n)$ should not be retrieved directly, because these locations are a tiny fraction of all 2^{n^2} locations in $C_{\text{Had}}(\beta)$.

[32] An alternative description may have each step repeat the corresponding check only once so that if the corresponding condition fails, then this step rejects with some (constant) positive probability. In this case, the analysis will only establish that the entire test rejects with some (constant) positive probability, and repetitions will be used to reduce the soundness error to $1/2$.

Locally Testable Codes over Large Alphabets. In Chapter 3 we presented low-degree tests for degree $d \ll |\mathcal{F}|$ and functions $f : \mathcal{F}^m \to \mathcal{F}$ as picking $d + 2$ points over a random line (in $\mathcal{F}^m$) and checking whether the values of f on these points fits a degree d univariate polynomial. We also commented that such a test can be viewed as a PCP of Proximity that test whether f is of degree d by utilizing a proof-oracle (called a *line oracle*) that provides the univariate degree d polynomials that describe the value of f on every line in $\mathcal{F}^m$.[33] (When queried on $(\bar{x}, \bar{h}) \in \mathcal{F}^m \times \mathcal{F}^m$, this proof-oracle returns the $d + 1$ coefficients of a polynomial that supposedly describes the value of f on the line $\{\bar{x} + i\bar{h} : i \in \mathcal{F}\}$, and the verifier checks that the value assigned by this polynomial to a random $i \in \mathcal{F}$ matches $f(\bar{x} + i\bar{h})$.)

Taking another step, we note that given access only to a "line oracle" $L : \mathcal{F}^m \times \mathcal{F}^m \to \mathcal{F}^{d+1}$, we can test whether L describes the restrictions of a single degree d multivariate polynomial to all lines. This is done by selecting a random pair of intersecting lines and checking whether they agree on the point of intersection. Friedl and Sudan [120] and Rubinfeld and Sudan [246] proposed to view each valid L as a codeword in a locally testable code over the alphabet $\Sigma = \mathcal{F}^{d+1}$. This code maps each m-variate polynomial of degree d to the sequence of univariate polynomials that describe the restrictions of this polynomial to all possible lines; that is, the polynomial p is mapped to $L_p : \mathcal{F}^m \times \mathcal{F}^m \to \mathcal{F}^{d+1}$ such that, for every $(\bar{x}, \bar{h}) \in \mathcal{F}^m \times \mathcal{F}^m$, it holds that $L_p(\bar{x}, \bar{h})$ is (or represents) a univariate polynomial that describes the value of p on the line $\{\bar{x} + i\bar{h} : i \in \mathcal{F}\}$. The corresponding 2-query tester of $L : \mathcal{F}^m \times \mathcal{F}^m \to \mathcal{F}^{d+1}$ will just select a random pair of intersecting lines and check whether they agree on the point of intersection.[34] The analysis of this tester reduces to the analysis of the corresponding low-degree test, undertaken in [24, 228].

The question at this point is what are the parameters of the foregoing code, denoted $\mathcal{C}$: $\Sigma^k \to \Sigma^n$, where $\Sigma = \mathcal{F}^{d+1}$ (and $n = |\mathcal{F}^m|^2$).[35] This code has distance $(1 - d/|\mathcal{F}|) \cdot n = \Omega(n)$, since different polynomials agree with probability at most $d/|\mathcal{F}|$ on a random point (and ditto on a random line). Since Σ^k corresponds to all possible m-variate polynomials of degree d over $\mathcal{F}$ (which have $\binom{m+d}{d}$ possible monomials), it follows that $\Sigma^k = |\mathcal{F}|^{\binom{m+d}{d}}$, which implies

$$k = \frac{\binom{m+d}{d}}{d+1} \approx \frac{(d/m)^m}{d} = \frac{d^{m-1}}{m^m} \tag{13.4}$$

where the approximation presumes $m \ll d$ (which is the preferred setting here (see next)). Note that $n = |\mathcal{F}^m|^2$, which (by Eq. (13.4)) means that

$$n \approx \left(\frac{m^m \cdot k}{d^{m-1}}\right)^2 \cdot |\mathcal{F}|^{2m} = d^2 \cdot m^{2m} \cdot (|\mathcal{F}|/d)^{2m} \cdot k^2 \gg k^2, \tag{13.5}$$

since $|\mathcal{F}| > d$. Lastly,

$$|\Sigma| = |\mathcal{F}|^{d+1} > k^{(d+1)/(m-1)} \gg k, \tag{13.6}$$

---

[33] This comment appears as footnote 18 in Chapter 3. Recall that PCPs of Proximity were defined in Section 13.2.3.3.

[34] That is, it select uniformly at random $\bar{x}_1, \bar{x}_2, \bar{h}_1, \bar{h}_2 \in \mathcal{F}^m$ and $i_1, i_2 \in \mathcal{F}$ such that $\bar{x}_1 + i_1\bar{h}_1 = \bar{x}_2 + i_2\bar{h}_2$, and checks whether the value of the polynomial $L(\bar{x}_1, \bar{h}_1)$ at i_1 equals the value of the polynomial $L(\bar{x}_2, \bar{h}_2)$ at i_2.

[35] Indeed, it would have been more natural to present the code as a mapping from sequences over $\mathcal{F}$ to sequences over $\Sigma = \mathcal{F}^{d+1}$. Following the convention of using the same alphabet for both the information and the codeword, we just pack every $d + 1$ elements of $\mathcal{F}$ as an element of Σ.

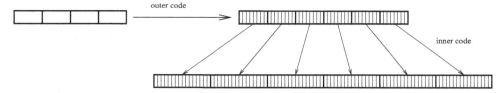

Figure 13.2: Concatenated codes. The outer (resp., inner) encoding is depicted by the horizontal arrow (resp., vertical arrows).

since $k < d^{m-1} < |\mathcal{F}|^{m-1}$. Hence, the smaller m, the better the rate (i.e., relation of n to k), but this comes at the expense of using a relatively larger alphabet. In particular, we consider two instantiations, where in both $|\mathcal{F}| = \Theta(d)$:

1. Using $d = m^m$, we get $k \approx (m^m)^{m-1}/m^m = m^{m^2-2m}$ and $n = O(d)^{2m} = m^{2m^2+o(m)}$, which yields $n \approx \exp(\sqrt{\log k}) \cdot k^2$ and $\log|\Sigma| = \log|\mathcal{F}|^{d+1} \approx d \log d \approx \exp(\sqrt{\log k})$.
2. Letting $d = m^c$ for any constant $c > 1$, we get $k \approx m^{(c-1)m-c}$ and $n = m^{2cm+o(m)}$, which yields $n \approx k^{2c/(c-1)}$ and $\log|\Sigma| \approx d \log d \approx (\log k)^c$.

In both cases, we obtain a locally testable code of polynomial length, but this code uses a large alphabet, whereas we seek codes over binary alphabet.

Alphabet Reduction. A natural way of reducing the alphabet size of codes is using the well-known paradigm of *concatenated codes* [117]: A concatenated code is obtained by encoding the symbols of an "outer code" (using the coding method of the "inner code"). Specifically, let $\mathcal{C}_1 : \Sigma_1^{k_1} \to \Sigma_1^{n_1}$ be the outer code and $\mathcal{C}_2 : \Sigma_2^{k_2} \to \Sigma_2^{n_2}$ be the inner code, where $\Sigma_1 \equiv \Sigma_2^{k_2}$. Then, the concatenated code $\mathcal{C}' : \Sigma_2^{k_1 k_2} \to \Sigma_2^{n_1 n_2}$ is obtained by letting $\mathcal{C}'(x_1, \ldots, x_{k_1}) = (\mathcal{C}_2(y_1), \ldots, \mathcal{C}_2(y_{n_1}))$, where $x_i \in \Sigma_2^{k_2} \equiv \Sigma_1$ and $(y_1, \ldots, y_{n_1}) = \mathcal{C}_1(x_1, \ldots, x_{k_1})$. That is, first $\mathcal{C}_1$ is applied to the k_1-long sequence of k_2-long blocks (of symbols in Σ_2), which are viewed as symbols of Σ_1, and then $\mathcal{C}_2$ is applied to each of the resulting n_1 blocks, which is now viewed as k_2-long sequences over Σ_2 (see Figure 13.2, where $k_1 = 4$, $n_1 = 6$, $k_2 = 8$ and $n_2 = 16$). Using a good inner code for relatively short sequences, allows to transform good codes for a large alphabet into good codes for a smaller alphabet.

The problem, however, is that concatenated codes do not necessarily preserve local testability. Here, we shall use special features of the specific tester used for the outer codes presented in the penultimate paragraph. Specifically, observe that, for each of the two queries made by the tester of the line-oracle $\mathcal{C} : \Sigma^k \to \Sigma^n$, the tester does not need the entire polynomial represented in $\Sigma = \mathcal{F}^{d+1}$, but rather only its value at a specific point. Thus, encoding Σ by an error-correcting code that supports recovery of the said value while using a constant number of probes will do.[36]

In particular, for integers h, e such that $d + 1 = h^e$, Goldreich and Sudan used an encoding of the elements of $\Sigma = \mathcal{F}^{d+1} = \mathcal{F}^{h^e}$ by sequences of length $|\mathcal{F}|^{eh}$ over $\mathcal{F}$ (i.e., this inner code mapped h^e-long $\mathcal{F}$-sequences to $|\mathcal{F}|^{eh}$-long $\mathcal{F}$-sequences), and provided testing and recovery procedures (for this inner code) that make $O(e)$ queries [157, Sec. 3.3]. Note that the case of $e = 1$ and $|\mathcal{F}| = 2$ corresponds to the Hadamard code,

---

[36] Indeed, this property is related to locally decodable codes (to be briefly discussed in Section 13.4.4). Here we need to recover one out of $|\mathcal{F}|$ specific linear combinations of the encoded $(d + 1)$-long sequence of $\mathcal{F}$-symbols. In contrast, locally decodable refers to recovering one out of the $\mathcal{F}$-symbols of the original $(d + 1)$-long sequence.

and that a bigger constant e allows for shorter codes (e.g., for $|\mathcal{F}| = 2$, we have length $2^{eh} = 2^{e \cdot t^{1/e}}$, where $t = h^e$ denotes the length of the encoded information). The resulting concatenated code, denoted $C' : \mathcal{F}^{(d+1) \cdot k} \to \mathcal{F}^{n'}$, is a locally testable code over $\mathcal{F}$, and has length $n' = n \cdot |\mathcal{F}|^{ed} = n \cdot \exp((e \log d) \cdot d^{1/e})$. Using a constant $e = 2c \in \mathbb{N}$ and setting $d = m^c \approx (\log k)^c$, we get $n' \approx k^{2c/(c-1)} \cdot \exp(d^{1/e}) \approx k^{2c/(c-1)} \cdot \exp(\widetilde{O}(\log k)^{1/2})$ and $|\mathcal{F}| = O(d) = \text{poly}(\log k)$, which means that we have reduced the alphabet size considerably (from $|\mathcal{F}|^{d+1}$ to $|\mathcal{F}|$, where $d = \Theta(|\mathcal{F}|)$).

Finally, a *binary* locally testable code is obtained by concatenating $C' : \mathcal{F}^k \to \mathcal{F}^{n'}$ with the Hadamard code (which is used to encode elements of $\mathcal{F}$), while noting that the latter supports a "local recovery" property that suffices to emulate the tester for C'. In particular, the tester of C' merely checks a linear (over $\mathcal{F}$) equation referring to a constant number of $\mathcal{F}$-elements, and for $\mathcal{F} = GF(2^\ell)$, this can be emulated by checking *related* random linear combinations of the bits representing these elements, which in turn can be locally recovered (or rather self-corrected) from the Hadamard code. The final result is a *locally testable (binary) code of nearly quadratic length*; that is, the length is $n' \cdot 2^\ell = n' \cdot \text{poly}(\log k)$, whereas the information contents is $k' \cdot \ell > k$ (and $n' \approx k^{2c/(c-1)} \cdot \exp(\widetilde{O}(\log k)^{1/2})$).[37] We comment that a version of this tester may use three queries, whereas 2-query locally testable *binary* codes are essentially impossible (cf., [46]).

13.3.2.2. Locally Testable Proofs of Polynomial Length: The PCP Theorem

The case of proofs is far more complex than that of codes: Achieving locally testable proofs of polynomial length is essentially the contents of the celebrated PCP Theorem of Arora, Lund, Motwani, Sudan and Szegedy [24], which asserts that *every set in $\mathcal{NP}$ has a PCP system of constant query complexity and logarithmic randomness complexity*.[38] The construction is analogous to (but far more complex than) the one presented in the case of codes:[39] First we construct locally testable proofs over a large alphabet, and next we compose such proofs with corresponding "inner" proofs (over a smaller alphabet, and finally over a binary one).

Teaching Note: This subsection is significantly more complex than the rest of this section, and some readers may prefer to skip it and proceed directly to Section 13.3.3. Specifically, we proceed in four steps:

1. Introduce an NP-complete problem, denoted PVPP.
2. Present a PCP over a large alphabet for PVPP.
3. Perform alphabet (and/or query complexity) reduction for PCPs.
4. Discuss the proof composition paradigm, which underlies the prior step.

(The presentation of Steps 1–3 (which follows [256, Apdx. C] and [44]) is different from the standard presentation of [24].) The second and third steps are most imposing and complex, but

---

[37] Actually, the aforementioned result is only implicit in [157], since Goldreich and Sudan apply these ideas directly to a truncated version of the low-degree–based code.

[38] Recall that the proof complexity of PCPs is exponential in their randomness complexity (and linear in their query complexity).

[39] Our presentation reverses the historical order in which the corresponding results (for codes and proofs) were achieved. That is, the constructions of locally testable proofs of polynomial length predated the coding counterparts.

the reader may benefit from the discussion of the proof composition paradigm (Step 4) even when skipping all prior steps. Our presentation of the composition paradigm follows [44], rather than the original presentation of [25, 24]. For further details regarding the proof composition paradigm, the reader is referred to [131, Sec. 9.3.2.2].

The Partially Vanishing Polynomial Problem (PVPP). As a preliminary step, we introduce the following NP-complete problem, for which we shall present a PCP. The input to the problem consists of a finite field $\mathcal{F}$, a subset $H \subset \mathcal{F}$ of size $|\mathcal{F}|^{1/15}$, an integer $m < |H|$, and a $(3m + 4)$-variant polynomial $P : \mathcal{F}^{3m+4} \to \mathcal{F}$ of total degree $3m|H| + O(1)$. The problem is to determine whether there exists an m-variant ("assignment") polynomial $A : \mathcal{F}^m \to \mathcal{F}$ of total degree $m|H|$ such that $P'(x, y, z, \tau) \overset{\text{def}}{=} P(x, y, z, \tau, A(x), A(y), A(z))$ vanishes on $H^{3m} \times \{0, 1\}^3$; that is,

$$P(x, y, z, \tau, A(x), A(y), A(z)) = 0 \text{ for every } x, y, z \in H^m \text{ and } \tau \in \{0, 1\}^3 \subset H. \quad (13.7)$$

Note that the instance (i.e., the polynomial P) can be explicitly described by a sequence of $|\mathcal{F}|^{3m+4} \log_2 |\mathcal{F}|$ bits, whereas the solution sought can be explicitly described by a sequence of $|\mathcal{F}|^m \log_2 |\mathcal{F}|$ bits. We comment that the NP-completeness of the aforementioned problem can be proved via a reduction from 3SAT, by identifying the variables of the formula with H^m (for $m = |H| / \log |H|$) and essentially letting P be a low-degree extension of a function $f : H^{3m} \times \{0, 1\}^3 \to \{0, 1\}$ that encodes the structure of the formula (by considering all possible 3-clauses).[40] In fact, the resulting P has degree $|H| - 1$ in each of the first $3m$ variables and constant degree in each of the other variables, and this fact can be used to improve the parameters below (but not in a fundamental way).

A PCP over Large Alphabet for PVPP. The proof that a given input P satisfies the condition in Eq. (13.7) consists of an m-variant polynomial $A : \mathcal{F}^m \to \mathcal{F}$ (which is supposed to be of total degree $m|H|$) as well as $3m + 1$ auxiliary polynomials $A_i : \mathcal{F}^{3m+1} \to \mathcal{F}$, for $i = 1, \ldots, 3m + 1$ (each supposedly of degree $(3m|H| + O(1)) \cdot m|H|$). The polynomial A is supposed to satisfy Eq. (13.7); that is, $P(x, z, y, \tau, A(x), A(y), A(z)) = 0$ should hold for every $x, y, z \in H^m$ and $\tau \in \{0, 1\}^3 \subset H$. Furthermore, $A_0(x, y, z, \tau) \overset{\text{def}}{=} P(x, z, y, \tau, A(x), A(y), A(z))$ should vanish on H^{3m+1} (i.e., $A_0(x, y, z, \tau) = 0$ for every $x, y, z \in H^m$ and $\tau \in H$). The auxiliary polynomials are given to assist the verification of the latter condition. In particular, A_i should vanish on $\mathcal{F}^i H^{3m+1-i}$, a condition that is easy to test for A_{3m+1} (assuming that A_{3m+1} is a low-degree polynomial). The point is that if, for each $i \in [3m - 1]$, the polynomials A_i and A_{i-1} agree on the H-segment of each axis-parallel line in the ith direction (i.e., for every $(u, v) \in \mathcal{F}^{i-1} \times \mathcal{F}^{3m+1-i}$ and $h \in H$, it holds that $A_i(uhv) = A_{i-1}(uhv)$), then the fact that A_i vanishes on $\mathcal{F}^i H^{3m+1-i}$ implies that A_{i-1} vanishes on $\mathcal{F}^{i-1} H^{3m+1-i+1}$.

Hence, a valid proof consists of a polynomial A that satisfies Eq. (13.7) and a sequence of polynomials $(A_1, \ldots, A_{3m-1})$ such that A_i vanishes on $\mathcal{F}^i H^{3m+1-i}$. Verifying that A_{i-1} agrees with A_i on $\mathcal{F}^{i-1} H^{3m+1-(i-1)}$, for $i = 1, \ldots, 3m + 1$, and that all A_i's are low-degree polynomials, establishes the claim for A_0. Thus, testing an alleged proof $(A, A_1, \ldots, A_{3m+1})$ is performed as follows:

---

[40] Specifically, $f(x, y, z, \mu\nu\xi) = 1$ if and only if $x^\mu \vee y^\nu \vee z^\xi$ appears as a clause in the given formula, where x^μ denotes x if $\mu = 0$ and $\neg x$ otherwise. The construction of low-degree extensions is reviewed in Exercise 3.1.

1. Testing that A is a polynomial of total degree $m|H|$.

   (This is a low-degree test. Recall that it can be performed by selecting a random line through $\mathcal{F}^m$, and testing whether A restricted to this line agrees with a degree $m|H|$ univariate polynomial).

2. Testing that, for $i = 1, \ldots, 3m + 1$, the polynomial A_i is of total degree $d \overset{\text{def}}{=} (3m|H| + O(1)) \cdot m|H|$.

   (Here we select a random line through $\mathcal{F}^{3m+1}$, and test whether A_i restricted to this line agrees with a degree d univariate polynomial.)

3. Testing that, for $i = 1, \ldots, 3m + 1$, the polynomial A_i agrees with A_{i-1} on $\mathcal{F}^{i-1} H \mathcal{F}^{3m+1-i}$, which implies that A_i agrees with A_{i-1} on $\mathcal{F}^{i-1} H^{3m+1-(i-1)}$.

   This is done by uniformly selecting $r' = (r_1, \ldots, r_{i-1}) \in \mathcal{F}^{i-1}$ and $r'' = (r_{i+1}, \ldots, r_{3m+1}) \in \mathcal{F}^{3m+1-i}$, and comparing $A_{i-1}(r', e, r'')$ to $A_i(r', e, r'')$, for every $e \in H$. In addition, we check that A_i, when restricted to the axis-parallel line $(r', \cdot, r'')$, agrees with a univariate polynomial of degree at most d.[41]

   We stress that the values of A_0 are computed according to the given polynomial P by accessing A at the appropriate locations (i.e., by definition $A_0(x, z, z, \tau) = P(x, z, y, \tau, A(x), A(y), A(z))$).

4. Testing that A_{3m+1} vanishes on $\mathcal{F}^{3m+1}$.

   This is done by uniformly selecting $r \in \mathcal{F}^{3m+1}$, and testing whether $A_{3m+1}(r) = 0$.

The foregoing tester may be viewed as making $O(m|\mathcal{F}|)$ queries to an oracle of length $|\mathcal{F}|^m + (3m + 1) \cdot |\mathcal{F}|^{3m+1}$ over the alphabet $\mathcal{F}$, or alternatively, as making $O(m|\mathcal{F}| \log |\mathcal{F}|)$ binary queries to a binary oracle of length $O(m \cdot |\mathcal{F}|^{3m+1} \log |\mathcal{F}|)$. We mention that the foregoing description (which follows [256, Apdx. C]) is somewhat different than the original presentation in [24], which in turn follows [29, 28, 107].[42]

Note that we have already obtained a highly nontrivial tester. It makes $\widetilde{O}(m|\mathcal{F}|)$ queries to a proof of length $\widetilde{O}(m \cdot |\mathcal{F}|^{3m+1})$ in order to verify a claim regarding an input of length $n \overset{\text{def}}{=} |\mathcal{F}|^{3m+4} \log_2 |\mathcal{F}|$. Using $m = \Theta(\log n / \log \log n)$, $|H| = \log n$ and $|\mathcal{F}| = \text{poly}(\log n)$, which satisfies $m < |H| = |\mathcal{F}|^{1/15}$, we have obtained a *tester of polylogarithmic query complexity and polynomial proof complexity* (equivalently, logarithmic randomness complexity).[43]

Although the foregoing tester is highly nontrivial, it falls short from our aim, because it employs a *nonconstant number of queries to a proof-oracle over a nonconstant alphabet*. Of course, we can convert the latter alphabet to a binary alphabet by increasing the number of queries, but actually the original proof of the PCP Theorem went in the opposite direction and reduce the number of queries by "packing" them into a constant number of queries to an oracle over an even larger alphabet (see the "parallelization technique" below). Either way, we are faced with the problem of *reducing the total amount of information obtained from the oracle*.

---

[41] Thus, the values of A_{i-1} at $\{r' h r'' : h \in H\}$, which equal the values of A_i at these points, are consistent with the values of A_i on the entire line $(r', \cdot, r'')$, whereas the latter sequence of values constitutes a codeword (of an error-correcting code that has a large distance). This means that the values of A_i at $\{r' f r'' : f \in \mathcal{F}\}$ provides a "robust" encoding of the values of A_{i-1} at $\{r' h r'' : h \in H\}$.

[42] The point is that the sum-check, which originates in [202], is replaced here by an analogous process (which is nonsequential in nature).

[43] In fact, the proof complexity is sublinear, since $\widetilde{O}(m \cdot |\mathcal{F}|^{3m+1}) = o(n)$.

Alphabet (and/or Query Complexity) Reduction for PCPs. To further reduce the query complexity, we invoke the "proof composition" paradigm, introduced by Arora and Safra [25] (and further discussed at the end of the current subsection). Specifically, we compose an "outer" tester (e.g., the foregoing tester) with an "inner" tester that locally checks the residual condition that the "outer" would have checked (regarding the answers it would have obtained). That is, rather than letting the "outer" verifier read (small) portions of the proof-oracle and decide accordingly, we let the "inner" verifier probe these portions and check whether the "outer" verifier would have accepted based on them. This composition is not straightforward, because we wish the "inner" tester to perform its task without reading its entire input (i.e., the answers to the "outer" tester). This seems quite paradoxical, since it is not clear how the "inner" tester can operate without reading its entire input. The problem can be resolved by using a "proximity tester" (i.e., a PCP of Proximity)[44] as an "inner" tester, provided that it suffices to have such a proximity test (for the answers to the "outer" tester). Thus, the challenge is to reach a situation in which the "outer" tester is "robust" in the sense that, when the assertion is false, the answers obtained by this tester are far from being convincing (i.e., far from any sequence of answers that is accepted by this tester). Two approaches toward obtaining such robust testers are known.

- One approach, introduced in [24], is to convert the "outer" tester into one that makes a constant number of queries over some larger alphabet, and furthermore have each answer be presented in an error-correcting format. Thus, robustness is guaranteed by the fact that the answers are presented as a sequence consisting of a constant number of codewords, which implies the uniqueness of a properly formatted sequence that is close to a fixed sequence.

  The implementation of this approach consists of two steps. The first step is to convert the "outer" tester that makes $t = \mathrm{poly}(\log \ell)$ queries to an oracle $\pi : [\ell] \to \{0, 1\}$ into a tester that makes a constant number of queries to an oracle that maps $[\mathrm{poly}(\ell)]$ to $\{0, 1\}^{\mathrm{poly}(t)}$. This step uses the so-called *parallelization technique*, which replaces each possible t-sequence of queries by a (low-degree) curve that passes through these t queries as well as through a random point (cf. [196, 24]). The new proof-oracle answers each such curve C with a (low-degree) univariate polynomial p_C that is supposed to describe the values of (a low-degree extension π' of) π at all $\mathrm{poly}(t)$ points that reside on C (i.e., $p_C(i) = \pi'(C(i))$). The consistency of these p_C's with π is checked by selecting a random curve C, and comparing the value that p_C assigns a random point on C to the value assigned to this point by π' (i.e., the low-degree extension of π).[45]

---

[44] See Section 13.2.3.3.

[45] **Advanced comment:** Specifically, we associate $[\ell]$ with H^m, where H resides in a finite field $\mathcal{F}$ such that $|\mathcal{F}| = \mathrm{poly}(t, |H|)$ and $|\mathcal{F}|^m = \mathrm{poly}(\ell)$. (We stress that m, H and $\mathcal{F}$ used here are different from those used in the foregoing description of the PCP for PVPP, although here too $m = |H|/\log|H|$ will do.) For every sequence of queries $\bar{q} = (q_1, \ldots, q_t) \in (H^m)^t$ made by the original verifier and every $r \in \mathcal{F}^m$, we consider the degree $t + 1$ curve $C_{\bar{q},r} : \mathcal{F} \to \mathcal{F}^m$ such that $C_{\bar{q},r}(0) = r$ and $C_{\bar{q},r}(i) = q_i$ for every $i \in [t] \subset \mathcal{F}$. Hence, the set of curves corresponds to $\Omega \times \mathcal{F}^m$, where Ω is the set of all possible outcomes of the internal coin tosses of the original verifier. The new proof-oracle consists of a function $\pi' : \mathcal{F}^m \to \mathcal{F}$, which is supposed to be a degree $m|H|$ extension of the original proof π, viewed as a Boolean function $\pi : H^m \to \{0, 1\}$, as well as univariate polynomials of degree $m|H| \cdot (t + 1)$ that are supposed to represent the restrictions of π' to all $|\Omega \times \mathcal{F}^m|$ curves (i.e., the polynomial $p_C : \mathcal{F} \to \mathcal{F}$ that corresponds to the curve C is supposed to satisfy $p_C(i) = \pi'(C(i))$ for every $i \in \mathcal{F}$). The new verifier will

In the second step, an error-correcting code is applied to the poly(t)-bit long answers provided by the foregoing oracle, while assuming that the "inner (proximity) verifier" can handle inputs that are presented in this format (i.e., that it can test an input that is presented in a constant number of parts, where each part is encoded separately).[46]

- An alternative approach, pursued and advocated in [44], is to take advantage of the specific structure of the queries, "bundle" the answers together (into a constant number of bundles), and show that the "bundled" answers are "robust" in a sense that fits proximity testing. (Furthermore, the robustness of individual bundles is inherited by any constant sequence of bundles.) Hence, the (generic) parallelization step is replaced by a closer analysis of the specific (outer) tester, which establishes the robustness of individual subtests, and the ability to bundle these subtests (i.e., use the same sequence of queries when emulating the different subtests). The bundling is captured by Eq. (13.8), and the text that follows it explains how to emulate the various subtests using a constant number of queries to these bundles.

Hence, while the first approach relies on a general technique of parallelization (and, historically (see footnote 46), also on the specifics of the inner verifier), the second approach refers explicitly to the notion of robustness and relies on the specifics of the outer verifier. An advantage of the second approach is that it almost preserves the length of the proofs (whereas the first approach may square this length). We will outline the second approach next, but warn that this terse description may be hard to follow.

First, we show how the queries of the foregoing *tester for PVPP* can be "bundled" such that the $O(m)$ subtests of this tester can be performed by inspecting a constant number of bundles. In particular, we consider the following "bundling" that accommodates the $3m + 1$ different subtests performed in Step (3): Consider $B : \mathcal{F}^{3m+1} \to \mathcal{F}^{3m+1}$ such that

$$B(x_1, \ldots, x_{3m+1})$$

$$(13.8)$$

$$\stackrel{\text{def}}{=} (A_1(x_1, x_2, \ldots, x_{3m+1}), A_2(x_2, \ldots, x_{3m+1}, x_1), \ldots, A_{3m+1}(x_{3m+1}, x_1, \ldots, x_{3m}))$$

and perform all $3m + 1$ tests of Step (3) by selecting uniformly $(r_2, \ldots, r_{3m+1}) \in \mathcal{F}^{3m}$ and querying B at $(e, r_2, \ldots, r_{3m+1})$ and $(r_2, \ldots, r_{3m+1}, e)$ for all $e \in \mathcal{F}$. Thus, all $3m + 1$ tests of Step (3) can be performed by retrieving the $2 \cdot |\mathcal{F}|$ values of B on two *axis parallel*

1. Test that π' has degree $m|H|$;
2. Test that π' matches the univariate polynomials by selecting a random point $i \in \mathcal{F}$ on a random curve C and comparing the value given by the corresponding univariate polynomial p_C to the value given by π' (i.e., checking that $p_C(i) = \pi'(C(i))$ holds);
3. Select a random curve $C = C_{\bar{q},r}$ and emulate the original tester based on the values $p_C(1), \ldots, p_C(t)$ obtained from the polynomial that corresponds to this curve.

Due to the randomization of the curves via their value at zero, it holds that a random point on a random curve is distributed almost uniformly in $\mathcal{F}^m$, where the possible slackness is due to the first t points on the curve. The analysis is based on the fact that if π' has degree $m|H|$ and the polynomial that corresponds to a curve does not agree with it at some point, then they disagree on most of the points.

[46] The aforementioned assumption holds trivially in case one uses a general-purpose "proximity tester" (e.g., a PCP of Proximity (a.k.a. an Assignment Tester) for sets in $\mathcal{P}$) as done in [94]. But the aforementioned approach can be applied (and, in fact, was originally applied) using a specific "proximity tester" that can handle only inputs presented in one specific format (cf. [24]).

random line through $\mathcal{F}^{3m+1}$ (i.e., the lines $(\cdot, r_2, \ldots, r_{3m+1})$ and $(r_2, \ldots, r_{3m+1}, \cdot)$).[47] Likewise, all $3m + 1$ tests of Step (2) can be performed by retrieving the $|\mathcal{F}|$ values of B on a single (arbitrary) random line through $\mathcal{F}^{3m+1}$. (The test of Step (1), which refers to A, remains intact, whereas the test of Step (4) is conducted on B rather than on A_{3m+1}.) Lastly, observe that these tests are "robust" in the sense that if, for some i, the function A_i is (say) 0.01-far from satisfying the condition (i.e., being low-degree or agreeing with A_{i-1}), then with constant probability the $|\mathcal{F}|$-long sequence of values of A_i on an appropriate random line will be far from satisfying the corresponding predicate. This robustness feature is inherited by B, since each symbol of B encodes the corresponding values of all A_i's. Hence, we have bundled $O(m)$ tests that refer to $O(m)$ different functions (i.e., the A_i's and A) into four tests that refer to two functions (i.e., B and A), where each of these tests queries one (or both) of the functions for its value at $O(|\mathcal{F}|)$ points.[48]

Next, we encode the symbols of B (resp., of A) by a good binary error-correcting code, and obtain a binary function B' (resp., A') that preserves the robustness up to a constant factor (which equals the relative distance of the code). Specifically, we may replace $A : \mathcal{F}^m \to \mathcal{F}$ and $B : \mathcal{F}^{3m+1} \to \mathcal{F}^{3m+1}$ by $A' : \mathcal{F}^m \times [O(\log |\mathcal{F}|)] \to \{0, 1\}$ and $B' : \mathcal{F}^{3m+1} \times [O(\log |\mathcal{F}|^{3m+1})] \to \{0, 1\}$, and conduct all tests by making $O(m^2 |\mathcal{F}| \log |\mathcal{F}|)$ queries to A' and B' (since each query to $A : \mathcal{F}^m \to \mathcal{F}$ (resp., to $B : \mathcal{F}^{3m+1} \to \mathcal{F}^{3m+1}$) is replaced by $O(\log |\mathcal{F}|)$ queries to A' (resp., $O(m \log |\mathcal{F}|)$ queries to B')). The resulting *robustness feature* asserts that if the original polynomial P had no solution (i.e., an A satisfying Eq. (13.7)), then the answers obtained by the tester will be far from satisfying the residual decision predicate of the tester.

Now, if the robustness feature of the resulting ("outer") tester fits the proximity testing feature of the "inner tester" (i.e., the threshold determining what is "far" w.r.t. robustness is greater than or equal to the threshold of "far" w.r.t. proximity), then composition is possible. Indeed, we compose the "outer" tester with an "inner tester" that checks whether the residual decision predicate of the "outer tester" is satisfies. The benefit of this composition is that the query complexity is reduced from polylogarithmic (in n) to polynomial in a double-logarithm function (in n). At this point we can afford the Hadamard-based proof tester (because the overhead in the proof length will only be exponential in poly$(\log \log n) = O(\log n)$), and obtain a locally testable proof of polynomial (in n) length. That is, we compose the poly$(\log \log)$-query tester (acting as an outer tester) with the Hadamard-based tester (acting as an inner tester), and obtain a locally testable proof of polynomial length (as asserted by the PCP Theorem).

On the Proof Composition Paradigm. The PCP Theorem asserts a PCP system for $\mathcal{NP}$ that simultaneously achieve the minimal possible randomness and query complexity (up to a multiplicative factor).[49] The foregoing construction obtains this remarkable result by

---

[47] Indeed, the values of $B(e, r_2, \ldots, r_{3m+1})$ and $B(r_2, \ldots, r_{3m+1}, e)$ yield the values of $A_i(r_i, \ldots, r_{3m+1}, e, r_2, \ldots, r_{i-1})$ and $A_{i-1}(r_i, \ldots, r_{3m+1}, e, r_2, \ldots, r_{i-1})$ for every $i \in [3m + 1]$. Recall, however, that the values of A_0 are determined based on A. Hence, for emulating the first of these tests (i.e., the test corresponding to $i = 1$), we use both B and A.

[48] Actually, the fourth test (corresponding to Step (4)) queries B at a single point. Recall that Step (1) queries A on a random line, Step (2) queries B on a random line, and Step (3) queries B (and A) on two random axis-parallel lines.

[49] The claim of minimality assumes that $\mathcal{P} \neq \mathcal{NP}$. Furthermore, the claim that the randomness complexity is at least logarithmic refers to low query complexity (e.g., query complexity that is smaller than the square root of the length of the NP-witness). The point is that a PCP system of randomness complexity $r(n)$ and query complexity $q(n)$ yields an NP-proof system that utilizes proofs of length $2^{r(n)} \cdot q(n)$.

combining two different PCPs: the first PCP obtains logarithmic randomness but uses polylogarithmically many queries, whereas the second PCP uses a constant number of queries but has polynomial randomness complexity. We stress that *each of these two PCP systems is highly nontrivial and very interesting by itself*. We also highlight the fact that these PCPs are combined using a very simple composition method (which refers to auxiliary properties such as robustness and proximity testing). Details follow.[50]

Loosely speaking, the proof composition paradigm refers to composing two proof systems such that the "inner" verifier is used for probabilistically verifying the acceptance criteria of the "outer" verifier. That is, the combined verifier selects coins for the "outer" verifier, determines the corresponding locations that the "outer" verifier would have inspected (in the proof), and verifies that the "outer" verifier would have accepted the values that reside in these locations. The latter verification is performed by invoking the "inner" verifier, *without reading the values residing in all the aforementioned locations*. Indeed, the aim is to conduct this ("composed") verification while using much fewer queries than the query complexity of the "outer" proof system. In particular, the inner verifier cannot afford to read its input, which makes the composition more subtle than the term suggests.

In order for the proof composition to work, the verifiers being combined should satisfy some auxiliary conditions. Specifically, the *outer* verifier should be robust in the sense that its soundness condition guarantee that, with high probability, the oracle answers are "far" from satisfying the residual decision predicate (rather than merely not satisfying it).[51] The *inner* verifier is given oracle access to its input and is charged for each query made to it, but it is only required to reject (with high probability) inputs that are far from being valid (and, as usual, accept inputs that are valid). That is, the inner verifier is actually a verifier of proximity (i.e., a PCP of Proximity, as defined in Section 13.2.3.3).

Composing two such PCPs yields a new PCP, where the new proof-oracle consists of the proof-oracle of the "outer" system and a sequence of proof-oracles for the "inner" system (one "inner" proof per each possible random-tape of the "outer" verifier). The resulting verifier selects coins for the outer-verifier and uses the corresponding "inner" proof in order to verify that the outer-verifier would have accepted under this choice of coins. Note that such a choice of coins determines locations in the "outer" proof that the outer-verifier would have inspected, and the combined verifier provides the inner-verifier with oracle access to these locations (which the inner-verifier considers as its input) as well as with oracle access to the corresponding "inner" proof (which the inner-verifier considers as its proof-oracle).

The quantitative effect of such a composition is easy to analyze. Specifically, composing an outer-verifier of randomness-complexity r' and query-complexity q' with an inner-verifier of randomness-complexity r'' and query-complexity q'' yields a PCP of randomness-complexity $r(n) = r'(n) + r''(q'(n))$ and query-complexity $q(n) = q''(q'(n))$, because $q'(n)$ represents the length of the input (oracle) that is accessed by the inner-verifier. Thus, assuming $q''(m) \ll m$, the query-complexity is significantly decreased (from $q'(n)$ to $q''(q'(n))$), while the increase in the randomness-complexity is moderate provided that $r''(q'(n)) \ll r'(n)$. Furthermore, the verifier resulting from the

---

[50] Our presentation of the composition paradigm follows [44], rather than the original presentation of [25, 24]. A more detailed overview of the composition paradigm is available in [131, Sec. 9.3.2.2].

[51] Furthermore, the latter predicate, which is well defined by the nonadaptive nature of the outer verifier, must have a circuit of size that is at most polynomial in the number of queries.

composition inherits the robustness features of the inner-verifier, which is important in case we wish to compose the resulting verifier with another inner-verifier.

The proof composition paradigm is reminiscent of the paradigm of concatenated codes that was used for alphabet reduction in the context of locally testable codes (cf. Section 13.3.2.1). We stress that the classical presentations of the paradigm of concatenated codes do not address the issue of local testability, which is the core of the proof composition paradigm. Recall that local testability of concatenated codes was shown in Section 13.3.2.1 based on some local decodability features of the outer code, whereas local testability of the outer and inner codes does not seem to suffice. In contrast, the proof composition paradigm is tailored for the preservation of local testability.

13.3.3. Locally Testable Codes and Proofs of Nearly Linear Length

We now move on to even *shorter* codes and proofs; specifically, codes and proofs of *nearly linear length*. The latter term has been given quite different interpretations, and we start by sorting these out. Currently, this taxonomy is relevant mainly for second-level discussions and review of some past works.[52]

Types of Nearly Linear Functions. A few common interpretations of the term "nearly linear" are listed below (going from the most liberal to the most strict one).

T1-nearly linear: A very liberal notion, which seems at the verge of an abuse of the term, refers to a sequence of functions $f_\epsilon : \mathbb{N} \to \mathbb{N}$ such that, for every $\epsilon > 0$, it holds that $f_\epsilon(n) \leq n^{1+\epsilon}$. That is, each function is actually of the form $n \mapsto n^c$, for some constant $c > 1$, but the sequence as a whole can be viewed as approaching linearity.

The PCP of Polishchuk and Spielman [228] and the simpler locally testable code of Goldreich and Sudan [157, Thm. 2.4] have nearly linear length in this sense. The locally testable (binary) code presented in Section 13.3.2.1 has *nearly quadratic* length in an analogous sense.

T2-nearly linear: A more reasonable notion of nearly linear functions refers to individual functions f such that $f(n) = n^{1+o(1)}$. Specifically, for some function $\epsilon : \mathbb{N} \to [0, 1]$ that tends to zero, it holds that $f(n) \leq n^{1+\epsilon(n)}$. Common subtypes include the following:

1. $\epsilon(n) = 1/\log\log n$.
2. $\epsilon(n) = 1/(\log n)^c$ for some constant $c \in (0, 1)$.
   The locally testable codes and proofs of [157, 49, 44] have nearly linear length in this sense. Specifically, in [157, Sec. 4–5] and [49] any $c > 1/2$ will do, whereas in [44] any $c > 0$ will do.
3. $\epsilon(n) = \frac{\exp((\log\log n)^c)}{\log n}$ for some constant $c \in (0, 1)$.
   Note that $\mathrm{poly}(\log\log n) \ll \exp((\log\log n)^c) \ll (\log n)^{\Omega(1)}$, for any constant $c \in (0, 1)$.
4. $\epsilon(n) = \frac{\mathrm{poly}(\log\log n)}{\log n}$, which corresponds to $f(n) = q(\log n) \cdot n$, where $q(m) = \exp(\mathrm{poly}(\log m))$.

---

[52] Things were different when the original version of this text [130] was written. At that time, only T2-nearly linear length was know for $O(1)$-local testability, and the T3-nearly linear result achieved later by Dinur [92] seemed a daring conjecture (which was, nevertheless, stated in [130, Conj. 3.3]).

Here near-linearity means *linearity up to a quasi-polylogarithmic factor*, and one is tempted to view it as a relaxation of the following type (T3).

Indeed, the case in which $\epsilon(n) = \frac{O(\log\log n)}{\log n}$ deserves a special category, presented next.

T3-nearly linear: The strongest notion interprets near-linearity as *linearity up to a polylogarithmic factor*; that is, $f(n) = \widetilde{O}(n) \stackrel{\text{def}}{=} \text{poly}(\log n) \cdot n$, which corresponds to the case of $f(n) \leq n^{1+\epsilon(n)}$ with $\epsilon(n) = O(\log\log n)/\log n$.
The results of [48, 92, 267, 268], reviewed in Section 13.3.3.1, refer to this notion.

We note that while [48, 92, 267, 268] achieve T3-nearly linear length, the low-error results of [210, 93] only achieve T2-nearly linear length.

13.3.3.1. Local Testability with Nearly Linear Length

The celebrated gap amplification technique of Dinur [92] is best known for providing an alternative proof of the PCP Theorem (which asserts that *every set in* $\mathcal{NP}$ *has a PCP system of constant query complexity and logarithmic randomness complexity*). However, applying this technique to a PCP that was (previously) provided by Ben-Sasson and Sudan [48] yields locally testable codes and proofs of T3-nearly linear length. In particular, the overhead in the code and proof length is only polylogarithmic in the length of the primal object (which establishes [130, Conj. 3.3]).

Theorem 13.11 (Dinur [92], building on [48]): *There exists a constant q and a polylogarithmic function* $f : \mathbb{N} \to \mathbb{N}$ *such that there exist q-locally testable codes and proofs* (for SAT) *of length* $f(k) \cdot k$, *where k denotes the length of the primal information* (i.e., the encoded information in case of codes and the assertion in case of proofs).

The PCP system asserted in Theorem 13.11 is obtained by applying the gap amplification method of Dinur [92] (reviewed in Section 13.3.3.2) to the PCP system of Ben-Sasson and Sudan [48]. We mention that the PCP system (for NP) of Ben-Sasson and Sudan [48] is based on the NP-completeness of a certain code (of length $n = \widetilde{O}(k)$), and on a randomized reduction of testing whether a given n-bit long string is a codeword to a constant number of similar tests that refer to $\sqrt{n}$-bit long strings. Applying this reduction $\log\log n$ times yields a PCP of query complexity $\text{poly}(\log n)$ and length $\widetilde{O}(n)$; actually, this reduction yields a 3-query "weak PCP with soundness error $1 - 1/\text{poly}(\log n)$" (which is the construct to which we apply the gap amplification method).

The PCP system of Theorem 13.11 can be adapted to yield a PCP of Proximity with the same parameters, which (as shown in Section 13.2.3.3) yields a (weak) locally testable code with similar parameters (i.e., constant number of queries and length $n = \widetilde{O}(k)$). Recall that this transformation of PCP of Proximity to locally testable codes works only for the weak version of the latter notion. A strong locally testable code with similar parameters was only obtained later (by Viderman [267, 268]).[53]

---

[53] Viderman's code is based on a refined analysis of the locally testable code of [48], which can be viewed as a PCP of Proximity, and on the effect of applying gap amplification to PCP of Proximity systems. In particular, an essential conceptual step is separating the lower-bounding of the rejection probability of a PCP of Proximity system in terms of its input-oracle from its lower-bounding in terms of its proof-oracle, and observing that gap amplification acts differently on the two parameters that capture these two relations.

Is a polylogarithmic overhead the best one can get? In the original version of this chapter [130], we conjectured that a polylogarithmic (length) overhead is inherent to local testability (or, at least, that linear length $O(1)$-local testability is impossible). We currently have mixed feelings with respect to this conjecture (even when confined to proofs), and thus rephrase it as an open problem.

Open Problem 13.12 (Local testability in linear length): *Determine whether there exist locally testable codes and proofs of linear length.*

13.3.3.2. The Gap Amplification Method

Essentially, Theorem 13.11 is proved by applying the gap amplification method (of Dinur [92]) to the (weak) PCP system constructed by Ben-Sasson and Sudan [48]. The latter PCP system has length $\ell(k) = \widetilde{O}(k)$, but its soundness error is $1 - 1/\text{poly}(\log k)$ (i.e., its rejection probability is at least $1/\text{poly}(\log k)$). Each application of the gap amplification step *doubles the rejection probability while essentially maintaining the initial complexities*. That is, in each step, the constant query complexity of the verifier is preserved and its randomness complexity is increased only by a constant term (and so the length of the PCP oracle is increased only by a constant factor). Thus, starting from the system of [48] and applying $O(\log \log k)$ amplification steps, we essentially obtain Theorem 13.11. (Note that a PCP system of polynomial length can be obtained by starting from a trivial "PCP" system that has rejection probability $1/\text{poly}(k)$, and applying $O(\log k)$ amplification steps.)[54]

In order to rigorously describe the aforementioned process we need to *redefine PCP systems so as to allow arbitrary soundness error*. In fact, for technical reasons, it is more convenient to describe the process in terms of an iterated reduction of a "constraint satisfaction" problem to itself. Specifically, we refer to systems of 2-variable constraints, which are readily represented by (labeled) graphs such that the vertices correspond to (non-Boolean) variables and the edges are associated with constraints.

Definition 13.13 (CSP with 2-variable constraints): *For a fixed finite set Σ, an instance of CSP consists of a graph $G = (V, E)$, which may have parallel edges and self-loops, and a sequence of 2-variable constraints $\Phi = (\phi_e)_{e \in E}$ associated with the edges, where each constraint has the form $\phi_e : \Sigma^2 \to \{0, 1\}$. The value of an assignment $\alpha : V \to \Sigma$ is the number of constraints satisfied by α; that is, the value of α is $|\{(u, v) \in E : \phi_{(u,v)}(\alpha(u), \alpha(v)) = 1\}|$. We denote by $\text{vlt}(G, \Phi)$ (standing for violation) the fraction of unsatisfied constraints under the best possible assignment; that is,*

$$\text{vlt}(G, \Phi) = \min_{\alpha:V \to \Sigma} \left\{ \frac{|\{(u, v) \in E : \phi_{(u,v)}(\alpha(u), \alpha(v)) = 0\}|}{|E|} \right\} \tag{13.9}$$

For various functions $\tau : \mathbb{N} \to (0, 1]$, we will consider the promise problem $\text{gapCSP}^{\Sigma}_{\tau}$, having instances as above, such that the YES-instances are fully satisfiable instances (i.e., $\text{vlt} = 0$) and the NO-instances are pairs (G, Φ) for which $\text{vlt}(G, \Phi) \geq \tau(|G|)$ holds, where $|G|$ denotes the number of edges in G.

---

[54] See Exercise 13.8.

Note that 3SAT (over m clauses) is reducible to $\text{gapCSP}^{\Sigma_0}_{\tau_0}$ for $\Sigma_0 = \{F, T\}^3$ and $\tau_0(m) = 1/m$ (e.g., replace each clause of the 3SAT instance by a vertex, and use edge constraints that enforce mutually consistent and satisfying assignments to each pair of clauses).[55] Furthermore, the PCP system of [48] yields a reduction of 3SAT to $\text{gapCSP}^{\Sigma_0}_{\tau_1}$ for $\tau_1(m) = 1/\text{poly}(\log m)$ where the size of the graph is T3-nearly linear in the length of the input formula.

Our goal is to reduce $\text{gapCSP}^{\Sigma_0}_{\tau_0}$ (or rather $\text{gapCSP}^{\Sigma_0}_{\tau_1}$) to $\text{gapCSP}^{\Sigma}_{c}$, for some fixed finite Σ and constant $c > 0$, where in the case of $\text{gapCSP}^{\Sigma_0}_{\tau_1}$ we wish the reduction to preserve the length of the instance up to a polylogarithmic factor.[56] The PCP Theorem (resp., a PCP of T3-nearly linear length) follows by showing a simple PCP system for $\text{gapCSP}^{\Sigma}_{c}$ (e.g., the PCP verifier selects a random edge and checks whether the pair of values assigned to its endpoints by the alleged proof satisfies the constraint associated with this edge).[57] As noted before, the reduction is obtained by repeated applications of an amplification step that is captured by the following lemma.

Lemma 13.14 (An amplifying reduction of gapCSP to itself): *For some finite Σ and constant $c > 0$, there exists a polynomial-time computable function f such that, for every instance (G, Φ) of gapCSP^{Σ}, it holds that $(G', \Phi') = f(G, \Phi)$ is an instance of gapCSP^{Σ} and the two instances are related as follows:*

1. *If $\text{vlt}(G, \Phi) = 0$, then $\text{vlt}(G', \Phi') = 0$.*
2. *$\text{vlt}(G', \Phi') \geq \min(2 \cdot \text{vlt}(G, \Phi), c)$.*
3. *$|G'| = O(|G|)$.*

That is, satisfiable instances are mapped to satisfiable instances, whereas instances that violate a ν fraction of the constraints are mapped to instances that violate at least a $\min(2\nu, c)$ fraction of the constraints. Furthermore, the mapping increases the number of edges (in the instance) by at most a constant factor. We stress that both Φ and Φ' consists of Boolean constraints defined over Σ^2. Thus, by iteratively applying Lemma 13.14 for a logarithmic (resp., double-logarithmic) number of times, we reduce $\text{gapCSP}^{\Sigma}_{\tau_0}$ (resp., $\text{gapCSP}^{\Sigma}_{\tau_1}$) to $\text{gapCSP}^{\Sigma}_{c}$.

Teaching Note: The rest of this subsection is also quite complex, and some readers may prefer to skip it and proceed directly to Section 13.4.

Outline of the Proof of Lemma 13.14: Before turning to the proof, let us highlight the difficulty that it needs to address. Specifically, the lemma asserts a "violation amplifying

---

[55] That is, given the instance $\wedge_{i \in [m]} \psi_i$, we construct a graph $G = ([m], E)$ such that vertices i and j are connected by an edge if and only if ψ_i and ψ_j have some common variable. In this case the constraint $\phi_{(i,j)} : \Sigma_0^2 \to \{0, 1\}$ is such that $\phi_{(i,j)}(\sigma, \tau) = 1$ if and only if $\psi_i(\sigma) = \psi_j(\tau) = 1$ and the values assigned to the common variable are identical. For example, if $\psi_i = x \vee y \vee z$ and $\psi_j = u \vee \neg x \vee \neg v$, then $\phi_{(i,j)}(\sigma, \tau) = 1$ if and only if $\sigma_1 \vee \sigma_2 \vee \sigma_3 = \tau_1 \vee \neg \tau_2 \vee \neg \tau_3 = T$ and $\sigma_1 = \tau_2$.

[56] Hence, for some fixed Σ and constant $c > 0$, the problem $\text{gapCSP}^{\Sigma}_{c}$ is NP-complete. As shown in Exercise 13.9, this cannot be the case if $|\Sigma| = 2$, unless $\mathcal{P} = \mathcal{NP}$.

[57] For $\Sigma = \{0, 1\}^{\ell}$, given a gapCSP^{Σ} instance (G, Φ), consider the PCP oracle $\pi : [n] \times [\ell] \to \{0, 1\}$, where n denotes the number of vertices in G. The verifier selects a random edge (u, v) in G, obtains $\sigma = \pi(u, 1) \cdots \pi(u, \ell)$ and $\tau = \pi(v, 1) \cdots \pi(v, \ell)$, and checks whether $\phi_{(u,v)}(\sigma, \tau) = 1$.

effect" (i.e., Items 1 and 2), while maintaining the alphabet Σ and allowing only a moderate increase in the size of the graph (i.e., Item 3). Waiving the latter requirements allows a relatively simple proof that mimics (an augmented version of) the "parallel repetition" of the corresponding PCP. Thus, the challenge is significantly decreasing the "size blow-up" that arises from parallel repetition and maintaining a fixed alphabet. The first goal (i.e., Item 3) calls for a suitable derandomization, and indeed we shall use a "pseudorandom" generator based on random walks on expander graphs. The second goal (i.e., fixed alphabet) can be handled by using the proof composition paradigm, which was outlined at the end of Section 13.3.2.2.

The lemma is proved by presenting a three-step reduction. The first step is a preprocessing step that makes the underlying graph suitable for further analysis (e.g., the resulting graph will be an expander). The value of vlt may decrease during this step by a constant factor. The heart of the reduction is the second step, in which we can increase vlt by any desired constant factor. This is done by a construction that corresponds to taking a random walk of constant length on the current graph. The latter step also increases the alphabet Σ, and thus a post-processing step is employed to regain the original alphabet (by using any inner PCP systems; e.g., the one presented in Section 13.3.1.2). Details follow.

We first stress that the aforementioned Σ and c, as well as the auxiliary parameters d and t (to be introduced in the following two paragraphs), are fixed constants that will be determined such that various conditions (which arise in the course of our argument) are satisfied. Specifically, t will be the last parameter to be determined (and it will be made greater than a constant that is determined by all the other parameters).

We start with the pre-processing step. Our aim in this step is to reduce the input (G, Φ) of gapCSP$^\Sigma$ to an instance (G_1, Φ_1) such that G_1 is a d-regular expander graph.[58] Furthermore, each vertex in G_1 will have at least $d/2$ self-loops, the number of edges will be preserved up to a constant factor (i.e., $|G_1| = O(|G|)$), and vlt$(G_1, \Phi_1) = \Theta(\text{vlt}(G, \Phi))$. This step is quite simple: essentially, the original vertices are replaced by expanders of size proportional to their degree, and a big (dummy) expander is "superimposed" on the resulting graph. (The constraints associated with the edges of the former expanders mandate equality, whereas the the constraints associated with the edges of the latter expander are trivial (i.e., require nothing).)

The main step is aimed at increasing the fraction of violated constraints by a sufficiently large constant factor. The intuition underlying this step is that the probability that a random (t-edge long) walk on the expander G_1 intersects a fixed set of edges is closely related to the probability that a random sample of (t) edges intersects this set. Thus, we may expect such walks to hit a violated edge with probability that is at least $\min(\Theta(t \cdot v), c)$, where v is the fraction of violated edges. Indeed, the current step consists of reducing the instance (G_1, Φ_1) of gapCSP$^\Sigma$ to an instance (G_2, Φ_2) of gapCSP$^{\Sigma'}$ such that the edges of G_2 correspond to t-step walks on G_1 and $\Sigma' = \Sigma^{d^t}$ (equiv., $\Sigma' = \{f : [d]^t \to \Sigma\}$). Specifically, G_2 and Φ_2 are defined as follows.

1. The vertex set of G_2 is identical to the vertex set of G_1, and each t-edge long path in G_1 is replaced by a corresponding edge in G_2, which is thus a d^t-regular graph.

---

[58] A graph is d-regular if each of its vertices has exactly d incident edges. Loosely speaking, an expander graph has the property that each cut (i.e., partition of its vertex set) has relatively many edges crossing it. An equivalent definition, also used in the actual analysis, is that all the eigenvalues of the corresponding adjacency matrix, except for the largest one (which equals d), have an absolute value that is bounded away from d.

Since there are self-loops on each vertex in G_1, each two vertices that are at distance $t' \leq t$ in G_1 are connected by an edge in G_2 (which corresponds to a t-step walk that takes t' real steps, and remains in place in $t - t'$ steps).

2. The constraints in Φ_2 treat each element of Σ' as a Σ-labeling of the ("distance $\leq t$") neighborhood of a vertex (i.e., the label $\alpha'_v \in \Sigma'$ of vertex v is viewed as a function from the t-neighborhood of v to Σ). Each constraint mandates that the two corresponding labelings (of the endpoints of the G_2-edge) are consistent as well as satisfy Φ_1. That is, the following two types of conditions are enforced by the constraints of Φ_2:

(consistency): If vertices u and w are connected in G_1 by a path of length at most t and vertex v resides on this path, then the Φ_2-constraint associated with the G_2-edge between u and w mandates the equality of the entries corresponding to vertex v in the Σ'-labeling of vertices u and w (i.e., $\alpha'_u(v) = \alpha'_w(v)$, where $\alpha'_x : [d]^t \to \Sigma$ is the Σ'-label of vertex x).

(satisfying Φ_1): If the G_1-edge (v, v') is on a path of length at most t starting at u, then the Φ_2-constraint associated with the G_2-edge that corresponds to this path enforces the Φ_1-constraint that is associated with (v, v').

Clearly, $|G_2| = d^{t-1} \cdot |G_1| = O(|G_1|)$, because d is a constant and t will be set to a constant. (Indeed, the relatively moderate increase in the size of the graph corresponds to the low randomness complexity of selecting a random walk of length t in G_1.)

Turning to the analysis of this step, we note that $\text{vlt}(G_1, \Phi_1) = 0$ implies $\text{vlt}(G_2, \Phi_2) = 0$. The interesting fact is that the fraction of violated constraints increases by a factor of $\Omega(\sqrt{t})$; that is, $\text{vlt}(G_2, \Phi_2) \geq \min(\Omega(\sqrt{t} \cdot \text{vlt}(G_1, \Phi_1)), c)$. Here we merely provide a rough intuition and refer the interested reader to [92]. We may focus on any Σ'-labeling of the vertices of G_2 that is consistent with some Σ-labeling of G_1, because relatively few inconsistencies (among the Σ-values assigned to a vertex by the Σ'-labeling of other vertices) can be ignored, while relatively many such inconsistencies yield violation of the "consistency constraints" of many edges in G_2. Intuitively, relying on the hypothesis that G_1 is an expander, it follows that the set of violated edge-constraints (of Φ_1) with respect to the aforementioned Σ-labeling causes many more edge-constraints of Φ_2 to be violated (because each edge-constraint of Φ_1 is enforced by many edge-constraints of Φ_2). The point is that *any set F of edges of G_1 is likely to appear on a $\min(\Omega(1) \cdot |F|/|G_1|, \Omega(1))$ fraction of the edges of G_2* (i.e., t-paths of G_1). (Note that the claim would have been obvious if G_1 were a complete graph, but it also holds for an expander.)[59]

The factor of $\Omega(\sqrt{t})$ gained in the second step makes up for the constant factor lost in the first step (as well as the constant factor to be lost in the last step). Furthermore, for a suitable choice of the constant t, the aforementioned gain yields an overall constant factor amplification (of vlt). Note, however, that so far we obtained an instance of $\text{gapCSP}^{\Sigma'}$ rather than an instance of gapCSP^{Σ}, where $\Sigma' = \Sigma^{d^t}$. The purpose of the last step is to reduce the latter instance to an instance of gapCSP^{Σ}. This is done by viewing the instance of $\text{gapCSP}^{\Sigma'}$ as a PCP-system,[60] and composing it with an inner-verifier using the proof composition paradigm outlined in Section 13.3.2.2. We stress

---

[59] We mention that, because of a technical difficulty, it is easier to establish the claimed bound of $\Omega(\sqrt{t} \cdot \text{vlt}(G_1, \Phi_1))$ rather than $\Omega(t \cdot \text{vlt}(G_1, \Phi_1))$.

[60] The PCP-system referred to here has arbitrary soundness error (i.e., it rejects the instance (G_2, Φ_2) with probability $\text{vlt}(G_2, \Phi_2) \in [0, 1]$).

that the inner-verifier used here needs handle only instances of constant size (i.e., having description length $O(d^t \log |\Sigma|)$), and so the verifier presented in Section 13.3.1.2 will do. The resulting PCP system uses randomness $r \overset{\text{def}}{=} \log_2 |G_2| + O(d^t \log |\Sigma|)^2$ and a constant number of binary queries, and has rejection probability $\Omega(\text{vlt}(G_2, \Phi_2))$, *where the constant in the Ω-notation is independent of the choice of the constant t.* Moving back to the world of gapCSP, for $\Sigma = \{0, 1\}^{O(1)}$, we can obtain an instance of gapCSP$^\Sigma$ that has a $\Omega(\text{vlt}(G_2, \Phi_2))$ fraction of violated constraints. Furthermore, the size of the resulting instance (which is used as the output (G', Φ') of the three-step reduction) is $O(2^r) = O(|G_2|)$, where the equality uses the fact that d and t are constants. Recalling that $\text{vlt}(G_2, \Phi_2) \geq \min(\Omega(\sqrt{t} \cdot \text{vlt}(G_1, \Phi_1)), c)$ and $\text{vlt}(G_1, \Phi_1) = \Omega(\text{vlt}(G, \Phi))$, this completes the (outline of the) proof of the entire lemma. ∎

Reflection. In contrast to the proof outlined in Section 13.3.2.2, which combines *two remarkable constructs* by using a *simple composition method*, the current proof of the PCP Theorem is based on a *powerful amplification method* that improves the quality of the single system to which it is applied. The amplification method, captured by Lemma 13.14, improves the quality of the system in a moderate manner, and so it is applied iteratively many times. Hence, remarkable results are obtained by a gradual process of many moderate amplification steps. (In contrast, the composition applied in Section 13.3.2.2, does not improve the quality of the systems to which it is applied but rather inherits the best aspects of the two systems (i.e., it inherits the randomness complexity of the "outer" system and the query complexity of the "inner" system).)

13.4. Chapter Notes

The term "locally testable proof" was introduced in [130] with the intention of matching the term "locally testable codes." As stated at the end of Section 13.2.2, the term "locally testable proofs" seems more fitting than the standard term "probabilistically checkable proofs" (abbreviated PCPs), because it stresses the positive aspect (of locality) rather than the negative aspect (of being probabilistic). The latter perspective has been frequently advocated by Leonid Levin.

13.4.1. Historical Notes

The celebrated story of the PCP Theorem is well known; still we provide a brief overview of this story and refer the interested reader to the account in [127, Sec. 2.6.2] (partially reproduced in the chapter notes of [131, Chap. 9]).

The *PCP model* was suggested by Fortnow, Rompel, and Sipser [118] as a model capturing the power of the (related) model of multiprover interactive proofs, which was introduced by Ben-Or, Goldwasser, Kilian, and Wigderson [43] as a generalization of the model of interactive proofs (introduced by Goldwasser, Micali, and Rackoff [161]).

The *PCP Theorem* itself is a culmination of a sequence of works, starting with Babai, Fortnow, and Lund [29], who showed that (unrestricted) PCPs (which are merely restricted by the verification time) captured the class $\mathcal{NEXP}$, continuing with the different "scale downs"[61] of that result to the polylogarithmic query complexity level (by

---

[61] The term "scale down" is meant to capture the conceptual contents of moving from $\mathcal{NEXP}$ to $\mathcal{NP}$. It is certainly not meant to diminish the impressive technical achievement involved.

Babai, Fortnow, Levin and Szegedy [28] and Feige, Goldwasser, Lovász, Safra and Szegedy [107]), and culminating with the PCP characterizations of $\mathcal{NP}$ (by Arora and Safra [25] and Arora, Lund, Motwani, Sudan and Szegedy [24]). These developments were inspired by the discovery of the power of interactive proof systems and made use of techniques developed towards this end (by Lund, Fortnow, Karloff, Nisan, and Shamir [202, 253]). The alternative proof of the PCP Theorem was found by Dinur [92] more than a decade later.

The model of *PCPs of Proximity* was introduced by Ben-Sasson, Goldreich, Harsha, Sudan and Vadhan [44], and is almost identical to the notion of Assignment Testers introduced independently by Dinur and Reingold [94].[62] We believe that the proof composition paradigm (of [25]) becomes much more clear when explicitly referring to the inner verifiers as PCPs of Proximity (and to the outer verifiers as being robust). In retrospect, the work of [28] should be viewed as a PCP of Proximity of polylogarithmic verification time for statements that are encoded using a specific error correction code.

There is a fair amount of confusion regarding credits for the introduction of the notion of *locally testable codes* (LTCs). This definition (or at least a related notion)[63] is arguably implicit in [28] as well as in subsequent works on PCP. However, as discussed in Section 13.2.4, these implicit definitions do not differentiate between the actual notion and related ones (see, e.g., footnote 63). The definition of locally testable codes has appeared independently in the works of Friedl and Sudan [120] and Rubinfeld and Sudan [246] as well as in the PhD thesis of Arora [23]. The distinction between the weak and strong notions (see Definition 13.7) is due to Goldreich and Sudan [157], who initiated a systematic study of these notions.

As stated in footnote 39, our presentation reverses the historical order in which the corresponding results (for codes and proofs) were achieved. That is, the constructions of locally testable proofs of polynomial length, captured in the PCP Theorem [25, 24], predated the coding counterparts.

13.4.2. On Obtaining Superfast testers

Our motivation for studying locally testable codes and proofs referred to superfast testing, but our actual definitions have focused on the query complexity of these testers. While the query complexity of testing has a natural appeal, the hope is that low query complexity testers would also yield superfast testing. Indeed, in the case of codes, it is typically the case that the testing time is related to the query complexity. However, in the case of proofs there is a seemingly unavoidable (linear) dependence of the verification time on the input length. This (linear) dependence can be avoided if one considers PCP of Proximity (see Section 13.2.3.3) rather than standard PCP. But even in this case, additional work is needed in order to derive testers that work in sublinear time. The interested reader is referred to [45, 205].

---

[62] Both notions are (important) special cases of the general definition of a "PCP spot-checker" formulated before by Ergün *et al.* [102].

[63] The related notion refers to the following relaxed notion of codeword testing: For two fixed good codes $C_1 \subseteq C_2 \subset \{0, 1\}^n$, one has to accept (with high probability) every codeword of C_1, but reject (with high probability) every string that is far from being a codeword of C_2. Indeed, our definitions refer to the special (natural) case that $C_2 = C_1$, but the more general case suffices for the construction of PCPs (and is implicitly achieved in most of them). See further discussion in [157, Sec. 5.2].

13.4.3. The Alternative Regime: LTCs of Linear Length

It is quite conceivable that there is a trade-off between the level of locality (i.e., number of queries) and length of the object being tester (i.e., code or proof). At least, the currently known results exhibit such a trade-off.

As stated previously, we have focused on one extreme of the query-versus-length trade-off: We have insisted on a constant number of queries and sought to minimize the length of the code (or proof). The opposite extreme is to insist on codes (or proofs) of linear length, and to seek to minimize the number of queries. In the case of codes, the state of the art in this regime was set by Kopparty, Meir, Ron-Zewi, and Saraf [191, 192], who obtained codes of optimal rate (with respect to their distance) that can be tested using quasi-polylogarithmically number of queries. Specifically, for any constant $\delta, \eta > 0$ and a sufficiently large finite set Σ, they obtain codes from Σ^k to Σ^n, where $k = (1 - \delta - \eta) \cdot n$, that have relative distance δ and can be tested using $(\log k)^{O(\log \log k)}$ queries. We briefly review their ideas next.[64]

A Warm-up: The Prior State-of-the-Art. For every constant $c > 0$, a folklore construction, which may be traced to [28], achieves a code of constant rate (i.e., $n = O(k)$) that can be tested using k^c queries. For any constant $m \in \mathbb{N}$, the construction identifies $[k]$ with H^m, and uses a finite field $\mathcal{F}$ of size $O(|H|)$. The code maps m-variate functions $f : H^m \to \{0, 1\}$ to their low-degree extension; that is, f is mapped to the polynomial $p : \mathcal{F}^m \to \mathcal{F}$ of individual degree $|H| - 1$ that agrees with f on H^m. This code has relative distance $1 - \frac{m \cdot (|H|-1)}{|\mathcal{F}|} > \frac{1}{2}$, rate $(|H|/|\mathcal{F}|)^m = \exp(-O(m))$, and it can be checked by inspecting the values of the purported codeword $w : \mathcal{F}^m \to \mathcal{F}$ on $O(m)$ random axis-parallel lines, which means making $O(m) \cdot |\mathcal{F}| = O(m) \cdot k^{1/m}$ queries. (A binary code can be obtained by encoding the symbols of $\mathcal{F}$ via a good binary error-correcting code.)

Note that we can use the foregoing construction with $m = 1$ and $|\mathcal{F}| = (1 + \eta(k)) \cdot k$, for a vanishing function η (e.g., $\eta(k) = 1/\sqrt{k}$). In this case, we obtain a code with very low relative distance (i.e., the relative distance is $\eta(k)/(1 + \eta(k)) \approx \eta(k)$) such that testing is performed by reading the entire purported codeword. Still, such simple codes (which have very poor distance but very high rate) will be an ingredient in the following construction. A crucial tool that allows their usage is distance amplification, which is actually the pivot of the entire construction.

Distance Amplification. Our aim here is to amplify the relative distance of locally testable codes while preserving their local testability. Specifically, starting with a code of relative distance δ, we can obtain a code of any desired relative distance $\delta' \in (0, 1)$, while increasing the query complexity (of codeword testing) by a factor of $\text{poly}(1/\delta)$, and decreasing the rate by only a factor of $1 - \delta' - o(\delta')$. (We shall be using $\delta' = \sqrt{\delta}$ for a small δ.) Denoting the initial code by $C : \Sigma^\ell \to \Sigma^{s \cdot m}$, where $s = (1 - \delta' - o(\delta')) \cdot t$ and $t = \text{poly}(1/\delta)$, we derive a code $C' : \Sigma^\ell \to \Gamma^m$, where $\Gamma \equiv \Sigma^t$, as follows. Toward this end, we shall use an auxiliary encoding $E : \Sigma^s \to \Sigma^t$ (of rate $1 - \delta' - o(\delta')$ and relative distance $\delta' + o(\delta')$) and a permutation $\pi : [m \cdot t] \to [m \cdot t]$, The codeword $C'(x)$

---

[64] Our presentation uses extracts from [192, Sec. 1.2], and we thank the authors for permission to use these extracts. We omit the credits for various ingredients of the construction, and refer the interested reader to [192, Sec. 1.2].

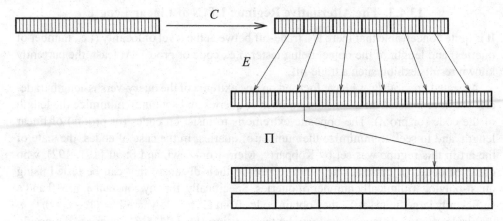

Figure 13.3: Distance amplification for a code $C : \Sigma^{40} \to \Sigma^{48}$, when using the encoding $E : \Sigma^8 \to \Sigma^{12}$, and a random permuation $\pi : [72] \to [72]$, yields a code $C' : \Sigma^{40} \to \Gamma^6$.

is obtained by partitioning $C(x)$ into m equal-length blocks, denoted $y_1, y_2, \ldots, y_m \in \Sigma^s$, encoding each block via E, permuting the resulting $m \cdot t$-long sequence $E(y_1) \cdot E(y_2) \cdots E(y_m) \in (\Sigma^t)^m$ according to π, and viewing each block of t consecutive Σ-symbols (in the result) as a symbol of Γ (see Figure 13.3). That is, the ith symbol of $C'(x)$ equal the t-tuple

$$((E(y_1) \cdot E(y_2) \cdots E(y_m))_{\pi((i-1)\cdot t+1)}, \ldots, (E(y_1) \cdot E(y_2) \cdots E(y_m))_{\pi(i\cdot t)}) \quad (13.10)$$

where $y_1 \cdot y_2 \cdots y_m = C(x)$ such that $|y_1| = \cdots = |y_m| = s$.

If π is "sufficiently random" (e.g., the permutation defined by the edge-set of a t-regular m-vertex expander will do)[65], then this construction amplifies distances (see next) although the alphabet size is increased (which is an issue that we already dealt with in other parts of this chapter).[66] To see why the distance is increased by Eq. (13.10), consider any $x \neq x'$. Recall that the $(s \cdot m$-long) codewords $y_1 \cdots y_m = C(x)$ and $y'_1 \cdots y'_m = C(x')$, where $y_1, \ldots, y_m, y'_1, \ldots, y'_m \in \Sigma^s$, are at relative distance at least δ, which implies that $|\{i \in [m] : y_i \neq y'_i\}| \geq \delta m$, whereas the encoding E maps blocks of different values (i.e., $y_i \neq y'_i$) to blocks (i.e., $E(y_i)$ and $E(y'_i)$) that are at relative distance at least $\delta' + o(\delta')$. The key observation is that for a sufficiently large t (i.e., $t = \text{poly}(1/\delta)$), the permutation π "distributes" any $(\delta' + o(\delta')) \cdot t$ symbols of any δm blocks among at least $\delta' m$ blocks (see footnote 65), which yields the claimed relative distance of δ'. Testing the codewords of C' is done by checking the validity of the E-encodings of the Σ-blocks and emulating ($O(t)$ executions of) the codeword tester of C, where in both cases we need to retrieve the encoded Σ-blocks from the locations to which they were mapped by π. (Recall that the

[65] Specifically, we consider the permutation that maps $(u, i) \in [m] \times [t] \equiv [mt]$ to (v, j) if $\{u, v\}$ is both the ith edge incident at u and the jth edge incident at v. We shall use the fact that in the underlying t-regular m-vertex expander, for each set S of $\delta' m$ vertices, at most δm vertices have at least $(\delta' + o(\delta'))t$ neighbors in S.

[66] Such an alphabet reduction involves using another auxiliary encoding of the form $E' : \Sigma^t \to \Sigma^{t/(1-\delta')}$, which means that it decreases the distance by a factor of δ'. Hence, wishing to obtain a relative distance of δ'', we actually use $\delta' = \sqrt{\delta''}$, which means that we decrease the rate by a factor of $(1 - \sqrt{\delta''})^2$. We comment that the actual parameter setting in [192] is different, since additional slackness has to be created in order to handle complications that arise from the use of tensor codes.

encoding of each symbol of the C-codeword is distributed among up to t symbols of the C'-codeword.)[67]

The Iterative Construction. With these preliminaries in place, we turn to the heart of the construction (of [192]), which is an iterative process. The process starts with a code of very small length, which can be tested simply by reading the entire purported codeword. Then, the length is increased iteratively, while the rate, relative distance, and query complexity (of codeword testing) are not harmed too much. Specifically, when wishing to obtain a code with length n, we start with a code of length $\text{poly}(\log n)$, rate $1 - (1/\text{poly}(\log n))$, and relative distance $1/\text{poly}(\log n)$. In each iteration (to be described next), the length and the rate are (roughly) squared, the relative distance is maintained, and the query complexity is increased by a factor of $\text{poly}(\log n)$. Thus, after approximately $\log \log n$ iterations, we obtain a code of length n, constant rate (since $(1 - (1/\text{poly}(\log n)))^{2^{\log \log n}} = 1 - o(1)$), relative distance $1/\text{poly}(\log n)$, and query complexity $(\log n)^{O(\log \log n)}$. Using the foregoing distance-amplification (which is also used inside the iterative process), this gives a code of high rate with constant relative distance and query complexity $(\log n)^{O(\log \log n)}$, as asserted upfront.

A Single Iteration. Suppose that iteration i begins with a code C_i that has length n_i, rate r_i, relative distance δ_i, and query complexity q_i. The iteration consists of two steps.

- *Tensor product*: First, we take the tensor product of C_i, denoted C_i^2, where the tensor product of C_i consists of all $n_i \times n_i$ matrices such that each of the rows and columns of the matrix is a codeword of C_i. The code C_i^2 has length n_i^2, rate r_i^2, and relative distance δ_i^2. Using additional features of the code C_i, which are preserved in the iterations, one can show that C_i^2 is testable with query complexity $q_i \cdot \text{poly}(1/\delta_i)$.
- *Distance amplification*: Next, we apply the foregoing distance-amplification to the code C_i^2, and amplify the relative distance from δ_i^2 to δ_i. The resulting code, denoted C_{i+1}, has length $n_{i+1} = O(n_i^2)$, relative distance $\delta_{i+1} = \delta_i = \delta_1$, rate $r_{i+1} = (1 - \delta_1) \cdot r_i^2 = (1 - \delta_1)^{2^i - 1} \cdot r_1^{2^i}$, and query complexity $q_{i+1} = q_i \cdot \text{poly}(1/\delta_1) = \text{poly}(1/\delta_1)^i \cdot q_1$.

Indeed, a crucial detail that we refrained from addressing is the testing of the tensor code. The interested reader is referred to [192].

13.4.4. Locally Decodable Codes

Locally *decodable* codes are in some sense complimentary to local *testable* codes. Here, one is given a slightly corrupted codeword (i.e., a string close to some unique codeword), and is required to recover individual bits of the encoded information based on a constant number of probes (per recovered bit).[68] That is, a code is said to be locally decodable if whenever relatively few location are corrupted, the decoder is able to recover each information-bit, with high probability, based on a constant number of probes to the (corrupted) codeword.

---

[67] The ith symbol of C' contains a part of the encoding of the pth block of C if there exists $j, q \in [t]$ such that $\pi((i-1) \cdot t + j) = (p-1) \cdot t + q$.

[68] The aim in this case is to minimize the length of the code. A dual regime refers to allowing only linear length codes and minimizing the query complexity (cf. [191]).

The best known locally decodable codes are of strictly subexponential length. Specifically, k information bits can be encoded by codewords of length $n = \exp(k^{o(1)})$ that are locally decodable using three bit-probes (cf. [100], building on [274]). It is also known that locally testable codes cannot be T2-nearly linear: Recovery based on q queries requires length at least $k^{1+(2/(q-1))}$ (cf. [179, 185]). Indeed, the gap between the known upper and lower bounds is huge. (We mention that locally decodable codes are related to schemes of (information theoretic) Private Information Retrieval, introduced in [79].)

A natural relaxation of the definition of locally decodable codes requires that, whenever few location are corrupted, the decoder should be able to recover most of the individual information bits (based on a constant number of queries), and for the rest of the locations the decoder may output a special failure symbol (but not the wrong value). That is, the decoder must still avoid errors (with high probability), but on a few bit locations it is allowed to say "don't know." This relaxed notion of local decodability can be supported by codes that have length $\ell(k) = k^c$ for any constant $c > 1$ (cf. [44, Sec. 4.2]).[69]

An obvious open problem is to separate locally decodable codes from relaxed locally decodable codes (or to refute this conjectured separation). This separation may follow if one establishes a $k^{1+\ell(q)}$ lower bound on the length of q-query locally decodable codes and a $k^{i+u(k)}$ upper bound on the length of the relaxed counterparts such that $\ell(q) > u(q)$, but currently we have $\ell(q) = 2/(q-1)$ and $u(q) = O(1/\sqrt{q})$. A more ambitious goal is to determine whether there exist locally decodable codes of polynomial length.

13.4.5. Exercises

Exercise 13.1 (ϵ-testing a code of relative distance 0.99ϵ): Show that, for every $\epsilon \in (0, 0.001)$, there exists a code of relative distance 0.99ϵ and constant rate that can be ϵ-tested with $O(1/\epsilon)$ queries.

> **Guideline:** We start with any code $C_0 \subset \{0, 1\}^n$ of constant rate, distance $d = 0.499n$ and covering radius smaller than d. (Such a code can be obtained by iteratively adding to the code any n-bit string that is (d/n)-far from the current code.) Now, for $m = 1.001d/\epsilon$, consider the code $C(x) = C_0(x) \cdot 0^m$, and note that C has relative distance greater than $d/(n + m) > 0.99\epsilon$ whereas any string that is ϵ-far from C contains at least $\epsilon \cdot (n + m) - d = \Omega(\epsilon m)$ nonzeros in its m-bit long suffix. Hence, codewords can be ϵ-tested by merely checking if this suffix is the all-zero string, and the claim follows.

Exercise 13.2 (On the weak version of Definition 13.7): Suppose that $\mathcal{C} = \{C_k : \{0, 1\}^k \to \{0, 1\}^{n(k)}\}_{k \in K}$ is locally testable in the *(weaker)* sense of Section 13.2.3.1; that is, for every constant $\epsilon > 0$ and all sufficiently large k, the tester accepts C_k and rejects strings that are ϵ-far from C_k. Show that, for some $q' : (0, 1] \to \mathbb{N}$, the code $\mathcal{C}$ is universally q'-locally testable (per the weak version of Definition 13.7).

> **Guideline:** For each $\epsilon > 0$, let k_ϵ be such that for every $k \geq k_\epsilon$ the tester accepts C_k and rejects strings that are ϵ-far from C_k. Consider a tester that on input parameters (k, ϵ), determines k_ϵ, activates the original tester if $k \geq k_\epsilon$, and reads the entire input-oracle otherwise. This yields $q'(\epsilon) = \max(q(\epsilon), k_\epsilon)$.

---

[69] That is, relaxed locally decodable codes of T1-nearly linear length are known [44]. In contrast, by [179], there exist no (nonrelaxed) locally decodable codes of T2-nearly linear length.

Exercise 13.3 (Obtaining a PCP from a PCP of Proximity for a corresponding set of codewords): For constant $\epsilon > 0$ and $\rho : \mathbb{N} \to \mathbb{N}$, suppose that C is an efficiently computable code of relative distance greater than $\epsilon > 0$ and rate ρ, and that V is a PCP of Proximity for $T \stackrel{\text{def}}{=} \{C(x) : x \in S\}$ with proximity parameter ϵ, query complexity q and proof complexity p. Present a PCP for S with query complexity $q'(n) = q(n/\rho(n))$ and proof complexity $p'(n) = p(n/\rho(n))$.

> **Guideline:** On input x and access to an alleged proof π, the verifier computes $w = C(x)$, and invokes $V^{w,\pi}(1^{|w|})$; that is, the verifier emulates queries to w by itself and answers queries to π by querying its own oracle. The point is that if $x \notin S$, then $C(x)$ is ϵ-far from T.

Exercise 13.4 (From PCP of Proximity to a locally testable code): Let $\mathcal{C}_0 : \{0, 1\}^k \to \{0, 1\}^n$ be an efficiently computable code of constant rate. Suppose that V is a PCP of Proximity for the set of all $\mathcal{C}_0$-codewords with proximity parameter ϵ, query complexity q, and proof complexity p. Construct a q-locally 3ϵ-testable code of length $O(p(n)/\epsilon)$ and relative distance that approximately equals that of $\mathcal{C}_0$. Show that the weak version of Definition 13.7 can be met, by using $\epsilon = \epsilon(k)$ that tends to zero with k.

> **Guideline:** Let $C(x) = \mathcal{C}_0(x)^t \pi(x)$, where $\pi(x)$ is the (canonical) proof that $\mathcal{C}_0(x)$ is a codeword of $\mathcal{C}_0$, and $t = O(\epsilon^{-1}|\pi(x)|/|\mathcal{C}_0(x)|)$. On input $w^{(1)} \cdots w^{(t)} \pi$, the 3ϵ-tester for C checks that $w^{(1)} \cdots w^{(t)}$ consists of t repetitions of the n-bit string $w^{(1)}$, and invokes V while providing it access to $w^{(1)}$ (as main input) and to π (as an alleged proof). The key observation is that if $w^{(1)} \cdots w^{(t)} \pi$ is 3ϵ-far from C, then $w^{(1)} \cdots w^{(t)}$ is 2ϵ-far from C_0^t. Hence, either $w^{(1)} \cdots w^{(t)}$ is ϵ-far from $w^{(1)} \cdots w^{(1)}$ or $w^{(1)}$ is ϵ-far from $\mathcal{C}_0$. Finally, note that using $\epsilon = \epsilon(k) = o(1)$ requires using a PCP of Proximity that works with this value of the proximity parameter, and constructing a code of length that is inversely proportional to $\epsilon(k)$. (We mention that such PCP of Proximity that have query complexity $\text{poly}(1/\epsilon(k))$ are known.)

Exercise 13.5 (Interactive proofs yield PCPs): Suppose that S has an interactive proof system in which the prover sends b bits. Show that S has a PCP of query complexity b.

> **Guideline:** The queries correspond to possible partial transcripts of the interaction of the verifier with the prover.

Exercise 13.6 (Satisfiability of quadratic systems over GF(2)): Prove that the following problem is NP-complete. An instance of the problem consists of a system of quadratic equations over GF(2), and the problem is to determine whether there exists an assignment that satisfies all the equations.

> **Guideline:** Start by showing that the corresponding problem for cubic equations is NP-complete, by a reduction from 3SAT that maps the clause $x \vee \neg y \vee z$ to the equation $(1 - x) \cdot y \cdot (1 - z) = 0$. Reduce the problem for cubic equations to the problem for quadratic equations by introducing auxiliary variables; that is, given an instance with variables $x_1, \ldots, x_n$, introduce the auxiliary variables $x_{i,j}$'s and add equations of the form $x_{i,j} = x_i \cdot x_j$.

Exercise 13.7 (On testing equality of matrices): Prove that for Boolean n-by-n matrices $A \neq B$, when $r, s \in \text{GF}(2)^n$ are uniformly selected vectors, it holds that $\mathbf{Pr}_s[As = Bs] = 2^{-\text{rank}(A-B)}$ and it follows that $\mathbf{Pr}_{r,s}[rAs = rBs] \leq 3/4$.

Guideline: The second assertion follows from the first one by observing that if $(u_1, \ldots, u_n) \neq (v_1, \ldots, v_n) \in GF(2)^n$, then $\mathbf{Pr}_r[\sum_i r_i u_i = \sum_i r_i v_i] = 1/2$, when $r = (r_1, \ldots, r_n)$ is uniformly distributed in $GF(2)^n$. The first assertion is proved by a generalization of the latter argument.[70]

Exercise 13.8 (A trivial PCP with large soundness error): Present a three-query PCP of logarithmic radomness complexity and soundness error $1 - (1/m)$ for 3SAT, where m denotes the number of clauses.

Guideline: View the proof-oracle as a truth assignment to the input formula.

Exercise 13.9 (On the complexity of $gapCSP_c^{\{0,1\}}$): Show that for every function $\tau : \mathbb{N} \to (0, 1]$, the problem $gapCSP_\tau^{\{0,1\}}$ is solvable in polynomial time.

Guideline: Reduce solving $gapCSP_\tau^{\{0,1\}}$ to deciding the satisfiability of 2CNF formulae.

---

[70] To analyze $\mathbf{Pr}_r[\sum_i r_i u_i = \sum_i r_i v_i] = 1/2$, consider $(w_1, \ldots, w_n) = (u_1, \ldots, u_n) - (v_1, \ldots, v_n)$, and show that $\mathbf{Pr}_r[\sum_i r_i w_i = 0] = 1/2$, by observing that $\sum_{i \in [n]} r_i w_i = \sum_{i : w_i = 1} r_i$. Similarly, prove that $\mathbf{Pr}_s[Ds = 0] = 2^{-\mathrm{rank}(D)}$, by showing that for any full rank k-by-k submatrix D' and any $v' \in GF(2)^k$ it holds that $\mathbf{Pr}_{s'}[D's' = v'] = 2^{-k}$.

Probabilistic Preliminaries

Summary: This appendix presents background from probability theory, which is used extensively throughout the book. This background and preliminaries include conventions regarding random variables, basic notions and facts, and three useful probabilistic inequalities (i.e., Markov's Inequality, Chebyshev's Inequality, and Chernoff Bound).

A.1. Notational Conventions

We assume that the reader is familiar with the basic notions of probability theory. In this section, we merely present the probabilistic notations that are used throughout the book.

Throughout the entire text we refer only to *discrete* probability distributions. Actually, we shall typically consider finite probability distributions (i.e., distributions supported by a finite probability space). Specifically, the underlying probability space consists of the set of all strings of a certain length ℓ, taken with uniform probability distribution. That is, the sample space is the set of all ℓ-bit long strings, and each such string is assigned probability measure $2^{-\ell}$. Traditionally, *random variables* are defined as functions from the sample space to the reals. Abusing the traditional terminology, we use the term random variable also when referring to functions mapping the sample space into the set of binary strings. One important case of such a random variable is the output of a randomized process (e.g., a probabilistic oracle machine).

We often do not specify the probability space, but rather talk directly about some random variables. For example, we may say that X is a 0-1 random variable such that $\Pr[X = 0] = \frac{1}{4}$ and $\Pr[X = 1] = \frac{3}{4}$, without specifying the underlying probability space. (Indeed, this random variable may be defined over the sample space $\{0, 1\}^2$, such that $X(11) = 0$ and $X(00) = X(01) = X(10) = 1$.)

Many probabilistic statements refer to random variables that are defined beforehand. Typically, we may write $\Pr[\chi(X)]$, where X is a random variable defined beforehand and χ is a predicate (e.g., we may write $\Pr[f(X) = v]$, when $f : \mathbb{R} \to \mathbb{R}$ is a function and $v \in \mathbb{R}$). In other cases, we may write $\Pr_{x \sim D}[\chi(x)]$, meaning that x is drawn according to a predetermined distribution D. In case D is the uniform distribution over some finite set S, we may write $\Pr_{x \in S}[\chi(x)]$ instead of $\Pr_{x \sim D}[\chi(x)]$.

A.2. Some Basic Notions and Facts

We shall often use the following notions and facts.

Union Bound. An obvious fact regarding finite sets is that the size of their union is upper-bounded by the sum of their sizes; that is, if $S_1, \ldots, S_t$ are finite sets, then $|\cup_{i \in [t]} S_i| \le \sum_{i \in [t]} |S_i|$. It follows that

$$\mathbf{Pr}_{r \in U} \left[r \in \cup_{i \in [t]} S_i \right] \le \sum_{i \in [t]} \mathbf{Pr}_{r \in U} [r \in S_i],$$

where $S_1, \ldots, S_t \subseteq U$. Recalling that events over a probability space are merely subsets of that space, and considering the events $E_1, \ldots, E_t$, it holds that $\mathbf{Pr}[\vee_{i \in [t]} E_i] \le \sum_{i \in [t]} \mathbf{Pr}[E_i]$.

Independent Random Variables. A sequence of random variables, $X_1, \ldots, X_n$, is called independent if for every $x_1, \ldots, x_n$ it holds that

$$\mathbf{Pr}\left[(X_1, \ldots, X_n) = (x_1, \ldots, x_n)\right] = \prod_{i \in [n]} \mathbf{Pr}[X_i = x_i].$$

This is often written in terms of conditional probabilities; namely, by writing $\mathbf{Pr}[X_{i+1} = x_{i+1} | (X_1, \ldots, X_i) = (x_1, \ldots, x_i)] = \mathbf{Pr}[X_{i+1} = x_{i+1}]$ (for all $i \in [n-1]$), which implies that $\mathbf{Pr}[(X_1, \ldots, X_i) = (x_1, \ldots, x_i) | X_{i+1} = x_{i+1}] = \mathbf{Pr}[(X_1, \ldots, X_i) = (x_1, \ldots, x_i)]$. The latter assertion is based on Bayes' Law, which asserts that, for any two events A and B, it holds that

$$\mathbf{Pr}[A|B] = \frac{\mathbf{Pr}[B|A] \cdot \mathbf{Pr}[A]}{\mathbf{Pr}[B]}$$

(which holds since both sides equal $\frac{\mathbf{Pr}[A\&B]}{\mathbf{Pr}[B]}$).

Statistical Difference. The statistical distance (a.k.a. variation distance) between the random variables X and Y is defined as

$$\frac{1}{2} \cdot \sum_v |\mathbf{Pr}[X = v] - \mathbf{Pr}[Y = v]| = \max_S \{\mathbf{Pr}[X \in S] - \mathbf{Pr}[Y \in S]\}. \tag{A.1}$$

(The equality can be verified by considering the set $S = \{v : \mathbf{Pr}[X = v] > \mathbf{Pr}[Y = v]\}$.) We say that X is δ-close to Y (resp., δ-far from Y) if the statistical distance between A and Y is at most (resp., greater than) δ. A useful fact is that statistical distance may only decrease when the same function (or even the same random process) is applied to both random variables.

Claim A.1 (Statistical distance is non-increasing): *Let X and Y be random variables, and A be an arbitrary randomized algorithm. Then, the statistical distance between $A(X)$ and $A(Y)$ is upper-bounded by the statistical distance between X and Y.*

Proof: We first prove the claim for a deterministic algorithm or rather any function, denoted f. In that case

$$\sum_v |\mathbf{Pr}[f(X) = v] - \mathbf{Pr}[f(Y) = v]| = \sum_v \left| \sum_{z \in f^{-1}(v)} \mathbf{Pr}[X = z] - \sum_{z \in f^{-1}(v)} \mathbf{Pr}[Y = z] \right|$$

$$\leq \sum_v \sum_{z \in f^{-1}(v)} |\mathbf{Pr}[X = z] - \mathbf{Pr}[Y = z]|$$

$$= \sum_z |\mathbf{Pr}[X = z] - \mathbf{Pr}[Y = z]| \, .$$

We next observe that the statistical distance is preserved when appending an *independent* random variable to a given pair of random variables; that is, *let Z be a random variable independent of both X and Y, then*

$$\sum_{v,w} |\mathbf{Pr}[(X, Z) = (v, w)] - \mathbf{Pr}[(Y, Z) = (v, w)]|$$

$$= \sum_{v,w} |\mathbf{Pr}[X = v] \cdot \mathbf{Pr}[Z = w] - \mathbf{Pr}[Y = v] \cdot \mathbf{Pr}[Z = w]|$$

$$= \sum_{v,w} \mathbf{Pr}[Z = w] \cdot |\mathbf{Pr}[X = v] - \mathbf{Pr}[Y = v]|$$

$$= \sum_v |\mathbf{Pr}[X = v] - \mathbf{Pr}[Y = v]| \, .$$

Finally, letting $f(z, r)$ denote the output of a randomized algorithm A on input z when using internal coins r, we observe that the random variable $A(z)$ is represented by $f(z, R)$, where R is a random variable representing the internal coin tosses of A. Denoting the statistical distance by Δ, we have

$$\Delta(A(X), A(Y)) = \Delta(f(X, R), f(Y, R))$$

$$\leq \Delta((X, R), (Y, R))$$

$$= \Delta(X, Y),$$

establishing the claim. ∎

A.3. Basic Facts Regarding Expectation and Variance

Throughout the rest of this appendix, we refer to random variables that are assigned real values. Typically, we shall consider only random variables that are supported by a finite probability space. In this case, the expectation and variance of these random variables are always well defined (or "exist"). We first recall these two standard notions.

Definition A.2 (Expectation and variance): *The* expectation *of a random variable* $X \in \mathbb{R}$, *denoted* $\mathbb{E}[X]$, *is defined as* $\sum_{x \in \mathbb{R}} \mathbf{Pr}[X = x] \cdot x$, *and its* variance, *denoted* $\mathbb{V}[X]$, *is defined as* $\mathbb{E}[(X - \mathbb{E}[X])^2]$.

To see that the expectation and variance are well defined, replace the summation over $\mathbb{R}$ by a summation over the support of X, where the support of X is the set of values v such that $\mathbf{Pr}[X = v] > 0$. Three useful facts that we often use without reference follow.

Fact 1: Linearity of expectation. For every sequence of (possibly dependent) random variables, $X_1, \ldots, X_n$, it holds that

$$\mathbb{E}\left[\sum_{i \in [n]} X_i\right] = \sum_{i \in [n]} \mathbb{E}[X_i].$$

This holds by commutativity of summation.

Fact 2: Variance versus the expectation of the square. For every random variable X, it holds that $\mathbb{V}[X] = \mathbb{E}[X^2] - \mathbb{E}[X]^2$.
This follows by $\mathbb{E}[(X - \mathbb{E}[X])^2] = \mathbb{E}[X^2 - 2 \cdot \mathbb{E}[X] \cdot X + \mathbb{E}[X]^2]$ and linearity of expectation.
Notable consequences of this fact include $\mathbb{V}[X] \le \mathbb{E}[X^2]$ and $\mathbb{E}[X^2] \ge \mathbb{E}[X]^2$.

Fact 3: Functions of independent random variables are independent. If $X_1, \ldots, X_n$ are independent random variables, then for every sequence of functions $f_1, \ldots, f_n : \mathbb{R} \to \mathbb{R}$ it holds that $f_1(X_1), \ldots, f_n(X_n)$ are independent random variables.

This follows by writing $\mathbf{Pr}[(f_1(X_1), \ldots, f_n(X_n)) = (v_1, \ldots, v_n)]$
as $\sum_{(x_1, \ldots, x_n) \in (f_1^{-1}(v_1) \times \cdots \times f_n^{-1}(v_n))} \mathbf{Pr}[(X_1, \ldots, X_n) = (x_1, \ldots, x_n)]$.

The following two additional facts will be used in this appendix, but we shall use them less often outside this appendix.

Fact 4: The expectation of the product of independent random variables. For every sequence of independent random variables $X_1, \ldots, X_n$, it holds that

$$\mathbb{E}\left[\prod_{i \in [n]} X_i\right] = \prod_{i \in [n]} \mathbb{E}[X_i].$$

This holds by distributivity of multiplication.

Fact 5: Linearity of the variance of independent random variables. For every sequence of independent random variables $X_1, \ldots, X_n$, it holds that

$$\mathbb{V}\left[\sum_{i \in [n]} X_i\right] = \sum_{i \in [n]} \mathbb{V}[X_i].$$

This can be shown by letting $\overline{X}_i = X_i - \mathbb{E}[X_i]$, and using

$$\mathbb{V}\left[\sum_{i \in [n]} X_i\right] = \mathbb{E}\left[\left(\sum_{i \in [n]} \overline{X}_i\right)^2\right] \qquad \text{[Fact 1]}$$

$$= \mathbb{E}\left[\sum_{i, j \in [n]} \overline{X}_i \overline{X}_j\right]$$

$$= \sum_{i,j\in[n]} \mathbb{E}[\overline{X}_i\overline{X}_j] \qquad \text{[Fact 1]}$$

$$= \sum_{i\in[n]} \mathbb{E}[\overline{X}_i^2] + \sum_{i,j\in[n]:i\neq j} \mathbb{E}[\overline{X}_i\overline{X}_j]$$

$$= \sum_{i\in[n]} \mathbb{V}[X_i] + \sum_{i,j\in[n]:i\neq j} \mathbb{E}[\overline{X}_i]\cdot\mathbb{E}[\overline{X}_j] \qquad \text{[Fact 4]}$$

$$= \sum_{i\in[n]} \mathbb{V}[X_i],$$

where the last equality holds since $\mathbb{E}[\overline{X}_i] = 0$ and the one before it uses the fact that X_i and X_j are independent.

The trick of considering $\overline{X}_i = X_i - \mathbb{E}[X_i]$ is good to bear in mind. We also observe that the latter proof only relied on the fact that each two variables are independent. For the sake of future reference, let us state the consequence of this fact.

Claim A.3 (Linearity of the variance of pairwise independent random variables): *Let $X_1, \ldots, X_n$ be a sequence of random variables such that every two variables in the sequence are independent; that is, for every $i \neq j$ and every y, z it holds that $\mathbf{Pr}[(X_i, X_j) = (y, z)] = \mathbf{Pr}[X_i = y] \cdot \mathbf{Pr}[X_j = z]$. Then,*

$$\mathbb{V}\left[\sum_{i\in[n]} X_i\right] = \sum_{i\in[n]} \mathbb{V}[X_i].$$

Indeed, a sequence as in the hypothesis of Claim A.3 is called *pairwise independent*.

A.4. Three Inequalities

The following probabilistic inequalities are very useful. They provide upper bounds on the probability that a random variable deviates from its expectation.

A.4.1. Markov's Inequality

The most basic inequality is Markov's Inequality that applies to any random variable with bounded maximum or minimum value. For simplicity, this inequality is stated for random variables that are lower-bounded by zero, and reads as follows.

Theorem A.4 (Markov's Inequality): *Let X be a nonnegative random variable and v be a positive real number. Then*

$$\mathbf{Pr}[X \geq v] \leq \frac{\mathbb{E}(X)}{v} \qquad (A.2)$$

Equivalently, $\Pr[X \geq t \cdot \mathbb{E}(X)] \leq \frac{1}{t}$. The proof amounts to the following three lines:

$$\mathbb{E}(X) = \sum_{x} \Pr[X = x] \cdot x$$

$$\geq \sum_{x < v} \Pr[X = x] \cdot 0 + \sum_{x \geq v} \Pr[X = x] \cdot v$$

$$= \Pr[X \geq v] \cdot v.$$

A.4.2. Chebyshev's Inequality

Using Markov's Inequality, one gets a potentially stronger bound on the deviation of a random variable from its expectation. This bound, called Chebyshev's Inequality, is useful when having additional information concerning the random variable (specifically, a good upper bound on its variance).

Theorem A.5 (Chebyshev's Inequality): *Let X be a random variable, and $\delta > 0$. Then*

$$\Pr\left[|X - \mathbb{E}(X)| \geq \delta\right] \leq \frac{\mathbb{V}(X)}{\delta^2}. \tag{A.3}$$

Proof: Defining a random variable $Y \overset{\text{def}}{=} (X - \mathbb{E}(X))^2$, and applying Markov's Inequality to it, we get

$$\Pr\left[|X - \mathbb{E}(X)| \geq \delta\right] = \Pr\left[(X - \mathbb{E}(X))^2 \geq \delta^2\right]$$

$$\leq \frac{\mathbb{E}[(X - \mathbb{E}(X))^2]}{\delta^2},$$

and the claim follows. ∎

Pairwise Independent Sampling: Chebyshev's Inequality is particularly useful in the analysis of the error probability of approximation via repeated sampling. It suffices to assume that the samples are picked in a pairwise independent manner, where $X_1, X_2, \ldots, X_n$ are pairwise independent if for every $i \neq j$ and every α, β it holds that $\Pr[X_i = \alpha \wedge X_j = \beta] = \Pr[X_i = \alpha] \cdot \Pr[X_j = \beta]$. Then, as a corollary to Chebyshev's Inequality, we get

Corollary A.6 (Pairwise independent sampling): *Let $X_1, X_2, \ldots, X_n$ be pairwise independent random variables with identical expectation, denoted μ, and identical variance, denoted σ^2. Then, for every $\epsilon > 0$, it holds that*

$$\Pr\left[\left|\frac{\sum_{i \in [n]} X_i}{n} - \mu\right| \geq \epsilon\right] \leq \frac{\sigma^2}{\epsilon^2 n}. \tag{A.4}$$

Using $\epsilon = \gamma \cdot \mu$ and $m = n \cdot \mu$, we obtain a ("multiplicative") bound of the form

$$\Pr\left[\left|\sum_{i \in [n]} X_i - m\right| \geq \gamma \cdot m\right] \leq \frac{\sigma^2/\mu}{\gamma^2 m}, \tag{A.5}$$

where we used $\epsilon n = \gamma \mu n = \gamma m$ and $\frac{\sigma^2}{(\gamma \mu)^2 n} = \frac{\sigma^2/\mu}{\gamma^2 m}$. Assuming that $\sigma^2 \leq \mu$ (which always holds when $X_i \in [0, 1])$[1], the probability bound of Eq. (A.5) simplifies to $1/\gamma^2 m$.

Proof: Combining Chebyshev's Inequality with Claim A.3, we get

$$\mathbf{Pr}\left[\left|\sum_{i\in[n]} X_i - n \cdot \mu\right| \geq n \cdot \epsilon\right] \leq \frac{\mathbb{V}\left[\sum_{i\in[n]} X_i\right]}{(n\epsilon)^2}$$

$$= \frac{\sum_{i\in[n]} \mathbb{V}[X_i]}{(n\epsilon)^2}$$

$$= \frac{n \cdot \sigma^2}{n^2 \epsilon^2}$$

and the claim follows. (Note that if the X_i's were not pairwise independent, then $\mathbb{V}[\sum_{i\in[n]} X_i] = \Omega(n^2)$ could hold.) ∎

Sampling by t-Wise Independent Points: A sequence of random variables is called t-wise independent if every t variables in it are totally independent. While we shall not use the following result in this book, we find it useful in many other setting and believe that its derivation highlights the ideas that underlie the proof of Corollary A.6. For simplicity, we consider the case that the random variable range over $[0, 1]$; a generalization to other bounded ranges can be derived similarly to the way this is done in the proof of Theorem A.11 (in the next section).

Theorem A.7 (2k-Wise independent sampling): *For $k \leq n/2$, let $X_1, X_2, \ldots, X_n \in [0, 1]$ be 2k-wise independent random variables and $\mu = \sum_{i\in[n]} \mathbb{E}[X_i]/n$. Suppose that $\mathbb{V}[X_i] \leq \beta$ for every $i \in [n]$. Then, for every $\epsilon > 0$, it holds that*

$$\mathbf{Pr}\left[\left|\frac{\sum_{i\in[n]} X_i}{n} - \mu\right| \geq \epsilon\right] < \left(\frac{3k\beta}{n\epsilon^2}\right)^k, \tag{A.6}$$

Recall that for any random variable Z ranging in $[0, 1]$, it holds that $\mathbb{V}[Z] \leq \mathbb{E}[Z]$. Hence, if the X_i's have identical expectation (which equals μ), then we may use $\beta = \mu$.

Proof: Define the random variables $\overline{X}_i \stackrel{\text{def}}{=} X_i - \mathbb{E}(X_i)$. Note that the $\overline{X}_i$'s are 2k-wise independent, and each has zero expectation. Mimicking the proof of Chebyshev's Inequality, we have

$$\mathbf{Pr}\left[\left|\sum_{i\in[n]} \frac{X_i}{n} - \mu\right| \geq \epsilon\right] \leq \frac{\mathbb{E}\left[\left(\sum_{i\in[n]} \overline{X}_i\right)^{2k}\right]}{\epsilon^{2k} \cdot n^{2k}}. \tag{A.7}$$

---

[1] Since in that case $\mathbb{E}[X_i^2] \leq \mathbb{E}[X_i]$, whereas $\mathbb{V}[X] \leq \mathbb{E}[X^2]$ always holds.

The rest of the proof is devoted to upper-bounding the numerator in the r.h.s. of Eq. (A.7). This is done by generalizing the proof of Claim A.3. We start with

$$\mathbb{E}\left[\left(\sum_{i\in[n]}\overline{X}_i\right)^{2k}\right] = \mathbb{E}\left[\sum_{i_1,\ldots,i_{2k}\in[n]}\prod_{j\in[2k]}\overline{X}_{i_j}\right]$$

$$= \sum_{i_1,\ldots,i_{2k}\in[n]}\mathbb{E}\left[\prod_{j\in[2k]}\overline{X}_{i_j}\right].$$

Now, the key observation is that each term (in this sum) that *contains a random variable that appears in it with multiplicity 1* equals zero. More generally, for each sequence $\bar{i} = (i_1,\ldots,i_{2k})$ and $j \in [n]$, denoting by $m_j(\bar{i})$ the multiplicity of j in $\bar{i}$, we have

$$\mathbb{E}\left[\prod_{j\in[2k]}\overline{X}_{i_j}\right] = \mathbb{E}\left[\prod_{j\in[n]}\overline{X}_j^{m_j(\bar{i})}\right]$$

$$= \prod_{j:m_j(\bar{i})>0}\mathbb{E}\left[\overline{X}_j^{m_j(\bar{i})}\right],$$

where the last equality is due to the independence of the random variables in the sequence $(\overline{X}_i)_{j:m_j(\bar{i})>0}$. Denoting by S the set of $2k$-long sequences over $[n]$ in which no element appears with multiplicity 1 (and recalling that $\mathbb{E}[\overline{X}_j] = 0$), we get

$$\mathbb{E}\left[\left(\sum_{i\in[n]}\overline{X}_i\right)^{2k}\right] = \sum_{(i_1,\ldots,i_{2k})\in S}\prod_{j\in[n]}\mathbb{E}\left[\overline{X}_j^{m_j(i_1,\ldots,i_{2k})}\right]. \qquad (A.8)$$

Note that the maximum number of elements that may appear in any sequence $(i_1,\ldots,i_{2k}) \in S$ is k, since each element that appears in $(i_1,\ldots,i_{2k})$ must appear in it with multiplicity at least 2. This already yields an upper bound of $|S| \leq \binom{n}{k}\cdot k^{2k} < (nk^2)^k$ on Eq. (A.8). A better upper bound can be obtained by partitioning S into $(S_1,\ldots,S_k)$ such that $S_t \subset S$ contains all sequences such that each sequence contains exactly t elements. Then:

$$\sum_{(i_1,\ldots,i_{2k})\in S}\prod_{j\in[n]}\mathbb{E}\left[\overline{X}_j^{m_j(i_1,\ldots,i_{2k})}\right] = \sum_{t\in[k]}\sum_{(i_1,\ldots,i_{2k})\in S_t}\prod_{j\in[n]}\mathbb{E}\left[\overline{X}_j^{m_j(i_1,\ldots,i_{2k})}\right]$$

$$\leq \sum_{t\in[k]}|S_t|\cdot\max_{i\in[n]}\left\{\mathbb{E}\left[\overline{X}_i^2\right]^t\right\} \qquad (A.9)$$

$$< \sum_{t\in[k]}(en/k)^t\cdot t^{2k}\cdot\beta^t,$$

where the first inequality uses the fact that for every $m > 2$ and $Z \in [-1,1]$ it holds that $\mathbb{E}[Z^m] \leq \mathbb{E}[Z^2]$, and the last inequality uses $|S_t| \leq \binom{n}{t}\cdot t^{2k} < (en/t)^t\cdot t^{2k}$ (for

$t \leq n/2$). Combining Eqs. (A.7)–(A.9), we get

$$\mathbf{Pr}\left[\left|\sum_{i\in[n]}\frac{X_i}{n} - \mu\right| \geq \epsilon\right] \leq \frac{\mathbb{E}\left[\left(\sum_{i\in[n]}\overline{X}_i\right)^{2k}\right]}{\epsilon^{2k}\cdot n^{2k}}$$

$$< \frac{\sum_{t\in[k]}(en/k)^t \cdot t^{2k} \cdot \beta^t}{\epsilon^{2k}\cdot n^{2k}}$$

$$< \frac{k^{2k}\cdot\sum_{t\in[k]}(\beta en/k)^t}{\epsilon^{2k}\cdot n^{2k}}$$

$$< \frac{k^{2k}\cdot 2\cdot(\beta en/k)^k}{\epsilon^{2k}\cdot n^{2k}}$$

$$< \left(\frac{3k\beta}{n\epsilon^2}\right)^k,$$

as required. ∎

A.4.3. Chernoff Bound

Note that when using pairwise independent sample points, the error probability of the approximation decreases linearly with the number of sample points (see Eq. (A.4)). In contrast, when using totally independent sample points, the error probability in the approximation can be shown to decrease exponentially with the number of sample points. Probability bounds supporting the latter statement are commonly referred to as Chernoff Bounds. We present such bounds next.

The bound that we present first is not the most popular bound, but it is a better starting point for deriving the popular bounds (and other useful bounds), as we shall do later. In particular, the following bound considers independent random variables ranging arbitrarily in $[0, 1]$, where these random variables are not necessarily identical.

Theorem A.8 (A Chernoff Bound): *Let $X_1, X_2, \ldots, X_n$ be independent random variables ranging in $[0, 1]$, and $\beta > 0$. Let $\mu = \sum_{i\in[n]}\mathbb{E}[X_i]$ and suppose that $\sum_{i\in[n]}\mathbb{V}[X_i] \leq \beta$. Then, for every $\alpha \in (0, 2\beta]$, it holds that*

$$\mathbf{Pr}\left[\left|\sum_{i\in[n]}X_i - \mu\right| > \alpha\right] < 2\cdot e^{-\alpha^2/4\beta}. \tag{A.10}$$

Note that $\sum_{i\in[n]}\mathbb{V}[X_i] \leq \sum_{i\in[n]}\mathbb{E}[X_i^2] \leq \mu$, where the last inequality uses the fact that $\mathbb{E}[X^2] \leq \mathbb{E}[X]$ holds for every random variable $X \in [0, 1]$. Hence (assuming $\mu > 0$)[2], we can always use $\beta = \mu$, and obtain a meaningful bound whenever $\alpha > 2\sqrt{\mu}$.

Proof: We upper-bound $\mathbf{Pr}[\sum_{i\in[n]}X_i > \mu + \alpha]$, and $\mathbf{Pr}[\sum_{i\in[n]}X_i < \mu - \alpha]$ is bounded similarly (or, alternatively, by letting $Y_i = 1 - X_i$ and using the bound on $\mathbf{Pr}[\sum_{i\in[n]}Y_i > (n - \mu) + \alpha]$). Letting $\overline{X}_i \stackrel{\text{def}}{=} X_i - \mathbb{E}(X_i)$, we apply Markov's

---

[2] Note that $\mu = 0$ implies that each X_i is identically zero.

Inequality to the random variable $e^{\lambda \sum_{i=1}^{n} \overline{X}_i}$, where $\lambda \in (0, 1]$ will be determined to optimize the expression that we derive. Specifically, we get

$$\Pr\left[\sum_{i \in [n]} \overline{X}_i > \alpha\right] = \Pr\left[e^{\lambda \sum_{i \in [n]} \overline{X}_i} > e^{\lambda \alpha}\right]$$

$$\leq \frac{\mathbb{E}\left[e^{\lambda \sum_{i \in [n]} \overline{X}_i}\right]}{e^{\lambda \alpha}}$$

$$= e^{-\lambda \alpha} \cdot \mathbb{E}\left[\prod_{i \in [n]} e^{\lambda \overline{X}_i}\right]$$

$$= e^{-\lambda \alpha} \cdot \prod_{i \in [n]} \mathbb{E}\left[e^{\lambda \overline{X}_i}\right],$$

where the last equality is due to the independence of the random variables. Now, using $e^x \leq 1 + x + x^2$ for every $x \in [-1, 1]$, and observing that $\mathbb{E}[\overline{X}_i] = 0$, we get $\mathbb{E}[e^{\lambda \overline{X}_i}] \leq 1 + \lambda^2 \cdot \mathbb{E}[\overline{X}_i^2]$, which equals $1 + \lambda^2 \cdot \mathbb{V}[X_i]$. Hence,

$$\Pr\left[\sum_{i \in [n]} \overline{X}_i > \alpha\right] \leq e^{-\lambda \alpha} \cdot \prod_{i \in [n]} \mathbb{E}\left[e^{\lambda \overline{X}_i}\right]$$

$$\leq e^{-\lambda \alpha} \cdot \prod_{i \in [n]} \left(1 + \lambda^2 \cdot \mathbb{V}[X_i]\right)$$

$$\leq e^{-\lambda \alpha} \cdot \prod_{i \in [n]} e^{\lambda^2 \cdot \mathbb{V}[X_i]}$$

$$= e^{-\lambda \alpha} \cdot e^{\lambda^2 \cdot \sum_{i \in [n]} \mathbb{V}[X_i]},$$

where the last inequality is due to using $1 + y \leq e^y$ for every $y \in [0, 1]$. Recalling that $\sum_{i \in [n]} \mathbb{V}[X_i] \leq \beta$ and optimizing at $\lambda = \alpha/2\beta \in (0, 1]$, we obtain

$$\Pr\left[\sum_{i \in [n]} \overline{X}_i > \alpha\right] \leq e^{-\lambda \alpha + \lambda^2 \beta}$$

$$= e^{-\alpha^2/4\beta},$$

and the claim follows. ∎

The Popular Chernoff Bounds. The popular bounds refer to the case that all X_i's are indentical (and range in $[0, 1]$) and consider the average of the random variables (i.e., $\sum_{i \in [n]} X_i/n$) rather than their sum (i.e., $\sum_{i \in [n]} X_i$). The most popular version refers to an additive deviation of $\epsilon > 0$.

Corollary A.9 (A standard ("additive") Chernoff Bound): *Let $X_1, X_2, \ldots, X_n$ be identical independent random variables ranging in $[0, 1]$, and let $p = \mathbb{E}[X_1]$. Then,* *for every $\epsilon \in (0, 2(1 - p)p]$, it holds that*

$$\mathbf{Pr}\left[\left|\frac{1}{n} \cdot \sum_{i \in [n]} X_i - p\right| > \epsilon\right] < 2 \cdot e^{-\epsilon^2 n/(4p(1-p))} < 2 \cdot e^{-\epsilon^2 n} \qquad (A.11)$$

and, for every $\epsilon \in (0, 1]$, it holds that

$$\mathbf{Pr}\left[\left|\frac{1}{n} \cdot \sum_{i \in [n]} X_i - p\right| > \epsilon\right] < 2 \cdot e^{-\epsilon^2 n/4}. \qquad (A.12)$$

Proof: We invoke Theorem A.8 with $\mu = n \cdot p$ and $\alpha = n \cdot \epsilon$. For Eq. (A.11) we use $\beta = n \cdot (1 - p)p$, while noting that $\mathbb{V}[X_i] \le \mathbb{E}[X_i] - \mathbb{E}[X_i]^2 = (1 - p)p$ (since $X_i \in [0, 1]$ implies $\mathbb{E}[X_i^2] \le \mathbb{E}[X_i]$). For Eq. (A.11) we use $\beta = n \cdot p \le n$, while assuming without loss of generality that $p \ge 1/2$ (which allows for $\epsilon \in (0, 1]$, and considering the $1 - X_i$'s otherwise). ∎

Corollary A.10 (A standard multiplicative Chernoff Bound): *Let $X_1, X_2, \ldots, X_n$ be identical independent random variables ranging in $[0, 1]$, and let $p = \mathbb{E}[X_1]$. Then, for every $\gamma \in (0, 2]$, it holds that*

$$\mathbf{Pr}\left[\left|\frac{1}{n} \cdot \sum_{i \in [n]} X_i - p\right| > \gamma \cdot p\right] < 2 \cdot e^{-\gamma^2 pn/4}. \qquad (A.13)$$

Proof: We invoke Theorem A.8 with $\mu = n \cdot p$ and $\alpha = \gamma \cdot \mu$, and use $\beta = \mu$ (while relying on $\mathbb{V}[X_i] \le \mathbb{E}[X_i]$). ∎

Generalization to an Arbitrary Bounded Range. The case that the X_i's range in an arbitrary interval can be handled by using a linear transformation that maps this interval to $[0, 1]$.

Theorem A.11 (Theorem A.8, generalized): *Let $X_1, X_2, \ldots, X_n$ be independent random variables ranging in $[a, b]$, and $\beta > 0$. Let $\mu = \sum_{i \in [n]} \mathbb{E}[X_i]$ and suppose that $\sum_{i \in [n]} \mathbb{V}[X_i] \le \beta$. Then, for every $\alpha \in (0, 2\beta/(b - a)]$, it holds that*

$$\mathbf{Pr}\left[\left|\sum_{i \in [n]} X_i - \mu\right| > \alpha\right] < 2 \cdot e^{-\alpha^2/4\beta}. \qquad (A.14)$$

Note that in this case (i.e., of independent X_i's ranging in $[a, b]$) it holds that $\sum_{i \in [n]} \mathbb{V}[X_i] \le (b - a) \cdot (\mu - n \cdot a)$, where the inequality uses $\mathbb{V}[X_i] = \mathbb{V}[X_i - a] = (b - a)^2 \cdot \mathbb{V}[(X_i - a)/(b - a)]$ and the fact that $(X_i - a)/(b - a) \in [0, 1]$.[3] Hence, we may use $\beta = (b - a) \cdot (\mu - n \cdot a)$.

Before proving Theorem A.11, we note that a multiplicative version of Theorem A.11 can be obtained by letting $\gamma = \alpha/(\mu - n \cdot a)$ and using $\beta = (b - a) \cdot (\mu - n \cdot a)$. Hence,

---

[3] Hence, $\mathbb{V}[X_i] \le (b - a)^2 \cdot \mathbb{E}[(X_i - a)/(b - a)]$, whereas $\mathbb{E}[(X_i - a)/(b - a)] = (\mathbb{E}[X_i] - a)/(b - a)$. It follows that $\sum_{i \in [n]} \mathbb{V}[X_i]$ is upper-bounded by $(b - a) \cdot \sum_{i \in [n]} (\mathbb{E}[X_i] - a)$.

for every $\gamma \in (0, 2]$, it holds that

$$\Pr\left[\left|\sum_{i\in[n]} X_i - \mu\right| > \gamma \cdot (\mu - n \cdot a)\right] < 2 \cdot e^{-\gamma^2(\mu - n \cdot a)/4(b-a)}. \tag{A.15}$$

For $a = 0$, the bound simplifies to $2 \cdot e^{-\gamma^2\mu/4b}$.

Proof: We consider the random variables $X_1', \dots, X_n'$ such that $X_i' = (X_i - a)/(b - a) \in [0, 1]$. Let $\alpha' = \alpha/(b - a)$ and $\beta' = \beta/(b - a)^2$, and note that $\sum_{i\in[n]} \mathbb{V}[X_i'] = \sum_{i\in[n]} \mathbb{V}[X_i]/(b - a)^2 \le \beta'$ and that $\alpha' \in (0, 2\beta']$. Invoking Theorem A.8 (with parameters α' and β', while noting that $\sum_{i\in[n]} \mathbb{E}[X_i'] = (\mu - na)/(b - a)$), we get

$$\Pr\left[\left|\sum_{i\in[n]} X_i' - \frac{\mu - na}{b - a}\right| > \frac{\alpha}{b - a}\right] < 2 \cdot e^{-(\alpha/(b-a))^2/4(\beta/(b-a)^2)}$$

and the claim follows. ∎

A.4.4. Pairwise Independent versus Totally Independent Sampling

Totally independent samples will be our first choice, since (except in Section 13.3) we do not care about the randomness complexity of testers. We shall resort to pairwise independent sampling (or to "almost pairwise independent sampling") only when this is imposed on us by the application (see, e.g., the proofs of Claim 9.21.3 and Lemma 11.4). Still, for sake of a wider perspective, we mention that the advantage of totally independent samples over pairwise independent ones is (only) in the dependency of the number of samples on the error probability.

In order to make the discussion more clear, we consider the problem of estimating the average value of a function $f : \Omega \to [0, 1]$. In general, we say that a random variable Z provides an (ϵ, δ)-approximation of a value v if $\Pr[|Z - v| > \epsilon] \le \delta$. By Chernoff Bound (e.g., Corollary A.9), the average value of f evaluated at $n = O((\epsilon^{-2} \cdot \log(1/\delta))$ *independent* samples (selected uniformly in Ω) yield an (ϵ, δ)-approximation of $\mu = \sum_{x\in\Omega} f(x)/|\Omega|$. Thus, the number of sample points is polynomially related to ϵ^{-1} and logarithmically related to δ^{-1}. In contrast, by Corollary A.6 an (ϵ, δ)-approximation by n *pairwise independent* samples calls for setting $n = O(\epsilon^{-2} \cdot \delta^{-1})$. We stress that, *in both cases the number of samples is polynomially related to the desired accuracy of the estimation (i.e., ϵ). The only advantage of totally independent samples over pairwise independent ones is in the dependency of the number of samples on the error probability (i.e., δ).*

A Mini-Compendium of General Results

Summary: This appendix restates several general results that were presented in the main body of this book, including

1. deriving standard testers from POTs;
2. positive results on the algebra of property testing;
3. reducing testing to learning;
4. the randomness complexity of testers;
5. archetypical application of self-correction;
6. the effect of local reductions.

While most results in the area of property testing refer to specific properties or to classes of properties (which at best are characterized in terms of invariances), there are a handful of *general* results that apply to property testing at large (with the exception of distribution testing). These results are restated in this appendix, while referring to their prior statement in the text, which also provides their proofs.

Deriving Standard Testers from Proximity-Oblivious Testers. We refer to the (very basic) notions of property testers and proximity-oblivious testers (i.e., POTs) as presented in Section 1.3.

Theorem B.1 (Deriving standard testers from POTs – Theorem 1.9): *Let Π be a property of functions.*

1. *If Π has a one-sided error POT of query complexity q with detection probability ϱ, then Π has a one-sided error tester of query complexity q' such that $q'(\epsilon) = O(q/\varrho(\epsilon))$.*
2. *If Π has a POT of query complexity q with threshold probability $\tau \in (0, 1)$ and detection probability ϱ, then Π has a tester of query complexity q' such that $q'(\epsilon) = O(q/\varrho(\epsilon)^2)$.*

The time complexity of the derived tester relates to that of the POT in a similar manner. If the POT is nonadaptive, then so is the derived tester.

On the Algebra of Property Testing. In Section 1.3.4 we show that natural classes of testable properties are closed under union but not under intersection (and complementation). That is, if Π' and Π'' are testable within some complexity bounds, then so is $\Pi' \cup \Pi''$ (up to a constant factor), but $\Pi' \cap \Pi''$ may be much harder to test.[1]

Theorem B.2 (Testing the union of properties – Theorem 1.10): *Let Π' and Π'' be properties of functions.*

1. *If Π' and Π'' are each testable within query complexity q, then $\Pi' \cup \Pi''$ is testable within query complexity $O(q)$. Furthermore, one-sided error testing is preserved.*
2. *Suppose that Π' has a q-query one-sided error POT with detection probability $\varrho : (0, 1] \to (0, 1]$, and ditto for Π''. Then, $\Pi' \cup \Pi''$ has a $2q$-query one-sided error POT with detection probability ϱ^2.*

Furthermore, the time complexity is preserved up to a constant factor.

We say that $\Pi \subseteq \{0, 1\}^*$ is **monotone** if for every $x \in \Pi$ and $w \in \{0, 1\}^{|x|}$ it holds that $x \vee w = (x_1 \vee w_1, \dots, x_n \vee w_n)$ is in Π; that is, Π is preserved under resetting some bits to 1. We first mention that the discrepancy between the complexity of testing a property and the complexity of testing its complement is maintained also for monotone properties (see Exercise 1.16). More importantly, in contrast to Theorem 1.12, we have

Theorem B.3 (Testing the intersection of monotone properties – Theorem 1.13): *Let Π' and Π'' be monotone properties.*

1. *If Π' and Π'' are testable within query complexity q' and q'', respectively, then, for every $\epsilon' \in (0, \epsilon)$, the property $\Pi' \cap \Pi''$ is ϵ-testable within query complexity $q(n, \epsilon) = O(q'(n, \epsilon') + q''(n, \epsilon - \epsilon'))$. Furthermore, one-sided error testing is preserved.*
2. *Suppose that Π' has a q-query one-sided error POT with detection probability $\varrho : (0, 1] \to (0, 1]$, and ditto for Π''. Then, $\Pi' \cap \Pi''$ has a $2q$-query one-sided error POT with detection probability $\varrho'(\delta) = \varrho(\delta/2)$.*

Furthermore, the time complexity is preserved up to a constant factor.

Testing via Learning. A general observation is that property testing reduces to learning. This observation is rarely used, because typically one seeks testers that are more efficient than the corresponding learners. Still, for sake of perspective, we detail the said connection. We refer to the definitions of general and proper learning as presented in Section 1.3.5.

Theorem B.4 (Learning implies testing – Theorem 1.15): *Let $\Pi = \cup_{n \in \mathbb{N}} \Pi_n$ be a set of functions, and suppose that Π can be learned within query complexity $q(n, \epsilon)$. Then, Π can be tested within query complexity $q'(n, \epsilon) = q(n, 0.3\epsilon) + O(1/\epsilon)$. Furthermore, if the learning algorithm is proper, runs in time $t(n, \epsilon)$ and outputs descriptions of functions such that, with respect to that representation, evaluating these functions and checking their membership in Π can be done in time $T(n)$, then*

---

[1] This is a general result that refers to all possible Π' and Π''. In contrast, in some cases, both $\Pi' \cup \Pi''$ and $\Pi' \cap \Pi''$ may be much easier to test than Π' and Π''.

Π *can be tested within query complexity* $q'(n, \epsilon) = q(n, 0.7\epsilon) + O(1/\epsilon)$ *and time complexity* $t'(n, \epsilon) = t(n, 0.7\epsilon) + O(T(n)/\epsilon)$.

We mention that similar results hold with respect to a variety of models including sample-based learning and testing and distribution-free learning and testing. Note that in the case of nonproper learning we invoke the learner with a proximity parameter that is strictly smaller than $\epsilon/2$, whereas in the case of proper learning we may use a proximity parameter that is larger than $\epsilon/2$ (as long as it is strictly smaller than ϵ). More importantly, the stated bound on time complexity (i.e., $t'(n, \epsilon) = t(n, 0.7\epsilon) + O(T(n)/\epsilon)$) does not hold in the case of nonproper learning (see [140, Sec. 3.2]).

On the Randomness Complexity of Testers. The following result is a special case of Exercise 1.21, which refers to arbitrary oracle machines. For simplicity, we assume that the given tester has error probability at most $1/4$, and derive a tester of error probability $1/3$. This discrepancy can be eliminated using error reduction, while increasing the query complexity by a fixed constant.

Theorem B.5 (Upper bound on the randomness complexity of property testing – a special case of Exercise 1.21): *Let* Π *be a property of functions from* $[n]$ *to* R, *and suppose that* Π *can be* ϵ-*tested using* q *queries with error probability at most* $1/4$. *Then,* Π *can be* ϵ-*tested using* q *queries with error probability at most* $1/3$, *while tossing at most* $\log_2 n + \log \log |R| + O(1)$ *coins.*

We warn that the randomness-efficient tester derived here is not necessarily computationally efficient.

An Archetypical Application of Self-correction. We refer to the notion of random self-reducibility as defined in Section 5.2.3 and to the notion of solving a promise problem. Recall that a promise problem is specified by two sets, P and Q, where P is the promise and Q is the question. The problem, denoted (P, Q), is define as *given an input in P, decide whether or not the input is in Q* (where standard decision problems use the trivial promise in which P consists of the set of all possible inputs). Equivalently, the problem consists of distinguishing between inputs in $P \cap Q$ and inputs in $P \setminus Q$.

Theorem B.6 (Testing intersection with a self-correctable property – Theorem 5.11): *Let* Π' *and* Π'' *be sets of functions over* $[n]$. *Suppose that functions in* Π' *are randomly self-reducible by* q *queries, that* Π' *is* ϵ-*testable using* $q'(\epsilon)$ *queries, and that the promise problem* (Π', Π'') *can be solved in query complexity* q'' *(i.e., a probabilistic* q''-*query oracle machine can distinguish between inputs in* $\Pi' \cap \Pi''$ *and inputs in* $\Pi' \setminus \Pi''$). *Then,* $\Pi' \cap \Pi''$ *is* ϵ-*testable using* $O(q'(\min(\epsilon, 1/3q))) + q \cdot O(q'')$ *queries.*

We stress that Theorem 5.11 does not employ a tester for Π'', but rather employs a decision procedure for the promise problem (Π', Π''). However, as shown in Exercise 5.5, such a decision procedure is implied by any $(1/q)$-tester for Π'', since Π' has distance at least $1/q$ (see Exercise 5.4).

The Effect of Local Reductions. We refer to the notion of a randomized local reduction as defined in Section 7.4.

Theorem B.7 (Randomized local reductions preserve testability – Exercise 7.10):
Let $\Pi = \cup_{n\in\mathbb{N}}\Pi_n$ and $\Pi' = \cup_{n'\in\mathbb{N}}\Pi'_{n'}$ be sets of functions, and suppose that Π is randomly q-local (ϵ, ϵ')-reducible to Π' with length function L. Then, if Π' can be ϵ'-tested with $q'(n', \epsilon')$ queries, then Π can be ϵ-tested with $q(n) \cdot \widetilde{O}(q'(L(n), \epsilon'))$ queries. Furthermore, if the reduction is deterministic, then Π can be ϵ-tested with $q(n) \cdot q'(L(n), \epsilon')$ queries.

An Index of Specific Results

Summary: This appendix provides an index to all results regarding specific properties that were presented in this book. For each property, we provide references only to the sections (or statements) in which relevant results can be found.

The properties are partitioned into five main groups, whereas in each group the listing is by alphabetic order. The first list contains all properties of objects that are most naturally described as functions or sequences. The next three lists refer to the three models of testing graph properties, which were studied in Chapters 8–10. The last list refers to properties of distributions, which were studied in Chapter 11.

Properties of Functions. Such properties were studied mostly in Chapters 2–6.

affine functions: Last paragraph of Chapter 2.
affine subspaces: Section 5.2.2.2 as well as Exercises 5.9–5.11.
codewords: Chapter 13.
  - For the Hadamard code see also linearity.
  - For general linear codes see Proposition 1.11.
  - For the Long Code see also dictatorship.
  - For the Reed–Muller code see also low-degree polynomials.
dictatorship: Section 5.2.
homomorphism (a.k.a. group homomorphism): Chapter 2.
junta: Section 5.3 and Corollary 7.20.
linearity: Special case of homomorphism.
low-degree polynomials: Chapter 3.
majority: Proposition 1.1.
monomials: Section 5.2.2 as well as Corollaries 6.4 and 6.7.
monotonicity: Chapter 4. See also sorted.
proofs: Chapter 13.
sparse (low-degree) polynomials (and linear functions): Corollary 7.12.
sorted: Proposition 1.5 and 1.8. See also monotonicity.

Graph Properties (in the Dense Graph Model). All in Chapter 8.

biclique: Proposition 8.6.
bipartiteness: Section 8.3.1.

colorability (by fixed number of colors): Theorem 8.13.
degree regularity: Theorem 8.5.
induced subgraph freeness: Theorem 8.20.
max-clique: Special case of Theorem 8.12.
max-cut: Special case of Theorem 8.12.
min-bisection: Special case of Theorem 8.12.
subgraph freeness: Section 8.4.2.

Recall that properties of sparse graphs (e.g., planarity) and properties that are close to any graph (e.g., connectivity) are easy to test in this model.

Graph Properties (in the Bounded-Degree Graph Model). All in Chapter 9.

bipartiteness: Sections 9.3.1 and 9.4.1.
colorability (by three colors): Theorem 9.19.
connectivity: Section 9.2.3. See Section 9.2.4 for t-connectivity.
cycle-freeness: Section 9.2.5, Theorem 9.17, and Section 9.4.2.
degree regularity: Section 9.2.2.
Eulerian: See the last paragraph in Section 9.2.2 and the last paragraph in Section 9.2.3.
expansion: Theorem 9.18.
planarity: Special case of Theorem 9.25.
subgraph freeness: Theorem 9.4.

Graph Properties (in the General Graph Model). All in Chapter 10.

bipartiteness: Sections 10.2.2 and 10.4.
connectivity: Section 10.2.1.
cycle-freeness: Theorem 10.15.
degree regularity: Theorem 10.15.
subgraph freeness: Theorem 10.15.

The tasks of estimating the average degree and selecting random edges are studied in Section 10.3.

Properties of Distributions. All in Chapter 11.

equality (between two unknown distributions): Section 11.3.
identity (a.k.a. equality to a fixed distribution): Section 11.2.
uniformity (a.k.a. equality to the uniform distribution): Section 11.2.1.

References

[1] J. Acharya, H. Das, A. Orlitsky, and A.T. Suresh. A unified maximum likelihood approach for optimal distribution property estimation. *ECCC*, TR16-186, 2016.

[2] J. Acharya, C. Daskalakis, and G. Kamath. Optimal testing for properties of distributions. arXiv:1507.05952 [cs.DS], 2015.

[3] J. Acharya, A. Orlitsky, and S. Pan. The maximum likelihood probability of unique-singleton, ternary, and length-7 patterns. In *IEEE Symposium on Information Theory*, pp. 1135–1139, 2009.

[4] L.M. Adleman. A subexponential algorithm for the discrete logarithm problem with applications to cryptography, In *20th IEEE Symposium on Foundations of Computer Science*, pp. 55–60, 1979.

[5] N. Ailon, B. Chazelle, S. Comandur, and D. Liu. Property-preserving data reconstruction. *Algorithmica*, Vol. 51 (2), pp. 160–182, 2008.

[6] N. Alon. Testing subgraphs of large graphs. *Random Structures and Algorithms*, Vol. 21, pp. 359–370, 2002.

[7] N. Alon, S. Dar, M. Parnas, and D. Ron. Testing of clustering. *SIAM Journal on Discrete Mathematics*, Vol. 16 (3), pp. 393–417, 2003.

[8] N. Alon, E. Fischer, M. Krivelevich and M. Szegedy. Efficient testing of large graphs. *Combinatorica*, Vol. 20, pp. 451–476, 2000.

[9] N. Alon, E. Fischer, I. Newman, and A. Shapira. A combinatorial characterization of the testable graph properties: It's all about regularity. In *38th ACM Symposium on the Theory of Computing*, pp. 251–260, 2006.

[10] N. Alon and J. Fox. Easily testable graph properties. *Combinatorics, Probability and Computing*, Vol. 24 (4), pp. 646–657, 2015.

[11] N. Alon, T. Kaufman, M. Krivelevich, S. Litsyn, and D. Ron. Testing low-degree polynomials over GF(2). In *7th RANDOM*. Lecture Notes in Computer Science, Vol. 2764, Springer, pp. 188–199, 2003.

[12] N. Alon, T. Kaufman, M. Krivelevich, and D. Ron. Testing triangle freeness in general graphs. In *17th ACM-SIAM Symposium on Discrete Algorithms*, pp. 279–288, 2006.

[13] N. Alon and M. Krivelevich. Testing *k*-Colorability. *SIAM Journal on Discrete Mathematics*, Vol. 15 (2), pp. 211–227, 2002.

[14] N. Alon, M. Krivelevich, I. Newman, and M. Szegedy. Regular languages are testable with a constant number of queries. *SIAM Journal on Computing*, Vol. 30 (6), pp. 1842–1862, 2001.

[15] N. Alon, Y. Matias, and M. Szegedy. The space complexity of approximating the frequency moments. *Journal of Computer and System Science*, Vol. 58 (1), pp. 137–147, 1999. Preliminary version in *28th STOC*, 1996.

[16] N. Alon, P.D. Seymour, and R. Thomas. A separator theorem for graphs with an excluded minor and its applications. In *22nd ACM Symposium on the Theory of Computing*, pp. 293–299, 1990.

[17] N. Alon and A. Shapira. Testing subgraphs in directed graphs. *Journal of Computer and System Science*, Vol. 69, pp. 354–482, 2004.

[18] N. Alon and A. Shapira. Every monotone graph property is testable. In *37th ACM Symposium on the Theory of Computing*, pp. 128–137, 2005.

[19] N. Alon and A. Shapira. A Characterization of the (natural) graph properties testable with one-sided error. In *46th IEEE Symposium on Foundations of Computer Science*, pp. 429–438, 2005.

[20] N. Alon and A. Shapira. A characterization of easily testable induced subgraphs. *Combinatorics Probability and Computing*, Vol. 15, pp. 791–805, 2006.

[21] N. Alon and A. Shapira. A separation theorem in property testing. *Combinatorica*, Vol. 28 (3), pp. 261–281, 2008.

[22] N. Alon and J.H. Spencer. *The Probabilistic Method*. John Wiley & Sons, 1992. Third edition, 2008.

[23] S. Arora. *Probabilistic checking of proofs and the hardness of approximation problems*. PhD thesis, UC Berkeley, 1994.

[24] S. Arora, C. Lund, R. Motwani, M. Sudan and M. Szegedy. Proof verification and intractability of approximation problems. *Journal of the ACM*, Vol. 45, pp. 501–555, 1998. Preliminary version in *33rd FOCS*, 1992.

[25] S. Arora and S. Safra. Probabilistic checkable proofs: A new characterization of NP. *Journal of the ACM*, Vol. 45, pp. 70–122, 1998. Preliminary version in *33rd FOCS*, 1992.

[26] S. Arora and M. Sudan. Improved low-degree testing and its applications. *Combinatorica*, Vol. 23 (3), pp. 365–426, 2003. Preliminary version in *29th STOC*, 1997.

[27] L. Avigad and O. Goldreich. Testing graph blow-up. In *Studies in complexity and cryptography*, Springer, pp. 156–172, 2011.

[28] L. Babai, L. Fortnow, L. Levin, and M. Szegedy. Checking computations in polylogarithmic time. In *23rd ACM Symposium on the Theory of Computing*, pp. 21–31, 1991.

[29] L. Babai, L. Fortnow, and C. Lund. Non-deterministic exponential time has two-prover interactive protocols. *Computational Complexity*, Vol. 1, No. 1, pp. 3–40, 1991. Preliminary version in *31st FOCS*, 1990.

[30] M. Balcan, E. Blais, A. Blum, and L. Yang. Active property testing. In *53rd IEEE Symposium on Foundations of Computer Science*, pp. 21–30, 2012.

[31] B. Barak. How to go beyond the black-box simulation barrier. In *42nd IEEE Symposium on Foundations of Computer Science*, pp. 106–115, 2001.

[32] T. Batu, S. Dasgupta, R. Kumar, and R. Rubinfeld. The complexity of approximating the entropy. *SIAM Journal on Computing*, Vol. 35 (1), pp. 132–150, 2005.

[33] T. Batu, F. Ergun, J. Kilian, A. Magen, S. Raskhodnikova, R. Rubinfeld, and R. Sami. A sublinear algorithm for weakly approximating edit distance. In *35th ACM Symposium on the Theory of Computing*, pp. 316–324, 2003.

[34] T. Batu, E. Fischer, L. Fortnow, R. Kumar, R. Rubinfeld, and P. White. Testing random variables for independence and identity. In *42nd IEEE Symposium on Foundations of Computer Science*, pp. 442–451, 2001.

[35] T. Batu, L. Fortnow, R. Rubinfeld, W.D. Smith, P. White. Testing that distributions are close. In *41st IEEE Symposium on Foundations of Computer Science*, pp. 259–269, 2000.

[36] M. Bellare, D. Coppersmith, J. Hastad, M.A. Kiwi, and M. Sudan. Linearity testing in characteristic two. *IEEE Transactions on Information Theory*, Vol. 42 (6), pp. 1781–1795, 1996.

[37] M. Bellare, O. Goldreich and M. Sudan. Free bits, PCPs and non-approximability – towards tight results. *SIAM Journal on Computing*, Vol. 27, No. 3, pp. 804–915, 1998. Extended abstract in *36th FOCS*, 1995.

[38] M. Bellare, S. Goldwasser, C. Lund and A. Russell. Efficient probabilistically checkable proofs and applications to approximation. In *25th ACM Symposium on the Theory of Computing*, pp. 294–304, 1993.

[39] A. Belovs and E. Blais. A polynomial lower bound for testing monotonicity. In *48th ACM Symposium on the Theory of Computing*, pp. 1012–1032, 2016.

[40] M. Bender and D. Ron. Testing acyclicity of directed graphs in sublinear time. *Random Structures and Algorithms*, pp. 184–205, 2002.

[41] I. Benjamini, O. Schramm, and A. Shapira. Every minor-closed property of sparse graphs is testable. In *40th ACM Symposium on the Theory of Computing*, pp. 393–402, 2008.

[42] I. Ben-Eliezer, T. Kaufman, M. Krivelevich, and D. Ron. Comparing the strength of query types in property testing: The case of testing k-Colorability. In *19th ACM-SIAM Symposium on Discrete Algorithms*, pp. 1213–1222, 2008.

[43] M. Ben-Or, S. Goldwasser, J. Kilian and A. Wigderson. Multi-prover interactive proofs: How to remove intractability. In *20th ACM Symposium on the Theory of Computing*, pp. 113–131, 1988.

[44] E. Ben-Sasson, O. Goldreich, P. Harsha, M. Sudan, and S. Vadhan. Robust PCPs of proximity, shorter PCPs, and applications to coding. *SIAM Journal on Computing*, Vol. 36 (4), pp. 889–974, 2006. Extended abstract in *36th STOC*, 2004.

[45] E. Ben-Sasson, O. Goldreich, P. Harsha, M. Sudan and S. Vadhan. Short PCPs verifiable in polylogarithmic time. In *20th IEEE Conference on Computational Complexity*, pp. 120–134, 2005.

[46] E. Ben-Sasson, O. Goldreich and M. Sudan. Bounds on 2-query codeword testing. In *7th RANDOM*, Lecture Notes in Computer Science, Vol. 2764, Springer, pp. 216–227, 2003.

[47] E. Ben-Sasson, P. Harsha, and S. Raskhodnikova. 3CNF properties are hard to test. *SIAM Journal on Computing*, Vol. 35 (1), pp. 1–21, 2005.

[48] E. Ben-Sasson and M. Sudan. Short PCPs with polylog query complexity. *SIAM Journal on Computing*, Vol. 38 (2), pp. 551–607, 2008. Preliminary version in *37th STOC*, 2005.

[49] E. Ben-Sasson, M. Sudan, S. Vadhan, and A. Wigderson. Randomness-efficient low degree tests and short PCPs via epsilon-biased sets. In *35th ACM Symposium on the Theory of Computing*, June 2003, pp. 612–621.

[50] P. Berman, S. Raskhodnikova, and G. Yaroslavtsev. Lp-testing. In *46th ACM Symposium on the Theory of Computing*, pp. 164–173, 2014.

[51] A. Bhattacharyya, S. Kopparty, G. Schoenebeck, M. Sudan, and D. Zuckerman. Optimal testing of Reed–Muller codes. In *IEEE Symposium on Foundations of Computer Science*, pp. 488–497, 2010.

[52] E. Blais. Testing juntas almost optimally. In *ACM Symposium on the Theory of Computing*, pp. 151–158, 2009.

[53] E. Blais. Testing juntas: A brief survey. In [134].

[54] E. Blais, J. Brody, and K. Matulef. Property testing lower bounds via communication complexity. *Computational Complexity*, Vol. 21 (2), pp. 311–358, 2012. Extended abstract in *26th CCC*, 2011.

[55] E. Blais, C. Canonne, T. Gur. Alice and Bob show distribution testing lower bounds (They don't talk to each other anymore). *ECCC*, TR016-168, 2016.

[56] A. Bhattacharyya and Y. Yoshida. Property testing. Forthcoming.

[57] E. Blais and Y. Yoshida. A characterization of constant-sample testable properties. *ECCC*, TR016-201, 2016.

[58] M. Blum and S. Kannan. Designing programs that check their work. In *21st ACM Symposium on the Theory of Computing*, pp. 86–97, 1989.

[59] M. Blum, M. Luby and R. Rubinfeld. Self-testing/correcting with applications to numerical problems. *Journal of Computer and System Science*, Vol. 47, No. 3, pp. 549–595, 1993. Extended abstract *22nd STOC*, 1990.

[60] A. Bogdanov and F. Li. A better tester for bipartiteness? `arXiv:1011.0531 [cs.DS]`, 2010.

[61] A. Bogdanov, K. Obata, and L. Trevisan. A lower bound for testing 3-Colorability in bounded-degree graphs. In *43rd IEEE Symposium on Foundations of Computer Science*, pp. 93–102, 2002.

[62] A. Bogdanov and L. Trevisan. Lower bounds for testing bipartiteness in dense graphs. In *19th IEEE Conference on Computational Complexity*, pp. 75–81, 2004.

[63] B. Bollobas, P. Erdos, M. Simonovits, and E. Szemeredi. Extremal graphs without large forbidden subgraphs. *Annals of Discrete Mathematics*, Vol. 3, pp. 29–41, 1978.

[64] C. Borgs, J. Chayes, L. Lovász, V.T. Sós, B. Szegedy, and K. Vesztergombi. Graph limits and parameter testing. In *38th ACM Symposium on the Theory of Computing*, pp. 261–270, 2006.

[65] J. Briet, S. Chakraborty, D. Garcia-Soriano, and A. Matsliah. Monotonicity testing and shortest-path routing on the cube. *Combinatorica*, Vol. 32 (1), pp. 35–53, 2012.

[66] R. Canetti, G. Even and O. Goldreich. Lower bounds for sampling algorithms for estimating the average. *Information Processing Letters*, Vol. 53, pp. 17–25, 1995.

[67] R. Canetti, O. Goldreich, S. and Halevi. The random oracle methodology, revisited. In *30th ACM Symposium on the Theory of Computing*, May 1998, pp. 209–218.

[68] C.L. Canonne. A survey on distribution testing: your data is big. But is it blue? *ECCC*, TR015-063, 2015.

[69] C.L. Canonne, T. Gouleakis, and R. Rubinfeld. Sampling Correctors. In *7th Innovations in Theoretical Computer Science*, pp. 93–102, 2016.

[70] C.L. Canonne, D. Ron, and R. Servedio. Testing probability distributions using conditional samples. *SIAM Journal on Computing*, Vol. 44 (3), pp. 540–616, 2015.

[71] D. Chakrabarty and C. Seshadhri. A o(n) monotonicity tester for Boolean functions over the hypercube. In *45th ACM Symposium on the Theory of Computing*, pp. 411–418, 2013.

[72] D. Chakrabarty and C. Seshadhri. Optimal bounds for monotonicity and Lipschitz testing over hypercubes and hypergrids. In *45th ACM Symposium on the Theory of Computing*, pp. 419–428, 2013.

[73] S. Chan, I. Diakonikolas, P. Valiant, and G. Valiant. Optimal algorithms for testing closeness of discrete distributions. In *25th ACM-SIAM Symposium on Discrete Algorithms*, pp. 1193–1203, 2014.

[74] B. Chazelle, R. Rubinfeld, and L. Trevisan. Approximating the minimum spanning tree weight in sublinear time. In *19th International Colloquium on Automata, Languages and Programming*, pp. 190–200, 2001.

[75] X. Chen, A. De, R.A. Servedio, and L. Tan. Boolean function monotonicity testing requires (almost) $n^{1/2}$ non-adaptive queries. In *47th ACM Symposium on the Theory of Computing*, pp. 519–528, 2015.

[76] X. Chen, R.A. Servedio, and L. Tan. New algorithms and lower bounds for monotonicity testing. In *55th IEEE Symposium on Foundations of Computer Science*, pp. 286–295, 2014.

[77] D. Cheng, R. Kannan, S. Vempala, and G. Wang. A divide-and-merge methodology for clustering. In *24th Symposium on Principles of Database Systems*, pp. 196–205, 2005.

[78] B. Chor and O. Goldreich. On the power of two–point based sampling. *Journal of Complexity*, Vol 5, pp. 96–106, 1989.

[79] B. Chor, O. Goldreich, E. Kushilevitz and M. Sudan. Private information retrieval. *Journal of the ACM*, Vol. 45, No. 6, pp. 965–982, 1998.

[80] G. Cormode and S. Muthukrishnan. Combinatorial algorithms for compressed sensing. In *40th Annual Conference on Information Sciences and Systems*, pp. 198–201, 2006.

[81] A. Czumaj, O. Goldreich, D. Ron, C. Seshadhri, A. Shapira, and C. Sohler. Finding cycles and trees in sublinear time. *Random Structures and Algorithms*, Vol. 45 (2), pp. 139–184, 2014.

[82] A. Czumaj, M. Monemizadeh, K. Onak, and C. Sohler. Planar graphs: Random walks and bipartiteness testing. In *52nd IEEE Symposium on Foundations of Computer Science*, pp. 423–432, 2011.

[83] A. Czumaj, P. Peng, and C. Sohler. Relating two property testing models for bounded degree directed graphs. In *48th ACM Symposium on the Theory of Computing*, pp. 1033–1045, 2016.

[84] C. Daskalakis, I. Diakonikolas, and R.A. Servedio. Learning *k*-modal distributions via testing. *Theory of Computing*, Vol. 10, pp. 535–570, 2014.

[85] R. David, I. Dinur, E. Goldenberg, G. Kindler, and I. Shinkar. Direct sum testing. In *6th Innovations in Theoretical Computer Science*, pp. 327–336, 2015.

[86] R.A. DeMillo and R.J. Lipton. A probabilistic remark on algebraic program testing. *Information Processing Letters*, Vol. 7 (4), pp. 193–195, June 1978.

[87] L. Devroye. The equivalence of weak, strong and complete convergence in L1 for kernel density estimates. *Annals of Statistics*, Vol. 11 (3), pp. 896–904, 1983.

[88] I. Diakonikolas, T. Gouleakis, J. Peebles, and E. Price. Collision-based testers are optimal for uniformity and closeness. *ECCC*, TR16-178, 2016.

[89] I. Diakonikolas and D. Kane. A new approach for testing properties of discrete distributions. In *57th IEEE Symposium on Foundations of Computer Science*, pp. 685–694, 2016.

[90] I. Diakonikolas, D. Kane, V. Nikishkin. Testing identity of structured distributions. In *26th ACM-SIAM Symposium on Discrete Algorithms*, pp. 1841–1854, 2015.

[91] I. Diakonikolas, H.K. Lee, K. Matulef, K. Onak, R. Rubinfeld, R.A. Servedio, and A. Wan. Testing for concise representations. In *48th IEEE Symposium on Foundations of Computer Science*, pp. 549–557, 2007.

[92] I. Dinur. The PCP Theorem by gap amplification. *Journal of the ACM*, Vol. 54 (3), Art. 12, 2007. Extended abstract in *38th STOC*, 2006.

[93] I. Dinur and P. Harsha. Composition of low-error 2-query PCPs using decodable PCPs. *SIAM Journal on Computing*, Vol. 42 (6), pp. 2452–2486, 2013. Extended abstract in *50th FOCS*, 2009.

[94] I. Dinur and O. Reingold. Assignment-testers: Towards a combinatorial proof of the PCP-Theorem. *SIAM Journal on Computing*, Vol. 36 (4), pp. 975–1024, 2006. Extended abstract in *45th FOCS*, 2004.

[95] I. Dinur and S. Safra. The importance of being biased. In *34th ACM Symposium on the Theory of Computing*, pp. 33–42, 2002.

[96] Y. Dodis, O. Goldreich, E. Lehman, S. Raskhodnikova, D. Ron, and A. Samorodnitsky. Improved testing algorithms for monotonicity. *ECCC*, TR99-017, 1999. Extended abstract in *3rd RANDOM*, 1999.

[97] E. Dolev and D. Ron. Distribution-free testing for monomials with a sublinear number of queries. *Theory of Computing*, Vol. 7 (1), pp. 155–176, 2011.

[98] P. Drineas, A. Frieze, R. Kannan, S. Vempala, V. Vinay. Clustering in large graphs and matrices. In *10th ACM-SIAM Symposium on Discrete Algorithms*, pp. 291–299, 1999.

[99] T. Eden, D. Ron, and C. Seshadhri. Sublinear time estimation of degree distribution moments: The arboricity connection. arXiv:1604.03661 [cs.DS], 2016.

[100] K. Efremenko. 3-query locally decodable codes of subexponential length. In *41st ACM Symposium on the Theory of Computing*, pp. 39–44, 2009.

[101] F. Ergun, S. Kannan, R. Kumar, R. Rubinfeld, and M. Viswanathan. Spot Checkers. *Journal of Computer and System Science*, Vol. 60, pp. 717–751, 2000. Extended abstract in *30th STOC*, 1998.

[102] F. Ergün, R. Kumar, and R. Rubinfeld. Fast approximate PCPs. In *31st ACM Symposium on the Theory of Computing*, pp. 41–50, 1999.

[103] G. Even, M. Medina, and D. Ron. Best of two local models: Local centralized and local distributed algorithms. CoRR abs/1402.3796, 2014.

[104] S. Even. *Graph Algorithms*. Computer Science Press, 1979. Second edition (edited by G. Even), Cambridge University Press, 2011.

[105] S. Even, A.L. Selman, and Y. Yacobi. The complexity of promise problems with applications to public-key cryptography. *Information and Control*, Vol. 61, pp. 159–173, 1984.

[106] U. Feige. On sums of independent random variables with unbounded variance, and estimating the average degree in a graph. *SIAM Journal on Computing*, Vol. 35 (4), pp. 964–984, 2006.

[107] U. Feige, S. Goldwasser, L. Lovász, S. Safra, and M. Szegedy. Approximating clique is almost NP-complete. *Journal of the ACM*, Vol. 43, pp. 268–292, 1996. Preliminary version in *32nd FOCS*, 1991.

[108] E. Fischer. On the strength of comparisons in property testing. *Information and Computation*, Vol. 189 (1), pp. 107–116, 2004.

[109] E. Fischer and L. Fortnow. Tolerant versus intolerant testing for Boolean properties. *Theory of Computing*, Vol. 2 (9), pp. 173–183, 2006.

[110] E. Fischer, Y. Goldhirsh, and O. Lachish. Partial tests, universal tests and decomposability. In *5th Innovations in Theoretical Computer Science*, pp. 483–500, 2014. Full version posted on *ECCC*, TR13-082, 2013.

[111] E. Fischer, G. Kindler, D. Ron, S. Safra and A. Samorodnitsky. Testing juntas. *Journal of Computer and System Science*, Vol. 68 (4), pp. 753–787, 2004. Extended abstract in *44th FOCS*, 2002.

[112] E. Fischer, O. Lachish, and Y. Vasudev. Trading query complexity for sample-based testing and multi-testing scalability. In *56th IEEE Symposium on Foundations of Computer Science*, pp. 1163–1182, 2015.

[113] E. Fischer, E. Lehman, I. Newman, S. Raskhodnikova, R. Rubinfeld, and A. Samorodnitsky. Monotonicity testing over general poset domains. In *34th ACM Symposium on the Theory of Computing*, pp. 474–483, 2002.

[114] E. Fischer and A. Matsliah. Testing graph isomorphism. In *17th ACM-SIAM Symposium on Discrete Algorithms*, pp. 299–308, 2006.

[115] E. Fischer, A. Matsliah, and A. Shapira. Approximate hypergraph partitioning and applications. In *48th IEEE Symposium on Foundations of Computer Science*, pp. 579–589, 2007.

[116] E. Fischer and I. Newman. Testing versus estimation of graph properties. In *37th ACM Symposium on the Theory of Computing*, pp. 138–146, 2005.

[117] G.D. Forney. *Concatenated Codes*. MIT Press, 1966.

[118] L. Fortnow, J. Rompel, and M. Sipser. On the power of multi-prover interactive protocols. *Theoretical Computer Science*, Vol. 134 (2), pp. 545–557, 1994. Extended abstract in *3rd IEEE Symp. on Structural Complexity*, 1988.

[119] J. Fox. A new proof of the graph removal lemma. *Annals of Mathematics*, Vol. 174 (1), pp. 561–579, 2011.

[120] K. Friedl and M. Sudan. Some improvements to total degree tests. In *3rd Israel Symposium on Theory of Computing and Systems*, pp. 190–198, 1995. Revision posted on *CoRR*, 1307.3975, 2013.

[121] A. Frieze and R. Kannan. The regularity lemma and approximation schemes for dense problems. In *37th IEEE Symposium on Foundations of Computer Science*, pp. 12–20, 1996.

[122] A. Frieze and R. Kannan. Quick approximation to matrices and applications. *Combinatorica*, Vol. 19 (2), pp. 175–220, 1999.

[123] A. Frieze, R. Kannan, and S. Vempala. Fast Monte-Carlo algorithms for finding low-rank approximations. *Journal of the ACM*, Vol. 51 (6), pp. 1025–1041, 2004. Extended abstract in *39th FOCS*, 1998.

[124] P. Gemmell, R.J. Lipton, R. Rubinfeld, M. Sudan, and A. Wigderson. Self-testing/correcting for polynomials and for approximate functions. In *23rd Symposium on the Theory of Computing*, pp. 32–42, 1991.

[125] L. Gishboliner and A. Shapira. Removal Lemmas with Polynomial Bounds. arXiv: 1611.10315 [math.CO], 2016.

[126] D. Glasner and R.A. Servedio. Distribution-free testing lower bound for basic Boolean functions. *Theory of Computing*, Vol. 5 (1), pp. 191–216, 2009.

[127] O. Goldreich. *Modern Cryptography, Probabilistic Proofs and Pseudorandomness*. Algorithms and Combinatorics, Vol. 17, Springer, 1998.

[128] O. Goldreich. *Foundation of cryptography – Basic tools*. Cambridge University Press, 2001.

[129] O. Goldreich. On Promise Problems: In memory of Shimon Even (1935–2004). *ECCC*, TR05-018, 2005. See also in *Theoretical Computer Science: Essays in memory of Shimon Even*, Lecture Notes in Computer Science, Festschrift, Vol. 3895, Springer, 2006.

[130] O. Goldreich. Short locally testable codes and proofs (survey). ECCC Technical Report TR05-014, 2005.

[131] O. Goldreich. *Computational Complexity: A Conceptual Perspective*. Cambridge University Press, 2008.

[132] O. Goldreich. Short locally testable codes and proofs: A survey in two parts. In [134].

[133] O. Goldreich. Introduction to testing graph properties. In [134].

[134] O. Goldreich (ed.). *Property Testing: Current Research and Surveys*. Lecture Notes in Computer Science, Vol. 6390, Springer, 2010.

[135] O. Goldreich. On multiple input problems in property testing. In *18th RANDOM*, pp. 704–720, 2014.

[136] O. Goldreich. On the communication complexity methodology for proving lower bounds on the query complexity of property testing. *ECCC*, TR13-073, 2013.

[137] O. Goldreich. The uniform distribution is complete with respect to testing identity to a fixed distribution. *ECCC*, TR16-015, 2016.

[138] O. Goldreich. Reducing testing affine subspaces to testing linearity. *ECCC*, TR16-080, 2016.

[139] O. Goldreich, S. Goldwasser, E. Lehman, D. Ron, and A. Samorodnitsky. Testing monotonicity. *Combinatorica*, Vol. 20 (3), pp. 301–337, 2000. Extended abstract in *39th FOCS*, 1998.

[140] O. Goldreich, S. Goldwasser, and D. Ron. Property testing and its connection to learning and approximation. *Journal of the ACM*, pp. 653–750, 1998. Extended abstract in *37th FOCS*, 1996.

[141] O. Goldreich, T. Gur, and I. Komargodski. Strong locally testable codes with relaxed local decoders. In *30th IEEE Conference on Computational Complexity*, pp. 1–41, 2015.

[142] O. Goldreich, T. Gur, and R. Rothblum. Proofs of proximity for context-free languages and read-once branching programs. In *42nd International Colloquium on Automata, Languages and Programming*, pp. 666–677, 2015.

[143] O. Goldreich and T. Kaufman. Proximity oblivious testing and the role of invariances. In *15th RANDOM*, pp. 579–592, 2011.

[144] O. Goldreich, M. Krivelevich, I. Newman, and E. Rozenberg. Hierarchy theorems for property testing. *Computational Complexity*, Vol. 21 (1), pp. 129–192, 2012.

[145] O. Goldreich and L.A. Levin. A hard-core predicate for all one-way functions. In *21st ACM Symposium on the Theory of Computing*, pp. 25–32, 1989.

[146] O. Goldreich, S. Micali and A. Wigderson. Proofs that yield nothing but their validity or all languages in NP have zero-knowledge proof systems. *Journal of the ACM*, Vol. 38, No. 3, pp. 691–729, 1991. Preliminary version in *27th FOCS*, 1986.

[147] O. Goldreich and D. Ron. Property testing in bounded degree graphs. *Algorithmica*, pp. 302–343, 2002. Extended abstract in *29th STOC*, 1997.

[148] O. Goldreich and D. Ron. A sublinear bipartite tester for bounded degree graphs. *Combinatorica*, Vol. 19 (3), pp. 335–373, 1999. Extended abstract in *30th STOC*, 1998.

[149] O. Goldreich and D. Ron. On testing expansion in bounded-degree graphs. *ECCC*, TR00-020, 2000.

[150] O. Goldreich and D. Ron. Approximating average parameters of graphs. *Random Structures and Algorithms*, Vol. 32 (3), pp. 473–493, 2008.

[151] O. Goldreich and D. Ron. Algorithmic aspects of property testing in the dense graphs model. *SIAM Journal on Computing*, Vol. 40, No. 2, pp. 376–445, 2011.

[152] O. Goldreich and D. Ron. On proximity oblivious testing. *SIAM Journal on Computing*, Vol. 40, No. 2, pp. 534–566, 2011. Extended abstract in *41st STOC*, 2009.

[153] O. Goldreich and D. Ron. On sample-based testers. In *6th Innovations in Theoretical Computer Science*, pp. 337–345, 2015.

[154] O. Goldreich and D. Ron. On the relation between the relative earth mover distance and the variation distance (an exposition). Available from http://www.wisdom.weizmann. ac.il/~oded/p_remd.html

[155] O. Goldreich and O. Sheffet. On the randomness complexity of property testing. *Computational Complexity*, Vol. 19 (1), pp. 99–133, 2010.

[156] O. Goldreich and I. Shinkar. Two-sided error proximity oblivious testing. *ECCC*, TR12-021, 2012. (See Revision 4, 2014.)

[157] O. Goldreich and M. Sudan. Locally testable codes and PCPs of almost-linear length. *Journal of the ACM*, Vol. 53 (4), pp. 558–655, 2006. Extended abstract in *43rd FOCS*, 2002.

[158] O. Goldreich and L. Trevisan. Three theorems regarding testing graph properties. *Random Structures and Algorithms*, Vol. 23 (1), pp. 23–57, August 2003.

[159] O. Goldreich, S. Vadhan, and A. Wigderson. On interactive proofs with a laconic prover. *Computational Complexity*, Vol. 11 (1–2), pp. 1–53, 2002.

[160] S. Goldwasser and S. Micali. Probabilistic encryption. *Journal of Computer and System Science*, Vol. 28, No. 2, pp. 270–299, 1984. Preliminary version in *14th STOC*, 1982.

[161] S. Goldwasser, S. Micali and C. Rackoff. The knowledge complexity of interactive proof systems. *SIAM Journal on Computing*, Vol. 18, pp. 186–208, 1989. Preliminary version in *17th STOC*, 1985. Earlier versions date to 1982.

[162] M. Gonen and D. Ron. On the benefit of adaptivity in property testing of dense graphs. *Algorithmica* (special issue for RANDOM and APPROX 2007), Vol. 58 (4), pp. 811–830, 2010.

[163] M. Gonen, D. Ron, U. Weinsberg, and A. Wool. Finding a dense-core in Jellyfish graphs. *Computer Networks*, Vol. 52 (15), pp. 2831–2841, 2008. Preliminary version in *5th International Workshop on Algorithms and Models for the Web-Graph*.

[164] T. Gowers. Lower bounds of tower type for Szemeredi's uniformity lemma, *GAFA*, Vol. 7, pp. 322–337, 1997.

[165] A. Guo, E. Haramaty, and M. Sudan. Robust testing of lifted codes with applications to low-degree testing. *ECCC*, TR15-043, 2015.

[166] T. Gur and R. Rothblum. Non-interactive proofs of proximity. *ECCC*, TR13-078, 2013.

[167] S. Halevy and E. Kushilevitz. Distribution-free property testing. In *7th RANDOM*, pp. 341–353, 2003.

[168] E. Haramaty, A. Shpilka, and M. Sudan. Optimal testing of multivariate polynomials over small prime fields. *SIAM Journal on Computing*, Vol. 42 (2), pp. 536–562, 2013. Preliminary version in *52nd FOCS*, 2011.

[169] A. Hassidim, J. Kelner, H. Nguyen, and K. Onak. Local graph partitions for approximation and testing. In *50th IEEE Symposium on Foundations of Computer Science*, pp. 22–31, 2009.

[170] J. Hastad. Clique is hard to approximate within $n^{1-\epsilon}$. *Acta Mathematica*, Vol. 182, pp. 105–142, 1999. Preliminary versions in *28th STOC* (1996) and *37th FOCS* (1996).

[171] J. Hastad. Getting optimal in-approximability results. *Journal of the ACM*, Vol. 48, pp. 798–859, 2001. Extended abstract in *29th STOC*, 1997.

[172] D. Hochbaum (ed.). *Approximation Algorithms for NP-Hard Problems*. PWS, 1996.

[173] M. Jha and S. Raskhodnikova. Testing and reconstruction of Lipschitz functions with applications to data privacy. *SIAM Journal on Computing*, Vol. 42 (2), pp. 700–731, 2013. Extended abstract in *52nd FOCS*, 2011.

[174] C. S. Jutla, A. C. Patthak, A. Rudra, and D. Zuckerman. Testing low-degree polynomials over prime fields. *Random Structures and Algorithms*, Vol. 35 (2), pp. 163–193, 2009. Preliminary version in *45th FOCS*, 2004.

[175] S. Kale and C. Seshadhri. Testing expansion in bounded degree graphs. In *35th International Colloquium on Automata, Languages and Programming*, pp. 527–538, 2008. (Preliminary version appeared as TR07-076, *ECCC*, 2007.)

[176] B. Kalyanasundaram and G. Schintger. The probabilistic communication complexity of set intersection. *SIAM Journal on Discrete Mathematics*, Vol. 5 (4), pp. 545–557, 1992.

[177] R. Kannan, S. Vempala, and A. Vetta. On clusterings: Good, bad and spectral. *Journal of the ACM*, Vol. 51 (3), pp. 497–515, 2004. Preliminary version in *41st FOCS*, 2000.

[178] D. Karger. Global min-cuts in $\mathcal{RNC}$ and other ramifications of a simple mincut algorithm. In *4th ACM-SIAM Symposium on Discrete Algorithms*, pp. 21–30, 1993.

[179] J. Katz and L. Trevisan. On the efficiency of local decoding procedures for error-correcting codes. In *32nd ACM Symposium on the Theory of Computing*, pp. 80–86, 2000.

[180] T. Kaufman, M. Krivelevich, and D. Ron. Tight bounds for testing bipartiteness in general graphs. *SIAM Journal on Computing*, Vol. 33 (6), pp. 1441–1483, 2004.

[181] T. Kaufman, S. Litsyn, and N. Xie. Breaking the epsilon-soundness bound of the linearity test over GF(2). *SIAM Journal on Computing*, Vol. 39 (5), pp. 1988–2003, 2010.

[182] T. Kaufman and D. Ron. Testing polynomials over general fields. *SIAM Journal on Computing*, 35 (3):779–802, 2006. Preliminary version in *45th FOCS*, 2004.

[183] T. Kaufman and M. Sudan. Algebraic property testing: The role of invariance. In *40th ACM Symposium on the Theory of Computing*, pp. 4-3–412, 2008.

[184] M.J. Kearns and U.V. Vazirani. *An Introduction to Computational Learning Theory*. MIT Press, 1994.

[185] I. Kerenidis and R. de Wolf. Exponential lower bound for 2-query locally decodable codes via a quantum argument. *Journal of Computer and System Science*, Vol. 69 (3), pp. 395–420, 2004. Preliminary version in *35th STOC*, 2003.

[186] S. Khot. On the power of unique 2-prover 1-round games. In *34th ACM Symposium on the Theory of Computing*, pp. 767–775, 2002.

[187] S. Khot, G. Kindler, E. Mossel, and R. O'Donnell. Optimal inapproximability results for MAX-CUT and other 2-variable CSPs? *SIAM Journal on Computing*, Vol. 37 (1), pp. 319–357, 2007. Extended abstract in *44th FOCS*, 2004.

[188] S. Khot, D. Minzer, and S. Safra. On monotonicity testing and Boolean Isoperimetric type theorems. *ECCC*, TR15-011, 2015.

[189] S. Khot and O. Regev. Vertex cover might be hard to approximate to within 2-epsilon. *Journal of Computer and System Science*, Vol. 74 (3), pp. 335–349, 2008. Extended abstract in *18th CCC*, 2003.

[190] J. Kilian. A note on efficient zero-knowledge proofs and arguments. In *24th ACM Symposium on the Theory of Computing*, pp. 723–732, 1992.

[191] S. Kopparty, O. Meir, N. Ron-Zewi, and S. Saraf. High rate locally-correctable and locally-testable codes with sub-polynomial query complexity *ECCC*, TR15-068, 2015.

[192] S. Kopparty, O. Meir, N. Ron-Zewi, and S. Saraf. High-rate locally-testable codes with quasi-polylogarithmic query complexity. *ECCC*, TR15-110, 2015.

[193] S. Korman, D. Reichman, and G. Tsur. Tight approximation of image matching. *CoRR*, abs/1111.1713, 2011.

[194] S. Korman, D. Reichman, G. Tsur, and S. Avidan. FAsT-Match: Fast affine template matching. *International Journal of Computer Vision*, Vol. 121 (1), pp. 111–125, 2017.

[195] E. Kushilevitz and N. Nisan. *Communication Complexity*. Cambridge University Press, 1997.

[196] D. Lapidot and A. Shamir. Fully parallelized multi prover protocols for NEXP-time. In *32nd IEEE Symposium on Foundations of Computer Science*, pp. 13–18, 1991.

[197] R. Levi and D. Ron. A quasi-polynomial time partition oracle for graphs with an excluded minor. *ACM Transactions on Algorithms*, Vol. 11 (3), pp. 24:1–24:13, 2015.

[198] R. Levi, D. Ron, and R. Rubinfeld. Local algorithms for sparse spanning graphs. In *18th RANDOM*, LIPIcs, Vol. 28, Schloss Dagstuhl – Leibniz-Zentrum fuer Informatik, pp. 826–842, 2014.

[199] L.A. Levin. One-way functions and pseudorandom generators. In *17th ACM Symposium on the Theory of Computing*, pp. 363–365, 1985.

[200] L. Lovász and N. Young. Lecture notes on evasiveness of graph properties. Technical Report TR–317–91, Princeton University, Computer Science Department, 1991.

[201] A. Lubotzky, R. Phillips, and P. Sarnak. Ramanujan graphs. *Combinatorica*, Vol. 8, pp. 261–277, 1988.

[202] C. Lund, L. Fortnow, H. Karloff, and N. Nisan. Algebraic methods for interactive proof systems. *Journal of the ACM*, Vol. 39, No. 4, pp. 859–868, 1992. Extended abstract in *31st FOCS*, 1990.

[203] S. Marko and D. Ron. Distance approximation in bounded-degree and general sparse graphs. *Transactions on Algorithms*, Vol. 5 (2), Art. 22, 2009.

[204] O. Meir. Combinatorial construction of locally testable codes. *SIAM Journal on Computing*, Vol. 39 (2), pp. 491–544, 2009. Extended abstract in *40th STOC*, 2008.

[205] O. Meir. Combinatorial PCPs with efficient verifiers. In *50th IEEE Symposium on Foundations of Computer Science*, pp. 463–471, 2009.

[206] R. Merkle. *Secrecy, authentication, and public key systems*. PhD dissertation, Department of Electrical Engineering, Stanford University 1979.

[207] S. Micali. Computationally sound proofs. *SIAM Journal on Computing*, Vol. 30 (4), pp. 1253–1298, 2000. Preliminary version in *35th FOCS*, 1994.

[208] M. Mihail. Conductance and convergence of Markov chains – A combinatorial treatment of expanders. In *30th IEEE Symposium on Foundations of Computer Science*, pp. 526–531, 1989.

[209] N. Mishra, D. Ron, and R. Swaminathan. A new conceptual clustering framework. *Machine Learning*, Vol. 56 (1–3), pp. 115–151, 2004.

[210] D. Moshkovitz and R. Raz. Two-query PCP with subconstant error. *Journal of the ACM*, Vol. 57 (5), 2010. Extended abstract in *49th FOCS*, 2008.

[211] E. Mossel, R. O'Donnell, and K. Oleszkiewicz. Noise stability of functions with low influences: Invariance and optimality. In *46th IEEE Symposium on Foundations of Computer Science*, pp. 21–30, 2005.

[212] R. Motwani and P. Raghavan. *Randomized Algorithms*. Cambridge University Press, 1995.

[213] S. Muthukrishnan. Data streams: Algorithms and applications. *Foundations and Trends in Theoretical Computer Science*, Vol. 1 (2), pp. 117–236, 2005.

[214] A. Nachmias and A. Shapira. Testing the expansion of a graph. TR07-118, *ECCC*, 2007.

[215] I. Newman. Testing membership in languages that have small width branching programs. *SIAM Journal on Computing*, Vol. 31 (5), pp. 1557–1570, 2002.

[216] I. Newman. Property testing of massively parametrized problems – A Survey. In [134].

[217] I. Newman and C. Sohler. Every property of hyperfinite graphs is testable. *SIAM Journal on Computing*, Vol. 42 (3), pp. 1095–1112, 2013.

[218] K. Onak. *New sublinear methods in the struggle against classical problems*. PhD thesis, Massachusetts Institute of Technology, 2010.

[219] A. Orlitsky, N. Santhanam, K. Viswanathan, and J. Zhang. On modeling profiles instead of values. In *20th Uncertainity in Artificial Intelligence*, pp. 426–435, 2004.

[220] A. Orlitsky, N. Santhanam, and J. Zhang. Always Good Turing: Asymptotically optimal probability estimation. *Science*, Vol. 302, Nr. 5644, pp. 427–431, 2003.

[221] L. Paninski. A coincidence-based test for uniformity given very sparsely-sampled discrete data. *IEEE Transactions on Information Theory*, Vol. 54, pp. 4750–4755, 2008.

[222] M. Parnas and D. Ron. Testing the diameter of graphs. *Random Structures and Algorithms*, Vol. 20 (2), pp. 165–183, 2002.

[223] M. Parnas and D. Ron. Approximating the minimum vertex cover in sublinear time and a connection to distributed algorithms. *Theoretical Computer Science*, Vol. 381 (1–3), pp. 183–196, 2007.

[224] M. Parnas, D. Ron, and R. Rubinfeld. On testing convexity and submodularity. *SIAM Journal on Computing*, Vol. 32 (5), pp. 1158–1184, 2003.

[225] M. Parnas, D. Ron, and R. Rubinfeld. Tolerant property testing and distance approximation. *Journal of Computer and System Science*, Vol. 72 (6), pp. 1012–1042, 2006.

[226] M. Parnas, D. Ron, and A. Samorodnitsky. Testing basic Boolean formulae. *SIAM Journal on Discrete Mathematics and Algebra*, Vol. 16 (1), pp. 20–46, 2002.

[227] L. Pitt and L.G. Valiant. Computational limitations on learning from examples. *Journal of the ACM*, Vol. 35 (4), pp. 965–984, 1988.

[228] A. Polishchuk and D.A. Spielman. Nearly-linear size holographic proofs. In *26th ACM Symposium on the Theory of Computing*, 1994, pp. 194–203.

[229] J. Pollard. Monte Carlo methods for index computations (mod p). *Mathematics of Computation*, Vol 32, pp. 918–924, 1978.

[230] S. Raskhodnikova. Approximate testing of visual properties. In *7th RANDOM*, Lecture Notes in Computer Science, Vol. 2764, pp. 370–381, Springer, 2003.

[231] S. Raskhodnikova. Transitive closure spanners: A survey. In [134].

[232] S. Raskhodnikova, D. Ron, A. Shpilka, and A. Smith. Strong lower bounds for approximating distribution support size and the distinct elements problem. *SIAM Journal on Computing*, Vol. 39 (3), pp. 813–842, 2009. Extended abstract in *48th FOCS*, 2007.

[233] S. Raskhodnikova and A. Smith. A note on adaptivity in testing properties of bounded degree graphs. *ECCC*, TR06-089, 2006.

[234] R. Raz. A parallel repetition theorem. *SIAM Journal on Computing*, Vol. 27 (3), pp. 763–803, 1998. Extended abstract in *27th STOC*, 1995.

[235] R. Raz and S. Safra. A sub-constant error-probability low-degree test, and a sub-constant error-probability PCP characterization of NP. In *29th ACM Symposium on the Theory of Computing*, pp. 475–484, 1997.

[236] O. Reingold, G. Rothblum, R. Rothblum. Constant-round interactive proofs for delegating computation. In *48th ACM Symposium on the Theory of Computing*, pp. 49–62, 2016.

[237] N. Robertson and P.D. Seymour. Graph minors. I. Excluding a forest. *Journal of Combinatorial Theory, Series B*, Vol. 35 (1), pp. 39–61, 1983.

[238] N. Robertson and P.D. Seymour. Graph minors. XIII. The disjoint paths problem. *Journal of Combinatorial Theory, Series B*, Vol. 63 (1), pp. 65–110, 1995.

[239] N. Robertson and P. D. Seymour. Graph Minors. XX. Wagner's conjecture. *Journal of Combinatorial Theory, Series B*, Vol. 92 (1), pp. 325–357, 2004.

[240] V. Rodl and R. Duke. On graphs with small subgraphs of large chromatic number. *Graphs and Combinatorics*, Vol. 1, pp. 91–96, 1985.

[241] D. Ron. Property testing: A learning theory perspective. *Foundations and Trends in Machine Learning*, Vol. 1 (3), pp. 307–402, 2008.

[242] D. Ron. Algorithmic and analysis techniques in property testing. *Foundations and Trends in Theoretical Computer Science*, Vol. 5, pp. 73–205, 2010.

[243] D. Ron and G. Tsur. Testing properties of sparse images. *ACM Transactions on Algorithms*, Vol. 10 (4), pp. 17:1–17:52, 2014. Extended abstract in *51st FOCS*, 2010.

[244] G. Rothblum, S. Vadhan, and A. Wigderson. Interactive proofs of proximity: Delegating computation in sublinear time. In *45th ACM Symposium on the Theory of Computing*, pp. 793–802, 2013.

[245] R. Rubinfeld and M. Sudan. Self-testing polynomial functions efficiently and over rational domains. In *3rd ACM-SIAM Symposium on Discrete Algorithms*, pp. 23–32, 1992.

[246] R. Rubinfeld and M. Sudan. Robust characterization of polynomials with applications to program testing. *SIAM Journal on Computing*, Vol. 25 (2), pp. 252–271, 1996. Unifies and extends part of the results contained in [124] and [245].

[247] R. Rubinfeld, G. Tamir, S. Vardi, and M. Xie. Fast local computation algorithms. In *2nd Innovations in (Theoretical) Computer Science*, pp. 223–238, 2011.

[248] M. Saks and C. Seshadhri. Local monotonicity reconstruction. *SIAM Journal on Computing*, Vol. 39 (7), pp. 2897–2926, 2010.

[249] A. Samorodnitsky and L. Trevisan. A PCP characterization of NP with optimal amortized query complexity. In *32nd ACM Symposium on the Theory of Computing*, pp. 191–199, 2000.

[250] J.T. Schwartz. Fast probabilistic algorithms for verification of polynomial identities. *Journal of the ACM*, Vol. 27 (4), pp. 701–717, October 1980.

[251] R. Servedio. Testing by implicit learning: A brief survey. In [134].

[252] C. Seshadhri, J. Vondrak. Is submodularity testable? *Algorithmica*, Vol. 69 (1), pp. 1–25, 2014. Extended abstract in *2nd Innovations in (Theoretical) Computer Science*, 2011.

[253] A. Shamir. IP = PSPACE. *Journal of the ACM*, Vol. 39, No. 4, pp. 869–877, 1992. Preliminary version in *31st FOCS*, 1990.

[254] A. Shpilka and A. Wigderson. Derandomizing homomorphism testing in general groups. *SIAM Journal on Computing*, Vol. 36 (4), pp. 1215–1230, 2006.

[255] D. Spielman. *Computationally efficient error-correcting codes and holographic proofs*. PhD thesis, Massachusetts Institute of Technology, June 1995.

[256] M. Sudan. *Efficient checking of polynomials and proofs and the hardness of approximation problems*. PhD thesis, Computer Science Division, University of California at Berkeley, 1992. Also appears as Lecture Notes in Computer Science, Vol. 1001, Springer, 1996.

[257] M. Sudan. Invariances in property testing. In [134].

[258] E. Szemerédi. Regular partitions of graphs. In *Proceedings Colloque International CNRS*, pp. 399–401, 1978.

[259] R. Tell. On being far from far and on dual problems in property testing. *ECCC*, TR15-072, 2015. (Revision 1, Aug. 2015.)

[260] R. Tell. A note on tolerant testing with one-sided error. *ECCC*, TR16-032, 2016.

[261] G.J. Valiant. *Algorithmic approaches to statistical questions*. PhD thesis, University of California at Berkeley, 2012.

[262] L.G. Valiant. A theory of the learnable. *Communications of the ACM*, Vl. 27 (11), pp. 1134–1142, 1984.

[263] G. Valiant and P. Valiant. Estimating the unseen: An n/log(n)-sample estimator for entropy and support size, shown optimal via new CLTs. In *43rd ACM Symposium on the Theory of Computing*, pp. 685–694, 2011. Full version in *ECCC*, TR10-179 and TR10-180, 2010.

[264] G. Valiant and P. Valiant. Instance-by-instance optimal identity testing. *ECCC*, TR13-111, 2013.

[265] G. Valiant and P. Valiant. Instance optimal learning of discrete distributions In *48th ACM Symposium on the Theory of Computing*, pp. 142–155, 2016.

[266] P. Valiant. *Testing symmetric properties of distributions*, PhD thesis, Massachusetts Institute of Technology, 2012.

[267] M. Viderman. Strong LTCs with inverse poly-log rate and constant soundness. In *54th IEEE Symposium on Foundations of Computer Science*, pp. 330–339, 2013.

[268] M. Viderman. Explicit strong LTCs with inverse poly-log rate and constant soundness. *ECCC*, TR15-020, 2015.

[269] J. von Neumann. Various techniques used in connection with random digits. *Applied Math Series*, Vol. 12, pp. 36–38, 1951. Reprinted in *von Neumann's Collected Works*, Vol. 5, pp. 768–770, Pergamon, 1963.

[270] D.P. Woodruff. Sketching as a tool for numerical linear algebra. *Foundations and Trends in Theoretical Computer Science*, Vol. 10 (1–2), pp. 1–157, 2014.

[271] Y. Wu and P. Yang. Chebyshev polynomials, moment matching, and optimal estimation of the unseen. `arXiv:1504.01227 [math.ST]`, 2015.

[272] A.C.C. Yao. Probabilistic complexity: Towards a unified measure of complexity. In *18th IEEE Symposium on Foundations of Computer Science*, pp. 222–227, 1977.

[273] A.C.C. Yao. Lower bounds by probabilistic arguments. In *24th IEEE Symposium on Foundations of Computer Science*, pp. 420–428, 1983.

[274] S. Yekhanin. Towards 3-query locally decodable codes of subexponential length. In *39th ACM Symposium on the Theory of Computing*, pp. 266–274, 2007.

[275] Y. Yoshida and H. Ito. Property testing on k-vertex-connectivity of graphs. *Algorithmica*, Vol. 62 (3), pp. 701–712, 2012.

[276] R.E. Zippel. Probabilistic algorithms for sparse polynomials. In *EUROSAM '79: International Symposium on Symbolic and Algebraic Manipulation*, E. Ng (Ed.), Lecture Notes in Computer Science, Vol. 72, Springer, pp. 216–226, 1979.

Index

Subject Index